Second Edition

The Historical Guide to North American Railroads

KALMBACH
BOOKS

Printed in Canada

02 03 04 05 06 07 08   10 9 8 7 6 5 4 3 2

Visit our website at
http://kalmbachbooks.com
Secure online ordering available

Publisher's Cataloging-in-Publication
(Provided by Quality Books, Inc.)
The historical guide to North American
    railroads — 2nd ed.
        p. cm.
        Includes bibliographical references.
        ISBN: 0-89024-356-5

        1. Railroads—United States. 2. Railroads—
Canada. 3. Railroads—Mexico.

TF23.D74 1999   385'.097
                    QBI99-861

Book design: Sabine Beaupré
Cover design: Kristi Ludwig
Cover photo: Linn H. Westcott

Contents

Introduction to the Second Edition

A book describing *all* the railroads that have vanished would be the size of an unabridged dictionary—hardly handy for quick reference. The two principal criteria for inclusion in this book are that the railroad disappeared after 1930 and was more than 50 miles long.

The year 1930 represents the end of the Roaring Twenties and is a historical watershed. Railroads had already reached their greatest extent and were feeling the competition of automobiles, trucks, paved highways, and airplanes; they would soon be affected by the events of Black Tuesday—October 29, 1929—and the Great Depression. The diesel was a novelty and streamlining was in the future.

Canada's railroad history does not divide nicely at 1930, so the first edition of this book included an entry on the railroads that became Canadian National Railways, which was a going concern by the early 1920s. Those railroads broke down the date barriers for the inclusion in this edition of some significant railroads that disappeared before the cutoff date, such as Hocking Valley, Nevada-California-Oregon, El Paso & Southwestern—railroads whose steam locomotives lasted for a number of years after they were orphaned.

Length was only part of the other criterion. Was the railroad more than an incidental part of the continent's rail network, or was it in the position of—to quote one railroad's advertising slogan—"serving an entire continent through connections"? To the 50-mile minimum we added the requirement of significance or conspicuousness. We also considered longevity. Some of the short lines created to operate castoffs of the Rock Island and Conrail sprouted, flourished, withered, and died in a single season.

What is a railroad?

Railroads have four components: fixed plant, which is track, right of way, and buildings; rolling stock; human organization; and financial structure. The human organization operates the rolling stock over the fixed plant, and the financial structure supports the operation. What we call a railroad does not necessarily have all four components. Amtrak began operation with a financial structure and a handful of employees; it rented cars, locomotives, and operating space from other railroads. For years the Buffalo, Rochester & Pittsburgh had only financial structure and fixed plant; Baltimore & Ohio provided the rolling stock and the people. The Clinchfield Railroad was an unincorporated organization of people and rolling stock that operated the Carolina, Clinchfield & Ohio Railway for its joint lessees, Atlantic Coast Line and Louisville & Nashville.

Among the reasons for separating the components are state laws and financial and operational convenience. Remembering that the components are separable may make it easier to understand the more complex railroad organizations.

Subsidiaries are generally with their parents, unless those subsidiaries had a long-lived distinctive identity. we omitted most of the interurbans. The electric railway industry was well into decline by 1930 and it has been extensively documented.

We included a few entities that were not railroads but were important factors in North American railroad development, such as the Pullman Company and the Interstate Commerce Commission. A few railroads not meeting the criteria sneaked in anyway. Union Pacific is in the book by reader demand, even though it is very much alive and still doing business at 1416 Dodge Street in Omaha.

What about the railroads?

The entry for each railroad begins with its history. A railroad's history is not necessarily proportional to its length or its life span. The Great Northern, largely the creation of one man, James J. Hill, built its line through territory far distant from any competitor. For its right of way over Marias Pass it did not have to fight the Santa Fe—only bears and topography. The Western

Pacific was involved with the Gould empire early on but had a simple existence afterward. The New Haven dated from 1831, endured a succession of flamboyant and shady managements, and had more history per route-mile than any three western roads put together.

We have tried to follow a middle path between the financial history that gives details of every stock and bond issue and the anecdotal history that tells the story of the railroad from the point of view of the locomotive engineer, the station agent, or the canal boat captain whose business the railroad took away. Enthusiasts of those types of history will find plenty of each out there.

Following the history are a number of data elements, facts, and statistics. The primary information sources were:

• Railroad name and location of headquarters: *The Official Guide*, January 1930. We have omitted "Company" and "Corporation," and have used the ampersand (&) instead of "and," whether or not the railroad did.

• Miles of railroad operated and number of locomotives and cars: *Poor's Railroads* and *Moody's Transportation Manual* up to about 1990, thereafter *The Pocket List of Railroad Officials*. The figures are as of December 31 of the year shown. *The Official Railway Equipment Register*, *The Pocket List*, and Poor and Moody often disagree on the figures, but for consistency we've stuck with Poor and Moody (and within those books quite often the figures as reported to the ICC, owned, and in service disagree). For railroads that turned over passenger service to Amtrak, final passenger car counts are as of December 31, 1970. Cabooses are included with freight cars; business cars are included with company service equipment. In later years Moody lumped together the figures for freight and company service cars. *The Pocket List* gives a total rolling stock count, the significance of which is the number of couplers divided by 2.

• Reporting marks: *The Official Railway Equipment Register*. For roads without officially assigned reporting marks we have shown the initials used on the cars. In recent years the ampersand has disappeared from the official reporting marks, even if it lingers on the occasional car side.

• Notable named passenger trains: Trains that had a nice matched set of streamlined equipment had a better chance of nomination.

• Historical and technical society: The February 1998 issue of *Model Railroader*. The addresses change frequently, but you can find current information at *MR*'s web site (http://www.model-railroader.com/).

• Recommended reading: We have cited what we think are the best books for further information on the railroad. Some are long out of print but can be found in libraries or used-book stores. we have tried to give the current or last-known address of the publisher.

• Subsidiaries and affiliated railroads: These are shown as of the end of the railroad's existence. We included major line-haul railroads and omitted most terminal and switching roads.

• Successors: This generally means corporate successor.

• Portions still operated: The top two information sources were the 5th edition (1996) of Edward A. Lewis's *American Shortline Railway Guide*, which is also part of Kalmbach's Railroad Reference Series, and the *Professional Railroad Atlas of North America* (1998 edition), published by DeskMap Systems, 3701 Executive Center Drive, Austin TX 78731, with the latter taking precedence because it is newer. For the most part, we have listed major main lines and branches. Omission of this entry means either "none" or "most lines are still in operation"—the text should make clear which.

• Map and photo: The map shows the railroad as it was in 1930 or the year it came into being. The purpose of the map is to show where the railroad fit into the North American railroad scene, not to document every station and curve. A few connecting railroads are shown to help clarify matters; dashed lines indicate segments that need to be differentiated. The photo is representative, not exhaustive. One photo is as inadequate as one sentence to describe a railroad.

The omission of a data item can usually be interpreted as "none;" in a few instances it means we couldn't find anything.

As you read this book you will want to have handy a standard atlas or map showing rivers, mountains, cities, and towns—the *Rand McNally Road Atlas*, for instance—and also a railroad atlas, such as an older edition of the *Rand McNally Handy Railroad Atlas* (all long out of print, unfortunately).

A Brief History of North American Railroading

North America's railroads did not develop in isolation. They connected with each other, shared many characteristics, and were shaped by the events of their time. A review of North America's railroad history furnishes a framework for the individual railroad histories and affords an understanding of why and when things happened.

First blossom, 1827–1860

Completion of the Erie Canal gave a boost to the city of New York and made other Atlantic port cities recognize the need for improved transportation to the interior. Baltimoreans could see that a canal to the west would be impractical and therefore chartered the Baltimore & Ohio Railroad on February 28, 1827, to build to the Ohio River and funnel commerce to Baltimore. The B&O was the first railroad in the U. S.—"railroad" meaning an incorporated common carrier offering freight and passenger service on regular schedules rather than a simple mine or quarry tramway. Ground was broken for the road on July 4, 1828, by Charles Carroll, last surviving signer of the Declaration of Independence.

In 1828 the commonwealth of Pennsylvania chartered the Main Line of Public Works (an ancestor of the Pennsylvania Railroad), a line of railroads and canals from Philadelphia to the Ohio River. Within a decade railroads pushed inland from Boston and Charleston, South Carolina, and west from Albany along the Erie Canal.

Railroad development along the coast was almost as rapid. By 1838 it was possible to travel from New York to Washington by a combination of boats and trains.

In 1852 the B&O attained its goal, the Ohio River, at Wheeling, West Virginia, and the Pennsylvania Railroad reached the Ohio at Pittsburgh. By early 1854 rails reached from the East Coast to the Mississippi River at Rock Island, Illinois. Three years later a rail route was opened from Charleston, S. C., to Memphis, Tennessee.

To the Pacific! 1850–1885

California joined the United States in 1850. A railroad was necessary to connect it to the rest of the nation and to bring to the marketplaces of the East Coast the legendary wealth of the Orient (then, jade, spices, and silk; later, Toyotas). Five routes were surveyed between 1853 and 1855: a northern route, later followed by Northern Pacific and Great Northern, a central route from Omaha to San Francisco following the Platte River across Nebraska and passing through Salt Lake City, the route ultimately chosen (and later followed by highway I-80); a route from Kansas City to San Francisco across southern Colorado and Utah (where the survey party was massacred), then north over Tehachapi Pass into the San Joaquin Valley; a route from Fort Smith, Arkansas, to Los Angeles, followed by the Rock Island and the Santa Fe (and later, I-40); and a route across central Texas through El Paso to Los Angeles, followed by the Texas & Pacific and the Southern Pacific.

The Civil War settled the question of the route. When the South seceded the advocates of the southern routes went with it. On July 1, 1862, President Abraham Lincoln signed an act authorizing the construction of a railroad from the Missouri River to the Pacific, and in 1863 he signed another setting its track gauge at 4 feet 8½ inches, later to become standard for North America.

"Standard gauge" was not standard in the beginning. Early railroads were built to almost any track gauge. The most common gauge in the North was 4 feet 8½ inches; railroads in the South were usually built to a 5-foot gauge (they were changed to standard gauge in 1886). Narrower gauges, such as 3 feet and 2 feet, were chosen for reasons of economy; wider gauges, such as the 6-foot gauge of the Erie, were adopted for more obscure reasons. Sometimes the reason for choosing a different gauge was so cars could not be interchanged with neighboring railroads. It took time for railroads to realize that interchanging cars was easier than transloading freight.

Central Pacific broke ground in Sacramento in January 1863, and Union Pacific did the same near Omaha at the end of that year. Construction went slowly because of the lack of capital and because of the Civil War, which was occupying the resources of the nation.

The American Civil War is considered the first modern war, and it was the first war in which railroads were strategically and tactically important. Junctions were captured: The First Battle of Bull Run centered on the junction of the Orange & Alexandria and Manassas Gap railroads, and Chattanooga was fought over for more than a year because lines from Richmond to Memphis and from Nashville to Atlanta crossed there. Equipment was seized: The Confederates made two raids on the Baltimore & Ohio at Martinsburg, West Virginia, and dragged locomotives and cars home along dirt roads behind teams of horses. Railroads were destroyed to prevent their use: This was General William T. Sherman's specialty, and destruction was the purpose of James J. Andrews' capture of a Western & Atlantic train at Big Shanty, Ga. (it resulted mostly in a much-described chase of two locomotives, the *General* and the *Texas)*. The railroads moved troops, and on April 2, 1865, less than a week before Lee's surrender at Appomattox, the Richmond & Danville evacuated the Confederate government from Richmond to Danville, Virginia.

The railroads of the South were built primarily to tie inland areas to the coast rather than form a railroad network. Southern railroads seemed loath to arrange through service or even use joint stations in a city—matters that had to be hastily corrected during the war.

Construction of the Union Pacific got under way with the laying of the first rails in July 1865. By then Central Pacific had progressed east out of the foothills and into the Sierra Nevada. The last spike, a gold one, was driven on May 10, 1869, at Promontory, Utah. The first transcontinental railroad was complete. (The term "transcontinental" in U. S. railroad usage refers only to the west half or third of the continent—Omaha to Sacramento, for example, or even Salt Lake City to Oakland, as in the case of the Western Pacific.)

Many of the railroads that opened the West received grants of alternate sections of federally owned land along their route. Attackers of the railroads have pounced on this seeming magnanimity of the government, but the nation got its money's worth. The land was almost valueless without railroads, but with transportation available, the government could double the price of the land it retained. The grants stipulated that the railroads had to provide reduced-rate transportation for government property, mail, and employees, a provision not repealed until 1946. By then the government had received more than ten times the value of the land it had granted.

The 1870s and 1880s saw a tremendous increase in railroad mileage. Every town needed a railroad; two were better than one. If capital were not available locally, it was in Europe, especially from prosperous industrial England, which had more capital than it could invest at home. The railroads of the western U. S. and Canada got more than capital in Europe—they also recruited colonists to inhabit the land they were opening.

Several rail routes to the Pacific were completed in the early 1880s. The Santa Fe met the Southern Pacific at Deming, New Mexico, in 1881. Three routes were completed in 1883: Santa Fe's own route across northern New Mexico and Arizona, SP's line between New Orleans and Los Angeles, and the Northern Pacific from Duluth, Minnesota, to Portland, Oregon. A year later the Union Pacific route to Oregon opened. Canadian Pacific's route across Canada was completed in 1885—and this is a good time for brief summaries of Canadian and Mexican railroad history.

Canada

Canada's first railroad was the Champlain & St. Lawrence Railroad, opened in 1836 between the south bank of the St. Lawrence at Laprairie and St. Johns, Quebec, head of open-water navigation on the Richelieu River, which drains Lake Champlain. Railroads soon spread down the St. Lawrence River Valley into the Maritime Provinces and westward into Ontario.

When British Columbia joined the confederation in 1871, the Canadian government promised a railroad to link the new province with the rest of the country. The principal railroad in Quebec and Ontario, the Grand Trunk, was not interested in a western extension, so the Canadian Pacific Railway was incorporated in 1881 to build from Callander, Ont., near North Bay, to the Pacific at what is now Vancouver. The builders of the railroad were faced with 1,300 miles of wilderness across northern Ontario, 1,000 miles of prairie, and 500 miles of rugged mountains. Construction of the line along the north shore of Lake Superior was extremely difficult, but nationalistic feeling precluded a detour through the U. S. The crossing of the Rockies called for 4.5 percent grades, replaced later by a pair of spiral tunnels. The line was completed on November 7, 1885.

Even while it was constructing its line to the west, the CPR (initials of Canadian roads almost invariably include the "R" for "Railway") was extending eastward to Ottawa and Montreal. By 1890 the road's eastern lines stretched from Windsor, Ont., opposite Detroit, through Montreal and across the state of Maine to Saint John, New Brunswick. CPR spread an extensive network of branches across the wheatlands between Winnipeg and Calgary after 1900, and in 1916 opened a secondary main line through the Kootenay region of southern British Columbia. Part of that line was financed by the government in exchange for a permanent reduction in grain shipping rates—the Crows Nest Pass Agreement of 1897, only recently amended.

Most of eastern Canada's railroads were part of one predecessor or another of Canadian National Railways. Financial difficulty brought these roads under government control between 1915 and 1923. The 3-foot-6-inch gauge Newfoundland Railway was added to CNR in 1949 when Newfoundland joined the confederation. In recent years CNR has built several lines north into the subarctic.

The provinces of Ontario and British Columbia are in the railroad business through ownership of the Ontario Northland Railway and BC Rail. The province of Alberta owned several railroads that were purchased by CNR and CPR jointly in 1929 to form Northern Alberta Railways, now part of CNR.

Mexico

Mexico's railroads have been owned by the government, and the National Railways of Mexico (Ferrocarriles Nacionales de Mexico) has operated most of the country's rail mileage—privatization has begun there. Mexico's first major railroad was one of the last to be nationalized (in 1946), the Ferrocarril Mexicano. It was built between 1864 and 1873 by British interests to connect Mexico City with the Gulf of Mexico at Veracruz. To counteract FCM's monopoly, Mexican president Porfirio Diaz offered concessions or subsidies to railroads between the interior and the coast, preferring for a few years to avoid connections with U. S. railroads.

National Railways of Mexico was incorporated in 1908 as successor to the National Railroad of Mexico, a company in which the Mexican government held a majority interest. National Railways of Mexico acquired the Mexican Central in 1909. During the late 1930s, a period of governmental upheaval, control of the railroad was tossed back and forth among the government, a syndicate of railroad workers, and the railroad's own management.

Both of NdeM's main lines from the U. S. border to Mexico City were built by companies receiving concessions from the government. NdeM's main line south from Ciudad Juarez, across the Rio Grande from El Paso, Tex., through Chihuahua, Torreon, Aguascalientes, and Queretaro, was built by Santa Fe interests as the Mexican Central. It was completed in 1884.

The line from Laredo was begun in 1881 as the 3-foot gauge Mexican National by Gen. William Jackson Palmer, builder of the Denver & Rio Grande. It was completed to Mexico City in 1888 via Monterrey, Saltillo, San Luis Potosi, Acambaro, and Toluca, with branches from Monterrey to Matamoros and from Acambaro to Uruapan. It was standard-gauged as far south as Escobedo in 1903 and a new line was built through Queretaro to Mexico City, roughly parallel to the Mexican Central. National of Mexico operates the two Queretaro–Mexico City lines as double track; both lines were recently replaced by a new double-track electrified line, but the electrification has been abandoned.

The line through Toluca was widened to standard gauge in 1949. The line from Mexico City to Veracruz, on the Gulf of Mexico, via Orizaba, is the former Ferrocarril Mexicano; the Mexico City–Veracruz line via Jalapa is the former 3-foot-gauge Ferrocarril Interoceanico, standard-gauged in 1948.

Three lines on the West Coast only recently became part of NdeM. The Region Pacifico of NdeM, until recently the Ferrocarril del Pacifico, from Nogales, on the Arizona border, to Guadalajara, is the former Southern Pacific of Mexico, completed in 1927. The Region Norte, the former Chihuahua Pacific—before that the Kansas City, Mexico & Orient—cuts diagonally across northwestern Mexico from Ojinaga on the Texas border to Los Mochis on the Gulf of California. It was completed in 1961. NdeM's Baja California Division, from Mexicali to a connection with the Region Pacifico at Benjamin Hill, was built as the Sonora-Baja California Railway by the government and opened in 1948.

United Southeastern Railways, which was formed by the 1969 merger of the United Railways of Yucatan (UdeY) and the Southeastern Railway, has also become part of NdeM. The first portion of the UdeY was opened in 1881; the road developed a system of standard and narrow gauge lines linking much of the state of Yucatan with its capital, Merida, and extending southwest into the neighboring state of Campeche. The UdeY was isolated until the government completed the Southeastern Railway from Allende in the state of Veracruz to the city of Campeche in 1950.

Narrow gauge fever, 1870–1890

The narrow gauge boom, part of the overall railroad boom, ran from roughly 1870 to 1890. The reason usually given for preferring narrow gauge to standard gauge was economy: Smaller locomotives and cars cost less. Another view is that narrow gauge railroads were fresh and new at a time when standard gauge railroads had fallen out of favor with the public (the 6-foot gauge Erie was worst of all).

The advantage of standard gauge was that it was standard (in 1886 the railroads of the South, which had been built to a 5-foot gauge were converted to standard gauge). Financially successful narrow gauge railroads were soon standard-gauged, unless the cargo carried would have to be transloaded anyway or the terrain made the cost of standard-gauging greater than any benefits of through operation.

Time of technology, 1870–1910

The basic items of railroading, rails and rolling stock, came first and refinements later. The first rails were strap iron on top of wooden stringers. Iron rails were introduced in 1830, and steel rails were first used in 1863. The first cars were basically stagecoaches and wagons on flanged wheels. The first double-truck car is sometimes credited to Ross Winans of the Baltimore & Ohio in 1831, but Gridley Bryant constructed one for the Granite Railroad in Quincy, Massachusetts, in 1826. The first locomotives were simple four-wheel machines; one of the first improvements was the lead truck, which helped guide the locomotive around curves.

The pioneers of railroading were more concerned with going than with stopping. Steam-operated locomotive brakes and hand brakes on the cars were a considerable advance over what the first trains used, which included sticks thrust between wheel spokes. George Westinghouse patented an air brake in 1869, others had previously done so. Westinghouse's most significant contribution, a later refinement, was the triple valve that made the system fail-safe.

The first trains were held together by chains. Chains were succeeded by the link-and-pin coupler, which required a man to hold a link in position as the cars came together and remove his hand at the right instant, lest the couplers do so. Eli Janney's automatic coupler of 1873, approved by the Master Car Builders' Association in 1887 made railroading a much safer occupation.

In the 1880s steam heat and electric lights began to replace stoves and oil and gas lamps, which were ready sources of fire in case of an accident—cars were constructed almost entirely of wood. Automatic block signals and electric locomotives appeared in the 1890s, and all-steel cars came in the early 1900s.

Nor was technology limited to the railroads. A few minutes difference in sun time between neighboring cities made little difference when the cities were a day's travel apart. Railroads reduced the time between cities to hours, and the telegraph provided instant communication. To eliminate the confusion caused by a railroad having to use the time of city A in city B, in 1883 the railroads divided the U. S. into four zones with uniform times an hour apart. Gradually others adopted the standard time of the railroads.

Robber barons and regulation, 1880–1920

The U. S. was fast becoming an industrial nation in the late 1800s. Ambitious men who would let nothing block them built industrial empires. Jay Gould, E. H. Harriman, and others assembled railroad systems, buying connecting lines to extend their systems, buying parallel lines to control competition, and sometimes just buying up railroads for the parts. The amount of publicity accorded these titans of industry (or robber barons) is due to the fact that railroads were larger, more conspicuous businesses than anything else—industrial empires and their leaders occupied newspapers and magazines the way rock stars now fill TV screens.

Regulation had its roots in the Midwest and West, where farmers were more dependent on railroads to move their products to market than in the East. The farmers complained that railroad rates were unfair. Favored shippers received rebates, and rates were often higher where one railroad had a monopoly.

Illinois passed legislation in 1871 and 1873 regulating freight rates and passenger fares, and Minnesota did so in 1874. By 1880 pressure for regulation, particularly from the Grange—the National Grange of the Patrons of Husbandry—had shifted to the national level and resulted in the Interstate Commerce Act of 1887.

At first stagecoaches and canal and river boats were the railroads' only competition. The first practical electric streetcar appeared in 1888 and quickly evolved into the electric interurban railway. It was what we now call light rail technology: rolling stock smaller than standard railroad dimensions, track sometimes in the streets and sometimes on private right of way, and emphasis on local service. The steam railroads were suddenly paralleled by competing electric railways. A few roads recognized that the electric lines were going after local traffic, the service steam roads found most expensive to operate, and encouraged neighboring electric lines, but for the most part hostility existed between the two types of railroads.

The interurban wasn't the sole competition for long. Paved highways took away the interurbans' business—the interurban era was over by 1930—then began eating into the traffic of the steam railroads. Many railroads responded by forming bus and truck lines; a few even offered air service.

USRA and the Roaring Twenties, 1917–1930

The U. S. entered World War I on April 6, 1917. Five days later a group of railroad executives pledged their cooperation in the war effort, creating the Railroad War Board. Among the problems the board had to deal with were labor difficulties, a patriotic rush of employees to join the Army, and a glut of supplies for the war effort choking East Coast yards and ports.

The efforts of the board were not enough for the government. On December 26, 1917, President Woodrow Wilson placed U. S. railroads under the jurisdiction of the United States Railroad Administration, whose director was William G. McAdoo, Secretary of the Treasury, Wilson's son-in-law, and, some years previous, builder of the Hudson & Manhattan Railroad (now the Port Authority Trans-Hudson line

between New York, Hoboken, and Newark). The government guaranteed the railroads a rental based on their net operating income for the previous three years. Essentially the government was renting the railroads as one would rent a house, with responsibility for anything lost or damaged. Among McAdoo's acts were the discharge of all railroad presidents, elimination of all rail competition, and a flat $20 wage increase for all employees earning less than $46 a month. The USRA ordered and assigned to railroads more than 2,000 locomotives and 50,000 freight cars of standardized design.

USRA control ended March 1, 1920. The USRA's net operating income for the 26 months of control fell short of the guaranteed payments by $714 million; damage claims were an additional $677 million. One happy legacy of the USRA was its set of 12 standardized locomotive designs, to which locomotives were built as late as 1944.

In 1920 Congress asked the ICC to prepare a plan for merging the railroads of the U. S. into a limited number of systems, preserving competition and existing routes of trade and, where possible, grouping the railroads so the cost of transportation on competing routes would be the same—or in the ICC's words, to equitably parcel out the weak sisters. In 1929 the ICC published its recommendations. Generally, subsidiaries would stay with their parents, short lines would be assigned to the connecting trunk line, and affiliates of the Canadian roads would stay with Canadian National and Canadian Pacific. A few railroads were assigned jointly to more than one system. The systems would have been:

1. **Boston & Maine**; Maine Central; Bangor & Aroostook; Delaware & Hudson

2. **New Haven**; New York, Ontario & Western; Lehigh & Hudson River; Lehigh & New England

3. **New York Central**; Rutland; Virginian; Chicago, Attica & Southern

4. **Pennsylvania**; Long Island

5. **Baltimore & Ohio**; Central of New Jersey; Reading; Buffalo & Susquehanna; Buffalo, Rochester & Pittsburgh; Detroit, Toledo & Ironton (½); Detroit & Toledo Shore Line (½); Monon (½); Chicago & Alton

6. **Chesapeake & Ohio-Nickel Plate**; Hocking Valley; Erie; Pere Marquette; Delaware, Lackawanna & Western; Bessemer & Lake Erie; Chicago & Illinois Midland; Detroit & Toledo Shore Line (½)

7. **Wabash-Seaboard Air Line**; Lehigh Valley; Wheeling & Lake Erie; Pittsburgh & West Virginia; Western Maryland; Akron, Canton & Youngstown; Norfolk & Western; Detroit, Toledo & Ironton (½); Toledo, Peoria & Western; Ann Arbor; Winston-Salem Southbound (½)

8. **Atlantic Coast Line**; Louisville & Nashville; Nashville, Chattanooga & St. Louis; Clinchfield; Atlanta, Birmingham & Coast Gulf, Mobile & Northern; New Orleans Great Northern; Monon (¼), Winston-Salem Southbound (½)

9. **Southern**; Norfolk Southern; Tennessee Central (east of Nashville); Florida East Coast; Monon (¼)

10. **Illinois Central**; Central of Georgia; Minneapolis & St. Louis; Tennessee Central (west of Nashville); Cotton Belt; Atlanta & St. Andrews Bay

11. **Chicago & North Western**; Chicago & Eastern Illinois; Litchfield & Madison; Mobile &

Ohio; Columbus & Greenville; Lake Superior & Ishpeming

12. Great Northern-Northern Pacific; Spokane, Portland & Seattle; Butte, Anaconda & Pacific (½)

13. Milwaukee Road; Escanaba & Lake Superior; Duluth, Missabe & Northern; Duluth & Iron Range; Butte, Anaconda & Pacific (½); trackage rights on SP&S to Portland

14. Burlington; Colorado & Southern; Fort Worth & Denver; Green Bay & Western; Missouri-Kansas-Texas; Trinity & Brazos Valley (½); Oklahoma City-Ada-Atoka

15. Union Pacific; Kansas City Southern

16. Southern Pacific

17. Santa Fe; Chicago Great Western; Kansas City, Mexico & Orient; Missouri & North Arkansas; Midland Valley; Minneapolis, Northfield & Southern

18. Missouri Pacific; Texas & Pacific; Kansas, Oklahoma & Gulf; Denver & Rio Grande Western; Denver & Salt Lake; Western Pacific; Fort Smith & Western

19. Rock Island-Frisco; Alabama, Tennessee & Northern; Trinity & Brazos Valley (½); Louisiana & Arkansas; Meridian & Bigbee

The plan caused great discussion, usually beginning with "The Pennsylvania is already big enough." No one, not even the creators of the plan, was happy with all facets of it. By 1932 most of the Wabash-Seaboard system had been reassigned to others, because both principals had entered receivership (Seaboard was left unallocated)—and most of the railroads in the Wabash-Seaboard system were controlled by the Pennsylvania. Any tinkering to correct an imbalance here resulted in three imbalances there. Congress withdrew the matter in 1940.

Depression and the diesel, 1930–1939

The Great Depression was no easier for the railroads than for anyone else. As business declined, railroads had less freight and fewer passengers to carry. Locomotives and cars were stored or scrapped. Dozens of railroads declared bankruptcy, including such major lines as Frisco, Missouri Pacific, Milwaukee Road, and New Haven. Only the strongest survived unscathed.

During the 1920s a few railroads and a few locomotive builders had experimented with internal combustion engines in gas-electric passenger cars and diesel-electric switch engines. The former could replace a two-or three-car local passenger train and be operated with fewer men; the latter had the advantages over steam of cleanliness and instant availability—it could be turned on and off as needed. In both, an internal combustion engine (gasoline or diesel) drove a generator, which in turn produced electric current for traction motors that drove the wheels.

In the early 1930s two railroads and two carbuilders ventured combinations of internal combustion and streamlining. Two trains emerged in 1934, Union Pacific's aluminum *M-10000*, built by Pullman-Standard, and Burlington's stainless steel *Zephyr*, built by Budd. Both had power plants built by Electro-Motive Corporation, a subsidiary of General Motors: the UP train a spark-ignition distillate engine, the Burlington train a diesel. Both trains toured the country, and the *Zephyr* made a dawn-to-dark run from Denver to Chicago. They captured the attention of the public and the railroad industry.

UP and Burlington quickly acquired fleets of diesel streamliners, and so did other railroads. The streamliners were of lighter-weight construction than conventional passenger trains; two mechanical innovations they included were air-conditioning and roller bearings on the axles. The use of roller bearings soon spread to freight cars. The diesel proved to be separable from the train. In 1935 Baltimore & Ohio and Santa Fe bought diesels from Electro-Motive to pull conventional trains, and EMC passenger diesels became the usual power for the new streamliners.

In 1939 Electro-Motive produced a four-unit, 5400-horsepower freight diesel demonstrator, No. 103, a locomotive *Trains* editor David P. Morgan called "the most significant piece of motive power since Stephenson's *Rocket*." (*Rocket's* success in the trials at Rainhill in 1830 led the directors of the infant Liverpool & Manchester Railway to choose the steam locomotive to power their trains.) More than any other locomotive, EMC 103 was responsible for the dieselization of American railroads.

War and wither away, 1940–1960

During World War II U. S. railroads remained in control of their affairs. Freight traffic doubled and passenger business quadrupled. Then the war was over. Detroit set out to satisfy a populace that hadn't seen a new automobile in four years, and the railroads tried to erase the memory of wartime travel conditions with new trains and new cars and innovations like the Vista-Dome.

By the mid-1950s the automobile had killed the local passenger train, and the Interstate highway system and the passenger jet airplane would soon start the decline of the long-distance train.

Losses from passenger trains caused the railroads to cut back services and discontinue trains; the public responded by riding less and less. The decline accelerated in the late 1960s when the Post Office withdrew mail from most passenger trains in favor of trucks, planes, and a new sorting system. By 1970 train riding was only for the most determined.

On May 1, 1971, the National Railroad Passenger Corporation, doing business under the name Amtrak, took over most of the nation's passenger trains. The government company immediately discontinued approximately two-thirds of the remaining passenger trains and set out to beef up business on those that remained.

The Interstate highway system was as beneficial for trucks as it was for cars. The railroads soon lost their less-than-carload merchandise traffic, though much of that was picked up by freight forwarders who filled trailers and towed them across town to the railroad's trailer-on-flat-car terminal. Perishable and livestock traffic declined.

Innovative equipment, though, increased other categories of freight business. The railroads had long since lost the new-automobile business, but they brought it back, using bilevel and trilevel rack cars twice as long and half again as high as the automobile box cars they replaced. Boxcars the same size as the rack cars were developed for auto parts, which are light but bulky. Grain began to move in huge covered hopper cars, easier to load and unload than box cars, and like coal, it moved in unit trains, solid trains moved intact from origin to destination. Piggyback traffic, trailers and containers on flat cars, became the hottest commodity the railroads moved.

The merger era, 1957–1985

Some date the modern merger era from the spring of 1947, when three mergers occurred: Gulf, Mobile & Ohio and Alton; Denver & Rio Grande Western and Denver & Salt Lake; and Chesapeake & Ohio and Pere Marquette. Others choose as the kickoff date August 30, 1957, when Louisville & Nashville merged Nashville, Chattanooga & St. Louis. At first it seemed only the smaller, regional roads were disappearing. Then in 1963 Chesapeake & Ohio acquired control of Baltimore & Ohio. C&O had traditionally been associated with Erie and Nickel Plate. A year later the Norfolk & Western merged the Nickel Plate, leased the Wabash and the Pittsburgh & West Virginia, and acquired control of the Akron, Canton & Youngstown. N&W and Wabash had long been affiliates of the Pennsylvania. Then N&W and C&O announced the possibility of merger.

As confirmation that traditional alliances were out, rivals Pennsylvania and New York Central announced their impending merger to form Penn Central. In 1964 Union Pacific, which had relied on Chicago & North Western and later Milwaukee Road to forward its streamliners to and from Chicago, proposed merger with the Rock Island. The ICC proceedings on the UP-RI merger were the longest in history, and by the time they were done, the Rock Island was in such poor shape that UP didn't want it.

Penn Central lasted little more than two years before becoming the biggest single bankruptcy in U. S. history. From its wreckage and that of several smaller roads the federal government formed Consolidated Rail Corporation on April 1, All Fools' Day, 1976. Conrail lived down

its birthday and began to show profits in 1981.

Other major recent mergers include Southern and Norfolk & Western to form Norfolk Southern; Seaboard System and Chessie System (themselves both products of mergers) to form CSX Transportation; Burlington Northern and Santa Fe; and Union Pacific, which in the past two decades has merged Western Pacific, Missouri Pacific, Missouri-Kansas-Texas, Chicago & North Western, and Southern Pacific (which included Denver & Rio Grande Western).

Spinoffs and regionals, 1976–1990

Conrail did not include all the lines of its predecessors. Many branch and secondary lines were sold to become locally operated short lines. The demise of the Rock Island and the shrinkage of the Milwaukee Road similarly occasioned the creation of several new short lines. In the early 1980s it appeared the U. S. would soon have a handful of huge railroads and a great many short lines. Then Illinois Central Gulf began to turn itself into a lean north-south railroad by spinning off secondary lines and east-west routes to form regional railroads, railroads in the 100-to-1000-mile range. Soo Line in effect bought the Milwaukee Road, moved in, and sold its own lines east of the Twin Cities to form the Wisconsin Central. Most of the large railroads spun off branch and secondary lines to form regional railroads (of a size that used to be considered Class 1) and short lines.

Deregulation and renaissance, 1980–2000

On October 14, 1980, President Jimmy Carter signed into law the Staggers Rail Act (named for Rep. Harley O. Staggers of West Virginia). It was massive deregulation of the railroads, including provisions to raise any rate that falls below 160 percent of out-of-pocket costs (later 180 percent) and to enter into contracts with shippers to set price and service, both without ICC approval.

Railroads are no less important and no less interesting now than they were in 1930. Even though the railroads' share of the intercity freight business has dropped in the intervening years from three-quarters to a bit more than one-third, ton-miles have doubled—railroads are carrying the same amount of cargo twice as far (or twice the amount the same distance). Statistics comparing U. S. Class 1 railroads in 1930 and 1980 shed light on the nature of the changes. (More recent statistics cannot be compared because of changes in reporting criteria after 1980.)

	1930	1980	Notes
Trackage operated (miles)	429,883	290,000	1
Number of employees	1,660,850	458,994	
Locomotives in service	56,582	28,396	
Freight cars in service	2,276,867	1,710,827	
Average freight car capacity (tons)	46.6	80.4	
Loaded freight cars moved	45,877,974	21,613,063	
Revenue ton-miles (millions)	383,450	918,621	
Passenger cars in service	52,130	4,347	2
Revenue passenger miles (millions)	26,815	11,500	
Average trip per passenger (miles)	38.11	37.97	3
Average trip per Amtrak passenger (miles)		216.7	

Notes:

1. 1980 figure includes sidings, yards, and additional main tracks.

2. 1980 figure does not include several hundred commuter cars.

3. Figures are for all classes of railroads.

This says that railroads of today are using a little more than half the hardware they did in 1930 to create more than twice as much of their product, which is ton-miles. The commuter business dominates the passenger statistics; the passenger-car count reflects the sleeping car of 1930, which held 27 passengers if all the upper berths were sold (and usually they weren't), and today's commuter coach of 1980, which seats 100 passengers or more.

There are fewer railroad companies today than in 1930, but they are just as fascinating and colorful. The Atlantic Coast Line and the New Haven and the Rock Island are gone. Start turning the pages to find out where they went and what they were—and perhaps how much remains of them.

Akron, Canton & Youngstown Railway

The Akron, Canton & Youngstown Railway was incorporated in 1907 and completed a line from Mogadore to Akron, Ohio, 8 miles, in 1913. In 1920 the AC&Y obtained control of the Northern Ohio Railway from the Lake Erie & Western. The Northern Ohio had a 161-mile route from Akron west to Delphos, Ohio. AC&Y also purchased outright a 9-mile portion of the Northern Ohio from Akron to Copley Junction.

Akron was noted for the manufacture of tires, and over the years tires and inner tubes moving from Akron to Detroit via the Detroit, Toledo & Ironton interchange at Columbus Grove constituted a significant part of AC&Y's freight traffic.

On January 14, 1944, the AC&Y and the Northern Ohio were consolidated as the Akron, Canton & Youngstown Railroad. In 1947 AC&Y considered extending its line east to Youngstown for access to the steel industry there and also to serve as a route around the congestion of Cleveland, but nothing came of it.

In 1949 AC&Y's president proposed a 130-mile Ohio River-to-Lake Erie two-way

Two Akron, Canton & Youngstown hood units, both products of Fairbanks-Morse, assemble a train at Carey, Ohio, about 1963. Photo by Roger Meade.

	1929	1964
Miles of railroad operated:	171	171
Number of locomotives:	25	18
Number of passenger cars:	5	
Number of freight cars:	223	
Number of company service cars:	28	
Number of freight and company service cars:	1,687	

Location of headquarters: Akron, Ohio
Reporting marks: ACY
Historical and technical society: Akron, Canton & Youngstown Historical Society, P. O. Box 196, Sharon Center, OH 44274-0096
Subsidiaries and affiliated railroads, 1964: Akron & Barberton Belt (25%)
Successors: Norfolk & Western, Wheeling & Lake Erie
Portions still operated: Wheeling & Lake Erie: Mogadore—Carey

conveyor belt. AC&Y was, understandably, the only railroad to support the proposal or to advocate passage of bills by the Ohio legislature granting right of eminent domain to the conveyor belt company.

Norfolk & Western purchased the AC&Y in 1964 at the time it merged with the Nickel Plate and leased the Wabash. N&W dissolved the AC&Y on January 1, 1982. The Wheeling & Lake Erie Railway (the 1990 company) purchased the remaining portion of the AC&Y in 1990.

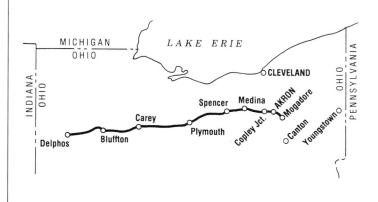

Alabama, Tennessee & Northern Railroad

The Carrollton Short Line Railway was chartered in 1897. By 1906, when its name was changed to Alabama, Tennessee & Northern Railroad, it had built a line from Reform, Ala., through Carrollton to Aliceville and was pushing slowly down the western edge of Alabama toward the Gulf of Mexico. The company underwent foreclosure and reorganization in 1918, and by 1920 the road reached south to Calvert, Ala., where the Southern Railway offered a connection to Mobile.

In 1928 AT&N completed its own line from Calvert to Mobile and that same year entered into an agreement with the Saint Louis-San Francisco Railway (which had just built a line from Aberdeen, Mississippi, to Pensacola, Florida, making a connection with the AT&N at Aliceville) for joint handling of through traffic between the Port of Mobile and points on the Frisco.

AT&N's finances were again reorganized in October 1944. On December 28, 1948, Frisco purchased 97.2 percent of AT&N's common stock (later increasing its holdings to 100 percent) and unified AT&N's operations with its own. The Alabama, Tennessee & Northern was merged with the Frisco on January 1, 1971. Frisco itself became part of Burlington

Burdened by the enormous volume of wartime traffic moving through the Port of Mobile, AT&N obtained War Production Board clearance for diesel purchases. Eleven Alco RS-1s like No. 102 and two small GE switchers allowed the road to completely dieselize by 1946, one of the first roads its size to do so. Photo by Grady W. Robarts Jr.; collection of Louis A. Marre.

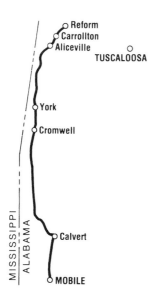

	1929	1970
Miles of railroad operated:	224	214
Number of locomotives:	19	1
Number of passenger cars:	14	
Number of freight cars:	419	1
Number of company service cars:	8	17

Location of headquarters: Mobile, Alabama
Reporting marks: AT&N

Historical and technical societies:
Frisco Modelers Information Group, 1212 Finnean's Run, Arnold, MD 21012-1876; http://www.frisco.org/fmig /fmig.htm

Frisco Railroad Museum, 54 Commercial St., Springfield, MO 65803-2945; http://www.frisco. org/frisco/ frisco.html

Successors:
St. Louis-San Francisco
Burlington Northern

Northern on September 21, 1980. The line was abandoned in the 1980s in favor of trackage rights to Mobile on Norfolk Southern rails. AT&N's terminal trackage in Mobile is still in operation.

Algoma Central & Hudson Bay Railway

The Algoma Central Railway was chartered in 1899 to build into the Ontario wilderness north of Sault Ste. Marie. Its purpose was to bring out pulpwood and iron ore. In 1901 the ambitions of its founder added "& Hudson Bay" to the corporate title. The line reached Hawk Junction, 165 miles north of Sault Ste. Marie, in 1912. From there a branch ran west through an iron-mining district to Michipicoten Harbor on Lake Superior. In 1914 the railroad was completed to a junction with the National Transcontinental Railway (a predecessor of Canadian National Railways) at Hearst, 297 miles from Sault Ste. Marie.

In recent decades the Algoma Central was known for its excursion trains from Sault Ste. Marie to the Agawa River canyon, where the railroad developed a park. The name of the company reverted to Algoma Central Railway in 1965, and in 1990 the company was renamed Algoma Central Corporation, with the railway as a subsidiary. The company also had shipping, trucking, real estate, and land and forest subsidiaries.

The expanding Wisconsin Central purchased the Algoma Central in January 1995.

An early affiliate of the Algoma Central was the Algoma Eastern Railway, which ran west from Sudbury, Ont., through Drury and Espan-ola to Little Current, on Manitoulin Island, 86.9 miles. For nearly 50 miles it paralleled Canadian Pacific's Sudbury–Sault Ste. Marie line. Canadian Pacific leased the Algoma Eastern in 1930.

	1929	1994
Miles of railroad operated:	324	322
Number of locomotives:	22	23
Number of passenger cars:	12	45
Number of freight cars:	1,133	947
Number of company service cars:	81	133

Reporting marks: AC, ACIS
Location of headquarters: Sault Ste. Marie, Ontario
Recommended reading:
Algoma Central Railway, by O. S. Nock, published in 1975 by A & C Black Limited, London (ISBN 0-7136-1571-0)
The Algoma Central Story, by Dale Wilson, published in 1984 by Nickel Belt Rails, P. O. Box 483, Station B, Sudbury, ON P3E 4P6 (ISBN 0-920356-05-2)
Successors: Wisconsin Central
Portions still operated: Wisconsin Central: Sault Ste. Marie–Hearst, Hawk Junction–Michipicoten

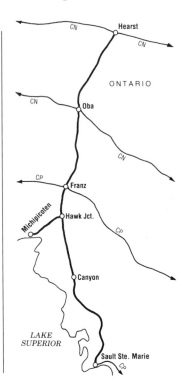

Alton Railroad

The Alton & Sangamon Railroad was chartered in 1847 to build a railroad connecting the agricultural area centered on Springfield, Illinois, with Alton, on the east bank of the Mississippi River 20 miles north of St. Louis. The railroad opened in 1851. During the ensuing decade it built a line north through Bloomington to Joliet and was renamed the St. Louis, Alton & Chicago Railroad. The Chicago & Alton Railroad was organized in 1861 to purchase the StLA&C.

In 1864 the Chicago & Alton leased the Joliet & Chicago Railroad to gain access to Chicago. Timothy B. Blackstone, president of the Joliet & Chicago, became president of the C&A. In 1870 the C&A leased the Louisiana & Missouri River Railroad (Louisiana, Mo., to the north bank of the Missouri River opposite Jefferson City) and in 1878 it leased the Kansas City, St. Louis & Chicago Railroad (Mexico, Mo.–Kansas City), creating the shortest Chicago–Kansas City route. (In 1888 the Santa Fe completed a Chicago–Kansas City route that was 32 miles shorter.)

By the end of the nineteenth century the Chicago & Alton had attracted the notice of Gould, Rockefeller, and Harriman, each of whom could find a place in his rail empire for the road. Harriman formed a syndicate of railroad financiers who were able to meet Blackstone's terms (basically $175 per $100 share of

Alton's motive-power policy was doubtless influenced by that of its parent, Baltimore & Ohio, one of the first railroads to use diesels in passenger service. Alton's E7s, built in early 1945, were among the very first of that model. Two are shown here soon after they arrived on the property bringing the southbound *Ann Rutledge* across the tracks of the Peoria & Eastern (nearer the camera) and the Nickel Plate into Bloomington, Illinois. Photo by Henry J. McCord.

common stock and $200 per share for preferred; Blackstone controlled one-third of the stock), and in 1899 the syndicate purchased 95 percent of the stock. The Chicago & Alton then issued bonds, which the stockholders bought cheap and resold dear to the public, and the railroad used the proceeds of the bond sale to issue a 30 percent cash dividend on its stock.

The Chicago & Alton Railway was incorporated April 2, 1900, to take over a line from Springfield to Peoria, and on the following day it leased the Chicago & Alton Railroad. The two companies were consolidated as the Chicago & Alton Railroad in 1906. In 1904 control passed to the Union Pacific and the Rock Island, and in 1907 to the Toledo, St. Louis & Western (the Clover Leaf, later part of the Nickel Plate).

In 1912 the Chicago & Alton began a string of deficit years that continued almost unbroken to 1941. It lost much of the coal traffic it had carried to Chicago, and the cattle trade from Kansas City disappeared (Blackstone had been one of the developers of the Chicago Union Stockyards). In 1922 the Chicago & Alton entered receivership.

The Baltimore & Ohio, perhaps in an expansionist mood brought on by the Interstate Commerce Commission's proposal to consolidate the railroads of the U. S. into 19 systems, purchased the road at a foreclosure sale in 1929. B&O incorporated the Alton Railroad on January 7, 1931, and on July 18 of that year the Alton purchased the property of the Chicago & Alton Railroad. For 12 years the Alton was operated as part of the B&O, but on March 10, 1943, B&O restored its independence. Several midwestern railroads considered purchasing the Alton but declined; Gulf, Mobile & Ohio offered merger. In 1945 GM&O paid B&O approximately $1.2 million for all its claims against the Alton and all its Alton stock. The effective date of the merger was May 31, 1947.

	1929	1945
Miles of railroad operated:	1,028	959
Number of locomotives:	292	193
Number of passenger cars:	232	112
Number of freight cars:	13,066	5,362
Number of company service cars:	571	391

Location of headquarters: Chicago, Illinois

Reporting marks: C&A

Notable named passenger trains: *Alton Limited, Abraham Lincoln, Ann Rutledge* (Chicago–St. Louis)

Historical and technical society: Gulf, Mobile & Ohio Historical Society, P. O. Box 2457, Joliet, IL 60434-2457; http://www.tfs.net/~jashaw/rhs/gmo.html

Recommended reading: *The Gulf, Mobile & Ohio*, by James Hutton Lemly, published in 1953 by Richard D. Irwin, Inc., Homewood, IL 60430

GM&O North, by Robert P. Olmsted, published in 1976 by Robert P. Olmsted

Successors:
Gulf, Mobile & Ohio
Illinois Central Gulf
Chicago, Missouri & Western
Gateway Western
SPCSL
Union Pacific

Portions still operated:
Gateway Western: Springfield, Ill.–Kansas City; Godfrey–Roodhouse, Ill.; Murrayville–Jacksonville, Ill.; Mexico–Fulton, Mo.
Union Pacific: Chicago–East St. Louis

Ann Arbor Railroad

The history of the Ann Arbor began with two companies organized in 1869 and 1872 to build a railroad between Toledo, Ohio, and Ann Arbor, Michigan, about 45 miles. The Panic of 1873 killed one of those two companies; it took another 20 years and 12 companies, most of them named Toledo, Ann Arbor & something, for the railroad to reach the eastern shore of Lake Michigan at Frankfort, Mich. (The Toledo–Frankfort line was the road's sole route until the late 1960s, when it acquired its only branch, a 4-mile New York Central remnant from Pittsfield to Saline, Mich.) From Elberta, across a small inlet from Frankfort, the Ann Arbor operated car ferry lines to Kewaunee and Manitowoc, Wisconsin, and Menominee and Manistique, Mich.

The Ann Arbor Railroad was incorporated in 1895 as a reorganization of the Toledo, Ann Arbor & North Michigan Railroad. The Detroit, Toledo & Ironton obtained control of the Ann Arbor in 1905 but sold its interests in 1910. In 1911 the Ann Arbor purchased all the capital stock of the Manistique & Lake Superior Railroad, which extended north from Manistique, Mich., to connections with the Duluth, South Shore & Atlantic and the Lake Superior & Ishpeming.

In 1925 the Wabash, which was controlled by Pennsylvania Railroad interests, acquired control of the Ann Arbor. By 1930 it held more than

Behind a pair of Alco FA-2s painted like those of parent Wabash, a local freight works north out of Ann Arbor bound for Owosso, the road's operating headquarters, in 1952. Photo by Robert A. Hadley.

97 percent of Ann Arbor's stock. Ann Arbor was in receivership from December 4, 1931, to January 1, 1943, but did not reorganize.

Never a major passenger carrier, Ann Arbor discontinued its last passenger train in 1950 and gave its full attention to freight service, largely through traffic using the Lake Michigan ferries to bypass Chicago. The road was completely dieselized by 1951.

In 1963 Wabash sold the Ann Arbor to the Detroit, Toledo & Ironton (which was owned by the Wabash and the Pennsy). The Manistique & Lake Superior and the connecting 100-mile car ferry route were abandoned in 1968. In 1970 the ICC authorized abandonment of the ferry route between Frankfort and Menominee (80 miles) and the facilities at Menominee.

On October 16, 1973, Ann Arbor declared

	1929	1972
Miles of railroad operated:	294	300
Miles of car ferry route:	319	139
Number of locomotives:	50	15
Number of passenger cars:	25	
Number of freight cars:	2,082	
Number of company service cars:	97	
Number of freight and company service cars:		454
Number of car ferries:	6	3

Location of headquarters: Toledo, Ohio
Reporting marks: AA
Historical and technical society: Ann Arbor Technical and Historical Association, P. O. Box 51, Chesaning, MI 48616-0051
Successors:
Michigan Interstate
Michigan Northern
Tuscola & Saginaw Bay
Ann Arbor Railroad (1988)
Portions still operated:
Ann Arbor: Toledo–Ann Arbor, Pittsfield–Saline, Mich.
Tuscola & Saginaw Bay: Ann Arbor–Thompsonville

bankruptcy. On April 1, 1976, it ceased operation as a railroad and Conrail took over its operation. The state of Michigan then purchased the railroad from the DT&I and arranged for its operation by Michigan Interstate Railway. The remaining car ferry lines from Frankfort to Manitowoc (79 miles) and Kewaunee (60 miles) ceased operation in April 1982.

In 1983 because of disputes over terms and payments, operation of the former Ann Arbor was split among three railroads: Michigan Interstate, Tuscola & Saginaw Bay, and Michigan Northern. In 1984 T&SB took over Michigan Northern's portion of the Ann Arbor. A new Ann Arbor Railroad was incorporated in 1988 to operate the line between Toledo and Ann Arbor.

Atchison, Topeka & Santa Fe Railway

By the mid-1600s the city of Santa Fe was established as the seat of government of the Spanish colony of New Mexico and as a trading center. Trade between the United States and New Mexico began in 1822, and a trail was established between Independence, Missouri, just east of Kansas City, and Santa Fe. It ran west to what is now La Junta, Colorado, south over Raton Pass, then west over the Sangre de Cristo Mountains to Santa Fe.

The Atchison & Topeka Railroad was chartered in 1859 to join the towns of its title and continue southwest toward Santa Fe. "Santa Fe" was added to the corporate name in 1863. Construction started in 1869; by the end of 1872 the road extended to the Kansas-Colorado border, opening much of Kansas to settlement and carrying wheat and cattle east to markets. The railroad temporarily set aside its goal of Santa Fe and continued building west, reaching Pueblo, Colorado, in 1876, just in time for the silver rush at Leadville.

In 1878 the railroad resumed construction toward Santa Fe: southwest from La Junta to Trinidad, then south over Raton Pass. It chose that route instead of an easier route south across the plains from Dodge City because of hostile Indians and a lack of water on the southerly route and and coal deposits near Trinidad, Colorado, and Raton, New Mexico.

Mikado 4023 leads a freight at Syracuse, Kansas, on October 8, 1941. Photo by John W. Maxwell.

The Denver & Rio Grande was also aiming at Raton Pass, but Santa Fe crews arose early one morning in 1878 and were hard at work with picks and shovels when the Rio Grande crews showed up after breakfast. At the same time the two railroads skirmished over occupancy of the Royal Gorge of the Arkansas River west of Canon City, Colo.; the Rio Grande won that battle.

The Santa Fe reached Albuquerque in 1880 (because of geography the city of Santa Fe found itself at the end of a short branch from Lamy, N. M.) and connected with the Southern Pacific at Deming, N. M., in 1881. The Santa Fe then built southwest from Benson, Arizona, to Nogales, on the Mexican border. There it connected with the Sonora Railway, which Santa Fe interests had constructed north from the Mexican port of Guaymas.

Atlantic & Pacific

The Atlantic & Pacific Railroad was chartered in 1866 to build west from Springfield, Missouri, through Amarillo, Texas, and Albuquerque, New Mexico, to a junction with the Southern Pacific at the Colorado River. The infant A&P had no rail connections. The line that was to become the St. Louis-San Francisco Railway (the Frisco) wouldn't reach Springfield for another 4 years, and SP did not build east from Mojave to the Colorado River until 1883. The A&P started construction in 1868, built southwest into what would become Oklahoma, and entered receivership. As an operating railroad the A&P dropped out of sight briefly, but not as a charter and corporate structure.

In 1879 the A&P struck a deal with the Santa Fe and the Frisco: Those railroads would jointly build and own the A&P west of Albuquerque. Construction began at Albuquerque, and in 1883

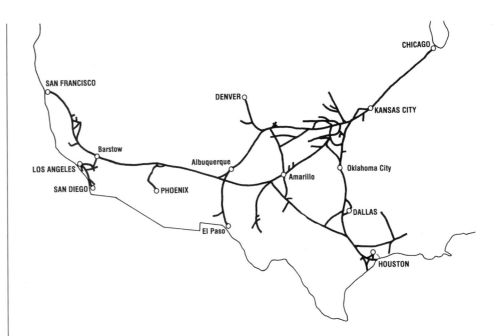

the A&P reached Needles, California, and a connection with the SP. Construction still hadn't begun on the Tulsa-Albuquerque portion of the Atlantic & Pacific.

Expansion

The Santa Fe began to expand:
• a line from Barstow, Calif., to San Diego in 1885 and to Los Angeles in 1887

• control of the Gulf, Colorado & Santa Fe (Galveston to Fort Worth) in 1886 and construction of a line between Wichita and Fort Worth in 1887
• lines from Kansas City to Chicago, from Kiowa, Kansas, to Amarillo, Texas, and from Pueblo to Denver (paralleling the Denver & Rio Grande) in 1888
• purchase of the Frisco and the Colorado Midland in 1890

No railroad image is better known than Santa Fe's red-and-silver "Warbonnet" diesel paint scheme. A four-unit set of F3s displays the colors as it pulls train 20, the Los Angeles–Chicago *Chief*, up Glorieta Pass between Lamy and Las Vegas, New Mexico on October 4, 1947. Photo by R. H. Kindig.

The depression of 1893 had the same effect on the Santa Fe that it had on many other railroads: financial problems and subsequent reorganization. In 1895 Santa Fe sold the Frisco and the Colorado Midland and wrote off the losses, but it retained control of the Atlantic & Pacific, and purchased it in 1898.

The Santa Fe still wanted to reach California on its own rails (it leased the Southern Pacific line from Needles through Barstow to Mojave),

and the state of California eagerly courted the Santa Fe in order to break SP's monopoly. In 1897 the Santa Fe traded the Sonora Railway to Southern Pacific for the SP line between Barstow and Mojave, giving the Santa Fe its own line from Chicago to the Pacific—Santa Fe all the way.

Subsequent expansion of the Santa Fe encompassed:
• a line from Amarillo to Pecos in 1899
• a line from Ash Fork, Ariz., to Phoenix in 1901
• the Belen Cutoff from the Pecos line at Texico to Isleta, south of Albuquerque, bypassing the grades of Raton Pass in 1907)
• the Coleman Cutoff, from Texico to Coleman, Texas, near Brownwood in 1912

In 1907 Santa Fe and Southern Pacific jointly formed the Northwestern Pacific Railroad, which took over several short railroads and built new lines connecting them to form a route from San Francisco north to Eureka. In 1928 Santa Fe sold its half of the NWP to Southern Pacific.

Also in 1928 the Santa Fe purchased the U. S. portion of the Kansas City, Mexico & Orient Railway as a way to reach the oilfields of west Texas. Post–World War II construction projects included an entrance to Dallas from the north and relocation of the main line across northern Arizona.

Because long stretches of its main line traversed areas without water, Santa Fe was one of the first purchasers of diesel locomotives for road freight service. The road was known for its passenger trains, notably the Chicago-Los Angeles *Super Chief*, and for the on-line eating houses and dining cars operated by Fred Harvey.

	1929	1994
Miles of railroad operated:	13,157	7,800
Number of locomotives:	1,993	1,696
Number of passenger cars:	1,511	510*
Number of freight cars:	87,060	29,947
Number of company service cars:	5,913	1,696

Location of headquarters: Chicago until 1991, then Schaumburg, Illinois

Reporting marks: ATSF

Notable named passenger trains: *Chief, Super Chief, El Capitan* (Chicago-Los Angeles), *Texas Chief* (Chicago-Houston)

Historical and technical society: Santa Fe Historical and Modeling Society, 9847 S. Spring Hill Lane, Highlands Ranch, CO 80126

Recommended reading:
History of the Atchison, Topeka and Santa Fe Railway, by Keith L. Bryant, Jr., published in 1974 by Macmillan Publishing Co., New York (ISBN 0-02-517920-9)

Golden Years of Railroading: Santa Fe in the Mountains, by George H. Drury, published in 1995 by Kalmbach Publishing Co., P. O. Box 1612, Waukesha, WI 53187 (ISBN 0-89024-229-1)

Successor: Burlington Northern & Santa Fe

*(1970)

Mergers

In 1960 the Santa Fe bought the Toledo, Peoria & Western Railroad, then sold a half interest to the Pennsylvania Railroad. The TP&W cut straight east across Illinois from near Fort Madison, Iowa, to a connection with the Pennsy at Effner, Indiana, forming a bypass around Chicago for traffic moving between the two lines. The TP&W route didn't mesh with the traffic pattern Conrail developed after 1976, so Santa Fe bought back the other half, merged the TP&W in 1983, then sold it back into independence in 1989.

During the 1960s the Santa Fe explored merger with the Frisco and the Missouri Pacific with no success. By 1980 Santa Fe, which had been the top road in route mileage in the 1950s, was surrounded by larger railroads. It was well managed and profitable, and it had the best route between the Midwest and Southern California, but its neighbors were larger, and friendly connections had been taken over by rival railroads. Southern Pacific was in the same situation. In 1980 Santa Fe and SP proposed merger. Approval seemed certain, but in 1986 the Interstate Commerce Commission denied permission because the merger would create a railroad monopoly in New Mexico, Arizona, and California.

The Santa Fe, suddenly the smallest of the Super Seven freight railroads, began spinning off branches and secondary lines and became primarily a conduit for containers and trailers moving between the Midwest and Southern California. In June 1994 Santa Fe and Burlington Northern announced their intention to merge—BN would buy Santa Fe. The deal was consummated in 1995.

Atlanta & West Point Rail Road
Western Railway of Alabama, Georgia Railroad

The Atlanta & West Point and the Western Railway of Alabama were together known as the West Point Route. They were affiliated with the Georgia Railroad, which was not a corporation but rather the representative of the Louisville & Nashville and the Atlantic Coast Line as lessees of the railroad properties of the Georgia Railroad & Banking Co. The Georgia Railroad & Banking Co. held substantial interests in the two West Point Route railroads. (Ownership and control of these three railroads was particularly convoluted; for most purposes it is sufficient to say they were in the Atlantic Coast Line family.) The West Point Route and the Georgia shared officers and *Official Guide* pages and were for most purposes considered a single entity.

Georgia Railroad

The Georgia Railroad was chartered in 1833 and amended its name to include "& Banking Company" in 1836. Its charter specified exemption from state and local taxation except for a small tax on net earnings. Construction was begun at Augusta, Ga., in 1835, and chief engineer J. Edgar Thomson completed the 171-mile 5-foot-gauge main line to Atlanta in 1845. (Two

Atlanta & West Point 427, a light Mikado of USRA design, leads a northbound freight between semaphore signals near Newnan, Georgia, in March 1949. Photo by R. D. Sharpless.

years later Thomson became chief engineer of the Pennsylvania Railroad.) In 1878 the Georgia Railroad absorbed the Macon & Augusta, which formed a branch from Camak to Macon.

The Georgia Railroad acquired stock in the Atlanta & West Point and in 1875 purchased the Western of Alabama jointly with the Central Railroad & Banking Co. of Georgia. In May 1881 William Wadley leased the Georgia Railroad and its holdings in the West Point Route. He assigned

Georgia Railroad train 1 rolls west through Robinson, Georgia, on its run between Augusta and Atlanta, two days after Christmas 1965. Mail, baggage, and express revenue obviously will outstrip passenger receipts today. Photo by Victor Hand.

the lease jointly to the Louisville & Nashville and the Central of Georgia. CofG's interest later passed to the L&N, which assigned it to Atlantic Coast Line.

Atlanta & West Point

The Atlanta & La Grange Rail Road was chartered in 1847. In 1854 it opened a 5-foot-gauge line from East Point, Ga., 6 miles from Atlanta, through La Grange to West Point, Ga., on the Alabama state line. It obtained trackage rights into Atlanta on the Macon & Western. In 1857 the road was renamed Atlanta & West Point.

Early in its existence the road contracted with the Georgia Railroad to maintain its rolling stock at Georgia's Atlanta shops. When the Georgia Railroad concentrated its facilities at Augusta, A&WP took over Georgia's shops for a few years before arranging with the Western Railway of Alabama for maintenance. In 1889 the A&WP constructed its own line from East Point to Atlanta, and in 1909 made an agreement with Central of Georgia, successor to the Macon & Western, to operate Atlanta & West Point's and Central of Georgia's East Point-Atlanta lines as paired track.

Western Railway of Alabama

The Montgomery Rail Road was organized in 1834 to build from Montgomery, Ala., east to West Point, Ga. It built 32 miles of standard gauge track (rather than 5-foot gauge, which was almost universal in the South) before running into financial problems. It was taken over in 1843 by the Montgomery & West Point Rail Road. The remainder of the 88-mile route between Montgomery and West Point was constructed by slave labor and opened in 1851. A branch from Opelika to Columbus, Ga., was opened in 1854.

During the Civil War the track gauge kept the road's rolling stock at home. An attack by Union forces in 1864 did not put the road out of business, but another in 1865 a few days after Lee's surrender destroyed enough equipment to shut down the railroad. Reconstruction began, and the road converted to 5-foot gauge in 1866. In 1870 the company was taken over by the Western Rail Road of Alabama.

The Western of Alabama had opened a line from Montgomery west to Selma, 44 miles, and acquisition of the line to West Point more than tripled its size. Financial troubles continued, and in 1875 the road was sold under foreclosure jointly to the Georgia Railroad & Banking Co. and the Central Railroad & Banking Co. of Georgia.

In 1881 the WofA came under control of the Central Railroad and Banking Co. when William Wadley leased the Georgia Railroad and its interests in the A&WP and WofA. That same year the Opelika-Columbus branch was leased to the Columbus & Western; it later became part of the Central of Georgia.

In 1883 the Western Rail Road of Alabama was reorganized as the Western Railway of Alabama to untangle the various leases. During the 1890s the Central of Georgia (Central Railroad & Banking Co.) interests in the Wadley lease passed to the Louisville & Nashville, which assigned them to Atlantic Coast Line, but CofG retained ownership of some WofA stock until 1944.

The roads were standard-gauged in 1886, as were most railroads in the South. By the turn of the century they were firmly in the Atlantic Coast Line-Louisville & Nashville family, serving a rich agricultural area and working as a bridge route. For many years Southern Railway's premier train, the New York–New Orleans *Crescent Limited*, was operated between Atlanta and New Orleans not on Southern's own rails but over those of the West Point Route between Atlanta and Montgomery and Louisville & Nashville between Montgomery and New Orleans. Georgia Railroad's passenger service was plebian, but its mixed trains lasted until 1983, when the newly formed Seaboard System bought the Georgia Railroad from the bank and merged it.

Atlanta & West Point	1929	1981
Miles of railroad operated:	91	91
Number of locomotives:	24	11
Number of passenger cars:	26	4*
Number of freight cars:	581	400
Number of company service cars:	46	19
Reporting marks: A&WP, AWP		

Western Railway of Alabama	1929	1981
Miles of railroad operated:	133	133
Number of locomotives:	29	14
Number of passenger cars:	21	11*
Number of freight cars:	852	298
Number of company service cars:	44	13
Reporting marks: WofA, WA		

Georgia Railroad	1929	1981
Miles of railroad operated:	329	329
Number of locomotives:	68	31
Number of passenger cars:	72	2*
*(1970)		
Number of freight cars:	1,512	810
Number of company service cars:	70	57

Reporting marks: GA

Location of headquarters: (all three railroads) Atlanta, Georgia

Notable named passenger trains: *Crescent Limited* (New York–New Orleans, operated north of Atlanta by Southern and Pennsylvania and south of Montgomery by Louisville & Nashville)

Recommended reading: *Steam Locomotives and History: Georgia Railroad and West Point Route*, by Richard E. Prince, published in 1962 by Richard E. Prince

Successors:
Seaboard System
CSX Transportation

Portions still operated:
CSX: Augusta–Atlanta–West Point–Montgomery–Selma
Georgia Woodlands Railroad: Washington–Barnet
Great Walton Rail: Social Circle–Monroe

Atlanta, Birmingham & Coast Railroad

The Waycross Air Line Railroad was incorporated as a logging railroad in 1887. By the end of 1904 it had become the Atlantic & Birmingham Railway, a common carrier with a line from Brunswick to Montezuma, Georgia, and branches to Thomasville and Waycross, Ga. At Montezuma the Central of Georgia offered connections to Macon, Atlanta, and Birmingham.

In 1906 the newly-created Atlanta, Birmingham & Atlantic Railroad absorbed the Atlantic & Birmingham. The new road built westward to Manchester, Ga., and from there to Atlanta and to Birmingham, reaching Atlanta in 1908 and Birmingham in 1910. By then the AB&A was in receivership, largely because of the cost of the marine terminal it had built at Brunswick.

The Atlanta, Birmingham & Atlantic Railway took over the operation at the beginning of 1916, but it fared little better financially. It was in receivership by 1921. The Atlanta, Birmingham & Coast Railroad was incorporated November 22, 1926, to acquire the Atlanta, Birmingham & Atlantic. The Atlantic Coast Line was firmly in control. AB&C offered ACL entries to Atlanta and Birmingham and a chance to participate more fully in Midwest-to-Florida traffic. ACL merged the AB&C on December 31, 1945.

In 1936 AB&C began hosting Chicago–Florida passenger trains. The streamlined *Dixie Flagler* inaugurated in 1940 called for a streamlined engine. AB&C's Fitzgerald shops shrouded a former Florida East Coast 4-6-2 for the every-third-day train. On other days No. 79 was available for duties such as train 1, an all-day Atlanta–Waycross mixed train. Photo by David W. Salter.

	1929	1945
Miles of railroad operated:	640	639
Number of locomotives:	30	59
Number of passenger cars:	51	39
Number of freight cars:	1,948	908
Number of company service cars:	128	129
Location of headquarters: Atlanta, Georgia		
Reporting marks: AB&C		
Historical Society: Atlantic Coast Line and Seaboard Air Line Historical Society, P. O. Box 325, Valrico, FL		

33595-0325; http://www.visuallink.net/ACLSAL

Recommended reading: *Atlantic Coast Line Railroad Steam Locomotives, Ships, and History,* by Richard E. Prince, published in 1966 by Richard E. Prince

Successors:
Atlantic Coast Line
Seaboard Coast Line
Seaboard System
CSX Transportation

Portions still operated: CSX: Waycross–Cordele, Ga.

Atlantic & Danville Railway

The Atlantic & Danville Railway was chartered in 1882 and completed its line from Portsmouth to Danville, Virginia, in 1890. Short branches from main line led to West Norfolk, Hitchcock Mills, and Buffalo Lithia Springs, Va., and a 50-mile narrow gauge line ran from Emporia, junction with the Atlantic Coast Line, northeast to Claremont on the James River.

In 1899 the Southern Railway leased the Atlantic & Danville for 50 years. The A&D provided a good connection from Southern's Washington–Atlanta main line at Danville to the port area of Norfolk and Portsmouth. The narrow gauge branch was abandoned in 1934, and the Hitchcock Mills and Buffalo Lithia Springs branches were taken up in the early 1940s, but the main line and the West Norfolk branch remained intact.

When the lease expired in 1949, Southern weighed the cost of operating the A&D and the limitations of its track, mostly 60- and 85-pound rail, against the cost of trackage rights over Atlantic Coast Line from Selma, North Carolina, to Norfolk, and chose not to renew the lease.

Atlantic & Danville resumed operation on its own August 1, 1949. It filed for bankruptcy on January 19, 1960, after the ICC turned down its request to guarantee a loan for capital expenditures and the purchase of freight cars.

Atlantic & Danville scheduled a single daily freight train in each direction. Here the two trains, both powered by Alco RS-2s, meet at Franklin, Virginia. Photo by Mallory Hope Ferrell.

	1949	1961
Miles of railroad operated:	203	203
Number of locomotives:	8	7
Number of freight cars:	139	271
Number of company service cars:	8	8

Location of headquarters: Norfolk, Virginia
Reporting marks: AD
Recommended reading: *The Atlantic and Danville Railway Company*, by William E. Griffin, Jr., published in 1987 by William E. Griffin, Jr. LCC 87-90852.
Successors:
Norfolk, Franklin & Danville
Norfolk & Western
Norfolk Southern
Portions still operated:
Norfolk Southern: Norfolk–Emporia, Va.
Commonwealth Railway: West Norfolk–Suffolk

On October 31, 1962, the railroad was purchased at auction by the Norfolk & Western, which organized the Norfolk, Franklin & Danville Railway, a wholly owned subsidiary, to operate it. The merger of Norfolk & Western and Southern rendered the Norfolk-Danville route redundant. The western third of the NF&D was abandoned in early 1983, and the remainder was absorbed by the N&W on December 30, 1983.

Atlantic & East Carolina Railway

The Atlantic & North Carolina Railroad was organized at New Bern, North Carolina, in 1854. It was to be the eastern portion of a state-owned system of three railroads that would cross North Carolina from west to east, tapping the commerce and agriculture of the state for the port of Morehead City—trade that the rivers of the area were taking to Norfolk, Virginia, and Charleston, South Carolina.

Morehead City never became the rival of New York, Baltimore, and Norfolk that its boosters predicted, and the three railroads continued as separate entities. The North Carolina Railroad and the Western North Carolina Railroad both became part of the Southern Railway family, and in 1904 the Atlantic & North Carolina was leased to the Norfolk & Southern.

The lease was forfeited in 1934 for nonpayment of rent and the A&NC began operating on its own in November 1935. On April 20, 1939, the stockholders voted to lease the road to H. P. Edwards, who organized the Atlantic & East Carolina Railway to operate the railroad. Within two years the A&EC was making a profit. The road dieselized in 1946 with two Electro-Motive F2s, an SW1, and a General Electric 44-ton switcher.

In February 1957 the Interstate Commerce Commission authorized the Southern Railway to purchase all the capital stock of the A&EC. By

The newness of Electro-Motive F2 No. 401 contrasts with the antiquity of the wood cars as the daily train crosses the Trent River at New Bern, North Carolina. A&EC photo.

January 1958 the A&EC was listed under the Southern Railway in *The Official Guide*, and it still exists as a subsidiary of Norfolk Southern. The Atlantic & North Carolina also still exists; 70 percent of its stock is held by the state of North Carolina. The Beaufort & Morehead Railroad, an independent short line at one time in the fold of the old Norfolk Southern, is essentially a 3-mile extension of the A&EC from Morehead City to Beaufort.

	1939	1956
Miles of railroad operated:	96	96
Number of locomotives:	11	7
Number of passenger cars:	10	9
Number of freight cars:	41	128
Number of company service cars:	5	7

Location of headquarters: New Bern, North Carolina

Reporting marks: AEC
Predecessor railroads in this books: Norfolk Southern
Successors:
Southern Railway
Norfolk Southern (1982)
Portions still operated: Norfolk Southern: Goldsboro–Morehead City
Map: See page 33

Atlantic & Yadkin Railway

The Cape Fear & Yadkin Valley Railway was an 1879 reorganization of the Western Railroad of North Carolina, which opened in 1860 from Fayetteville to Cumnock, 6 miles north of Sanford. By 1890 the CF&YV had a line from Wilmington through Fayetteville, Sanford, and Greensboro to Mount Airy and another from Fayetteville southwest to Bennettsville, South Carolina. The company entered receivership in 1894.

In 1899 it was sold at foreclosure and split between the Atlantic Coast Line, which acquired the Wilmington–Sanford and Fayetteville–Bennettsville lines, and the Southern Railway, which organized the Atlantic & Yadkin Railway to take over the remainder, from Sanford to Mount Airy. The Atlantic & Yadkin was operated by the Southern Railway, which controlled it, until July 1, 1916, when it assumed its own operation. The Southern merged the company and resumed operation of the road on January 1, 1950.

Atlantic & Yadkin Ten-Wheeler No. 113, shown at Sanford in 1936, was acquired from the Richmond, Fredericksburg & Potomac in 1929. Photo by Richard E. Prince, Jr.

	1929	1949
Miles of railroad operated:	163	152
Number of locomotives:	24	13
Number of passenger cars:	6	
Number of freight cars:	10	11
Number of company service cars:	10	7

Location of headquarters: Greensboro, North Carolina

Historical and technical societies:
Southern Railway Historical Association, P. O. Box 33, Spencer, NC 28159

Southern Railway Historical Society, P. O. Box 204094, Augusta, GA 30917-4094

Successors:
Southern Railway
Norfolk Southern (1982)

Portions still operated:
Norfolk Southern: Sanford–Gulf
Yadkin Valley Railroad: Walnut Cove–Rural Hall–Mount Airy

Map: See page 33

Atlantic Coast Line Railroad

ACL's history begins in 1830 with the organization of the Petersburg Railroad, which opened in 1833 between its namesake city in Virginia and the north bank of the Roanoke River opposite Weldon, North Carolina. In 1838 it made a rail connection with the newly opened Richmond & Petersburg Railroad.

In 1840 the Wilmington & Raleigh Railroad was opened from Wilmington, N. C., north 161 miles to Weldon. Its destination had been Raleigh initially, but the citizens of the state capital were not interested in the project. The railroad was renamed Wilmington & Weldon in 1855. The Wilmington & Manchester Railroad from Wilmington west into South Carolina opened in 1853. The North Eastern Railroad opened in 1857 from Florence, S. C., south to Charleston.

After the Civil War William T. Walters of Baltimore acquired control of the Petersburg, Richmond & Petersburg, Wilmington & Weldon, Wilmington & Manchester, and North Eastern railroads, forming a route from Richmond to Charleston known as the Atlantic Coast Line—an association of more or less independent railroads. The five railroads acquired a number of smaller railroads and the Wilmington & Weldon undertook a major piece of construction between 1885 and 1892, the

ACL's first streamliner was the New York–Miami *Champion,* inaugurated in 1939 in conjunction with the Pennsylvania, Florida East Coast, and Richmond, Fredericksburg & Potomac railroads. In 1946 the train was joined by the *West Coast Champion* to Tampa and St. Petersburg. The postwar equipment is shown here on a publicity run for the press. ACL photo.

Fayetteville Cutoff between Wilson, N. C., and Pee Dee, S. C. Sixty-two miles shorter than the line through Wilmington, it became the main route of the Atlantic Coast Line. In 1889 Walters formed a holding company to control them; it was renamed the Atlantic Coast Line Company in 1893.

In 1898 the Richmond & Petersburg merged the Petersburg and was renamed the Atlantic Coast Line Railroad of Virginia. In April 1900 it merged the Norfolk & Carolina (Norfolk, Va.–Tarboro, N. C.), the Wilmington & Weldon, and the ACL of South Carolina (a group of five railroads between Wilmington and Charleston) and was renamed the Atlantic Coast Line Railroad. The new railroad stretched from Richmond and Norfolk, Va., to Charleston, S. C., and Augusta, Georgia.

The Plant System

ACL's lines south and west of Charleston, S. C., were part of the Plant System, which ACL purchased in 1902. Henry B. Plant had been superintendent of Adams Express at the beginning of the Civil War. In 1861 he organized Southern Express (it became a component of American Railway Express during World War I). In 1879 Plant acquired the Atlantic & Gulf Railroad, which had a main line from Savannah southwest to Bainbridge, Ga., and a branch to Live Oak, Fla. He reorganized the company as the Savannah, Florida & Western Railway and constructed several lines: west from near Bainbridge to Chattahoochee, Fla., to connect with a Louisville & Nashville predecessor; southeast from Waycross, Ga., to Jacksonville, Fla.; and south from Live Oak to Gainesville.

In 1893 the Plant System absorbed the South Florida Railroad (Sanford–Port Tampa) and in 1899, the Jacksonville, Tampa & Key West (Jacksonville–Sanford). It merged three more railroads, the Charleston & Savannah, the Brunswick & Western (Brunswick through Waycross to Albany, Ga.), and the Alabama Midland (Bainbridge to Montgomery, Alabama) in 1901. That same year the Plant System built a cutoff from Jesup to Folkston, Ga., bypassing Waycross.

Charleston & Western Carolina

Another member of ACL's family was the Charleston & Western Carolina (Port Royal, S. C., through Augusta, Ga., to Anderson, Greenville, and Spartanburg, S. C., connecting with the Clinchfield at Spartanburg). The first portion of the road, between Augusta and the coast, was financed by the Georgia Railroad & Banking Co. However, the Central Railroad & Banking Co. (Central of Georgia) gained control in 1881 to tap inland South Carolina for the port of Savannah. Central of Georgia lost the C&WC in 1894; ACL gained control in 1897.

By 1930 the C&WC shared officers with parent ACL. ACL attempt to merge the C&WC in 1930, but neighboring roads protested. Although the C&WC was operated independently, it looked like Atlantic Coast Line—secondhand ACL steam locomotives, including Pacifics for freight service, and silver-and-purple diesels. ACL finally merged the Charleston & Western Carolina in 1959. Connecting with the C&WC at Laurens, S. C., was another ACL family member, the Columbia, Newberry & Laurens Railroad, a 75-mile line joining the three cities of its name.

Interlocking relationships

In 1902 ACL acquired control of the Louisville & Nashville Railroad, which in turn controlled the Nashville, Chattanooga & St. Louis Railway. Later ACL and L&N jointly leased the Carolina, Clinchfield & Ohio Railway and formed the Clinchfield Railroad to operate it. ACL and L&N also leased the railroad property of the Georgia Railroad & Banking Company (closely affiliated with the Atlanta & West Point and the Western Railway of Alabama) and formed the Georgia Railroad to operate it.

In 1926 ACL formed Atlanta, Birmingham & Coast Railroad to acquire the Atlanta, Birmingham & Atlanta. The AB&C had lines from Waycross to Atlanta and Birmingham, where it connected with L&N. ACL merged the Atlanta, Birmingham & Coast in 1945.

Typical of Atlantic Coast Line is this Baldwin-built copy of a USRA Pacific on a southbound freight leaving Richmond, Virginia, in March 1950. Photo by August A. Thieme, Jr.

Atlantic Coast Line was considered one of the three strong roads of the South (the other two were the Louisville & Nashville and the Southern). It carried the majority of Florida-bound passengers, turning Miami passengers over to Florida East Coast at Jacksonville but carrying west-coast passengers all the way—to Tampa, St. Petersburg, Sarasota, Fort Myers, and Naples. ACL also participated in most of the Midwest-to-Florida passenger routes. The opening of ACL's Perry Cutoff in 1928 between Thomasville, Ga., and Dunellon, Fla., shortened considerably the route between the Midwest and west coast points.

Atlantic Coast Line advertised itself as the Standard Railroad of the South, and its route between Richmond and Jacksonville was fully signalled and mostly double track, much more than parallel Seaboard Air Line could boast. As with the Pennsylvania, which advertised itself as the standard railroad of the world, there were some nonstandard items. Two are notable. ACL was one of few railroads to consider the Pacific a dual-purpose engine, but the profile of its main line was such that a 4-6-2 could move freight at good speed. ACL was particularly taken with the USRA light Pacific, which was the equal of a mid-size 2-8-0 in tractive effort and considerably better in the matter of speed. The other was the color choice for its diesels—purple (president Champion McDowell Davis liked purple). The 4-6-2s yielded to Es for passengers and Fs for freight, and purple on the diesels eventually gave way to black.

In 1958 Atlantic Coast Line and Seaboard Air Line announced they were considering merger, and in 1960 they petitioned to merge as the Seaboard Coast Line Railroad. The two roads served much the same territory, and they had 75 common points. The principal argument for merger was the elimination of duplicate lines and facilities. The merger was approved and took effect on July 1, 1967.

	1929	1966
Miles of railroad operated:	5,155	5,743
Number of locomotives:	1,007	629
Number of passenger cars:	786	361
Number of freight cars:	32,644	31,284
Number of company service cars:	1,852	

Location of headquarters: Wilmington, North Carolina, until 1961; then Jacksonville, Florida

Reporting marks: ACL

Notable named passenger trains: *Florida Special* and *Champion* (New York–Miami; operated north of Richmond by Pennsylvania and Richmond, Fredericksburg & Potomac, and south of Jacksonville by Florida East Coast), *West Coast Champion* (New York–Tampa–St. Petersburg)

Historical and technical society: Atlantic Coast Line and Seaboard Air Line Historical Society, P. O. Box 325, Valrico, FL 33595-0325; http://www.visuallink.net/ACLSAL

Recommended reading: *Atlantic Coast Line Railroad Steam Locomotives, Ships, and History*, by Richard E. Prince, published in 1966 by Richard E. Prince

Subsidiaries and affiliated railroads, 1965:
Clinchfield (50%, jointly with Louisville & Nashville)
Columbia, Newberry & Laurens
Louisville & Nashville
Georgia Railroad
Atlanta & West Point
Western Railway of Alabama
Winston-Salem Southbound (50%, jointly with Norfolk & Western)
Richmond-Washington Co.—which owned the controlling interest in the Richmond, Fredericksburg & Potomac (16.7%)

Predecessor railroads in this book: Atlanta Birmingham & Coast

Successors:
Seaboard Coast Line
Seaboard System
CSX Transportation

Portions still operated:
A list of all lines that have been trimmed would be cumbersome; the major routes that have been cut at one point or another are: Suffolk, Va.–Tarboro, N. C.; Wilmington–Fayetteville–Sanford, N. C.; Wilmington, N. C.–Pee Dee, S. C.; Bennettsville–Sumter, S. C.; Wadesboro, N. C.–Florence, S. C.; McCormick–Anderson, S. C. (ex-C&WC); Brunswick–Sessoms, Ga. (ex-AB&C); Fitzgerald–Moultrie, Ga. (ex-AB&C); Jacksonville–St. Petersburg, Fla.

Baltimore & Ohio Railroad

The most important U. S. seaports in the early 1800s were Boston, New York, Philadelphia, Baltimore, and Charleston. Baltimore had an advantage in being farther inland than the others, almost at the head of navigation on Chesapeake Bay, the estuary of the Susquehanna River. New York gained an advantage in 1825 with the opening of the Erie Canal, permitting navigation all the way to Lake Erie, and in 1826 the commonwealth of Pennsylvania chartered a system of canals to link Philadelphia with Pittsburgh. Baltimore responded to the competition of the other cities by chartering the Baltimore & Ohio Railroad on February 28, 1827.

The B&O was to build a railroad from Baltimore to a suitable point on the Ohio River. It was to be the first common carrier railroad in the U. S., the first to offer scheduled freight and passenger service to the public. Such a project would be challenging today—and we know where the Ohio River is, we know something about the intervening territory, and we know what a railroad is. Today's equivalent of the chartering of the B&O might be the establishment of a company to operate scheduled freight and passenger service to the moon. Baltimore's only alternative was a canal, and the only route for that was south to Washington and up the Potomac, where the Chesapeake & Ohio canal was already under construction. Such a canal,

Baltimore & Ohio's early construction was characterized by heavy stone viaducts, the most impressive of which was (and is) the Thomas Viaduct at Relay, Maryland. A trio of Electro-Motive EAs and EBs, the first streamlined passenger diesels that were separate from the train, leads a typical heavyweight and partly streamlined B&O passenger train across the viaduct in 1952. Photo by James P. Gallagher.

too, would lead quickly to the Allegheny Mountains, where construction and operation of a canal would be difficult.

Ground was broken for the railroad with great celebration on July 4, 1828. The first stone was laid by 90-year-old Charles Carroll of Carrollton,

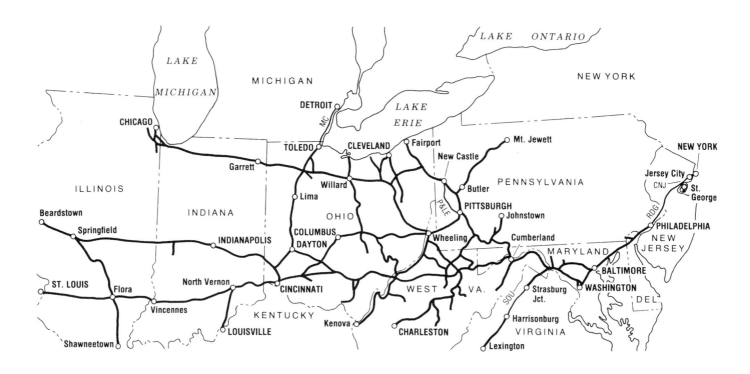

Maryland, the last signer of the Declaration of Independence still alive then. A route was laid out to follow the Patapsco and Monocacy rivers to the Potomac, and work began.

The line was opened for scheduled service to Ellicott's Mills on May 24, 1830. On December 1, 1831, the road was opened to Frederick, 60 miles. The B&O opened a branch from Relay (then called Washington Junction) to Washington in August 1835. Two years later a bridge was completed across the Potomac to Harpers Ferry, West Virginia (The separation of the western portion of Virginia did not occur until 1863, but for clarity I'll use present state names.) At Harpers Ferry the B&O connected with the Winchester & Potomac, forming the first junction of two railroad companies in the U. S.

B&O's line continued west through Cumberland, Md., to Grafton, W. Va., where it turned northwest to reach the goal of its charter at Wheeling, W. Va., 379 miles from Baltimore, on January 1, 1853, almost 25 years after commencing construction. Another line was pushed west from Grafton to reach the Ohio at Parkersburg, W. Va., in 1856.

The railroad continued westward in 1866 by leasing the Central Ohio Railroad, a line from Bellaire, Ohio, across the Ohio River from Wheeling, through Newark to Columbus, and in 1869 by leasing a line from Newark to Sandusky, Ohio. From a point on that line called Chicago Junction (now Willard) a subsidiary company, the Baltimore & Ohio & Chicago, built west to Chicago between 1872 and 1874.

Battle with the Pennsylvania

Under the leadership of John W. Garrett the B&O continued to expand. In 1871 the Pittsburgh & Connellsville Railroad completed a line from Cumberland to Pittsburgh and leased it to the B&O the following year. B&O opened the Metropolitan Branch, from Washington northwest to a connection with the main line at Point of Rocks, Md., in 1873.

The Pennsylvania Railroad considered Pittsburgh its exclusive territory. B&O's Cumberland–Pittsburgh route eventually resulted in another B&O incursion into Pennsy territory, a line from Baltimore to Philadelphia. New York–Washington trains in the 1870s were operated jointly by the Pennsylvania Railroad (Jersey City–Philadelphia), the Philadelphia,

B&O's assault on the Alleghenies required far more massive locomotives than rivals Pennsylvania and New York Central. Engine 7170, a 2-8-8-0, shown here climbing Newburg Grade near Austen, West Virginia, in July 1949 with a 54-car coal train, has help from two similar Mallets pushing at the rear. Photo by R. H. Kindig.

Wilmington & Baltimore (Philadelphia to Baltimore), and the B&O (Baltimore to Washington). The B&O was less than cooperative in the matter of through ticketing of passengers and through billing of freight. Moreover, B&O had a monopoly on Washington, and its charter protected its monopoly status. In 1872 the Pennsylvania built a slightly roundabout but legal line from Baltimore to Washington. B&O moved its New York trains off the Pennsy and onto the Philadelphia & Reading-Central of New Jersey route east of Philadelphia.

The Philadelphia, Wilmington & Baltimore was figuratively and literally in the middle. Both the B&O and the Pennsy wanted it, and in 1881 the Pennsylvania secured control. In retaliation B&O proposed its own line from Baltimore to Philadelphia and its own terminal facilities on Staten Island. The Pennsy responded in 1884 by refusing to handle B&O trains east of Baltimore. B&O completed its own line from Baltimore to Philadelphia, parallel to the PB&W and no more than a few miles from it, in 1886.

Garrett died in 1884 and was succeeded by his son Robert for two years, Samuel Spencer for one, and then Charles F. Mayer. Mayer undertook to improve the road and at the same time keep its financial situation from crumbling. The most significant improvements were control of the Pittsburg & Western (Pittsburgh–Akron), construction of a line from Akron, Ohio, to Chicago Junction; control of a route from Parkersburg, W. Va., through Cincinnati to St. Louis (the Baltimore & Ohio Southwestern, which included the former Ohio & Mississippi, completed in 1857); construction of the Baltimore Belt line through, around, and under Baltimore to connect the Philadelphia route with the rest of the B&O; and electrification of the Baltimore Belt, the first mainline electrification in North America.

The financial situation was more difficult. B&O had a large debt. Freight and passenger rates were low and revenues were dropping—in 1889 B&O handled 31 percent of the country's tidewater soft coal traffic; by 1896, that had dropped to just 4 percent because of competition from other railroads. The B&O cut back on expenditures for maintenance and quickly acquired a reputation for unreliability. B&O entered receivership in 1896.

Baltimore & Ohio came out of receivership in 1899 still under its original charter, which included tax exemption privileges. In 1901 the Pennsylvania bought a large block of B&O stock and appointed Leonor F. Loree president of the road. He undertook a line improvement program that reduced grades and curves and added many miles of double track, and he secured for B&O a large interest in the Reading, which in turn controlled the Central Railroad of New Jersey. The Pennsylvania sold some of its B&O stock to Union Pacific in 1906 and traded the remainder to UP for Southern Pacific stock in 1913. UP eventually distributed its Baltimore & Ohio stock as a dividend to its own stockholders.

The Willard era and after

Daniel Willard became president of the B&O in 1910. More than anyone else he is responsible for the road's conservative, courteous personality in the mid-twentieth century. Further expansion included the purchase in 1910 of the Chicago Terminal Transfer Railroad, a belt line that was renamed the Baltimore & Ohio Chicago Terminal; the acquisition in 1917 of the Coal & Coke Railway from Elkins to Charleston, W. Va.; and acquisition that same year of portions of the Cincinnati, Hamilton & Dayton and its leased lines to form a route from Cincinnati to Toledo.

In 1927 B&O celebrated its centennial with the Fair of the Iron Horse, a pageant and exhibition at Halethorpe, Md. Much of the rolling stock exhibited there was from B&O's museum collection, which formed the nucleus of the B&O Museum in Baltimore, one of the earliest and best railroad museums.

The Interstate Commerce Commission merger plan of the 1920s put B&O into an expansionist mood. In 1926 B&O purchased the Cincinnati, Indianapolis & Western's line from Hamilton, Ohio, to Springfield, Illinois. In 1927 it acquired an 18 percent interest in the Wheeling & Lake Erie and began to purchase Western Maryland stock. In 1929 B&O bought the Chicago & Alton Railroad, reorganized it as the Alton Railroad, and operated it as part of the B&O. (Alton regained independence in 1943 and merged with Gulf, Mobile & Ohio in 1947.) In 1932 B&O acquired the Buffalo, Rochester & Pittsburgh from the Van Sweringens in exchange for B&O's interest in the W&LE and also purchased the Buffalo & Susquehanna.

In 1934 B&O arranged for trackage rights on Pittsburgh & Lake Erie's water-level route between McKeesport and New Castle, Pa., bypassing the curves and grades of its own route (which remained in service for local business). B&O's through passenger trains moved to P&LE's Pittsburgh station across the Monongahela River from the B&O station.

For many years B&O competed with Pennsylvania and New York Central in the New York–Chicago and New York–St. Louis passenger markets. B&O's trains were slower, partly because of their longer route through Washington, but they were dieselized a decade before the competition. B&O competed with Pennsy on the New York–Washington run, compensating for the Pennsylvania's terminal in Manhattan with a network of buses that received passengers at trainside in Jersey City, crossed the Hudson by ferry, and fanned out through New York. Many preferred B&O's New York–Washington trains to Pennsy's, but the most frequently stated reason for preferring B&O—"You could always get a seat"—was the reason B&O dropped its passenger service east of Baltimore in 1958.

C&O, Chessie, and CSX

In 1960 Chesapeake & Ohio began to acquire B&O stock. New York Central made a competing bid, but B&O's stockholders approved C&O control, and on May 1, 1962, so did the ICC. By early 1964 C&O owned 90 percent of B&O's stock. In 1967 the ICC authorized C&O and B&O to control Western Maryland; B&O's WM stock had long been held in a nonvoting trust.

On June 15, 1973, B&O, C&O, and WM were made subsidiaries of the newly created Chessie System. There was no great surge of track abandonment, because in most areas B&O and C&O were complementary rather than competitive. In 1981 B&O leased the former Rock Island track from Blue Island to Henry, Ill.

B&O continued to exist within Chessie System. On May 1, 1983, B&O took over operation of the Western Maryland. Four years later, on April 30, 1987, C&O merged B&O, and four months after that, CSX Transportation merged C&O.

	1929	1972
Miles of railroad operated:	5,658	5,491
Number of locomotives:	2,364	995
Number of passenger cars:	1,732	23
Number of freight cars:	102,072	
Number of company service cars:	3,092	

Number of freight and company service cars: 56,305

Location of headquarters: Baltimore, Maryland

Reporting marks: BO

Notable named passenger trains: *Capitol Limited* (New York–Chicago), *National Limited* (New York–St. Louis), *Royal Blue* (New York–Washington), *Cincinnatian* (Baltimore–Cincinnati, later Detroit–Cincinnati)

Historical and technical society: Baltimore & Ohio Historical Society, P. O. Box 13578, Baltimore, MD 21203-3578

Recommended reading:

Impossible Challenge, by Herbert H. Harwood, Jr., published in 1979 by Barnard, Roberts & Co.

History of the Baltimore & Ohio Railroad, by John F. Stover, published in 1987 by Purdue University Press, South Campus Courts–D, West Lafayette, IN 47907 (ISBN: 0-911198-81-4)

Subsidiaries and affiliated railroads, 1972:

Baltimore & Ohio Chicago Terminal (100%)

Staten Island Rapid Transit Railway (100%)

Reading Company (38.3%)

Western Maryland (43.3%)

Washington Terminal (50%, jointly with Penn Central, formerly Pennsylvania)

Richmond-Washington Co. (16.7%)

Monongahela (33.3%)

Predecessor railroads in this book:

Buffalo & Susquehanna

Buffalo, Rochester & Pittsburgh

Successors:

Chessie System

CSX Transportation

Boston & Maine Railroad

In recent years much of Boston & Maine's track has been abandoned or sold, either to the Massachusetts Bay Transportation Authority for commuter service or to short lines. The railroad itself is now a subsidiary of Guilford Transportation Industries (and the Guilford image dominates), and for a period recently, most or all of the railroad was operated by a subsidiary, Springfield Terminal.

The Boston & Maine grew for the most part by acquisition, not by construction. The oldest component of the B&M was the line between Boston and Lowell, Massachusetts, 25 miles, opened by the Boston & Lowell Railroad on June 24, 1835, but not acquired until much later. It is easiest to deal with B&M's nineteenth-century history route by route (using early-1950s names).

Portland Division

The Boston & Maine's earliest corporate predecessor was the Andover & Wilmington Railroad, opened in August 1836 from Andover, Massachusetts, south to a junction with the Boston & Lowell at Wilmington, about 7 miles. The line was extended north 10 miles to Bradford, on the south bank of the Merrimac River opposite Haverhill, the next year. Construction continued north, reaching North Berwick, Maine, in 1843, by which time the three com-

Mogul 1455, built by Manchester in 1907, leads eight wood cars full of homebound commuters at West Medford, Massachusetts, on a spring evening in 1946. Photo by Albert G. Hale.

panies involved (one for each state) had been consolidated using the name of the New Hampshire company, Boston & Maine Railroad. At North Berwick, the B&M connected with the Portland, Saco & Portsmouth Railroad, opened in 1842 between the cities of its name and leased in 1847 jointly by the B&M and the Eastern

Railroad (Boston to Portsmouth, N. H., opened in 1840).

B&M was dissatisfied with using the Boston & Lowell and in 1845 opened its own line from North Wilmington through Reading to Boston. There followed a boom in railroad construction in eastern Massachusetts. Towns not on a railroad wanted one; towns already on a railroad wanted a second one, for the benefits of competition. Each of the three major companies, B&M, Boston & Lowell, and Eastern, bought up smaller railroads as they were built to keep the other two railroads from getting them. Soon the Boston & Lowell had branches from Wilmington to Lawrence and from Lowell to Salem; the Eastern had a branch from Salem to Lawrence, plus several branches to coastal towns east of its main line; and the B&M had branches from Andover to Lowell and from Wakefield to Newburyport and to Peabody (the Eastern soon got that last one and found it nearly useless).

Competition between the B&M and the Eastern for Boston–Portland traffic was fierce. The Eastern route was a few miles shorter but reached Boston by a ferry from East Boston until 1854, when the Eastern built a line into Boston from the north. The B&M carried most of the traffic. In 1869 the Eastern and the Maine Central cahooted up to control the traffic, with the upshot that the Portland, Saco & Portsmouth canceled the joint lease and leased itself to the Eastern. The Eastern in turn obtained control of the Maine Central. Just about that same time B&M built a line of its own line from South Berwick to Portland.

The new lease of the PS&P, the cost of control of the Maine Central, and several disastrous accidents nearly exhausted the Eastern. In the early 1870s the Eastern made merger overtures to the B&M, which was unwilling to assume the Eastern's debt. The two roads reached an agreement in 1874 to end the worst of the competition, and in 1883 B&M leased the Eastern, acquiring control of the Maine Central.

The Worcester, Nashua & Rochester had an inland route northeast from Worcester to Rochester, New Hampshire, a back-door route to Maine. Several railroads wanted it, not so much for itself as to prevent another railroad from acquiring it. The Boston & Albany didn't want the Old Colony to get it; the B&M didn't want the B&A to get it; and the Boston & Lowell didn't want the B&M to get it. B&M, which already controlled the Portland & Rochester leased the Worcester, Nashua & Rochester in 1886 and became the dominant (and only) railroad in southern Maine.

New Hampshire Division

Lowell, Massachusetts, was one of America's first industrial cities, combining the power of a fall in the Merrimac River with power textile loom technology. It began its rise in 1822, and it needed year-round transportation to Boston. The Middlesex Canal, opened in 1803 to connect Boston with the Merrimac River, froze in the winter, and the roads were inadequate. The Boston & Lowell Railroad was built parallel to the canal and soon took its business.

In 1838, three years after the B&L opened, the Nashua & Lowell Railroad began operating from Lowell north alongside the Merrimac River to Nashua, N. H., 18 miles. By 1850 the Nashua & Lowell included branches west to Ayer, Mass., and Wilton, N. H., both intended primarily to block construction by the Fitchburg Railroad. In 1857 the Boston & Lowell and the Nashua & Lowell agreed to operate as a unit.

By then another textile mill city, Manchester, was growing on the banks of the Merrimac north of Nashua. The Manchester & Lawrence Rail-

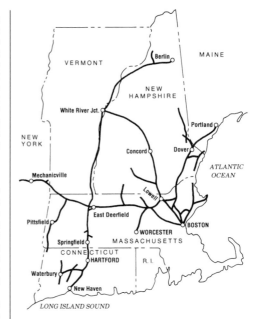

road linked Manchester with Lawrence, Mass., on the Boston & Maine, competing with the Concord Railroad-Nashua & Lowell-Boston & Lowell route to Boston. The five railroads involved formed a pooling agreement, but then the Concord leased the Manchester & Lawrence. The B&L proposed consolidation with the Nashua & Lowell and the Concord; the B&M, of course, opposed such a move. In 1869 the Great Northern Railroad was chartered. It was to include the three roads plus the Northern (Concord, N. H., to White River Junction, Vermont). It required the approval of the New Hampshire legislature, which it did not get. The B&L was equally unsuccessful with a proposal to consolidate with the Fitchburg, and it had a falling out with the Nashua & Lowell.

In 1880 the B&L leased the Nashua & Lowell and acquired control of the Massachusetts Central, under construction between Boston and Northampton, Mass., on the Connecticut River. In 1884 it leased the Northern and the Boston, Concord & Montreal, acquired control of the St. Johnsbury & Lake Champlain, and came head to head with the Concord Railroad (Nashua to Concord, N. H.), kicking off a railroad war in the legislature and courts of New Hampshire. The Boston & Lowell leased itself to the Boston & Maine in 1887, and let the B&M (which was incorporated in New Hampshire) do battle with the Concord Railroad.

The B&M and the Concord eventually reached accord, primarily because the B&M had the Concord surrounded, except for one poorly built branch from Nashua south to Concord, Mass., where it connected with the Fitchburg and the Old Colony. In 1895 the B&M, which by then had acquired control of the Concord & Montreal (the consolidation of the Concord and the Boston, Concord & Montreal), leased the C&M and became the dominant railroad in New Hampshire.

Fitchburg Division

B&M's line to the West was built by several companies over a period of 30 years. The Fitchburg Railroad was opened from Boston to Fitchburg, Mass., 50 miles northwest, in 1845. It soon acquired several branches but did not choose to extend its line westward.

The Vermont & Massachusetts built west from Fitchburg over a range of hills to the Connecticut River at Grout's Corner (later Millers Falls), near Greenfield, then turned north, reaching Brattleboro, Vt., in 1850.

As early as 1819 there was a proposal for a canal across northern Massachusetts, using a tunnel to penetrate Hoosac Mountain, which stood between the valleys of the Deerfield and Hoosic rivers. The proposal for a canal became a proposal for a railroad from Boston to the Great Lakes at Oswego or Buffalo, N. Y. The tunnel was begun in 1851 by the Commonwealth of Massachusetts.

The state also built the Troy & Greenfield Railroad west from Greenfield to the Hoosac Tunnel and leased it to the Fitchburg and the Vermont & Massachusetts in 1868. In 1870 the Vermont & Massachusetts sold its Grout's Corner–Brattleboro line to the Rutland; the line later became part of the Central Vermont.

The Troy & Boston Railroad was opened in the early 1850s from Troy, N. Y., north to the Hoosic River, then east and south to connections at Eagle Bridge and White Creek with two railroads north to Rutland, Vt. By 1859 the Troy & Boston, the Southern Vermont (8 miles across the southwest corner of Vermont), and the 7-mile-long western portion of the Troy & Greenfield formed a route from Troy to North Adams, Mass.

Two railroad-consolidation petitions came before the Massachusetts legislature in 1873, one to allow consolidation of the Fitchburg, Vermont & Massachusetts, Troy & Greenfield, and Troy & Boston railroads and the Hoosac Tunnel (then nearly complete), and the other to consolidate the Boston & Lowell with the Fitchburg. In response a legislative committee proposed consolidating all the railroads in both petitions. The railroads rejected the idea; the sole result of the proposal was that the Fitchburg leased the Vermont & Massachusetts.

As the Hoosac Tunnel neared completion in 1875 two other railroads were started: the Massachusetts Central and the Boston, Hoosac Tunnel & Western. The Massachusetts Central was projected west from Boston to a connection with the Troy & Greenfield near the Hoosac Tunnel; the Boston, Hoosac Tunnel & Western Railroad was to run west from the tunnel to Oswego, N. Y.

The Massachusetts Central built west from Boston through sparsely populated territory about halfway between the lines of the Fitchburg and the Boston & Albany and crossing nine other railroads along the way. It ran out of breath when it reached the Connecticut River at Northampton. The BHT&W was built from the Vermont-Massachusetts state line near Williamstown, Mass., parallel to the Troy & Boston and crossing it several times, then west from Johnsonville, N. Y., to Mechanicville and Rotterdam.

In spite of the financial problems of both roads, the combination of the Massachusetts Central and the Boston, Hoosac Tunnel & Western constituted a competitive threat to the Fitchburg. The solution was control of the state-owned Hoosac Tunnel. The state would allow that only if the Fitchburg had its own route to the Hudson River. Accordingly, in 1887 the Fitchburg consolidated with Troy & Boston and the state-owned Troy & Greenfield and in 1892 with the Boston, Hoosac Tunnel & Western.

In 1899 the New York Central was seeking access to Boston and considered leasing either the Boston & Albany or the Fitchburg—or both. The B&A served larger cities; the Fitchburg had the easier crossing of the mountains of western Massachusetts. NYC doubted it could get state approval to lease both railroads and chose the B&A. The Boston & Maine offered to lease the Fitchburg and in 1900 did so.

Connecticut River line

The Connecticut River line connected with all the routes running west and northwest from Boston: Boston & Albany at Springfield, Mass.; Massachusetts Central at Northampton; Fitchburg at Greenfield; Vermont & Massachusetts at East Northfield; Cheshire Railroad and Rutland at Bellows Falls, Vt.; Concord & Claremont at Claremont, N. H.; Northern Railroad and Central Vermont at White River Junction, Vt.; and Boston, Concord & Montreal and Montpelier & Wells River at Wells River, Vt.; plus the Portland & Ogdensburg and the St. Johnsbury & Lake Champlain at St. Johnsbury, Vt. It consisted of six railroad companies: Connecticut River Railroad from Springfield to East Northfield; Vermont & Massachusetts to Brattleboro; Vermont Valley to Bellows Falls; Sullivan County to Windsor; Central Vermont to White River Junction; and Connecticut & Passumpsic Rivers Railroad from White River Junction to the Canadian border at Newport, Vt. They were all under the control of the Con-

The Fitchburg Division was B&M's heavy-duty freight route to the West. Rock-ballasted double track and centralized traffic control are evident in this scene of FTs working upgrade at Shelburne Falls, Massachusetts, in 1948. Photo by Virginia H. Parkinson.

necticut River Railroad (except for the Central Vermont), as was the St. Johnsbury & Lake Champlain.

By 1893 the lines north of White River Junction had been leased to the B&M, and the New Haven was ready to lease what remained, but during the few months of control of the B&M by the Philadelphia & Reading, A. A. MacLeod, president of the P&R, secured control of the Connecticut River Railroad, leased it to the B&M, and signed an agreement with the New Haven to divide New England along the line of the Boston & Albany. (New Haven already had several branches that reached north of the B&A

almost to the New Hampshire border; B&M had none south of the B&A.)

Twentieth century

In the early twentieth century B&M and its controlled lines reached from Boston west to the Hudson River at Troy and Mechanicville, N. Y., and the Mohawk River at Rotterdam Junction; northwest to Lake Champlain at Maquam, Vt.; north to Sherbrooke and Lime Ridge, Quebec; and northeast to Vanceboro and Eastport, Maine. East of the Connecticut River, north of the Boston & Albany, and south of the Canadian border there were only two railroads of any consequence not under B&M control: the Bangor & Aroostook and the Grand Trunk route from Montreal and Sherbrooke to Portland, Maine.

The New Haven, expanding under the leadership of Charles S. Mellen, acquired control of the B&M in 1907. In 1914 the New Haven's B&M stock was placed in the hands of trustees for eventual sale, and that same year B&M sold its Maine Central stock. B&M was placed in receivership in 1916.

In 1919 B&M simplified its corporate structure by consolidating with itself the Fitchburg, Boston & Lowell, Connecticut River, and Concord & Montreal railroads. B&M returned to independent operation several roads it had been operating: Suncook Valley in 1924, St. Johnsbury & Lake Champlain in 1925, and Montpelier & Wells River in 1926. Also in 1926 B&M leased its lines north of Wells River, Vt., to the Canadian Pacific and CPR subsidiary Quebec Central. About that same time B&M abandoned some of the weakest of its redundant branch lines.

B&M opened a new North Station in Boston in 1928, replacing the adjacent B&M, Boston & Lowell, and Fitchburg stations, which had been operated as a unit. In 1930 B&M acquired control of the Springfield Terminal Railway, an electric line between Charlestown, N. H., and Springfield, Vt., 6 miles.

From 1932 to 1952 B&M shared officers with Maine Central in a voluntary arrangement that provided many of the benefits of consolidation or merger. Floods in 1936 and a hurricane in 1938 caused the abandonment of several branches. In 1939 B&M disposed of its interest in the Mount Washington Cog Railway. In 1946 B&M purchased the Connecticut & Passumpsic

Rivers Railroad south of Wells River, Vt.; Canadian Pacific and its subsidiaries purchased the line north of Wells River. Samuel M. Pinsly bought several branches to form short lines: the branch from Mechanicville to Saratoga, N. Y., became the Saratoga & Schuylerville in 1945; the Rochester, N. H.–Westbrook, Maine, line became the Sanford & Eastern in 1949; and the Concord–Claremont, N. H., branch became the Claremont & Concord Railroad in 1954.

B&M dieselized quickly, except for suburban passenger trains, and it was an early user of Centralized Traffic Control. In 1950 it was a well-run, progressive railroad—in a region that was losing its heavy industry and beginning to build superhighways. In 1956 Patrick B. McGinnis became president of the B&M, bringing in a new image—not just blue replacing maroon on the locomotives and cars but a new way of doing things: deficits, deferred maintenance, kickbacks on the sale of B&M's streamlined passenger cars.

B&M amassed the world's largest fleet of Budd Rail Diesel Cars, using them for all passenger service except the New York–Montreal trains operated in conjunction with the New Haven and the Central Vermont. By the mid-1960s only suburban passenger service remained, operated for the Massachusetts Bay Transportation Authority.

In 1958 B&M posted a deficit on its ledgers, and the deficits continued in the following years. B&M asked to be included in the Norfolk & Western, but N&W was reluctant to take on what was rapidly becoming a charity case. On March 23, 1970, B&M declared bankruptcy. By the end of the year, B&M's trustees had chosen John W. Barriger III to be chief executive officer. Barriger

retired at the end of 1972, having made a start at rerailing the B&M.

Rather than split the B&M among its connections or ask for its inclusion in Conrail, B&M's trustees decided to reorganize independently. Under the leadership of Alan Dustin, the B&M bought new locomotives, rebuilt its track, and changed its attitude. The revived B&M went after new business and expanded its operations. It sold the tracks and rolling stock used by its commuter operations to Massachusetts Bay Transportation Authority in 1975, but retained freight rights on those lines and continued to operate the trains for MBTA. In 1977 it took over the operation of commuter trains on the former New Haven and Boston & Albany lines out of Boston's South Station, and in 1982 it purchased several lines in Massachusetts and Connecticut from Conrail.

A revived Boston & Maine was purchased in 1983 by Timothy Mellon's Guilford Transportation Industries, which had bought the Maine Central in 1981 and in 1984 would buy the Delaware & Hudson. Guilford began operating the three railroads as a unified system, selling unprofitable lines, closing redundant yards and shops, and eliminating jobs. Employees went on strike. Guilford leased most of the B&M and the Maine Central to the Springfield Terminal to take advantage of work rules. Track degenerated to the point that Amtrak discontinued the *Montrealer*, which operated on B&M rails between Springfield, Mass., and Windsor, Vt. (Central Vermont acquired and rebuilt the Brattleboro–Windsor line, and Amtrak restored the *Montrealer*, rerouting it on CV rails south of Brattleboro.)

In 1990 the principal point of interchange with Conrail was shifted from Rotterdam Junction, N. Y., west of Schenectady, to Ayer, Mass., removing all through freight traffic from the former Fitchburg Division line through Hoosac Tunnel. B&M's problem for years had been that its routes were so short that its share of revenue on a freight move was small; those routes became 173 miles shorter. It seems likely that B&M's shrinkage will continue.

	1929	1982
Miles of railroad operated:	2,077	1,508
Number of locomotives:	787	151
Number of passenger cars:	1,275	
Number of freight cars:	11,062	3,112
Number of company service cars:	1,130	293

Location of headquarters: Boston, Massachusetts; moved during the 1970s to North Billerica, Massachusetts

Reporting marks: BM

Notable named passenger trains: *Flying Yankee* (Boston–Bangor, Maine; operated east of Portland by Maine Central)

Historical and technical society: Boston & Maine Railroad Historical Society, Box 2936, Middlesex-Essex GMF, Woburn, MA 01888-2936

Recommended reading:

Boston and Maine: Three Colorful Decades of New England Railroading, by Robert Willoughby Jones, published in 1991 by Trans-Anglo Books, P. O. Box 6444, Glendale, CA 91225 (ISBN: 0-87046-101-X)

Bluebirds and Minutemen, by Tom Nelligan, published in 1986 by McMillan Publications, 2921 Two Paths Drive, Woodridge, IL 60517-4512 (ISBN 0-934228-15-9)

The Formation of the New England Railroad Systems, by George Pierce Baker, published in 1937 by Harvard University Press, Cambridge, MA 02138

Subsidiaries and affiliated railroads, 1984:

Northern Railroad (82%)

Springfield Terminal Railway (100%)

Stony Brook (62%)

Vermont & Massachusetts (36%)

Successor: Guilford Transportation Industries

Portions still operated:

Claremont Concord: Claremont Jct.–Claremont, N. H.

Guilford: Portland, Me.–Rotterdam Jct., N. Y.; Rockingham Jct.–Portsmouth–Seabrook, N. H.; Boston–Salem–Danvers, Mass.; Wilmington, Mass.– Lawrence, Mass.–Salem, N. H.; Boston–Lowell, Mass.–Manchester, N. H.; Nashua–Wilton, N. H.; Boston–Ayer, Mass.; Worcester–Ayer, Mass.; Springfield–East Northfield, Mass.; Amherst–Northampton, Mass.; Adams–North Adams, Mass. (ex-Boston & Albany route); Springfield, Mass.–New Haven, Conn.; Derby–Torrington, Conn.; Waterbury–Newington, Conn. (routes in and to Connecticut are ex-New Haven)

Massachusetts Bay Transportation Authority: Boston to Rockport, Ipswich, Haverhill, Lowell, and Fitchburg, Mass.

Massachusetts Central: Bondsville–Forest Lake, Mass.

Milford-Bennington: Milford–Bennington, N. H.

New England Central: Brattleboro–Windsor, Vt.

New England Southern: Manchester–North Woodstock, N. H., Concord–Penacook, N. H., Chicopee–Chicopee Falls, Mass.

New Hampshire & Vermont: Groveton–Littleton, N. H.

New Hampshire North Coast: Dover–Ossipee, N. H.

Providence & Worcester: Worcester–Gardner, Mass.

Boston, Revere Beach & Lynn Railroad

The shoe-manufacturing city of Lynn, Massachusetts, 12 miles from Boston on the main line of the Eastern Railroad, was growing rapidly in the 1860s. The time was right for land developer Alpheus Blake to propose a second railroad between Boston and Lynn—along the shore, where Blake owned land.

The Boston, Revere Beach & Lynn Railroad was chartered in May 1874. Blake chose a track gauge of 3 feet for the usual reason—economy. Small trains cost less. Construction began exactly a year after the charter was granted and went quickly. The only major engineering works were a pair of 500-foot tunnels in East Boston and several pile trestles across marshes and the Saugus River.

The line opened on July 22, 1875. It was an immediate success and cut sharply into the local passenger business of the Eastern Railroad, despite the necessity for a ferry crossing to Boston from the terminus of the narrow gauge in East Boston. In 1885 the company acquired two lines to the town of Winthrop.

Electrification

In 1911 the New York, New Haven & Hartford Railroad proposed to purchase the BRB&L and convert it to a standard gauge electrically operated line. The BRB&L began to develop its own plans to electrify—it had the highest traffic density in the United States. In 1919, though, the company reported a deficit, and it was worse in 1920. Operating costs had risen. Competition was coming from the automobile and from new bus lines that were invading the territory. Over public protest the railroad reduced off-peak service to half-hour headways.

By the mid-1920s the BRB&L was back in the black, and in late 1927 control of the company was purchased by a New York City engineering company. The new management proceeded to convert the line to electric operation. Catenary was erected, automatic block signals were installed, and the wood open-platform coaches were motorized. The last day of steam operation was December 2, 1928. All but one of the Mason-bogie 2-4-4Ts were scrapped.

The Depression hit less than a year later, and the BRB&L was in financial trouble. The opening of the Sumner Tunnel between Boston and East Boston in 1934 made automobile commuting easier and gave competing bus companies a considerable advantage over the narrow gauge. That same year a bill before the Massachusetts legislature proposed purchase of the narrow gauge by the Boston Elevated Railway, conversion to standard gauge, and access to the subway station in East Boston. That proposal did not pass, but the Boston El did purchase competing streetcar lines into Revere.

The BRB&L filed for reorganization in 1937. In 1938 the elevated line that served the ferry terminal in Boston was abandoned, and in July 1939 the railroad requested permission to abandon. The last day of operation for both the trains and the ferries was January 27, 1940; the company was dissolved July 19, 1940.

In January 1952 the Metropolitan Transit Authority, successor to the Boston Elevated Railway, opened the first phase of the Revere extension of its East Boston subway line, built on the right of way of the BRB&L. The line was extended to Wonderland Station in January 1954.

	1927	1939
Miles of railroad operated:	13	13
Number of steam locomotives:	26	1
Number of passenger cars:	98	71
Number of ferryboats:	4	3
Number of company service cars:	27	8

Location of headquarters: Boston, Massachusetts

Recommended reading: *Narrow Gauge*, by Robert C. Stanley, published in 1980 by the Boston Street Railway Association, P. O. Box 102, Cambridge MA 02138

Buffalo & Susquehanna Railroad

 In 1885 Frank Goodyear, a fuel and lumber dealer in Buffalo, New York, bought a large tract of timberland in northwest Pennsylvania. He organized the Sinnemahoning Valley Railroad to build a line from Keating Summit (on what later became the Pennsylvania Railroad line to Buffalo) to Austin, Pa., where he had a sawmill. Goodyear formed a partnership with his brother Charles in 1887 and began to expand their empire. By 1893 their railroad system reached east to Galeton and Ansonia, and the various railroad companies were consolidated as the Buffalo & Susquehanna Railroad. At the beginning of 1896 the B&S had a line northwest from Galeton to Wellsville, N. Y., In 1898 the Goodyears purchased the Addison & Pennsylvania, a former narrow gauge line from Galeton northeast to Addison, N. Y.

The Goodyears pushed their railroad southwest through Du Bois to Sagamore, Pa., with the thought of continuing to Pittsburgh. Coal became the mainstay of the south end of the railroad, and lumber and leather (many tanneries were located on the line) were the principal commodities carried at the north end. The Goodyear lumber and railroad empire prospered, and by the early 1900s it included lumber mills in the South and the New Orleans Great Northern Railroad.

When Baltimore & Ohio took over Buffalo & Susquehanna, B&S's Atlantics remained at the head of the passenger trains, though with new B&O numbers. The engineer oils around No. 1485 at Addison, New York, on June 22, 1946. Photo by Mike Runey.

In 1906 the Goodyears built the Buffalo & Susquehanna Railway from Wellsville to Buffalo, nearly 90 miles. A year later Frank Goodyear died; his brother Charles died in 1911, and the Goodyear empire began to fall apart. The expense of constructing the line to Buffalo began to cause financial difficulty, and the road laid aside plans to extend its line to Pittsburgh and to relocate its line to eliminate the four switchbacks over the mountains between Galeton and Wharton. The Buffalo & Susquehanna Railway leased the Buffalo & Susquehanna Railroad, but that didn't forestall receivership. After a brief period of operation as the Wellsville & Buffalo, the Buffalo extension was scrapped in 1916. The remainder of the system was reorganized as the Buffalo & Susquehanna Railroad Corporation.

In 1932 the Baltimore & Ohio purchased the B&S with the thought of using the Du Bois–Sinnemahoning portion as part of a new freight line across Pennsylvania. In July 1942 a flood washed out much of the line south of Galeton. B&O abandoned the line between Sinnemahoning and Burrows, just south of Galeton, isolating the Wellsville–Galeton–Addison portion from the rest of the B&O.

Because of the problems of isolation and declining traffic, B&O considered selling or abandoning the northern part of the B&S, and to simplify sale, in 1954 B&O merged the B&S and two smaller roads that it had leased since the turn of the century.

On January 1, 1956, B&O sold the northern portion of the former Buffalo & Susquehanna to Murray M. Salzberg, who organized the Wellsville, Addison & Galeton Railroad to operate it. The WA&G was abandoned in stages, with the last piece going in 1979. The last portion of the south end of the B&S, B&O's branch from Du Bois to Weedville, disappeared from B&O's map in the 1970s. None of Buffalo & Susquehanna's lines remains in service.

	1929	1931
Miles of railroad operated:	254	254
Number of locomotives:	47	46
Number of passenger cars:	12	12
Number of freight and company service cars:	2,833	1,482

Location of headquarters: Wellsville, New York
Reporting marks: B&S
Historical and technical society: Baltimore & Ohio Railroad Historical Society, P. O. Box 13578, Baltimore, MD 21203-3578
Recommended reading: *The History of the Buffalo & Susquehanna*, by Paul Pietrak, published by Paul Pietrak, North Boston, NY 14110
Successors:
Baltimore & Ohio
Wellsville, Addison & Galeton
Map: See page 56

Buffalo, Rochester & Pittsburgh Railway

Rochester, New York, had a well-developed flour-milling industry in 1869. The Genesee River furnished power to drive the mills, and wheat came from the fertile Genesee Valley south of Rochester in boats on the Genesee Valley Canal. To provide better grain transportation and, more important, to bring coal from Pennsylvania, the Rochester & State Line Railroad was incorporated in 1869. It was to build south up the valley of Genesee to the Pennsylvania state line—the destination was later changed to the town of Salamanca, N. Y.

The railroad was completed in 1878. Most of its stock was owned by William H. Vanderbilt, of the New York Central system. However, Vanderbilt lost interest in the railroad about the time it began having financial difficulties, and he sold his stock to a New York syndicate.

The road was reorganized as the Rochester & Pittsburgh Railroad in 1881. It extended its line south to Punxsutawney, Pa., and contracted with the Pennsylvania Railroad for access to Pittsburgh. At the same time the Buffalo, Rochester & Pittsburgh Railroad was organized to build a branch to Buffalo.

In 1884 the R&P was sold to Adrian Iselin, a New York financier also connected with the Mobile & Ohio. After some corporate manipulations he consolidated the railroads as the Buffalo,

The year is 1945 and 2-6-6-2 7533 lugging 105 cars through Lewis Run, Pennsylvania, a few miles south of Bradford, carries Baltimore & Ohio identification, but the line and the locomotive are both former Buffalo, Rochester & Pittsburgh property. Photo by Gordon R. Roth.

Rochester & Pittsburgh Railway in 1887. The BR&P built branches into the coalfields of western Pennsylvania and constructed a line north from Rochester to the shore of Lake Ontario to connect with a car ferry to Cobourg, Ont.

In 1893 BR&P opened a branch to Clearfield,

Pa., and a connection with the New York Central and, via NYC, the Reading. In 1898 the Allegheny & Western Railroad was incorporated to extend the BR&P from Punxsutawney west to Butler, Pa., and a connection with the Pittsburgh & Western (Baltimore & Ohio). Trackage rights from Butler to New Castle and Pittsburgh were included in the arrangement with the B&O. The new line opened in 1899, and BR&P finally linked the cities of its name.

BR&P developed into a well-run coal hauler. After the Interstate Commerce Commission merger plan of the 1920s was published, both Delaware & Hudson and Baltimore & Ohio petitioned for control of the BR&P. The ICC approved B&O's application in 1930, but in the meantime the Van Sweringen brothers (who owned the Nickel Plate and controlled the Chesapeake & Ohio) had bought the BR&P. B&O still wanted it, and the Van Sweringens wanted the Wheeling & Lake Erie, in which B&O held a minority interest. They traded on January 1, 1932. Baltimore & Ohio wanted to assemble a Chicago–New York shortcut that would use BR&P from Butler to Du Bois, Buffalo & Susquehanna to Sinnemahoning, and a new line connecting with the Reading west of Williamsport (a railroad equivalent of Interstate 80). The Great Depression was not an auspicious time for railroad construction, and the project was shelved.

Chessie System sold the Rochester branch to the Genesee & Wyoming Railroad in 1986 to become the Rochester & Southern Railroad, and in April 1988 the remainder of the BR&P became the Buffalo & Pittsburgh Railroad, also a G&W subsidiary. The Rochester line has been abandoned between Machias and Silver Lake Junction, but most of the rest of the BR&P is still in service.

	1929	1931
Miles of railroad operated:	602	601
Number of locomotives:	272	262
Number of passenger cars:	96	94
Number of freight cars:	11,152	
Number of company service cars:	359	
Number of freight and company service cars:		10,356

Location of headquarters: Rochester, New York

Reporting marks: BR&P

Historical and technical societies: Baltimore & Ohio Railroad Historical Society, P. O. Box 13578, Baltimore, MD 21203-3578

Recommended reading: *The Buffalo, Rochester & Pittsburgh Railway,* by Paul Pietrak, published in 1979 by Paul Pietrak, North Boston, NY 14110

Successors:
Baltimore & Ohio
Chessie System
Buffalo & Pittsburgh
Rochester & Southern

Portions still operated:
Buffalo & Pittsburgh: Buffalo, N. Y.–Eidenau, Pa.; Machias–Ashford, N. Y.; Du Bois–Clearfield, Pa.; Punxsutawney–Clarksburg, Pa., Creekside Junction–Graceton, Pa.
Rochester & Southern: Rochester–Silver Lake Junction

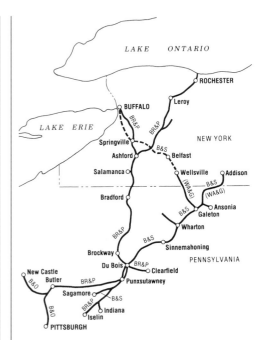

Burlington Northern Railroad

BN had a greater extent than any other U. S. railroad: Vancouver, British Columbia, to Pensacola, Florida. If you crossed North America from east to west, you had to cross BN rails or get your feet wet in the Gulf of Mexico or find your way around the north side of the city of Winnipeg. It was created on March 2, 1970, by the merger of the Northern Pacific Railway, the Great Northern Railway, the Chicago, Burlington & Quincy Railroad, and the Spokane, Portland & Seattle Railway. It was during most of its existence the longest railroad in North America, edging past the previous title-holder, Canadian National Railways.

Great Northern and Northern Pacific covered most of Minnesota north and west of the Twin Cities and the eastern third of North Dakota. West of there, the main lines of the two roads were as much as 200 miles apart, coming together at Spokane but separating again to cross Washington. The two roads were instrumental in settling much of the northern Great Plains, and they pretty much divided the northern tier of the country from the Mississippi River to Puget Sound between them (as the Milwaukee Road eventually learned).

The Chicago, Burlington & Quincy's main axis was its Chicago–Denver route. Branch lines covered much of western Illinois, southern Iowa,

Burlington Northern became the top coal hauler in the U. S. because of the development of coalfields in the Powder River Basin of eastern Wyoming. Four BN units, led by SD60M 9289, lug coal uphill at East Coal Creek, Wyo., in 1991. Photo by Wesley Fox.

northern Missouri, and southern Nebraska, and long branchless lines reached to Paducah, Kentucky, St. Paul, Minnesota, and Billings, Montana. Despite its image of diesels and stainless-steel *Zephyrs*, it was a very conservative railroad.

The Spokane, Portland & Seattle was built to give the Great Northern and the Northern Pacific access to Portland, Oregon, from the east. It was owned equally by GN and NP, which acted more like stingy uncles than loving parents.

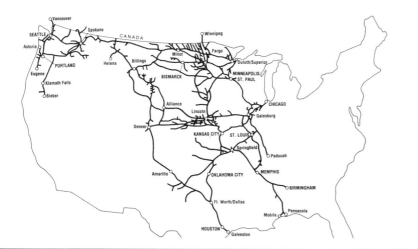

Burlington Northern existed in a way long before the merger formalities of 1970. In 1901 Great Northern and Northern Pacific each acquired almost 49 percent of the stock of the Chicago, Burlington & Quincy, assuring a connection to Chicago from St. Paul, eastern terminus of GN and NP. At the same time NP came under the control of GN. In 1905 GN and NP organized and constructed the Spokane, Portland & Seattle Railway. In 1927 the Great Northern Pacific Railway was organized to consolidate GN and NP and lease the CB&Q and the SP&S. The Interstate Commerce Commission would approve it only without the inclusion of the CB&Q. The companies resumed merger studies in 1956, and in 1960 the directors of GN and NP approved the terms. Government approval and actual merger took another decade.

	1970	1994
Miles of railroad operated:	23,609	28,937
Number of locomotives:	1,973	2,957
Number of passenger cars:	1,171	
Number of freight cars:	116,491	88,858
Number of company service cars:	8,250	9,593

Location of headquarters: St. Paul, Minn.; after 1984, Fort Worth, Texas

Reporting marks: BN

Notable named passenger trains: *Empire Builder* and *North Coast Limited* (Chicago to Portland and Seattle), *Denver Zephyr* (Chicago–Denver)

Historical and technical society: Friends of the Burlington Northern, P. O. Box 271, West Bend, WI 53095-0271; http://www.getnet.com/~dickg/nmra/sigs/ FOBNR /FOBNR.html

Recommended reading:
Burlington Northern and Its Heritage, by Steve Glischinski, published in 1992 by Andover Junction Publications, P. O. Box 1160, Andover, NJ 07821 (ISBN 0-944119-08-5)
Burlington Northern Diesel Locomotives, by Paul D. Schneider, published in 1993 by Kalmbach Publishing Co. (ISBN: 0-89024-143-0)

Predecessor railroads in this book:
Alabama, Tennessee & Northern
Burlington-Rock Island
Chicago, Burlington & Quincy
Colorado & Southern
Fort Worth & Denver
Great Northern
Northern Pacific
St. Louis-San Francisco
Spokane, Portland & Seattle
Successors: Burlington Northern & Santa Fe
Portions still operated: See the predecessor railroads.

BN merged the St. Louis-San Francisco Railway (the Frisco) in 1980. At the end of 1981 BN absorbed the Colorado & Southern, which had been a CB&Q subsidiary, and transferred C&S's Denver–Texline route to the Fort Worth & Denver, a C&S subsidiary. On January 1, 1983, FW&D was also merged into BN.

BN developed into the nation's top coal-hauler because of the development of the coal-fields in the Powder River Basin of eastern Wyoming. It slimmed down by spinning off several large chunks of its network, including strategic segments of the former Northern Pacific main line.

Meanwhile, BN's neighbor to the south, Union Pacific, was expanding: acquiring Western Pacific, Missouri Pacific, Missouri-Kansas-Texas, and partial ownership of Chicago & North Western. By 1990 UP was almost as big as BN.

The proposed Southern Pacific-Santa Fe merger would have created a three-railroad situation between the Midwest and the Pacific—SPSF across the south, Union Pacific across the middle, and BN across the north. After the Interstate Commerce Commission ruled against the SP-Santa Fe merger, the Denver & Rio Grande Western acquired SP, leaving Santa Fe on its own.

Gradually the western railroad situation shook out and settled down. In June 1994 after some months of denying rumors of impending merger, Santa Fe and Burlington Northern announced their intention to merge—BN would buy Santa Fe. The deal was consummated in 1995. As this book went to press in mid-1999, the two railroads were still separate, but locomotives had been painted and lettered for Burlington Northern & Santa Fe.

Burlington-Rock Island Railroad

Looking like a purely Burlington operation, the *Sam Houston Zephyr* arrives Fort Worth from Houston behind E5 9909. Photo by R. S. Plummer.

The Trinity & Brazos Valley Railway was chartered by the state of Texas on October 17, 1902. By the beginning of 1904 it had a line open between Cleburne and Mexia, Texas.

In 1905 the Colorado & Southern purchased control of the T&BV, and in 1906 it sold a half interest in the road to the Rock Island. The T&BV filled out its map in 1907: Mexia to Houston;

Rock Island, jointly built the Galveston Terminal Railway. The T&BV constituted a Fort Worth–Houston–Galveston extension of the Burlington system and the Rock Island.

Texas in those days was not a booming petrochemical complex. Business did not meet expectations, and the T&BV entered receivership in 1914. During the receivership it lost its Santa Fe and Katy trackage rights; only the Fort Worth–Houston line via Waxahachie survived.

The Trinity & Brazos Valley emerged from receivership in July 1930 with a new name: Burlington-Rock Island Railroad (Chicago, Burlington & Quincy had gained control of the Colorado & Southern in 1908). It re-established trackage rights from Waxahachie to Dallas over the Katy and from Cleburne to Fort Worth on the Santa Fe and acquired rights to Galveston over the Texas & New Orleans (Southern Pacific).

In 1931 the Rock Island and the Fort Worth & Denver City (C&S) jointly leased the Dallas–Teague segment of the railroad and began operating it in alternate 5-year periods. In 1932 B-RI abandoned its line from Hillsboro to Cleburne and dropped the Santa Fe trackage rights to Fort Worth. By 1942 the branch, the original T&BV line, was cut back to Mexia.

On June 1, 1950, B-RI ceased operation and its two parents made a new joint lease of the entire line with alternate 5-year operating periods. The Fort Worth & Denver and the Rock Island purchased the property of the B-RI in April 1964, and the corporation was dissolved in April 1965. Upon the demise of the Rock Island in 1980, the Burlington Northern assumed sole operation.

trackage rights over Gulf, Colorado & Santa Fe from Houston to Galveston and from Cleburne north to Fort Worth; Teague to Waxahachie; trackage rights from Waxahachie to Fort Worth on Houston & Texas Central (Southern Pacific); and trackage rights from Waxahachie to Dallas on the Missouri-Kansas-Texas. The T&BV purchased a quarter interest in the Houston Belt & Terminal Railway, and T&BV's parents, C&S and

	1929	1949
Miles of railroad operated:	367	228
Number of locomotives:	37	
Number of passenger cars:	20	3
Number of freight cars:	721	
Number of company service cars:	186	36

Location of headquarters: Houston, Texas

Reporting marks: BRI

Notable named passenger trains: *Sam Houston Zephyr, Texas Rocket* (Fort Worth–Dallas–Houston)

Historical and technical societies:
Burlington Route Historical Society, P. O. Box 456, LaGrange, IL 60525-0456; BRHS@KKTV.com; http://www.burlingtonroute.com/
Rock Island Technical Society, c/o David J. Engle, 11519 N. Wayne Ave., Kansas City, MO 64155-2914; http://storm.simpson.edu/~RITS/

Recommended reading: *The Colorado Road,* by F. Hol Wagner Jr., published in 1970 by Intermountain Chapter, National Railway Historical Society, P. O. Box 5181, Denver, CO 80217

Successors:
Burlington Northern
Burlington Northern & Santa Fe
Chicago, Rock Island & Pacific
Fort Worth & Denver

Portions still operated: Burlington Northern & Santa Fe: Dallas–Galveston

Butte, Anaconda & Pacific Railway

The Butte, Anaconda & Pacific was incorporated in 1892 and opened in 1893. It connected copper mines at Butte, Montana, with a smelter at Anaconda. The mines, the smelter, and the railroad were all owned by Marcus Daly.

By 1911 the Anaconda Copper Mining Co., Daly's company, had acquired considerable expertise using electric motors to drain and ventilate its mines. The BA&P electrified its line to take advantage of the economies that would result from electric operation of that aspect of the business as well. BA&P was the first road to electrify for purely economic reasons; moreover, the electrification project would demonstrate uses of the copper produced by its parent. The road was the first to use General Electric's 2400-volt DC system. Electric locomotives started hauling trains in 1913.

In 1957 two electric locomotives were added to the original fleet of 28; a few years earlier BA&P had replaced its few remaining steam locomotives with diesels for service on non-electrified track. In 1958 BA&P began operation over the Northern Pacific between Butte and Durant under a joint trackage agreement. Electric operation continued until 1967, when the installation of a new ore concentrator at Butte changed the road's traffic pattern. The seven GP7s and GP9s that had been working the non-electrified trackage took over all of BA&P's operation.

A trio of Butte, Anaconda & Pacific boxcabs brings a long train of empties along the main line near Silver Bow, west of Butte. Photo by Donald Sims.

The 1980 closing of Anaconda's smelter in Anaconda again changed the road's traffic pattern—indeed, eliminated most of it—and BA&P's operations changed from daily to "as required." The mines themselves closed in 1983, and the railroad all but ceased operation. In 1984 owner Anaconda Minerals petitioned for abandonment and in March 1985 agreed to sell and donate the railroad properties to the state of Montana for operation by the Rarus Railway Co., a new short line.

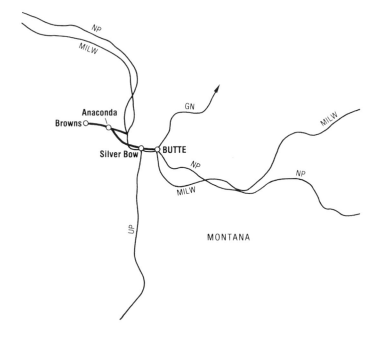

	1929	1982
Miles of railroad operated:	69	43
Number of steam locomotives:	7	
Number of electric locomotives:	28	
Number of diesel locomotives:		9
Number of passenger cars:	8	
Number of freight cars:	1,422	
Number of company service cars:	22	
Number of freight and company service cars:		674

Location of headquarters: Anaconda, Montana
Reporting marks: BAP
Recommended reading: "Montana Copper Carrier," a chapter of *When The Steam Railroads Electrified,* by William D. Middleton, published in 1974 by Kalmbach Publishing Co. (ISBN 0-89024-028-0)
Portions still operated: Rarus Railway: Butte—Anaconda

Predecessors of Canadian National Railways

The two principal railroads in Canada today are Canadian National Railways, formerly government owned and then privatized, and privately owned Canadian Pacific Railway. A few paragraphs on Canadian Pacific are a necessary preface to the history of Canadian National—and a few sentences on Canadian history are necessary to explain Canadian Pacific.

The Dominion of Canada was created on July 1, 1867, by the union of the provinces of New Brunswick, Nova Scotia, and Canada (whose two parts, Upper and Lower Canada, became present-day Ontario and Quebec, respectively). Canada's population was anything but homogeneous: Immigrants came from England, Scotland, Ireland, France, Germany, and the United States, and they settled along the seacoast, the St. Lawrence River, and the shores of Lake Ontario and Lake Erie. North and west of Toronto lay a thousand miles of rocky forested wilderness, and beyond that were the prairies and the Rockies.

In 1871 when British Columbia joined the confederation (it included Manitoba by then), the Canadian government promised a railway to link British Columbia with the rest of Canada. The Canadian Pacific Railway was incorporated in 1881 to build from Callander, Ont., near North Bay, to the Pacific at what is now Vancouver. The company received extensive land

Grand Trunk Railway 4-6-2 No.1108 leads the first Grand Trunk Pacific train up to the Canadian Pacific station at Saskatoon on October 7, 1918. CN photo.

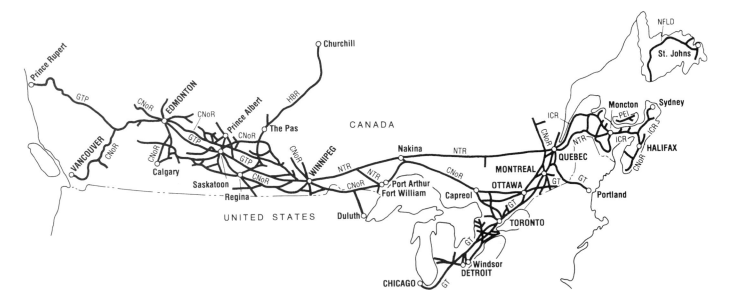

grants and subsidies from the Canadian government in exchange for unifying Canada.

CPR completed its main line on November 7, 1885, and then began to spread an extensive network of branches across the wheatlands between Winnipeg and Calgary. It became the dominant railroad on the prairies. In eastern Canada, though, Canadian Pacific was the minority railroad, with little more than a line east through Montreal and across Maine to Saint John, N. B., and another route southwest through Toronto to Windsor, Ont.

Canadian National Railways was not built—it was gathered and assembled. Its five major components were Intercolonial Railway, National Transcontinental Railway, Canadian Northern Railway, Grand Trunk Pacific Railway, and Grand Trunk Railway. All five were brought into CNR because they were in financial difficulty.

Intercolonial Railway

The maritime provinces had far more communication and commerce with New England than with Quebec and Ontario. The government deemed a rail link necessary to tie the Maritimes to the rest of Canada and was willing to finance that railroad. A commission headed by Sandford Fleming surveyed a route from Moncton, N. B., northwest to Mont Joli, Que., and then southwest along the south bank of the St. Lawrence to a connection with the Grand Trunk at Riviere du Loup, Que. For military reasons Fleming chose a route as far as possible from the U. S. border.

The Intercolonial began operation between Halifax and Riviere du Loup in 1876, and in 1879 it assumed operation of Grand Trunk's line from Riviere du Loup to just west of Levis, across the St. Lawrence from Quebec City. Canadian Government Railways took over operation of the Intercolonial in 1913.

Canadian Northern Railway

In the late 1890s William Mackenzie and Donald Mann began assembling the Canadian Northern system. It included a new line across the prairies from Winnipeg through Edmonton to Vancouver (not completed until 1915), several lines in Manitoba leased from the Northern Pacific, and lines in Ontario, Quebec, and Nova Scotia. By 1916 Canadian Northern had a main line from Toronto west to Vancouver via Sudbury, Capreol, and Port Arthur-Fort William (now Thunder Bay), Ont.; Warroad, Minnesota; Winnipeg and Dauphin, Man.; Canora (named for the railroad), Warman, and North Battleford, Saskatchewan; Edmonton and Jasper, Alberta; and the canyons of the Thompson and Fraser rivers. Another main line ran from Toronto to Quebec City via Napanee and Ottawa, Ont., and Joliette and Garneau, Que. A Capreol–Ottawa line was completed in 1917, and a line into Montreal via the Mount Royal Tunnel in 1918.

The Canadian Northern system included two orphan lines in Nova Scotia (the Halifax & Southwestern along the south shore, and a line to Inverness on Cape Breton Island); a tentacle north to Chicoutimi, Que.; an extensive network of branches covering the prairies between Winnipeg and the Rockies; and the Duluth, Winnipeg & Pacific Railway from Fort Frances, Ont., to Duluth, Minn.

Canadian Northern ran out of money. The mother country couldn't help—World War I had stopped the export of capital from Britain. Because of loans and land grants the Canadian government found itself CNoR's major creditor. On September 6, 1917, CNoR management resigned and a new board appointed by the government took over. On December 20, 1918, all government-owned railways were brought under the new CNoR management, to be known as "Canadian National Railways."

National Transcontinental Railway

In the first few years of the twentieth century the Grand Trunk Railway, prompted by a spirit of expansionism, tried to team up first with Canadian Pacific and then with Canadian Northern. Neither attempt succeeded, so GT proposed constructing a rail line from Callander, Ont., to Winnipeg well north of the Canadian Pacific line, then continuing west to the Pacific.

The Canadian Pacific was a product of Canada's Conservative Party. The Liberals, who came into power in 1896, decided to make their reputation with another transcontinental railroad. They seized GT's proposal, extended it east to Moncton, N. B., and laid out as direct a route as possible to Winnipeg, passing far to the north of Montreal, Ottawa, and Toronto. Except near Quebec City there was neither settlement nor population along the route (there is little more now), and the terrain was largely swamps and bare rock. The major engineering work on the NTR was the St. Lawrence River bridge at Quebec City, which collapsed twice during construction.

The line was to be constructed by Grand Trunk Pacific, a subsidiary of Grand Trunk, on behalf of the government. GTP would lease it from the government upon completion. The rental was to be based on the cost of construction—and that proved to be more than twice the estimate. Grand Trunk Pacific, already in financial trouble because of the cost of its own line west of Winnipeg, refused to take over the National Transcontinental upon its completion. Canadian Government Railways, which was already operating the Intercolonial, took over the National Transcontinental in 1915.

Grand Trunk Pacific

The Grand Trunk Pacific Railway was incorporated in 1903 to build from Winnipeg to the Pacific at Prince Rupert, B. C., the Canadian port nearest the Orient. GTP's route through Saskatoon to Edmonton lay between the Canadian Pacific and the Canadian Northern lines. From Edmonton to Yellowhead Pass, 250 miles, GTP and CNoR were parallel. During World War I part of GTP's line west of Edmonton was dismantled so the rails could be used in France. GTP was given running rights on CNoR's track, portions of which were later relocated on the GTP roadbed. From Yellowhead Pass GTP's line reached 700 miles northwest to Prince Rupert. The line was completed in 1914.

Prince Rupert never developed into a major seaport. Land transportation rates were higher than those to and from Vancouver, and there was almost no population to provide local business in the area between Prince Rupert and the Rockies. On the prairies GTP was as deficient in branches as Canadian Northern was prolific. GTP entered receivership in 1919 and came under the Canadian National umbrella in 1920.

Grand Trunk Railway

The Grand Trunk (whose lines included the former Champlain & St. Lawrence, Canada's first railway—1836) was the last major addition to Canadian National Railways. It was conceived as a Canadian main line from Montreal through Toronto to Sarnia, Ont., where it would connect with a railroad to Chicago and in Chicago with a railroad to the Canadian West. At the time it was believed that the terrain north of Lake Superior would force any route to western Canada through Michigan. The project included two lines east from Montreal, one to the year-round port of Portland, Maine, and the other down the St. Lawrence to connect with a line from Halifax.

The Grand Trunk Railway was incorporated in 1852. By 1856 it was in operation between Quebec City (more accurately, Levis, on the south bank of the St. Lawrence River) and Windsor, Ont. In 1859 GT opened the Victoria Bridge across the St. Lawrence at Montreal—at a cost which sent GT to the government for funds.

At the time of confederation in 1867 it was proposed to extend the Grand Trunk west to the Pacific and east to New Brunswick and Nova Scotia at public expense. Public feeling was against the idea because of GT's debt and mismanagement. Nor was GT interested, because it could see little connection, either figurative or physical, between the existing GT system and the line to Vancouver. GT stuck to its original goal of Chicago, which it reached in 1880 by purchasing several short railroads (in the process outfoxing William H. Vanderbilt). The Michigan lines were connected to the rest of the system by ferry until the completion of the St. Clair Tunnel in 1890.

In 1882 GT absorbed the Great Western, which had opened in January 1854 from Niagara Falls through Hamilton to Windsor, Ont. In the 1880s Grand Trunk acquired Central Vermont stock as part of a traffic agreement. It increased its CV holdings to fend off advances into New England by Canadian Pacific and northward expansion by Boston & Maine. By 1900 Grand Trunk owned a majority interest in the Central Vermont. In 1904 GT purchased the Canada Atlantic Railway, which had a line from Alburgh, Vt., at the north end of Lake Champlain, through Coteau, Ottawa, and Algonquin National Park to the shores of Georgian Bay near Parry Sound.

Grand Trunk incurred an enormous debt for the construction of its subsidiary, Grand Trunk Pacific. Grand Trunk had an opportunity to turn over the GTP to the government, but GT's British board of directors rejected the government proposal. GT badly botched its own defense, and on May 21, 1920, the Canadian government took formal possession of Grand Trunk and Grand Trunk Pacific. Grand Trunk Pacific became part of Canadian National Railways almost immediately; Grand Trunk was absorbed in 1923. At that time GT's U. S. lines became separate companies: Grand Trunk Western (Port Huron and Detroit to Chicago) and Grand Trunk (Island Pond, Vt., to Portland, Me.).

Canadian National

Canadian National Railways was incorporated on June 6, 1919; the name had been in use for six months to conveniently refer to the combined Canadian Northern and Canadian Government railways. CNR also included two minor railways, the Prince Edward Island Railway, which the Canadian government had bailed out when Prince Edward Island joined the Confederation in 1873, and the Hudson Bay Railway, a line constructed to carry grain from the prairies north across the tundra to the Hudson Bay port (usable only three months each year) of Churchill, Man. The Newfoundland Railway became part of CNR when Newfoundland joined Canada in 1949.

Historical and technical society: Canadian National Lines Special Interest Group, 101 Elm Park Road, Winnipeg, Manitoba R2M 0W3; http://129.93. 226.138/rr/cnr/cnlines.htm
Recommended reading: *History of the Canadian National Railways*, by G. R. Stevens, published in 1973 by The Macmillan Company, 866 Third Avenue, New York, NY 10022

Central New England Railway

The Central New England had its beginnings in the Hartford & Connecticut Western Railroad, opened in 1871 from Hartford northwest to Millerton, New York. There it connected with the Harlem Division of the New York Central, giving Hartford a route to Albany and the West. The intention of the Hartford & Connecticut Western was to meet the Dutchess & Columbia Railroad, but the Boston, Hartford & Erie got control of the Dutchess & Columbia and blocked alliance with the HC&W.

The HC&W found two other outlets to the Hudson. The more northerly was the Rhinebeck & Connecticut, a 42-mile line from State Line north to Boston Corners, then southwest to Rhinecliff (airline distance, about 24 miles). In 1881 the H&CW bought the bankrupt Rhinebeck & Connecticut, creating a line under one management from Hartford to the Hudson—and more important, to the Hudson directly opposite the eastern terminal of the Delaware & Hudson Canal.

HC&W's other outlet to the Hudson was the Poughkeepsie & Eastern, from Poughkeepsie northeast 37 miles to Boston Corners. In the 1880s a bridge over the Hudson at Poughkeepsie was proposed by Philadelphia interests, who saw a market for Pennsylvania anthracite in New England. The Poughkeepsie & Eastern would have been the ideal connection between the bridge and the Hartford & Connecticut Western, but the owner of the Poughkeepsie & Eastern would have nothing to do with the idea. He changed the railroad's name to New York & Massachusetts and proposed to extend it east to a connection with the Central Massachusetts near Springfield. The bridge company built a parallel railroad, the Poughkeepsie & Connecticut, from Poughkeepsie to a connection with the HC&W.

The Poughkeepsie bridge opened in 1888, and soon afterward the Poughkeepsie & Connecticut and the Hudson Connecting Railroad (Poughkeepsie to Campbell Hall) were consolidated as the Central New England & Western Railroad. That company leased the HC&W and also the Dutchess County Railroad, from Poughkeepsie southeast to a connection with the New York & New England. In 1892 the CNE&W was consolidated with the Poughkeepsie Bridge & Railroad Company as the Philadelphia, Reading & New England Railroad, under the control of the Philadelphia & Reading. Within months the Philadelphia & Reading controlled the New York & New England and the Boston & Maine, and within two months more the bankruptcy of the Philadelphia & Reading caused the whole empire to collapse.

The PR&NE was reorganized as the Central New England Railway in 1898. In 1904 the New Haven bought control of the Central New England for the Poughkeepsie Bridge and the connections at Maybrook and Campbell Hall. The Central New England continued to exist until January 1, 1927, when the New Haven merged it. Nearly all of the CNE east of the bridge was abandoned in 1938.

	1926
Miles of railroad operated:	264
Number of locomotives:	58
Number of passenger cars:	50
Number of freight cars:	1,015
Number of company service cars:	22

Location of headquarters: New Haven, Connecticut

Reporting marks:

Historical and technical society: New Haven Railroad Historical and Technical Association, P. O. Box 122, Wallingford, CT 06492

Recommended reading: *The Formation of the New England Railway Systems*, by George Pierce Baker, published in 1937 by the Harvard University Press

Successors: New York, New Haven & Hartford

Portions still operated: Guilford Transportation Industries: Hartford–Griffins, Ct.

Central of Georgia Railway

CENTRAL OF GEORGIA The opening in 1830 of the South Carolina Railroad between Charleston, S. C., and Augusta, Georgia, diverted traffic from the port of Savannah, Ga., to Charleston. To recapture that business, the citizens of Savannah organized the Central Rail Road & Canal Company in 1833 to build a railroad toward Macon. Routes were surveyed and construction began in December 1835, about the same time the company's name was changed to Central Rail Road & Banking Company of Georgia. The railroad reached Macon, 191 miles from Savannah, in October 1843. By the Civil War the road had purchased or leased lines to Augusta and Eatonton.

In 1869 the CofG leased the South Western Railroad, which it had earlier helped finance, gaining lines from Macon to Columbus, Fort Gaines, and Albany, Ga., and Eufala, Alabama. In 1872 the road acquired a Savannah–New York steamship line and in 1875 purchased the Western Rail Road of Alabama jointly with the Georgia Railroad. The year 1879 saw the CofG enter Montgomery, Ala., through purchase of a controlling interest in the Montgomery & Eufala.

In 1881 the Georgia Railroad and its interests in the Western of Alabama and the Atlanta & West Point were leased to William Wadley, president of the Central of Georgia. Wadley assigned half the

In the summer of 1947 Central of Georgia inaugurated with great success two coach streamliners. In this July 1947 scene 4 miles out of Atlanta the *Nancy Hanks II* (left) has just begun its evening return to Savannah and the *Man o' War* (right) is nearly at the midpoint of its second daily Columbus–Atlanta round trip. CofG photo.

lease to the CofG and half to the Louisville & Nashville. At the same time, CofG gained control of the Port Royal & Augusta and began development of a system to reach into western South Carolina, but encountered hostility from the government of the state of South Carolina. In that same era the CofG extended lines northwest from Columbus to Birmingham, Ala., and north through Rome to Chattanooga, Tennessee.

In 1888 the 2,600-mile CofG came under control of the Richmond Terminal and was leased to the Georgia Pacific Railway, a subsidiary of the Richmond & Danville (a predecessor of the Southern Railway). In 1892 CofG entered receivership. It lost the Port Royal system (which became the Charleston & Western Carolina, a member of the Atlantic Coast Line family) and the Georgia Railroad and its affiliates.

Reorganization

Sold at foreclosure and reorganized as the Central of Georgia Railway, the new CofG included several former subsidiary companies, two leased railroads, the South Western and the Augusta & Savannah, and what was called the Auxiliary System—a land company, the steamship line, and several short lines. In 1900 the company opened a line southwest through Dothan and Hartford to Florala, Ala.; spurs of this line reached into Florida. In 1901 CofG regained its Chattanooga line, which had operated independently since the foreclosure sale, and acquired a branch from Dover west to Brewton, Ga. In 1905 the line from Columbus to Greenville, Ga., was widened from 3-foot gauge to standard and extended to Newnan, forming a direct Columbus–Atlanta route in conjunction with the Atlanta & West Point.

E. H. Harriman and the Illinois Central

In 1907 E. H. Harriman gained control of the Central of Georgia. His system already included Union Pacific, Southern Pacific, and Illinois Central. None of those railroads connected directly with the CofG, so Harriman assembled a Jackson, Tenn.–Birmingham line for IC from 129 miles of trackage rights over Mobile & Ohio, Southern, and Frisco and 80 miles of new construction. In 1909 Harriman sold his interest in the CofG to the Illinois Central.

The Depression cut into CofG's traffic, and the relocation of textile mills from New England to the South eliminated much of the business in cotton moving through the port of Savannah. The road entered receivership at the end of 1932 and was reorganized in 1948, out from under IC control. In 1951 CofG purchased the Savannah

& Atlanta and in 1962 consolidated operations with the S&A between Savannah and Waynesboro, Ga., to allow abandonment of part of each road's line between those points.

Southern Railway ownership

The Central of Georgia was a desirable and strategic property. In 1956 the Frisco purchased control, subject to Interstate Commerce Commission approval—but the ICC disapproved and ordered the Frisco to sell its interest in 1961. The ICC approved of Southern Railway's acquisition of CofG, and on June 17, 1963, the Central of Georgia Railway became a subsidiary of the Southern. The Central of Georgia Railroad was incorporated June 1, 1971, and immediately merged the Central of Georgia Railway and three smaller lines: the Georgia & Florida, the Savannah & Atlanta, and the Wrightsville & Tennille. The new CofG quickly lost its identity in the Southern system, but it survives on paper as part of the Norfolk Southern.

	1929	1970
Miles of railroad operated:	1,944	1,729
Number of locomotives:	331	131
Number of passenger cars:	262	30
Number of freight cars:	9,693	
Number of company service cars:	477	
Number of freight and company service cars:		8,296

Location of headquarters: Savannah, Georgia
Reporting marks: CG
Notable named passenger trains: *Nancy Hanks II* (Atlanta–Savannah), *Man o' War* (Atlanta–Columbus)

Historical and technical society: Central of Georgia Historical Society, c/o William L. Pippin Jr., P. O. Box 9966, Atlanta, GA 30319
Recommended reading: *Central of Georgia Railway and Connecting Lines*, by Richard E. Prince, published in 1976 by Richard E. Prince
Subsidiaries and affiliated railroads, 1970:
Savannah & Atlanta
Wrightsville & Tennille
Successors:
Southern Railway
Norfolk Southern

Central Railroad of New Jersey

The earliest railroad ancestor of the Central of New Jersey was the Elizabethtown & Somerville Railroad, incorporated in 1831 and opened from Elizabethport to Elizabeth, N. J., in 1836. Horses gave way to steam in 1839, and the road was extended west, reaching Somerville at the beginning of 1842. The Somerville & Easton Railroad was incorporated in 1847 and began building westward. In 1849 it purchased the Elizabethtown & Somerville and adopted a new name: Central Railroad Company of New Jersey. The line reached Phillipsburg, on the east bank of the Delaware River, in 1852. It was extended east across Newark Bay to Jersey City in 1864, and it acquired branches to Flemington, Newark, Perth Amboy, Chester, and Wharton.

The New Jersey Southern began construction in 1860 at Port Monmouth. The railroad worked its way southwest across lower New Jersey and reached Bayside, on the Delaware River west of Bridgeton, N. J., in 1871. The NJS came under the control of the Central of New Jersey in 1879. CNJ's influence briefly extended across the Delaware River in the form of the Baltimore & Delaware Bay Railroad from Bombay Hook, Del., east of Townsend, to Chestertown, Maryland. That line became part of the Pennsylvania Railroad family in 1901.

The Camelback locomotive was designed on the premise that the wide firebox necessary for slow-burning anthracite would restrict the forward view from a cab in the conventional location. The engineer of a Camelback rode in a cab astride the boiler (the right side of the cab was for the engineer; the left side of the cab was primarily for symmetry), and the fireman had a minimal shelter attached to the rear of the firebox. Central of New Jersey used Camelbacks later than any other major railroad, and the Camelback 4-6-0, as shown here on a local passenger train leaving Jersey City, was almost as much a CNJ trademark as the Statue of Liberty emblem. Photo by William R. Frutchey.

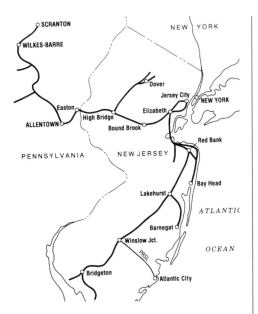

The New Jersey Southern was connected to the CNJ by the New York & Long Branch Railroad, which was completed in 1881 between Perth Amboy and Bay Head Junction. The NY&LB, at least in modern times, had no equipment of its own; CNJ and the Pennsylvania, joint owners of the Long Branch, both operated on it by trackage rights.

CNJ's lines in Pennsylvania were built by the Lehigh Coal & Navigation Co. as the Lehigh & Susquehanna Railroad. The main line was com-pleted from Phillipsburg, N. J., to Wilkes-Barre in 1866. A notable feature of the line was the Ashley Planes, a steep stretch of line (maximum grade, 14.65 percent) operated by cables driven by stationary engines. The Ashley Planes remained in service until after World War II.

Central of New Jersey leased the Lehigh & Susquehanna in 1871. The line was extended to Scranton in 1888 by a subsidiary of the L&S, the Wilkes-Barre & Scranton. Most of the traffic on the Pennsylvania lines was anthracite coal, much of it from mines owned by subsidiaries of the railroad, until the Commodities Clause of the Interstate Commerce Act of 1920 forbade railroads to haul freight in which they had an interest.

Reading control

From 1883 to 1887 the CNJ was leased to and operated by the Philadelphia & Reading, with which it formed a Jersey City–Philadelphia route. CNJ resumed its own management after a reorganization in 1887. In 1901 the Reading Company, successor to Philadelphia & Reading, acquired control of the CNJ through purchase of a majority of its stock, and at about that same time Baltimore & Ohio acquired control of the Reading.

CNJ's *Blue Comet*, inaugurated in 1929, was the forerunner of the coach streamliners that blossomed nationwide in the late 1930s and the 1940s. It was a deluxe coach train operating twice daily between Jersey City and Atlantic City, and its refurbished cars offered more comfort than the usual day coach of the era. It was painted blue from the pilot of its 4-6-2 to the rear of its observation car. It succumbed to automobile competition in 1941.

In 1929 CNJ purchased a 30 percent interest in the Raritan River Railroad, a short line from Perth Amboy to New Brunswick. In 1931 it acquired total ownership of the Wharton & Northern and a partial interest in the Mount Hope Mineral Railroad from Warren Foundry & Pipe Corp.

CNJ maintained a small carfloat terminal in the Bronx. It was the site of the first successful Class 1 railroad diesel operation.

Postwar woes

The years after World War II were not kind to the Central of New Jersey. Passenger traffic was almost entirely commuter business, requiring great amounts of rolling stock for two short periods five days a week. Three-fourths of CNJ's freight traffic terminated on line—the road was essentially a terminal carrier. In addition, heavy taxes levied by the state of New Jersey ate up much of CNJ's revenue.

Between 1946 and 1952 CNJ's lines in Pennsylvania were operated as the Central Railroad of Pennsylvania in an effort to escape taxation by the state of New Jersey. CNJ resumed its own operation of the Pennsylvania lines at the end of 1952.

When the Lehigh & New England Railroad was abandoned in 1961 CNJ acquired a few of its branches and organized them as the Lehigh & New England Railway. In 1963 Lehigh Coal & Navigation sold its railroad properties to the Reading, but the lease to the CNJ continued. In 1965 CNJ and Lehigh Valley consolidated their lines along the Lehigh River in Pennsylvania and portions of each road's line were abandoned; the anthracite traffic that had supported both roads had largely disappeared. CNJ operations in Pennsylvania ended March 31, 1972.

Over the years CNJ maintained an extensive marine operation on New York Bay, including a steamer line to Sandy Hook. CNJ's last marine service, the ferry line between Manhattan and CNJ's rail terminal at Jersey City, made its final run on April 30, 1967. It was also the last day for the terminal itself; the next day CNJ passenger trains began originating and termi-nating at the Pennsylvania Railroad station in Newark, where New York passengers could transfer to either PRR or Port Authority Trans-Hudson trains.

Although the state of New Jersey began subsidizing commuter service in 1964 and the tax situation changed in 1966, CNJ entered bankruptcy proceedings on March 22, 1967. The merger between Chesapeake & Ohio and Norfolk & Western that was proposed in 1965 to counter the impending Pennsylvania-New York Central merger was to have included CNJ, but the bankruptcy of Penn Central killed that prospect.

CNJ drafted elaborate plans for reorganization; they came to naught as neighboring railroads collapsed. Conrail took over the railroad properties and freight operations of the Central of New Jersey on April 1, 1976; NJ Transit purchased the lines over which it now operates commuter service.

	1929	1974
Miles of railroad operated:	693	526
Number of locomotives:	535	101
Number of passenger cars:	917	157
Number of freight cars:	22,978	2,232
Number of company service cars:	674	51

Location of headquarters: New York, New York

Reporting marks: CNJ

Notable named passenger trains: *Blue Comet* (Jersey City–Atlantic City)

Historical and technical society: Anthracite Railroads Historical Society, P. O. Box 519, Lansdale, PA 19446-0519

Recommended reading: *Jersey Central Album*, by Warren B. Crater, published in 1963 by Warren B. Crater, 270 West Colfax Avenue, Roselle Park, NJ 07204

Subsidiaries and affiliated railroads:
Central Railroad of Pennsylvania (1946–1952)
Lehigh & New England Railway (1961–1976)

Successors:
Conrail
NJ Transit

Portions still operated:
Conrail: East Ferry Street (Newark)–Elizabethport–Perth Amboy; Red Bank–Toms River
Morristown & Erie: Bartley–Lake Junction–Rockaway
NJ Transit: Elizabethport–High Bridge; Perth Amboy–Bay Head
Southern Railroad of New Jersey: Winslow Junction–Vineland
Winchester & Western: Vineland–Mauricetown, Bridgeton Junction–Seabrook

Central Vermont Railway

The Vermont Central Railroad was opened in 1849 between Windsor and Burlington, Vermont. Its builders found a relatively easy route over the divide between the Connecticut River and Lake Champlain by following the valleys of the White and Winooski rivers. Like many New England railroads of the time, it aimed to capture traffic moving between Boston and the Great Lakes. By 1850 connections were in place at each end, creating a through route from Boston to Ogdensburg, New York, on the St. Lawrence River.

By 1871 the Vermont Central rail system reached from New London, Connecticut, north to Montreal and west to Ogdensburg. It included the Rutland Railroad and steamship lines from New London to New York and from Ogdensburg to Chicago. In 1873 the Vermont Central was reorganized as the Central Vermont Railroad.

After the financial panic of 1893 the Central Vermont surrendered its leases of the Rutland and the Ogdensburg & Lake Champlain. The company was reorganized again in 1898 as the Central Vermont Railway, with Canada's Grand Trunk Railway as its majority stockholder. Control passed from Grand Trunk to Canadian National Railways in 1923. A flood in 1927 wiped out almost all of CV's main line across the

Central Vermont's 2-10-4s were the largest steam locomotives in New England. Engine 703 is shown rolling freight south through the Connecticut Valley on Boston & Maine rails north of Brattleboro, Vermont, in December 1952. Photo by Philip R. Hastings.

middle of Vermont; Canadian National funded the rebuilding of the line.

CV was in receivership between 1927 and 1929. It trimmed back several branch lines during the Depression, and it discontinued its New London–New York steamship service after

World War II. In the mid-1950s it abandoned its own line to Montreal in favor of trackage rights on parent CN. The railroad dieselized relatively late, in 1957.

In 1971 Canadian National Railways placed all its U. S. subsidiaries under the control of the

Grand Trunk Corporation, headquartered in Detroit. Later in the 1970s CV regained a measure of independence and local control. However, traffic and revenues diminished—most of CV's traffic was received from CN and Conrail and terminated on line.

In 1983 the CV was briefly offered for sale, but there were no buyers. CV made several attempts to build up business: a piggyback train, a unit train carrying wood chips to a power plant, a unit train carrying lumber and building materials, and a TankTrain (linked tank cars). None of those attempts was outstandingly successful.

The middle portion of CV's main line, between Windsor and Brattleboro, Vt., consisted of track-age rights on Boston & Maine's Connecticut River line. B&M's track deteriorated in the 1980s to such an extent that in 1987 Amtrak suspended the operation of its Washington–Montreal *Montrealer* and used its condemnation powers to take ownership of the Brattleboro–Windsor route. Amtrak transferred the line to CV, which rehabilitated the track, and the *Montrealer* resumed operation in 1989 on a new route—the entire length of CV's main line, from New London, Conn., to East Alburgh, Vt.

In the early 1990s CV was again for sale. It was purchased by RailTex, Inc., which took over operations on February 4, 1995 as the New England Central Railroad.

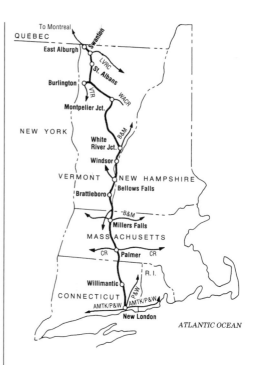

	1929	1992
Miles of railroad operated:	469	366
Number of locomotives:	68	20
Number of passenger cars:	128	
Number of freight cars:	3,350	223
Number of company service cars:	148	

Location of headquarters: St. Albans, Vermont

Reporting marks: CV

Notable named passenger trains: *Montrealer* and *Washingtonian* (Washington–Montreal, operated jointly with Pennsylvania, New Haven, Boston & Maine, and Canadian National)

Historical and technical society: Central Vermont Railway Historical Society, c/o John Haropulos, 1070 Belmont Street, Manchester, NH 03104

Recommended reading:
The Central Vermont Railway, by Robert C. Jones, published in 1981 and 1982 by Sundance Publications, Silverton, CO 81433 (ISBN 0-913582-27-1, -28-X, -29-8, -30-1, -31-X, and 32-8)

"Central Vermont . . . a survivor," by Scott Hartley, in *Trains* Magazine, February 1991, pages 30–42

Successors: New England Central Railroad

Portions still operated: New England Central: New London, Conn.–East Alburgh, Vt., Essex Junction–Burlington, Vt.

Chesapeake & Ohio Railway

The rivers and the ocean were the primary avenues of transportation in Virginia in the 1830s. The few early railroads in the state connected the coast with inland points. One of these was the Louisa Railroad, chartered in 1836 to run from Taylorsville, on the Richmond, Fredericksburg & Potomac just south of what is now Doswell, to points in Louisa County. At first the RF&P operated the railroad, but in 1847 the Louisa Railroad acquired its own rolling stock and took over its own affairs. By 1850 the railroad had been extended west to Charlottesville. That year it became the Virginia Central Railroad, and in 1851 over the protests of the RF&P it built its own line from Taylorsville to Richmond.

The state of Virginia undertook construction of the Blue Ridge Railroad west from Charlottesville and on completion leased it to the Virginia Central (which later purchased it). Meanwhile, the Virginia Central leapfrogged its rails ahead to Clifton Forge. In 1853 the state chartered the Covington & Ohio Railroad to connect the Virginia Central Railroad and the James River & Kanawha Canal at Covington with the Ohio River.

The Civil War halted the westward expansion of the railroad, even though the line would have been valuable to the Confederacy. During the latter part of the war the Virginia Central pulled up parts of its line for supplies to maintain other parts. However, by 1865 the entire line was back in service. The Virginia Central and the Covington & Ohio were consolidated as the Chesapeake & Ohio Railroad in 1868.

A trainload of coal, Chesapeake & Ohio's principal commodity, leaves Ronceverte, West Virginia, behind a 2-6-6-6; another Allegheny is pushing at the rear of the train. Photo by William P Price.

C. P. Huntington

In 1869 the C&O came under the control of C. P. Huntington, builder of the Central Pacific and the Southern Pacific. The C&O had run out of money, and its officers asked Huntington if he could finance the westward construction of the road. Huntington and his associates subscribed to mortgage bonds, and the C&O was reorganized with Huntington as its president.

On January 29, 1873, the C&O was completed from Richmond to the Ohio River a few miles east of its confluence with the Big Sandy (which forms the border between West Virginia and Kentucky). The western terminus of the road was the new city of Huntington, W. Va. In 1875 C&O entered receivership and was foreclosed and reorganized as the Chesapeake & Ohio Railway; another reorganization followed in 1888.

Huntington envisioned the C&O as the eastern portion of a transcontinental system. He organized the Chesapeake, Ohio & Southwestern Railroad in 1877 to take over the Memphis, Paducah & Northern Railroad, a line from Elizabethtown and Louisville through Paducah, Ky., to Memphis. Huntington's Louisville, New Orleans & Texas Railway provided the connection between Memphis and New Orleans, the eastern terminus of the Southern Pacific. In 1884 Huntington formed the Newport News & Mississippi Valley Co. to hold the C&O, the CO&SW, and the Elizabethtown, Lexington & Big Sandy (opened in 1872 from the Big Sandy River to Lexington, Ky., with trackage rights on the Louisville & Nashville to Louisville)

C&O's line along the Ohio River to Cincinnati opened in 1888 with the completion of the Maysville & Big Sandy Railroad from Ashland to Covington, Ky., opposite Cincinnati (the second Covington on C&O's main line), and the Covington & Cincinnati Elevated Railroad & Transfer & Bridge Co.—one of few three-ampersand railroads in the U. S. Both the M&BS and the C&CER&T&B were proprietary companies of the C&O.

The Vanderbilt years

Huntington's empire fell apart in 1888. The C&O was taken over and reorganized by Vanderbilt interests. It soon acquired the Elizabethtown, Lexington & Big Sandy and its Lexington–Louisville trackage rights. Illinois Central, by then under the control of E. H. Harriman, purchased the Chesapeake, Ohio & Southwestern and the Louisville, New Orleans & Texas, consolidating the latter with the Yazoo & Mississippi Valley.

During the presidency of Melville Ingalls (also president of the Cleveland, Cincinnati, Chicago & St. Louis), C&O undertook expansion at its eastern end. In 1882 it constructed a line east from Richmond to a new tidewater terminal at Newport News. In 1888 it leased (and later purchased) the Richmond & Allegheny Railroad, which followed the towpath of the James River & Kanawha Canal from Richmond through Lynchburg to Clifton Forge. Two years later the road arranged for access to Washington over the Virginia Midland Railway (later Southern Railway) from Gordonsville.

Expansion into Ohio and Indiana

By the turn of the century C&O had become a major coal hauler, and the Midwest was becoming a better market for coal than the East. In 1903 the majority of the stock of the Hocking Valley Railroad (Toledo–Columbus–Athens and Gallipolis, Ohio) was purchased jointly by the C&O, Baltimore & Ohio, Erie, Lake Shore & Michigan Southern (New York Central), and Pennsylvania railroads. In addition, C&O and LS&MS jointly acquired the Kanawha & Michigan from the Hocking Valley (the K&M ran from Charleston, W. Va., through Gallipolis and Athens, Ohio, to Columbus), and LS&MS purchased most of the stock of the Toledo & Ohio Central (Toledo–Columbus–Corning). By 1911 C&O had acquired control of the Hocking Valley. To satisfy antitrust legislation, C&O was required to sell its interest in the Kanawha & Michigan to the Toledo & Ohio Central in 1914.

To gain access to the Hocking Valley, C&O incorporated the Chesapeake & Ohio Northern Railway to build north from Limeville, Ky., a few miles southeast of Portsmouth, Ohio. C&ON bridged the Ohio, built north to Waverly, Ohio, and arranged for trackage rights over Norfolk & Western for 62 miles to Valley Crossing, south of Columbus. The C&ON was opened in 1917.

In the 1920s because of a limitation on the number of trains C&O could run on the N&W line and because grades on the N&W were steeper than those on C&O's main line, C&O constructed a parallel line—the Chesapeake & Hocking Valley Railway—between Greggs, near Waverly, and Valley Crossing. C&O leased the C&HV in 1926 and merged it (and also merged the Hocking Valley Railroad) in 1930.

In 1910 C&O purchased the Chicago, Cincinnati & Louisville Railroad, a line from Cincinnati to Hammond, Ind., and reorganized it as the Chesapeake & Ohio Railway of Indiana. About that same time C&O bought a one-sixth interest in the Richmond-Washington Co., operator of the Richmond, Fredericksburg & Potomac. In 1918 C&O bought White Sulphur Springs, Inc.— C&O had controlled the company since 1910— operator of the Greenbrier, a resort hotel at White Sulphur Springs, W. Va.

The Van Sweringen era

In 1923 Orris Paxton Van Sweringen and his brother Mantis James Van Sweringen, Cleveland real estate developers, purchased 30 percent of C&O's stock. The principal item in the Van Sweringens' empire was the Nickel Plate (more formally, the New York, Chicago & St. Louis Railroad), and they drafted proposals to merge C&O, NKP, Erie, Hocking Valley, and Pere Marquette to form a fourth eastern system of the magnitude of New York Central, Pennsylvania, and Baltimore & Ohio.

By 1929 the Van Sweringens also hoped to include the Wheeling & Lake Erie, the Lackawanna, and the Chicago & Eastern Illinois, the last to furnish a connection with the Missouri Pacific, in which they held a sizable interest. Later that year the Van Sweringens withdrew their applications as their empire began to collapse. Meanwhile, in 1928 C&O had received permission to control the Pere Marquette. In 1930 C&O and PM unified their operations.

In the depths of the Great Depression C&O inaugurated an all-air-conditioned passenger train, the *George Washington*, from Washington and Newport News to Louisville and Cincinnati. In 1933 C&O's advertising introduced the figure of a sleeping kitten. "Chessie" quickly became one of the best-known advertising symbols in the country.

Robert R. Young

In 1937 Robert R. Young acquired 43 percent of the stock of Alleghany Corporation (a holding company that controlled the Chesapeake Corporation, a holding company that controlled the C&O). By 1942 Young was chairman of the board of C&O. In 1945 he proposed a merger of C&O, Pere Marquette, Nickel Plate, and Wheeling & Lake Erie, with the idea of adding western connections (likely prospects were Missouri Pacific, Rio Grande, and Western Pacific) to make a coast-to-coast railroad. The Nickel Plate objected to the proposal. As it fell out, C&O merged Pere Marquette on June 6, 1947, Nickel Plate purchased C&O's Wheeling & Lake shares about the same time, and C&O distributed its NKP shares to C&O stockholders as a dividend later that year.

Young also proposed takeovers of the Association of American Railroads and the Pullman Company. He pushed for coast-to-coast through sleeping car service with his famous ad headed "A hog can cross America without changing trains—but you can't!"

Young intended to make C&O the top passenger railroad in the country. To this end he ordered a steam-turbine-powered Vista-Dome streamliner, the *Chessie*, for daylight service between Washington and Cincinnati, and he sent an order to Pullman-Standard for 289 passenger cars, enough to completely re-equip all of C&O's other trains. By the time the *Chessie* arrived from the Budd Company, C&O had discovered (possibly by counting the passengers on Baltimore &

Ohio's new *Cincinnatian*) that there was no market for a daytime Washington–Cincinnati train. Most of the *Chessie* cars were sold to other U. S. railroads; a dozen went to Argentina. Nearly half of the Pullman-Standard order was canceled or diverted to other railroads.

While all that was happening, in 1947 C&O became NYC's largest stockholder. Young proposed a merger of C&O, NYC, and the Virginian Railway. Young left the C&O in 1954 to take over management of the New York Central.

B&O, Western Maryland, and Chessie System

In 1960 C&O turned its attention to neighbor Baltimore & Ohio and offered to purchase its stock. The Interstate Commerce Commission approved C&O control of B&O at the end of 1962, and the actual exchange of C&O stock for B&O took place in February 1963. By 1973 C&O owned more than 90 percent of B&O's stock. B&O in turn owned nearly half the stock of Western Maryland and controlled Reading Company; the Reading controlled the Central Railroad of New Jersey. In 1966 the ICC approved C&O control of the Chicago South Shore & South Bend, an interurban-turned-commuter-carrier with tracks through the industrial area just south of Lake Michigan.

The Chessie System was incorporated in 1973 to own the C&O. C&O in turned controlled B&O, and the two of them held more than 90 percent of Western Maryland's stock. C&O, B&O, and WM did not merge immediately but became the Chessie System Railroads: They traded their identities and colors for new paint and a new emblem featuring C&O's cat, Chessie. South Shore did not become a Chessie System Railroad but remained a stray in the alley behind Chessie's house until 1984, when it was purchased by the Venango River Corporation.

	1929	1972
Miles of railroad operated:	2,740	4,994
Number of locomotives:	946	1,030
Number of passenger cars:	427	92*
Number of freight cars:	53,518	74,962
Number of company service cars:	1,641	1,850

Location of headquarters: Richmond, Virginia, and Cleveland, Ohio

Reporting marks: CO

Notable named passenger trains: *George Washington* (Washington/Newport News–Cincinnati/Louisville) ; *Chessie*

Historical and technical society: Chesapeake & Ohio Historical Society, P. O. Box 79, Clifton Forge, VA 24422; http://cohs.marshall.edu

Subsidiaries and affiliated railroads, 1972:

Baltimore & Ohio

*(1970)

Western Maryland

Chicago South Shore & South Bend

Predecessor railroads in this book:

Pere Marquette

Hocking Valley

Successors:

Chessie System

CSX Transportation

Portions still operated: The C&O is for the most part still intact. Among the longer branches and secondary lines that have been abandoned are: Lindsay–Strathmore, Va.; Covington–Hot Springs, Va.; Covington–Bess, Va.; North Caldwell–Durbin, W. Va.; Hocking Valley lines east of Diamond and south of Dundas, Ohio; C&O of Indiana between Cincinnati and Fernald, Ohio, and between Malden and Hammond, Ind. (that is, both ends of the Cincinnati–Hammond route; and Pere Marquette north of Baldwin, Mich.

Chessie System Railroads

Chessie System The Chessie System was incorporated on February 26, 1973. At that time, the Chesapeake & Ohio Railway controlled the Baltimore & Ohio, and C&O and B&O between them held more than 90 percent of Western Maryland's stock. On June 15, 1973, B&O, C&O, and WM were made subsidiaries of the Chessie System. A new image appeared using C&O's cat, Chessie, as the emblem, but the individual railroads continued in existence and rolling stock continued to carry the initials of the railroads. (The Chicago South Shore & South Bend, controlled by Chesapeake & Ohio since 1967, remained an orphan outside the Chessie System. Venango River Corporation purchased it in 1984.)

On November 1, 1980, Chessie System and Seaboard Coast Line Industries, the parent of the Seaboard Coast Line Railroad, merged to form CSX Corporation. At the time the intention was for the subsidiary railroads to maintain their identities.

On May 1, 1983, Baltimore & Ohio took over operation of the Western Maryland, reducing Chessie System to two railroads. Four years later, on April 30, 1987, Chesapeake & Ohio merged B&O, becoming the sole Chessie System Railroad. On August 31, 1987, CSX Transportation, a subsidiary of CSX Corporation, merged C&O.

The Chessie image is evident on the four GP40s of the *St. Louis Jet* as it rolls through the valley of West Virginia's Cheat River on February 26, 1984. Tie plates lying between the two tracks indicate recent track work. Not long afterward, B&O's Washington–St. Louis route was downgraded and cut in two locations between Parkersburg, W. Va., and Cincinnati. Photo by Thomas A. Biery.

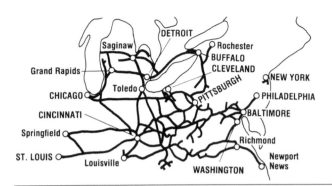

	1973	1985
Miles of railroad operated:	11,289	10,920
Number of locomotives:	2,093	1,759
Number of freight cars:	135,513	84,957
Number of company service cars:	3,239	3,022

Location of headquarters: Cleveland Ohio
Reporting marks: BO, CO, WM
Historical and technical societies:
Baltimore & Ohio Historical Society, P. O. Box 13578, Baltimore, MD 21203-3578
Chesapeake & Ohio Historical Society, P. O. Box 79, Clifton Forge, VA 24422; http://cohs.marshall.edu
Chesapeake System Historical Society, P. O. Box 206, Amesville, OH 45711; schs@opnet.nshore.org;http://pw2.netcom.com/~peake/mf.htm
Western Maryland Railway Historical Society, P. O. Box 395, Union Bridge, MD 21791
Subsidiaries and affiliated railroads, 1986:
Richmond-Washington Company (40%)

Predecessor railroads in this book:
Baltimore & Ohio
Buffalo & Susquehanna
Buffalo, Rochester & Pittsburgh
Chesapeake & Ohio
Hocking Valley
Pere Marquette
Western Maryland
Successor: CSX Transportation
Segments abandoned: Between 1973 and 1986 Chessie System sold or abandoned the following major portions of its network:

Baltimore & Ohio
Knox–Mt. Jewett, Pa. (now operated by the Knox & Kane); Belpre–Chillicothe, Ohio (Chillicothe to Red Diamond and Fire Brick operated by Indiana & Ohio Eastern); Greenfield–Midland City, Ohio (operated by Indiana & Ohio Central); North Vernon–Charlestown, Ind.; Beardstown–Springfield–Shawneetown, Ill.

(Springfield–Shawneetown operated by Prairie Trunk 1979–1984); Dayton–Washington Court House, Ohio; Mansfield–Fredericktown, Ohio; Zanesville–Relief, Ohio; Willard–Sandusky, Ohio; North Baltimore–Tontogany, Ohio
Chesapeake & Ohio
Lindsay–Strathmore, Va.; Covington–Hot Springs; Ronceverte–Durbin–Bartow, W. Va.; Columbus–Logan–Minerton and Logan–Athens, Ohio (Columbus–Logan operated by Indiana & Ohio Central); Cincinnati–Fernald, Ohio; Malden–Hammond, Ind.; Bad Axe–Port Huron, Mich. (Bad Axe–Croswell and branches now operated by Huron & Eastern, which later acquired the Saginaw–Bad Axe segment); Remus–Greenville, Mich.; Manistee–Bay View, Mich. (short portions now operated by Tuscola & Saginaw Bay)
Western Maryland
Emory Grove–Highfield, Md. (now operated by Maryland Midland); Big Pool–Cumberland, Md.–Connellsville, Pa.; Henry–Elkins, W. Va.

Chicago & Eastern Illinois Railway

The earliest ancestor of the Chicago & Eastern Illinois was the Evansville & Illinois, chartered in 1849 to build north from Evansville, Indiana, on the Ohio River. Its line reached Vincennes in 1853 and Terre Haute in 1854. By 1877 it had gone through several identities and was named the Evansville & Terre Haute Railway. That railroad controlled the Evansville & Indianapolis, a consolidation of several lines forming a second Evansville–Terre Haute route through Washington and Worthington, Ind., to the east of E&TH's own line.

Lines north and west of Terre Haute

The Evansville, Terre Haute & Chicago Railroad was chartered in 1869 and opened its line from Terre Haute to Danville, Illinois, in 1871. The Chicago, Danville & Vincennes Railroad, chartered in 1865, built south from Dolton, Ill., just south of Chicago, to Danville, completing the line in 1872. In 1873 it defaulted and in 1877 was sold at foreclosure to become the Chicago & Eastern Illinois Railroad. In 1880 the C&EI leased the Evansville, Terre Haute & Chicago and began to build southwest from Danville. By the turn of the century C&EI had by construction and purchase put together a line from Chicago to the Mississippi River at Thebes, Ill.

A new Chicago & Eastern Illinois Railroad

The *Whippoorwill* leaves Danville northbound for Chicago during its brief tenure (1946–1951) on the Evansville–Chicago route. The E7 on the point is crossing the Detroit–St. Louis line of the Wabash; the roof of C&EI's Danville station is visible above the coaches. Union Switch & Signal photo.

was incorporated June 6, 1894, as a consolidation of the previous C&EI and the Chicago & Indiana Coal Railway. The latter road had a line from Momence, Ill., on C&EI's main line, to Brazil, Ind., with a branch from Percy Junction to La Crosse, Ind. The C&IC leased the Chicago & West Michigan (later Pere Marquette) line from La Crosse to New Buffalo, Mich.

In the next five years Chicago & Eastern Illinois purchased the Evansville, Terre Haute & Chicago, which it had previously leased; the Chicago, Paducah & Memphis Railroad (Mt. Vernon to Marion, Ill., about 40 miles); the Eastern Illinois & Missouri River Railroad (Marion to Thebes); and the Indiana Block Coal Railroad (Terre Haute to Brazil).

Frisco control

In 1902 B. F. Yoakum's expanding St. Louis & San Francisco acquired control of the C&EI. To connect with the Frisco at its closest point, the C&EI built a 20-mile line from Findlay Junction to Pana, Ill., and arranged for trackage rights on the Cleveland, Cincinnati, Chicago & St. Louis Railway (the Big Four, part of the New York Central System) from Pana to St. Louis. The C&EI also built a 62-mile line from Woodland Junction on the main line to Villa Grove, Ill., cutting off a dogleg through Danville for trains between Chicago and St. Louis.

In 1911 the C&EI absorbed the Evansville & Terre Haute and the Evansville Belt Railway, extending itself south from Terre Haute to the Ohio River. About that same time the road purchased a number of coal mines and coal lands in southern Illinois and Indiana. In 1913 the C&EI and its parent, the Frisco, entered receivership.

After 1920

The Chicago & Eastern Illinois Railway was organized on December 13, 1920, to acquire the properties and franchises of the Chicago & Eastern Illinois Railroad, except for the coal properties and the following lines: the former Evansville & Indianapolis (which became the Evansville, Indianapolis & Terre Haute and eventually part of the New York Central), the Evansville & Richmond (which became part of Milwaukee Road's Chicago, Terre Haute & Southeastern); and the former Chicago & Indiana Coal Railway

In 1940 nine roads announced they would inaugurate coach streamliner service between Chicago and Miami. The trains would operate every third day on their respective railroads, giving daily service from Chicago and Miami. Chicago & Eastern Illinois teamed up with Louisville & Nashville; Nashville, Chattanooga & St. Louis; Atlanta, Birmingham & Coast; Atlantic Coast Line; and Florida East Coast to operate the *Dixie Flagler*. The car had been built a year previously for Florida East Coast's *Henry M. Flagler*. C&EI sent Pacific No. 1008 to the shops to be streamlined for the train, shown here heading south on "the boulevard of steel." Photo by S. D. Warner.

(which was incorporated as the Chicago, Attica & Southern). The new C&EI had hardly begun existence when a coal strike in 1922 resulted in southern Illinois coal pricing itself out of a shrinking market, and C&EI's traffic, largely based on coal, began to fall off. In 1927 the C&EI purchased the Chicago Heights Terminal Transfer Railroad, a switching line at Chicago Heights.

In 1928 the Van Sweringen brothers of Cleveland acquired control of C&EI through their Chesapeake & Ohio but did little to integrate it with the remainder of their empire (Chesapeake & Ohio, Missouri Pacific, Nickel Plate, Erie, Pere Marquette, and Wheeling & Lake Erie). By 1933 the C&EI was in reorganization. Much of the plan for its reorganization was formulated by John W. Barriger III.

The Chicago & Eastern Illinois Railroad took over the business, assets, and property of the C&EI on December 31, 1940. At various times its leadership included John Budd (in his only period away from the Great Northern) and Downing B. Jenks, who later headed Missouri Pacific. In 1952 the CE&I acquired the Jefferson Southwestern, a 12-mile line at Mt. Vernon, Ill., and later transferred one-third of the shares to Missouri Pacific and one-third to Illinois Central. Through a lease agreement it acquired the abandoned St. Louis & O'Fallon in October 1954 for access to East St. Louis.

Missouri Pacific began merger discussions with C&EI in 1959. In 1961 both Mopac and Louisville & Nashville acquired C&EI stock and petitioned the ICC for permission to control the road; Illinois Central also petitioned for control. In 1963 the ICC ruled in favor of Mopac with the condition that MP negotiate in good faith for sale of the Evansville line to L&N. The Woodland Junction–Evansville line became L&N property in 1969. L&N purchased a half interest in the C&EI main line from there to Dolton Junction (Chicago) and half of C&EI's interests in the Chicago & Western Indiana and the Belt Railway of Chicago. L&N bought 48 diesel locomotives and 1,495 freight cars and cabooses from C&EI. Chicago & Eastern Illinois was merged with Missouri Pacific on October 15, 1976.

All-American railroad

Chicago & Eastern Illinois was sometimes cited as an all-American average railroad, but it did have distinctions. For years it carried the majority of Florida-bound passengers out of Chicago on what was essentially a northern extension of Louisville & Nashville's passenger service—trains such as the *Dixie Flyer*, *Dixie Limited*, and *Dixie Flagler*. C&EI's own passenger trains included two of the earliest and shortest-lived postwar streamliners, the *Whippoorwill* and the *Meadowlark*, on the Evansville–Chicago and Cypress–Chicago runs, respectively. C&EI's Chicago–St. Louis service succumbed shortly after World War II to the competition of Wabash, Illinois Central, and Gulf, Mobile & Ohio. Service to southern Illinois, spruced up in the 1930s with ACF motorcars and taken over in the 1950s by an RDC, endured into the 1960s.

C&EI discontinued passenger service south of Danville—the Evansville–Chicago portion of L&N's *Humming Bird* and *Georgian*—in 1968, shortly before L&N purchased the Evansville line. The last train, a Chicago–Danville local which briefly carried the name *Danville Flyer*, remained in service until the start of Amtrak in 1971, though as an L&N train, ironically.

No other railroad surpassed C&EI in slogans: The Danville Route, The Evansville Route, The Modern Route, The Noiseless Route, The Boulevard of Steel, and one that could have been applied to several dozen roads, The Chicago Line.

	1929	1975
Miles of railroad operated:	946	64
Number of locomotives:	334	49
Number of passenger cars:	284	
Number of freight cars:	14,818	
Number of company service cars:	561	
Number of freight and company service cars:		7,210

Location of headquarters: Chicago, Illinois

Reporting marks: CEI

Historical and technical societies:

Chicago & Eastern Illinois Historical Society, P. O. Box 606, Crestwood, IL 60445-0606; http://www2.justnet.com/cei/

Missouri Pacific Historical Society, P. O. Box 330427, Fort Worth, TX 76163

Subsidiaries and affiliated railroads, 1975:
Chicago Heights Terminal Transfer Railroad (100%)

Successors:
Missouri Pacific
Union Pacific

Portions still operated:
CSX and Union Pacific: Chicago–Woodland Junction, Ill.
CSX: Woodland Junction, Ill.–Evansville, Ind.
Union Pacific: Woodland Junction–St. Louis; Goodwine–Cissna Park, Ill.; Findlay–Vienna Junction, Ill.

Chicago & Northwestern Railway
Chicago, St. Paul, Minneapolis & Omaha Railway

For years the Chicago & North Western operated Chicago's most extensive commuter service. Its three routes were designated West, Northwest, and North. Those names also serve well to group C&NW's lines west, northwest, and north from Chicago.

West

The railroad capital of the United States, Chicago, saw its first locomotive in 1848: the *Pioneer* of the Galena & Chicago Union Rail Road. The G&CU, chartered in 1836, lay dormant for 12 years before construction began. By 1850, though, its rails reached west to the Fox River valley at Elgin and in 1853 to Freeport, where it connected with the Illinois Central Railroad.

In 1855 the Galena & Chicago Union completed a second line westward, from what is now West Chicago, reaching Fulton, Illinois, on the Mississippi River. By 1867 the Chicago, Iowa & Nebraska had built from Clinton, Iowa, to Cedar Rapids, and the Cedar Rapids & Missouri River Railroad had extended that line west across Iowa to a connection with the Union Pacific at

Chicago & North Western Mikado 2524 brings a train of refrigerator cars through West Chicago in September 1945. The left-hand running and the odd semaphore signals are both typical of the C&NW. Photo by Henry J. McCord.

Council Bluffs, on the east bank of the Missouri River (Chicago & North Western purchased those two companies in 1884).

That line was extended farther west, making a second connection with the Union Pacific at Fremont, Nebraska, and eventually reached Rapid City, South Dakota, and Casper, Wyoming. A dispute with the Union Pacific caused the North Western to project an extension from Casper over South Pass toward Salt Lake City and Ogden, Utah. By the time the railhead reached Lander, Wyo., the C&NW had come to an agreement with UP and construction stopped.

North

Railroads were chartered in Illinois and Wisconsin in 1855 to connect Chicago with Milwau-

kee. The line was completed in 1855, and in 1863 the two companies were consolidated as the Chicago & Milwaukee Railway. The company was leased by the Chicago & North Western in 1866 and was merged in 1883.

Two lines reached north from Milwaukee to Green Bay—one along the shore of Lake Michigan, a continuation of the line from Chicago, and the other northwest through the valley of the Fox River. (There are two Fox Rivers in eastern Wisconsin. One rises near Waukesha and flows south into the Illinois River. The other rises near Portage and flows north and northeast through several lakes into Lake Michigan at Green Bay.) The C&NW developed a dense network of branches in eastern Wisconsin and built lines into the mining area of Michigan's upper peninsula.

About 1906 C&NW constructed a second line from Chicago to Milwaukee for freight trains, a belt line around Milwaukee, and a long main line diagonally across Wisconsin from Milwaukee to a connection with the older Chicago–Twin Cities route at Wyeville.

Northwest

In 1855 the Chicago, St. Paul & Fond du Lac Rail Road was incorporated to extend an existing road northwest from Cary, Ill., through Madison and La Crosse, Wisconsin, to St. Paul, Minnesota, and north through Fond du Lac, Wisconsin, to the iron and copper country south of Lake Superior. The company was reorganized in 1859 as the Chicago & North Western Rail-

way. In 1864 the C&NW was consolidated with the Galena & Chicago Union. At that point the C&CU consisted of lines from Chicago to Freeport and to Fulton, Ill., from Belvidere, Ill., to Beloit, Wis., and from Elgin to Richmond, Ill., plus the east-west route across Chicago known as the St. Charles Air Line.

Omaha Road

Notable among C&NW's acquisitions was the Chicago, St. Paul, Minneapolis & Omaha Railway. The Omaha Road reached from west-central Wisconsin to the Twin Cities, and from there southwest to Omaha and northeast to Duluth and Superior. It maintained a separate corporate existence until 1972, 90 years after its acquisition by C&NW.

In 1857 the Minnesota legislature passed a bill vesting U. S. government land grants in four railroad corporations. One of them was the Root River & Southern Minnesota Railroad (later simply Southern Minnesota). Work on that line began in 1858, and the company was reorganized in 1862—still having only roadbed, no rail. In 1864 St. Paul businessmen incorporated the Minnesota Valley Railroad to take over the Southern Minnesota. It was renamed the St. Paul & Sioux City Railroad in 1869.

The Chicago, St. Paul, Minneapolis & Omaha was formed in 1880 by the consolidation of the Northern Wisconsin Railway, which reached north to Bayfield and Superior, Wis., and the Chicago, St. Paul & Minneapolis Railway, which had started out as a railroad chartered to build from Tomah, Wis., to Lake St. Croix. The CStPM&O was headquartered in Hudson, Wis., a few miles east of St. Paul, Minn. It intersected with the Chicago & North Western at 17 points. C&NW bought a majority of the Omaha Road's stock in 1882.

Chicago & North Western

In 1901 C&NW built a long line south from the Chicago–Council Bluffs line at Nelson, Illinois, through Peoria toward St. Louis. The primary purpose of the line was to carry coal from southern Illinois, but the line also carried Chicago–St. Louis merchandise traffic in cooperation with the Litchfield & Madison Railway, a 44-mile terminal road in the industrial area across the Mississippi River from St. Louis.

The Chicago & North Western was one of a very few railroads in North America whose trains kept to the left on double track. Reasons given for the practice range from a preponderance of British stockholders to (more likely) the position of the station buildings on the lines around Chicago—generally on the left for trains heading toward Chicago. When C&NW double-tracked its lines through the suburbs it assumed that Chicago-bound passengers would be more likely to use the depot buildings than homeward-bound suburbanites and made the track nearest the station the inbound line.

The North Western became Union Pacific's preferred connection at Council Bluffs. Until 1955 UP's yellow streamliners continued to Chicago on the C&NW. In 1955 Union Pacific surprised the railroad industry by switching its trains to the Milwaukee Road for the trip to Chicago. The North Western fell into a decline.

In the 1980s, the North Western once again became UP's favored connection, partly because C&NW thoroughly rebuilt its line be-

At Janesville, Wisconsin, October 12, 1956, the *Dakota 400* is arriving from Chicago behind a single E8, while a Madison to Chicago train waits for the 400 to clear. Power for the latter is C&NW's unique Baldwin half locomotive-half baggage car and a standard F7B. Photo by William D. Middleton.

tween Chicago and Council Bluffs and partly by default—most of the competing routes had been abandoned.

Latter-day expansion

In the late 1950s and 1960s C&NW merged several smaller railroads: Litchfield & Madison in 1958; Minneapolis & St. Louis in 1960; Chicago Great Western in 1968; and Des Moines & Central Iowa (which owned the Fort Dodge, Des Moines & Southern) in 1968. C&NW gradually dismantled the lines of most of these railroads, keeping only a few strategic segments in service. In 1972 C&NW joined with Missouri Pacific to purchase the Alton & Southern from

Alcoa, but a year later sold its half to St. Louis Southwestern.

There was also a change in corporate structure in 1972. The Chicago & North Western Transportation Company was incorporated in 1970 as the North Western Employees Transportation Co., owned by nearly 1,000 C&NW employees. In 1972 it purchased the transportation assets of the Chicago & North Western Railway and changed its name to Chicago & North Western Transportation Co. For some time thereafter the road's herald carried the words "Employee Owned." In 1989 Chicago & North Western Holdings Corp., which owns the transportation company, was formed by Blackstone

C&NW	1929
Miles of railroad operated:	8,459
Number of locomotives:	1,805
Number of passenger cars:	2,117
Number of freight cars:	69,418
Number of company service cars:	4,032
Number of freight and company service cars:	
Location of headquarters: Chicago, Illinois	
Reporting marks: CNW	

CStPM&O	1929
Miles of railroad operated:	1,747
Number of locomotives:	325
Number of passenger cars:	258
Number of freight cars:	10,507
Number of company service cars:	559
Number of freight and company service cars:	

Location of headquarters: Chicago, Illinois

Reporting marks: CMO

Notable named passenger trains: *400* (Chicago–Minneapolis) and the entire *400* fleet, which served C&NW's principal lines in Wisconsin and northern Illinois

Historical and technical society: Chicago & North Western Historical Society, P. O. Box 1436, Elmhurst, IL 60126-9998

Recommended reading: *The Northwestern,* by H. Roger Grant, published in 1996 by North Illinois University Press, DeKalb, IL 60115 (ISBN 0-87580-214-1)

Successors: Union Pacific

Capital Partners. It was privately held until 1992.

After the 1980 demise of the Rock Island the C&NW acquired Rock's Minneapolis–Kansas City "spine line," and by the mid-1980s abandoned the somewhat longer Chicago Great Western route between those cities.

The North Western's other major expansion was into the Powder River Basin of northeastern Wyoming. C&NW (through a subsidiary, Western Railroad Properties) and Burlington Northern jointly operated a line north into the coalfields from Orin and Shawnee, Wyoming (the line was constructed by BN between 1976 and 1979). In 1984 C&NW opened a new line along the Wyoming-Nebraska state line to a connection with Union Pacific's line along the North Platte River rather than rebuild more than 500 miles of its line across northern Nebraska.

The North Western spun off two major groups of lines to form regional railroads:
• Dakota, Minnesota & Eastern Railroad: Winona, Minn., to Rapid City, S. Dak., plus branches, 965 miles in all (September 1986)
• Fox River Valley Railroad: two lines from Green Bay to Granville and Cleveland, Wis., plus branches, 214 miles (December 9, 1988). Sale of the two main lines south of Green Bay had the effect of isolating C&NW's lines in northern Wisconsin and Michigan's Upper Peninsula from the rest of the system. Wisconsin Central later purchased those lines as well as the Fox River Valley Railroad.

By the 1990s most of Chicago & North Western's traffic was concentrated on two lines: Chicago to Council Bluffs, essentially an eastern extension of Union Pacific's transcontinental main line, and the Wyoming and Nebraska coal lines.

During the late 1980s the C&NW was the target of several hostile takeover attempts. Union Pacific was concerned about these—by then C&NW was its principal eastern connection. On March 17, 1995, Union Pacific announced its intention to buy the 70 percent of the C&NW that it did not already own.

Chicago, Attica & Southern Railroad

The Chicago, Attica & Southern was a descendant of the grandly named Chicago & Great Southern, which by the mid-1880s had put together a line in northwestern Indiana from Fair Oaks, on the Monon between Rensselaer and Shelby, to Brazil, between Indianapolis and Terre Haute.

The Chicago & Great Southern was reorganized as the Chicago & Indiana Coal Railway. The C&IC extended itself north to Wilder and La Crosse to connect with what in later years became the Erie, the Chesapeake & Ohio, and the Pennsylvania, and acquired trackage rights north to New Buffalo, Michigan.

The proprietor of the C&IC, Henry H. Porter, acquired control of the Chicago & Eastern Illinois and in 1888 constructed a connection between his two roads from Percy Junction, near

	1929	1946
Miles of railroad operated:	155	59
Number of locomotives:	6	6
Number of freight cars:	20	8
Number of company service cars:		7

Location of headquarters: Attica, Indiana

Reporting marks: CA&S

Recommended reading: *Ghost Railroads of Indiana*, by Elmer G. Sulzer, published in 1970 by Vane A. Jones Co., 6710 Hampton Drive East, Indianapolis, IN 46226

Predecessor railroads in this book: Chicago & Eastern Illinois

Map: See page 83

All of Chicago, Attica & Southern's power was bought used. Consolidation 320 came from the Buffalo, Rochester & Pittsburgh in November 1928. It was built by Brooks in 1904 as BR&P 320. A rebuilding in BR&P's shop resulted in the unusual combination of Southern valve gear and inside valves.

Goodland, Ind., northwest to Momence, Ill., on the C&EI main line. The C&EI leased and in 1894 merged the Chicago & Indiana Coal Railway. "Coal Road" continued as an unofficial name of that portion of the C&EI.

In 1921 as part of its reorganization C&EI offered the Coal Road for sale. Edmund P. Kelly picked it up for $15,000 and assigned it to Stoddard M. Stevens Jr. Stevens sold the Brazil–West Melcher portion to the Cincinnati, Indianapolis & Western for $137,500 and the remainder of the line to Charles F. Propst for $250,000.

Propst organized the Chicago, Attica & Southern Railroad, which began operation on December 7, 1922. Propst hoped for local business and also for bridge traffic as a Chicago bypass. However, the CA&S faced formidable competition and had no money to rehabilitate its track. In the late 1920s there was an effort to lease the CA&S to the New York Central, but the Central said the cost of rehabilitation would not be worth the revenue that might come from operating the road. The CA&S entered receivership on August 5, 1931.

In June 1942 C&EI abandoned the portion of the connecting line from Momence to the Illinois-Indiana state line, and in 1943 the Interstate Commerce Commission authorized abandonment of CA&S's portion of the connector plus the line from Percy Junction to La Cross and the line south of Veedersburg. What was left was a nowhere-to-nowhere (Morocco to Veedersburg) track that hung on through World War II only because of the war effort. In April 1946 the ICC granted permission to abandon the remains of the CA&S.

Chicago Aurora & Elgin Railroad

The Aurora, Elgin & Chicago Railway was incorporated in March 1901. By the autumn of 1902 it had built a line from Aurora, Illinois, to Laramie Avenue in Chicago and a branch to Batavia. In May 1903 it opened a branch from Wheaton to Elgin. The AE&C was unusual among interurbans in that current distribution was through a third rail rather than overhead wire, except in streets, yards, and terminals. In March 1905 the AE&C extended its service over the rails of the Metropolitan West Side Elevated (the "L") to a terminal on Chicago's famous Loop at Wells Street.

The company was consolidated with several streetcar lines in the Fox River Valley in 1906 to form the Aurora, Elgin & Chicago Railroad. In 1910 a subsidiary then built a line to West Chicago and Geneva; interurban cars continued

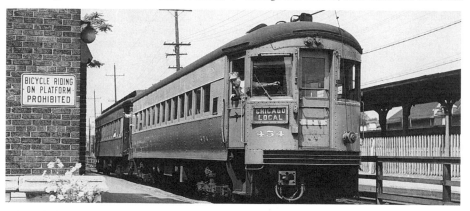

A Chicago local prepares to leave the Wheaton station. The head car is one of a batch of ten built by St. Louis Car Co. in 1945 — the last new cars CA&E purchased. Photo by William D. Middleton.

91

Samuel Insull acquired control of the CA&E in 1926. He proposed a new line to bypass the congestion and local stations on the main line, much like the Skokie Valley line that the Chicago North Shore & Milwaukee opened that same year. The project was soon killed by the Depression.

The CA&E entered another receivership in 1932. The West Chicago–Geneva–St. Charles line was abandoned in 1937 for lack of traffic. Private right of way and a new terminal in Aurora in 1939 replaced street running there, the last on the CA&E. The road was again in financial distress during World War II. The physical plant was in poor condition, and the road lacked the resources to rebuild it. Even with a reorganization as the Chicago Aurora & Elgin Railway in 1946, abandonment was inevitable.

The customary pattern of train operation was interesting. Originally local trains served Aurora and Elgin alternately; in the 1930s the service changed to alternate local trains to Wheaton and express trains with cars for Aurora, Elgin, and St. Charles—the expresses were divided and assembled at Wheaton. Shuttle cars operated between Batavia and Batavia Junction on the Aurora line. The road's business was primarily passengers—there was little industry on line and scant opportunity to participate in long-haul freight traffic.

The city of Chicago, Cook County, and state and federal highway administrations planned to build an expressway along the route of the "L" and move the Chicago Transit Authority tracks to its median strip. In September 1953 temporary track replaced the "L" so construction could begin. CA&E and CTA set up an interchange station at Des Plaines Avenue. The loss of one-seat service to downtown Chicago only aggravated the loss of passengers resulting from service cuts and the postwar increase in automobile ownership. Half of CA&E's riders switched to parallel railroads or their own cars by December 1953, and the opening of the new highway only made the situation worse.

CA&E applied to discontinue passenger service in 1955. After the customary hearings and proceedings, passenger service ceased at noon on July 3, 1957. Track and rolling stock remained in place, and there was thought of reviving service on the new CTA route. However, CA&E trains could not operate into the new subway that replaced the "L" and there was no terminal the CA&E could use. Freight service continued until June 9, 1959. Legal abandonment occurred on June 10, 1961.

	1929	1956
Miles of railroad operated:	66	54
Number of locomotives:	9	7
Number of passenger cars:	87	89
Number of company service cars:	2	
Location of headquarters: Wheaton, Illinois		
Historical and technical society: Shore Line Interurban Historical, Society, P. O. Box 720, Sheboygan, WI 53082-1230; http://www.cnwhs.org		
Recommended reading: The Great Third Rail, edited by George Krambles, published in 1961 by Central Electric Railfans' Association, P. O. Box 503, Chicago, IL 60690		

from Geneva to St. Charles on streetcar tracks.

The AE&C entered receivership in 1919. In 1922 the company's properties were separated into two parts: the Fox River Division, encompassing the streetcar lines in the Fox Valley between Aurora and Elgin, and the Third Rail Division, the four-pronged line from Chicago to Aurora, Batavia, Geneva, and Elgin. The latter was sold to the Chicago Aurora & Elgin Railroad, which took over the operation July 1, 1922.

Chicago, Burlington & Quincy Railroad

The Aurora Branch Railroad was chartered on February 12, 1849, to build a line from Aurora, Illinois, to a connection with the Galena & Chicago Union (forerunner of the Chicago & North Western) at Turner Junction (West Chicago). Service began with G&CU's first locomotive, the *Pioneer*.

In 1852 the road was renamed the Chicago & Aurora Railroad and received authority to build to Mendota, Ill., where it would connect with the Illinois Central. On February 14, 1855, it was again renamed, becoming the Chicago, Burlington & Quincy Railroad.

That same year a railroad was opened between Galesburg and the east bank of the Mississippi opposite Burlington, Iowa; a year later a string of railroads, including the CB&Q, linked Chicago with Quincy, Ill., via Galesburg. A Galesburg–Peoria line was opened in 1857. By 1865 the CB&Q had acquired all these lines, built its own line from Aurora to Chicago, and had undergone several consolidations to become the corporation that would endure until the Burlington Northern merger in 1970.

Beyond the Mississippi

West of the Mississippi expansion proceeded on two fronts. The Hannibal & St. Joseph, char-

The *Morning Zephyr*, train 22 from Minneapolis and St. Paul to Chicago, rolls alongside the Mississippi River at Fountain City, Wisconsin. CB&Q photo.

tered in 1847, began operation between its namesake cities in 1859. A short spur to a point opposite Quincy and a steamboat across the Mississippi created the first railroad from Chicago to the Missouri River. The Burlington & Missouri River Railroad began construction in 1855 at Burlington, Iowa, and followed an old Indian trail (later U. S. 34) straight across

Iowa—very slowly. Not until November 26, 1869, did it reach the east bank of the Missouri River opposite Plattsmouth, Nebraska (Chicago & North Western reached Council Bluffs in 1867 and the Rock Island got there on May 11, 1869). By then CB&Q had bridged the Mississippi at Burlington and Quincy, both in 1868, and the Missouri in 1869 at Kansas City, as part of a line

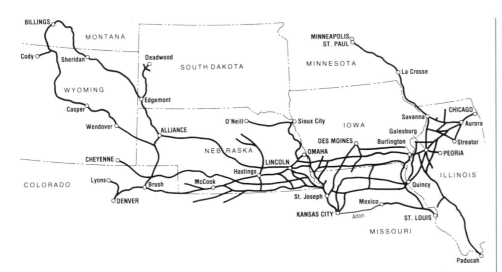

from Cameron, on the Hannibal & St. Joseph, to Kansas City.

The Burlington, in the form of the Burlington & Missouri River Rail Road In Nebraska, pushed beyond the Missouri River to Lincoln, Nebr., in 1870. It acquired the Omaha & South Western for access to Omaha and built west from Lincoln to a junction with the Union Pacific at Kearney. The road began a colonization program to increase the population along its lines and to sell off the lands it had been granted. CB&Q provided financial backing for the two B&MR (Iowa and Nebraska) companies and directors for their boards. Meanwhile the CB&Q was acquiring branch lines in Illinois and upgrading its plant: double track, steel rail to replace iron, and iron bridges to replace wood.

Jay Gould acquired control of the Hannibal & St. Joseph in 1871, and friction began to develop among the railroads in the Burlington family over such matters as routing of connecting traffic to and from the Union Pacific. To begin unifying the system, CB&Q leased the B&MR in 1872 and merged it in 1875. Gould gained control of Union Pacific in 1875 and then in quick succession got the Kansas Pacific (Kansas City–Denver), the Wabash (and extended it to Council Bluffs), and the Missouri Pacific. Burlington's Nebraska lines were surrounded by Gould lines, and the Wabash would be likely to get the largest share of eastbound traffic from the UP. In the summer of 1880 the CB&Q consolidated with the B&MR, acquired the Kansas City, St. Joseph & Council Bluffs, opened a bridge over the Missouri at Plattsmouth, and began an extension west to Denver, completed in May 1882.

In May 1883 the Q regained control of the Hannibal & St. Joseph and soon found itself with increased competition in the Chicago–Kansas City market: Milwaukee Road in 1887 and Santa Fe in 1888.

North to St. Paul and Minneapolis

In 1882 the growth of the Pacific Northwest and the construction of the Northern Pacific and the St. Paul, Minneapolis & Manitoba (later the Great Northern) prompted the Burlington to consider building a line up the east bank of the Mississippi River to St. Paul. The line would be 25 miles longer than the Milwaukee Road and Chicago & North Western lines between Chicago and the St. Paul, but the grades would be easier. The Q extended its Chicago & Iowa line west to Savanna; the Chicago, Burlington & Northern (the Q owned one-third of its stock) built the line along the river. It was opened in 1886. Considerable friction ensued between parent and child: The CB&N wanted to cut rates to secure business, and the CB&Q knew that retaliation by the Milwaukee and the North Western would be directed at CB&Q systemwide, not just at the CB&N. The matter was eventually settled when CB&Q increased its CB&N holdings in 1890 and absorbed the road in 1899.

Extensions and potential merger

Over the years the Burlington considered extension to the Pacific coast and merger with nearly every other railroad. Between 1883 and 1886 it made surveys west of Denver but did no construction. The arrival at Pueblo of the Missouri Pacific in 1887 and the Rock Island in 1888 (on trackage rights from Colorado Springs) put the Burlington at a competitive disadvantage. The Rio Grande received the same amount for moving freight from Salt Lake City to Pueblo as it did from Salt Lake City through Pueblo to Denver (the Dotsero Cutoff was still nearly five decades in the future). Naturally Rio Grande preferred to interchange at Pueblo—it received nothing additional for the 119-mile haul from Pueblo to Denver. There was thought of the Burlington's acquiring James J. Hill's St. Paul, Minneapolis & Manitoba and vice versa. Burlington considered merger with the Pennsylvania; the two roads purchased interests in the Toledo, Peoria & Western. In 1893 the Burlington looked eagerly at the Oregon Short Line and Oregon Railway & Navigation Co. when their parent, Union Pacific, was in receivership. Other merger partners considered were Northern Pacific, Yazoo & Mississippi Valley, Missouri-Kansas-Texas, Chicago Great Western, Denver & Rio Grande, Kansas City Southern, Minneapolis & St. Louis, Chicago & Eastern Illinois, and St. Louis-San Francisco. With one exception the Q was content for a while to stay within its boundaries, marked by corner stakes at Chicago, St. Louis, Kansas City, Denver, Omaha, Galesburg, and St. Paul. That exception was a line opened in 1894 from Alliance, Nebr., northwest through the coalfields of eastern Wyoming to Billings, Montana.

Merger—eventually

Perhaps the most important event in the Burlington's history was the purchase effective July 1, 1901, of nearly 98 percent of its stock jointly by the Great Northern and the Northern Pacific. James J. Hill, builder of the Great Northern, saw in the Burlington the connection he needed from St. Paul to Chicago—the Chicago & North Western was largely held by the New York Central, and the Milwaukee Road refused to consider the matter. At the same time Edward H. Harriman realized that the Burlington could bring his Union Pacific to Chicago from Omaha. Burlington recognized it would be better off with the northern lines because of their on-line resources of coal and lumber, both lacking on the Union Pacific-Southern Pacific route to San Francisco. The battle for control was brief and intense. Control of the Burlington essentially moved from Boston to St. Paul. That same year Hill, with the backing of J. P. Morgan, his banker, acquired control of Northern Pacific. The next logical step was merger of the three railroads, a process that took 69 years of off-and-on petitioning, protesting, and arguing.

The Chicago, Burlington & Quincy Railroad was leased to the Chicago, Burlington & Quincy Railway for 99 years on September 30, 1901; that lease lasted until June 30, 1907, when the railroad resumed its own management. The Railroad and Railway companies had a number of officers and directors in common. Of the railway company during those years Moody's railroad manual simply says "The company has decided not to issue a report."

In 1908 the Burlington acquired control of the Colorado & Southern, gaining a route from Denver to the Gulf of Mexico at Galveston, Texas, and a route from Denver north into Wyoming. CB&Q extended a line down from Billings, Mont., to meet the C&S in 1914. Other extensions were to the coalfields of southern Illinois and on across the Ohio River to Paducah, Kentucky, and a line from Ashland, Nebr., north to a connection with the Great Northern at Sioux City, Iowa, in 1916.

The Burlington's growth leveled off during the 1920s. In 1930 the ICC authorized merger of Great Northern and Northern Pacific on the condition that they relinquish control of the Burlington; GN and NP withdrew their merger application in 1931 in favor of retaining joint control of the Q.

Zephyr years

The year 1932 saw the beginning of two significant projects: the Rio Grande's Dotsero Cutoff, which would give Denver a direct rail line west, and Burlington's order for a stainless-steel streamlined train from the Budd Company. The cutoff opened June 16, 1934. The *Zephyr*, the country's first diesel-powered streamliner, was delivered in April 1934 and was prophetically the first train to traverse the Dotsero Cutoff.

A whole family of *Zephyrs* soon appeared on Burlington rails. In 1939 the Burlington teamed up with Rio Grande and Western Pacific to operate a through passenger train between Chicago and San Francisco via the Dotsero Cutoff—the *Exposition Flyer*. In 1945 Burlington built the first Vista-Dome coach. These elements achieved their ultimate synthesis in 1949 with the inauguration of the Vista-Dome-equipped *California Zephyr*, operated between Chicago and San Francisco by the Burlington, the Rio Grande, and the Western Pacific. The route was longer and slower than that of the competition, but the schedule took advantage of the scenery. The train was an immediate success and remained so through its life.

The Q was still aware of the shortcomings of its Chicago–Kansas City route across northern Missouri (the 1902 purchase of the Quincy, Omaha & Kansas City Railroad, a circuitous secondary line between Quincy and Kansas City, largely abandoned in 1939, appears to have been an act of mercy on the Burlington's part). The Burlington first proposed a four-way deal that would give Santa Fe a route to St. Louis; Gulf, Mobile & Ohio a route of its own to Chicago (Q president Ralph Budd had been a member of the board of directors of GM&O predecessor Gulf, Mobile & Northern); and the foundering Alton a good home. GM&O would get the Alton, less its St. Louis–Kansas City line, which didn't fit into GM&O's north-south pattern; Burlington would take that line and swap trackage rights into St. Louis to the Santa Fe for a shortcut across Missouri on Santa Fe's main line.

The other roads serving St. Louis protested. GM&O merged the Alton, but the rest of the plan did not come to fruition. In the early 1950s Burlington built a new line across Missouri and coupled it with Wabash trackage rights to shorten its Chicago–Kansas City route by 22 miles. The line was further improved in 1960 with a new bridge at Quincy.

Merger with Great Northern, Northern Pacific, and Spokane, Portland & Seattle (jointly owned by GN and NP) was proposed once again in 1960 and finally became reality on March 2, 1970, with the creation of Burlington Northern.

	1929	1969
Miles of railroad operated:	9,367	8,430
Number of locomotives:	1,575	665
Number of passenger cars:	1,225	624
Number of freight cars:	62,225	36,264
Number of company service cars:	4,579	3,087

Location of headquarters: Chicago, Illinois

Reporting marks: CBQ, RBBQ, RBBX, BREX

Notable named passenger trains: *Denver Zephyr* (Chicago–Denver), *California Zephyr* (Chicago–Denver–Salt Lake City–San Francisco; operated jointly with Denver & Rio Grande Western and Western Pacific), *Morning* and *Afternoon Zephyrs* (Chicago–Minneapolis)

Historical and technical society: Burlington Route Historical Society, P. O. Box 456, LaGrange, IL 60525-0456; http://www.burlingtonroute.com/

Recommended reading: *Burlington Route,* by Richard C. Overton, published in 1965 by Alfred A. Knopf, New York, New York

Golden Years of Railroading: Burlington Route Across the Heartland, by Jeff Wilson, published in 1999 by Kalmbach Publishing Co., P. O. Box 1612, Waukesha, WI 53187 (ISBN 0-89024-337-9)

Subsidiaries and affiliated railroads, 1969: Colorado & Southern (74%)

Successors:
Burlington Northern
Burlington Northern & Santa Fe

Chicago, Central & Pacific Railroad

The original route of the Illinois Central Railroad was from Cairo, at the southern tip of Illinois, north to Galena, in the northwest corner of the state. That line was completed in 1856, but the road's Centralia–Chicago branch proved to be more important than the main line to Galena. Nonetheless, the IC pushed the line west to the Mississippi River and across it into Iowa. In 1867 the Illinois Central leased the Dubuque & Sioux City Railroad; by 1870 that railroad had reached Sioux City. In the 1880s IC began serious expansion westward. It built branches to Cedar Rapids, Iowa, Sioux Falls, South Dakota, and Omaha, Nebraska, and a line from Chicago west to Freeport, Ill., connecting the Iowa lines with Chicago.

In the early 1980s Illinois Central Gulf (the product of the 1972 merger of IC and Gulf, Mobile & Ohio) decided to concentrate on its north-south main line and spin off its east-west routes. The first to be sold was the route to Omaha and Sioux City. In December 1985 Jack Haley's Chicago, Central & Pacific Railroad purchased ICG's Chicago–Omaha line and its branches to Sioux City and Cedar Rapids, Iowa, for $75 million. Haley had started his railroad empire in 1984 by purchasing ICG's Cedar Falls, Iowa–Albert Lea, Minnesota, branch and operating it as the Cedar Valley Railroad. In 1986 the road later bought Chicago & North

Red-and-white GP10 No. 1705 heads up a Chicago Central freight at New Hartford, Iowa, on September 5, 1991. Photo by Jim Shaw.

Western's line between Wall Lake and Ida Grove, Iowa, 24 miles.

The Chicago Central got off to a good start, but in 1987 General Electric Credit Corporation, which had provided the financing, became anxious when Haley fell behind in loan payments. Haley took the Chicago Central into bankruptcy on September 1, 1987, so he could retain control. The Chicago Central was released from bankruptcy in October under the leadership of Don

Wood, formerly executive vice-president for operations, of Burlington Northern. Wood trimmed the road's car fleet, reduced train miles, and lowered speed limits to save fuel and wear on the track. The CC undertook several track repair projects to recover from ICG's policy of deferred maintenance.

The Cedar Valley Railroad ceased operation on May 22, 1991, and the Interstate Commerce Commission let Chicago Central serve customers on the line. At the end of 1991 CC bought the Cedar Valley through a subsidiary, the Cedar River Railroad.

The Chicago Central turned profitable in 1988. The Burlington Northern considered acquiring the road for its line between Chicago and the Mississippi River at Portage Junction—it would relieve congestion on BN's single-track line west from Aurora. However, after its period of shrinkage, the Illinois Central decided to grow again. It saw the Chicago Central as a source of Iowa grain traffic and perhaps get some of the traffic moving east from the coalfields of Wyoming. In June 1996 IC purchased the Chicago Central for $157 million. Part of the deal was trackage rights for Burlington Northern & Santa Fe between Chicago and Portage Junction.

	1987	1995
Miles of railroad operated:	798	707
Number of locomotives:	98	88
Number of freight cars:	2,043	2,390
Number of company service cars:	75	

Location of headquarters: Waterloo, Iowa

Reporting marks: CC

Historical and technical society: Illinois Central Historical Society, 14818 Clifton Park Avenue, Midlothian, IL 60445

Recommended reading: "Seared, burned, but now cooking," by Steve Glischinski, in *Trains* Magazine, July 1992, pages 34–41

Subsidiaries and affiliated railroads, 1995: Cedar River Railroad

Predecessor railroads in this book: Illinois Central Gulf

Successors: Illinois Central

Portions still operated: Illinois Central: Chicago–Omaha; Manchester, Iowa–Cedar Rapids; Marion Junction–Marion; Fort Dodge–Sioux City; Wall Lake–Ida Grove

Chicago Great Western Railroad

By the late 1870s the Upper Midwest was spiderwebbed with the lines of four major railroads: the Burlington, the Milwaukee Road, the Chicago & North Western, and the Rock Island. Even so, people thought there was room for more. One of them was A. B. Stickney, who had been construction superintendent of the St. Paul, Minnesota, & Manitoba (forerunner of the Great Northern), general superintendent of the western portion of the Canadian Pacific, and an official of the Minneapolis & St. Louis. Stickney decided to build a railroad from St. Paul to Chicago. He acquired the franchise and outstanding stock of the Minnesota & Northwestern Railroad, which had been chartered in 1854 to build a line from Lake Superior through St. Paul toward Dubuque, Iowa. The charter was particularly enticing to Stickney because of a tax limitation clause it contained.

Construction of the road started at St. Paul in September 1884, and a year later the line was open to the Iowa state line, where it connected with a road the Illinois Central had leased. Stickney, however, was intent on having his own line, so even before the Minnesota & Northwestern was completed he acquired and merged with it the Dubuque & Northwestern. That railroad had been incorporated in 1883 to build from Dubuque to Vancouver, British Columbia, or at least to a con-

Chicago—Oelwein manifest freight 91 rolls along Burlington rails for a short distance between Galena Junction and Portage, Illinois, before crossing the Mississippi River to Dubuque, Iowa, on November 12, 1956. Photo by William D. Middleton.

nection with the Northern Pacific. The M&NW met the Dubuque & Northwestern near Oneida, Iowa, in October 1886.

Meanwhile the Minnesota & Northwestern of Illinois was building west from what is now Forest Park, Ill. Completed in early 1888, the engineering feat of the line was the longest tunnel in Illinois, the half-mile-long Winston Tun-

nel, named for the construction company that built the line.

Chicago, St. Paul & Kansas City

Stickney recognized that Minnesota & Northwestern was hardly an appropriate name for a railroad that began at St. Paul and went to Chicago. He renamed it the Chicago, St. Paul &

Kansas City and set out for Kansas City. He acquired the Dubuque & Dakota Railroad, a short line from Sumner, Iowa, through Waverly to Hampton, and the Wisconsin, Iowa & Nebraska Railway, a line from Waterloo, Iowa, to Des Moines. The WI&N was nicknamed "The Diagonal" for its direction across the state of Iowa. Stickney extended the WI&N east to connect with his main line at Oelwein and southwest to St. Joseph, Missouri, and Leavenworth, Kansas, arriving there in 1891. Trackage rights over a Missouri Pacific subsidiary carried CStP&KC trains to Kansas City.

Construction costs and rate wars began to adversely affect CStP&KC's financial situation—Stickney was an advocate of simplified freight rates and a practitioner of rate cutting. The road was reorganized in 1892 as the Chicago Great Western Railway. Stickney took advantage of depressed prices during the Panic of 1893 to rebuild the road and erect new shops at Oelwein, the hub of the railroad.

In 1901 the CGW leased the Wisconsin, Minnesota & Pacific Railroad, which had lines west out of Winona and Red Wing, Minn., and the Mason City & Fort Dodge Rail Road. The latter road (which had been controlled by James J. Hill since the late 1880s) served as a springboard for CGW's extension to Omaha. The route to Omaha, opened in 1903, led through largely unpopulated territory. A CGW subsidiary planned, developed, and sold towns at regular intervals along the line. About this same time the road planned and surveyed an extension to Sioux City but dropped the idea in 1906 because of the expense. CGW even set its sights briefly on Denver before turning its attention to a policy of

encouraging the short lines, both steam and electric, with which it connected.

The Felton era

The CGW entered receivership in 1908. J. P. Morgan purchased it and reorganized it as the Chicago Great Western Railroad in August 1909. Samuel M. Felton, well known as a rehabilitator of weak railroads, replaced Stickney as presi-

dent. During World War I, USRA control diverted much business from the CGW, but government payment for damages helped finance postwar improvements.

To cut passenger expenses, CGW replaced steam trains with motor cars. CGW had purchased several McKeen gasoline cars in the early 1900s, and it continued the motorization of its passenger trains with the purchase of

	1929	1967
Miles of railroad operated:	1,495	1,411
Number of locomotives:	237	139
Number of passenger cars:	185	
Number of freight cars:	7,363	
Number of company service cars:	646	
Number of freight and company service cars:		3,540
Location of headquarters: Chicago, Illinois		
Reporting marks: CGW		

Historical and technical society: Chicago & North Western Historical Society, P. O. Box 1436, Elmhurst, IL 60126-9998

Recommended reading: *The Corn Belt Route,* by H. Roger Grant, published in 1984 by Northern Illinois University Press, DeKalb, IL 60115 (ISBN 0-87580-095-5)

Successors:
Chicago & North Western
Union Pacific

Portions still operated: Union Pacific: Elmhurst–Fox River, Ill.; Oelwein–Coulter, Iowa; Mason City–Somers, Iowa

Electro-Motive's first gas-electric car. In the mid-1920s CGW teamed up with Santa Fe to offer through Pullman car service from the Twin Cities to Texas and Los Angeles. In 1929 CGW converted three old McKeen cars to a deluxe gas-electric train, the *Blue Bird,* for service between Minneapolis and Rochester, Minn.

Felton retired in 1929 when a syndicate of industrial traffic managers led by Patrick H. Joyce acquired control of the CGW. The new management completely revised the operational structure of the railroad, closed facilities, and discharged employees. The Joyce administration got involved in a stock manipulation scheme—it included the Van Sweringen brothers of Cleveland and the Kansas City Southern—that resulted in CGW's bankruptcy in February 1935. More noteworthy fruits of the Joyce era were three dozen 2-10-4s for freight service and the inauguration in 1936 of piggyback service.

A 1941 reorganization created the Chicago Great Western Railway, which included a number of previously separate subsidiaries. Immediately after World War II the road began to dieselize; dieselization was complete by 1950.

The Deramus era

In 1948 a group of Kansas City businessmen began to invest heavily in the CGW. Among them were William N. Deramus, president of Kansas City Southern, and his son, William N., III. Within a few months the younger Deramus was president of the CGW. Under his direction the road caught up on deferred maintenance and improved its physical plant.

Passenger service was reduced to a single coach-only train each way between the Twin Cities and Kansas City, the Twin Cities and Omaha, and Chicago and Oelwein. With the intent of reducing train-miles, CGW began to run enormously long freight trains behind sets of six or more F-units. Service suffered as trains were held to reach maximum tonnage and through trains performed local work. The road consoli-

dated its offices at Oelwein and Kansas City and closed its Chicago general offices. The last passenger trains, between the Twin Cities and Omaha, made their last runs on September 29, 1965. They lasted this long because of mail and express traffic inherited when Chicago & North Western dropped its Twin Cities–Omaha trains.

Chicago Great Western did reasonably well during the 1950s and 1960s, but it became clear that it would have to merge to survive. As early as 1946 there had been a proposal to merge CGW with Chicago & Eastern Illinois and Missouri-Kansas-Texas, and during the Deramus era it was generally thought that Kansas City Southern and CGW would team up. CGW investigated merger with Rock Island, Soo Line, and Frisco, but it was with the rapidly expanding Chicago & North Western that CGW merged on July 1, 1968. The North Western subsequently abandoned most of the CGW.

Chicago, Indianapolis & Louisville Railway

The New Albany & Salem Rail Road was organized in 1847 to build a railroad from New Albany, Indiana, on the north bank of the Ohio River opposite Louisville, Kentucky, to the shore of Lake Michigan. The line's founder, James Brooks, chose Salem, Ind., for the destination in the road's title to provide an appearance of conservatism to attract investors. The line was opened to Salem in 1851, to Bedford and Bloomington in 1853, and to Gosport in early 1854. A branch was begun from Gosport toward Indianapolis, but financial problems stopped work on it before the grading was completed. (It was eventually built as part of the Pennsylvania Railroad system.) Finances also halted progress on the main line.

Meanwhile the Michigan Central was stymied at Michigan City in its effort to build west from Detroit to Chicago. The charter of the New Albany & Salem allowed construction anywhere in Indiana, and Brooks did some trading. Michigan Central built its line to the Illinois border using NA&S's franchise and bought a block of NA&S stock, providing the capital Brooks needed to finish the NA&S between Gosport and Crawfordsville.

In 1852 NA&S took over the Crawfordsville & Wabash, which had a line from Crawfordsville to

Monon train 11, the southbound Chicago–Indianapolis *Tippecanoe,* crosses its namesake river at Monticello, Indiana, in April 1959, less than a week before the train's last run. Photo by J. P. Lamb Jr.

Lafayette, and in 1853 opened a line between Lafayette and Michigan City. The line was as level and straight (including a 65-mile tangent) as the south end of the NA&S was crooked and hilly.

A drought in 1856 adversely affected farming along the railroad and the Ohio River steamboats with which the railroad connected. The New Albany & Salem defaulted on its interest payments and entered receivership in 1858. It was reorganized in 1869 as the Louisville, New Albany & Chicago Railway under the leadership of John Jacob Astor. The reorganization was

declared illegal. There was another foreclosure sale to the same group of investors, and in 1873 the road made a second start as the Louisville, New Albany & Chicago Railway.

The road had lost any claim it might have had to Michigan Central's line into Chicago. The Indianapolis, Delphi & Chicago Railway was incorporated in 1865, then reincorporated in 1872 with the same name as part of a proposed railroad, the Chicago & South Atlantic, between Chicago and Charleston, South Carolina. It began construction in 1877 of a narrow gauge

railroad. The first portion was opened a year later from Bradford (renamed Monon in 1879) to Rensselaer. A new company, the Chicago & Indianapolis Air Line Railway, took over in 1881, and it was merged with the LNA&C in 1883. The line was converted to standard gauge in 1881, and Chicago–Indianapolis trains began operating in 1883. Access to Chicago was over the rails of the Chicago & Western Indiana and entrance to Indianapolis was on the Indianapolis Union Railway. About the same time LNA&C gained access to Louisville from New Albany over the rails of the Pennsylvania and the Louisville & Nashville.

The Monon Route

The LNA&C map now resembled an elongated X, with the Chicago–Indianapolis and Michigan City–Louisville lines crossing at the town of Monon. The "Monon Route" slogan was first used in 1882, and the nickname quickly eclipsed the official title of the road. The map showed few branch lines. In the 1880s the road acquired two, one from Orleans west to French Lick and the other from Bedford west toward (but not to) the western Indiana coalfields. In 1898 the Indiana Stone Railroad was incorporated to build a water-level bypass of the severe grades north of Harrodsburg—the old main line remained in service as a branch. A branch was constructed from Wallace Junction to Victoria to reach the coalfields that the branch from Bedford had stopped short of. It was built by the Indianapolis & Louisville Railroad as part of a proposed Indianapolis–Evansville line—Wallace Junction–Victoria was all that was built, though.

In 1889 and 1890 the Monon made an agreement to use the Kentucky & Indiana bridge over the Ohio River between New Albany and Louisville, facilitating connections with the Louisville Southern, which extended east from Louisville to the Cincinnati, New Orleans & Texas Pacific (Southern Railway System). The Monon built a branch of the LS to Lexington and also built the Richmond, Nicholasville, Irvine & Beattyville east toward the coalfields of eastern Kentucky.

Early in 1890 Astor died. Dr. William L. Breyfogle of New Albany pulled a shareholder coup, unseated the management, and aborted the extension into Kentucky. The Louisville Southern became part of the Southern system, and the RNI&B became part of the L&N. The Monon was reorganized as the Chicago, Indianapolis & Louisville Railway in 1897, and J. P. Morgan acquired control in 1899.

In 1902 the Southern and the Louisville & Nashville acquired most of the Monon's common stock and more than three-quarters of the preferred. At that time the road was doing well enough to consider double-tracking the line between Monon and Chicago. To that end it acquired the Chicago & Wabash Valley, a short line parallel to and east of the main line across northwestern Indiana. Nothing came of the project. In 1916 the Monon merged that line and two other roads that formed Monon branches, the Indiana Stone Railroad and the Indianapolis & Louisville.

Decline

By the 1920s the Monon had begun to stagnate. The road served little of the industrial area of Indianapolis, and the through business on the route was largely in conjunction with the ne'er-do-well Cincinnati, Hamilton & Dayton and its successor, the Cincinnati, Indianapolis & Western. Baltimore & Ohio acquired the CI&W in 1927, drying up connecting traffic—B&O could move Cincinnati–Chicago traffic on its own rails all the way via Deshler, Ohio.

The Indiana coalfields were at a competitive disadvantage with the Appalachian ones. The demand for building stone, which at times constituted nearly a quarter of Monon's freight traffic, diminished as construction activity dropped during the Depression. Both the railroads with which the Monon connected at Louisville, Southern and L&N, had more expeditious connections for Chicago business and did not particularly favor the Monon, even though they controlled it.

In an effort to avert bankruptcy, Monon applied to the Reconstruction Finance Corp. for a loan in December 1933. John W. Barriger III, head of the agency, recognized that the road's finances needed reorganization and refused the loan. The Monon filed for bankruptcy on December 30, 1933. It cut passenger service to the minimum and abandoned the branch west of Bedford and the former Chicago & Wabash Valley. The trustees even considered total abandonment—the Monon had the longest route between an Ohio River crossing and Chicago and was the hardest to operate—but the road struggled through World War II.

The Barriger era

On May 1, 1946, a new Chicago, Indianapolis & Louisville Railway took over, with John W. Barriger III as president. Barriger was an advocate of the Super Railroad—flat, straight, fast, multiple track, heavy duty—and the Monon was its antithesis. Nonetheless, Barriger replaced steam with diesel, purchased war-surplus hospital cars to convert to streamlined passenger cars (cheaper and quicker than ordering new cars), restored passenger trains, solicited freight business, bought freight cars by the hundreds, and caught up on 20 years of deferred maintenance. Concluding that the south end of the railroad needed to be totally relocated, which was impossible, he limited relocation efforts to replacement of the Wabash River bridge at Delphi and a bypass of a bottomless bog at Cedar Lake. He was unable to relocate the Monon out of city streets at New Albany, Bedford, Lafayette, and Monticello. Nonetheless, when Barriger departed at the end of 1952 to assume a vice-presidency of the New Haven he left behind a well-maintained and well-operated railroad with black ink on its ledgers.

Barriger was succeeded by Warren Brown, during whose tenure the railroad changed its official name to Monon Railroad. In 1959 the Monon dropped its Indianapolis passenger trains; the Chicago–Louisville train lasted until 1967, largely because of business generated by Purdue University at Lafayette and Indiana University at Bloomington.

When the Louisville & Nashville purchased the eastern half of the Chicago & Eastern Illinois in 1969, the Monon approached the Southern Railway on the matter of merger. Southern had just upgraded its line into Cincinnati and was content to interchange Chicago business there rather than acquire its own line north from the Ohio River. Louisville & Nashville was much more receptive to merger, seeing the Monon as a useful alternate route and also eyeing Monon's interests in Chicago & Western Indiana, Belt Railway of Chicago, and Kentucky & Indiana Terminal. The Louisville & Nashville merged the Monon on July 31, 1971.

	1929	1970
Miles of railroad operated:	648	541
Number of locomotives:	174	44
Number of passenger cars:	91	27*
Number of freight cars:	6,356	3,078
Number of company service cars:	256	98

Location of headquarters: Chicago, Illinois
Reporting marks: CIL, MON
Historical and technical society: Monon Railroad Historical & Technical Society, P. O. Box 68, Ladoga, IN 47954-0068; http://monon.indiana.edu
Recommended reading: *Monon Route,* by George W. Hilton, published in 1978 by Howell-North Books, 850 North Hollywood Way, Burbank CA 91505
Subsidiaries and affiliated railroads, 1970:
Chicago & Western Indiana (20%)
Belt Railway of Chicago (8.33%)
Kentucky & Indiana Terminal (33.3%)
Successors:
Louisville & Nashville
Seaboard System
CSX Transportation
Portions still operated: CSX: Chicago–Louisville; Monon–Delphi; Medaryville–Monon
*(1966)

Chicago, Milwaukee, St. Paul & Pacific Railroad

The Milwaukee & Waukesha Rail Road was chartered in 1847. Even before it laid its first rails in 1850, its name was changed to Milwaukee & Mississippi. In 1851 it reached Waukesha, Wisconsin, 20 miles west of Milwaukee. Its rails reached Madison in 1854 and Prairie du Chien, on the Mississippi River, in 1857.

In 1858 the La Crosse & Milwaukee Rail Road was completed between the cities of its name, forming a second route across Wisconsin between Lake Michigan and the Mississippi River. It was reorganized in 1863 as the Milwaukee & St. Paul, and in 1867 it purchased the Milwaukee & Prairie du Chien, successor to the Milwaukee & Mississippi.

The Milwaukee & St. Paul acquired in 1872 the St. Paul & Chicago, which had just completed a route down the west bank of the Mississippi from St. Paul to La Crescent, opposite La Crosse. In 1873 the M&StP completed a line from Milwaukee south to Chicago and a year later added "Chicago" to its name.

In the next few years the road built or bought lines from Racine, Wis., to Moline, Illinois; from Chicago to Savanna, Ill., and two lines west across southern Minnesota. The road reached Council Bluffs, Iowa, across the Missouri River from Omaha, in 1882, and reached Kansas City in 1887. In 1893 the CM&StP acquired the Mil-

Two "Little Joe" electric locomotives and a GP9 accelerate out of Three Forks, Montana, with westbound time freight 263, on July 25, 1964. Photo by William D. Middleton.

waukee & Northern, which reached from Milwaukee into Michigan's upper peninsula.

In 1900 the Chicago, Milwaukee & St. Paul was considered one of the most prosperous, pro-

gressive, and enterprising railroads in the U. S. Its lines reached from Chicago to Minneapolis, Omaha, and Kansas City. Secondary lines and branches covered most of the area between the

Omaha and Minneapolis lines in Wisconsin, Iowa, and Minnesota. Lines covered much of eastern South Dakota and reached the Missouri River at three places in that state: Running Water, Chamberlain, and Evarts. Except for the last few miles into Kansas City and operation over Union Pacific rails from Council Bluffs to Omaha, the Missouri River formed the western boundary of the CM&StP. ("Milwaukee Road" as a name or nickname did not come into use until the late 1920s; "St. Paul Road" was sometimes used as a nickname, but the railroad's advertising used the full name).

Pacific extension

The battle over control of the Northern Pacific and the Burlington in 1901 made the Milwaukee Road aware that without its own route to the Pacific it would be at its competitors' mercy—a commodity the railroad industry was singularly short of. At the same time the Milwaukee Road was experiencing a change in its traffic from dominance by wheat to a more balanced mix of agricultural and industrial products. Arguments against extension westward included the possibility of the construction of the Panama Canal and the presence of strong competing railroads: Union Pacific, Northern Pacific, and Great Northern. Arguments for the extension banked heavily on the growth of traffic to and from the Pacific Northwest.

In 1901 the president of the Milwaukee Road dispatched an engineer west to estimate the cost of duplicating Northern Pacific's line. His figure was $45 million. Such an expenditure required considerable thought; not until November 1905 did Milwaukee's board of directors authorize construction of a line west to Tacoma and Seattle.

In 1905 and 1906 the Milwaukee Road incorporated subsidiaries in South Dakota, Montana, Idaho, and Washington. The Washington company was renamed the Chicago, Milwaukee & Puget Sound Railway, and it took over the other three companies in 1908. It was absorbed by the CM&StP in 1912.

The extension began with a bridge across the Missouri River at Mobridge, 3 miles upstream from Evarts, S. Dak. Roadbed and rails pushed out from several points into unpopulated territory. The work went quickly, and the road was open to Butte, Mont., in August 1908.

The route from Harlowton to Lombard was that of the Montana Railroad, the "Jawbone." Its mortgage was held by James J. Hill and the Great Northern Railway. Taking advantage of Hill's absence on a trip to England, the Milwaukee Road advanced the owner the funds required to pay off the mortgage and bought the railroad through the CM&PS.

Construction was also under way eastward from Seattle. The last spike on the line was driven near Garrison, Mont., on May 14, 1909. Local passenger service was established later that year; through passenger service was inaugurated in May 1911.

In 1912 the Milwaukee Road decided to electrify much of the new line. The terrain (the Belt, Rocky, Bitter Root, Saddle, and Cascade mountain ranges), the possibility of hydroelectric

The craftsmanship of Milwaukee Road's shops in its home city is displayed in both the streamlined shroud on F1 Pacific No. 152 (originally built by Alco in 1910) and the passenger cars behind as train 21, the *Chippewa-Hiawatha*, accelerates through Milwaukee's north side. Photo by Jim Scribbins.

power, the difficulties associated with operating steam locomotives through tunnels and in severe winter weather, and an increase in traffic all suggested electrification. The section from Harlowton, Mont., to Avery, Idaho, was com-pletely turned over to electric operation in late 1916. Early in 1917 the road decided to electrify the portion of the line from Othello, Wash., to Tacoma. Electric operation on the Coast Division began in 1919, and overhead wires reached Seattle, on a 10-mile branch off the main line, in 1927. The electrification cost $23 million, but in 1925 the road reported that the savings over steam operation had already amounted to more than half that sum.

Financial difficulty

The cost of the Pacific Extension, $234 million, greatly exceeded estimates. Traffic on the new route came nowhere near the projections: The boom in the Pacific Northwest ended about 1910, and the Panama Canal opened in 1914. The debt incurred in building the Pacific Extension remained.

On top of that, in 1921 the Milwaukee leased the Chicago, Terre Haute & Southeastern and in 1922 acquired the Chicago, Milwaukee & Gary to gain access to the coalfields of southern Indiana. Both those roads were heavily in debt. The Milwaukee Road entered bankruptcy in 1925.

The company emerged from reorganization in 1928 as the Chicago, Milwaukee, St. Paul & Pacific Railroad. On June 29, 1935, it declared bankruptcy again. Despite the financial problems, the late 1930s and early 1940s were interesting times for Milwaukee Road. In May 1935 the road introduced the *Hiawatha*, a fast steam-powered streamlined train between Chicago and the Twin Cities. It was an immediate and overwhelming success. In the next few years the train was re-equipped, service was doubled, and *Hiawathas* appeared on other Milwaukee routes. The cars of the *Hiawatha*, like most of Milwaukee Road's freight and passenger cars and many of its steam locomotives, were products of the road's shops in Milwaukee.

The postwar boom brought the Milwaukee

Road out of bankruptcy, and the road remained reasonably healthy into the 1960s. In 1955 Union Pacific moved its streamliners from the Chicago & North Western to Milwaukee's Chicago–Council Bluffs, Iowa, route, and in the early 1960s Milwaukee Road modernized its Chicago suburban service and built a new station in Milwaukee. The road discussed merger with the Chicago & North Western and with the Rock Island. As a condition of the creation of Burlington Northern it was granted trackage rights on BN into Portland, Oregon; and as a condition of Louisville & Nashville's merger of the Monon, it received trackage rights over the former Monon line from Bedford, Indiana, to Louisville, Kentucky.

The longest branch line

Through this period there was little change in Milwaukee's lines west of the Missouri River. North America's longest electrification continued unchanged—in the same two disconnected portions, with steam and later diesel power hauling trains over the 212 miles of nonelectrified track between Avery, Idaho, and Othello, Wash. With dieselization of the Milwaukee Road after World War II it appeared that the electrification, by then 30 years old, would be dismantled, but the road purchased 12 electric locomotives that had been built by General Electric for Russia and embargoed because of international tensions. Milwaukee Road regauged the "Little Joes" from 5 feet to standard and equipped two with steam generators for passenger service. They went into service

between Harlowton and Avery.

The electrification soldiered on for another two decades, but diesels showed up under the wires more and more often, sometimes running in multiple with the electrics. By the early 1970s passenger service had long since been discontinued, many of the original electric locomotives had been scrapped, and much of the hardware of the electrification needed replacement. Traffic on the line was insufficient to justify rebuilding the electric plant—and the road did not have the funds to do so anyway. The Milwaukee Road de-energized the catenary over the Coast Division in 1972 and ended electric operation on the Rocky Mountain Division on June 16, 1974.

Financial difficulties again

Except for its double-track Chicago–Twin Cities main line, the Milwaukee Road was secondary railroading. It was not the first railroad you thought of between, say, Chicago and Kansas City or St. Paul and Seattle. Traffic on the Pacific Extension barely supported one freight train a day each way. The lightly constructed branch lines that spider-webbed across Wisconsin, Iowa, Minnesota, and South Dakota carried mostly products of agriculture.

Over the decades the road's management had made too many wrong decisions: building the Pacific Extension, not electrifying between the two electrified portions (or perhaps undertaking the electrification at all), purchasing the line into

Indiana, and choosing Flexivans instead of conventional piggyback.

After several money-losing years in the early 1970s, the Milwaukee Road voluntarily entered reorganization once again on December 19, 1977. The major result of the 1977 reorganization was the amputation of everything west of Miles City, Montana, to concentrate on a "Milwaukee II" system linking Chicago, Kansas City, Minneapolis-St. Paul, Duluth (on Burlington Northern rails from St. Paul), and Louisville.

By 1983 the Milwaukee's map consisted of the Chicago–Twin Cities main line; Chicago–Savanna–Kansas City; Chicago–Louisville (almost entirely on Conrail and Seaboard System rails), Milwaukee–Green Bay; New Lisbon–Tomahawk, Wis.; Savanna–La Crosse, along the west bank of the Mississippi; Marquette to Sheldon, Iowa, and Jackson, Minn.; Austin, Minn.–St. Paul; and St. Paul–Ortonville, Minn., plus a few branches.

Three railroads vied for the Milwaukee Road: the Chicago & North Western, financially none too solid itself; Canadian National subsidiary Grand Trunk Western, with an eye toward creating a route between eastern and western Canada south of the Great Lakes; and Canadian Pacific subsidiary Soo Line. Soo Line purchased the Milwaukee Road in February 1985 and merged it January 1, 1986. Soo subsequently sold the Milwaukee–Green Bay and New Lisbon–Tomahawk routes to Wisconsin Central.

	1929	1984
Miles of railroad operated:	11,248	3,023
Miles operated west of Mobridge, S. Dak.:	3,074	3,064*
Number of locomotives:	1,801	323
Number of passenger cars:	1,330	347†
Number of freight cars:	73,184	11,411
Number of company service cars:	3,704	1,492

Location of headquarters: Chicago, Illinois

Reporting marks: MILW

Notable named passenger trains: *Olympian, Olympian Hiawatha* (Chicago–Seattle–Tacoma); *Twin Cities Hiawatha* (Chicago–Minneapolis); Union Pacific *City* streamliners (Chicago–Council Bluffs)

Historical and technical societies:
Milwaukee Road Historical Association, P. O. Box 307, Antioch, IL 60002-0307; http://www.mrha.com/ Milwest, c/o Kevin McCray, 6 Park Place, Clancy MT 59634-9759

Recommended reading:
Milwaukee Road Remembered, by Jim Scribbins, published in 1990 by Kalmbach Publishing Co., P. O. Box 1612, Waukesha, WI 53187. ISBN 0-89024-075-2
*(1979)
†(1970)

The Electric Way Across the Mountains, by Richard Steinheimer, published in 1980 by Carbarn Press, Tiburon, CA 94920 (ISBN 0- 934406-00-6)

Subsidiaries and affiliated railroads, 1984: Indiana Harbor Belt (49%)

Successor:
Soo Line
Canadian Pacific

Portions still operated:
Burlington Northern: Council Bluffs–Bayard, Iowa; Canton–Mitchell, S. Dak.; Canton–Madison, S. Dak., Sioux City, Iowa–Aberdeen, S. Dak.; Ortonville, Minn.–Terry, Mont.; Lewistown to Heath and Moore, Mont.; Bovill, Idaho–Palouse, Wash.; Warden–Royal City, Wash.; Maple Valley–Snoqualmie Falls, Wash.

Cedar Rapids & Iowa City: Cedar Rapids–Middle Amana, Iowa

Chehalis Western: Tacoma–Chehalis Jct., Frederickson–Morton, Wash.

Chicago & North Western: Jefferson–Yale, Iowa; Herndon–Perry, Iowa; Woodward–Slater, Iowa

Central Montana Rail: Spring Creek Junction–Geraldine, Mont.

D&I Railroad: Dell Rapids S. Dak.–Sioux Falls–Sioux City, Iowa

Dakota Southern: Mitchell–Chamberlain–Kadoka, S. Dak.

Escanaba & Lake Superior: Green Bay, Wis.–Republic, Mich., and Channing–Ontonagon, Mich.

Kankakee, Beaverville & Southern: Hooper–Danville, Ill.

Northern Illinois Railroad Corporation (Mete): Chicago–Rondout–Fox Lake, Ill.

Pend Oreille Valley: Newport–Metaline Falls, Wash.

Potlatch Corp.: Avery–St. Maries, Idaho

Sisseton Milbank: Milbank–Sisseton, S. Dak.

Soo Line: Chicago–Milwaukee–St. Paul–Ortonville, Minn.; Sturtevant–Union Grove, Wis.; Watertown–Madison–Portage, Wis.; Chicago–Savanna, Ill.–Kansas City; Davis Jct., Ill.–Janesville, Wis.; Savanna–La Crescent, Minn.; Marquette–Sheldon, Iowa; Mason City, Iowa–St. Paul, Minn.; Ramsey–Jackson, Minn.; Chicago–Louisville (all but Terre Haute–Bedford, Ind., on trackage rights)

St. Maries River: Bovill–Plummer, Idaho

Washington Central: Warden–Royal City and Tiflis–Moses Lake

Wisconsin & Calumet: Madison–Janesville–Monroe, Wis.; Madison–Prairie du Chien; Milton Jct.–Waukesha; Bardwell–Elkhorn; and Janesville–Fox Lake, Ill.

Wisconsin & Southern: North Milwaukee to Cambria, Fox Lake, Markesan, and Oshkosh, Wis.

Wisconsin Central: North Milwaukee–Green Bay and New Lisbon–Tomahawk, Wis.

Chicago North Shore & Milwaukee Railroad

In 1891 the Waukegan & North Shore Rapid Transit Co. was incorporated—a trolley line for the city of Waukegan, Illinois, on the shore of Lake Michigan, 36 miles north of Chicago. In 1897, by which time it reached 6 miles south to Lake Bluff, it was sold and reorganized as the Chicago & Milwaukee Electric Railway. The line was extended south through the towns along the lake to Evanston, where it connected with a branch of the Milwaukee Road to Chicago. It also built a line west from Lake Bluff to Libertyville in 1903 and to what is now Mundelein in 1905.

Construction northward from Lake Bluff began in 1904 following steam-railroad standards of grade and curvature—the line to Evanston was typical of suburban trolley line construction. In December 1905 the line reached Kenosha, Wisconsin, where it connected with the Milwaukee Light, Heat & Traction Co. At the same time the Milwaukee Road connection at Evanston was replaced by the Northwestern Elevated Railroad. An all-electric Chicago–Milwaukee trip became possible—it took five hours, considerably more than on the parallel Chicago & North Western or Milwaukee Road, but the fare was less. The Chicago & Milwaukee pushed its own rails north, reaching Milwaukee (and bankruptcy) in 1908. Operation began, nonetheless, and immediately included

A two-car train of modernized "Silverliner" cars heads south toward Chicago near Racine, Wisconsin, on August 20, 1955. Photo by William D. Middleton.

limited-stop express trains with parlor car and dining service.

Enter Samuel Insull

In 1916 the Insull interests purchased the railroad, reorganized it as the Chicago North Shore & Milwaukee Railroad, and immediately began a modernization program. Business nearly doubled during the first year of new management. In 1919 the North Shore made arrangements to operate to the Loop in downtown Chicago over the rails of the elevated (the "L") and constructed new terminals in Chicago and Milwaukee. Business flourished on the 85-mile route, even with the competition of two very healthy steam roads. The North Shore quickly developed into the definitive interurban.

In the early 1920s traffic between Waukegan and Evanston reached the saturation point of the line, which was handicapped by stretches of street running. The railroad saw that a new line a few miles west along the right of way of one of Insull's power companies would be cheaper than just the construction of temporary track needed to rebuild the existing line. The first 5-mile portion of the new Skokie Valley Line was opened in

MILWAUKEE

RACINE

KENOSHA   *LAKE*

WISCONSIN
ILLINOIS   Zion

              MICHIGAN

              Waukegan
Libertyville   North Chicago Jct.
Mundelein

              Highwood

Skokie
(Dempster Street)   Evanston
                     Howard Street

              CHICAGO

	1929	1962
Miles of railroad operated:	138	107
Number of locomotives:	7	8
Number of passenger cars:	214	135
Number of motor freight cars:	42	7
Number of freight cars:	211	17
Number of company service cars:	58	32

Location of headquarters: Highwood, Illinois
Reporting marks: CNS&M
Notable named passenger trains: *Electroliner* (Chicago–Milwaukee)
Historical and technical society: Shore Line Interurban Historical Society, P. O. Box 1270, Sheboygan, WI 53082-1230
Recommended reading: *North Shore*, by William D. Middleton, published in 1964 by Golden West Books, P. O. Box 80250, San Marino, CA 91108
Portions still operated: Chicago Transit Authority: Howard Street, Chicago–Dempster Street, Skokie

1925 and was operated by Chicago Rapid Transit, which continued to operate local service until 1948. The entire line opened in 1926 and became the new main route. The Shore Line, as the orig-

inal route was termed, was relegated to local service. The new route was much faster, materially helping the North Shore compete with the steam roads. North Shore quickly became America's fastest interurban. In addition the North Shore emphasized its parlor and dining service—it was perhaps the only interurban to have much success with such operations.

Electroliners and abandonment

In 1931 the Great Depression finally got a grip on the North Shore. The line declared bankruptcy in September 1932. Even so, the road continued to operate fast, frequent trains. It cooperated with parallel Chicago & North Western and public agencies in a line relocation project through Glencoe, Winnetka, and Kenilworth, eliminating grade crossings and street running. In 1939 the North Shore ordered a pair of streamliners from St. Louis Car Co.: the *Electroliners*. No other trains of the streamliner era had such disparate elements in their specifications: 85-mph top speed (North Shore's schedules called for start-to-stop averages of 70 mph) and the ability to operate around the 90-foot radius curves of the Chicago "L." World War II brought increased traffic, and the North Shore emerged from bankruptcy in 1946—just as competition from automobiles and strikes by employees began to cut into the road's business. Waukegan and North Chicago streetcar services were taken over by buses in 1947, dining car service on trains other than the *Electroliners* was dropped in 1949, local streetcar service in Milwaukee was discontinued in 1951, and the Shore Line was abandoned in 1955.

By then the North Shore was owned by the Susquehanna Corporation, a holding company that found the road's losses useful for tax purposes— ditto for tax credits from abandonment. In 1959 an Interstate Commerce Commission examiner recommended abandonment, and the 1960 completion of the Edens Expressway took passengers away by the thousands. Protests and renewed petitions prolonged the struggles of the line until January 21, 1963.

North Shore's freight business consisted of less-than-carload traffic carried in merchandise despatch cars (motor baggage cars) and intermediate traffic, received from one steam road and delivered to another. North Shore inaugurated piggyback service in 1926, but improved parallel highways led to its discontinuance in 1947.

Remnants of the North Shore exist. Many of its standard steel passenger cars are in trolley museums across the country, and the two *Electroliners* are at Illinois Railway Museum at Union, Ill., and Shade Gap Electric Railway, Orbisonia, Pennsylvania, after several years of service on the Philadelphia & Western. North Shore's right of way is still visible, and part of the Shore Line has become a bicycle path. Chicago Transit Authority restored service to the south end of the Skokie Valley Route in 1964—the *Skokie Swift*, a nonstop service between Howard Street in Chicago and Dempster Street in Skokie.

Chicago, Rock Island & Pacific Railway

 In 1847 the Rock Island & La Salle Rail Road was chartered to build between Rock Island, Illinois, on the Mississippi River, and La Salle, where connections would be made with the Illinois & Michigan Canal to Chicago. Contractor Henry Farnam persuaded the organizers to extend the railroad all the way to Chicago to connect with other railroads. The charter was so amended, and the railroad was renamed the Chicago & Rock Island. Construction began in 1851. The first train ran southwest from Chicago to Joliet, 40 miles, on October 10, 1852. Its power was a 4-4-0 named *Rocket*.

The line was opened to Rock Island on February 22, 1854, and the contractors turned the line over to the corporation in July of that year. By then the railroad had an agreement with the Northern Indiana Railroad (later part of the New York Central) for joint terminal facilities in

A westbound *Rocket* powered by an Electro-Motive TA, a model unique to the Rock Island, overtakes a 2-8-2 and its freight train just east of Bureau, Illinois, September 1940. Photo by Paul Stringham.

offered a bonus if a train arrived by midnight, December 31, 1855. Muscatine got its railroad first, on November 20, 1855, but (if we are to believe contemporary accounts) a frozen locomotive was pushed over hastily laid and barely spiked rails into Iowa City as church bells rang in the New Year, securing the bonus and providing a perfect scenario for a multitude of grade-B novels and movies.

A bridge across the Mississippi was necessary to connect the Chicago & Rock Island and Mississippi & Missouri railroads. The Mississippi had not yet been spanned, and the immediate reaction to the proposed railroad bridge was that it would be a hazard to navigation. However, the bridge was built, and it was officially opened on April 21, 1856. On the evening of May 6 the steamboat *Effie Afton*, which usually plied the New Orleans–Louisville run, cleared the open draw span then veered aside, turned around, rammed one of the piers, and suddenly and suspiciously burst into flames. The case of the bridge soon became one of railroad advocates versus steamboat advocates. The latter felt that even a single bridge would set an unfortunate precedent and soon there would be bridges every 40 or 50 miles along the length of the river. The railroad's case, argued by Abraham Lincoln, went one way and the other in successive courts, but in 1866 the U. S. Supreme Court held for the railroad. Several other railroads immediately applied to bridge the Mississippi at other locations.

The Mississippi & Missouri, far behind its construction schedule, was sold to the newly incorporated Chicago, Rock Island & Pacific on July 9, 1866. On August 20 that company consolidated with the Chicago & Rock Island to

Chicago, and a branch from Bureau, Ill., south to Peoria was nearly complete (it opened in November 1854).

Beyond the Mississippi

The Mississippi & Missouri Railroad was chartered in Iowa to build a railroad from Davenport, across the Mississippi River from Rock Island, to Council Bluffs, with branches south through Muscatine and north through Cedar Rapids. Money to finance construction of the Mississippi & Missouri was hard to come by. Both Iowa City, then the state capital, and Muscatine wanted the railroad first. Iowa City

form a successor Chicago, Rock Island & Pacific Railroad. The line reached Des Moines a year later and arrived at Council Bluffs on May 11, 1869—one day after the completion of the Union Pacific and Central Pacific railroads from Council Bluffs to the West Coast. The Rock Island was not the first railroad into Council Bluffs; the Cedar Rapids & Missouri (later part of the Chicago & North Western) had reached there more than two years earlier and established ties with the Union Pacific.

To Missouri, Kansas, and beyond

In the 1870s the road extended its Muscatine line southwest across Iowa and northwestern Missouri to Leavenworth, Kansas, and later negotiated trackage rights over the Hannibal & St. Joseph from Cameron, Mo., to Kansas City. Also during the 1870s the road acquired a couple of "firsts"—the first dining cars and Jesse James's first train holdup.

The 1880s saw some corporate simplification, the acquisition of the Keokuk & Des Moines and the St. Joseph & Iowa, and control of the Burlington, Cedar Rapids & Northern, which had a line from Burlington, Iowa, through Cedar Rapids and Cedar Falls to Plymouth, near Mason City, with a branch through Iowa Falls and Estherville to Watertown, South Dakota. The BCR&N later acquired lines west out of Davenport and Clinton, Iowa, and lines to Decorah, Iowa, Worthington, Minn., and Sioux Falls, S. Dak.

On December 5, 1883, the Rock Island made a tripartite agreement with Union Pacific and the Milwaukee Road for interchange of business at Omaha. The Chicago & North Western, which had been UP's preferred connection, quickly became a party to the agreement, as did the Wabash, St. Louis & Pacific (a predecessor of the Wabash). The Burlington & Missouri River in Nebraska (part of the Burlington) protested the agreement. UP suddenly found itself in financial difficulties, and Rock Island decided to build its own extensions west rather than rely on interchange traffic with UP. Two years later the Chicago, Kansas & Nebraska Railroad was chartered to build from St. Joseph and Atchison southwest across Kansas to Wichita, and another railroad of the same name was incorporated in Nebraska to build from the southeast tip of the state to Kearney. The two companies merged and were leased to the St. Joseph & Iowa Railroad, a subsidiary of the Rock Island. A charter was approved for the extension of the southwest line from Wichita to Galveston, Texas, and from Liberal, Kans., to El Paso, Tex. By the end of 1887 rails reached to Caldwell, on the southern border of Kansas, and in February 1888 they reached Liberal. A year later the Rock Island had built west across northern Kansas and Colorado to Colorado Springs. RI made arrangements to use Denver & Rio Grande track north to Denver and south to Pueblo; in 1889 RI began using Union Pacific tracks from Limon, Colo., to Denver.

Rock Island's Chicago–Colorado route via St. Joseph was circuitous. To assemble a route through Omaha, RI constructed a line from Omaha to Lincoln and in 1890 traded the trackage rights from McPherson to Hutchinson, Kans., to Union Pacific for trackage rights on UP between Lincoln and Beatrice and use of UP's Missouri River bridge between Council Bluffs and Omaha. RI began Chicago–Colorado service via Omaha on August 16, 1891, and later built its own line west of Lincoln. Also in 1891 Rock Island acquired the property of the Chicago, Kansas & Nebraska. Subsidiary Chicago, Rock Island & Texas reached Fort Worth in 1893.

The Reid-Moore era

In 1901 control of the Rock Island was taken over by the Reid-Moore syndicate: Daniel G. Reed, William H. Moore, his brother James H. Moore, and William Leeds, men who had put together the National Biscuit, Diamond Match, and American Can companies. The road continued to burgeon. It acquired the Choctaw, Oklahoma & Gulf Railroad, a line from Memphis, Tennessee, through Little Rock, Arkansas, and Oklahoma City to Elk City in western Oklahoma, and the 70-mile St. Louis, Kansas City & Colorado Railroad (which the Santa Fe at one point had considered acquiring for an entrance to St. Louis). Expansion continued:
• 1902—lease of the Burlington, Cedar Rapids & Northern for 999 years, and extension of the southwestern line from Liberal to Santa Rosa, New Mexico, to connect with the El Paso & Northeastern, a Southern Pacific predecessor (the new track included the second longest stretch of straight track in the U. S., nearly 72 miles between Guymon, Okla., and Dalhart, Tex.)
• 1903—Chicago, Rock Island & Gulf completed a line between Fort Worth and Dallas
• 1904—the Choctaw line was extended west to Amarillo, Tex., and the Kansas City–St. Louis line was opened
• 1905—the road began assembling and constructing a line south from Little Rock to Eunice, Louisiana, with the intent of reaching New Orleans

Two GP7s wearing the new-image blue and white and lettered "The Rock" and two U25Bs in the old maroon livery lead a westbound freight across Iowa between Homestead and South Amana in September 1976. Photo by William J. Husa Jr.

• 1906—RI acquired a half interest in the Trinity & Brazos Valley Railway (Dallas–Houston–Galveston, later the Burlington-Rock Island Railroad) from the Colorado & Southern.

At the same time the controlling syndicate, which now included B. F. Yoakum, was busy acquiring control of the Chicago & Alton, the Chicago & Eastern Illinois, the Toledo, St. Louis & Western, and the St. Louis-San Francisco through holding companies and exchanges of stock. By 1909, though, the interest due on SLSF bonds far exceeded the dividends received on SLSF stock—none. B. F. Yoakum bought Rock Island's Frisco stock at a considerable loss to the Rock Island.

Financial difficulty

Rock Island created a Twin Cities–Kansas City route in 1913 by leasing the St. Paul & Kansas City Short Line Railroad and building a line between Allerton and Carlisle, Iowa, a few miles south of Des Moines. In 1914 red ink caused by debt interest appeared on Rock Island's ledgers, and on April 20, 1915, the road entered receivership. On June 22, 1917, the road was out of receivership and back in the hands of its stockholders. Shortly afterward the United States Railroad Administration took over management for the duration of World War I.

New management took over in the 1920s and placed considerable emphasis on paying of stock dividends to the detriment of maintaining the property. Edward N. Brown, chairman of the board of the Frisco, began to buy Rock Island stock with the thought of using dividends to bolster the Frisco's situation. Soon Brown was chairman of Rock Island's executive committee. In 1927 Rock Island declared a stock dividend of 5 percent; in 1928, 6 percent; and in 1929, 7 percent—even though Rock Island's annual interest on its debt was nearly $14 million. In 1930 Brown began to secretly acquire Frisco stock for the Rock Island. Revenues dropped as the depression deepened. Then Rock Island's territory was struck with wheat crop failures and dust storms. The Rock Island declared bankruptcy on June 7, 1933.

Edward M. Durham, vice-president of Missouri Pacific, took over as chief executive office in December 1935. He brought in John D. Farrington, general manager of the Fort Worth & Denver, as operating officer in May 1936. Farrington started a scrap drive to finance a rail relay program and purchased ten diesel switchers and six diesel-powered *Rocket* streamliners. His program included line relocations between Davenport and Kansas City and a new bridge over the Cimarron River just east of Liberal, Kans. The road turned a profit in 1941. Durham retired in July 1942, and Farrington took over as chief executive officer.

The Chicago, Rock Island & Pacific Railroad emerged from a long and acrimonious reorganization on January 1, 1948. Farrington was still leading the company and pursuing a program of dieselization, line improvement, and industrial development. Rock Island rolled on through the 1950s and into the 1960s doing decently although surrounded by stronger railroads. Its freight traffic was largely agricultural. Its passenger trains for the most part would take you anywhere the Burlington or the Santa Fe could, but not as quickly nor with quite as much style.

The fight over the Rock Island

In 1964 Ben Heineman, chairman of the Chicago & North Western, proposed merging the C&NW, the Rock Island, and the Milwaukee Road into an Upper Midwest system and selling the lines south of Kansas City to Santa Fe. Union Pacific made a counterproposal: merger, which would put the UP into Chicago. That year, 1964, was Rock Island's last year of profitability.

The proposal turned into the longest, most complicated merger case ever handled by the Interstate Commerce Commission. The other railroads west of Chicago protested one aspect or another of the merger, petitioned for inclusion, or asked for a piece of the Rock Island. In 1970 the Milwaukee Road, which had fallen on hard times, entered the case, asking for inclusion in Union Pacific or Southern Pacific. In 1973 the ICC proposed restructuring the railroads of the West into four systems: Union Pacific, Southern Pacific, Burlington Northern, and Santa Fe. The railroads involved in the merger case other than

the two principals petitioned the ICC to dismiss the case and start over.

The ICC finally approved the merger on November 8, 1974, with several conditions: Southern Pacific would be allowed to purchase the Kansas City–Tucumcari line (that had been part of the UP merger proposal from the beginning); the Omaha–Colorado Springs line would be sold to the Denver & Rio Grande Western; and Santa Fe would be permitted to buy the Choctaw Route (Memphis–Amarillo) only if it would absorb the bankrupt and decrepit Missouri-Kansas-Texas. Union Pacific said it would have to re-evaluate the merger, since the Rock Island of 1974 wasn't the Rock Island of 1964. Rock Island filed for bankruptcy on March 17, 1975, and on August 4 of that year UP withdrew its merger offer. The ICC dismissed the case on July 10, 1976.

Slow death

By then the Rock Island was in terrible shape. A new management headed by John W. Ingram did its best, introducing a new image of sky-blue and white and appointing John W. Barriger III, then 76 years old, as Senior Traveling Freight Agent (Barriger's own title) and consultant.

Rock Island's clerks walked off their jobs on August 28, 1979, over a pay dispute, and United Transportation Union members followed the next day. President Jimmy Carter issued an order September 20 creating an emergency board to settle the dispute. The UTU members then returned to their jobs, but members of the Brotherhood of Railway and Airline Clerks stayed off.

On September 26 the Kansas City Terminal was ordered by the ICC to operate the railroad. KCT's owners plus Denver & Rio Grande Western and Southern Pacific began operating the Rock Island. On March 2, 1980, the ICC refused to extend its directed service order, and the Rock Island ceased operation March 31, 1980.

The railroad industry had never before seen an abandonment of the magnitude of Rock Island. Other railroads had been abandoned in their entirety, but they were roads like the New York, Ontario & Western (541 miles, 1957; it had always been sickly and shouldn't have been built), Fort Smith & Western (250 miles, 1939; it didn't go anywhere and shouldn't have been built), and the Colorado Midland (338 miles, 1918; it had steep grades and shouldn't have been built—and 1918 was ancient history anyway).

The 7,000-mile Rock Island connected big cities like Chicago, Denver, Minneapolis, Houston, and Kansas City. It had no major operating handicaps, like mountains. It had long routes, so it wasn't another Reading or Central of New Jersey. Industry reaction to the abandonment ranged from "Someone has to take it over and run it" to "Can I have the Kansas City–Minneapolis line?"

When the dust began to settle it turned out that what was abandoned was the operating company and the financial structure, not the physical plant. Rock Island's sky-blue freight cars showed up with reporting marks like C&NW and BM underneath the slogan "The Rock," and the fixed plant of the railroad was parceled out to other railroads, as detailed on the next page.

	1929	1978
Miles of railroad operated:	8,158	7,021
Number of locomotives:	1,453	660
Number of passenger cars:	1,075	79
Number of freight cars:	43,751	
Number of company service cars:	3,489	
Number of freight and company service cars:		26,592

Location of headquarters: Chicago, Illinois

Reporting marks: RI, ROCK

Notable named passenger trains: *Golden State Limited* (Chicago–Kansas City–El Paso, Texas–Los Angeles; operated west of Tucumcari, N. Mex., by Southern Pacific); *Rockets* (Chicago–Peoria, Chicago–Des Moines–Omaha–Colorado Springs/Denver, Minneapolis–Kansas City–Dallas–Houston, and others)

Historical and technical society: Rock Island Technical Society, 11519 N. Wayne Ave., Kansas City, MO 64155-2914

Recommended reading: *Iron Road to Empire,* by William Edward Hayes, published in 1953 by Simmons-Boardman Publishing Corp.

Major portions still operated:

Chicago–Colorado route and branches:

Chicago–Joliet, Ill.: Regional Transportation Authority (passenger)

Chicago–Blue Island, Gresham–Pullman Jct.–Calumet Harbor, Ill.: Chicago Rail Link (La Salle & Bureau County)

Chicago–Omaha; branches to Pella, Audubon, and Oakland, Iowa: Iowa Interstate

Blue Island–Joliet–Bureau–Henry, Ill.: Chessie System (Baltimore & Ohio)

Peoria–Mossville, Peoria–Keller, Ill.: Peoria & Pekin Union

Iowa Junction (Peoria)–Hollis, Ill.: Chicago & North Western

Davenport–Iowa City: Milwaukee Road (trackage rights)

Clinton–Davenport–Muscatine–Washington, Iowa: Milwaukee Road

Cedar Rapids–Manly; Vinton–Dysart, Iowa: Iowa Northern

Iowa Falls–Estherville; Bricelyn–Estherville–Ocheyedan; Dows–Forest City; Palmer–Royal, Iowa: Chicago & North Western

Hallam–Fairbury, Nebr.: Union Pacific

Clay Center–Belleville, Kans.; Mahaska, Kans.–Limon, Colo.: Kyle Railroad

Limon–Cimarron Hills, Colo.: Cadillac & Lake City

Golden State route:

St. Louis–Owensville, Mo; Kansas City–Tucumcari, N. Mex.: Cotton Belt (Southern Pacific)

Tucumcari–Santa Rosa, N. Mex.: Southern Pacific (long operated by SP)

Liberal, Kans.–Stinnett, Tex.; Morse Jct.–Etter, Tex.: Texas Northwestern

Mid-Continent route:

Inver Grove, Minn.–Des Moines–Kansas City: Chicago & North Western

Salina–Herington–Wichita, Kans.–El Reno, Okla.–Fort Worth: Oklahoma, Kansas & Texas (subsidiary of Missouri-Kansas-Texas)

North Enid–Ponca City, Okla.: Enid Central

Fort Worth–Dallas: Missouri-Kansas-Texas

Dallas–Houston–Galveston: Burlington Northern (previously operated jointly with BN)

Choctaw route:

Memphis–Brinkley, Ark.: Cotton Belt

Hazen–Little Rock, Ark.: Missouri Pacific

Little Rock–Perry, Ark.: Little Rock & Western

McAlester–Council, Okla.: Missouri-Kansas-Texas

Shawnee–Oklahoma City: Atchison, Topeka & Santa Fe (trackage rights)

Weatherford–Elk City, Okla.: Farmrail Corp.

"Little Rock" lines:

Haskel–Hot Springs–Malvern, Ark.: Missouri Pacific

Fordyce–Whitlow Jct., Ark.: Fordyce & Princeton

El Dorado, Ark.–Lillie, La.: East Camden & Highland

Hodge–Winnfield–Alexandria, La.: Central Louisiana & Gulf

Chihuahua Pacific Railway

(Ferrocarril de Chihuahua al Pacifico)

On September 24, 1928, the Atchison, Topeka & Santa Fe purchased the Kansas City, Mexico & Orient Railway, which consisted of four separate lines:
• from Wichita, Kansas, southwest across Oklahoma and Texas, much of the way through barren, uninhabited territory where oil had recently been discovered
• from the city of Chihuahua, capital of the Mexican state of the same name, northwest toward the Rio Grande
• from Miñaca, Chih., southwest to Creel
• from Topolobampo, a port on the Gulf of California in the state of Sinaloa, northeast into the Sierra Madre

The Santa Fe was more interested in the oilfields of west Texas than in completing a line across the mountains of Mexico to an undeveloped port, so it sold the Mexican lines to B. F. Johnston and the United Sugar Company of Los Mochis.

Johnston combined the operations of the Orient with those of the Mexico North-Western Railway, which ran from Chihuahua to Ciudad Juarez in long loop that reached west to the mountains, in the process linking the two segments of the Orient.

Three Ch-P trains meet at Divisadero Barrancas at the rim of Copper Canyon April 30, 1971: a westbound pair of Fiat railcars (autovías), the eastbound Vista Train behind GP28 803, and an eastbound freight occupying the siding ahead of the Vista Train. Photo by Joe McMillan

Government ownership

In 1940 the Mexican government purchased the KCM&O and announced the line would be completed—across some of the roughest and wildest country in North America, Mexico's Sierra Madre. Some surveying and construction ensued. In 1952 the government took over the North-Western and in 1955 merged it with the KCM&O to form the Ferrocarril de Chihuahua al Pacifico. Construction resumed, and on November 23, 1961, the line was opened, finally completing the railroad Arthur Stilwell proposed in 1900.

Topolobampo never developed into a major port, and the rails of the Chihuahua Pacific carried little cargo from the heartland of the United States to waiting ships there, but the railroad opened the Copper Canyon area of northwest Mexico to tourism.

In 1987 the ChP was absorbed by the National Railways of Mexico. In the mid-1990s Mexico sought to privatize its railroad system. The first efforts to auction off the Chihuahua Pacific in late 1996 brought bids that were rejected because they were too low.

	1955	1986
Miles of railroad operated:	834	942
Number of locomotives:	63	57
Number of passenger cars:	60	48
Number of freight cars:	1,641	1,459
Number of company service cars:	16	

Location of headquarters: Chihuahua, Chih., Mexico

Reporting marks: CHP

Recommended reading: *Destination Topolobampo*, by John Leeds Kerr, published in 1968 by Golden West Books

Predecessor railroads in this book: Kansas City, Mexico & Orient
Mexico North-Western

Successors: National Railways of Mexico

Portions still operated: Ojinaga–Topolobampo, La Junta–Ciudad Juarez

Cincinnati & Lake Erie Railroad

The Ohio Electric Railway was formed in 1907 as a confederation of several companies. The main trunk of the system was a line from Cincinnati north through Dayton, Springfield, and Lima to Toledo; branches reached from Dayton to Richmond, Indiana, and Union City, Ohio, from Springfield through Columbus to Zanesville, and from Lima to Fort Wayne, Ind., and Defiance, Ohio. In 1918 the Cincinnati, Dayton & Toledo Railway pulled out of Ohio Electric and reorganized as the Cincinnati & Dayton Traction Co. Ohio Electric went bankrupt in 1921, and its other components resumed their own identities: Indiana, Columbus & Eastern; Dayton & Western; Columbus, Newark & Zanesville; Lima & Toledo, and Fort Wayne, Van Wert & Lima.

Dr. Thomas Conway, a professor of finance at the University of Pennsylvania's Wharton School of Finance, had become an expert in the electric railway industry and decided to put his theories to practice. In 1922 he took over the Chicago, Aurora & Elgin but quickly realized he wanted a system that had more growing room and offered greater challenge.

In 1926 he purchased the Cincinnati & Dayton Traction Co. and reorganized it as the Cincinnati, Hamilton & Dayton Railway (not to be confused with a steam railroad of the same

Running as the *Golden Eagle* to Columbus, Cincinnati & Lake Erie "Red Devil" 125, one of the 1929 lightweights, pauses to receive passengers at Osborn, Ohio, on August 2, 1936. Photo by George Krambles.

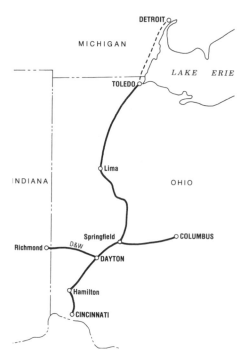

name that became part of the Baltimore & Ohio).

Conway began rebuilding the railroad, beginning with the purchase of ten new interurban cars and ten new suburban cars. Conway acquired control of the Indiana, Columbus & Eastern Traction Co. and the Lima-Toledo Railroad, both remnants of Ohio Electric, and he coordinated their operation with CH&D. In the summer of 1929 CH&D ordered 20 passenger cars of a new low-slung, lightweight design and within a short time ordered 15 new freight motors.

At the end of 1929 CH&D was reorganized as the Cincinnati & Lake Erie Railroad and acquired the properties of the Indiana, Columbus & Eastern and the Lima-Toledo. The new railroad consisted of a main line from Cincinnati to Toledo and a branch from Springfield to Columbus.

The new cars arrived and were tested. As a publicity stunt one of them raced an airplane over a mile and a half of specially groomed track. (The car won by a length.) The railroad began through service to Detroit in late 1930, but the connecting Eastern Michigan-Toledo Railway was abandoned in October 1932.

Meanwhile, the Depression was deepening. Ridership and freight traffic dropped. Connecting interurban lines were dying, and to protect one of its connections, C&LE took over operation of the bankrupt Dayton & Western in 1931. Conway instituted economies such as cuts in executive salaries and one-man train crews. A rash of accidents in 1932 began to eat away at C&LE's rolling stock, and revenues continued to slide. The company entered receivership in 1932 with Conway as receiver.

Automobile competition increased. C&LE was unable to take up the slack with freight because of franchise restrictions on street trackage. Several fatal accidents in 1935 and 1936 drove away timid riders. In 1936 operation of the Dayton & Western was turned over to the Indiana Railroad. In November 1937 C&LE abandoned its line between Springfield and Toledo. A road-widening project in 1938 caused the south end of the line to be cut back (C&LE's cars had never gone farther south than Cumminsville in northwestern Cincinnati, because Cincinnati's streetcar system was broad gauge and used dual overhead wires). In October of that year service ceased between Columbus and Springfield. The high-speed lightweights were sold to Lehigh Valley Transit and the Cedar Rapids & Iowa City. In May 1939 more service was abandoned, leaving only a suburban line in Dayton—and that was abandoned in September 1941. The company's bus affiliate continued in service and was purchased by Greyhound in 1947.

	1930
Miles of railroad operated:	270
Number of locomotives:	1
Number of passenger cars:	106
Number of freight motors:	40
Number of freight trailers:	175
Number of company service cars:	19
Location of headquarters: Dayton, Ohio	
Recommended reading: *Cincinnati & Lake Erie Railroad*, by Jack Keenan, published in 1974 by Golden West Books, P. O. Box 80250, San Marino, CA 91108	

Cincinnati, Indianapolis & Western Railroad

The Cincinnati, Hamilton & Dayton Railroad existed long before the period this book covers, but a brief description is necessary as a prelude to describing the Cincinnati, Indianapolis & Western, and also to distinguish it from an electric railway that used the same name in the same territory from 1926 to 1929.

	1926
Miles of railroad operated:	347
Number of locomotives:	60
Number of passenger cars:	34
Number of freight cars:	1,840
Number of company service cars:	84

Location of headquarters: Indianapolis, Indiana

Reporting marks:

Successors:

Baltimore & Ohio

Chessie System

CSX Transportation

Portions still operated: CSX Transportation: Hamilton, Ohio–Indianapolis; Hillsdale, Ind.–Decatur, Ill.

There are strong traces of Harriman influence in the design of CI&W Mikado 407, built by Lima in 1916. Lima Locomotive Works photo from the collection of the Allen County Historical Society.

The CH&D built north from Cincinnati to Dayton in 1851 and 1852 to connect with the Mad River & Lake Erie. Relations between the two railroads were not comfortable, and the CH&D leased the Dayton & Michigan Railroad, which was under construction from Dayton north to Toledo. By 1858 it had reached Lima and was already arranging trackage rights from Toledo to Detroit over a predecessor of the Pere Marquette. Between Cincinnati and Dayton the CH&D laid a third rail for the broad gauge trains of the Atlantic & Great Western, the southwestern extension of the Erie, and it acquired branches, among them lines from Dayton northwest through Delphos, from Findlay west through Ottawa to Fort Wayne, and from Dayton southeast through the coalfields to the Ohio River at Ironton. It also acquired the Cincinnati, Hamilton & Indianapolis and the Indianapolis, Decatur & Springfield railroads.

Around the turn of the century the CH&D fell on hard times. It acquired and leased the Pere Marquette in 1904. J. P. Morgan & Company purchased the two roads in 1905 and offered them to the Erie. Word got about that the Erie accepted them. F. D. Underwood, president of the Erie, hurried home from Europe, inspected the CH&D and PM, and rejected them. Morgan himself took them back, placed them in receivership, and offered them to the Baltimore & Ohio. B&O took them in 1909 on a 7-year trial basis.

Floods in Ohio in 1913 threw the CH&D back into financial trouble and receivership. It cast off the Pere Marquette and tore up some of its branches in western Ohio. It spun off the Hamilton–Springfield, Ill., line as the Cincinnati, Indianapolis & Western Railway. CH&D reorganized in 1916 as the Toledo & Cincinnati Railroad, and B&O acquired it in 1917.

Independence for the CI&W

The Cincinnati, Indianapolis & Western Railway was sold at foreclosure on September 9, 1915. The Cincinnati, Indianapolis & Western Railroad was incorporated on October 30 of that year as its successor, to be effective December 1, 1915. The new company took over the Hamilton, Ohio–Springfield, Illinois line plus trackage rights but spun off the line from Sidell to Olney, Illinois, as the Sidell & Olney Railroad, owned by the CI&W but operated separately. In 1919 that line was sold to become the Kansas & Sidell Railroad plus two short-lived companies that briefly operated the line from Kansas to Casey and from Casey to Yale.

At the beginning of 1922 the CI&W purchased the West Melcher–Brazil, Indiana, line of the Chicago & Indiana Coal Railway (the rest of the Coal Road became the Chicago, Attica & Southern). Baltimore & Ohio acquired control of the CI&W on June 1, 1927, and thereafter the CI&W was operated as part of the B&O.

The major role of the Cincinnati, Indianapolis & Western had been to serve as the Cincinnati extension of the Monon's Chicago–Indianapolis line. The B&O could move Chicago–Cincinnati traffic on its own rails all the way—east to Deshler, Ohio, on the Chicago–Pittsburgh main line, then south on the former CH&D. The route was about 80 miles longer than the direct routes—no passenger would choose that route unless he was trying to set a slow-play record. B&O acquisition of the CI&W had the effect of accelerating the Monon's decline and taking traffic off the CI&W. By 1941 passenger service on the line consisted of Hamilton–Indianapolis and Indianapolis–Decatur motor trains.

Clinchfield Railroad

 A railroad running north and south across the Blue Ridge Mountains in eastern Tennessee and western North Carolina had been proposed early in the railroad era, but until the end of the 1800s only bits and pieces of such a railroad were built. In 1900 the only piece of the future Clinchfield in existence was the Ohio River & Charleston, which meandered a few miles south from a connection with the South-ern Railway at Johnson City, Tennessee.

The South & Western Railroad was incorporated in 1905 and was almost immediately purchased by a syndicate as part of a plan to mine coal in western Virginia and eastern Tennessee. In 1908 it opened between Johnson City, Tenn., and Marion, North Carolina, and was renamed the Carolina, Clinchfield & Ohio Railway. By the end of 1909 the CC&O had been extended north from Johnson City to Dante, Va., and south from Marion to Spartanburg, South Carolina. In 1915 the road opened an extension north from Dante to a connection with the Chesapeake & Ohio at Elkhorn City, Kentucky.

In 1924 the Atlantic Coast Line and Louisville & Nashville railroads jointly leased the properties of the CC&O. The two lessees named the Clinchfield Railroad Company, an unincorporated entity, as the operating organization.

The Clinchfield's original mission was to haul

	1929	1982
Miles of railroad operated:	309	296
Number of locomotives:	86	98
Number of passenger cars:	38	
Number of freight cars:	7,562	
Number of company service cars:	87	
Number of freight and company service cars:		5,291
Location of headquarters: Erwin, Tennessee		
Reporting marks: CRR		
Successors:		
Seaboard System, CSX Transportation		

During World War II the Clinchfield turned to 4-6-6-4s to power its fast freights. The first batch followed Delaware & Hudson specifications; one of this group gets a northbound freight under way at Ridge, North Carolina, in August 1952. A second group of Challengers was built for Union Pacific, diverted to the Rio Grande by the War Production Board, and sold by Rio Grande to the Clinchfield. Photo by Floyd A. Bruner.

coal. Its strategic location and relatively easy grades and curves—the result of construction late enough to take advantage of modern construction machinery and methods—led to Clinchfield's development into a fast freight route between the Midwest and the Piedmont. At Spartanburg, S. C., it connected with the Southern Railway and Atlantic Coast Line's Charleston & Western Carolina subsidiary, and at Elkhorn City, Ky., it connected with C&O. The Clinchfield was unusual in that it had no significant branches, just the single main stem.

The creation of the Seaboard System Railroad on December 29, 1982, by the merger of Seaboard Coast Line and Louisville & Nashville rendered unnecessary a separate company to operate the Clinchfield. On January 1, 1983, the Clinchfield Railroad became the Clinchfield Division of the Seaboard System Railroad.

On March 1, 1984, the Clinchfield Division was abolished and the former Clinchfield Railroad split between the Corbin and Florence divisions of the Seaboard. The entire line is still in service.

Colorado & Southern Railway
Fort Worth & Denver City Railway

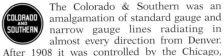

The Colorado & Southern was an amalgamation of standard gauge and narrow gauge lines radiating in almost every direction from Denver. After 1908 it was controlled by the Chicago, Burlington & Quincy; in its early years, however, it had no relation at all with the Burlington.

Lines west of Denver

The earliest part of the Colorado & Southern was the standard gauge line from Denver to Golden, which was opened in 1870 as the Colorado Central Railroad. From Golden it pushed a 3-foot-gauge line up Clear Creek Canyon to Georgetown (1877) and Central City. To allow its narrow gauge trains access to Denver, the road three-railed the Denver–Golden line in 1879. In 1881 the road made plans to continue west to Leadville. The few miles from Georgetown to Silver Plume required a complete loop—a much-publicized feat of engineering—in order to gain altitude. Work on a tunnel under the Continental Divide ceased soon after it began.

"Company service cars" includes the rolling stock that a railroad uses in maintaining its track and structures. An assortment of C&S company service cars trails 2-10-2 No. 900 at Boulder, Colorado, on July 20, 1959. Photo by Richard F. Lind.

Lines north of Denver

Meanwhile, with financial help from Union Pacific the road built a line north from Golden through Boulder. Although the goal of the line was Julesburg on the Union Pacific main line in the northeast corner of the state, construction halted at Longmont when the Panic of 1873 caused financial difficulty for the UP.

In 1877 UP resumed construction of the Colorado Central, this time with a line south from Cheyenne, and in 1879 leased the CC. In 1882 Colorado Central completed a line southwest from Julesburg to La Salle, where it connected with the Denver Pacific (UP's Denver–Cheyenne line). The Julesburg line gave UP a short route into Denver from the east, necessary to compete with the Burlington, whose rails reached Denver in May 1882.

Union Pacific built a connecting line between Greeley and Fort Collins in 1882, and in 1886 Colorado Central built a direct line between Denver and Boulder. Two portions of the CC that were considered roundabout and redundant were abandoned in 1889: the Colorado Central north of Fort Collins and most of the old Golden–Boulder line.

Cheyenne interests began building the Cheyenne & Northern Railway in 1886 to head off a Chicago & North Western subsidiary at Douglas. The North Western line reached Douglas the next year, and the Cheyenne & Northern stopped at Wendover, Wyoming. It was extended north to a connection with the C&NW at Orin Junction a few years later.

Lines southwest of Denver

In 1873 the Denver, South Park & Pacific began constructing a 3-foot-gauge line southwest from Denver. Progress was slowed by the Panic of 1873, and not until 1880 did the line reach the Arkansas River at Buena Vista. By then Jay Gould had gained control of Union Pacific and a half interest in the Denver & Rio Grande. He acquired control of the South Park in 1880 and sold it to Union Pacific.

The DSP&P bored Alpine Tunnel—1,805 feet long and the highest railroad tunnel in the U. S.—under the Continental Divide in 1881 to extend its line to Gunnison. Neither the South Park nor the Rio Grande was happy with the DSP&P's trackage rights over Rio Grande from

Buena Vista to Leadville, so in 1884 the South Park completed a Como–Leadville line that crossed the Continental Divide twice over Boreas and Fremont passes. The South Park entered receivership in 1889 and was reorganized as the Denver, Leadville & Gunnison Railway, still under UP control. Union Pacific itself entered receivership in 1893. DL&G regained independence as part of the UP reorganization in 1894.

Lines southeast of Denver

In 1881 John Evans, who had been the first governor of Colorado, incorporated the Denver & New Orleans Railroad to build a line to Fort Worth, Texas. The goal was later changed to a connection with Fort Worth & Denver City Railway, which had started construction northwest from Fort Worth. Evans's line built southeast from Denver through Parker, Elizabeth, and Fountain to Pueblo, with a 10-mile spur west to Colorado Springs from Manitou Junction.

The Denver, Texas & Fort Worth was organized to build south from Pueblo using trackage rights on the Denver & Rio Grande as far as Trinidad. In 1888 it met up with the Fort Worth & Denver City. Soon afterward the DT&FW, itself having come under UP control, acquired control of the FW&DC and the Denver, Texas & Gulf, a reorganization of the Denver & New Orleans.

The north-south roads were brought together in 1890, when the Union Pacific, Denver & Gulf was formed by the UP to consolidate the Colorado Central, the Cheyenne & Northern, the Denver, Texas & Gulf, the Denver, Texas & Fort Worth, and several short lines. When the Union Pacific entered receivership in 1893, a separate receiver was appointed for these lines, Frank

Trumbull, who was also to become receiver of the Denver, Leadville & Gunnison.

Colorado & Southern

The reorganization committees of the DL&G and the UPD&G (which by then owned the FW&DC) arranged for the sale of their roads at foreclosure in 1898, and they were consolidated as the Colorado & Southern Railway. The only portion of the predecessors that was not included was the Julesburg–La Salle line, which was sold to Union Pacific. C&S made agreements with Santa Fe for joint use of terminal facilities in Denver, Colorado Springs, and Pueblo, and for trackage rights between Denver and Pueblo, abandoning its own line from Manitou Junction to Pueblo.

The *Texas Zephyr* speeds south through Colorado foothill country on July 5, 1965. The 25-year-old E5As are still capable of making up time. Photo by Roger Meade.

C&S had its corporate eye on the boom town of Cripple Creek. Its plan was to extend the former South Park line south to a connection with the Colorado Midland, and to that end C&S acquired control of Colorado Midland jointly with Rio Grande Western in 1900. In 1905 C&S purchased control of the Colorado Springs & Cripple Creek District Railway, which operated a steam railroad between Colorado Springs and Cripple Creek and an electric line between Cripple Creek and Victor. Then the mining boom declined. C&S sold its Colorado Midland interest in 1912 (CM was abandoned in 1921), and the CS&CCD, which had remained a separate operation, was abandoned in 1922.

In the same era C&S organized an electric subsidiary, the Denver & Interurban, which built a line between Denver and Boulder and a streetcar system in Fort Collins. D&I entered receivership in 1918. The Denver–Boulder line was abandoned in 1926. The Fort Collins system was sold to the city; when service ended in 1951 it was the last city streetcar system in Colorado and the last in the U. S. to operate four-wheel Birney cars.

Control by the Burlington

In 1901 Great Northern and Northern Pacific acquired joint control of the Chicago, Burlington & Quincy. The three roads saw the C&S as an outlet to the Gulf of Mexico. In 1905 C&S bought control of the Trinity & Brazos Valley, gaining access to the port of Galveston (see the entry for Burlington-Rock Island), and in 1908 CB&Q bought nearly two-thirds of the common stock of the C&S. In the ensuing years, though, C&S and Fort Worth & Denver maintained a degree of independence, even if their image soon became that of the Burlington.

In 1911 C&S restored the abandoned Fort Collins–Cheyenne link and teamed up with the Denver & Rio Grande to build a new double-track line between Pueblo and Walsenburg. That year C&S abandoned the former South Park line west of Buena Vista. The mining industry was declining and paved highways were beginning to penetrate the Rockies. The last major portion of the South Park, between Denver and Climax, was abandoned in 1937. The Clear Creek lines to Idaho Springs and Black Hawk were torn up in 1941. The Leadville–Climax line, orphaned in 1937, was standard-gauged in 1943 and eventually was the home of C&S's last steam operation. Floods in May 1935 destroyed much of the original Denver & New Orleans line from Denver to Falcon, east of Colorado Springs, and that line was stubbed off outside Denver.

Fort Worth & Denver

The history of the Texas lines is considerably simpler. The Fort Worth & Denver City Railway was chartered in 1873, and construction began in 1881. The line reached Wichita Falls in 1882 and met up with the line from Colorado on March 14, 1888.

The Wichita Valley Railway was chartered in 1890 to build southwest from Wichita Falls. It developed into a Wichita Falls–Abilene main stem with several branches owned by different railroads, all operated as Wichita Valley Lines.

In 1939 the Burlington proposed leasing the Fort Worth & Denver City to the C&S and closing its offices and shops in favor of C&S's facilities in Denver. There was loud protest in Fort Worth and Childress, and the ICC denied the request.

In 1961 the Fort Worth & Denver ("City" was dropped in 1951) proposed leasing the C&S south of Denver (lines north of Denver would be leased to the Burlington) and routing traffic between Denver and Amarillo over the Santa Fe via Las Animas, Colo., to permit abandonment of the C&S line between Trinidad, Colo., and Folsom, N. M. Parent Burlington had its mind on the BN merger at the time and nothing came of the proposal.

FW&D and Rock Island purchased the Burlington-Rock Island in 1964; FW&D took over its operation upon the demise of the Rock Island.

Burlington Northern

Ownership of C&S was transferred to Burlington Northern when it was created in 1970, and by 1981 BN owned more than 92 percent of Colorado & Southern's stock. BN merged C&S on December 31, 1981, and C&S's line south of Denver was transferred to the Fort Worth & Denver. Exactly a year later BN merged the Fort Worth & Denver. Traffic on the former C&S line has increased in recent years: Coal moves on the main line from Wyoming to Texas and the branch to Golden serves the Coors brewery, which moves the bulk of its traffic by rail.

	1929	C&S, 1980	FW&D, 1980
Miles of railroad operated:	2,004	678	1,181
Number of locomotives:	255	235	24
Number of passenger cars:	164		
Number of freight cars:	10,093	2,329	1,443
Number of company service cars:	559	65	105

(1929 figures include Fort Worth & Denver and Wichita Valley Lines)

Location of headquarters: C&S, Denver, Colorado; FW&DC, Fort Worth, Texas

Reporting marks: C&S, CX, RBCS, FW&D, FWDX

Notable named passenger trains: *Texas Zephyr* (Denver–Dallas)

Historical and technical societies:
Burlington Route Historical Society, P. O. Box 456, LaGrange, IL 60525; BRHS@KKTV.com; http://www.burlingtonroute.com/
Colorado & Southern Narrow Gauge Historical Society, P. O. Box 3246, Littleton, CO 80161-3246

Recommended reading: *The Colorado Road,* by F. Hol Wagner Jr., published in 1970 by Intermountain Chapter, National Railway Historical Society, P. O. Box 5181, Denver, CO 80217

Subsidiaries and affiliated railroads, 1980:
Fort Worth & Denver (99.9%)
Galveston Terminal (50%, jointly with Rock Island)

Predecessor railroads in this book: Burlington-Rock Island

Successors:
Burlington Northern
Burlington Northern & Santa Fe

Portions still operated: Burlington Northern & Santa Fe: Orin Jct., Wyo.–Galveston, Tex.; Fort Collins–Greeley, Colo.; Denver–Golden; Denver–Sheridan; Estelline–Lubbock, Tex.; Sterley–Dimmitt, Tex.; Childress–Wellington, Tex.
Leadville-Climax Shortline: Leadville–Climax, Colo.
Southern Switching Co.: Abilene–Lanius, Texas

Conrail (Consolidated Rail Corporation)

Penn Central's bankruptcy in 1970 upset the entire railroad industry. Something had to be done, but what? Penn Central could not simply be liquidated. It operated one-third of the nation's passenger trains and was the principal freight carrier in the northeast quadrant of the nation. Without the railroad, the industries of the area would die. Penn Central's management proposed reorganizing the railroad under certain conditions—abandonment of 45 per cent of its track, reduction of its work force, and increased payment for operating Amtrak trains—but there was no confidence in PC management.

Carving up PC and parceling it out to its neighbors was out of the question (even if that's what was done ultimately—but that's getting ahead of the story), because PC's western neighbors wanted nothing to do with the railroad, and its eastern neighbors had problems of their own.

The Central Railroad of New Jersey had been bankrupt since 1967. Neither Chesapeake & Ohio nor Norfolk & Western wanted the Lehigh Valley. It entered bankruptcy on June 4, 1970, three days after Penn Central. The Reading entered bankruptcy November 23, 1971.

The creation of Erie Lackawanna and Penn Central changed traffic patterns, leaving the Lehigh & Hudson River with almost no business.

Four General Electric hood units lead a Selkirk–Weehawken freight south on the former New York Central West Shore route at Bear Mountain Bridge. Photo by Scott A. Hartley.

It declared bankruptcy April 18, 1972. Although a Norfolk & Western subsidiary purchased the Erie Lackawanna (and also the Delaware & Hudson) in 1968, N&W offered no assistance when the EL suffered $9 million worth of damage in a hurricane on June 22, 1972. EL entered bankruptcy on June 26, 1972. There were proposals to merge and reorganize the other bankrupt railroads to compete with Penn Central, but those railroads, like Penn Central, had no money for much-needed repairs to track and rolling stock.

A new USRA

The United States Railway Association, a federal government corporation, was formed to attempt a rescue. The USRA planned to parcel out portions of the Reading and Erie Lackawanna to Chessie System and Penn Central's lines along the DelMarVa Peninsula to the Southern Railway. A new railroad, Consolidated Rail Corporation, would acquire the rest. Neither Chessie nor Southern could reach agreement with the labor unions, so Consolidated Rail Corporation (first ConRail, then Conrail), took over the railroad properties and operations of Penn Central, Central of New Jersey, Erie Lackawanna, Lehigh & Hudson River, Lehigh Valley, Reading, and Pennsylvania-Reading Seashore Lines on April 1, 1976. PRSL alone among the seven railroads was not bankrupt, but it had almost no traffic and was on the verge of physical collapse. Those railroads and a number of their predecessors are described elsewhere in this book.

Conrail started out with $2.1 billion from the U. S. government, which purchased Conrail debentures and preferred stock, and perhaps $2.10 worth of confidence in its success—after all, six times bankrupt equals bankrupt, and the road was a department of the federal government (or so it was perceived). The new railroad operated 5,000 locomotives on 17,000 route-miles of railroad; it had 162,000 freight cars, 95,000 employees, and 278 different labor agreements. It had excess plant; it had labor-protection agreements; and it had extensive commuter train operations serving Boston, New York, and Philadelphia.

Conrail identified 6,000 miles of railroad it did not need and abandoned those lines or sold them to short lines and state and local operating authorities. Conrail transferred ownership of the Northeast Corridor (Boston–New York–Washington, Springfield–New Haven, and Philadelphia–Harrisburg) to Amtrak. It began to catch up on years of deferred maintenance, rebuilding track and buying new locomotives and rebuilding old ones. It eliminated duplicate facilities and won a few minor concessions from labor unions. In the second quarter of 1979 Conrail posted a modest net income, but an economic recession wiped out any chance of another quarter of profitability. Meanwhile, the USRA continued to consider Conrail's future.

In October 1980 U. S. president Jimmy Carter signed into law the Staggers Rail Act, which gave railroad companies freedom to set prices. Not long afterward the United States received a new president, Ronald Reagan, who intended to dismantle Conrail. Congress, however, allowed Conrail to discharge redundant employees and transfer its commuter services to state and regional authorities, giving Conrail a two-year reprieve.

Profit!

Freed of commuter services and able to set its own rates and abandon track it no longer needed, Conrail started to become a profitable freight railroad. L. Stanley Crane assumed the presidency of Conrail at the beginning of 1981, about the time the Reagan administration proposed selling the railroad. Crane continued to trim Conrail's physical plant and payroll. He took advantage of deregulation; he improved the quality of Conrail's service; he sharpened Conrail's image.

Conrail posted a profit for 1981, and kept doing better, even as almost every other railroad was (a) bidding to purchase it at a bargain price and (b) protesting anyone else's doing so. Santa Fe and Norfolk Southern both expressed interest in purchasing Conrail, but Santa Fe soon turned its attention to its proposed merger with Southern Pacific (which was denied). Norfolk Southern continued as the favorite and won the approval of the U. S. Department of Transportation. In February 1986 the U. S. Senate voted to sell Conrail to Norfolk Southern. Numerous other railroads, CSX notable among them,

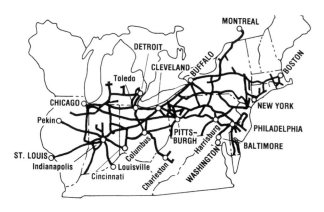

protested. In August 1986 Norfolk Southern withdrew its bid to purchase Conrail.

In October 1986 President Reagan signed a bill authorizing the sale of Conrail stock to the public. It went on sale March 25, 1987, at $28 a share, the largest single initial public stock offering in the history of the New York Stock Exchange. It netted the government $1.6 billion, plus $300 million of Conrail cash and a return of $2 billion worth of tax credits. Conrail settled down to a stable existence as one of America's "Super Seven" freight railroads.

Crane retired as chairman at the end of 1988 and was succeeded by Richard D. Sanborn, who had become president of Conrail in March 1988. Sanborn died suddenly of a heart attack after only 6 weeks as chairman; James Hagen was brought from CSX to succeed Sanborn.

During the recession of 1990 and 1991 Conrail

	May 1, 1977	1994	Erie
Miles of railroad operated:	17,000	17,368	Erie Lackawanna
Number of locomotives:	4,594	2,583	Lehigh & Hudson River
Number of freight cars:		89,128	Lehigh Valley
Location of headquarters: Philadelphia, Pennsylvania			New York Central
Reporting marks: CR plus the marks of its predecessors			New York, New Haven & Hartford
Historical and technical societies:			Penn Central
Conrail Historical Society, P. O. Box 38, Walnutport, PA 18088-0038; crts@worldnet.att.net			Pennsylvania
Conrail Technical Society, c/o John P. Krattinger, P. O. Box 7140, Garden City, NY			Pennsylvania-Reading Seashore Lines
11530-7140; http://www.rrhistorical.com/crts			Reading
Predecessor railroads in this book:			**Successors:**
Central Railroad of New Jersey			CSX Transportation
Delaware, Lackawanna & Western			Norfolk Southern

reacted quickly to the anticipated drop in revenue by cutting expenses, storing locomotives and cars, and restructuring its services, with the result that it was still able to declare a stock dividend. In 1990 Conrail bought back about one third of its common stock as part of a restructuring to thwart possible takeover bids. By the end of 1991 the price of Conrail stock had risen to $84.50 a share—an indicator of the company's robust health.

By 1995 the Super Seven had become five: Burlington Northern & Santa Fe and Union Pacific west of Chicago, CSX and Norfolk Southern in the Southeast, Conrail in the Northeast—and Conrail, CSX, and NS in the area between the Allegheny Mountains and Chicago. In 1995 Norfolk Southern again expressed an interest in purchasing Conrail, but nothing came of it. Then there was a surprising announcement on October 15, 1996, that Conrail and CSX planned to merge. Norfolk Southern immediately made a counteroffer. In January 1997 Conrail stockholders voted two to one to reject CSX's offer in favor of Norfolk Southern's. Then the executives of the three railroads met to discuss compromises.

The result was an announcement that CSX would buy Conrail, then sell approximately half of Conrail's routes to Norfolk Southern. CSX would get the eastern half of the former New York Central (Boston and New York through Albany and Buffalo to Cleveland) and the Cleveland–Indianapolis–St. Louis route (part NYC—or Big Four—and part PRR). NS would get the eastern portion of the Pennsylvania, the former New York Central from Cleveland through Toledo to Chicago), and what little remains of Michigan Central. CSX and Norfolk Southern have the task now of unmerging Conrail and remerging it.

Copper Range Railroad

The Copper Range Railroad was incorporated in 1899 as successor to the Northern Michigan Railroad. It was controlled by the Copper Range Corporation, second largest producer of copper in the Lake Superior district. The line was opened from Gay to McKeever, Mich., that same year.

The railroad was reorganized in 1930. In 1944 it reinstated passenger service (only mixed train service had been offered for some years) with a new train called the *Chippewa*. The *Chippewa* ran between Houghton and McKeever, where it connected with Milwaukee Road's *Chippewa*, providing daytime service

between the Keweenaw Peninsula and Chicago: The service was a wartime measure, and it was discontinued in late 1946.

The Copper Range Railroad made its last run on October 27, 1972, and the road was torn up soon after. Soo Line's ex-Duluth, South Shore & Atlantic line to Houghton lasted less than a decade longer.

	1929	1971
Miles of railroad operated:	108	53
Number of locomotives:	20	3
Number of passenger cars:	16	
Number of freight cars:	637	35
Number of company service cars:	11	
Location of headquarters: Houghton, Michigan		
Reporting marks: CR, COPR		
Map: See page 157		

Baldwin switcher No. 101 leads a train of pulpwood cars across the Firesteel River bridge north of McKeever, Michigan, in the summer of 1972, shortly before the railroad was abandoned. Photo by Clinton Jones Jr.

Copper River & Northwestern Railway

The gold rush in Alaska at the end of the 1890s was followed by the discovery of copper, coal, and oil. In 1905 the Copper River & Northwestern was incorporated to build a railroad from tidewater near the mouth of the Copper River to copper mines in southeastern Alaska. The road was completed on March 29, 1911, from Cordova to Kennecott. A week later the first trainload of ore moved over the railroad.

Copper mining peaked in 1916. There were proposals to extend branches to the Bering River coalfield and north to the Yukon River, but nothing came of them, nor of a proposal to sell the railroad to the U. S. government. By the early 1930s the copper mines had been worked out and the railroad had accumulated a long string of deficit years. Its owner, Kennecott Copper Corp., petitioned for abandonment, and the last train ran on November 11, 1938—except for a brief period during World War II when a few miles of the line at Cordova were reactivated for the construction of an airfield.

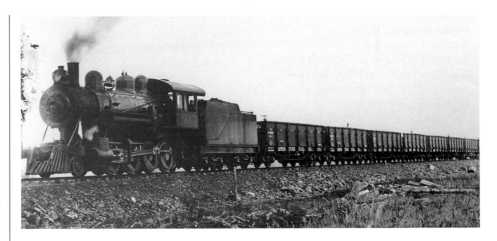

Consolidation No. 22 heads the first trainload of ore—20 cars—to travel the Copper River & Northwestern. Photo from the collection of A. E. Hegg.

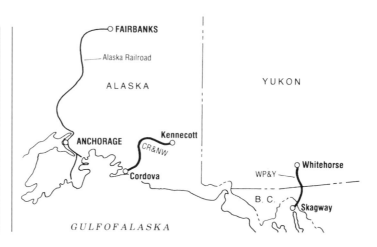

	1929	1936
Miles of railroad operated:	195	195
Number of locomotives:	15	13
Number of passenger cars:	6	6
Number of freight cars:	219	199
Number of company service cars:	132	128

Location of headquarters: Seattle, Washington
Recommended reading: *The Copper Spike,* by Lone E. Janson, published in 1975 by Alaska Northwest Publishing Co., Box 4-EKE, Anchorage, AK 99509 (ISBN 0-88240-066-5)

Cumberland & Pennsylvania Railroad

Between 1844 and 1846 the Mount Savage Railroad was built from Cumberland, Maryland, northwest to coal and iron mines at Mount Savage. In 1854 the properties of the railroad were conveyed to the recently incorporated Cumberland & Pennsylvania Railroad, and in 1860 the C&P became the property of Consolidation Coal Company. In 1863 the C&P bought the George's Creek Railroad, which had built northeast toward Mount Savage from the Potomac River at Westernport, Md., and Piedmont, West Virginia. The C&P began a long career of carrying coal down to the Baltimore & Ohio and the Western Maryland.

In 1845 and 1846 the Maryland Mining Co. constructed a railroad from Eckhart Mines to Cumberland Narrows. The mining company became the property of Consolidation Coal Co. in 1870, and its railroad became part of the C&P in

1915. In 1944 Consolidation Coal Co. was in financial difficulty and sold the Cumberland & Pennsylvania to the Western Maryland. WM quickly integrated C&P's operations into its own, but the smaller road's corporate existence continued until 1953, when it was merged into Western Maryland.

	1929	1944
Miles of railroad operated:	50	49
Number of locomotives:	16	11
Number of passenger cars:	11	
Number of freight cars:	933	5
Number of company service cars:		21

Location of headquarters: Cumberland, Maryland
Reporting marks: C&PA
Recommended reading: *Rails to the Big Vein,* by Deane Mellander, published in 1981 by Potomac Chapter, National Railway Historical Society, P. O. Box 235B, Kensington, MD 20895
Successors:
Western Maryland
Chessie System
CSX Transportation
Portions still operated: CSX Transportation: Lonaconing–Westernport

Cumberland & Pennsylvania 2-8-0 No. 33, built by the road's Mt. Savage shops in 1917, brings a train of hopper cars under Western Maryland's line near Cumberland in June 1944. Photo by C. A. Brown.

Delaware & Hudson Railroad

The D&H dates from 1823, when the Delaware & Hudson Canal Co. was chartered to build a canal from Honesdale, Pennsylvania, to Rondout, New York, on the Hudson River. The purpose of the canal was to carry anthracite coal from mines near Carbondale, Pennsylvania, to New York City. The mines would be served by a gravity railroad with stationary engines and cables for the uphill runs.

D&H imported four steam locomotives from England in 1829. They were too heavy for the track, but one of them, the *Stourbridge Lion*, earned D&H the distinction of operating the first steam locomotive in America.

D&H increased its coal holdings as the demand for anthracite grew. In 1863 the company proposed a railroad north from Carbondale to a connection with the Erie Railroad at Lanesboro. The Erie built the Carbondale–Lanesboro line in 1868, and three years later the D&H extended it north to a connection with the Albany & Susquehanna at Nineveh, New York. D&H leased the A&S for access to Albany and to keep it from falling into the hands of Jay Gould and Jim Fisk.

About that same time D&H built south to Scranton from Carbondale and found itself more a railroad than a canal company—a railroad with three track gauges. The gravity lines had a gauge of 4 feet 3 inches, the Albany & Susquehanna was built to the Erie's 6-foot gauge, and the Carbondale–Scranton line was standard gauge.

Challenger 1526 rolls southbound freight at 50 mph through Harpursville, New York, on February 1, 1947. Photo by Arthur F. Knauer.

Rensselaer & Saratoga

The Rensselaer & Saratoga Rail Road was chartered in 1832 to build a line from Troy, New York, north to a connection with the Saratoga & Schenectady, which was under construction from Schenectady north to Saratoga Springs. The R&S obtained control of the S&S in 1835.

Construction of the Saratoga & Washington Rail-Road began in 1836, but there was an 11-year hiatus in the work, and the railroad did not reach Whitehall, at the south end of Lake Champlain, until 1848. An eastward extension reached Rutland, Vermont, in 1850. The company endured some financial difficulty before being leased by the Rensselaer & Saratoga in 1865, the same year the R&S also leased the Troy & Rutland and Rutland & Washington railroads, which formed a route from Troy north along the New York-Vermont state line to Rutland.

North to Canada

The Hudson River and Lake Champlain formed a natural route from New York to Montreal, but it was unusable in winter. A rail route through Vermont was in place by 1849, but there was none on the New York shore of Lake Champlain. In 1852 the Plattsburgh & Montreal Rail Road and two Canadian roads were completed from Plattsburgh, almost at the north end of the lake, to Montreal. There was little local business to support it.

In 1866 the Whitehall & Plattsburgh Rail Road was chartered to join Whitehall and Plattsburgh. Two disconnected pieces of line were built, and the company was leased by the Rutland, which sought a route to northern New York and Canada that bypassed the Vermont Central. Soon afterward the Vermont Central leased the Rutland.

New York residents knew that power struggles by the two Vermont railroads would not get a railroad built through their area, and the Ver-

mont roads would funnel commerce to Boston, not to New York City. The D&H backed the local residents in organizing the New York & Canada Railroad, which absorbed the Whitehall & Plattsburgh and the Montreal & Plattsburgh (successor to the Plattsburgh & Montreal) in 1873. Marshy and mountainous areas along the shore of the lake made construction difficult, but the line was opened between Whitehall and Plattsburgh in 1875, completing an Albany–Montreal route.

In the 1880s the D&H built west from Plattsburgh to an iron-mining area at Lyon Mountain, then south to Lake Placid. By the turn of the century D&H's interests included hotels and steamboat lines on Lake Champlain and Lake George and a network of electric railways around Albany. In 1898 D&H sold its interests in the Rutland, escaping from the squabbles of the two principal railroads in Vermont. At the same time it sold the canal and converted the gravity railroad to standard-gauge.

Two roads in Canada came into the D&H family. In 1906 D&H purchased the Quebec, Montreal & Southern, which extended the border to St. Lambert, opposite Montreal, then northeast to Pierreville, Que. More important was the 28-mile Napierville Junction Railway, opened in 1907 from Rouses Point, N. Y., on the border, north to Delson and connections with Canadian Pacific and Canadian National (to use modern-era names).

The Loree era

Leonor F. Loree became president of the D&H in 1907 after working on the Pennsylvania and the Baltimore & Ohio. He undertook an upgrading

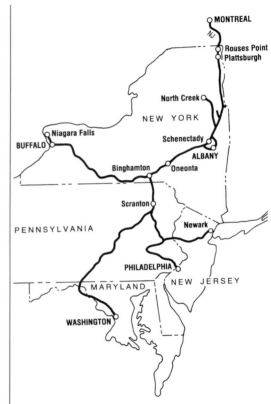

of the D&H, but he had definite ideas about locomotives. He shunned most advances in steam locomotive technology—the initial demonstration of Lima's Super-Power concept took place practically under his nose—and pushed the Consolidation type to its limit. The road's traffic was primarily coal—not a time-sensitive commodity—and speed was secondary to tractive effort.

By the time Loree retired in 1938, oil had begun to replace coal for heating, so D&H turned its attention to developing bridge traffic (traffic received from one railroad and passed to another) from the Midwest to New England and Canada. To accelerate its trains, D&H bought two groups of modern locomotives: 4-6-6-4s for freight and 4-8-4s for dual service. They arrived on the property just in time for the traffic increases of World War II.

D&H sold its hotels and steamboats in 1939, and abandoned its circuitous route to Lake Placid in 1946. In 1943 it simplified its corporate structure by merging the Rensselaer & Saratoga and the Albany & Susquehanna. D&H dieselized quickly in the early 1950s with utilitarian road-switchers instead of streamlined cab diesels.

Search for a merger partner

In 1957 D&H studied merger with Erie and Delaware, Lackawanna & Western, but was deterred by the long-term debt of those roads. D&H sold off its coal interests and asked to be including in the 1964 Norfolk & Western merger because the impending merger of the Pennsylvania and the New York Central would surround it.

Frederick Dumaine Jr. became president of the D&H in 1966. He upgraded the road's passenger trains for traffic to the 1967 world's fair at Mon-

The passenger renaissance of the Dumaine-era Delaware & Hudson was made possible, in a way, by passenger train discontinuances on the Santa Fe and the Rio Grande. The Montreal-bound *Laurentian* is shown at Whitehall, New York, on February 24, 1968. The paint on PA-1 No. 16 reflects Santa Fe painting diagrams if not color charts. The baggage-mail car, the diner-lounge, and the coaches are veterans of Rio Grande's Royal Gorge and Prospector. Photo by Jim Shaughnessy.

treal. He proposed two alternate courses for D&H: independence or inclusion in a merger of the major roads of New England. New management took over in 1968 after a proxy fight. Dereco, a subsidiary of N&W, acquired control of D&H, but it was never considered part of the N&W system. D&H entered a period of joint management with Erie Lackawanna, also owned by Dereco.

In the thrashing around that preceded the formation of Conrail, D&H acquired trackage rights to Buffalo, N. Y., Newark, New Jersey, and Alexandria, Virginia. It sought loans from the United States Railway Association to enable it to compete with Conrail, yet the USRA's mission was to ensure that Conrail succeeded. D&H's parent Norfolk & Western provided no help. Management changed with increasing frequency, and the company lost more and more money.

On January 4, 1984, Guilford Transportation Industries purchased the D&H and began to consolidate its operations with those of the Boston & Maine and the Maine Central. D&H entered bankruptcy in June 1988, and the New York, Susquehanna & Western was designated to operate it while Guilford put it up for sale.

CP Rail purchased the road in January 1991, eyeing D&H's trackage rights to Washington, Philadelphia, and Newark, New Jersey, in the light of the U. S.-Canada free trade pact of 1990. CP undertook a rehabilitation of the D&H and began regular freight service to Philadelphia and Newark.

The office functions of the D&H were combined with those of parent CP Rail in Montreal, then moved to Calgary, Alberta. The first D&H locomotive to be rehabilitated under the new ownerships was painted in D&H's traditional blue and gray—but by CP's Calgary shops rather than D&H's Colonie Shops near Albany. D&H's identity, like that of CP's other U. S. subsidiary, Soo Line, is rapidly giving way to that of CP Rail System—and CP is reverting to the Canadian Pacific name.

	1929	1983
Miles of railroad operated:	898	1,581
Number of locomotives:	445	134
Number of passenger cars:	374	
Number of freight cars:	15,735	4,341
Number of company service cars:	637	328

Location of headquarters: Albany, N. Y.

Reporting marks: DH

Notable named passenger trains: *Laurentian, Montreal Limited* (New York–Montreal), operated jointly with New York Central)

Historical and technical society: Bridge Line Historical Society, Box 7242, Capitol Station, Albany, N. Y. 12224; http://www.fileshop.com/personal/jashaw/rhs/blhs.html

Recommended reading: *Delaware & Hudson, Second Edition,* by Jim Shaughnessy, published in 1997 by Syracuse University Press, Syracuse, NY 13244-5160 (ISBN 8-8156-0455-6)

Successors: Canadian Pacific

Portions still operated:

Batten Kill Railroad: Eagle Bridge–Greenwich Junction, N. Y.

Clarendon & Pittsford: Rutland, Vt.–Whitehall, N. Y.

Canadian Pacific: Rouses Point–Binghamton, N. Y.; Schenectady–Mechanicville–Albany–Delanson, N. Y.; Saratoga Springs–North Creek, N. Y.; by trackage rights: Binghamton to Buffalo, Philadelphia, Newark, and Alexandria, Va.

Delaware-Lackawanna Railroad: Scranton–Carbondale, Pa.

Luzerne & Susquehanna: track in Wilkes-Barre and Scranton, Pa.

Delaware, Lackawanna & Western Railroad

The Lackawanna's history, like that of many Eastern railroads, is one of mergers, consolidations, and leases. The oldest portion was the Cayuga & Susquehanna Railroad, completed in 1834 between Owego and Ithaca, New York. Lackawanna's corporate structure dates from the incorporation of the Liggett's Gap Railroad in 1849. That line was built north from Scranton, Pennsylvania, to the Susquehanna River and a connection with the Erie at Great Bend, Pa. It was renamed the Lackawanna & Western in 1851, and it opened later that year.

Also incorporated in 1849 was the Delaware & Cobb's Gap Railroad, to build a line from the Delaware River over the Pocono Mountains to Cobb's Gap, near Scranton. It was consolidated with the Lackawanna & Western in 1853 to form the Delaware, Lackawanna & Western Railroad. It was completed in 1856 and almost immediately made a connection with the Central Railroad of New Jersey at Hampton, N. J., through the Warren Railroad, which was leased by the DL&W in 1857.

The Morris & Essex Railroad was chartered in 1835 to construct a line from Morristown, N. J., to New York Harbor. By 1860 it extended west to the Delaware River at Phillipsburg, N. J. The Lackawanna leased it in 1869 to acquire a

Reinforced concrete viaducts were the hallmark of Lackawanna's improvement program in the early 1900s. A Pocono (Lackawanna's name for the 4-8-4 type) hauls a freight across Martins Creek Viaduct. Photo by Wayne Brumbaugh.

line under its own control across New Jersey.

That same year the Lackawanna bought the Syracuse, Binghamton & New York Railroad, leased the Oswego & Syracuse, and incorporated the Valley Railroad to build a connection from Great Bend to Binghamton to avoid having to

use Erie tracks. In 1870 DL&W leased the Utica, Chenango & Susquehanna Valley and the Greene Railroad. Thus in the space of a couple of years the Lackawanna grew to extend from tidewater to Utica, Syracuse, and Lake Ontario.

On March 15, 1876, the Lackawanna converted

Gray-and-maroon E8s lead Lackawanna's *Phoebe Snow* through Milburn, New Jersey, on January 1, 1956. The train is about half an hour out of Hoboken on its run to Buffalo. The catenary wires overhead were used by electric suburban trains. Photo by Don Wood.

its lines from 6-foot gauge (chosen because of the Liggett's Gap Railroad's connection with the Erie) to standard gauge. That year also marked the beginning of a short period of financial difficulty—not enough to cause reorganization, receivership, or bankruptcy, but enough for suspension of dividend payments. In 1880 Jay Gould began buying Lackawanna stock. His empire reached as far east as Buffalo, east end of the Wabash, and he saw that the Lackawanna would be an ideal route to New York if the gap between Binghamton and Buffalo could be closed. Lackawanna management prevented Gould from acquiring control of the road, but Gould's pro-posed extension to Buffalo was built: The New York, Lackawanna & Western was incorporated in 1880 and leased to the DL&W in 1882, changing the DL&W from a regional railroad to a New York–Buffalo trunk line.

Diversification and upgrading

The 1880s brought diversification in Lackawanna's traffic. Anthracite, much of it from railroad-owned mines, had been the reason for the Lackawanna's existence. During the 1880s the coal traffic increased one-third, but Lackawanna's general merchandise traffic increased five times that amount. In addition the DL&W

was rapidly becoming a commuter carrier at its east end.

William H. Truesdale became president of the Lackawanna in 1899 and embarked on a rebuilding and upgrading program. The two major items were a new line north of Scranton and a 28-mile cutoff straight across western New Jersey between Slateford and Port Morris that bypassed some 40 miles of slow, curvy, hilly track. Both new lines were characterized by massive cuts and fills and graceful reinforced-concrete viaducts—Tunkhannock, Paulins Kill, Martins Creek, and Kingsley. Lackawanna's suburban territory came in for track elevation, grade-crossing elimination, and new stations, all as prelude to the 1930 electrification of lines to Dover, Gladstone, and Montclair.

Merger, eventually

By the late 1930s the New York Central had purchased 25 percent of the Lackawanna's stock, giving it working—but unexercised—control of the DL&W. During World War II the Lackawanna merged a number of its subsidiaries and leased lines for tax purposes. After the war the Lackawanna began to purchase Nickel Plate stock with an eye to possible merger, but Nickel Plate and New York Central were both opposed to it.

In 1949 Phoebe Snow returned to the Lackawanna. Early in the century she had been Lackawanna's symbol with a gown that stayed white from morn till night upon the Road of Anthracite—anthracite was much cleaner-burning than the bituminous coal used by other roads. Phoebe Snow's return to the road was in the form of a diesel-powered maroon-and-gray streamliner for daytime service between Hoboken and Buffalo.

In 1954 the Lackawanna and parallel rival Erie began to explore the idea of cooperation. The first results were the elimination of duplicate freight facilities at Binghamton and Elmira, and then in 1956 and 1957 the Erie moved its passenger trains from its old Jersey City terminal to Lackawanna's somewhat newer one at Hoboken. The two roads eliminated some duplicate track in western New York. The discussions of cooperation turned into merger talks, at first including the Delaware & Hudson.

Meanwhile DL&W's financial situation took a turn for the worse. Hurricanes in 1955 damaged Lackawanna's line through the Poconos. The cost of repairs no doubt contributed to the deficits of 1958 and 1959. DL&W threatened to discontinue all suburban passenger service if the state of New Jersey would not alleviate the losses and rectify the tax situation. The state responded with a minimal subsidy.

DL&W and Erie merged as the Erie-Lackawanna on October 17, 1960.

	1929	1959
Miles of railroad operated:	998	926
Number of locomotives:	683	212
Number of passenger cars:	899	610
Number of freight cars:	26,195	11,719
Number of company service cars:	872	437

Location of headquarters: New York, New York

Reporting marks: DLW

Notable named passenger trains: *Phoebe Snow* (Hoboken–Buffalo)

Historical and technical societies:
Anthracite Railroads Historical Society, P. O. Box 519, Lansdale, PA 19446-0519; http://www.rrhistorical.com/arhs
Erie Lackawanna Historical Society, c/o Bob Rose, 1 La Malfa Road, Randolph, NJ 07869; http:www.dnaco.net/~gelwood/

Recommended reading: *The Delaware, Lackawanna & Western Railroad in the Nineteenth Century,* by Thomas Townsend Taber, published in 1977, and *The Delaware, Lackawanna & Western Railroad in the Twentieth Century* (two volumes), by Thomas Townsend Taber and Thomas T. Taber III, published in 1980 by Thomas T. Taber III, 504 South Main Street, Muncy, PA 17756

Successors:
Erie Lackawanna
Conrail
NJ Transit

Portions still operated:
Bath & Hammondsport: Bath–Wayland, N. Y.
Conrail: Netcong–Phillipsburg, N. J., Martins Creek–Portland, Pa.; Pittston Jct.–Taylor, Pa.; Binghamton–Johnson City, N. Y.; Jamesville–Oswego, N. Y.; Painted Post–Bath, N. Y.; Greigsville–North Alexander, N. Y., Lancaster–East Buffalo, N. Y.
Delaware & Hudson: Taylor, Pa.–Binghamton, N. Y.
Delaware-Lackawanna Railroad: Pocono Summit–Scranton, Pa.
Genesee & Wyoming: Groveland–Greigsville, N. Y.
Morristown & Erie: Kenvil–Randolph, N. J.
New York, Susquehanna & Western: Binghamton–Jamesville; Chenango Forks–Utica, N. Y.
NJ Transit Hoboken–Morristown–Netcong; Roseville Avenue–Montclair; Summit–Gladstone; Hoboken–Clifton; Mountain View–Denville
North Shore: Northumberland–Hicks Ferry, Pa.
Pocono Northeast: Kingston–Pittston Jct. Pa.
Steamtown, U. S. A. (museum operation): Moscow–Scranton, Pa.

Map: See page 187

Denver & Rio Grande Western Railroad

The Denver & Rio Grande Railway was incorporated by William Jackson Palmer in 1870 to build a railroad from Denver south along the eastern edge of the Rockies to El Paso, Texas. Palmer, who had risen to the rank of brigadier general during the Civil War, chose a track gauge of 3 feet for reasons of economy.

The line was completed to the new town of Colorado Springs in 1871. In 1872 it was extended south to Pueblo, then west to tap coal deposits near Canon City, Colorado. There the railroad remained for a few years.

In 1878 the Rio Grande engaged in two railroad wars with the Santa Fe—perhaps "skirmishes" is more accurate than "wars." Palmer's forces narrowly lost Raton Pass in southern Colorado, but won occupancy of the Royal Gorge of the Arkansas River west of Canon City. Shortly afterward the D&RG was leased to the Santa Fe for a year.

In 1879 the Rio Grande was on its own again under the management of Palmer and Jay Gould. It made an agreement with the Santa Fe a year later to head in different directions: the Santa Fe south into New Mexico and the D&RG west into the Rockies. In 1881 the Rio Grande reached Gunnison and Durango, and, foreshadowing changes to come, it added a third rail for standard gauge trains to its tracks between Denver and Pueblo.

West to Utah

In 1882 D&RG leased the affiliated Denver & Rio Grande Western Railway, which was building and consolidating lines southeastward from Salt Lake City. In 1883 the two railroads met near Green River, Utah, forming a narrow gauge route from Denver to Salt Lake City via Pueblo and Marshall Pass. In the early 1880s the D&RG built a new route from Leadville north over Tennessee Pass (10,239 feet, the highest point reached by a standard gauge main line in North America), then along the Eagle and Grand rivers, reaching Glenwood Springs in 1887. Two years later the track was extended west to Rifle. From there to Grand Junction the line was built by the

The *San Juan,* running between Alamosa and Durango, Colorado, was the last narrow gauge train in the U. S. to offer first class service and the last narrow gauge passenger train west of the Mississippi River. Trains 115 and 116, the west- and eastbound *San Juans,* meet at Carracas, Colo., in 1952. Photo by Robert F. Collins.

Rio Grande Junction Railway, which was jointly owned with the standard gauge Colorado Midland Railway—which in 1890 came under the control of the Santa Fe. Meanwhile, D&RG had been adding a third rail to its line east of Leadville. The lines west of Grand Junction were converted to standard gauge, and by 1890 D&RG had standard gauge track all the way from Denver to Ogden, Utah.

At the same time D&RG's narrow gauge network continued to expand south and west of the Pueblo–Grand Junction main line. In 1880 a line was extended south from Antonito, Colo., to Española, N. M. Rails reached Silverton from Durango in 1882, and in 1890 a line was built north from Alamosa to connect with existing lines southwest of Salida. In 1886 the Texas, Santa Fe & Northern Railroad constructed a line north from Santa Fe to Española. The company was reorganized as the Santa Fe Southern in 1888, and the Rio Grande acquired it in 1895.

Financial difficulty

The Rio Grande was deeply involved in financing the construction of the Western Pacific Railway between Salt Lake City and San Francisco, completed in 1910. When WP entered bankruptcy in 1915, it pulled the Rio Grande in after it. The Rio Grande was sold in 1920 to interests affiliated with the WP and became the Denver & Rio Grande Western Railroad. It entered receivership in 1921 and emerged in 1924 under the joint ownership of Western Pacific and Missouri Pacific—and encumbered with debt that put it back in trusteeship again in 1935. There was a difference this time. The trustees were not East Coast bankers but local

Dates are those of abandonment, conversion to standard gauge, installation of third rail, or sale.

men: Wilson McCarthy of Salt Lake City and Henry Swan of Denver.

The Moffat Tunnel and Dotsero Cutoff

David Moffat's Denver, Northwestern & Pacific Railway had built westward from Denver over Rollins Pass. In 1912 it was reorganized as the Denver & Salt Lake Railroad, but it got no closer to the goal in its name than Craig, in northwestern Colorado. The city of Denver, which for decades had wanted a direct rail route to the west, constructed the 6-mile Moffat Tunnel under James Peak for the D&SL (and also to bring Western Slope water to Denver). The tunnel, opened in 1928, let D&SL avoid the steep and often snowy climb over Rollins Pass, but D&SL had little traffic to send through the tunnel.

At Bond, the D&SL was about 40 miles up the Colorado River from D&RGW's main line at Dotsero. Both railroads wanted to build a cutoff connecting the routes; the Interstate Commerce Commission gave the nod to the Rio Grande.

Black-and-yellow FTs are a few miles into their attack on the Front Range as they cross over Route 72 at Coal Creek on March 15, 1952. Merger with the Denver & Salt Lake is still five years in the future. Photo by John W. Maxwell.

The Dotsero Cutoff was opened in 1934 and the Rio Grande acquired trackage rights on the D&SL between Denver and Bond. Denver finally was on a transcontinental main line, and D&RGW's route between Denver and Salt Lake City was 175 miles shorter. The D&RGW came out of trusteeship and merged the D&SL on April 11, 1947.

The California Zephyr

In 1939 the D&RGW, Western Pacific, and Chicago, Burlington & Quincy teamed up to operate a through passenger train, the *Exposition Flyer*, between Chicago and San Francisco via Denver and the Moffat Tunnel. The *Flyer* did not set the world on fire with its speed, but westbound it offered magnificent views of the Rockies west of Denver and California's Feather River Canyon (eastbound it traversed most of the mountain country by night).

In 1949 the train became the *California Zephyr*. The *CZ* was slower than its competition, but it was scheduled and equipped—five Vista-Domes per train—to take advantage of the scenery. It was more than a train—it was a long-distance land cruise. It was an immediate success, and it continued to carry good loads even in the late 1960s. In 1970 the Western Pacific managed to disencumber itself of the passenger business, and the *CZ* degenerated into a triweekly Chicago–Salt Lake City–Ogden operation designated "California service."

When Amtrak took over the nation's passenger trains in 1971, the Rio Grande elected to continue operating its remnant of the *CZ*, the Denver–Salt Lake City *Rio Grande Zephyr*. D&RGW joined Amtrak in 1983, and the triweekly *RGZ* was replaced by Amtrak's daily three-pronged service from Chicago to San Francisco, Los Angeles, and Seattle.

Narrow gauge lines

By the 1920s Rio Grande had only two narrow gauge routes: from Salida west to Montrose via Marshall Pass, the original main line, then south to Ridgway and a connection with the Rio Grande Southern Railroad, which D&RG had controlled since 1893; and from Alamosa west to Durango. At Antonito the "Chili Line" branched south to Santa Fe, N. M.; at Durango branches headed for Farmington, N. M., and Silverton, and there was a second connection with the Rio Grande Southern. A narrow gauge line between Salida and Alamosa connected the two routes. It was possible to ride a complete circle on narrow gauge lines until a bus replaced the passenger trains on the Salida–Alamosa branch in the mid-1920s.

The Chili Line was abandoned in 1942 for lack of traffic, and the narrow gauge circle was broken at Cerro Summit on the Marshall Pass route in 1949. The pace of narrow gauge abandonments accelerated (a few short segments were standard-gauged), so that by the mid-1950s only the Alamosa–Durango–Farmington–Silverton line was left—and it remained operational until 1967. Two segments of that route, from

145

Antonito to Chama, N. M., and from Durango to Silverton, survive as tourist carriers.

Merger with Southern Pacific

Even though coal from mines in northwestern Colorado became increasingly important to the D&RGW, the road's principal role was that of a fast-freight bridge route between Denver and Pueblo on the east and Salt Lake City and Ogden on the west. Mergers and abandonments changed the railroad map in the 1980s. The Rock Island, a good source of interchange traffic at Denver, ceased operation. The Union Pacific acquired Rio Grande's principal eastern connection, the Missouri Pacific, and principal western connection, Western Pacific. D&RGW acquired trackage rights east over the former MP route to Kansas City as a condition of the UP-MP merger. Then Rio Grande's other western connection, Southern Pacific, began talking merger with Santa Fe. Had the SP-SF merger occurred, D&RGW would have gotten an exclusive lease of SP's line from Ogden west to Roseville, Calif., and Klamath Falls, Oregon, plus trackage rights to Bakersfield, Oakland, and Ogden.

Philip Anschutz, a Denver businessman, acquired control of D&RGW in 1984. When the Interstate Commerce Commission rejected the SP-Santa Fe merger, Anschutz submitted an offer to purchase SP, and the ICC approved it on August 9, 1988.

	1929 Standard gauge	1929 Narrow gauge	1987
Miles of railroad operated:	1,720	842	2,247*
Number of locomotives:	375	91	314
Number of passenger cars:	188	80	20†
Number of freight cars:	13,098	2,783	
Number of company service cars:	720	201	
Number of freight and company service cars:			11,361

Location of headquarters: Denver, Colorado

Reporting marks: DRGW

Notable named passenger trains: *California Zephyr* (Chicago–San Francisco, operated jointly with Burlington and Western Pacific), *Prospector, Royal Gorge* (Denver–Salt Lake City), *San Juan* (Alamosa–Durango)

Historical and technical society: Rio Grand Historical Society, P. O. Box 314, Parker, CO 80134

*666 miles by trackage rights on other railroads

†(1982)

Recommended reading:
Rebel of the Rockies, by Robert G. Athearn, published in 1962 by Yale University Press, New Haven, CT 06520 (LCC: 62-16560)
Rio Grande to the Pacific, by Robert A. Le Massena, published in 1974 by Sundance Ltd., 100 Kalamath St., Denver, CO 80223 (ISBN 0-913582-10-7)

Predecessor railroads in this book: Denver & Salt Lake

Successors:
Southern Pacific
Union Pacific

Portions still operated:
Cumbres & Toltec Scenic Railroad: Antonito, Colo.–Chama, N. M.
Durango & Silverton Narrow Gauge Railroad: Durango–Silverton, Colo.
Union Pacific: Denver–Salt Lake City; Bond–Craig, Colo.; Gypsum–Dotsero, Colo.; Glenwood Springs–Carbondale, Colo.; Grand Junction–Montrose, Colo.; Delta–Oliver, Colo.; Brendel–Potash, Utah; Mounds–Sunnyside, Utah; Colton–Scofield, Utah; Springville–Elberta, Utah; Midvale–Copperton–Magna, Utah; Denver–Pueblo–Trinidad, Colo.; Pueblo–Malta, Colo.; Walsenburg–South Fork, Colo.; Alamosa–Antonito, Colo.

Denver & Salt Lake Railway

When the Union Pacific pushed westward in the 1860s the city of Denver was the largest center of population between the Missouri River and the Pacific. The railroad to the Pacific did not pass through Denver, though, because the Rocky Mountains immediately west constituted an almost insurmountable barrier. Routes had been surveyed west from Denver, but all were at considerably higher elevations than the route UP selected across Wyoming—and all of them would require much tunneling in the bargain.

The Denver Pacific Railroad was organized to connect Denver with Cheyenne, Wyoming, on the UP line; treasurer of the enterprise was David H. Moffat, a Denver businessman and banker. Its first train arrived in Denver on June 24, 1870, drawn by a locomotive named for Moffat. For the next 30 years Moffat was involved at one time or another with most of Denver's railroads as he tried to plan and build a railroad directly west from Denver.

Denver, Northwestern & Pacific

In 1902 Moffat decided to build a railroad west from Denver to serve as a connection from the Burlington and the Rock Island at Denver to the San Pedro, Los Angeles & Salt Lake at Salt Lake City. Construction of the Denver, Northwestern & Pacific Railway began almost imme-

Low-drivered Ten-Wheeler No. 302 leads train 1, the Denver–Craig local, at Tolland, a few miles east of the Moffat Tunnel, in November 1939. Photo by R. H. Kindig.

diately. The line was and is one of the most spectacular in North America.

In June 1904 the DNW&P began operating trains to Tolland and almost simultaneously was ousted from Denver Union Station, which was controlled by the Union Pacific and the Denver & Rio Grande. By September of that year rails had reached the top of Rollins Pass on what was intended to be a temporary line until a tunnel could be bored under the divide.

Later that autumn Moffat met a foe far more formidable than either the UP or the D&RG—snow. The summit of the pass was 11,680 feet above sea level, and it was reached by 4 percent grades and tight curves. The road was shut down for much of that winter after its new rotary snowplow became snowbound.

Late in the summer of 1905 DNW&P rails reached Hot Sulphur Springs, and soon afterward Moffat ran out of money. (Earlier Moffat had met with E. H. Harriman to discuss takeover of the road, but he co.uld not accept Harriman's terms.) In 1907 a group of Denver men formed a company to construct an extension of the road to Steamboat Springs, which was completed in December 1908. A more important goal was the coalfields near Oak Creek, because the D&NWP penetrated largely unpopulated territory with little potential for freight traffic. Moffat by then had exhausted his fortune. On March 17, 1911, he received a promise of financial support and, a day later, word of withdrawal of that support. The turn of events killed Moffat.

In July 1912 the Moffat Road was reorganized as the Denver & Salt Lake Railroad. The new company entered receivership in January 1913. In November 1913 D&SL rails reached Craig, in northwestern Colorado. They were to go no farther. The D&SL struggled along and entered receivership again in 1917. In 1918 the employees went on strike for seven months after years of low, and sometimes unpaid, wages. Things got worse. A tunnel fire and the subsequent collapse of the tunnel in South Boulder Canyon in March 1922 threatened to shut down the road permanently.

The Moffat Tunnel

The city of Denver recognized the importance of the road and pressed for the construction of a tunnel under the Continental Divide. The state legislature passed a bill in 1922 that provided funds for the 6-mile tunnel.

The authorization of the tunnel (which would take six years to build) wasn't an immediate help—wrecks, rockslides, and fires continued to plague the line—but finally, as northwestern Colorado developed, freight traffic began to increase. The D&SL made a profit for the first time in 1925, and capital was becoming less scarce. The road emerged from reorganization as the Denver & Salt Lake Railway in 1926. The Moffat Tunnel opened on February 26, 1928, vastly improving the operation of the railroad and shortening the route by approximately 23 miles. The line over the pass was abandoned.

Thought was given to the road's goal of Salt Lake City. A more practical route than one west from Craig was to follow the Colorado River 38 miles downstream to a connection with the Denver & Rio Grande Western at Dotsero, where the Eagle River joins the Colorado. The D&SL incorporated the project in 1924 as the Denver & Salt Lake Western, but the Rio Grande fought for the right to build the new cutoff, knowing that the owner of the cutoff would control the route.

The Interstate Commerce Commission, after considering the financial condition of both roads, granted the right to the Rio Grande. Construction began in late 1932, and in June 1934 the route was opened, cutting 175 miles out of D&RGW's Denver–Salt Lake City route. The east end of the cutoff was at Orestod (Dotsero spelled backwards), and a new station named Bond was designated on the cutoff just west of Orestod. The Rio Grande acquired trackage rights on the D&SL from Denver to Orestod. D&RGW began to acquire D&SL stock and merged the D&SL on April 11, 1947. The entire line is still in service, and coal traffic from mines along the western portion of the line has increased in recent years.

	1929	1945
Miles of railroad operated:	238	232
Number of locomotives:	58	39
Number of passenger cars:	25	9
Number of freight cars:	1,020	590
Number of company service cars:	164	179
Location of headquarters: Denver, Colorado		
Reporting marks: D&SL		

Recommended reading: *Rails That Climb,* by Edward T. Bollinger, published in 1979 by the Colorado Railroad Historical Foundation, P. O. Box 10, Golden, CO 80401

Successors:
Denver & Rio Grande Western
Southern Pacific
Union Pacific

Portions still operated: Union Pacific: Denver–Craig

Map: See page 144

Detroit & Toledo Shore Line Railroad

The Pleasant Bay Railway was incorporated in Toledo, Ohio, on March 29, 1898. A year later it purchased the Toledo & Ottawa Beach Railway, acquiring a substantial debt along with it, and was renamed Detroit & Toledo Shore Line Railroad. Plans were to create a fast electric line between Detroit and Toledo.

The track reached from Toledo north to Trenton, Michigan, about three-fourths of the distance to Detroit, when the stockholders sold the line jointly to the Grand Trunk and the Toledo, St. Louis & Western (the Clover Leaf) in 1902. The acquisition was a logical one for both roads, giving Grand Trunk a connection to Toledo and the Clover Leaf a connection to Detroit. The road was opened in 1903.

Detroit & Toledo Shore Line carried no passengers and originated little freight—it was principally a bridge route for its owners. The two principal commodities it carried were automobiles and coal to fuel Detroit's automobile factories.

The Clover Leaf half interest passed to the Nickel Plate in 1923 and then to Norfolk & Western when N&W merged NKP in 1964. In April 1981 Grand Trunk Western purchased Norfolk & Western's half interest in the D&TSL, merged the road, and integrated D&TSL operations with its own.

	1929	1980
Miles of railroad operated:	50	50
Number of locomotives:	31	16
Number of freight cars:	402	
Number of company service cars:	68	
Number of freight and company service cars:		604
Location of headquarters: Detroit, Michigan		
Reporting marks: D&TS		
Successors: Grand Trunk Western		
Portions still operated: Grand Trunk Western: Detroit–Toledo		
Map: See page 151		

A pair of Detroit & Toledo Shore Line diesel switchers pushes a cut of cars over the hump at Lang Yard in Toledo, Ohio, in September 1979. Photo by John Uckley.

Detroit, Toledo & Ironton Railroad

In May 1905 two bankrupt railroads, the Detroit Southern and the Ohio Southern, merged to form the Detroit, Toledo & Ironton Railway. The Detroit Southern, previously the Detroit & Lima Northern, extended southwest from Detroit to Lima, Ohio. Ohio Southern's antecedents included the Springfield, Jackson & Pomeroy, a 3-foot-gauge coal hauler that was intended to become part of a narrow gauge system stretching from Toledo, Ohio, to Mexico City. The new railroad then took control of the Ann Arbor to gain entry to Toledo. Ann Arbor regained independence in 1910, and the DT&I was reorganized in 1914 as the Detroit, Toledo & Ironton Railroad.

In 1920 Henry Ford wanted to straighten the shipping channel through which Great Lakes freighters reached his new River Rouge plant at Dearborn, Michigan. The project included a new bridge for DT&I, and the railroad suggested that Ford lend them the money in exchange for DT&I bonds. Ford decided instead to purchase the railroad.

He rebuilt it, instituted some unusual labor practices (wages considerably higher than average, white caps and clean overalls required, beards and mustaches not allowed, and no trains on Sundays), electrified a 17-mile portion between the Rouge Plant and Carleton, Mich., and

Mikado 801, built by Lima in 1940, has freight in tow at St. Paris, Ohio. DT&I's Mikes are a rare example of a railroad reverting in its motive power policy: The Berkshires that Lima furnished in 1935 and 1939 verged on being more locomotive than the railroad needed or could handle. Photo by Dick Acton Sr., collection of David Oroszi.

built a 46-mile cutoff between Dundee, Mich., and Malinta, Ohio. In 1929 Ford sold the railroad to the Pennroad Corporation, which was closely associated with the Pennsylvania Railroad. The 1930s saw the end of passenger service, except for a Springfield–Jackson, Ohio, mixed train that

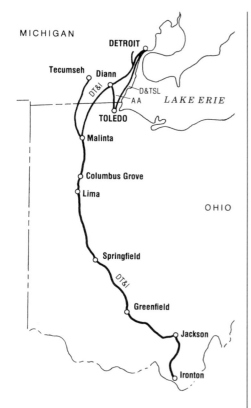

MICHIGAN

DETROIT

Tecumseh Diann

DT&I

D&TSL

A A   LAKE ERIE

TOLEDO

Malinta

Columbus Grove

Lima   OHIO

Springfield

DT&I

Greenfield

Jackson

Ironton

lasted until 1955. Dieselization began in the late 1940s and was complete by the end of 1955.

In 1951 the Pennsylvania Company, a subsidiary of the Pennsylvania Railroad, and the Wabash Railroad purchased Pennroad's stock in DT&I; in 1965 Wabash sold its share, 18 percent, to the Pennsylvania Company (which held 87 percent of the stock of the Wabash). In 1963 DT&I purchased the Ann Arbor Railroad from the Wabash. Ann Arbor went bankrupt in 1973, and portions of its line were sold to the state of Michigan; DT&I retained trackage rights from Diann, Mich., to Toledo.

With the formation of Conrail in 1976 DT&I acquired trackage rights over Conrail from Springfield, Ohio, to Cincinnati. The Pennsylvania Company, by then a subsidiary of Penn Central, put the DT&I up for sale. Grand Trunk Western, a subsidiary of Canadian National Railways, offered to purchase the DT&I, and Chessie System and Norfolk & Western offered a joint counterproposal. The ICC approved the sale to Grand Trunk; the sale was consummated on June 24, 1980.

The south end of the DT&I, from Jackson to Ironton, Ohio, was abandoned in 1982, and the line was dismantled. That same year the line from Washington Court House to Waverly was abandoned in favor of trackage rights on former Baltimore & Ohio and Chesapeake & Ohio lines; two year later, in 1984 the line was abandoned south of Washington Court House, including the recently acquired trackage rights.

In 1990 GTW sold the DT&I line between Springfield and Washington Court House to the Indiana & Ohio, and in 1997 sold the Diann–Springfield portion to the I&O.

	1929	1981
Miles of railroad operated:	517	623
Number of locomotives:	67	72
Number of passenger cars:	11	
Number of freight cars:	2,746	
Number of company service cars:	133	
Number of freight and company service cars:		3,778

Location of headquarters: Dearborn, Michigan
Reporting marks: DTI
Successors: Grand Trunk Western
Portions still operated:
Blue Rock Transportation: Blue Rock Limestone Quarry–Thrifton, Ohio
Grand Trunk Western: Detroit–Diann, Mich.
Indiana & Ohio Central: Diann, Mich.–Springfield–Washington Court House, Ohio

Duluth & Iron Range Railroad

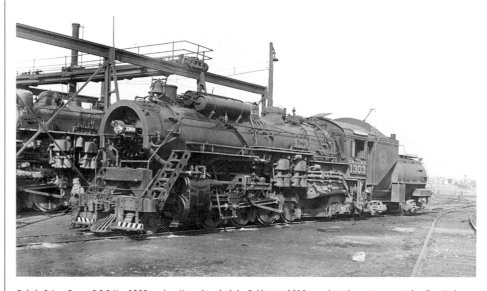

In the late 1860s gold was discovered—so the reports said—at Vermilion Lake in the wilderness north of Duluth, Minnesota. The gold turned out to be iron pyrites, often called fool's gold, but it led to a more important discovery—an immense deposit of high-grade iron ore, the Vermilion Range.

The Duluth & Iron Range Rail Road was chartered on December 21, 1874, to build a line from Duluth to Babbitt. The Minnesota legislature granted the company land through the wilderness, but the railroad remained no more than a charter.

The iron ore interested two Philadelphians, Charlemagne Tower and George C. Stone. Stone acquired ore lands from the public domain for Tower's Minnesota Iron Co., and Tower formed the Duluth & Iron Mountain Railroad in 1881. Tower was unable to get a land grant for his railroad, so he acquired control of the D&IR and vested its ownership in the Minnesota Iron Co.

Surveys and construction got under way, and the company built an ore dock at Agate Bay (now Two Harbors). The first trainload of iron ore rolled down to the docks at Two Harbors on July 31, 1884. In 1886 the road constructed a 26-mile extension southwest along the shore of Lake Superior to Duluth.

Duluth & Iron Range 2-8-2 No. 1303, a class N machine built by Baldwin in 1913, stands in the engine terminal at Two Harbors on July 10, 1937. Among the modifications made by its owners since Baldwin delivered it in 1913 are a Coffin feedwater heater on the smokebox front, a large sandbox on the pilot beam supplementing the sand dome, and air reservoirs mounted atop the boiler. Photo by Lewis Buttles.

Illinois Steel Co. developed a mine at Ely, 20 miles northeast of the Minnesota Iron Co. operation, and proposed to build a railroad from Duluth. Tower sold Minnesota Iron and the D&IR to Illinois Steel, whose backers included Henry H. Porter, Marshall Field, Cyrus McCormick, and John D. Rockefeller. (Porter had built the Chicago & Illinois Coal Railway and acquired control of the Chicago & Eastern Illinois for Illinois Steel.) The discovery of the iron ore deposits of the Mesabi Range in 1890 spurred D&IR to construct a branch from Allen Jct. west to the city of Virginia and several short branches to mines.

Illinois Steel was succeeded by Federal Steel, and Federal Steel by United States Steel Corporation. In 1901 U. S. Steel acquired the Duluth & Iron Range and also its neighbor to the west, the Duluth, Missabe & Northern. The two railroads retained their autonomy at first but gradually began to move toward unification, starting by sharing officers. On January 1, 1930, the DM&N leased the D&IR and immediately consolidated operations with an eye toward the economies that would result from joint use of equipment and eliminating duplicate facilities. On March 22, 1938, the Duluth, Missabe & Iron Range Railway, successor to the DM&N, acquired the assets and property of the D&IR.

	1929
Miles of railroad operated:	308
Number of locomotives:	85
Number of passenger cars:	21
Number of freight cars:	5,313
Number of company service cars:	49

Location of headquarters: Duluth, Minnesota

Reporting marks: D&IR

Historical and technical society: Missabe Railroad Historical Society, 719 Northland Avenue, Stillwater, MN 55082-5208

http://www1.minn.net/~mspanton/mrhs.html

Recommended reading:
The Missabe Road, by Frank A. King, published in 1972 by Golden West Books, P. O. Box 80250, San Marino, CA 91108 (ISBN 87095-040-1)

Locomotives of the Duluth, Missabe & Iron Range, by Frank A. King, published in 1984 by Pacific Fast Mail, P. O. Box 57, Edmonds, WA 98020 (ISBN 0-915713-11-X)

Successors:
Duluth, Missabe & Northern
Duluth, Missabe & Iron Range

Portions still operated:
Duluth, Missabe & Iron Range: Two Harbors–Embarrass; Wales–Jordan; Allen Jct.–Gilbert
North Shore Scenic Railroad: Duluth–Two Harbors

Map: See page 154

Duluth, Missabe & Northern Railway

The iron mines of Minnesota's Vermilion Range had been in production for more than 20 years when the mammoth deposits of high-grade hematite ores of the Mesabi Range were discovered in 1890. (There are several spellings of "Mesabi," a Chippewa word meaning "giant.") Neither of the nearby railroads, the Duluth & Iron Range to the east and the Duluth & Winnipeg (later Great Northern) to the southwest, was interested in extending to the Mesabi Range, so on June 3, 1891, the Merritt brothers of Duluth, who had acquired tracts of land at Mountain Iron and Biwabik, incorporated their own railroad, the Duluth, Missabe & Northern Railway.

Surveying and construction soon began, and on October 18, 1892, the first carload of Mesabi ore rolled into Duluth. The Merritts contracted with the Duluth & Winnipeg to use its line south of Brookston and its ore docks at Allouez (Superior), Wisconsin, but in 1893 they decided to build their own line into Duluth and construct ore docks there. The Merritts incurred

Duluth, Missabe & Northern 90–93 were the heaviest ten-coupled switchers in the world when Baldwin built them in 1928. The tender boosters were removed in 1930. Collection of H. L. Broadbelt.

considerable debt in doing so, and the Panic of 1893 didn't help matters. By February 1894 John D. Rockefeller was in control of their Lake Superior Consolidated Iron Mines and the DM&N.

Business rebounded. The Mesabi Range quickly outstripped the Vermilion Range, and DM&N, located at the center of the range, prospered. Traffic required a second ore dock at Duluth, then a third. In 1901 Rockefeller sold the DM&N to the newly formed United States Steel Corporation, which in the same year acquired the Duluth & Iron Range. DM&N entered an era of improving its physical plant: steel ore cars, Mallet locomotives, double track, extensions to other mines.

At first U. S. Steel made no moves to consolidate its two railroads, but after tentative steps in that direction, on January 1, 1930, DM&N leased the D&IR and integrated the operations of the two roads. The economies that resulted from sharing equipment and eliminating duplicate facilities were welcome during the Depression, when ore traffic almost disappeared.

On July 1, 1937, the DM&N consolidated with the Spirit Lake Transfer Railway, part of a short connecting line from Adolph, Minn., to Itasca, Wis., to form the Duluth, Missabe & Iron Range Railway (DM&N had leased the Spirit Lake line since 1915). On March 22, 1938, DM&IR acquired the assets and property of the Duluth & Iron Range and the Interstate Transfer Railway (the other portion of the connecting line, also leased by DM&N since 1915). The names of the two predecessors survived as designations for the two divisions of the DM&IR, Iron Range and Missabe.

	1929	1937
Miles of railroad operated:	313	539
Number of locomotives:	101	131
Number of passenger cars:	29	22
Number of freight cars:	8,917	
Number of company service cars:	128	
Number of freight and company service cars:		13,759

1937 figures reflect combined DM&N and D&IR operations.
Location of headquarters: Duluth, Minnesota
Reporting marks: DM&N
Historical and technical society: Missabe Railroad Historical Society, 719 Northland Avenue, Stillwater, MN 55082-5208;

http://www1.minn.net/~mspanton/mrhs.html
Recommended reading:
The Missabe Road, by Frank A. King, published in 1972 by Golden West Books, P. O. Box 80250, San Marino, CA 91108 (ISBN 87095-040-1)
Locomotives of the Duluth Missabe & Iron Range, by Frank A. King, published in 1984 by Pacific Fast Mail, P. O. Box 57, Edmonds, WA 98020 (ISBN 0-915713-11-X)
Subsidiaries and affiliated railroads, 1937: Duluth & Iron Range
Successor: Duluth, Missabe & Iron Range
Portions still operated: DM&IR: Duluth–Mountain Iron; Wolf–Virginia; Iron Junction–Gilbert; Keenan–Hibbing; Adolph, Minn.–South Itasca, Wis.

Duluth, South Shore & Atlantic Railway

The backers of the Duluth, South Shore & Atlantic Railway proposed to build a railroad from Duluth, Minnesota, east through the iron country of Wisconsin and the Upper Peninsula of Michigan to Sault Ste. Marie, with branches to St. Ignace, Mich., on the Straits of Mackinac, and Houghton, Mich., in the copper-mining country of the Keweenaw Peninsula. The DSS&A was incorporated in 1887 as a consolidation of several railroads serving the iron ore region of Michigan's Upper Peninsula: Mackinaw & Marquette, Sault Ste. Marie & Marquette; Wisconsin, Sault Ste. Marie & Mackinac; and Duluth, Superior & Michigan. The first-named, the Mackinaw & Marquette, was successor to the Detroit, Mackinac & Marquette, which opened a line in 1881 between St. Ignace and Marquette.

The DSS&A reached Sault Ste. Marie in September 1887 and Duluth in September 1888, the latter by using Northern Pacific tracks west of Iron River, Wis. About the same time it acquired control of the Mineral Range Railroad, which reached north from Hancock to Calumet and Lake Linden. Canadian Pacific acquired control of the DSS&A in 1888.

DSS&A extended its own rails west from Iron River to Superior in 1892. When the Lake Superior & Ishpeming arrived in the iron-mining area in 1896 it took much of the ore business away

Duluth, South Shore & Atlantic train 1 (Mackinaw City to Houghton and Hancock) arrives in St. Ignace in September 1951. The cars are ferried across the Straits of Mackinac on the *Chief Wawatam;* RS-1 No. 107 will power the train onward from St. Ignace. The two New York Central baggage cars carry mail from Detroit. Photo by A. C. Kalmbach.

	1929	1960
Miles of railroad operated:	574	544
Number of locomotives:	62	24
Number of passenger cars:	58	
Number of freight cars:	2,709	
Number of company service cars:	154	
Number of freight and company service cars:		1,720

Location of headquarters: Minneapolis, Minnesota

Reporting marks: DSS&A, DSA

Historical and technical society: Soo Line Historical & Technical Society, 2253 N. 70th Street, Wauwatosa, WI 53213

Recommended reading: *Wisconsin Central*, by Otto P. Dobnick and Steve Glischinski, published in 1997 by Kalmbach Publishing Co. (ISBN 0-89024-562-2)

Successors:
Soo Line Railroad
Wisconsin Central Ltd.

Portions still operated:
Escanaba & Lake Superior: Sidnaw–Nestoria, Mich. Wisconsin Central Ltd.: Marengo, Wis.–White Pine, Mich.; Baraga–Nestoria–Humboldt, Mich; Ishpeming–Trout Lake, Mich.

from the South Shore, leaving it largely dependent upon forest products. The road carried on—several issues of *Moody's Railroads* refer to it as "one of the least prosperous of the Canadian Pacific Railway's subsidiaries." By 1930 the road was sharing officers with Soo Line, also a CPR subsidiary. South Shore filed for bankruptcy in 1937, emerging in 1949 as the Duluth, South Shore & Atlantic Railroad, which included the old South Shore and the Mineral Range Railroad (which ran from Houghton to Calumet and Lake Linden). In the late 1930s the South Shore abandoned its main line west of Marengo, Wis., in favor of trackage rights from there to Ashland on Soo Line and from Ashland to Superior on Northern Pacific. Passenger service dwindled to a St. Ignace–Marquette round trip, operated with an RDC, discontinued in 1958, and the

north end of the Chicago–Calumet *Copper Country Limited*, operated in conjunction with the Milwaukee Road.

On January 1, 1961, the Soo Line Railroad was created by the merger of the DSS&A, the Minneapolis, St. Paul, & Sault Ste. Marie (the old Soo Line), and the Wisconsin Central Railway, which had long been operated by the Soo Line. The new railroad used DSS&A's corporate structure.

Durham & Southern Railway

The Durham & Southern was incorporated in 1906 as a reorganization and extension of the Cape Fear & Northern Railway. A lumber company had built the CF&N between Apex and Dunn, North Carolina, and the D&S would extend the line north to Durham. The purpose of the road was to connect Durham with the main lines of Atlantic Coast Line and Seaboard Air Line.

The Duke family was associated with the railroad from the beginning, and in 1930 control passed to the Duke Power Co., which also owned the Piedmont & Northern. The two roads were put under the same management, and a connection between the two was proposed, but it was rejected by the Interstate Commerce Commission. In 1954 management of the two roads was separated, and Durham & Southern came under the control of the Nello Teer Co., a Durham construction company.

The Durham & Southern was noteworthy from the standpoint of motive power: an assortment of Decapods, including one of only two common-carrier steam locomotives built in the U. S. during 1933, and an ex-Norfolk & Western Twelve Wheeler in steam days; an array of Baldwin diesel road-switchers; and finally orthodoxy in the form of four GP38-2s.

Seaboard Coast Line bought the railroad in 1976 and dissolved the corporation on September 15, 1981.

	1929	1980
Miles of railroad operated:	59	59
Number of locomotives:	9	4
Number of passenger cars:	9	
Number of freight cars:	1	50
Number of company service cars:	11	

Location of headquarters: Durham, North Carolina
Reporting marks: DS
Successors: Seaboard Coast Line, Seaboard System, CSX Transportation
Portions still operated: Dunn-Erwin Railway: Erwin–Dunn, N. C.
Map: See page 33

Durham & Southern 2-10-0 No. 202, which was built by Baldwin in 1933, rolls into Apex, North Carolina, with a freight train from Durham in September 1952. Photo by Philip R. Hastings.

East Broad Top Railroad & Coal Co.

The East Broad Top was the last narrow gauge common carrier in the U. S. east of the Mississippi. It was better known than most other roads of its size and remoteness. Strictly speaking it should not be in this book, because it still exists; it just barely qualifies on length.

The East Broad Top Railroad & Coal Company was chartered in 1856 to mine and transport coal from Broad Top Mountain, a plateau in Pennsylvania south of the Juniata River about halfway between Philadelphia and Pittsburgh. Construction did not begin until 1872, after the road's directors had chosen a track gauge of 3 feet. The line was opened from Mount Union, on the main line of the Pennsylvania Railroad, south to Orbisonia in 1873 and extended farther south to Robertsdale in 1874. By then the Rockhill Iron & Coal Company had been organized by the same management.

The Shade Gap Railroad was incorporated in 1884 to handle business that was sure to result from the construction of the South Pennsylvania Railroad, a line across the state backed by New York Central interests. A year later the Pennsylvania Railroad and the New York Central called a truce, and the half-dug tunnels of the South Penn were abandoned for the next 50 years.

The East Broad Top had a long career of car-

Loaded and empty East Broad Top coal trains meet at Kimmel, Pennsylvania, between Saltillo and Robertsdale, in March 1956, shortly before the line was abandoned. Photo by John Krause.

rying mostly coal but also limestone, lumber, and bark; its history is peppered with strikes by mine workers and flooding rivers and creeks. The EBT hit on hard times in the 1890s and was rehabilitated in the early 1900s. The road adopted automatic couplers in 1908 and air brakes in 1913; in 1912 it ordered its first all-steel hopper cars. In 1919 the road was purchased by Madeira, Hill & Co., a coal mining firm. The chief improvements under that management were a coal-cleaning plant at Mount Union and

facilities for changing the trucks of standard gauge cars so they could move on the EBT. In 1934 Madeira, Hill underwent voluntary bankruptcy and in 1937 went bankrupt again.

In 1938 the road's bondholders bought the East Broad Top and the mining company and reorganized them as the Rockhill Coal Company. The Shade Gap branch finally got the traffic for which it had been built when the long-abandoned roadbed of the South Penn was used as the foundation for the Pennsylvania

	1929	1955
Miles of railroad operated:	51	38
Number of locomotives:	12	8
Number of passenger cars:	18	4
Number of freight cars:	402	311
Number of company service cars:	20	8

Historical and technical society: Friends of the East Broad Top, c/o Ruth H. Kosowski, RD 1, Box 966, Three Springs, PA 17264; febtmemship@aol.com;http://www.usaor.net/users/vagelk/febthome.htm

Recommended reading: *East Broad Top,* by Lee Rainey and Frank Kyper, published in 1982 by Golden West Books, P. O. Box 80250, San Marino, CA 91108 (ISBN 0-87095-078-9)

Portions still operated:
East Broad Top Railroad: Orbisonia–Colgate Grove Rockhill Trolley Museum (standard gauge): short stretch of track at Orbisonia

Turnpike, construction of which began in 1939.

After World War II rising labor costs and shorter work days increased EBT's operating expenses, and frequent strikes called by John L. Lewis, head of the United Mine Workers, resulted in less coal moving over the railroad (and decreased revenue). However, the road remained in business and went so far as to ask General Electric about diesel power.

The demand for coal dropped as oil and gas took its place in homes and industries. The Rockhill Coal Co. decided to close its mines and offered the EBT to the Pennsylvania Railroad at scrap prices, but Pennsy declined the offer. The Interstate Commerce Commission approved abandonment effective March 31, 1956, and the last train ran on April 13, 1956, just three days short of the centennial of the chartering of the railroad. Nothing was scrapped immediately; the locomotives and cars were stored on the property.

The railroad and the coal company were purchased by Kovalchick Salvage Co., a scrap dealer. Nick Kovalchick, its president, petitioned to postpone dismantling the railroad and the mine facilities, and mining activity resumed in 1957, but the coal moved in trucks. In 1960 Kovalchick was asked if the railroad could be reactivated for the celebration of the bicentennial of Orbisonia. It could, and the East Broad Top reopened on August 13, 1960.

EBT has operated since then as a tourist railroad during the summer season. In 1963 standard gauge tracks were laid on a short portion of the Shade Gap branch by Railways to Yesterday, which operates a trolley museum at Orbisonia.

East Tennessee & Western North Carolina Railroad

The East Tennessee & Western Carolina Railroad was chartered in 1866 and built a few miles of 5-foot gauge track (then standard for the South) before stopping for breath and refinancing. In 1879 a group of investors led by Ario Pardee (who was connected with the East Broad Top Railroad) bought the line and resumed construction with a track gauge of 3 feet. The line was opened in 1882 between Johnson City, Tennessee, and Cranberry, North Carolina. At Cranberry were mines that produced high-grade ore used in the production of tool steel.

In 1913 the ET&WNC purchased the Linville River Railway, a logging railroad with which it connected at Cranberry. The line was extended a few miles at a time until it reached Boone, 33 miles from Cranberry, in 1918. In the 1930s ET&WNC turned to tourism to fill its trains—the mountains had been logged off, the mines were running out, and highways were taking passengers away. The mountains and the Doe River Gorge attracted excursionists, and during that era the road received its nickname, "Tweetsie." In 1940 rains washed out much of the Linville River line, and it was abandoned in 1941.

The ET&WNC kept busy during World War II because of the increased demand for steel and because of gasoline and tire rationing. At the end of the war the mines were depleted, and without the ore traffic there was little need for the narrow

Ten-Wheeler No. 11 and a short train cross the Doe River after emerging from a tunnel on August 5, 1941. Photo by Robert B. Adams.

gauge railroad. The last narrow gauge train ran on October 16, 1950.

The railroad had installed a third rail for standard gauge traffic between Johnson City and Elizabethton in 1906. That portion of the railroad remained in service after the narrow gauge line was abandoned and was operated with steam locomotives until 1967, when the last two Consolidations, Nos. 207 and 208, were replaced with a pair of Alco road-switchers from the Southern Railway. The two Consolidations returned to the Southern, their former owner, and regained their old numbers, 630 and 722, for Southern's steam excursion service.

In September 1983 the East Tennessee Railway Corporation took over operation of the line between Johnson City and Elizabethton.

	1929	1949
Miles of railroad operated:	36	34
Number of locomotives:	7	6
Number of passenger cars:	18	
Number of freight cars:	278	
Number of company service cars:	21	
Number of cars:		69

Location of headquarters: Johnson City, Tennessee
Historical and technical society: East Tennessee & Western North Carolina Historical Society, c/o John R. Waite, 8 Hickory Hills, DeSoto, MO 63020

Recommended reading: *Tweetsie Country,* by Mallory Hope Ferrell, published in 1976 by Pruett Publishing Co., 3235 Prairie Avenue, Boulder, CO 80301 (ISBN 0-87108-082-6)
Successor: East Tennessee Railway
Portions still operated: East Tennessee Railway: Johnson City–Elizabethton
Map: See page 124

Erie Railroad

When the Erie Canal was built across upstate New York between Albany and Buffalo, DeWitt Clinton, governor of New York, promised the people of the Southern Tier of the state some kind of avenue of commerce by way of appeasement. William Redfield proposed a direct route from the mouth of the Hudson to the Great Lakes, but it was Eleazar Lord who was instrumental in the chartering of the New York & Erie Railroad by the New York state legislature in April 1832. Among the conditions of the charter were that the railroad lie wholly within New York and that it not connect with any railroads in New Jersey or Pennsylvania without permission of the legislature. A track gauge of 6 feet ensured that even if it did connect, its cars and locomotives would not stray onto foreign rails.

The terminals were fixed: The town of Dunkirk offered land for a terminal on Lake Erie, and Lord lived at Piermont, on the Hudson River just north of the New Jersey state line. The New York & Harlem was willing to extend a line north to a point opposite Piermont, which would have given the New York & Erie an entrance to Manhattan, but the new road refused the offer. The surveyed route included two detours into Pennsylvania, one because the Delaware & Hudson Canal had already occupied the New York side of the Delaware River above Port Jervis, and the other to follow the Susquehanna River to maintain an easy grade.

Compared to its rivals in the New York–Chicago trade, the Erie was basically a freight railroad and one concerned more with through traffic than with local business. Here a fast freight rolls down the Delaware Valley west of Port Jervis, New York, bound for Jersey City, behind one of Erie's massive Berkshires. Erie photo.

Ground was broken on November 7, 1835, near Deposit, N. Y. Shortly afterwards fire destroyed much of New York and wiped out the fortunes of many of the road's supporters; then a business panic struck the nation.

Construction got under way in 1838, and the first train ran in 1841. Much of the railroad was built on low trestlework rather than directly on the ground; the resulting construction and maintenance costs drove the railroad into bankruptcy soon after it opened. Construction continued, however. The line that had been built east a few miles from Dunkirk was taken up to provide rails for the extension from Goshen, N. Y., to Middle-

town. Standard-gauging the line was proposed while it would still be relatively inexpensive to do so, but the road chose to stay with its broad gauge.

The New York & Erie reached Port Jervis, N. Y., on the Delaware River 74 miles from Piermont, on December 31,1847; just a year later it was into Binghamton. The whole road from Piermont to Dunkirk was opened in May 1851 with an inspection trip for dignitaries from U. S. President Millard Fillmore and Secretary of State Daniel Webster on down and the customary eating, drinking, and speechifying.

The road acquired branches: at the east end to Newburgh, N. Y., on the Hudson, and at the west

end to Rochester and to Buffalo, which soon replaced Dunkirk as the principal western terminal of the road.

In 1833 the Paterson & Hudson River Rail Road was chartered to build between Paterson, N. J., and Jersey City, and the Paterson & Ramapo Railroad north to the New York state line at Suffern. The two lines provided a shortcut between New York City and the New York & Erie at Suffern, even though they did not connect directly—passengers walked the mile between the two. The New York & Erie fought the situation until 1852, when it leased the two railroads, built a connecting track, and made that the main route, supplanting the original line to Piermont.

Hard times

The New York & Erie came upon hard times in the 1850s. Cornelius Vanderbilt and Daniel Drew both lent the road money. In 1859 it entered receivership and was reorganized as the Erie Railway. Drew and two associates, James Fisk and Jay Gould, engaged in some machinations, with the result that in the summer of 1868 Drew, Fisk, and Vanderbilt were out and Gould was in as president of the Erie.

In 1874 the Erie leased the Atlantic & Great Western, which had been opened 10 years earlier between Salamanca, N. Y., on the Erie, and Dayton, Ohio. The A&GW entered Cincinnati over the Cincinnati, Hamilton & Dayton, which laid a third rail to accommodate A&GW's broad gauge equipment. At Cincinnati the A&GW connected with the broad gauge Ohio & Mississippi to St. Louis. (The CH&D and the Ohio & Mississippi later became part of Baltimore & Ohio.)

The lease to the Erie did not last long. A&GW

entered receivership and was reorganized as the New York, Pennsylvania & Ohio. To obtain access to Cleveland and Youngstown, the NYP&O leased the Cleveland & Mahoning Valley in 1880. The Erie leased the Nypano (as it was known) in 1883, acquired all its capital stock in 1896, and acquired its properties in 1941.

Hugh Jewett became president of the Erie in 1874. His first task was to lead the road through reorganization; it became the New York, Lake Erie & Western Railroad. On June 22, 1880, the entire system was converted to standard gauge. That same year the Chicago & Atlantic was completed between Hammond, Indiana, and Marion, Ohio, where it connected with the Atlantic & Great Western. Access to Chicago was over the rails of the Chicago & Western Indiana, a terminal road. Jewett also double-tracked the Erie from Jersey City to Buffalo. The road was bankrupt again by 1893 and reorganized in 1895 as the Erie Railroad.

The Underwood era

In 1899 Frederick Underwood began a 25-year term as president of the Erie. He had been associated with James J. Hill, and he was a friend of E. H. Harriman. Both Hill and Harriman had considered the Erie as a possible eastern extension of their respective systems. Neither man did much toward acquiring it, although Harriman became a member of Erie's board of directors and arranged financing for it. In 1905 the Erie briefly acquired the Cincinnati, Hamilton & Dayton and the affiliated Pere Marquette from J. P. Morgan, Erie's banker. Investigation revealed that CH&D's financial condition was not as advertised, so Underwood asked Morgan to take the

Erie fielded only three passenger trains between New York and Chicago: the *Erie Limited,* which served the eastern half of its route by day; the *Lake Cities,* which served the western half of the route by day, and the *Atlantic* and *Pacific Expresses,* which were primarily mail trains on a late evening to late evening schedule. The *Lakes Cities* is shown departing from Chicago's Dearborn Station behind new E8s in March 1951. Photo by Robert Milner.

two roads back—which he did. Two days later the CH&D and the PM entered receivership.

Underwood is remembered for rebuilding the Erie. His projects included double-tracking the remainder of the main line and building several freight bypasses with lower grades, making the line east of Meadville, Pa., largely a water-level route. In 1907 Erie electrified passenger operations on its branch between Rochester and Mount Morris, N. Y. Electric operation lasted until 1934.

In the 1920s the Van Sweringen brothers began buying Erie stock, seeing the road as a logical eastern extension of their Nickel Plate Road.

By the time they were done, they owned more than 55 percent of Erie's stock along with their interests in Chesapeake & Ohio, Pere Marquette, and Hocking Valley.

The Erie family included several short lines. The Erie began to buy New York, Susquehanna & Western stock in 1898 and leased the line that same year. The Susquehanna entered bankruptcy in 1937 and resumed life on its own in 1940. Bath & Hammondsport was controlled by the Erie from 1903 to 1936, when it was sold to local businessmen. Much of Erie's commuter business out of Jersey City was over subsidiary lines that Erie operated as part of its own system: New York & Greenwood Lake, Northern Railroad of New Jersey, and New Jersey & New York.

The Erie held its own against the Great Depression until January 18, 1938, when it entered bankruptcy. Its reorganization, accomplished in December 1941, included purchase of the leased Cleveland & Mahoning Valley, swapping high rent for lower interest payments, and purchase of subsidiaries and leased lines. To the surprise of many, Erie began paying dividends. Prosperity continued until the mid-1950s, but then began to decline. Erie's 1957 income was less than half that for 1956; in 1958 and 1959 the road posted deficits.

The business recession of the 1950s prompted Erie to explore the idea of cooperation with Delaware, Lackawanna & Western. The first results were the elimination of duplicate freight facilities at Binghamton and Elmira, and in 1956 and 1957 Erie moved its passenger trains from its old Jersey City terminal to Lackawanna's newer one at Hoboken. The discussions of cooperation turned into merger talks, at first including the Delaware & Hudson. An agreement was worked out with the Lackawanna, and the two roads merged as the Erie-Lackawanna on October 17, 1960.

	1929	1959
Miles of railroad operated:	2,316	2,215
Number of locomotives:	1,122	484
Number of passenger cars:	1,368	535
Number of freight cars:	44,916	20,028
Number of company service cars:	1,619	605

Location of headquarters: New York, New York; after 1931 Cleveland, Ohio

Reporting marks: ERIE

Notable named passenger trains: *Erie Limited* (Jersey City–Chicago)

Historical and technical society: Erie Lackawanna Historical Society, c/o Bob Rose, 1 La Malfa Road, Randolph, NH 07869

Recommended reading: *Men of Erie,* by Edward Hungerford, published in 1946 by Random House, New York, N. Y.

Subsidiaries and affiliated railroads, 1959:
Akron & Barberton Belt (25%)
Buffalo Creek (50%, jointly with Lehigh Valley)
Niagara Junction (25%)
New Jersey & New York (84%)

Successors:
Erie Lackawanna
Conrail
NJ Transit

Portions still operated:
Ashland Railway: Mansfield–Ashland–West Salem, Ohio
Bradford Industrial Rail: East Bradford–Bradford, Pa.
Buffalo Southern: Buffalo–Gowanda, N. Y.
Conrail: Jersey City, N. J.–Rittman, Ohio; Burbank–Ontario, Ohio; Kenton–Alger, Ohio; Aurora–Cleveland, Ohio; Maitland–Dayton, Ohio; Jersey City–Orangeburg, N. Y.; Hornell–Buffalo, N. Y.; Carrolton, N. Y.–Bradford, Pa.; Meadville–Oil City, Pa.
JK Lines: North Judson–Monterey, Ind.
Livonia, Avon & Lakeville: Avon–Lakeville, N. Y
New York & Lake Erie: Gowanda–Waterboro, N. Y.; Dayton–Salamanca, N. Y.
New York, Susquehanna & Western: Passaic Junction, N. J.–Campbell Hall, N. Y.–Binghamton (trackage rights)
NJ Transit: Hoboken, N. J.–Port Jervis, N. Y.; Hoboken–Spring Valley, N. Y.
Stourbridge: Lackawaxen–Honesdale, Pa.

Map: See page 167

Erie Lackawanna Railroad

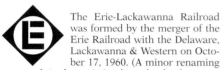

The Erie-Lackawanna Railroad was formed by the merger of the Erie Railroad with the Delaware, Lackawanna & Western on October 17, 1960. (A minor renaming occurred in late 1963 when the hyphen was dropped.) The new railroad took after its parent Erie; the greatest amount of Lackawanna influence seemed to be paint. Both of EL's parents entered the merger with recent deficits on their books, and EL continued their record, except for 1965 and 1966.

EL quickly consolidated its passenger services, with most trains following the ex-Lackawanna route east of Binghamton and the ex-Erie route west. Long-distance passenger trains were gradually cut back during the 1960s, and the last Hoboken–Chicago train was discontinued in 1970, leaving EL with a single daily commuter round trip between Cleveland and Youngstown and its extensive New Jersey commuter services. In 1967 the state of New Jersey began subsidizing the commuter service and in 1970 began to acquire new cars and locomotives for the trains on the ex-Erie routes and the nonelectrified Lackawanna lines (the Lackawanna electric cars would continue running until 1984). The Cleveland–Youngstown train lasted until 1977.

In 1960 Chesapeake & Ohio began acquiring Baltimore & Ohio stock, and in November 1961

Symbol freights CX-99 and NE-74, Erie Lackawanna's hottest westbound and eastbound freights, meet at Rood's Creek, New York, in the early 1970s. Two SD45s are in charge of NE-74. Photo by J. J. Young, Jr.

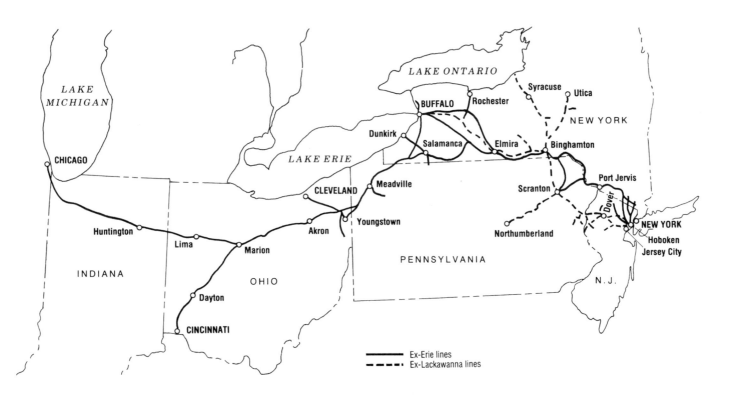

LAKE MICHIGAN

LAKE ONTARIO

LAKE ERIE

CHICAGO

BUFFALO

Rochester

Syracuse

Utica

NEW YORK

Dunkirk

Salamanca

Elmira

Binghamton

Meadville

CLEVELAND

Port Jervis

Scranton

Dover

Youngstown

Huntington

Akron

NEW YORK

Lima

Marion

Northumberland

Hoboken

Jersey City

INDIANA

Dayton

OHIO

PENNSYLVANIA

N. J.

CINCINNATI

———— Ex-Erie lines
– – – – Ex-Lackawanna lines

New York Central and Pennsylvania announced their intention to merge. In 1964 Norfolk & Western teamed up with Nickel Plate, Wabash, Pittsburgh & West Virginia, and Akron, Canton & Youngstown. Erie Lackawanna was suddenly surrounded, or thought it would be when all the mergers were approved, and asked to be included in the Norfolk & Western system. In 1965 Norfolk & Western and Chesapeake & Ohio announced their merger plan, which would include EL, and several other smaller eastern railroads, to be held by a wholly owned subsidiary holding company named Dereco.

The N&W-C&O merger didn't take place, but on March 1, 1968, Dereco and the Erie Lackawanna Railway were both incorporated. Dereco exchanged its shares for Erie Lackawanna Railway's 1,000 shares. On April 1, 1968, the Erie Lackawanna Railway merged with the Erie Lackawanna Railroad. Stockholders of the Erie Lackawanna Railroad received Dereco shares. To put it in simpler language, Norfolk & Western bought the Erie Lackawanna at arm's length.

Hurricane Agnes hit the East on June 22, 1972. After estimating that damage to the railroad, principally between Binghamton and Salamanca, N. Y., amounted to $9.2 million, EL filed for bankruptcy on June 26, 1972. During the reorganization of the eastern railroads, it was thought that EL might be able to reorganize on its own, and there was a proposal by Chessie System to buy a portion of the EL. However, Chessie canceled the agreement and EL asked to be included in Conrail.

Consolidated Rail Corporation took over EL's operations on April 1, 1976. Conrail's map excluded most of the former Erie main line west of Marion, Ohio. The Erie Western was formed to operate the 152 miles from Decatur to Hammond, Indiana, with subsidy from the state of Indiana. The road operated for a brief period in 1978 and 1979, but the subsidy was withdrawn and on-line traffic wasn't sufficient to support the operation. Other shortline operators have taken over various parts of EL with more success; they are listed in the entries for the Erie and the Lackawanna. As an odd valedictory for EL, parent Norfolk & Western donated its 1,000 shares of Erie Lackawanna stock and the corporate records to the University of Virginia in 1983.

	1960	1975
Miles of railroad operated:	3,189	2,807
Number of locomotives:	695	516
Number of passenger cars:	1,098	407
Number of freight and company service cars:	29,905	19,162

Location of headquarters: Cleveland, Ohio
Reporting marks: EL
Historical and technical society: Erie Lackawanna Historical Society, c/o Bob Rose, 1 La Malfa Road, Randolph, NH 07869
Recommended reading:
Erie Lackawanna East, by Karl R. Zimmermann, published in 1975 by Quadrant Press, 19 West 44th Street, New York, NY 10036 (ISBN 0-915276-12-7)
Erie Lackawanna: Death of an American Railroad, 1938–1992, by H. Roger Grant, published in 1994 by Stanford University Press, Stanford, Calif. (ISBN 0-8047-2357-5)
Subsidiaries and affiliated railroads, 1975:
Akron & Barberton Belt (25%)
Buffalo Creek (50%, jointly with Lehigh Valley)
Chicago & Western Indiana (20%)
Lackawanna & Wyoming Valley (86%)
New Jersey & New York (84%)
Predecessor railroads in this book:
Delaware, Lackawanna & Western, Erie Railroad
Successors: Conrail, NJ Transit
Portions still operated: See entries for Delaware, Lackawanna & Western and Erie

Florida East Coast Railway – Key West Extension

When Henry M. Flagler's Florida East Coast Railway reached Miami from the north in 1896, Flagler was not content to rest. The Florida Keys, a string of islands, reach more than 100 miles southwest from the southern tip of mainland Florida to the outermost island, Key West, only 90 miles from Havana, Cuba. Until the 1950s there was a great deal of freight and passenger traffic between the U. S. and Cuba; in addition Key West was nearer the Panama Canal, then under construction, than any other U. S. port. In 1904 Flagler decided to extend his railroad to Key West.

The construction problems were formidable and labor turnover was high. On the portion of the line from Homestead to Key Largo, the dredging of canals to drain the swamp provided material for the roadbed. Along Key Largo the problem was not terrain but insects. Worse than terrain or insects was the weather: A hurricane in September 1906 destroyed the initial work on the Long Key Viaduct and killed more than 100 laborers. In 1907 the opening of Long Key Viaduct, more than 2 miles of concrete arches (it became FEC's trademark), allowed service to Knights Key, where a marine terminal was built.

Hurricanes in 1909 and 1910 wiped out much of the completed railroad. After both hurricanes,

A northbound train pauses at Long Key in March 1929. In charge is 4-8-2 No. 431, built by Alco in 1926. FEC photo.

169

work resumed at a faster pace—Flagler was getting old and wanted to ride all the way to Key West on his railroad. He did so on January 22, 1912. Regular service began the next day, with through sleepers between New York and Key West and connections at Key West with passenger steamers and carferries for Havana.

A hurricane on September 2, 1935, washed away 40 miles of the Key West Extension. Florida East Coast was unwilling to repair a line that had never repaid its construction cost—an unknown figure only hinted at by the federal valuation of $12 million. The concrete viaducts survived to become the bridges of U. S. Highway 1, and the railroad was cut back to Florida City, 30 miles south of Miami. In recent years that line has been cut back to Miami.

Miles of railroad operated in 1929: 156
Notable named passenger trains: *Havana Special* (New York–Key West, operated north of Jacksonville by Atlantic Coast Line, Richmond, Fredericksburg & Potomac, and Pennsylvania Railroad)
Recommended reading:
The Railroad That Died At Sea, by Pat Parks, published in 1968 by the Stephen Greene Press, Brattleboro, VT 05301
Speedway to Sunshine, by Seth Bramson, published in 1984 by Boston Mills Press, 98 Main Street, Erin, Ontario N0B 1T0, Canada (ISBN 0919783-12-0)

Fort Dodge, Des Moines & Southern Railroad

In 1893 the Boone Valley Coal & Railroad Company was formed to build a railroad from coalfields northwest of Des Moines, Iowa, to a connection with the Minneapolis & St. Louis Railway. Within a decade it was part of the Newton & Northwestern Railroad, a line from Newton, Iowa, northwest to Rockwell City. A notable feature of the line was a long, high trestle near Boone over Bass Point Creek, a tributary of the Des Moines River.

The Fort Dodge, Des Moines & Southern Railroad was incorporated in 1906 and built three lines branching off the Newton & Northwestern: from Hope north to Fort Dodge, from Midvale south to Des Moines, and from Kelly to Ames. The road purchased streetcar companies in Fort Dodge and Ames, and made a connection with the Inter-Urban Railway (later part of the Des Moines & Central Iowa) for access to downtown Des Moines. The Des Moines and Fort Dodge lines were electrified from the beginning, and trolley wires were erected over the Newton & Northwestern between Midvale and Hope.

The N&NW entered receivership in 1908 and was purchased in 1909 by the FDDM&S; a year later the FDDM&S also entered receivership, which lasted until 1913, when the road was sold at foreclosure to another company of the same name. The Rockwell City line was electrified, and the line from Midvale to Newton was dismantled in 1917 after several years of disuse. About that same time the FDDM&S built and acquired lines from Fort Dodge east to Webster City and Lehigh to tap coal and gypsum mines.

From the beginning the railroad was primarily a freight carrier. The road was listed in the 1930 edition of Poor's—unusual for an electric line—which said, "Road is electrically operated, but is of standard steam railroad construction . . . and operates under the steam railroad laws of Iowa." Passenger service on the branches was discontinued in the 1920s, and by 1930 mainline passenger service was down to four trips a day in each direction. That was reduced to two each way from 1935 until the early 1940s, when four trips were again scheduled.

The Fort Dodge, Des Moines & Southern Railroad entered receivership again in 1930; the Fort Dodge, Des Moines & Southern Railway took over the property in 1943. The Iowa Commerce Commission permitted abandonment of passenger service in 1952, but the passenger trains continued to operate until 1955. Dieselization began in 1949, and the road was temporarily totally dieselized for three months in the summer of 1954 because of floods. Electric operation ended when passenger service ceased.

The Des Moines & Central Iowa was the successor in 1922 to the Inter-Urban Railway. Its main lines ran from Des Moines east to Colfax and northwest to Perry. It abandoned the Colfax line and went bankrupt in 1946. In 1949 it was

Car 72 operating as train 2 from Fort Dodge to Des Moines crosses the Fort Dodge Line's famous high bridge near Boone, Iowa, in April 1955. Photo by William D. Middleton.

purchased by Murray Salzberg, who ended passenger service on the Perry line and dieselized the road. Chicago & North Western acquired control in 1969.

In 1954 control of the FDDM&S was acquired by the Des Moines & Central Iowa. Most of the Fort Dodge Line's branches were abandoned in the 1960s. C&NW leased the FDDM&S in 1971 and quickly took over its operations. In 1983 most of the main line was abandoned. The Boone Railroad Historical Society purchased 11 miles of the line from Boone to Wolf Crossing, including the famous High Bridge, for operation as the Boone & Scenic Valley Railroad, a tourist carrier.

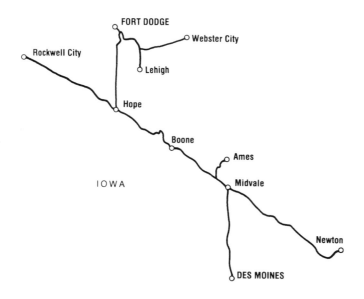

FORT DODGE

Webster City

Rockwell City

Lehigh

Hope

Boone

Ames

IOWA

Midvale

Newton

DES MOINES

	1929	1970
Miles of railroad operated:	151	112
Number of locomotives:	12	9
Number of passenger cars:	19	
Number of freight cars:	683	202
Number of company service cars:	23	17

Location of headquarters: Boone, Iowa
Reporting marks: FtDDM&S
Historical and technical society:
Boone Railroad Historical Society, 1024 Eighth
Street, Boone, IA 50036
Chicago & North Western Historical Society, P. O. Box
1436, Elmhurst, IL 60126-9998
Recommended reading: *Iowa Trolleys,* edited by
Norman Carlson, published in 1975 by Central Electric Railfans' Association, P. O. Box 503, Chicago, IL
60690
Successor: Chicago & North Western
Portions still operated: Boone & Scenic Valley
Railroad: Boone–Wolf Crossing

Fort Smith & Western Railway

The Fort Smith & Western Railroad was incorporated in Arkansas in 1899. It opened its first 20 miles of line between Coal Creek and McCurtain, Oklahoma, at the end of 1901. (The road used trackage rights on Kansas City Southern from Fort Smith, Ark., headquarters of the company, to Coal Creek.) The end of 1903 saw the entire line open between Coal Creek and a connection with the Santa Fe at Guthrie, Okla., at that time the territorial capital. The line served no major population centers, and the lack of business put the road into receivership.

In 1915 FS&W acquired trackage rights on the Missouri-Kansas-Texas from Fallis, Okla., to Oklahoma City, which had become the state capital in 1910. The road teamed up with the Missouri, Oklahoma & Gulf, with which it connected at Dustin, to offer passenger service between Oklahoma City, Muskogee and Joplin, Mo. A major portion of the road's freight traffic was metallurgical-grade coal from mines near McCurtain and cotton.

The Fort Smith & Western Railway was incorporated on January 10, 1921, to purchase and operate the property of the Fort Smith & Western Railroad. It began operation on February 1, 1923. The early 1920s were good years for the FS&W. Oil was discovered near Okemah, and the road made a successful effort to solicit

Fort Smith & Western's freight was moved by light Mikados like Baldwin-built No. 25. Air reservoirs atop the boiler were an FS&W trait. Photo by Charles E. Winters.

bridge traffic—traffic received from one railroad and delivered to another. Prosperity, however, managed to elude FS&W's grasp. On June 1, 1931, the Central United National Bank of Cleveland, Ohio, brought suit for foreclosure and the appointment of a receiver (corporate headquarters of the FS&W were in Cleveland, and several of the road's directors were connected with the Nickel Plate Road).

The Great Depression had the same effect on the FS&W that it did on other roads; in addition, droughts during the early 1930s destroyed much of the agriculture along the FS&W. The road faced other problems too: Its equipment was old and worn out; many of its management people, who had been with the road since its construction, were in the same condition; the approach to the Canadian River bridge was washed out twice in the late 1930s, requiring expensive repairs and detours over other railroads;

and Katy withdrew trackage rights into Oklahoma City.

Fort Smith & Western ceased operations on February 9, 1939, and received permission to abandon five months later. A Kansas City Southern subsidiary, the Fort Smith & Van Buren Railway, acquired the original portion of the road from Coal Creek to McCurtain.

From 1907 to 1922 the Fort Smith & Western controlled the St. Louis, El Reno & Western Railway, whose line from Guthrie to El Reno, Okla., gave the FS&W a connection with the Rock Island. It was dismantled in 1926.

	1929	1938
Miles of railroad operated:	250	250
Number of locomotives:	26	11
Number of passenger cars:	21	6
Number of freight cars:	1,063	136
Number of company service cars:	64	6
Location of headquarters: Fort Smith, Arkansas		
Reporting marks: FS&W		

Recommended reading: *Railroads in Oklahoma*, edited by Donovan L. Hofsommer, published in 1977 by the Oklahoma Historical Society, 2100 North Lincoln, Oklahoma City, OK 73105

Portions still operated: Kansas City Southern: Coal Creek–McCurtain, Okla.

Map: See page 240

Georgia & Florida Railroad

John Skelton Williams, former president of the Seaboard Air Line, proposed in 1906 to assemble a railroad from Columbia, South Carolina, to a port to be developed on the Gulf of Mexico in Florida. To form the Georgia & Florida Railway he acquired four short lines: the Augusta & Florida Railway (Keysville–Swainsboro, Ga.); the Millen & Southwestern Railroad (Millen–Pendleton–Vidalia, Ga.), the Douglas, Augusta & Gulf Railway (Hazlehurst–Nashville–Sparks, Ga.); and the Valdosta Southern Railway (Valdosta, Ga.–Madison, Fla.). In addition the four roads included several branches and leased lines. He connected these by constructing four

segments of track totaling 84 miles: Swainsboro–Pendleton, Vidalia–Hazlehurst, Garent–Douglas Junction, and Nashville–Valdosta. In addition, he secured trackage rights between Augusta and Keysville over the Augusta Southern.

By 1910 a line was complete between Augusta, Ga., and Madison, Fla. In 1911 the G&F reached Moultrie, Ga., by completion of a short branch and purchase of a few miles of trackage rights. In 1919 the road purchased the Augusta Southern at foreclosure, gaining a line to Sandersville and Tennille, Ga. In 1924 the road leased the Midland Railway of Georgia, which formed a branch to Statesboro (the Midland had begun life as a

Savannah–Chattanooga proposal and had gone through several identities).

The Georgia & Florida entered receivership in 1915. Skelton became receiver of the G&F in 1921, and it was reorganized as the Georgia & Florida Railroad shortly after Skelton's death in 1926. The road began construction of an extension north to Greenwood, S. C., completed in 1929. The cost of construction and the effects of the Depression put the G&F into receivership again in 1929.

In March 1954 the road sold the Valdosta–Madison line to the Valdosta Southern Railroad—a new company, not the one acquired by

Georgia & Florida's largest steam locomotives were three 4-8-2s originally built for New Orleans Great Northern in 1927 and purchased from Gulf, Mobile & Ohio in 1947. They proved too heavy for the track south of Augusta and were soon restricted to the South Carolina portion of the railroad. Photo by T. Blasingame.

	1929	1961
Miles of railroad operated:	502	321
Number of locomotives:	32	12
Number of passenger cars:	29	
Number of freight cars:	635	513
Number of company service cars:	49	43

Location of headquarters: Augusta, Georgia

Reporting marks: G&F

Recommended reading: *Central of Georgia Railway and Connecting Lines,* by Richard E. Prince, published in 1976 by Richard E. Prince

Successors: Southern Railway

Portions still operated:

Norfolk Southern: Adel—Moultrie, Ga.

Valdosta Southern: Valdosta—Clyatteville, Ga.

Skelton. In February 1962 the Southern Railway formed the Georgia & Florida Railway to acquire the road and sell it to three other roads controlled by the Southern: Live Oak, Perry & Gulf; Carolina & North Western, and South Georgia. Transfer of the G&F to the three roads occurred July 1, 1963. On June 1, 1971, the Georgia & Florida Railway was merged into the Central of Georgia Railroad, another subsidiary of the Southern. The South Carolina portion was abandoned in the early 1970s; most of the main line remains in service.

Georgia Northern Railway

In 1891 a private logging railroad that extended a few miles north from Pidcock, Georgia, was organized as the Boston & Albany Railroad of Georgia. Within two years it had been extended north to Moultrie and the company had entered receivership. J. N. Pidcock, who owned lumber mills in the area, purchased the railroad and reorganized it as the Georgia Northern Railway. In 1905 the railroad relocated the southern 4 miles of the line to terminate at Boston, east of Pidcock, and that same year completed the line north to Albany, 68 miles from Boston.

The Flint River & Northeastern was completed between Pelham and Ticknor, 23 miles, in 1904. By 1908 Pidcock had acquired an interest in the road and was operating it as part of the Georgia Northern. In 1922 Pidcock organized the Georgia, Ashburn, Sylvester & Camilla Railway to take over a 50-mile portion of a sub-subsidiary of the Southern Railway between Ashburn and Camilla.

The Albany & Northern was organized in 1895 to take over a 35-mile line between Albany and Cordele. In 1910 the Georgia, Southwestern & Gulf, which had been incorporated to build a line from Albany southwest to St. Andrews Bay on the Gulf of Mexico, purchased control of the Albany & Northern, leased it, and operated it as the Georgia, Southwestern & Gulf (The line to the Gulf never became reality.) The GSW&G

Georgia Northern SW8 No. 13 leads a Georgia, Ashburn, Sylvester & Camilla freight through a sea of dry grass between Camilla and Bridgeboro. Photo by Jim Boyd.

Georgia Northern	1929	1965
Miles of railroad operated:	68	68
Number of locomotives:	5	3
Number of passenger cars:	7	1
Number of freight cars:	49	3
Number of company service cars:	2	5
Location of headquarters: Moultrie, Georgia		

Georgia, Ashburn, Sylvester & Camilla	1929	1965
Miles of railroad operated:	50	51
Number of locomotives:	1	2
Number of cars:	10	1
Location of headquarters: Moultrie, Georgia		

Flint River & Northeastern	1929	1945
Miles of railroad operated:	23	23
Number of locomotives:	2	2
Number of cars:	4	3
Location of headquarters: Moultrie, Georgia		
Reporting marks: FR&N		

Georgia, Southwestern & Gulf	1929	1938
Miles of railroad operated:	35	35
Number of locomotives:	5	5
Number of passenger cars:	7	4
Number of freight cars:	13	9
Location of headquarters: Albany, Georgia		

Albany & Northern		1962
Miles of railroad operated:		35
Number of locomotives:		2
Number of freight cars:		2
Location of headquarters: Albany, Georgia		

Recommended reading: *Central of Georgia Railway and Connecting Lines*, by Richard E. Prince, published in 1976 by Richard E. Prince

Successors:
Southern Railway
Norfolk Southern

Portions still operated: Norfolk Southern: Pavo–Albany; Camilla–Sylvester

Map: See page 175

entered receivership in 1932, and Pidcock was appointed receiver in 1939. In 1942 the GSW&G was dissolved, the lease was canceled, and the Albany & Northern resumed its own operation.

The roads shared many officers. Georgia Northern, GAS&C, and FR&N were listed together in *The Official Guide* and shared general offices at Moultrie. Offices of the Albany & Northern and the Georgia, Southwestern & Gulf were at Albany.

Back in the Teens, the Georgia, Southwestern & Gulf and the Georgia Northern participated in operating a through passenger train, the Hampton Springs Special, which came down from Atlanta on the Atlanta, Birmingham & Atlantic and continued south of Moultrie on the Valdosta, Moultrie & Western and the South Georgia to Hampton, 6 miles west of Perry.

The Flint River and Northeastern was abandoned in 1946. Southern Railway acquired control of Georgia Northern, Albany & Northern, and GAS&C in 1966. The roads were merged on January 1, 1972; Georgia Northern exists today as a subsidiary of the Southern Railway. It operates the remains of the Pidcock system and also a short portion of the former Georgia & Florida Railroad extending from Moultrie to Adel, Ga.

Great Northern Railway

In 1857 the Minnesota & Pacific Railroad was chartered to build a line from Stillwater, Minnesota, on the St. Croix River, through St. Paul and St. Cloud to St. Vincent, in the northwest corner of the state. The company defaulted after completing a roadbed between St. Paul and St. Cloud, and its charter was taken over by the St. Paul & Pacific Railroad, which ran its first train between St. Paul and St. Anthony (now Minneapolis) in 1862.

For financial reasons the railroad properties were reorganized as the First Division of the St. Paul & Pacific. Both StP&P companies were soon in receivership, and Northern Pacific, with which the StP&P was allied, went bankrupt in the Panic of 1873.

In 1878 James J. Hill and an associate, George Stephen, acquired the two St. Paul & Pacific companies and reorganized them as the St. Paul, Minneapolis & Manitoba Railway (often referred to as "the Manitoba"). By 1885 the company had 1,470 miles of railroad and extended west to Devils Lake, North Dakota. In 1886 Hill organized the Montana Central Railway to build from Great Falls, Montana, through Helena to Butte, and in 1888 the line was opened, creating in conjunction with the StPM&M a railroad from St. Paul to Butte.

In 1881 Hill took over the 1856 charter of the

Great Northern re-equipped its Chicago–Seattle–Portland *Empire Builder* in 1951, only four years after the first set of streamlined equipment entered service. The 1947 equipment became the *Western Star*, running on a slower, three-night schedule between Chicago and the Pacific Northwest. The train is shown in Glacier National Park. GN photo.

Minneapolis & St. Cloud Railroad. He first used its franchises to build the Eastern Railway of Minnesota from Hinckley, Minn., to Superior, Wisconsin, and Duluth. Its charter was liberal enough that he chose it as the vehicle for his line to the Pacific. He renamed the road the Great Northern Railway; it then leased the Manitoba and assumed its operation.

Over the mountains to Puget Sound

Hill decided to extend his railroad from Havre, Mont., west to the Pacific, specifically to

Puget Sound at Seattle. He had briefly considered building to Portland, but it was already served by the Oregon-Washington Railroad & Navigation Co. and the Northern Pacific.

Hill's surveyors found an easy route through the Rockies over Marias Pass. Later there was considerable advocacy for creating a national park in the Rockies of northern Montana, and GN—in particular, Louis W. Hill, son of James J. and president of GN from 1907 to 1912 and 1914 to 1919—joined the forces urging the establishment of Glacier National Park. GN developed the park, and for many years furnished the only

transportation to it. The park, in turn, drew passengers to the railroad-owned hotels and provided the railroad with a herald, a Rocky Mountain goat (actually a species of antelope). GN sold its Glacier Park hotel properties in 1960.

The Cascade Range in the state of Washington was a far more formidable barrier to the Great Northern. The Northern Pacific had originally detoured to the south, using Oregon-Washington rails along the Columbia River. Hill, however, saw the vast stands of timber on the slopes of the mountains as a resource, and his engineer, John Stevens, found a pass (it now bears his name)

that could afford a route from the interior of Washington to the tidewater of Puget Sound.

The Great Northern was opened through to Seattle in 1893 using a temporary line over Stevens Pass. In 1900 the first Cascade Tunnel, 2.63 miles long, provided relief from the switchbacks and the 4 percent grades of the temporary line and lowered the summit of the line from 4,068 feet to 3,383 feet.

The tunnel was electrified with a 2-wire, 3-phase system in 1909. The electrification was replaced with a more conventional system in 1927 as a prelude to the opening of the 7.79-mile

The 69-inch drivers of Great Northern class O-8 Mikado 3381 have a freight train moving at a mile a minute across the prairie near Benson, Minnesota. Great Northern and the Pennsylvania Railroad were the only railroads in the U. S. that favored the Belpaire boiler on their steam locomotives. Photo by Frank A. King.

second Cascade Tunnel in 1929. The new tunnel, the longest in the Western Hemisphere, lowered the maximum elevation of the line to 2,881 feet and eliminated 8 miles of snowsheds and more than 5 complete circles of curvature. The tunnel project included other line relocations in the area and the extension of the electrified portion of the line east to Wenatchee and west to Skykomish.

Lines in Canada

Even before completion of the route from St. Paul, the Great Northern opened a line along the shore of Puget Sound between Seattle and Vancouver, British Columbia, in 1891. In the years that followed, Hill pushed a number of lines north across the international boundary into the mining area of southern British Columbia in a running battle with Canadian Pacific. In 1912 GN traded its line along the Fraser River east of Vancouver to Canadian Northern for trackage rights into Winnipeg.

GN gradually withdrew from British Columbia after Hill's death. In 1909 the Manitoba Great Northern Railway purchased most of the property of the Midland Railway of Manitoba (lines from the U. S. border to Portage la Prairie and to Morden), leaving the Midland, which was jointly controlled by GN and NP, with terminal properties in Winnipeg. The Manitoba Great Northern disposed of its rail lines in 1927. They were later abandoned.

Later expansion

In 1907 the Great Northern purchased the properties and assets of the St. Paul, Minneapolis & Manitoba and of a number of its proprietary companies, such as the Eastern Railway of Minnesota and the Montana Central. In 1928 there was another spate of such activity. The result was that GN was a large railroad with very few subsidiaries, unlike, for example, the Southern Railway.

Among the major branches and lines added to the system were

• the Surrey Cutoff between Fargo and Minot, N. Dak., shortening the route between St. Paul and Seattle by about 50 miles, opened in 1912
• an interurban system, the Spokane, Coeur d'Alene & Palouse, east and south from Spokane (absorbed by GN in 1943)
• an extension of the Oregon Trunk from Bend, Ore., south to a connection with the Western Pacific at Bieber, California, completed in 1931 (from Chemult to Klamath Falls, Ore., on Southern Pacific rails).

The Great Northern changed little in the modern era—from the 1920s through the 1960s—apart from the industry-wide change from steam to diesel. A ventilating system allowed dieselization of the Cascade Tunnel in 1956 and eliminated the electrification. In November 1970 the

Cascade Tunnel acquired a rival, the Flathead Tunnel, shorter by only 70 yards, as part of a line relocation necessitated by construction of a dam at Libby, Mont. Most of the construction was done by GN; only the last portion and the actual opening of the tunnel were done by Burlington Northern.

The 69-year merger

On July 1, 1901, the Great Northern and the Northern Pacific jointly purchased more than 97 percent of the stock of the Chicago, Burlington & Quincy to ensure a connection between St. Paul and Chicago. GN and NP backed construction of the Spokane, Portland & Seattle Railway from Spokane, Wash., to Portland, Ore. SP&S in turn sponsored the construction of the Oregon Trunk Railway from Wishram, Wash., on the Columbia River, south to Bend, Ore. GN got another route to Portland by acquiring trackage rights on Northern Pacific from Seattle.

Hill soon acquired control of Northern Pacific with the intent of merging GN, NP, Burlington, and SP&S into a single railroad. As a start, he formed Northern Securities as a holding company, but the Interstate Commerce Commission quickly ruled against such a merger.

In 1927 the Great Northern Pacific Railway was incorporated to merge GN and NP and lease SP&S and the Burlington. The ICC approved the merger upon the condition that GN and NP divest themselves of the Burlington—a condition the two Northerns were unwilling to meet. More than four decades passed before the merger went through on March 2, 1970—with the Burlington included and indeed half the name of the merged company.

	1929	1969
Miles of railroad operated:	8,368	8,274
Number of locomotives:	1,164	609
Number of passenger cars:	946	415
Number of freight cars:	55,777	36,300
Number of company service cars:	2,766	2,268

Location of headquarters: St. Paul, Minnesota

Reporting marks: GN

Notable named passenger trains: *Empire Builder* (Chicago to Seattle and Portland; operated east of St. Paul by the Chicago, Burlington & Quincy, and between Spokane and Portland by the Spokane, Portland & Seattle)

Historical and technical society: Great Northern Railway Historical Society, c/o Connie Hoffman, 1781 Griffith, Berkley, MI 48072; http://www.gnrhs.org/

Subsidiaries and affiliated railroads, 1969:

Spokane, Portland & Seattle (50%, jointly with Northern Pacific)

Chicago, Burlington & Quincy (48.59%)

Oregon, California & Eastern (50%, jointly with Southern Pacific)

Successors:

Burlington Northern

Burlington Northern & Santa Fe

Portions still operated: Only these major lines have been abandoned: Sioux Falls—Yankton, S. Dak.; Havre—Great Falls, Mont.; Basin—Butte, Mont.; Eureka—Ripley, Mont. (replaced by the Flathead Tunnel line); and most of the former Spokane, Coeur d'Alene & Palouse system. Parts of the secondary line from Minneapolis through St. Cloud and Alexandria to Fargo have been abandoned or sold. The remainder of the GN, except for short portions of a few branches, is operated by Burlington Northern & Santa Fe.

Dakota Rail: Wayzata—Hutchinson, Minn.

Otter Tail Valley: Fergus Falls—Moorhead, Minn.

Red River Valley & Westeren: Wahpeton—Casselton, N. D.

Green Bay & Western Railroad
Fox River Valley Railroad

GREEN BAY ROUTE

The Green Bay & Lake Pepin Railway was chartered in 1866 to build west from Green Bay, Wisconsin, to the Mississippi River. The road was to provide a Lake Michigan port for Minnesota's wheat and serve the growing lumber industry of northern Wisconsin. The first spike was driven in 1871, and the road reached the Mississippi at East Winona, Wis., in 1873. After several name changes and a period of control by the Lackawanna Iron & Coal Co., an affiliate of the Delaware, Lackawanna & Western, the road was reorganized as the Green Bay & Western Railway in 1896.

The railroad's eastern extension to Lake Michigan was incorporated in 1890 as the Kewaunee, Green Bay & Western Railroad, and opened in 1891. At Kewaunee it connected with the carferries that crossed Lake Michigan to Frankfort and Ludington, Mich. The KGB&W came under GB&W control in 1897. GB&W merged it on January 1, 1969, but one of the curiosities of the diesel era was that one of GB&W's Alco FA-1s was lettered for the KGB&W.

On November 30, 1990, a Green Bay & Western local freight pulled by Alco C424 No. 311 rolls through Luxemburg, Wisconsin, with two cars of grain for the Co-op at Kewaunee. Car ferry service to Kewaunee ended two weeks previously. Photo by Stanley H. Mailer.

Another subsidiary, the Ahnapee & Western branched off the KGB&W at Casco Junction and ran 33 miles northeast to Sturgeon Bay. GB&W sold the short line in 1947.

The importance of GB&W's bridge traffic diminished in the late 1970s—Ann Arbor's ferries from Frankfort ceased running in 1982, and Chesapeake & Ohio was down to a single Ludington–Kewaunee run. At the same time the importance of Wisconsin's paper industry increased to the point that Burlington Northern expressed interest in acquiring the GB&W.

The Itel Corporation acquired the Green Bay & Western in 1977 primarily as a place to store its box car fleet—traffic was down and the supply of cars was far in excess of demand.

Fox River Valley

In the downsizing of the late 1980s, the Chicago & North Western sought to sell its lines between Milwaukee and Green Bay—more specifically, from Granville, in the northwest corner of the city of Milwaukee, north through Fond du Lac and Appleton to Green Bay; from Cleveland, north of Sheboygan, to Duck Creek (a junction on the north side of Green Bay); and from Kaukauna South to New London. The Itel Corporation purchased the lines to form the Fox River Valley Railroad. It began operation December 9, 1988.

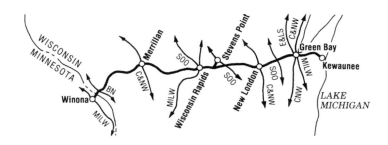

The new railroad was unable to earn enough money to pay the interest on the purchase price, and the business surge as the 1990s began meant Itel no longer needed a place to store its box cars.

Purchase by Wisconsin Central

In late 1991 Itel placed the GB&W and the Fox River Valley Railroad under the same management and approached Wisconsin Central about buying the two railroads. In January 1992 WC announced it was forming a subsidiary, Fox Valley & Western Ltd., to acquire those railroads. There were loud protests from the Chicago & North Western (which had sold those lines), Soo Line (which had sold most of its Wisconsin routes to WC), and from the labor unions. The Interstate Commerce Commission refuse to specify the traffic conditions C&NW and Soo requested but imposed conditions protecting the jobs of the employees affected. The ICC made its final ruling on August 27, 1993, and Wisconsin Central took possession of the two roads that day.

Green Bay & Western   1929   1992
Miles of railroad operated: 234   254
Number of locomotives: 31   25
Number of passenger cars: 32
Number of freight cars: 888   1,687
Number of company service cars: 42
Reporting marks: GBW
Location of headquarters: Green Bay, Wisconsin
Portions still operated: Wisconsin Central Ltd.: Green Bay–Scandinavia; Plover–East Winona, Wis. (GB&W's Mississippi River bridge at Winona burned in 1989)

Kewaunee, Green Bay & Western   1929   1968
Miles of railroad operated: 36   35
Number of locomotives: 12   4
Number of passenger cars: 9
Number of freight cars: 268   32
Reporting marks: KGBW
Location of headquarters: Green Bay, Wisconsin
Portions still operated: Wisconsin Central Ltd.: Green Bay–Kewaunee

Fox River Valley   1988   1992
Miles of railroad operated: 36   208
Number of locomotives: 12   36
Number of freight cars: 268   62
Reporting marks: FRVR
Location of headquarters: Green Bay, Wisconsin
Portions still operated: Wisconsin Central Ltd.: Granville–Green Bay; Cleveland, Wis.–Francis Creek; Denmark–Green Bay; Kaukauna–Appleton
Recommended reading:
Green Bay & Western, by Stan Mailer, published in 1989 by Hundman Publishing Inc., 5115 Monticello Drive, Edmonds, WA 98020 (ISBN 0-945434-01-4)
Wisconsin Central, by Otto P. Dobnick and Steve Glischinski, published in 1997 by Kalmbach Publishing Co. (ISBN 0-89024-562-2)
Successors: Wisconsin Central Ltd.

Gulf, Mobile & Northern Railroad

In 1890 the Mobile, Jackson & Kansas City Railroad was chartered to tap the longleaf-pine areas of southern Mississippi. In 1898 it opened the first 50 miles of line northwest from Mobile, Alabama, to the new town of Merrill, Miss., named for one of the promoters of the railroad, and in 1902 reached Hattiesburg, Miss.

New promoters bought the line and also purchased the 62-mile narrow gauge Gulf & Chicago between Middleton, Tennessee, and Pontotoc, Miss., then proceeded to fill in the 240 miles between the two railroads. The MJ&KC entered receivership in 1906 shortly after construction was completed; it emerged in 1909 as the New Orleans, Mobile & Chicago Railroad. In 1911 the Louisville & Nashville and the Frisco assumed joint control of the NOM&C with the thought of using the road as an entrance to New Orleans. In 1913 the railroad's finances collapsed again.

The Gulf, Mobile & Northern Railroad began operation on January 1, 1917, as a reorganization of the New Orleans, Mobile & Chicago. President of the road was Isaac B. Tigrett, a banker in Jackson, Tenn. One of the first items of business was to extend the road north 40 miles from Middleton, Tenn., to Jackson and connections with Illinois Central and Nashville, Chattanooga & St. Louis.

In 1926 GM&N began operating freight trains from Jackson, Tenn., north to Paducah,

Gulf, Mobile & Northern standardized on the 2-10-0 for freight power. In 1934 Decapods made up one-third of its steam roster. The arched, browlike device on the front of 261's smokebox is a Coffin feedwater heater. Photo by C. W. Witbeck.

Kentucky, on trackage rights over NC&StL. At Paducah GM&N connected with the Chicago, Burlington & Quincy, with which it made a preferential traffic agreement, forming a Chicago to Gulf route that did not require a competing road, such as Illinois Central, to short-haul itself in order to give traffic to GM&N. (IC had considered GM&N a friendly connection until GM&N extended itself to Jackson, Tenn.)

In 1928 GM&N merged with the 49-mile

Birmingham & Northwestern, which ran from Jackson, Tenn., northwest to Dyersburg, Tenn. It shared a president—Tigrett—with the smaller road and had controlled it since 1924. In 1929 GM&N merged with the Meridian & Memphis (from Union, Miss., east to Meridian) and the Jackson & Eastern (from Union west to Jackson, Miss.). Over the years the two Jacksons on GM&N's map, both of them important cities, must have created untold confusion for GM&N's ticket agents, traffic representatives, and historians. On December 30, 1929, GM&N acquired control of New Orleans Great Northern, whose line ran from Jackson, Miss., to New Orleans, and on July 1, 1933, GM&N leased the NOGN.

GM&N got through the Depression by reducing wages, services, and maintenance, but subsidiary New Orleans Great Northern defaulted on bond interest and had to reorganize. In 1935 GM&N upgraded its through passenger service with the *Rebel* trains, the first streamliners in the South. The *Rebels* and the various types of rail motor cars GM&N had been using gave the road an all-motorized passenger service. In 1936 GM&N organized Gulf Transport, a bus and truck subsidiary to supplement rail service and replace money-losing local passenger trains; GM&N had been operating highway services for several years under its own banner.

On June 1, 1933, GM&N moved its Jackson, Tenn.–Paducah freight trains from the NC&StL to Illinois Central rails on a route 34 miles shorter. In 1934 the road began to study acquisition of bankrupt Mobile & Ohio, whose line paralleled GM&N from Mobile to Jackson, Tenn., and continued north from Jackson to St. Louis. A line to St. Louis would bypass the need

for operating on the rails of competitor Illinois Central and would afford connections with railroads to the east, north, and west. Ralph Budd (who represented Burlington's stock interest, nearly 30 percent, on GM&N's board of directors) objected, because Burlington would lose its exclusive connection with GM&N and also collect a smaller portion of the freight revenue because its mileage on a through move would be less. M&O acquisition was given added impetus in 1936 when problems arose in connection

with GM&N crews operating over IC rails. On June 30, 1938, a decree was rendered—GM&N trains would have to use IC crews within 20 days. GM&N quickly executed a traffic agreement with Mobile & Ohio and ceased operating to Paducah.

Despite the objections of the Burlington and the Illinois Central—Illinois Central said that one day it would buy GM&N and M&O—the merger of Gulf, Mobile & Northern and Mobile & Ohio took place on September 13, 1940.

	1929	1940
Miles of railroad operated:	734	827
Number of locomotives:	77	55
Number of passenger cars:	39	31
Number of freight cars:	1,573	
Number of company service cars:	144	
Number of freight and company service cars:		1,647

Location of headquarters: Mobile, Alabama

Reporting marks: GM&N

Notable named passenger trains: *Rebel* (Jackson, Tenn.–Jackson, Miss.–New Orleans)

Historical and technical society: Gulf, Mobile & Ohio Historical Society, P. O. Box 2457, Joliet, IL 60434-2457; http://www.tfs.net/~jashaw/rhs/gmo.html

Recommended reading: *The Gulf, Mobile and Ohio,* by James Hutton Lemly, published in 1953 by Richard D. Irwin, Inc., Homewood, IL 60430

Subsidiaries and affiliated railroads, 1939:
Mississippi Export (25%)
New Orleans Great Northern (29%)

Predecessor railroads in this book: New Orleans Great Northern

Successors:
Gulf, Mobile & Ohio
Illinois Central Gulf

Portions still operated:
Illinois Central: Slidell, La.—Wanilla, Miss.;
Slidell—Covington, La.; Beaumont, Miss.—Mobile, Ala.
Kansas City Southern: Laurel—Ackerman, Miss.;
Woodland, Miss.—Middleton, Tenn.
Tennken Railroad: Dyersburg, Tenn.—Hickman, Ky.

Map: See page 188

Gulf, Mobile & Ohio Railroad

 The Gulf, Mobile & Ohio was incorporated in Mississippi on November 10, 1938, to acquire the properties of the Mobile & Ohio and the Gulf, Mobile & Northern. It acquired the M&O through foreclosure sale on August 1, 1940, and was consolidated with the GM&N on September 13, 1940. The new railroad extended from New Orleans, Louisiana, and Mobile and Montgomery, Alabama, north to St. Louis.

During World War II GM&O trimmed a few branches from its system, consolidated shop facilities, and otherwise tightened up the organization. In 1944 the road began to investigate acquiring the bankrupt Alton Railroad, which extended from St. Louis to Chicago and from Springfield, Illinois, west to Kansas City. On May 31, 1947, GM&O merged the Alton and became a Great Lakes-to-Gulf carrier.

Three GP30s and a GP35 lead a freight south through Scooba, Mississippi. GM&O's GP30s and 35s were distinctive on several counts: They rode on the trucks of traded-in Alco FAs, they wore an EMD-designed black and white paint scheme on a road traditionally associated with red and maroon liveries, and they seldom worked north of St. Louis before the ICG merger. Photo by J. Parker Lamb.

All lines north of St. Louis are former Alton lines. South of St. Louis, solid lines indicate former Gulf, Mobile & Northern routes, and dashed lines indicate former Mobile & Ohio routes.

At first GM&O planned to sell the Kansas City line, which was an east-west appendage to an otherwise north-south system. In 1948 GM&O, the Burlington, and the Santa Fe formulated a plan that would result in the sale of the Kansas City line to the Burlington, Santa Fe's use of that line and the connecting Burlington line at Mexico, Missouri, for access to St. Louis, and Burlington trackage rights over Santa Fe into Kansas City from the northeast. Several railroads serving St. Louis protested Santa Fe's part in the plan. As it fell out, Burlington acquired trackage rights over GM&O between Mexico and Kansas City and in 1952 opened 71 miles of new line across northern Missouri to shorten its own Chicago to Kansas City route. Santa Fe never gained access to St. Louis.

In 1949 and 1950 GM&O acquired the properties of three roads the Alton had leased, the Kansas City, St. Louis & Chicago Railroad; the Louisiana & Missouri River Railroad; and the Joliet & Chicago Railroad. GM&O inherited Mobile & Ohio's trackage rights on Southern and Illinois Central track between Memphis, Corinth, Miss., and Birmingham. In 1952 GM&O acquired trackage rights over Louisville & Nashville from Tuscaloosa to Birmingham and ceased use of the Corinth–Birmingham route.

GM&O was one of the first major railroads to dieselize completely. Its last steam operation was on October 7, 1949. By 1947 GM&O's passenger service south of St. Louis consisted of the *Rebel* trains, the first streamliners in the South, between St. Louis and New Orleans and the St. Louis–Mobile *Gulf Coast Rebel*. In addition subsidiary Gulf Transport operated an extensive bus system between St. Louis and the Gulf Coast. Rail passenger service to New Orleans ended in 1954, and the St. Louis–Mobile train was discontinued in 1958.

North of St. Louis GM&O took over an intensive passenger service from the Alton: seven trains daily between Chicago and St. Louis, a pair of St. Louis–Kansas City trains operated jointly with the Burlington, and a few motor-train locals and mixed trains on branches. The Bloomington, Ill.–Kansas City motor train run endured until 1960.

When Amtrak took over the nation's passenger trains, GM&O was operating three Chicago–St. Louis trains and a Chicago–Joliet commuter train. Amtrak continued the operation of the two daytime Chicago–St. Louis trains. The Chicago–Joliet train survived the startup of Amtrak and the ICG merger. Metra now operates two Chicago–Joliet commuter trains on the former GM&O route.

GM&O merged with Illinois Central on August 10, 1972, forming the Illinois Central Gulf Railroad. Successive events are properly part of ICG's history, but a summary here will not be amiss. ICG was trying hard to be a north-south railroad and realized it had eight east-west routes. In the 1980s it spun off those routes—indeed, spun off two-thirds of its mileage, including most of the former Gulf, Mobile & Ohio.

On July 10, 1985, Gulf & Mississippi purchased most of the former GM&O routes in Alabama, Mississippi, and Louisiana. On April 14, 1988, a subsidiary of MidSouth Rail (which had purchased ICG's Meridian–Shreveport route) bought the Gulf & Mississippi. Kansas City Southern acquired MidSouth in 1993. (For a few months in 1994, Illinois Central was intent on purchasing KCS, which would have started the whole cycle over again.)

The Chicago, Missouri & Western bought the Joliet–St. Louis and Springfield–Kansas City routes on April 28, 1987, essentially recreating the Alton Railroad. CM&W declared bankruptcy less than a year later.

On September 30, 1989, Southern Pacific purchased the Joliet–East St. Louis route from the CM&W, extending its Cotton Belt subsidiary to Chicago. The new operation was titled SPCSL (for Southern Pacific Chicago St. Louis). Union Pacific acquired the line as part of its merger of Southern Pacific.

On January 9, 1990, Gateway Western, an affiliate of the Santa Fe, purchased the Springfield–Kansas City and Godfrey–Roodhouse lines from CM&W. On May 5, 1997, Gateway Western became a subsidiary of the expanding Kansas City Southern.

	1929	1971
Miles of railroad operated:	1,808	2,734
Number of locomotives:	180	258
Number of passenger cars:	96	92
Number of freight and company service cars:	6,255	
Number of freight cars:		12,699

Location of headquarters: Mobile, Ala.

Reporting marks: GM&O

Notable named passenger trains: *Rebel* (Jackson, Tenn.–New Orleans; later St. Louis–New Orleans); *Abraham Lincoln, Ann Rutledge, Alton Limited* (Chicago–St. Louis)

Historical and technical society: Gulf, Mobile & Ohio Historical Society, P. O. Box 2457, Joliet, IL 60434-2457; http://www.tfs.net/~jashaw/rhs/gmo.html

Recommended reading:

The Gulf, Mobile and Ohio, by James Hutton Lemly, published in 1953 by Richard D. Irwin, Inc., Homewood, IL 60430

GM&O North, by Robert P. Olmsted, published in 1976 by Robert P. Olmsted

Subsidiaries and affiliated railroads, 1971:

New Orleans Great Northern (98.17%)

Mississippi Export (25.5%)

Predecessor railroads in this book:

Alton

Gulf, Mobile & Northern

Mobile & Ohio

New Orleans Great Northern

Successors:

Illinois Central Gulf

Illinois Central

Portions still operated:

Gateway Western: Springfield, Ill.–Kansas City; Godfrey–Roodhouse, Ill.; Murrayville–Jacksonville, Ill.; Mexico–Fulton, Mo.

Illinois Central: Jackson, Tenn.–Corinth, Miss.; Slidell, La.–Wanilla, Miss.; Slidell–Covington, La.; Beaumont, Miss.–Mobile, Ala.

Kansas City Southern: Corinth, Miss.–Mobile, Ala.; West Point, Miss.–Tuscaloosa, Ala.; Laurel–Ackerman, Miss.; Woodland, Miss.–Middleton, Tenn.

Norfolk Southern: Tuscaloosa–Montgomery, Ala.

Tennken Railroad: Dyersburg, Tenn.–Hickman, Ky.

Union Pacific: Chicago–East St. Louis

West Tennessee Railroad: Lawrence–Kenton, Tenn.

Hocking Valley Railway

The Columbus & Hocking Valley Railroad built a line from Columbus, Ohio, 50 miles southeast to Logan between 1869 and 1871. The lower half of the route followed the Hocking River. The line was extended first northwest, then southeast into the coalfields. In 1872 the Columbus & Toledo Railroad was incorporated by C&HV interests. Its line opened from Columbus to Marion, Ohio, on October 15, 1876, and reached Toledo on January 10, 1877. The Ohio & West Virginia Railway opened from Logan to Gallipolis, on the Ohio River, on October 15, 1880, and at the beginning of 1881 opened an extension from Gallipolis north along the river to Pomeroy. The three railroads were consolidated on August 20, 1881, as the Columbus, Hocking Valley & Toledo Railway.

The Hocking Valley Railway was chartered on February 25, 1899, to take over the Columbus, Hocking Valley & Toledo and the Hocking Coal & Railroad Co. The new company conveyed the coal properties to a subsidiary, the Buckeye Coal & Railway Co. The Hocking Valley came to control the Kanawha & Michigan Railway, which had a line from Charleston, W. Va., northwest through Gallipolis and Athens to Columbus, more or less parallel to its own lines, and the Toledo & Ohio Central, which had a line from Columbus to Toledo.

A Chesapeake & Ohio passenger train powered by a former Hocking Valley Ten-Wheeler, No. 98, meets a New York Central freight at Athens, Ohio. Photo by B. F. Cutler.

In June 1903 a majority block of Hocking Valley stock was acquired by five railroads: Pittsburgh, Cincinnati, Chicago & St. Louis (Pennsylvania Railroad), Baltimore & Ohio, Chesapeake & Ohio, Lake Shore & Michigan Southern (New York Central), and Erie. The PCC&StL acquired one-third of the stock and the other roads, one-sixth each.

In March 1910 Chesapeake & Ohio bought out the other five railroads and acquired full control of the Hocking Valley. About that same time the C&O and the LS&MS acquired control of the Kanawha & Michigan and LS&MS purchased nearly all the stock of the Toledo & Ohio Central. The Hocking Valley and the Kanawha & Michigan gave the C&O a good route to the Midwest for coal from the West Virginia coalfields.

In 1914 a U. S. district court, sniffing anti-trust problems in the air, ordered the C&O to divest itself of its interest in the Kanawha & Michigan, creating a gap between the Hocking Valley and the rest of the C&O system. The C&O moved quickly. In May of that year the C&O formed the Chesapeake & Ohio Northern Railway to build from Limeville, Kentucky, north up the valley of the Scioto River to a connection with the Norfolk & Western at Waverly. At the same C&O acquired trackage rights on the N&W to Columbus.

Soon C&O ran into limitations on the N&W: the number of trains it could run and the grades, which were steeper than on C&O's main line. C&O constructed the Chesapeake & Hocking Valley Railway north from Greggs, near Waverly, to Valley Crossing in Columbus. C&O leased the C&HV in 1926 and merged it and the Hocking Valley in 1930.

The effect of constructing the C&ON and the C&HV was to remove through traffic from the portion of the Hocking Valley southeast of Columbus. In the mid-1970s C&O began to abandon that line bit by bit from the south end.

	1929
Miles of railroad operated:	349
Number of locomotives:	119
Number of passenger cars:	56
Number of freight cars:	6,079
Number of company service cars:	273

Location of headquarters: Columbus, Ohio
Reporting marks: HV
Historical and technical society: Chesapeake & Ohio Historical Society, P. O. Box 79, Clifton Forge, VA 24422; http://cohs.marshall.edu/
Recommended reading: *Chessie's Road* (second edition), by Charles W. Turner, Thomas W. Dixon, Jr., and Eugene L. Huddleston, published in 1986 by the Chesapeake & Ohio Historical Society
Successors: Chesapeake & Ohio
Portions still operated:
CSX Transportation: Toledo–Columbus
Hocking Valley Scenic Railway: Logan–Nelsonville
Indiana & Ohio Central: Valley Crossing (Columbus)–Logan

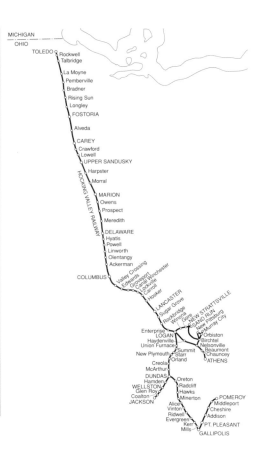

Hoosac Tunnel & Wilmington Railroad

The Deerfield River Railroad was chartered in Vermont in 1884; on July 4, 1885, it celebrated the opening of 11 miles of 3-foot-gauge track from Readsboro, Vt., south to a junction with the Fitchburg Railroad at the east portal of the Hoosac Tunnel in northwestern Massachusetts. In 1886 the proprietors of the railroad incorporated the Hoosac Tunnel & Wilmington Railroad in Massachusetts; it acquired the Massachusetts portion of the line and leased the Vermont part, with which it was consolidated in 1892. By then the line had been extended north from Readsboro to Wilmington, another 13 miles. The entire line was converted to standard gauge in 1913.

The New England Power Company purchased the road in 1922 and began construction of a dam across the Deerfield River that required relocation of the north end of the line—after an initial proposal by the power company to substitute a carferry on the lake that the dam would create. The power company sold the railroad to local interests in 1926.

The world's first organized railroad fan trip was held on the HT&W. Members of the Railroad Enthusiasts chartered a train to ride the length of the line on Sunday, August 26, 1934. They were the first rail passengers on the line since floods in 1927 had caused the substitution of bus service for the passenger trains.

Hoosac Tunnel & Wilmington No. 5 switches the Boston & Maine interchange track at Hoosac Tunnel, Massachusetts. The Mogul came to HT&W second-hand from the Washington, Brandywine & Point Lookout in 1938. Photo by R. E. Tobey.

After more floods in early 1936 the railroad was sold to the H. E. Salzberg Co.; ownership soon passed to Salzberg's son-in-law, Samuel M. Pinsly. He abandoned the line north of Readsboro but thought the remainder could be operated profitably. A hurricane did substantial damage to the HT&W in September 1938, but Pinsly rebuilt the line. In 1941 the Hoosac Tunnel & Wilmington made its first profit in 15 years, and it continued to be a profit maker. Pinsly dieselized the line in 1949.

Business fell off in the mid-1950s and profits

turned to deficits. In the late 1950s the HT&W received a new customer in the form of a nuclear power plant at Monroe Bridge. HT&W hauled in much of the material for construction of the plant. Another power plant, the Bear Swamp Project, would have required extensive relocation of the HT&W and resulted instead in abandonment on October 13, 1971.

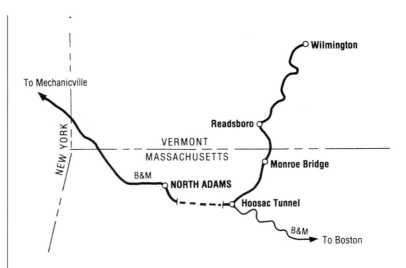

	1929	1970
Miles of railroad operated:	24	11
Number of locomotives:	3	2
Number of passenger cars:	5	
Number of freight cars:	25	4

Location of headquarters: Wilmington, Vermont, until 1937; then Readsboro, Vermont

Recommended reading: *Hoot Toot & Whistle*, by Bernard R. Carman, published in 1963 by the Stephen Greene Press, Brattleboro, VT 05301

Huntingdon & Broad Top Mountain Railroad & Coal Company

The Huntingdon & Broad Top Mountain was incorporated in 1852 to build a railroad into the coalfields along the west side of Broad Top Mountain south of Huntingdon, Pennsylvania. (The Pennsylvania Railroad had reached Huntingdon from Harrisburg two years before.) The first portion of the line opened that same year, and in 1864 the company was consolidated with the Bedford Railroad, which continued the line southward to Mount Dallas. From there to Bedford, eight miles, the H&BTM operated over Pennsylvania Railroad tracks.

The line was prosperous for many years, but by the end of World War II the road's future, which depended on coal mines, was doubtful. The road had last paid dividends on preferred stock in 1922 and on common stock in 1906. Reorganization began in 1949 but without much success; in December 1953 the Interstate Commerce Commission granted permission for abandonment on March 31, 1954.

Upon the abandonment of the H&BTM, the Everett Railroad was organized to take over the segment of the line from Mt. Dallas through Everett to Tatesville, about four miles. It has since ceased operation.

	1929	1953
Miles of railroad operated:	74	64
Number of locomotives:	15	6
Number of passenger cars:	9	
Number of freight cars:	659	70
Number of company service cars:	16	14
Location of headquarters: Philadelphia, Pennsylvania		
Reporting marks: H&BT		
Map: See page 160		

Consolidation No. 37 leads Huntingdon & Broad Top Mountain train 3, consisting of a combine (a depowered gas-electric car) and a milk car, out of Bedford, Pennsylvania. Photo by Philip R. Hastings.

Illinois Central Railroad
Illinois Central Gulf Railroad

Illinois Central was alive and doing business at the same old stand when this book was in preparation—that last qualifier is necessary because the railroad industry changes fast. What is it doing in a book about former railroads? In the past 25 years or so it has gone through more changes than most railroads, and a lot of what used to be Illinois Central isn't any more, and some of what was IC, then wasn't, is again. (Illinois Central Gulf is gone. There's no need to justify ICG's presence in the book.)

In the 1940s, '50s, and '60s the Illinois Central was as conservative and traditional a railroad as you could find. It stayed with steam for freight service longer than most railroads, it carried great quantities of coal from the coalfields of southern Illinois, and it ran fast merchandise freight trains up and down the Mississippi Valley. Its passenger operations included an intense electrified commuter service running south from Chicago and glossy brown-and-orange streamliners. During the passenger-train decline of the 1960s many considered IC's Chicago–New

A pair of SD20s, products of the diesel rebuilding program of ICG's Paducah Shop, leads a long train of empty coal cars south through Chebanse, Illinois, on ICG's main line in July 1982. Photo by R. B. Olson.

195

Orleans *Panama Limited* to be the best train in the country.

About 1970 something happened. To summarize in 23 words: Illinois Central got married, put on weight, had a bunch of kids, got divorced,

slimmed way down, and took its old name back. IC merged the parallel Gulf, Mobile & Ohio to become Illinois Central Gulf and bought a few short lines. Then it sold off lines (including nearly all the GM&O) to form shortline and regional railroads, shrinking to about 40 percent of its pre-1970 size. More recently it has bought back some of those lines.

Early history

The Illinois Central Railroad was chartered in 1851 to build a line from Cairo, at the southern tip of Illinois—the confluence of the Ohio and Mississippi rivers—to Galena, in the extreme northwestern corner of the state, with a branch to Chicago. A previous undertaking had resulted in a few miles of grading north of Cairo but nothing else.

The IC was aided, however, by a land-grant act signed by President Millard Fillmore in 1850. Finished in 1856, the line was a Y-shaped railroad with its junction just north of Centralia (named for the railroad). The IC gave Chicago an outlet to the Mississippi for north-south traffic, and the railroad operated a steamboat line between Cairo and New Orleans.

On the southern front, IC entered into a traffic agreement with the New Orleans, Jackson & Great Northern Railroad and the Mississippi Central Railway. The former had been opened in 1858 from New Orleans north through Jackson, Mississippi, to Canton, Miss.; the latter was completed in 1860 from Canton north to Jackson, Tennessee. IC completed its own line between Jackson, Tenn., and Cairo in 1873. (Traffic had previously used the Mobile & Ohio Rail Road between Jackson and Columbus, Kentucky, and

a riverboat between Columbus and Cairo.) In 1874 IC, the principal bondholder of the NOJ&GN and the Mississippi Central, took them over. The lines south of Cairo were built to the 5-foot track gauge that was standard in the South, and remained at that gauge until July 29, 1881.

In the 1870s railroads began to penetrate the fertile Yazoo Delta along the western edge of the state of Mississippi. IC's entry was the Yazoo & Mississippi Valley Railroad, incorporated in 1882 to build a railroad westward from Jackson, Miss. Meanwhile, a rival, the Louisville, New Orleans & Texas Railway, was under construction between Memphis and New Orleans via Vicksburg and Baton Rouge, west of IC's main line. That company obtained the backing of C. P. Huntington, who saw the route as a connection between his Southern Pacific at New Orleans and his Chesapeake, Ohio & Southwestern at Memphis. Huntington's forces completed the LNO&T in 1884, then purchased the Mississippi & Tennessee Railroad, whose line from Memphis to Grenada, Miss., funneled traffic to IC.

Saber-rattling ensued—in the form of canceled traffic agreements—but Huntington's empire was in financial trouble. IC purchased the LNO&T and the Mississippi & Tennessee and consolidated them with the Yazoo & Mississippi Valley. The acquisition increased IC's mileage by 28 percent and greatly expanded IC's presence in the South.

IC's southern lines were connected by rail to the northern part of the system in 1889 with the completion of the Ohio River bridge at Cairo. In 1893 IC purchased the Chesapeake, Ohio & Southwestern (Louisville to Memphis) and in 1895 built a line into St. Louis from the southeast.

Later expansion

IC's original line had been extended west of Galena to the Mississippi River, then across Iowa by leasing the Dubuque & Sioux City Railroad, which reached Sioux City in 1870. In the late 1880s under the leadership of E. H. Harriman the road undertook a westward expansion program. The Chicago, Madison & Northern was incorporated in 1886 to build from Chicago to a connection with the Centralia–Galena line at Freeport, Ill., then north to Madison and Dodgeville, Wisconsin. IC also constructed branches to Cedar Rapids, Iowa; Sioux Falls, South Dakota; and Omaha, Nebraska.

In 1906 the IC completed a line from Effingham, Ill., to Indianapolis, partly through new construction and partly through acquisition of narrow gauge lines. In 1908 it assembled a route from Fulton, Kentucky, to Birmingham, Alabama, largely on trackage rights, and in 1909 it acquired control of the Central of Georgia. In 1926 IC electrified its suburban line along the Chicago lakefront, and in 1928 it constructed a cutoff line between Edgewood, Ill., and Fulton, Ky., to bypass congestion at Cairo.

After World War II, IC began to simplify its corporate structure, absorbing the Yazoo & Mississippi Valley and the Gulf & Ship Island, purchasing the Chicago, St. Louis & New Orleans, and acquiring control of the Alabama & Vicksburg and Vicksburg, Shreveport & Pacific, which had been leased by the Y&MV. In the 1950s it purchased several short lines: Waterloo, Cedar Falls & Northern (jointly with the Rock Island through a subsidiary, the Waterloo Railroad); Tremont & Gulf; Peabody Short Line; Louisiana Midland; and the west end of the Tennessee Central.

Illinois Central Gulf

The Illinois Central and the Gulf, Mobile & Ohio railroads merged on August 10, 1972, to create the Illinois Central Gulf Railroad, a wholly owned subsidiary of Illinois Central Industries. At the same time ICG acquired three short lines, the Columbus & Greenville, the Bonhomie & Hattiesburg Southern, and the Fernwood, Columbia & Gulf.

The north-south lines of ICG's map resembled an hourglass. Driving across Mississippi and Illinois from east to west you could encounter as many as eight ICG lines.

The former IC system converged at Fulton, Kentucky, just north of the Tennessee line, and the former GM&O line was less than 10 miles west of Fulton at Cayce. In addition to the north-south lines, ICG had eight routes that ran generally east and west:
- Chicago to Omaha, Nebraska, and Sioux City, Iowa (ex-IC)
- Springfield, Ill., to Kansas City, Missouri (ex-GM&O)
- Indianapolis to Effingham, Ill. (ex-IC)
- Louisville to Paducah, Ky. (ex-IC)
- Birmingham, Alabama, through Corinth, Miss., to Memphis, Tenn. (ex-IC, mostly trackage rights on Southern and Frisco from Birmingham to Corinth, and ex-GM&O trackage rights on Southern from Corinth to Memphis)
- Montgomery, Ala., to Greenville, Miss. (ex-GM&O east of Columbus Miss., and ex-Columbus & Greenville west of there)
- Meridian, Miss., to Shreveport, Louisiana (ex-IC; previously Alabama & Vicksburg and Vicksburg, Shreveport & Pacific)
- Mobile, Ala., to Natchez, Miss. (a combination of former GM&O, Bonhomie & Hattiesburg Southern, and Mississippi Central lines)

Shrinkage

ICG soon decided that the east-west lines did not fit with a north-south railroad. Its 515-mile Chicago–Council Bluffs route was the longest of the six railroads connecting those cities. GM&O had tried to sell the Kansas City line to the Burlington in 1947, but it remained a long rural branch of the GM&O. The Louisville line, once the Chesapeake, Ohio & Southwestern, ultimately proved more valuable for its route to Memphis from the north than for the line east to Louisville. The Mobile–Natchez route had a ferry, not a bridge, at its west end, and the connecting railroads west of the Mississippi River led mostly to junctions with the Meridian–Shreveport line. In most cases, use of one of ICG's east-west routes as a bridge route required one of the connecting railroads to shorthaul itself (get less than the maximum possible haul and revenue from a carload of freight).

Regional railroads created from ICG lines
- July 10, 1985: Gulf & Mississippi purchased most of the former GM&O routes south of Tennessee.
- December 24, 1985: Chicago, Central & Pacific purchased the line from Chicago to Omaha and its branches to Cedar Rapids and Sioux City, Iowa.
- March 31, 1986: MidSouth Rail Corporation purchased the Meridian–Shreveport line (the former Alabama & Vicksburg and Vicksburg, Shreveport & Pacific) and the Hattiesburg–

Illinois Central	1929	1971
Miles of railroad operated:	6,712	6,760
Number of locomotives:	1,762	766
Number of passenger cars:	2,034	462*
Number of freight cars:	65,035	49,709
Number of company service cars:	2,334	2,161
Illinois Central Gulf	1972	1988
Miles of railroad operated:	9,658	2,900
Number of locomotives:	1,039	548
Number of passenger cars:	371	
Number of freight cars:	59,546	17,476
Number of company service cars:	2,586	1,297

Location of headquarters: Chicago, Illinois

Reporting marks: IC, ICG

Notable named passenger trains: *Panama Limited*, *City of New Orleans* (Chicago–New Orleans), *Green Diamond* (Chicago–St. Louis), *City of Miami* (Chicago-Miami)

Historical and technical society: Illinois Central Historical Society, 14818 Clifton Park Avenue, Midlothian, IL 60445

Predecessor railroads in this book:
Alton
Gulf, Mobile & Northern
*(1970)

Gulf, Mobile & Ohio
Mobile & Ohio
New Orleans Great Northern
Successors: Canadian National
Portions still operated:
Illinois Central: Chicago–Carbondale, Ill.–Memphis–Greenwood, Miss.–New Orleans; Chicago–Joliet, Ill.; Gilman–Springfield–East St. Louis–DuQuoin; Mattoon–Peoria, Ill.; Edgewood, Ill.–Fulton, Ky.; Memphis–Winona, Miss.–Jackson; Jackson, Miss.–Hattiesburg, Miss.; Mobile, Ala.–Natchez, Miss.; Wanilla, Miss.–Slidell, La.; New Orleans–Baton Rouge–Zee, La.; Hammond, La.–Baton Rouge; Chicago–Omaha, and Fort Dodge–Sioux City, Iowa.
Bloomer Line: Colfax–Kempton, Ill.
Cedar River: Waterloo, Iowa–Albert Lea, Minn.
Decatur Junction: Assumption–Decatur–Cisco, Ill.
Gloster Southern: Slaughter, La.–Gloster, Miss.
Great River: Rosedale–Great River Junction, Miss.
Indiana Rail Road: Newton, Ill.–Indianapolis, Ind.
Mississippi Delta: Swan Lake–Jonestown, Miss.
Paducah & Louisville: Paducah–Louisville, Ky.; Dawson–Central City; Kevil–Paducah–Clayburn
Redmont Railway: Corinth, Miss.–Red Bay, Ala.
Wisconsin & Calumet: Freeport, Ill.–Madison, Wis.

Gulfport, Miss., line (the southern half of the former Gulf & Ship Island).
• August 27, 1986: Paducah & Louisville purchased the Louisville–Paducah route plus branches west and south of Paducah, and the Paducah shops.
• April 28, 1987: Chicago, Missouri & Western purchased Joliet–St. Louis and Springfield–Kansas City routes, essentially re-creating the Alton Railroad (CM&W declared bankruptcy on April 1, 1988).
• April 14, 1988: A MidSouth subsidiary,

SouthRail, purchased the Gulf & Mississippi.
• 1988: Fulton, Ky.–Birmingham, Ala., route sold to Norfolk Southern (Southern Railway).
• September 30, 1989: ICC approved Southern Pacific purchase of the Joliet–East St. Louis route from CM&W to operate as Southern Pacific—Chicago–St. Louis Line (SPCSL).
• January 9, 1990: Gateway Western, a Santa Fe affiliate, purchased the Springfield–Kansas City and Godfrey–Roodhouse, Ill., routes from CM&W.

Short lines created from ICG lines
• March 28, 1974: ICG sold the Louisiana Midland, which it had purchased exactly seven years before.
• 1975: ICG sold the Columbus & Greenville, which it had acquired in September 1972.
• February 26, 1980: Chicago, Madison & Northern began operation between Freeport, Ill., and Madison, Wisconsin. The line was later operated by the Central Wisconsin Railroad; Wisconsin & Calumet began operation January 1, 1985.
• March 1982: Tradewater Railway purchased branches from Waverly to Princeton, Ky., and from Blackford to Providence, Ky.
• March 1, 1982: Natchez Trace Railroad began operation on the Grand Junction, Tenn.–Oxford, Miss., route.

• December 5, 1983: Tennken Railroad began operation on the Dyersburg, Tenn.–Hickman, Ky., route.
• August 1984: Gibson County Railroad Authority acquired 43 miles of the former Mobile & Ohio main line from Lawrence, Tenn., near Jackson, north to Kenton. It is operated by the West Tennessee Railroad, an affiliate of the Tennken Railroad.
• September 20, 1984: Cedar Valley Railroad purchased Waterloo, Iowa–Albert Lea, Minnesota, route.
• March 1986: Indiana Hi-Rail Corp. acquired the Henderson, Kentucky–Evansville, Indiana–Browns, Illinois route.
• March 19, 1986: Indiana Rail Road began operation on the Indianapolis line between Indianapolis and Sullivan, Ind.
• 1990: Indiana Railroad purchased the Sullivan, Ind.–Newton, Ill., and Newton-Browns, Ill., routes, and turned the latter over to Indiana Hi-Rail for operation.

IC's slimming down included not only routes but track and rolling stock. More than half its Chicago–New Orleans main line was double track; IC reduced it to single track with a computerized CTC system. IC scrapped its surplus freight cars and sold its excess locomotives. It turned its attention to long-haul business between Chicago and the Gulf of Mexico.

Illinois Central again
On February 29, 1988, the railroad changed its name back to Illinois Central, having divested itself of nearly all the former Gulf, Mobile & Ohio routes it acquired in 1972, when it added "Gulf" to its name. At the end of 1988 the Whitman Corporation (formerly IC Industries) spun off the IC, and in August 1989 control of the railroad was gained by the Prospect Group, which formerly controlled MidSouth Rail Corporation, another ICG spinoff.

In late 1990 Illinois Central made an offer to purchase MidSouth. MidSouth rejected the offer; then as stock prices changed, IC withdrew the offer. Kansas City Southern purchased MidSouth (plus SouthRail and MidLouisiana Rail) in 1993. The next year IC proposed merger with Kansas City Southern.

Then IC turned its eyes west, to the Chicago Central & Pacific, which it had sold for $75 million. It saw CC&P's route across northern Iowa as a source of grain traffic and perhaps a way to get some of the coal moving east from Wyoming. In June 1996 IC purchased the Chicago Central & Pacific for $157 million.

In February 1998 Canadian National Railway Co., recently privatized after more than 80 years of government ownership, agreed to purchase IC, creating a 19,000-mile railroad that would be the fifth largest in North America in revenue.

Illinois Terminal Railroad System

The Illinois Terminal had its beginning in the 1890 purchase of a streetcar system serving the neighboring towns of Urbana and Champaign, Illinois, by William B. McKinley, an Illinois congressman and utilities tycoon. He sold it in 1893, bought it again, and within two decades expanded it into an interurban system from Danville and Peoria through Springfield to East St. Louis and across the Mississippi River on its own bridge to St. Louis, Missouri. His empire also included an interurban line between Joliet and Princeton, Ill., that was intended to form a Chicago extension of the system.

When McKinley was elected to Congress in 1904 the railway system was placed in the hands of Illinois Traction Co. ITC early recognized the importance of freight service: It built bypasses around most of the major cities to avoid running freight trains on city streets, and in 1909 it established joint rates with Chicago & Eastern Illinois and Frisco—similar arrangements with other steam roads soon followed.

In 1923 ITC formed a subsidiary, Illinois Power & Light, to hold the railroad properties, which were then consolidated as Illinois Traction System (the various parts of the system had been built by different companies, though all under the same ownership). Manager of the system was

Car 270 loads passengers at Danville for the trip to Springfield in May 1950. It was the first interurban car in the U. S. to be air-conditioned (in 1935). Kalmbach Publishing Co. photo by David A. Strassman.

Clement Studebaker, of the South Bend, Indiana, automobile manufacturing family.

In 1925 Illinois Traction acquired two steam railroads serving the industrial area east of the Mississippi, the St. Louis & Illinois Belt and the St. Louis, Troy, & Eastern. At the beginning of 1928 Illinois Power & Light Corporation acquired all the common stock of the Illinois Terminal Railroad, a line from Edwardsville to Alton. Illinois Terminal then leased the two steam roads and Illinois Traction. In 1930 the Alton & Eastern, a remnant of the Chicago, Peoria & St. Louis, was brought into the family, which by then was known as the Illinois Terminal Railroad System.

Reorganization and purchase

The company was reorganized in 1937 as the Illinois Terminal Railroad Co. Most railroad reorganizations involved minor changes of name, usually "Railroad" to "Railway" or vice versa. IT's history is different in the matter of names. The Purchaser Railroad was incorporated in 1945 to acquire the Illinois Terminal Railroad Co. On December 14, 1945, the old IT became the Liquidating Railway and the Purchaser Railroad was renamed the Illinois Terminal Railroad.

In 1954 the Illinois-Missouri Terminal Railway was incorporated by nine railroads: Baltimore & Ohio; Chicago & Eastern Illinois; Chicago, Burlington & Quincy; Gulf, Mobile & Ohio; Litchfield & Madison; Illinois Central; Nickel Plate; Frisco; and Wabash. The Illinois-Missouri Terminal purchased the IT in June 1956, whereupon the Illinois-Missouri Terminal was renamed the Illinois Terminal Railroad Co.

and the previous Illinois Terminal was renamed the Liquidating Terminal. The Rock Island and the New York Central purchased interests in the IT later. IT could furnish the steam roads neutral access to the industrial area between East St. Louis and Alton.

Passenger service

IT was one of the last interurbans to offer passenger service. The 1930s saw the abandonment of branchline passenger service and the routing of mainline passenger trains off the streets of the major cities (except Bloomington) and onto the freight belt lines. IT discontinued all of its city streetcar services in 1936, except for those in Peoria, which lasted another decade.

IT's passenger service was notable for several features: sleeping cars, parlor cars, and streamliners. Only three interurbans operated sleeping cars: Interstate Public Service (Indianapolis–Louisville), Oregon Electric (Portland–Eugene), and IT. IT's service was much more extensive and longer-lived than the other two and was operated largely with private room cars. The principal sleeper route was between Peoria and St. Louis, a route with no steam-road competition. Peoria–St. Louis sleepers ran until 1940. For a short time a sleeper ran between Champaign and St. Louis, and a Springfield–St. Louis setout car lasted until 1934.

IT offered parlor-buffet car service on many of its day trains almost until the end of passenger service. After World War II the road purchased three streamliners (eight cars—three cab-baggage-coach cars, two coaches, and three buffet-parlor-observation cars) for St. Louis–Decatur and St. Louis–Peoria service. Streamliner service to Decatur was discontinued after less than two years, and it never reached Peoria. IT's tracks in Peoria could not handle the new trains, so streamliner service was offered only as far as East Peoria. The cars had to be uncoupled to be turned at East Peoria and St. Louis. The streamliners lost their names and their parlor-

	1929	1980
Miles of railroad operated:	484	413
Number of locomotives:	22 steam,	
	51 electric	46 diesel
Number of passenger cars:	124	
Number of freight and company service cars:		2,055
Number of freight cars:		2,624
Number of company service cars:	4	
Location of headquarters: St. Louis, Missouri		
Reporting marks: ITC		

Historical and technical society: Illinois Traction Society, 5903 Vollmer Lane, Godfrey, IL 62035

Recommended reading: *The Lincoln Land Traction,* by James D. Johnson, published in 1965 by The Traction Orange Co., P. O. Box 52, Wheaton, IL 60189

Successors:
Norfolk & Western
Norfolk Southern

Portions still operated: Norfolk Southern: St. Louis–Wood River, Ill.; Madison–Edwardsville–Wood River

buffet cars in 1951. In 1955 passenger service was dropped north and east of Springfield; less than a year later Springfield–St. Louis passenger service was dropped, leaving only the St. Louis–Granite City suburban service, which lasted until June 1958.

Shrinkage

In 1950 the IT began eliminating unproductive track, beginning with the line through Bloomington and most of the Granite City–Wood River–Alton–Grafton route. At the same time IT began dieselizing its freight service, and

by the end of 1955 only passenger service—what little remained of it—was operated electrically. By 1980 IT's main lines were about two-thirds trackage rights on parallel railroads and one-third owned. The major portions of IT's own lines remaining in service were the former steam-powered lines in East St. Louis. In addition, IT purchased a former Pennsylvania line between Maroa and Farmdale in 1976, creating a Decatur–East Peoria route. Norfolk & Western purchased Illinois Terminal September 1, 1981. IT's corporate existence ended on May 8, 1982.

Indiana Railroad

INDIANA RAILROAD In the early 1920s Samuel Insull owned large interests in electric power companies and electric railways in Indiana. Among the companies controlled by his Midland United Corporation were

• Interstate Public Service, which had an interurban line between Indianapolis and Louisville, Kentucky

• Northern Indiana Public Service Company, whose rail lines centered on Kokomo

• Winona Service Company, which had a single line connecting the interurbans of northern and central Indiana

• Gary Railways, which operated streetcars in Gary and interurban lines radiating from Gary

In 1925 Insull added the Chicago, Lake Shore & South Bend (predecessor of the Chicago South Shore & South Bend) and the Indiana Service Corporation, which had rail lines centered on Fort Wayne. That same year Insull proposed consolidating these companies. The Indiana Public Service Commission rejected the proposal.

In 1930 Insull acquired the property of the bankrupt Union Traction Company, which had lines north, northeast, and east from Indianapolis. Insull reorganized the Union Traction system as the Indiana Railroad on August 1, 1930, and coordinated its operations with the Northern Indiana, Indiana Service, and Interstate lines.

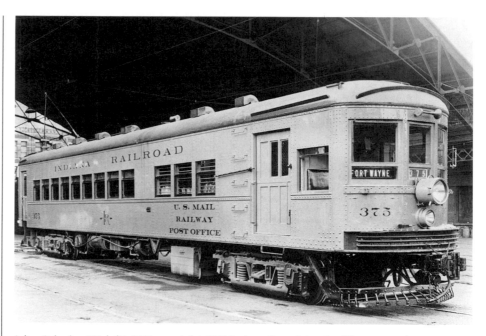

Indiana Railroad car 375, built in 1926, was rebuilt in 1935 for the road's new Railway Post Office route. It is shown at the Indianapolis terminal. Photo from the collection of Wilbourne B. Cox.

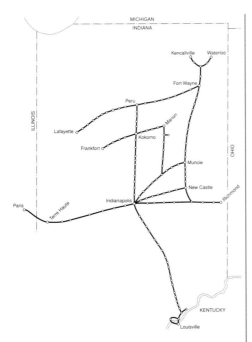

The new system covered almost 700 route miles.

Not included in the Indiana Railroad were the Winona, the only link with the northern tier of the state but a weak company; the Terre Haute, Indianapolis & Eastern, whose lines ran northwest, west, and southwest from Indianapolis (it was in receivership at the time the IR was formed); and the Fort Wayne-Lima Railroad.

The new railroad made a point of offering frequent, coordinated passenger train services and fast freight and package service, and it immediately ordered 35 high-speed lightweight cars to re-equip those services. Rebuilt track and new substations allowed schedules to be accelerated. The railroad dropped parlor and dining car service in late 1930—it was expensive to operate—and the Indianapolis–Louisville sleeping cars remained only 2 years longer.

The key to Indiana Railroad's success was—or would have been—the development of interline freight service, in particular coal to the electric generating plants around the system. IR's track, while adequate for lightweight passenger cars, was in no condition to handle heavy freight trains, and the typical interurban mix of sharp curves, steep grades, and street running precluded the operation of standard steam-railroad freight cars over much of the system.

In June 1931 the Indiana Railroad acquired the bankrupt Terre Haute, Indianapolis & Eastern. It abandoned the weaker lines but retained the routes east to Richmond and west to Terre Haute and Paris, Illinois. Then IR began to abandon the weakest of its lines as the Depression took hold. Insull was forced out of the management of the company in 1932, and the company entered receivership in 1933. The company struggled to keep the business it had, emphasizing its package freight service and even acquiring two Railway Post Office routes. In 1936 IR posted a net income. It was the only time it would do so.

The company began converting its rail lines to bus and truck routes. The last major rail route, Indianapolis–Fort Wayne, shut down on January 19, 1941. In June 1941 the company emerged from receivership as a bus and truck operator and remained in business several more years.

Recommended reading:
Indiana Railroad — The Magic Interurban, by George K. Bradley, published in 1991 by Central Electric Railfans' Association, P. O. Box 503, Chicago, IL 60690-0503 (ISBN 0-915348-28-4)
"Indiana Railroad: The All-American Interurban," by William D. Middleton, in *Vintage Rails,* No. 13 (July–August 1998), published by Pentrex Media Group, P. O. Box 379, Waukesha, WI 53187-0379
Portions still operated: Southern Indiana Railway: Watson–Speed, Ind.

Interstate Railroad

The Interstate was incorporated in 1896 and completed in 1909 from Stonega to Norton, Virginia, 16 miles. In 1913 it absorbed the Wise Terminal Co., and in 1923 it constructed a branch line from Norton to a connection with the Clinchfield near St. Paul, Va. That branch soon became the main line. Interstate's

	1929	1960
Miles of railroad operated (with branches and sidings):	83	88
Number of locomotives:	12	10
Number of passenger cars:	6	
Number of freight and company service cars:		3,052
Number of freight cars:		2,812
Number of company service cars:		11

Location of headquarters: Andover, Virginia

Reporting marks: INT

Successors:
Southern Railway
Norfolk Southern

Map: See page 124

With striping on its running boards and driver tires that it never had in its previous life on the Pennsylvania Railroad, Interstate Mikado 15 wheels a long freight through Tacoma, Virginia, on April 16, 1952. Photo by Henry L. Stuart Jr.

chief business was hauling coal for its parent, Virginia Coal & Iron Co. Whatever the goal implied by the name of the railroad, it never crossed the Virginia state line, though it got within a mile or two. The Southern Railway bought the Interstate in June 1961.

Interurbans

The railroad industry and its regulators (the Interstate Commerce Commission and the state commissions) differentiated between steam railroads and electric railways. The Santa Fe was a steam railroad; the Chicago North Shore & Milwaukee was an electric railway. The steam railroads were the genuine article. Electric railways were different, not so much in technology as in organization and ownership. More often than not they were a division of an electric power company or a city transit system. (The classification system wasn't logical—the Pennsylvania Railroad's New York–Washington line was a steam railroad, GG1s, 11,000-volt catenary, and all.)

The first practical electric streetcar appeared in 1888. City streetcars didn't remain confined within city limits for long. Lines were extended to the suburbs, to neighboring towns that would become suburbs, and then to the next good-sized cities in competition with the established steam railroads. The term "interurban" was applied to the lines that connected cities.

Interurban railways used streetcar technology. Their cars were generally longer, heavier, and more comfortable than streetcars, but still smaller and lighter than steam railroad cars. Interurbans usually used streetcar tracks to reach downtown terminals but beyond the built-up areas of cities they had their own private right

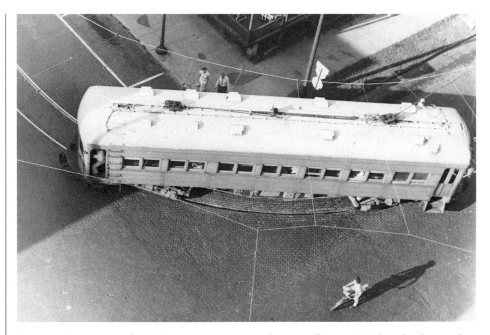

Illinois Terminal car 1202 turns from Market Street to Center Street in Bloomington, Illinois, in 1952. The track in the street, the brick pavement, the angle of the trucks to the solid-looking yet stubby carbody all say "interurban." Photo by George Isaacs.

of way, sometimes alongside highways, sometimes on their own.

Interurbans were soon found all over the country wherever there were population centers no more than 50 miles apart. In the Northeast interurbans were primarily suburban trolley lines because the steam railroads already had dense networks of branch lines. In California interurbans reached steam-railroad dimensions. The Pacific Electric had 575 miles of line throughout the Los Angeles Basin in 1929; the Sacramento Northern stretched 183 miles from San Francisco to Chico.

Interurbans reached fullest flower in the Upper Midwest, between the Alleghenies and the Missouri River. Ohio and Indiana had extensive networks of interurban lines. The Illinois Traction System had nearly 500 miles of routes from St. Louis, Missouri, to Peoria and Danville, Illinois.

In northeast Illinois were three interurbans that came under the management of Samuel Insull: the Chicago Aurora & Elgin Railroad, the Chicago North Shore & Milwaukee Railroad, and the Chicago South Shore & South Bend Railroad. All three are described elsewhere in this book.

Freight service

Most interurbans offered freight service. Sometimes it was package express service, like UPS offers today. In some instances several interurbans joined to offer such service over a network of lines.

Some interurbans offered carload freight service in interchange with steam railroads. This depended, of course, on a friendly connection. Some steam railroads worked with neighboring interurbans; others were openly hostile. Motive power for interurban freight trains ranged from passenger cars that could pull one or two freight cars to specialized locomotives—Illinois Terminal and Oregon Electric operated powerful eight-axle freight locomotives.

Generally speaking, the interurbans that were successful in the freight business were those that survived, usually as freight-only short lines.

Decline of interurbans

The interurban industry reached its peak in 1917. The public discovered that automobiles and trucks on newly paved highways were faster and more flexible. People could go to town when they wanted and return when they wanted without having to stop elsewhere. The Depression hastened the decline, World War II retarded it, and postwar prosperity—which manifested itself as new automobiles—doubled or tripled the pace of the decline.

By 1950 only a few interurbans remained in operation, and many of those became freight-only, diesel-operated short lines. Pacific Electric sold its passenger operations in 1953 to Metropolitan Coach Lines, and the last rail line (Los Angeles to Long Beach) shut down on April 8, 1961. The three lines operating into Chicago were considered the strongest in the industry, but the Chicago Aurora & Elgin fell victim to a highway construction project, and the North Shore, also a victim of highway construction, became a tax loss for a conglomerate.

After the death of the North Shore in 1963 the Chicago South Shore & South Bend was the last interurban still running electric-powered freight and passenger trains, and it looked more like an electrically operated steam railroad than an interurban. Heavy electric locomotives bought secondhand from the New York Central powered long freight trains through the industrial area along the south shore of Lake Michigan; heavy steel passenger cars of steam-road dimensions ran a busy suburban service. Diesels took over freight service in 1981, but passenger service continued to operate under wires, after 1990 under the aegis of the Northern Indiana Commuter Transportation District. It doesn't look much like an interurban any more—except in Michigan City, where NICTD trains still roll along the streets, and in the countryside between Michigan City and South Bend.

Recommended reading:

The Electric Interurban Railways in America, by George W. Hilton and John F. Due, published in 1960 by Stanford University Press, Standofd, Calif. (LCC 60-5383).

The Interurban Era, by William D. Middleton, published in 1961 by Kalmbach Publishing Co. (LCC 61-10728)

Kansas City, Mexico & Orient Railway

(Ferrocarril Kansas City, Mexico y Oriente)

Mexico North-Western Railway

(Ferrocarril Nor-Oeste de Mexico)

In the 1880s Albert Kimsey Owen proposed a railroad that would form a land bridge for traffic between Europe and the Far East. The two North American ports to be connected by the railroad were Norfolk, Virginia, and Topolobampo, Mexico. If you extend the Arizona-New Mexico border about 400 miles south, it will hit the Gulf of California just about at Topolobampo. Owen incorporated the Texas, Topolobampo & Pacific Railroad, but little more came of his proposal.

In 1897 Enrique Creel, who was governor of the Mexican state of Chihuahua, incorporated

A 2-8-0 once on Santa Fe's roster leads an eastbound way freight at Pichachos, between Chihuahua and Ojinaga. Photo by Edward C. Spalding.

the Ferrocarril Chihuahua al Pacifico, a railroad to run from the city of Chihuahua to the Pacific coast. The railroad opened its first section, 124 miles from Chihuahua to Minaca, on March 31, 1900.

The Rio Grande, Sierra Madre & Pacific Railroad was incorporated on June 11, 1897, to build a line between Ciudad Juarez, across the Rio Grande from El Paso, Texas, to the Pacific at Tijuana. The railroad worked southwest through Casas Grandes into timber country, eventually stopping at Madera, just west of the Continental Divide. The Chihuahua al Pacifico built a branch north from La Junta to Temosachic, and the ChP and the RGSM&P teamed up to organize the Sierra Madre & Pacific to construct the line between Madera and Temosachic, 54 miles. In 1909 the Sierra Madre & Pacific, the Rio Grande, Sierra Madre & Pacific, and the Chihuahua al Pacifico were consolidated as the Ferrocarril Nor-Oeste de Mexico (Mexico North-Western Railway). The entire route from Ciudad Juarez to Chihuahua (more than twice as long as National Railways of Mexico's direct route) was open by 1912.

Arthur E. Stilwell

Arthur E. Stilwell built the Kansas City, Pittsburg & Gulf Railroad (now the Kansas City Southern) from Kansas City directly south to the Gulf of Mexico at Port Arthur, Tex. Ousted by new management in 1899, he proposed a railroad from Kansas City to the nearest Pacific port, Topolobampo—to be called Port Stilwell. The rail distance would be less than 1,700 miles (Kansas City–Los Angeles via the Santa Fe was 1,780 miles). Creel granted Stilwell trackage

rights from Chihuahua to Minaca, 122 miles, and also the federal concessions of the Chihuahua al Pacifico. Stilwell met with Owen and secured the rights and lands of the Texas, Topolobampo & Pacific.

On April 30, 1900, Stilwell incorporated the Kansas City, Mexico & Orient Railway. By mid-1903 lines were open from Milton, Kansas, near Wichita, to Carmen, Oklahoma; from Chihuahua to a point 34 miles east; and from Topolobampo to El Fuerte. By early 1912 the U. S. portion of the line reached from Wichita to Girvin, Tex., on the Pecos River, traversing a barren, uninhabited area for most of its length.

Also by 1912 Mexico was deep in a revolution. Neither the desolate topography in the U. S. nor the situation in Mexico was conducive to revenue. The road entered receivership in March 1912, and Stilwell was once again a former railroad president.

The newly organized Kansas City, Mexico & Orient Railroad purchased the KCM&O on July 6, 1914. The first reorganization plan was rejected and a second receiver, William T. Kemper, was appointed in 1917. The Orient scraped along, building an extension to Alpine, Tex., where it connected with Southern Pacific. During World War I the USRA at first rejected the

KCM&O but later took over its operation at Kemper's request.

In the early 1920s things began to look better: The Mexican government said it would extend the line east from Chihuahua toward the border at Presidio to compensate for damage sustained during the revolution, and oil was discovered in west Texas.

Purchase by the Santa Fe

In 1924 a U. S. government loan came due. The KCM&O was unable to repay it, and the government directed that the railroad be sold at auction. Kemper was the successful bidder, and he organized the Kansas City, Mexico & Orient Railway, the second company of that name. However, pipelines had begun to cut into the Orient's oil traffic, and Kemper realized he could never afford to extend the line from Wichita to Kansas City, much less connect the three disjointed Mexican portions of the railroad. He sought a buyer, first in the Missouri Pacific, which had financial difficulties of its own, then the Santa Fe.

On September 24, 1928, the Santa Fe purchased the Orient (merger came on June 30, 1941, except for the Texas portion, which was merged in 1964). Santa Fe then sold the three Mexican portions of the road to B. F. Johnston and the United Sugar Co. of Los Mochis. Johnston combined the operations of the Mexican portion of the KCM&O with those of the Mexico North-Western, whose rails joined the eastern and middle portions of the KCM&O. In October 1930 the eastern portion of the line was opened to Ojinaga. The Santa Fe extended a line from Alpine to Presidio and bridged the Rio Grande that same year, opening a new gateway for traffic between the U. S. and Mexico.

Government ownership

In 1940 the operations of the KCM&O and the Mexico North-Western were separated. The Mexican government purchased the KCM&O from United Sugar and also purchased the La Junta–Minaca portion of the Mexico North-Western. The government announced that the two portions of the KCM&O would be connected.

Separating the two portions between Creel and San Pedro was Mexico's Sierra Madre range, some of the roughest and least known topography in North America. Surveys were made and some construction was undertaken, then suspended, then resumed, and so on.

In 1952 KCM&O took over operation of the Rio Mayo Railway, a 38-mile line from Yavaros, on the shore of the Gulf of California, to Navojoa, on the Southern Pacific of Mexico 86 miles north of Sufragio, where KCM&O crossed the SPdeM. Three years later the Rio Mayo line became part of the Ferrocarril del Pacifico, successor to SPdeM.

In 1952 the Mexico North-Western was taken over by the Mexican government and in 1955 it was merged with the Ferrocarril Kansas City, Mexico y Oriente to form the Ferrocarril de Chihuahua al Pacifico. The pace of construction accelerated. Laying of rail on the new line began in 1960, and the line connecting Chihuahua with the coast was opened by Mexico's president on November 23, 1961.

Kansas City, Mexico & Orient	1929	1954
Miles of railroad operated:	349	384
Number of locomotives:	11	15
Number of passenger cars:	11	18
Number of freight cars:	255	356
Number of company service cars:	15	15

Location of headquarters: El Paso, Texas; later Ciudad Juarez, Chihuahua; then Chihuahua, Chih.
Reporting marks: FKCM&O
Successors:
Atchison, Topeka & Santa Fe
Chihuahua Pacific

National Railways of Mexico
Portions still operated:
Chihuahua Pacific: Ojinaga, Chih.–Topolobampo, Sinaloa
Farmrail Corp.: Westhom–Altus–Elmer, Okla.
South Orient: San Angelo–Alpine–Presidio, Texas
Texas & Oklahoma: Sweetwater–Maryneal, Tex.

Mexico North-Western	1929	1954
Miles of railroad operated:	497	476
Number of locomotives:	27	41
Number of passenger cars:	21	32
Number of freight cars:	935	1,099
Number of company service cars:	8	81

Location of headquarters: Ciudad Juarez, Chihuahua
Reporting marks: N-OdeM
Successors:
Chihuahua Pacific
National Railways of Mexico
Portions still operated: National Railways of Mexico: Ciudad Juarez–La Junta, Chih.
Recommended reading: *Destination Topolobampo*, by John Leeds
Kerr and Frank P. Donovan Jr., published in 1968 by Golden West Books,
P. O. Box 80250, San Marino, CA 91108

Kettle Valley Railway

C anadian Pacific's main line across the prairies of Manitoba, Saskatchewan, and Alberta lies 50 to 100 miles north of the U. S. border. The line turns northwest at Medicine Hat, Alberta, to cross the Rockies and the Selkirks, runs generally westward, then turns sharply to follow the Thompson and Fraser rivers almost due south for about 100 miles. On a map it looks like a detour—and it is. The Kootenay district of southern British Columbia is an area of rugged mountain ranges running north and south, and watercourses useful to an east-west railroad are scarce.

In the late 1800s southern British Columbia was geographically and economically closer to the United States than to the rest of Canada. The discovery of silver near Nelson in 1887 and a desire to keep the region tied to Canada sparked the idea of a railroad across the southern part of British Columbia. Rails working north from Spokane, Washington, soon penetrated the area, adding impetus to the proposal; the Depression of 1893 and the repeal of the Silver Purchase Act in the U. S. made it unlikely the proposal would become reality.

Prosperity returned within a few years, and there were further incursions by U. S. railroads. It became more and more necessary to build a Canadian railroad into the area. The CPR already reached west from Medicine Hat to

211

Lethbridge, Alta. In 1898 it was extended west across the Rockies to Cranbrook, B. C. The Canadian government provided a cash grant for construction of the line in exchange for a permanent reduction in the rates for carry grain—the Crows Nest Pass Agreement of 1897 (the agreement proved expensive in the long run, and not until 1983 were matters remedied).

British Columbians who advocated the railroad as a way to connect the Kootenay region with Vancouver saw that the new railroad would connect the area instead to the East. There were several immediate proposals to build a railroad east from Vancouver, and the forces grouped into three factions: the Canadian Pacific, the provincially chartered Vancouver, Victoria & Eastern Railway, and James J. Hill of the Great Northern Railway, who was building and buying lines north into the area intending to continue west to Vancouver—and Hill got control of the Vancouver, Victoria & Eastern.

The Kettle River Valley Railway was incorporated in 1901 as part of a project to carry copper ore from Republic, Washington, north to a smelter in Grand Forks, B. C. James J. Hill saw it as an intrusion of his territory and squashed it. In 1907 Canadian Pacific opened a branch from Spences Bridge on the main line southeast to the coalfields at Merritt and Nicola. Hill meanwhile was expanding his presence in the area and once again proposing a line directly west to Vancouver. There ensued a series of skirmishes between Hill and the CPR. By 1909 Hill's line reached as far west as Princeton, B. C.

Canadian Pacific surveyed routes westward from Midway, where its track ended, recognizing that if it did not complete a line across southern British Columbia, the whole area would be under the control of the Great Northern—an American company—and the lines CPR had already constructed would be worthless. It met with the Kettle Valley Railway (the renamed Kettle River Valley in 1911) and worked out an arrangement in which Kettle Valley would build the required line, including an extremely difficult stretch from Merritt southwest over Coquihalla Pass to Hope. Hill's Vancouver, Victoria & Eastern was also aiming at Coquihalla Pass—and the topography would barely permit one railroad, let alone two. In 1913 the two railroads agreed to share a single line.

In October 1914 the two railroads had built enough track to create a rail route from the Kootenay area to a connection with the CPR main line at Spences Bridge—a roundabout route but not nearly as roundabout as going east to Lethbridge then back west through Calgary or going around Wenatchee and Seattle. On July 31, 1916, the Coquihalla Pass route was completed and CPR and Kettle Valley inaugurated passenger train service between Vancouver and Nelson.

James J. Hill died on May 29, 1916, and Great Northern management had no interest at all in rail lines in British Columbia. GN ran one inspection train over the Coquihalla Pass line and that was all.

On December 31, 1930, Canadian Pacific took over operation of the Kettle Valley Railway. The Kettle Valley corporation continued to exist until 1956. In 1938 CPR considered closing the Coquihalla Pass line, which was closed by snow for part of each winter, but changed its mind scant months before Canada entered World War II.

In November 1959 portions of the Coquihalla line washed out. After more than a year of inactivity, CPR announced it was abandoning that portion of the route. About that same time CPR began routing Kootenay–Vancouver freight over the Lake Windermere line between Cranbrook and Golden. Kettle Valley passenger service ended in 1964—the longer route through Spences Bridge and the lack of through service made the service unattractive to riders. In 1978 CPR abandoned the line between Midway and Penticton, the eastern portion of the Kettle Valley proper, and the Penticton–Spences Bridge line has since been abandoned.

Historical and technical society: Canadian Pacific Special Interest Group, 5 Grovenest Drive, Scarborough, ON, Canada M1E 4J2
Recommended reading: *McCulloch's Wonder*, by Barrie Sanford, published in 1978 by Whitecap Books, Vancouver, B. C. (ISBN 0-921061-25-0)

Lehigh & Hudson River Railway

The Warwick Valley Railroad was chartered in 1860 to build a line from Warwick, New York, to Greycourt, on the New York & Erie. It was opened in 1862, and until 1880, when it narrowed its tracks from 6 feet to standard gauge, it was operated with Erie cars and locomotives.

The line was extended southwest to serve iron mines, then all the way to the Delaware River at Belvidere, New Jersey, as the Lehigh & Hudson River Railroad. The two railroads were consolidated as the Lehigh & Hudson River Railway in 1882.

The construction of the Poughkeepsie Bridge across the Hudson River prompted a 10-mile extension from Greycourt to Maybrook, N. Y., opened in 1890. At the other end of the line, the Delaware River was bridged and the L&HR and the Pennsylvania traded trackage rights: L&HR over Pennsy between Belvidere and Phillipsburg, N. J., and Pennsylvania over L&HR to reach the Poughkeepsie Bridge.

Initially traffic was agricultural, but soon coal became predominant. The principal industry on the L&HR was a mine and crushing plant of the New Jersey Zinc Co. near Franklin. The purchase of the Central New England and its bridge at Poughkeepsie by the New Haven turned the L&HR into a bridge route. At the insistence of

Lehigh & Hudson River 94, a massive 2-8-0 with a wide firebox for burning anthracite and a 12-wheel tender for carrying it, brings a Maybrook–Allentown freight through Lake, New York, 5 miles northeast of Warwick. Photo by Donald W. Furler.

the New Haven, the L&HR was purchased in 1905 by several major railroads to ensure the New Haven's connections with those roads.

The only major change in ownership between 1929 and 1975 was that the 20 percent interest held by Lehigh Coal & Navigation Co., owner of the Lehigh & New England, passed more or less equally to Lehigh Valley and Pennsylvania about 1950. Ownership in 1975, just before the property passed to Conrail, was Central of New Jersey, 16.75 percent; Reading, 13.44 percent; Penn Central, 14.43 percent; Erie-Lackawanna, 32.73 percent; and Lehigh Valley, 22.16 percent.

Traffic patterns began to change in the 1960s. The merger of Erie and Lackawanna shifted traffic off the L&HR to the former Erie line, which connected directly with the New Haven. With the creation of Penn Central, traffic between New England and the South that had moved over the Poughkeepsie Bridge was rerouted through Selkirk, near Albany, via the ex-New York Central West Shore and Boston & Albany lines.

L&HR filed for bankruptcy protection on April 18, 1972. What little traffic remained disappeared when the Poughkeepsie Bridge burned in 1974. L&HR's property was transferred to Conrail on April 1, 1976.

	1929	1975
Miles of railroad operated:	97	90
Number of locomotives:	34	6
Number of passenger cars:	14	
Number of freight cars:	398	2
Number of company service cars:	66	9

Location of headquarters: Warwick, New York

Reporting marks: LHR

Historical and technical societies: Anthracite Railroads Historical Society, P. O. Box 519, Lansdale, PA 19446-0519 New Jersey Midland Railroad Historical Society, P. O. Box 6125, Parsippany, NJ 07054; http://ourworld.compuserve.com/homepages/njmidland

Recommended reading: *The Northeast Railroad Scene, Vol. 2: The Lehigh & Hudson River,* by Bob Pennisi, published in 1977 by Railroad Avenue Enterprises, P. O. Box 114, Flanders, NJ 07836

Successors: Conrail

Portions still operated: New York, Susquehanna & Western: East Hall, N. Y.–Sparta Junction, N. J.

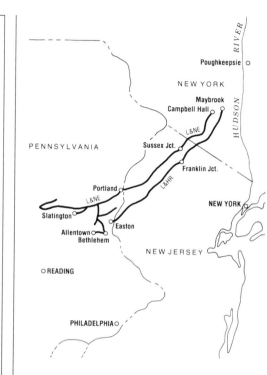

Lehigh & New England Railroad

The Lehigh & New England's oldest ancestor was the South Mountain & Boston, chartered in 1873 to construct a railroad between Harrisburg, Pennsylvania, and Boston, Massachusetts. Several reorganizations finally produced the Pennsylvania, Poughkeepsie & Boston, which completed a line from Slatington, Pa., on the Lehigh River, to Pine Island, New York, using the tracks of the New York, Susquehanna & Western between Hainesburg Jct. and Swartswood Jct., New Jersey. In 1891 the Philadelphia & Reading leased the road, but canceled the lease when the PP&B entered receivership in 1893. Yet another reorganization in 1895 produced the Lehigh & New England Railroad. After 1904 most of the L&NE's stock was owned by the Lehigh Coal & Navigation Co.

In 1926 the L&NE and the Reading agreed to a lease of the L&NE by the Reading, but the Interstate Commerce Commission denied the application. In 1929 the Baltimore & Ohio and the Chesapeake & Ohio both asked for four-way control of the L&NE by B&O, C&O, New York Central, and Pennsylvania; that same year the Wabash asked to control the road. All three applications were withdrawn in 1930. The ICC's merger plan of 1929 assigned the road to the New Haven.

Declining traffic, first in anthracite, then in cement, made the L&NE's fate obvious to its

Black-and-white Alco freight units wearing Lehigh & New England's "fried egg" herald lead a train of hopper cars through the Lehigh River Gorge. General Electric photo.

owner. In 1960 the L&NE, which was still solvent, petitioned for abandonment. The Central Railroad of New Jersey organized the Lehigh & New England Railway to buy and operate the portions of the line between Hauto and Tamaqua, Pa., and from Bethlehem and Allentown through Bath to Martins Creek, Pa., about 40 miles total. The remainder of the L&NE was abandoned in 1961. In 1972 CNJ transferred its own Pennsylvania lines to the Lehigh Valley but continued to operate the L&NE remnants. In 1974 the ICC assigned operation of the line out of Bethlehem to the LV and the Hauto–Tamaqua line to the Reading. Two years later both of those railroads were taken over by Conrail.

	1929	1960
Miles of railroad operated:	217	177
Number of locomotives:	61	32
Number of passenger cars:	12	
Number of freight cars:	3,457	
Number of company service cars:	63	
Number of freight and company service cars:		2,608

Location of headquarters: Philadelphia, Pennsylvania

Reporting marks: LNE

Historical and technical societies:
Anthracite Railroads Historical Society, P. O. Box 519, Lansdale, PA 19446-0519
New Jersey Midland Railroad Historical Society, P. O. Box 6125, Parsippany, NJ 07054;
http://ourworld.compuserve.com/homepages/njmidland

Recommended reading: *The Lehigh and New England Railroad*, by Ed Crist, published in 1980 by Carstens Publications, P. O. Box 700, Newton, NJ 07860

Successors:
Central Railroad of New Jersey
Lehigh Valley
Reading
Conrail

Portions still operated:
Conrail: Bethlehem–Bath–Stokertown, Pa.
Reading, Blue Mountain & Northern: Tamaqua–Lansford, Pa.

Map: See page 214

Lehigh Valley Railroad

Anthracite coal was discovered at Mauch Chunk, Pennsylvania, in 1791 (Mauch Chunk was renamed Jim Thorpe in 1954). The only practical means to transport the coal to a sizable market was to boat it down the often unnavigable Lehigh River. A canal was constructed, and by the 1820s the Lehigh Coal & Navigation Co. had a near-monopoly on the mining and transportation of coal in the region.

To break the monopoly and also to improve transportation, the Delaware, Lehigh, Schuylkill & Susquehanna Railroad was incorporated in 1846 to build a line from Mauch Chunk to Easton, Pa., where the Lehigh River flows into the Delaware. Construction did not begin until 1851; then with the management and the financing of Asa Packer work began in earnest. The railroad was renamed the Lehigh Valley Railroad in 1853, and it was opened from Easton to Mauch Chunk in September 1855.

The railroad began to grow both by new construction and by consolidating with existing railroads. In 1866, the year the Lehigh & Mahanoy merged with Lehigh Valley, Alexander Mitchell, master mechanic of the L&M, designed a freight locomotive with a 2-8-0 wheel arrangement and named it "Consolidation"—the name became the standard designation for that wheel arrangement.

In the late 1930s and early 1940s Lehigh Valley streamlined several of its named passenger trains and adopted a livery of black and Cornell red with white trim. Train 28, the eastbound *John Wilkes,* is shown near Glen Onoko, Pennsylvania, soon after its 1939 streamlining. Photo by Wayne Brumbaugh.

The Lehigh Valley reached north into the Wyoming Valley to Wilkes-Barre in 1867, the same year that Lehigh Coal & Navigation's Lehigh & Susquehanna Railroad, originally a White Haven-to-Wilkes-Barre line, opened a line south along the Lehigh River to Easton, in places on the opposite bank from the LV and in other places sharing the same bank.

In 1865 Packer purchased a flood-damaged canal, renamed it the Pennsylvania & New York Canal & Railroad, and used its towpath as roadbed. The P&NY was completed to a connection with the New York & Erie at Waverly New York, in 1869, giving the Lehigh Valley an outlet to the west. In 1876 Lehigh Valley furnished the material and the money necessary for Erie to lay a third rail to accommodate standard gauge trains on its line from Waverly to Buffalo, to eliminate the need to transfer freight and passengers at Waverly. Lehigh Valley leased the P&NY in 1888.

To New York and to Buffalo

At its eastern end Lehigh Valley saw its connecting routes taken over by rival railroads: The Lackawanna acquired the Morris & Essex in 1868, and the Central of New Jersey, formerly considered friendly, leased the Lehigh & Susquehanna in 1871, getting a line parallel to the Lehigh Valley from Easton to Wilkes-Barre.

LV bought the Morris Canal across New Jersey chiefly for its property on New York Harbor at Jersey City. It assembled a line to Perth Amboy in 1875, but not until 1899 did LV reach its Jersey City property on its own rails.

Lehigh Valley's use of Erie rails (more accurately, one of its own and one of Erie's) to reach

Buffalo was not completely satisfactory. In 1876 LV got control of the Geneva, Ithaca & Sayre Railroad, which put it into Geneva, N. Y. In the early 1880s LV built a terminal railroad and a station in Buffalo and established a Great Lakes shipping line (whose flag became the emblem of the railroad).

Construction of a line from Geneva to Buffalo and a freight bypass to avoid the steep grades on the Geneva, Ithaca & Sayre began in 1889. In 1890 LV merged the companies involved in building the new line as the Lehigh Valley Rail Way. The Buffalo extension was opened in September 1892.

LV lines in western New York included a branch from the new line to Rochester; the former Southern Central Railroad from Sayre to North Fair Haven on Lake Ontario; and the Elmira, Cortland & Northern Railroad, which meandered from Elmira through East Ithaca, Cortland, and Canastota to Camden—nothing came of a proposal to extend it to Watertown, N. Y. In 1896 LV opened a short bypass around Buffalo for traffic to and from Canada.

Alliance with the Reading

A few years earlier Archibald A. McLeod had started the Philadelphia & Reading on a course of expansion with the backing of financiers J. P. Morgan and Anthony Drexel. The Reading negotiated quietly with the Lehigh Valley, which had a Great Lakes outlet for Reading's anthracite as well as its own. The financial arrangement seemed beneficial to LV, too, which had just spent a lot of money getting to Buffalo and was noticing a decline in anthracite traffic. In February 1892 the Reading leased the Lehigh Valley

(and also the Central of New Jersey). Morgan and Drexel were suddenly alarmed by the growth of the Reading (it was pursuing the Boston & Maine by then) and withdrew their support. The Reading collapsed into receivership. The lease of the Lehigh Valley was terminated in August 1893.

J. P. Morgan agreed to fund the LV. He moved its general offices from Philadelphia to New York and began rebuilding the road. The independent stockholders of the line protested the diversion of money from dividends into physical plant and regained control in 1902. Several other railroads bought blocks of LV stock—New York Central, Reading, Erie, Lackawanna, and Central of New Jersey—and the road became part of William H. Moore's short-lived Rock Island system. In 1903 the company underwent some corporate simplification, merging and dissolving a number of subsidiaries.

In 1913 LV's passenger trains were evicted from the Pennsylvania Railroad's Jersey City terminal and moved to the Central of New Jersey station; in 1918 under the direction of the USRA they were moved into Pennsylvania Station in New York. It remained LV's New York terminus until the end of passenger service.

Several events during the teens adversely affected LV's revenues: a munitions explosion on Black Tom Island on the Jersey City waterfront in 1916, the divestiture of the Great Lakes shipping operation in 1917 (required by the Panama Canal Act), the divestiture of the coal mining subsidiary (required by the Sherman Antitrust Act), and a drop in anthracite traffic as oil and gas became the dominant home-heating fuels.

The ICC merger proposal of the 1920s called

for four major railroad systems in the East. The response of Leonor F. Loree, president of the Delaware & Hudson, was a proposal for a fifth system, to include D&H; LV; Wabash; Wheeling & Lake Erie; and Buffalo, Rochester & Pittsburgh. Loree purchased large amounts of LV stock but not enough to gain control. He was later able to sell his shares in Wabash and Lehigh Valley to the Pennsylvania Railroad, which suddenly found itself with 31 percent of LV's common stock, enough to keep LV from falling into the hands of the New York Central. However, the Pennsylvania Railroad exercised no noticeable influence on the policies and operations of the Lehigh Valley.

The Depression and aftermath

Lehigh Valley entered the Depression with its physical plant in good shape and with little debt of its own maturing in the next few years. However, the maturation of bonds of the Lehigh Valley Coal Co., New Jersey state taxes, and interest on debt soon had the railroad in debt to the federal government for nearly $8 million. Highways were taking away passenger and freight business. LV began to prune its branches, starting with the former Elmira, Cortland & Northern.

In the late 1930s LV made a valiant effort to attract passenger business by hiring designer Otto Kuhler to streamline its old cars and locomotives. World War II brought a surge of business to on-line Army bases and LV's port facilities, but LV's decline resumed when the war was over.

The route chosen for the New York State Thruway in Buffalo lay along LV's right of way, so after first considering renting facilities from another railroad LV constructed and opened a new terminal in Buffalo in 1955. That same year Hurricane Diane inflicted severe damage on much of LV's line in Pennsylvania, with attendant costs of rebuilding. The next year, 1956, was to be LV's last profitable year.

On the New York–Buffalo run LV's passenger trains competed with the newer and faster trains of the Lackawanna and the New York Central—to say nothing of the new Thruway. In May 1959 LV discontinued all but two of its mainline passenger trains, and those two, the New York–Lehighton *John Wilkes* and the New York–Toronto *Maple Leaf,* lasted less than two years longer. LV was one of the first major railroads to offer only freight service.

Relief from passenger losses made no difference. LV's financial situation continued to worsen. In 1961 the Pennsylvania Railroad bought all the outstanding stock to protect its previous investment in the Lehigh Valley. LV continued to prune branches and reduce double track to single and teamed up with Central of New Jersey to eliminate duplicate lines between Easton and Wilkes-Barre. In 1972 Lehigh Valley took over all of Central of New Jersey's operations in Pennsylvania.

One of the conditions of the creation of Penn Central was that Lehigh Valley be offered to Norfolk & Western and Chesapeake & Ohio. Neither wanted it. Penn Central declared bankruptcy on June 21, 1970, and Lehigh Valley filed for bankruptcy protection three days later. LV's situation got no better during the next six years, and its properties were taken over by Conrail on April 1, 1976. Most of the track west of Sayre, Pa., was considered redundant and abandoned.

	1929	1974
Miles of railroad operated:	1,362	988
Number of locomotives:	725	149
Number of passenger cars:	673	
Number of freight cars:	26,443	3,965
Number of company service cars:	1,578	161

Location of headquarters: New York, New York

Reporting marks: LV

Notable named passenger trains: *Black Diamond* (New York–Buffalo), *Asa Packer,* *John Wilkes* (New York–Wilkes-Barre–Pittston, Pa.)

Historical and technical societies:
Anthracite Railroads Historical Society, P. O. Box 519, Lansdale, PA 19446-0519
Cornell Railroad Historical Society, 3 Greystone Drive, Dryden, NY 13053

Recommended reading: *Lehigh Valley Railroad,* by Robert F. Archer, published in 1977 by Howell-North Books, 850 North Hollywood Way, Burbank, CA 91505

Subsidiaries and affiliated railroads, 1974:
Buffalo Creek Railroad (50%, jointly with Erie Lackawanna)
Ironton Railroad (50%, jointly with Reading)
Niagara Junction (25%)
Successors: Conrail
Portions still operated:
Conrail: Jersey City–Newark, N. J.–Easton–Allentown, Pa.–Pittston Junction, Pa.–Waverly–Ithaca–Ludlowville, N. Y. (Allentown to Pittston Junction is part former LV, part former Central of New Jersey); South Plainfield–Perth Amboy, N. J.; Penn Haven Junction–Hazleton–Jeddo, Pa.; Cayuga–Geneva, N. Y.
Ontario Central: Manchester–West Victor, N. Y.
Owego & Harford: Owego–Harford, N. Y.
Pocono Northeast: Pittston Junction–Kingston, Pittston Junction–Wilkes-Barre, Pa.
Towanda-Monroeton Shippers' Lifeline: Towanda–Monroeton, Pa.

Louisiana & Arkansas Railway

In 1882 the Vicksburg, Shreveport & Pacific missed the town of Minden, Louisiana, by 5 miles. Mindenites chartered a railroad to connect the town with the railroad; it opened in 1885 between Minden and Sibley. In 1897 the Arkansas, Louisiana & Southern Railway was chartered to build north from Minden.

Meanwhile, 50 miles or so north in Stamps, Arkansas, William Buchanan was getting involved in the lumber business. Part of that business was a logging railroad which on March 18, 1898, was incorporated by Buchanan as the Louisiana & Arkansas Railroad. The L&A pushed south, the AL&S pushed north, and they met on September 29, 1898. The AL&S bought the Minden–Sibley line, the L&A bought the AL&S, and the L&A had its charter amended to permit extensions to Alexandria, La., and Natchez, Mississippi.

In 1902 the Louisiana & Arkansas Railway was incorporated to take over and extend the L&A. Buchanan owned all but 11 of the 2500 shares of stock. In 1903 the railroad opened an extension north to Hope, Ark., to connect with predecessors of the Missouri Pacific and the Frisco, and in 1910 it reached Shreveport by buying, rebuilding, and extending a logging railroad. The Natchez extension opened in 1913.

Buchanan died in 1926. His heirs had little

Ten-Wheeler 394, inherited from Louisiana Railway & Navigation, wheels into Bossier City, Louisiana, with the overnight *Hustler* from New Orleans. Photo by C. W. Witbeck.

221

interest in the railroad and negotiated to sell it in 1928 to a syndicate headed by Harvey Couch.

Louisiana Railway & Navigation Company

In 1896 William Edenborn, who had made his fortune in the steel wire business, adopted railroading as a second career. He began building a railroad southeast from Shreveport, the Shreveport & Red River Valley Railway. The new railroad followed the east bank of the Red River. The only other railroad in the area was Texas & Pacific's New Orleans–Shreveport line a few miles to the south on the other side of the river. Train service began between Shreveport and Coushatta in 1898.

Edenborn's initial purpose was to improve local transportation in the area, but he decided to push his railroad farther. In October 1901 the line reached Pineville, across the Red River from Alexandria. Edenborn continued to push his railroad southeast, crossing the Mississippi by ferry just north of its confluence with the Red River. The line reached New Orleans in 1906, and New Orleans–Shreveport passenger service began on April 14, 1907.

The new railroad developed well, and Edenborn was influential in persuading industries, oil refineries in particular, to locate along the line. The railroad operated at a deficit, unable to pay interest and dividends, but the major—almost sole—creditor and stockholder was Edenborn.

In 1923 the LR&N purchased a Missouri-Kansas-Texas branch that reached west from Shreveport to McKinney, Texas, about 20 miles north of Dallas, and in 1924 it opened its own station on Rampart Street in New Orleans (previously it had used Terminal Station). About that time Edenborn began negotiations to sell the LR&N to the Kansas City Southern. The Mississippi ferry crossing was a handicap to the sale, so in 1925 the road undertook to relocate its line, build a bridge over the Atchafalaya River, and establish a much shorter Mississippi River ferry crossing. Edenborn died in 1926, shortly before the new line and bridge were ready. Edenborn's widow sought a purchaser for the railroad and found it in Harvey Couch of the Louisiana & Arkansas. The L&A purchased the LR&N in 1928.

The enlarged L&A

The L&A was a well-maintained property that didn't go much of anywhere; the LR&N suffered from lack of maintenance but looked good on a map; and LR&N's Texas line made the rest of the LR&N look good. The railroad began to upgrade its properties and inaugurated two name trains: the Shreveport–Hope *Shreveporter*, which carried a St. Louis sleeper, and the overnight Shreveport–New Orleans *Hustler*. The company remained in the black through the Depression.

Kansas City Southern

During the 1930s Harvey Couch acquired an interest in the Kansas City Southern Railway, which had been seeking a route to New Orleans. In 1939 the Interstate Commerce Commission approved control of the L&A by the KCS. Operation of the two roads was unified, but L&A maintained a separate corporate existence until 1992. Major post-1939 events in L&A's history included the opening of a Mississippi River bridge at Baton Rouge in 1940, inauguration of the diesel-powered, streamlined Kansas City–New Orleans *Southern Belle* that same year, and sale of the Packton–Ferriday branch (the Natchez line) to the Louisiana Midland Railway in 1945.

Location of headquarters: Shreveport, Louisiana
Reporting marks: L&A
Notable named passenger trains: *Southern Belle* (Kansas City–New Orleans, operated jointly with Kansas City Southern)
Historical and technical society: Kansas City Southern Historical Society, P. O. Box 5332, Shreveport, LA 71135-5332
Recommended reading: *The Louisiana and Arkansas Railway*, by James R. Fair, published in 1997 by Northern Illinois University Press, 320 Williston Hall, DeKalb, IL 60115 (ISBN 0-87580-219-2)
Successor: Kansas City Southern
Portions still operated: Kansas City Southern: New Orleans–Alexandria–Shreveport (via LR&N)–Greenville, Texas; Sibley–Minden, La., Shreveport–Minden–Springhill, La.

Louisville & Nashville Railroad

In the 1840s Louisville, Kentucky, was developing into a river port and distribution center—except during seasons of low water in the Ohio River. The growing city needed more dependable transportation. Tennessee was already building railroads from Memphis and Nashville to Chattanooga, and the Western & Atlantic Railroad opened from Chattanooga to Atlanta, Georgia, in 1850.

Nashville interests proposed a railroad north toward but not into Louisville to capture the trade that moved through Louisville. That proposal spurred Louisville to action: In 1850 the Kentucky legislature chartered the Louisville & Nashville Railroad to build between the cities of its name, with branches to Lebanon, Ky., and Memphis, Tenn. The state of Tennessee issued a charter for the southern portion of the line, with the condition that the railroad come no closer to Nashville than the north bank of the Cumberland River—any freight for Nashville would have to enter the city by wagon.

Work went slowly because of problems with financing, disputes over the route, and low water that kept materials from arriving at Louisville. In March 1850 the road was opened between Louisville and Lebanon. The segment between Nashville and Bowling Green opened in August 1859, and two months later the line was completed,

A single E6 leads the Cincinnati–New Orleans *Humming Bird* through Turner, Kentucky, in 1948. A rebuilt heavyweight sleeping car trails the original six lightweight cars of the streamliner. L&N photo.

including a bridge across the Cumberland into Nashville and another over the Green River at Munfordville, Ky., that was the longest iron bridge in America at the time. The line to Memphis opened in April 1861. It was a joint effort by the L&N, the Memphis & Ohio, and the Memphis, Clarksville & Louisville railroads.

By then the Civil War had begun, with Kentucky on one side and Tennessee on the other. During the war Union and Confederate forces fought up and down the L&N, destroying as they went. By mid-1863 the major action of the war had moved to the Southeast. L&N began to pick up the pieces and get back to business—and there was enough business that L&N prospered.

Postwar expansion

With the war over, L&N began to find its territory invaded by competing railroads. On the west the Evansville, Henderson & Nashville was completed in 1872 and sold to the St. Louis & Southeastern Railway, and to the east the city of Cincinnati was busy planning and building the Cincinnati Southern Railway (now operated by the Southern Railway but still owned by the city).

To the south, though, L&N faced little competition. By 1860 several railroad companies had put together a line from Nashville to Decatur, Alabama—they were consolidated in 1866 as the Nashville & Decatur Railroad—and by 1870 a rail line was open from Montgomery, Ala., through Mobile to New Orleans. The Nashville & Decatur proposed a lease to the L&N if L&N would guarantee the completion of the South & North Alabama, which was under construction from Mobile north through the infant industrial center of Birmingham to Decatur. The

Louisville–Montgomery route was completed in 1872. L&N also began extending its Lebanon branch southeastward toward Knoxville and Cumberland Gap.

In 1875, therefore, L&N had a main line from Louisville to Montgomery and branches from Lebanon Junction to Livingston, Ky., from Richmond Junction to Richmond, Ky., and from Bowling Green, Ky., to Memphis. L&N began expanding in earnest. It purchased the Evansville, Henderson & St. Louis at foreclosure in 1879, gaining a second route from the Ohio River to Nashville. EH&StL's owner, the St. Louis & Southeastern, had been in receivership since 1874; its line from East St. Louis to Evansville was purchased by the Nashville, Chattanooga & St. Louis.

On the southern front, L&N purchased the Montgomery & Mobile and the New Orleans, Mobile & Texas, obtaining a route to New Orleans; along with the Montgomery & Mobile came routes into western Florida. L&N was alarmed at the sudden expansion of the NC&StL that promised a bridge over the Ohio, a link between Owensboro and Evansville, and leases of the Western & Atlantic and Central of Georgia. L&N began buying NC&StL stock, soon acquiring virtual control over its rival. L&N quickly took over NC&StL's East St. Louis–Evansville line and added it to its own system.

One of L&N's major acquisitions was the "Short Line" between Louisville and Cincinnati. The Louisville & Frankfort and Lexington & Frankfort railroads completed a line from Louisville to Lexington in 1851. There were proposals to extend that line from Lexington to Cincinnati and to build a new short, direct line

from Louisville to Cincinnati. The latter was built in 1869 by the Louisville & Frankfort in the face of rivalry between the cities of Louisville and Cincinnati, debate over the gauge (and thus over which city would have the freight transfer business), and even the route into Louisville—the city council advocated a route that the railroad said could be damaged by floods, and when the railroad knuckled under to the city and sent surveyors out, they found the proposed route deep under water. The two railroads consolidated in 1869 to form the Louisville, Cincinnati & Lexington Railroad, over the protests of the city of Frankfort that it would become simply a way station. L&N purchased the Louisville, Cincinnati & Lexington in 1881.

Another major acquisition was the Kentucky Central Railway, purchased from the C. P. Huntington interests in 1892. The road consisted of a main line from Covington, Ky., across the Ohio River from Cincinnati south to a junction with L&N's Lebanon Branch just north of Livingston, Ky., and a line from Lexington to Maysville, Ky., crossing the main line at Paris, Ky.

L&N had made a connection with the Southern Railway at Jellico, Tenn., for traffic to and from Knoxville, but shortly after the turn of the century decided to build its own line south to Knoxville and Atlanta. In 1902 L&N acquired the Knoxville Southern and the Marietta & North Georgia railroads, which formed a line from Knoxville to Marietta, Gal, 20 miles northwest of Atlanta on the Western & Atlantic. This line ran through an area rich in copper and marble—and through mountainous territory that required a pair of sharp curves between Whitestone and Talking Rock, Ga.—the "Hook"—and a complete loop between Farner and Appalachia, Tenn.—the Hiwassee Loop or "Eye." In 1906 L&N constructed a line with easier grades and curves between Etowah, Tenn., and Cartersville, Ga., west of the Hook & Eye line.

Affiliations

In 1898 L&N became the sole lessee of the Georgia Railroad and the affiliated Western Railway of Alabama and Atlanta & West Point but almost immediately assigned a half interest in the lease to Atlantic Coast Line.

In April 1902 Edwin Hawley and John W. Gates acquired a large block of L&N stock which they sold within a few weeks to J. P. Morgan & Co. Before the year was over Morgan sold his L&N interest—51 percent—to the Atlantic Coast Line Railroad. In May 1902 L&N and Southern, both under J. P. Morgan's control, jointly purchased the Chicago, Indianapolis & Louisville (Monon). Many pieces of the Seaboard System were in place 80 years before the creation of that railroad.

L&N was one of only a few railroads to build its own locomotives in any great numbers. Between 1905 and 1923 L&N's South Louisville Shops constructed more than 400 Consolidations, Pacifics, Mikados, and Eight-Wheel switchers. Although L&N was the largest coal hauler south of Virginia it began dieselizing relatively early. At the beginning of World War II L&N purchased 14 Berkshires for freight and passenger service and simultaneously began dieselizing passenger trains with a fleet of Electro-Motive E6s. L&N had already purchased its first road freight diesels, albeit for helper service, when 22 more 2-8-4s came from Lima in 1949

The year and the engine number are the same—1954—as one of L&N's M-1-class Berkshires leads an Atlanta-bound freight out of Decoursey (Kentucky) Yard a few miles south of Cincinnati. L&N photo.

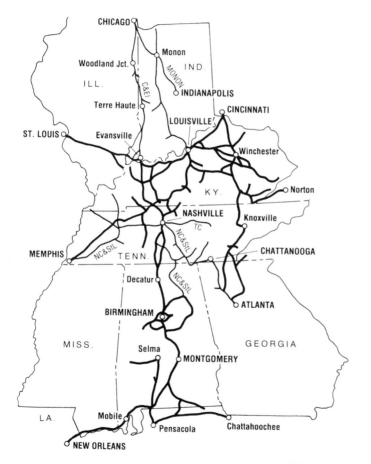

for service in the eastern Kentucky coalfields at a time when L&N was undertaking a great deal of branchline construction in that area. In 1950 L&N began to dieselize freight service in earnest, finishing the job by the end of 1956.

Passenger trains

The upgrading of passenger service after World War II centered on two coach streamliners, the Cincinnati-New Orleans *Humming Bird* and the St. Louis-Atlanta *Georgian,* placed in service in 1946. Both trains soon acquired sleeping cars and through cars to Chicago via the Chicago & Eastern Illinois—Chicago traffic on the *Georgian* quickly outstripped that on its original route.

The New York–New Orleans *Crescent Limited,* considered the premier train of the Southern Railway, but operated between Montgomery and New Orleans by L&N, was streamlined in 1950. In 1949 L&N and Seaboard teamed up to offer the Jacksonville–New Orleans *Gulf Wind.* L&N was a key link in the busiest Chicago–Florida passenger route, the "Dixie Route" (C&EI-L&N-NC&StL-ACL), and also forwarded the Pennsylvania Railroad's Chicago–Florida trains south of Louisville.

Mergers

L&N merged the Nashville, Chattanooga & St. Louis on August 30, 1957—a date some consider the beginning of the modern railroad merger era (others say it began a decade earlier when Pere Marquette, Denver & Salt Lake, and Alton were merged into larger systems). In 1969 L&N purchased the Woodland, Ill.–Evansville, Indiana, line of the Chicago & Eastern Illinois and

	1929	1982
Miles of railroad operated:	5,250	10,396
Number of locomotives:	1,350	1,086
Number of passenger cars:	1,006	113*
Number of freight cars:	64,134	53,095
Number of company service cars:	2,584	1,554

Location of headquarters: Louisville, Kentucky

Reporting marks: LN

Notable named passenger trains: *Pan-American, Humming Bird* (Cincinnati–New Orleans), *Crescent Limited* (New York–New Orleans, operated north of Montgomery, Ala., by West Point Route, Southern Railway, and Pennsylvania Railroad), *South Wind* (Chicago–Miami, operated jointly with Pennsylvania Railroad, Atlantic Coast Line, and Florida East Coast), *Georgian* (Chicago/St. Louis–Atlanta, operated jointly with Chicago & Eastern Illinois and Nashville, Chattanooga & St. Louis)

*(1970)

Historical and technical society: Louisville & Nashville Historical Society, P. O. Box 17122, Louisville, KY 40217; http://www.rrhistorical.com/lnhs

Recommended reading: *Louisville & Nashville Railroad, 1850–1963*, by Kincaid A. Herr, published in 1964 by the Public Relations Department, Louisville & Nashville Railroad, Louisville, Ky.

Predecessor railroads in this book:
Chicago, Indianapolis & Louisville (Monon)
Nashville, Chattanooga & St. Louis

Successors:
Seaboard System
CSX Transportation

Portions still operated: The only major routes of the "old" L&N (before the NC&StL merger) that have been cut or abandoned are the Bowling Green–Memphis line and some redundant lines between Louisville and Winchester and Richmond, Ky. For the status of Monon, NC&StL, and Tennessee Central see the entries for those roads.

acquired 140 miles of the abandoned Tennessee Central from Nashville to Crossville, Tenn. In 1971 L&N merged the Monon Railroad to obtain a second route from the Ohio River to Chicago. (L&N's financial interest in the Monon had been eliminated in Monon's 1946 reorganization.)

L&N's ownership by Atlantic Coast Line included a joint lease of the Carolina, Clinchfield & Ohio Railway (operated by the Clinchfield Railroad) and the railroad properties of the Georgia Railroad & Banking Co. (Georgia Railroad, Western Railway of Alabama, and Atlanta & West Point Rail Road). Atlantic Coast Line merged with Seaboard Air Line in 1967 to form Seaboard Coast Line Railroad.

In the mid-1970s SCL began to refer to the "Family Lines" in its advertising, and the ad usually included a list of the members. It wasn't an official railroad name, but it indicated probable merger in the future. On November 1, 1980, Seaboard Coast Line Industries, parent of Seaboard Coast Line Railroad, merged with Chessie System to form CSX Corporation, and on December 29, 1982, Seaboard Coast Line Railroad merged with L&N to form the Seaboard System Railroad.

Macon, Dublin & Savannah Railroad

The Macon, Dublin & Savannah began construction southeast from Macon, Georgia, in 1885, the year of its incorporation. The line reached Dublin in 1891 and the decision was made not to build all the way to Savannah but only to Vidalia, where the MD&S could connect with the Georgia & Alabama Railway. The Georgia & Alabama became part of the Seaboard Air Line in 1900, forming its Savannah–Montgomery line, and the MD&S served as a Macon branch of that route.

In 1904 the Atlantic Coast Line purchased the outstanding stock and bonds of the MD&S but soon realized that the railroad was many miles from the nearest ACL track, an orphan. In 1906 ACL sold its holdings to the Seaboard. In 1930 SAL owned somewhat less than half of MD&S's stock but in the mid-1940s acquired the remainder. SAL absorbed the MD&S on March 1, 1958. The Georgia Central Railway purchased the line in 1990. The entire line is still in operation.

	1929	1957
Miles of railroad operated:	94	93
Number of locomotives:	11	8
Number of passenger cars:	7	
Number of freight cars:	21	
Number of company service cars:	11	
Number of freight and company service cars:		107

Location of headquarters: Macon, Georgia
Reporting marks: MD&S
Successors:
Seaboard Air Line
Seaboard System
CSX Transportation
Georgia Central
Portions still operated: Georgia Central: Macon–Vidalia
Map: See page 386 (Seaboard Air Line)

In 1946 Macon, Dublin & Savannah acquired an ex-Western Maryland Pacific from its parent Seaboard Air Line. The much-traveled Baldwin is shown at Dublin, Georgia, on the daily passenger train. MD&S's diesel fleet comprised a Baldwin VO1000 and seven Alco RS-2s. Photo by Truman Blasingame.

Maine Central Railroad

A recurring theme in the history of railroad development in Maine is the establishment of a year-round Atlantic seaport for Canada—the St. Lawrence River freezes over in winter. Numerous railroads were chartered in Maine with Montreal or Quebec as their destinations. Several more were proposed to build from the coast to the shore of Moosehead Lake, a large lake about halfway between Bangor and Quebec.

The Maine Central didn't get caught up in the push to Canada, but the first of the railroads that did, the Atlantic & St. Lawrence, provided the jumping-off place for two predecessors of the

Maine Central. Construction of the A&StL began in 1846, but it went slowly. The line was completed from Portland to Montreal in 1853, and it was immediately leased by the Grand Trunk Railway of Canada.

From Danville, 27 miles north of Portland on the A&StL, the Androscoggin & Kennebec began construction of a line to Waterville. At the same time the Penobscot & Kennebec, which had the same backers, was under construction from Waterville to Bangor. Both roads, like the Atlantic & St. Lawrence, were built with a track gauge of 5 feet 6 inches.

Meanwhile the standard gauge Kennebec &

Portland was under construction from Yarmouth, 12 miles from Portland on the A&StL, east to Brunswick, then north along the Kennebec River to Augusta, the state capital, where it connected with (and operated and later leased) the Somerset & Kennebec to Waterville and Skowhegan. In 1850 the Kennebec & Portland built its own line into Portland from Yarmouth.

By the late 1850s there were four railroads in the area between Portland, Waterville, and Bangor, all with "Kennebec" in their names. Two were broad gauge and two were standard gauge. In the same territory was the broad gauge Androscoggin Railroad, opened in 1855 between

Two GP7s cross the Kennebec River at Fairfield, Maine, on February 14, 1976, with freight bound for Dover-Foxcroft. Photo by Ronald N. Johnson.

Leeds Junction on the Androscoggin & Kennebec east of Lewiston, and Farmington. In 1861 after discussions with the A&K fell apart, the Androscoggin Railroad built an extension south to the Kennebec & Portland at Brunswick and narrowed its track to standard gauge. The Eastern Railroad added to the confusion by taking sides with the standard gauge lines in a dispute over through fares. There were all the makings of a railroad war, or at least a railroady sort of Russian novel adapted to the stage by Gilbert and Sullivan.

Maine Central gathers them in

The Maine Central was incorporated in 1862 to consolidate the Androscoggin & Kennebec and Penobscot & Kennebec railroads. In 1870 it leased the Portland & Kennebec (the reorganized Kennebec & Portland) and in 1871 leased the Androscoggin Railroad. That same year Maine Central converted its own lines to standard gauge. It absorbed the leased lines soon after and came under the control of the Eastern Railroad. That control passed to the Boston & Maine in 1884.

With a monopoly established in the territory between Bangor and Portland, the Maine Central began expanding. In 1882 MEC leased the European & North American Railway. The E&NA had been conceived as a rail line to the farthest tip of Nova Scotia (cutting the steamship time to Europe to a minimum) and as part of a rail route between Montreal and the Maritime Provinces. It opened from Bangor to Vanceboro, on the New Brunswick border, in 1871; consolidated with its Canadian counterpart (Vanceboro to Saint John); leased the Bangor &

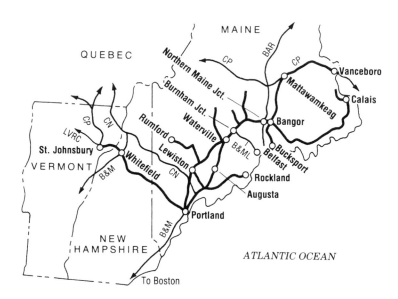

Piscataquis and Bucksport & Bangor railroads; then slipped into receivership in 1875, losing most of its acquisitions. Construction in 1884 extended the Maine Central through Ellsworth to Mount Desert Ferry.

Maine Central leased the Portland & Ogdensburg in 1888. The P&O was the Maine and New Hampshire portion of a series of railroads from Portland to Lake Ontario. Control of the other segments by other railroads reduced the line to local status (the other pieces became the St. Johnsbury & Lake Champlain and the western portion of the Rutland).

In 1890 MEC leased the Upper Coos Railroad and the Hereford Railway, which together formed a route along the upper reaches of the Connecticut River and north across the Canadian border to a connection with the Quebec Central.

In 1891 MEC leased the Knox & Lincoln Railway, which ran from Woolwich, across the

	1929	1981
Miles of railroad operated:	1,121	818
Number of locomotives:	201	73
Number of passenger cars:	246	66*
Number of freight cars:	6,698	4,523
Number of company service cars:	410	215

Location of headquarters: Portland, Maine

Reporting marks: MEC

Notable named passenger trains: *Flying Yankee* (Boston–Bangor; operated west of Portland by Boston & Maine)

*(1959)

Historical and technical society: The 470 Club, Inc., P. O. Box 641, Portland, ME 04104

Subsidiaries and affiliated railroads, 1981: Portland Terminal Company

Successor: Guilford Transportation Industries

Portions still operated:

Guilford: Portland–Lewiston–Waterville–Bangor–Mattawamkeag; Royal Junction–Brunswick–Lewiston Lower; Augusta–Waterville; Leeds Junction–Rumford; Oakland–North Anson; Fairfield–Hinckley; Bangor–Bucksport

Maine Coast Railroad: Brunswick–Rockland; Brunswick–Augusta

New Brunswick Southern: Mattawamkeag–Vanceboro; Calais–St. Croix Junction–Woodland

New Hampshire Central Railroad: North Stratford–Columbia Bridge, N. H.

Twin State Railroad: Whitefield, N. H.–St. Johnsbury, Vt.

Kennebec River from Bath, east to Rockland. In 1904 it acquired control of the Washington County Railroad, built in 1893 from Ellsworth east to Calais and Eastport. In 1907 MEC acquired control of the Somerset Railroad, which stretched north along the Kennebec River from Oakland, west of Waterville, to Moosehead Lake; that same year MEC leased the Portland & Rumford Falls Railway, which ran from Auburn west to Poland and Mechanic Falls, then north to Kennebago.

In 1911 the Portland Terminal Company was created as a wholly owned subsidiary of the MEC. It acquired MEC's and Boston & Maine's terminal properties in and around Portland.

Maine's most prosperous 2-foot-gauge railroads, the Sandy River & Rangeley Lakes and the Bridgton & Saco River, came under the control of the Maine Central in 1911 and 1912. The prosperity soon evaporated, and the narrow gauge lines regained their independence in 1923 and 1927, respectively.

Pruning the tree

The lease of the Hereford Railway was terminated in 1925. Part of its line was abandoned; part sold to Canadian Pacific. The Belfast & Moosehead Lake Railroad, which MEC had leased since its opening in 1871, began independent operation in 1926. In 1927 the state of Maine opened a rail and highway bridge across the Kennebec between Bath and Woolwich, replacing the ferry which had been the Rockland Branch's connection to the rest of the railroad.

Two long branches reaching northward were abandoned in the 1930s: the former Somerset Railroad from Austin Junction, near Bingham, to Kineo Station on the shore of Moosehead Lake, and the Portland & Rumford Falls north of Rumford in 1935 and 1936. Most of the remainder of the Portland & Rumford Falls was abandoned in 1952.

Control of the Maine Central by the Boston & Maine ended in 1914, but in 1933 MEC entered an agreement with the B&M for joint employment of some officers and personnel. The cooperative arrangement, which provided the benefits of merged operation, continued until 1952, when MEC took steps to resume its independence. Separation from B&M was completed on December 29, 1955.

Passenger service on the Maine Central ceased in 1960, though the trains remained in service for a while as mail and express carriers (handicapped somewhat by the decision of Boston & Maine, MEC's principal passenger connection, to drop all mail and express service and concentrate on carrying passengers).

In 1974 Maine Central sold the former European & North American line between Mattawamkeag and Vanceboro, 57 miles, to Canadian Pacific, retaining trackage rights—essentially swapping positions on that stretch of track, which was part of CPR's Montreal–Saint John line.

Two years later MEC sold its North Stratford, N. H.–Beecher Falls, Vt., line to the state of New Hampshire. The North Stratford Railroad began operating the line in 1977. In the late 1970s Maine Central upgraded the track on its Mountain Division, the former Portland & Ogdensburg line from Portland through the White Mountains to St. Johnsbury, Vt. Even though local business had decreased, traffic interchanged with Canadian Pacific at St. Johnsbury was still at a good level.

Purchase of the Maine Central

In December 1980 U. S. Filter Corporation purchased the railroad. Almost immediately Ashland Oil took over U. S. Filter and in June 1981 sold the railroad to Guilford Transportation Industries. Suddenly it made more sense to route traffic to and from the west via Boston & Maine and Delaware & Hudson, and the Mountain Division was out of a job. Through freight service ceased, and Mattawamkeag replaced St. Johnsbury as the interchange with CPR. By the mid-1980s the Portland–St. Johnsbury line was all but abandoned. MEC abandoned the Rockland and Calais branches about the same time and petitioned to abandon most of the "Lower Road," the Portland–Augusta–Waterville route, leaving the railroad with a main line from Portland through Lewiston, Waterville, and Bangor to Mattawamkeag and a few branches.

Guilford management has had about as much success with Maine Central as it has had with Boston & Maine. For a while the entire railroad was leased to the Springfield Terminal to take advantage of labor agreements. Guilford's future appears uncertain.

Mexican Railway (Ferrocarril Mexicano)

The Mexican Railway was projected as early as 1837. It was chartered in 1855 as a transcontinental line from Veracruz, on the Gulf of Mexico, through Mexico City to Acapulco, on the Pacific, a straight-line distance of approximately 300 miles. The first piece of the line, three miles out of Mexico City, opened in 1857. The route to Veracruz was then surveyed, and by 1861 a few miles of track had been laid west from Veracruz.

Then Mexico defaulted on the interest payments on its European debts. Great Britain and Spain joined with France to collect the debts by force. Britain and Spain withdrew their troops from Mexico, but the French remained. Napoleon III of France established a monarchy in Mexico and placed the emperor Maximilian on the throne in 1864. Mexico demanded that France withdraw, and at the end of the U. S. Civil War the U. S. government moved troops to the border to support Mexico's demands. Napoleon III withdrew, leaving Maximilian to face capture and execution.

The situation stabilized sufficiently that the railway could attract British capital, and it was registered in England as the Imperial Mexican Ry. Co., Ltd. Construction resumed and at the end of 1872 the road was opened from Veracruz to Mexico City, 264 miles. It was never extended beyond Mexico City.

Ferrocarril Mexicano 32, an 0-6-6-0 named Orizava, was built in 1872. The plate on the tank at the far end reads "Fairlie's Patent." Photo from the collection of Gerald M. Best.

The Maltrata Incline

The line was notable for its engineering. In the 48 miles from Veracruz to Paso del Macho the line climbed from sea level to 1,560 feet. That averages to a little over 30 feet a mile; FCM's maximum grade there was 1.7 percent. From Mexico City east to Esperanza (elevation 8,045 feet) the line lay across a plateau, with grades of no more than 1.5 percent. But in the 64 miles between Esperanza and Paso del

	1929	1959
Miles of railroad operated:	490	292
Number of steam locomotives:	93	75
Number of electric locomotives:	12	12
Number of passenger cars:	110	59
Number of freight cars:	1,153	644
Number of company service cars:	110	59

Location of headquarters: Mexico City, Mexico

Reporting marks: FCM

Recommended reading:
Mexican Narrow Gauge, by Gerald M. Best, published in 1968 by Howell-North Books, 850 North Hollywood Way, Burbank, CA 91505

Successors: National Railways of Mexico

Portions still operated: National Railways of Mexico: Mexico City–Veracruz; Apizaco–Puebla

Mexicano B-B-B electric 1011 helps a pair of National of Mexico F units lift the Veracruz–Mexico City day train to the top of the Orizaba–Esparanza grade in 1961. Photo by Jim Shaughnessy.

Macho included a difference in elevation of 6,485 feet. The steepest part of the line, the Maltrata Incline, had ruling grades of 4.7 percent and curves of 16.5 degrees (radius, 347 feet).

Mexicano's initial solution to the problem of motive power that could cope with such grades was the Fairlie articulated: a pair of swiveling engine units beneath a double-ended center-firebox boiler. The second solution was to electrify the line. The first segment of the electrification, between Orizaba and Esperanza, was opened in 1923, and the wires were extended east to Paso del Macho by 1928. The electrification was still in service as late as the end of 1968, but it was discontinued in the early 1970s. Other noteworthy locomotives were a group of 3-cylinder Pacifics, 4 built in 1928 by Alco and 3 in 1938 by Montreal, and 10 2-8-0s turned out by Baldwin in 1946.

Narrow gauge lines

The Mexicano had five principal branch lines with four different gauges. Two were purchased in 1909, the 34-mile, 30-inch-gauge Zacatlan Railway and the 20-mile, 2-foot-gauge Cordoba Huatusco Railway. In 1913 FCM bought the 57-mile, 3-foot-gauge San Marcos & Huajuapan De Leon Railway. The Huatusco Branch was abandoned in 1951, and the Zacatlan and Huajuapan branches were abandoned in 1958. All three narrow gauge branches were named for towns they never reached.

The standard gauge line from Apizaco to Puebla remains in service; the standard gauge branch from Xalta to Pachuca, opened in 1890, was abandoned in 1956. In 1921 FCM began construction of the line between Pachuca and Tampico that would cut in half the distance from Mexico City to Tampico; the project was abandoned in 1931 after two short stubs out of Pachuca and Tampico had been constructed.

A 6-mile branch from Santa Ana, on the Puebla Branch, to Tlaxcala, was operated in 1930 with Ford motor cars according to Moody's manual for that year. That branch was abandoned in 1944.

The Mexicano was purchased by the Mexican government in 1946. In 1959 it ceased to exist as a separate company and its operations were merged with National Railways of Mexico. The main line is still in service, but the Orizaba–Esperanza section of the line is being augmented by a new line with easier grades. The new line will have the highest double-track railroad bridge in the world.

Midland Terminal Railway

The name "Midland Terminal" refers to the road's original purpose as a switching road between mines at Cripple Creek and a mainline railroad, the Colorado Midland—and also refers to the terminal phase of the Colorado Midland's existence. A brief history of the CM is a necessary prelude to discussion of the Midland Terminal.

Colorado Midland

In 1883 a line drawn through Denver, Pueblo, and Trinidad, Colo., would have been the demarcation between standard gauge and narrow gauge railroading in the state. It was surprising, therefore, when a standard gauge railroad from Colorado Springs over Ute Pass into the South Park was proposed and incorporated in November 1883—the Colorado Midland Railway, to build from Colorado Springs to Leadville and Salida. It was to be primarily a local railroad, the Rock Island's line into Colorado Springs from the east was still five years in the future.

Financial backing for the new railroad came from James J. Hagerman, who had been instructed by his physician to find a climate better for his health than that of Milwaukee. Hagerman owned mines near Aspen and Glenwood Springs, and he proposed building a western extension of the CM first because of the traffic

Midland Terminal bought six 0-6-0s from the U. S. Army in 1946 and rebuilt three of them as Moguls. All three are shown here with an ore train near Bull Hill in October 1948. Photo by Donald Duke.

those mines would furnish. When the two established roads in Colorado, the Denver & Rio Orande and the Union Pacific, doubled their rates on rails carried to Leadville, Hagerman decided to start from Colorado Springs. Construction of the hastily surveyed route over Ute Pass began in 1886, and the line was completed to Glenwood Springs in December 1887. It included the Hagerman Tunnel west of Leadville, 2,060 feet long at an elevation of 11,530 feet.

By then Grand Junction, Colo., and Ogden, Utah, were CM's goals. (The rail route west from Grand Junction was the independent Denver & Rio Grande Western Railway at the time.) CM continued its line down the south bank of the Grand River (the pre-1921 name of the Colorado River east of Grand Junction), reaching New Castle about the time the Denver & Rio Grande on the north bank did. The two roads formed the Rio Grande Junction Railway to build the line to Grand Junction. In 1890 that line was completed, Denver & Rio Grande finished standard-gauging its main line, and Santa Fe purchased the Colorado Midland.

Midland Terminal Railway is born

Also in 1890 gold was discovered west of Pikes Peak. Colorado Midland proposed a branch south from the main line at the summit of Hayden Divide to Midland, there to connect with a new 2-foot-gauge line, the Midland Terminal Railway, to go the last few miles to Victor and Cripple Creek. The Midland Terminal built the whole line from Divide to Cripple Creek. The knowledge that the narrow gauge Florence & Cripple Creek was building north from a connection with the narrow gauge Denver & Rio Grande caused a change to standard gauge, since MT's only connection would be the standard gauge CM. The line was opened to Victor in December 1894 and to Cripple Creek a year later. Traffic was outbound ore for processing in the mills at Colorado Springs and inbound merchandise and supplies.

The panic of 1893 was caused in part by the closing of the mints of India to silver coinage. The resulting silver glut was doubly hard on Colorado: The U. S. was on a bimetallic money standard (until silver was demonetized in late 1893), and silver mining was one of Colorado's major industries. CM's traffic fell off. The company defaulted on its bond interest and soon found itself in receivership. Reorganization occurred in 1897.

Also in 1893 the Busk-Ivanhoe Tunnel under Hagerman Pass was opened, eliminating 575 feet of elevation and more than five complete circles from CM's line. The tunnel was owned by a separate company, and after a dispute over tolls in 1897 CM reopened its old line over the pass. Blizzards in early 1899 tied up the Leadville-Glenwood end of the road for more than two months. CM purchased the Busk-Ivanhoe Tunnel in 1899.

Colorado Midland purchased

That same year the Colorado & Southern and the Rio Grande Western jointly purchased the Colorado Midland, two years later Denver & Rio Grande, CM's principal competitor, bought the RGW and with it RGW's half interest in the Colorado Midland. Initially CM's fears that its traffic would be diverted to the D&RG proved groundless. Rio Grande routed traffic over CM while rebuilding and upgrading its own line, but took the traffic itself once it had the capacity to move it. Colorado & Southern was purchased by the Burlington, which was in turn part of the Hill empire—of which the CM was an insignificant piece. CM defaulted on its Rio Grande Junction obligations, Rio Grande bought CM's half interest, and CM entered receivership again in 1912.

Colorado Midland abandoned

In 1917 Albert E. Carlton purchased the Colorado Midland at foreclosure. He proposed an extension to Utah, using the Uintah Railway as part of the new line (but bypassing the 7.5-percent grades and 66-degree curves of Baxter Pass). During World War I the USRA noted on its maps CM's short route across Colorado and routed a great deal of traffic over the line—until the road choked up and the USRA withdrew all traffic.

The road closed down in August 1918. Carlton delayed dismantling the line while the Santa Fe considered purchasing it, but scrapping began in 1921. Carlton gave the right of way to the state for highways, except for the Busk-Ivanhoe Tunnel, which became first a toll highway tunnel, then a conduit to bring western slope water into the Arkansas Valley for irrigation.

For a few years in the late teens all the railroads in Cripple Creek—the Midland Terminal, the Colorado Springs & Cripple Creek District, and the remains of the Florence & Cripple Creek—were united as the Cripple Creek & Colorado Springs under Carlton. Upon the demise of the Colorado Midland, the Midland Terminal took over the CM line from Divide to Colorado Springs. Within a few years it was the sole railroad serving the dying mining industry of Cripple Creek. There was a brief revival in 1933 when the government revised gold prices, but for the most part the trend was just as much downhill as the journey the ore made from Cripple Creek and Victor to the mill at Colorado Springs. Finally a new mill near Victor removed the last reason for the existence of the railroad. The Midland Terminal ceased operation in February 1949.

	1929	1948
Miles of railroad operated:	56	56
Number of locomotives:	9	7
Number of passenger cars:	15	
Number of freight cars:	240	279
Number of company service cars:	25	20

Location of headquarters: Colorado Springs, Colorado

Historical and technical society: Colorado Midland Railway, c/o E. M. McFarland, 475 Ocelot Drive, Colorado Springs, CO 80919

Recommended reading: *The Cripple Creek Road,* by Edward M. "Mel" McFarland, published in 1984 by Pruett Publishing Co., 3235 Prairie Avenue, Boulder, CO 80301 (ISBN 0-87108-647-6)

Midland Valley Railroad

Kansas, Oklahoma & Gulf Railway
Oklahoma City-Ada-Atoka Railway

These three railroads were controlled by the Muskogee Company and were operated jointly; in later years most of the rolling stock was lettered for all three roads. Muskogee also owned the Foraker Co., which in turn owned the 18-mile Osage Railway, which connected with the Midland Valley at Foraker in northern Oklahoma. The Osage was abandoned in 1953.

Midland Valley

The Midland Valley was incorporated in 1903 and completed its line from Hoye, Arkansas, south of Fort Smith, through Muskogee and Tulsa, Oklahoma, to Wichita, Kansas, in 1906. MV reached Fort Smith by exercising trackage rights over the Frisco; the road owned

Kansas, Oklahoma & Gulf 2-10-2 No. 500 brings a freight over the Katy crossing at Durant, Oklahoma, in December 1948. Photo by Preston George.

considerable coal land in that area of Arkansas and adjoining Oklahoma. In 1926 MV made a joint facility and operation agreement with the Kansas, Oklahoma & Gulf and in 1930 did the same with the Oklahoma City-Ada-Atoka. In 1930 the Muskogee Company acquired control of the MV.

Kansas, Oklahoma & Gulf

The Kansas, Oklahoma & Gulf was incorporated in 1918 as a successor to the Missouri, Oklahoma & Gulf The MO&G was built between 1903 and 1913 from Muskogee northeast to Joplin, Mo., and southwest to Denison, Texas. The only major town it served was Muskogee, and at nearly every town it faced competition from the long-established Frisco and Katy. It was proposed to extend the MO&G north to Pittsburg, Kans., then to Kansas City on trackage rights over Kansas City Southern to form a connection between the Union Pacific at Kansas City and the Houston & Texas Central (Southern Pacific) at Denison. The proposed extension was mentioned well into the 1920s, but it was never built. The MO&G was sold at foreclosure and reorganized as the Kansas, Oklahoma & Gulf in July 1919.

The KO&G entered receivership in 1924 and was acquired by Midland Valley interests in 1925. The KO&G and MV worked out joint facility agreements, and KO&G developed into a bridge route for Kansas–Texas traffic between the Missouri Pacific and the Texas & Pacific. About 1960 MP and T&P rerouted such traffic to remain on MP and T&P rails all the way, drying up much of KO&G's traffic. In 1962 KO&G abandoned the northern 105 miles of its line

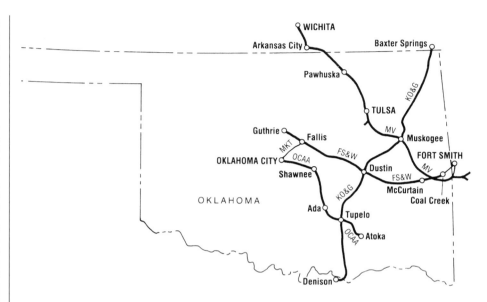

between Baxter Springs, Kans., and Okay (North Muskogee), Okla.

Oklahoma City-Ada-Atoka

The Oklahoma City-Ada-Atoka was incorporated in 1923 to acquire the Shawnee Division of the Missouri-Kansas-Texas, which was undergoing reorganization. The line ran from Oklahoma City to Atoka, Okla. In 1930 OCAA acquired the Oklahoma City–Shawnee Interurban Railway. Muskogee Co. acquired control in 1929.

Purchase by Texas & Pacific

In 1962 the Muskogee Co. authorized the sale of all its railroad stocks to the Texas & Pacific. In September 1964 T&P acquired control of the three Muskogee roads but immediately sold the OCAA to the Santa Fe. OCAA was merged with Santa Fe on December 1, 1967. Midland Valley was merged into T&P on April 1, 1967, and the same happened to KO&G exactly three years later. The Muskogee Company was dissolved in 1964 after its properties were sold.

Midland Valley

	1929	1966
Miles of railroad operated:	363	333
Number of locomotives:	26	
Number of passenger cars:	19	
Number of freight cars:	295	
Number of company service cars:	73	2

Location of headquarters: Muskogee, Oklahoma
Reporting marks: MV
Portions still operated:
Osage Railroad (1990): Tulsa–Barnsdall, Okla.
Union Pacific: Muskogee–Tulsa, Okla.

Kansas, Oklahoma & Gulf

	1929	1969
Miles of railroad operated:	327	206
Number of locomotives:	28	15
Number of passenger cars:	3	
Number of freight cars:	255	
Number of company service cars:	48	
Number of freight and company service cars:		46

Location of headquarters: Muskogee, Oklahoma
Reporting marks: KO&G
Portions still operated: Union Pacific: Muskogee–Okay, Okla.

Oklahoma City-Ada-Atoka

	1929	1966
Miles of railroad operated:	129	101
Number of passenger cars:	7	
Number of company service cars:	6	

Location of headquarters: Muskogee, Oklahoma
Recommended reading: Railroads in Oklahoma, edited by Donovan L. Hofsommer, published in 1977 by the Oklahoma Historical Society, 2100 North Lincoln, Oklahoma City, OK 73105
Successors:
Texas & Pacific
Missouri Pacific
Atchison, Topeka & Santa Fe

MidSouth Rail Corporation

MIDSOUTH

The Clinton & Vicksburg Railroad was incorporated in 1833. By 1840 it had been renamed the Vicksburg & Jackson and was operating between the Mississippi cities of its name. Across the Mississippi River from Vicksburg, the Vicksburg, Shreveport & Texas had a line as far west as Monroe, Louisiana. The Civil War destroyed both roads, but they were rebuilt. By 1890 both had new corporate structures and new names (Alabama & Vicksburg Railway and Vicksburg, Shreveport & Pacific Railway) and were part of the Queen & Crescent System, a group of affiliated railroads reaching from Cincinnati to New Orleans and from Meridian, Miss., west to Shreveport, La.

The Cincinnati–New Orleans portion of the Queen & Crescent eventually became part of the Southern Railway system, and Illinois Central acquired the Vicksburg Route in 1926. A bridge over the Mississippi River at Vicksburg was opened in 1930, eliminating the need for a train ferry.

As part of Illinois Central Gulf's slimming down in the 1980s, on March 31, 1986, MidSouth Rail Corporation purchased ICG's line from Meridian to Shreveport, plus short branches north and south from Vicksburg (remnants of ICG's Memphis–Baton Rouge

A MidSouth local freight returns to Vicksburg from a trip to a paper mill at Redwood, Mississippi. Photo by Louis R. Saillard.

line) and a line not connected with the others extending from Hattiesburg to Gulfport, Miss., once part of the Gulf & Ship Island Railroad.

Illinois Central Gulf had operated a single daily train each way. MidSouth increased that to two trains a day over much of its main line, and scheduled those to minimize delay to cars delivered to the railroad. Pulpwood, paper, and

chemicals constituted more than 60 percent of the road's traffic. About one-third of MidSouth's traffic originated on line; another third was received from other roads and terminated on line; and the remainder was bridge or overhead traffic.

At the end of 1991 MidSouth purchased through a new subsidiary, TennRail, the Corinth & Counce Railroad, a 16-mile line from Corinth, Miss., to Counce, Tennessee.

In the 1990s Illinois Central decided to grow. In December 1990 it offered to buy MidSouth, perhaps starting the whole cycle over again. It's worth noting that IC chairman and CEO Edward Moyers was instrumental in starting MidSouth. MidSouth considered the offer unso-

licited and inadequate. IC asked the Interstate Commerce Commission for approval, then almost immediately dropped its request. Kansas City Southern was also growing and in September 1991 announced its offer to purchase MidSouth. In early 1993 Illinois Central dropped its opposition, and the ICC approved KCS's proposal on June 4, 1993.

MidLouisiana Rail Corporation

On September 8, 1987, MidSouth purchased the 40-mile North Louisiana & Gulf Railroad, with which it connected at Gibsland, La. The NL&G was incorporated in 1906 and was owned by Continental Can Co., which has a large paper mill at Hodge, La. Along with the NL&G came a 25-mile subsidiary, the Central Louisiana & Gulf Railway, which in 1980 acquired a short segment of former Rock Island track between Hodge and Winnfield, La. MidSouth renamed its acquisition Mid-Louisiana Rail Corporation.

SouthRail Corporation

Even before MidSouth was created, ICG spun off most of its ex-Gulf, Mobile & Ohio lines in Mississippi and Alabama to the Gulf & Mississippi Railroad on July 10, 1985. The new road was handicapped by poor track conditions and competition from ICG and Burlington Northern lines. It was facing bankruptcy when a MidSouth subsidiary, SouthRail Corporation, acquired it on April 14, 1988.

MidSouth	1986	1993
Miles of railroad operated:	474	1,197
Number of locomotives:	58	117
Number of freight cars:	1,571	4,694
Reporting marks: MSRC, MDR, SR		
North Louisiana & Gulf	1987	
Miles of railroad operated:	65	
Number of locomotives:	6	
Number of freight cars:	1,141	
Reporting marks: NLG		
Gulf & Mississippi	1987	
Miles of railroad operated:	732	
Number of locomotives:	46	
Number of freight cars:	897	
Reporting marks: GMSR		
Location of headquarters: Jackson, Mississippi		
Recommended reading: "Rebirth of the Vicksburg Route," by Louis R. Saillard, in *Trains* Magazine, April 1989, pages 30–41		
Predecessor railroads in this book:		
Gulf, Mobile & Northern		
Gulf, Mobile & Ohio		
Illinois Central Gulf		
Mobile & Ohio		
Successor: Kansas City Southern		

Minneapolis & St. Louis Railroad

The Minneapolis & St. Louis began with the chartering of the Minnesota Western Railroad in 1853. The name was changed to Minneapolis & St. Louis Railway in 1870, and the company built a line that reached from White Bear, Minn., south through Minneapolis to Albert Lea and by 1881 to Fort Dodge, Iowa. By 1884 a tentacle stretched west from Minneapolis to Watertown, South Dakota, and in 1900 a line was opened from Winthrop, Minn., on the Watertown line, south to Storm Lake, Iowa. In 1905 the Minnesota, Dakota & Pacific Railway extended the Watertown line west to Leola and Le Beau, S. Dak., with the thought of eventual extension to the Pacific. M&StL purchased the MD&P in 1912.

Meanwhile the Iowa Central after reorganizations and renamings, had assembled a railroad from Albia east through Oskaloosa to Peoria, Illinois, and from Oskaloosa north across Iowa to a connection with the M&StL at Northwood, Iowa, south of Albert Lea.

Edwin Hawley

In 1896 Edwin Hawley became president of the M&StL and soon afterward president of the Iowa Central. Hawley also became involved with the Alton and the Toledo, St. Louis & Western (the Clover Leaf), and for a brief season around 1911 the four roads were under common man-

After World War II M&StL's passenger trains consisted of mail-baggage gas-motor cars pulling Budd-built streamlined coaches. One such train is shown at Albert Lea, Minnesota, next to Alco RS-1 No. 546 in July 1953. M&StL numbered its diesels for the month and year of delivery. Photo by Dale Bufkin.

agement. Hawley also invested in the Chesapeake & Ohio, the Missouri-Kansas-Texas, and the Kansas City, Mexico & Orient in the hope of assembling a coast-to-coast railroad system.

Such a system never materialized—the only thing to come out of it was the purchase of the Iowa Central by the M&StL on January 1, 1912, a month before Hawley's death.

The third major portion of the M&StL was the Des Moines & Fort Dodge–Des Moines Valley system, a route from Des Moines through Perry and Fort Dodge to Ruthven, Iowa, and by trackage rights over Milwaukee Road to Spencer, on M&StL's Winthrop–Storm Lake line. Later, trackage rights over the Burlington between Oskaloosa and Des Moines connected the south end with the rest of the M&StL.

Sprague rescues the M&StL

The M&StL ran into financial trouble and entered receivership in 1923. The bondholders elected Walter Colpitts of Coverdale & Colpitts, the railroad engineering firm, as chairman of their reorganization committee. He appointed Lucian Sprague as receiver. Sprague took over at the beginning of 1935 in the face of numerous proposals to dismember, parcel out, and abandon the M&StL. He sold antiquated rolling stock as scrap to realize immediate cash, modernized the road's locomotives, and opened traffic offices and began soliciting business at a time when other railroads were pulling back.

In 1942 the road was sold—after 42 previous efforts to auction it off—to Coverdale & Colpitts, the firm that had managed its reorganization. The reorganized M&StL encompassed a new Railway Company (the main lines), a new Railroad Corporation (the branches), and the old Railroad Company, all titled Minneapolis & St. Louis. The separation of the branch lines was found unnecessary by 1944. The M&StL began dieselization in 1938 and was fully dieselized by 1950.

Ben Heineman and the C&NW

In May 1954 a group of stockholders led by attorney Ben Heineman took over the M&StL, and Heineman replaced Sprague as chairman of the board. Heineman's only previous railroad experience was in representing a group of stockholders in a dividend case against the Chicago Great Western. Heineman revived an old idea of a belt route around Chicago and began negotiating to purchase Toledo, Peoria & Western stock. His purchase of a block of Monon stock apparently alerted the Santa Fe and the Pennsylvania, which jointly purchased the TP&W to block Heineman.

In 1956 the M&StL acquired all the stock of the Minnesota Western Railway (Minneapolis to Gluek, Minn., 115 miles; a 1924 reorganization of the Electric Short Line Railway and a sometime affiliate of the Minneapolis, Northfield & Southern) and renamed it the Minneapolis Industrial Railway. It was abandoned in the early 1970s.

Heineman gave the M&StL a modern-thinking, aggressive management before he moved on to the Chicago & North Western in 1956. Chicago & North Western purchased the railroad assets of the M&StL on November 1, 1960.

	1929	1959
Miles of railroad operated:	1,628	1,391
Number of locomotives:	218	74
Number of passenger cars:	122	10
Number of freight cars:	6,581	4,178
Number of company service cars:	310	116

Location of headquarters: Minneapolis, Minnesota

Reporting marks: M&StL, MSTL

Historical and technical society: Chicago & North Western Historical Society, P. O. Box 1436, Elmhurst, IL 60126-9998

Recommended reading: *Mileposts on the Prairie,* by Frank P. Donovan, published in 1950 by Simmons-Boardman Publishing Corporation, 1809 Capitol Avenue, Omaha, NE 68102

Successors:

Chicago & North Western

Union Pacific

Portions still operated:

Dakota, Minnesota & Eastern: Albert Lea—Waseca, Minn.

Minnesota Central: Norwood—Hanley Falls, Minn.

Union Pacific: Peoria—Middle Grove, Ill.; Albia, Iowa—Albert Lea, Minn.; Montgomery—Minneapolis, Minn.; Belmond—Kanawha, Iowa; Des Moines—Rippey, Iowa; Grand Jct.—Mallard, Iowa

Minneapolis, Northfield & Southern Railway

The Minneapolis, Northfield & Southern was incorporated in 1907 as the Minneapolis, St. Paul, Rochester & Dubuque Electric Traction Company. One of its incorporators was Col. Marion W. Savage, a livestock feed tycoon who bought Dan Patch, one of the most famous race horses of all time. Savage had a farm a few miles south of Minneapolis and sought to improve the transportation system in the area.

The new railroad was known as the "Dan Patch Electric Line," and it was like other interurban lines of the era with one major difference: no trolley wire. Its passengers rode in General Electric gas-electric cars. The road inaugurated service between the outskirts of Minneapolis and Antlers Park on July 4, 1910, and the line was extended to Northfield, Minn., 37 miles from Minneapolis, later that year.

The MStPR&D inaugurated freight service in 1913 using a GE gas-electric locomotive, and was the first railroad in the world to operate freight and passenger service exclusively with internal-combustion power. It negotiated trackage rights over the Chicago Great Western from Northfield to Mankato and operated through service between Minneapolis and Mankato, 107 miles, using gas-electric cars. Additional local trains ran as far as Faribault and Randolph on

Minneapolis, Northfield & Southern favored Baldwin diesels like DRS-6-6-1500 switching the yard at Auto Club Junction on September 22, 1958. Photo by William D. Middleton.

the CGW. The railroad built a second route into Minneapolis and bought more locomotives, both gas-electric and steam, and large fleet of passenger and freight cars. Col. Savage purchased land for a suburban housing development. The road's listing in the June 1916 issue of *The Official Guide* proudly advertised "Freight Handled by Steam Power."

The company was overextended, and in late 1916 it entered bankruptcy. In 1918 its properties were purchased by the newly organized Minneapolis, Northfield & Southern. The new company concentrated on freight, aided by a route map that constituted a belt line most of the way around Minneapolis. It developed a healthy business moving freight between other railroads, bypassing the congestion of downtown Minneapolis. It did so well that in 1938 the Chicago Great Western and the Rock Island led a campaign to have all through freight rates via the MN&S canceled. There was considerable protest from labor and shippers, and the Interstate Commerce Commission ruled in favor of the MN&S. In June 1982 Soo Line purchased the MN&S.

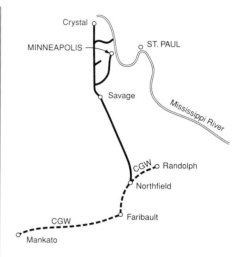

	1929	1979
Miles of railroad operated:	140	82
Number of locomotives:	12	13
Number of passenger cars:	8*	
Number of freight cars:	53	716
Number of company service cars:	35	

Location of headquarters: Minneapolis, Minnesota
Reporting marks: MNS
Successors:
Soo Line
Canadian Pacific
Portions still operated: Canadian Pacific: Crystal–Northfield, Minn.
*(4 motor cars)

Missisippi Central Railroad

In 1896 the Pearl & Leaf Rivers Railroad was incorporated. It was a logging road from Hattiesburg to Sumrall, Mississippi, 19 miles. The western goal of the railroad was Natchez, across the state on the Mississippi River. In 1905 after a reorganization the railroad was renamed the Mississippi Central Railroad, and the line was completed in 1908 (the western portion was built by the Natchez & Eastern Railway, absorbed by Mississippi Central in 1909).

The road's plans to extend its line to the Gulf of Mexico were never fulfilled, but in 1921 MSC leased a branch of the Gulf, Mobile & Northern from Hattiesburg to Beaumont and acquired trackage rights to Mobile over GM&N. In 1924 GM&N sold off the branch, which became the Bonhomie & Hattiesburg Southern, and MSC pulled back to Hattiesburg.

Mississippi Central ran its last passenger train in 1941. Just before the beginning of World War II the Army announced it would reopen Camp Shelby, south of Hattiesburg. Mississippi Central had torn up its branch line to Camp Shelby some years previously, but the road hastily relaid 7 miles of track in the interests of national defense and freight revenue.

MSC's business held up well after the war, and the road participated in east-west bridge traffic in cooperation with the Louisiana Midland, a

Mississippi Central 2-8-2 No. 131 assists in the cleanup of a mishap at Cobbs, west of Brookhaven. The Mike has two bells, a characteristic of the road's steam locomotives — and both are nicely polished. Photo by C. W. Witbeck.

new road created from a Louisiana & Arkansas branch west of the Mississippi River. The route was a joint Louisiana & Arkansas-Louisiana Midland-MSC project using the name "Natchez Route." Profits turned to deficits in the early 1960s and MSC looked for a buyer. At first Illinois Central rejected the offer, but the prospect of a new paper mill between Wanilla and Silver Creek changed the situation. IC purchased the Mississippi Central on March 29, 1967. Illinois Central Gulf still operates the entire line.

	1929	1966
Miles of railroad operated:	151	148
Number of locomotives:	21	9
Number of passenger cars:	19	
Number of freight cars:	698	165
Number of company service cars:	69	18

Location of headquarters: Hattiesburg, Mississippi

Reporting marks: MSC

Recommended reading: *Natchez Route — A Mississippi Central Railroad Album,* by David S. Price and Louis R. Saillard published in 1975 by Mississippi Great Southern Chapter, National Railway Historical Society, 306 Bay Street, Hattiesburg, MS 39401

Successor: Illinois Central

Portions still operated: Illinois Central: Natchez—Hattiesburg

Missouri & North Arkansas Railway

After the Civil War, Eureka Springs in northwest Arkansas developed as a health resort. IN 1882 to provide access to the resort the St. Louis & San Francisco chartered the Missouri & Arkansas Railroad to build from Seligman, Mo., to Beaver, Ark., on the White River, a distance of 13 miles. That same year the Eureka Springs Railway was chartered to build 5 miles of railroad from the M&A to Eureka Springs, and the two railroads were consolidated under the Eureka Springs name. The line was completed in February 1883.

Ozark towns beyond Eureka Springs were clamoring for rail service, so in May 1899 the St. Louis & North Arkansas Railroad was chartered to purchase the Eureka Springs and extend it east to Harrison. It reached there in March 1901. In 1906 the road was reorganized as the Missouri & North Arkansas Railroad. It arranged for trackage rights on the Frisco between Seligman and Wayne, Mo., and on the Kansas City Southern between Neosho and Joplin, Mo. It built a line from Wayne to Neosho, 32 miles, and started construction southeast across Arkansas to Helena, on the Mississippi River.

The M&NA hoped to serve as a bridge route between the KCS and Frisco and the Yazoo & Mississippi Valley (Illinois Central) for traffic

The Missouri & Arkansas purchased a pair of ACF Motorailers in 1938 to revive passenger service along the line. Car 705, named Thomas C. McRae (governor of Arkansas from 1921 to 1925) pauses at Harrison, the road's headquarters, while running as train 202 from Kensett, Ark., to Neosho, Mo. Photo by M. B. Cooke.

moving between Kansas City and New Orleans. There were proposals to change M&NA's eastern terminus from Helena to Little Rock or to Memphis and to extend construction to Pensacola, but the management of the road stuck with Helena.

The line was completed from Neosho to Helena in 1909. By then Frisco had a Kansas City–Memphis line that connected directly with IC, and KCS reached the Gulf of Mexico at Port Arthur, Texas—routing traffic on the M&NA would require that the connecting roads shorthaul themselves. In addition, the M&NA lay between two Missouri Pacific routes. It soon became clear that the Missouri & North Arkansas would have to rely on local business, and there wasn't much of that. The road entered receivership in 1912.

On August 5, 1914, a southbound M&NA gas-electric car collided with a KCS passenger train just south of Joplin on KCS rails. It was the first recorded accident involving a gas-electric. The car's fuel tanks contained more than 100 gallons of gasoline, and 47 people were crushed or burned in the resulting fire. The financial loss to the railroad was considerable.

The United States Railroad Administration took over operation of the M&NA in 1918 and raised employee wages to industry standards. M&NA requested and got release from USRA control, then quickly returned the railroad to the agency until 1920. Upon release from the USRA, management returned wages to their old levels, and the employees walked out on February 26, 1921. During the 23-month work stoppage the railroad was plagued with bridge fires, track damage, and acid in its locomotive boil-

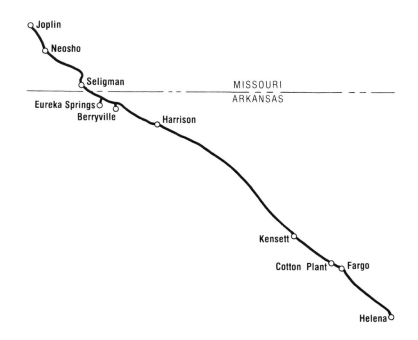

ers, and at least one employee was murdered.

The railroad was reorganized as the Missouri & North Arkansas Railway in 1922. It entered receivership in 1927 and was sold at foreclosure in 1935 to become the Missouri & Arkansas Railway. The new railroad managed to turn a profit for a few years, but fires in 1941 destroyed the offices and shops, and floods in 1945 wiped out

part of the south end of the railroad. In 1946 the employees demanded a wage increase and threatened a strike. Management retaliated with the threat of abandonment. The employees walked out on September 6, 1946, and the Missouri & Arkansas was abandoned.

The Arkansas & Ozarks Railway was incorporated on March 4, 1949, to operate the line

The fancy paint and striping on the wood caboose matches that on the 70-ton diesel pulling an Arkansas & Ozarks freight past the spur to the Eureka Springs station. Photo by Johnnie M. Gray.

	1929	1945
Miles of railroad operated:	365	365
Number of locomotives:	32	22
Number of passenger cars:	14	11*
Number of freight cars:	394	53
Number of company service cars:	53	46

Location of headquarters: Harrison, Arkansas

Reporting marks: M&NA (Missouri & North Arkansas), MA (Missouri & Arkansas)

Recommended reading: The North Arkansas Line, by James R. Fair Jr., published in 1969 by Howell-North Books, 850 North Hollywood Way, Burbank, CA 91505

Successors:
Missouri & Arkansas
Arkansas & Ozarks
Helena & Northwestern
Cotton Plant-Fargo

Portions still operated: Eureka Springs & North Arkansas (tourist railroad): a short piece of track at Eureka Springs

*(3 motor cars)

between Seligman, Mo., and Harrison, Ark., the oldest part of the M&A. It began operations in February 1950 and was abandoned in April 1961, because of flooding and also condemnation of part of the line by the U. S. Army Corps of Engineers for dam construction.

The portion of the line from Cotton Plant, Ark., to Helena was revived as the Helena & Northwestern Railway. Operation began in September 1949; after a foreclosure suit the last train operated on October 18, 1951. The Cotton Plant-Fargo Railway was chartered in February 1952 to operate the six miles of line between those two towns. It ceased operation in 1977.

Missouri-Kansas-Texas Railroad

The Katy was incorporated in 1865 as the Union Pacific Railway, Southern Branch (it had no corporate connection with the Union Pacific proper) to build south from Junction City, Kansas, along the Neosho River through Emporia and Parsons to New Orleans. It received a land grant, and construction began in 1869.

The railroad changed its name to Missouri, Kansas & Texas Railway the following year, and late in 1870 it reached the southern boundary of Kansas at Chetopa ahead of two rival lines, earning the right to build south through what is now Oklahoma. Also in 1870 the MK&T absorbed the Tebo & Neosho, a line from Sedalia, Missouri, southwest to Parsons, Kan.

Katy rails reached Denison, Texas, in 1872. Other significant events about that time were a battle with the Atlantic & Pacific (a Frisco predecessor) over a crossing at Vinita, Okla., in 1871; extension of the road from Sedalia to a junction with the Burlington at Hannibal, Mo., in 1873; and control of the road by Jay Gould, who saw it as a feeder to his Missouri Pacific system.

The Katy reached Dallas and Fort Worth in 1881, the latter on trackage rights over the Texas & Pacific from Whitesboro, Texas. That same year the Katy purchased the International & Great Northern, another Gould road. The lines of the MK&T, building south, and I&GN, build-

The Katy's steam locomotives were characterized by generous amounts of white trim on running board edges and driver and lead truck tires and red and white enameled heralds on the tenders. Pacific 385 is shown south of Dallas on the *Katy Limited* in February 1948. Equally characteristic were the yellow-painted express boxcars carried on most of the through passenger trains. Photo by C. W. Witbeck

ing north, met at Taylor, Texas, in 1882. In 1883 the Katy purchased the Galveston, Houston & Henderson, which Gould leased to the I&GN.

In 1886 MK&T built north from Parsons, Kan., to Paola, and negotiated trackage rights from Paola to Kansas City over the Kansas City, Fort Scott & Gulf (later part of the Frisco). In 1888 Jay Gould lost financial control of the Katy. Missouri Pacific's lease of the Katy was canceled, and control of I&GN passed to Missouri Pacific.

In 1891 the Missouri, Kansas & Texas of Texas was created to hold all the Katy's Texas properties to comply with a law the state of Texas had passed in 1886 requiring railroads operating in Texas to maintain general offices there.

Expansion and reorganization

The MK&T emerged from receivership in 1891 and began a period of expansion which put its rails into Houston (1893), St. Louis (1896), Shreveport (1900), San Antonio (1900), Tulsa (1903), and Oklahoma City (1904). In 1910 Katy acquired the Texas Central, which reached out toward Abilene from Waco, and in 1911 took over the Wichita Falls & Northwestern and the Wichita Falls & Southern. By 1915 the sprawling system had 3,865 miles of railroad that reached south from St. Louis, Hannibal, Kansas City, and Junction City to Galveston and San Antonio, east to Shreveport, and west into the Oklahoma panhandle.

In 1923 the Katy was reorganized as the Missouri-Kansas-Texas Railroad. It leased the Moberly–Hannibal portion of the Hannibal branch to the Wabash, sold the Shreveport line to the Louisiana Railway & Navigation Co. (now part of the Kansas City Southern), and sloughed off the Oklahoma City line to become the Oklahoma City-Ada-Atoka Railway (after 1929 part of the Muskogee group; later Santa Fe). In 1931 Katy purchased the Beaver, Meade & Englewood, which reached almost to the west end of the Oklahoma panhandle.

World War II and decline

Through the 1930s and into World War II Katy's image was one of classic American railroading tempered with individuality—red and

More symbolic of the pre-Barriger Katy is this string of wheat-laden boxcars moving behind a single GP7 near Mouser, Oklahoma, out toward the west end of the former Beaver, Meade & Englewood. Photo by Don Hofsommer.

white heralds on the tenders of its Pacifics and Mikados; bright yellow cabooses and boxcars. The war brought increased traffic to the Katy. Oil moving north became an exception to Katy's predominantly southbound traffic.

Not everything associated with the war was beneficial. The increased traffic was hard on the track, and in a three-month period in 1945 Katy's top three officers died. Dieselization helped the road briefly—it had not purchased new locomotives since 1925—but Katy's diesel maintenance program was insufficient. Track deterioration continued, and drought in the 1950s held traffic down. Suddenly in 1957 Katy was in the red. William N. Deramus III was brought in from the Chicago Great Western to become Katy's president. He rationalized the locomotive roster, repowering non-EMD units with EMD engines; abandoned the Junction City branch, Katy's original line; trimmed the payroll; consolidated offices at Denison, Texas (the St. Louis offices were moved over a weekend; employees received notice of the closure by encountering locked doors Monday morning); and cut most of the road's passenger service.

Barriger revives the Katy

Katy's decline resumed in a few years. In 1965 John W. Barriger III was brought in to save the railroad. In the 1940s he had rebuilt the Monon; more recently he had retired after several years as president of the Pittsburgh & Lake Erie. Barriger faced the same situation that he had on the Monon: almost complete deterioration of the physical plant and equally complete lack of employee morale. Barriger set to work as traveling freight agent and president (his own description of his job) and did what he had done before

and would do again (for Boston & Maine and Rock Island). He reopened the railroad's office in St. Louis; discontinued the remaining passenger service (on June 30, 1965); and found money for a rehabilitation program by liquidating bonds, applying for loans that had been approved but not made, and even cleaning up scrap around the railroad. His program included rebuilding the track, purchasing new locomotives, and purchasing and leasing new freight cars. After a long period of economizing itself to death, Katy spent more than a year's gross receipts for new equipment.

The railroad embarked on a program of diversification in 1967 with the incorporation of Katy Industries, which acquired much of the stock of the railroad in exchange for its own stock. A lean, rejuvenated Katy returned to profitability in 1971 under the leadership of Reginald Whitman. Upon the demise of the Rock Island in 1980 a Katy subsidiary, the Oklahoma, Kansas & Texas Railway, acquired RI's line from Abilene, Kan., south through Herington, Wichita, and El Reno, Okla., to Dallas.

Merger

Much of Katy's business in the 1970s and 1980s was unit trains of grain and coal moving south from connections. Since more than 70 percent of Katy's traffic was interline, the mergers taking place around Katy (Missouri Pacific into Union Pacific and Frisco into Burlington Northern) were of great concern to Katy's management. The initial reaction to the UP-MP-WP merger was to protest it as unjustified. As a condition of that merger, Katy received trackage rights on UP to Omaha, Council Bluffs, Lincoln, and Topeka.

	1929	1987
Miles of railroad operated:	3,189	3,130
Number of locomotives:	515	237
Number of passenger cars:	411	66*
Number of freight cars:	20,140	3,566
Number of company service cars:	1,731	76

Location of headquarters: Dallas, Texas

Reporting marks: MKT, MKTT, BKTY, OKKT

Notable named passenger trains: *Texas Special* (St. Louis–San Antonio; operated by the St. Louis-San Francisco north of Vinita, Okla.)

Historical and technical society: Katy Railroad Historical Society, P. O. Box 1784, Sedalia, MO 65302; http://web2.airmail.net/rvjack2

*(1964)

Recommended reading: *Katy Power*, by Joe G. Collias and Raymond B. George, Jr., published in 1986 by MM Books, P. O. Box 29319, Crestwood, MO 63126 (ISBN 0-9612366-1-2)

Subsidiaries and affiliated railroads, 1987:

Galveston, Houston & Henderson (50%)

Oklahoma, Kansas & Texas Railway (100%)

Successor: Union Pacific

Portions still operated:

Dallas, Garland & Northeastern: Trenton–Greenville–Garland, Texas

Georgetown Railroad: Smith–Belton, Texas

Hollis & Eastern: Duke–Altus, Okla.

Northwestern Oklahoma: 5 miles at Woodward, Okla.

Wichita, Tillman & Jackson: Wichita Falls, Texas–Altus, Okla.

Union Pacific did not abandon any Katy track that was in operation at the time of purchase.

In early 1985 the Katy announced that it was receptive to merger or sale, and in mid-1985 Union Pacific made a bid, which it soon withdrew, restructured, and resubmitted in mid-1986. Katy and UP already shared operations on several lines through trackage rights, the longest such route being from Wagoner, Okla., east of Tulsa, to San Marcos, Texas, northeast of San Antonio. Indeed, by 1987, 939 miles (32 percent) of Katy's operation was on tracks of other roads, and other roads used 598 miles of Katy track. As a condition of the deal, the trackage rights between Kansas City and Omaha that Katy had used were granted to Kansas City Southern, apparently to preserve access to Omaha by a railroad otherwise terminating at Kansas City. The Interstate Commerce Commission approved the purchase of the Katy by the Missouri Pacific Railroad (a subsidiary of UP) on May 16, 1988. UP absorbed the Katy's operations on August 12, 1988.

Missouri Pacific Railroad

The history of the Missouri Pacific Railroad is easier to understand if the railroad is considered in three parts: the lines west of St. Louis, the lines south and southwest of St. Louis, and the lines in Texas and Louisiana.

Lines west of St. Louis

Ground was broken for the Pacific Railroad at St. Louis, Missouri, on July 4, 1851, the nation's 75th birthday. The road had been chartered two years previously to build west from St. Louis through Jefferson City, Mo., to the Pacific. The first four miles of the railroad were opened in 1852, and its train was the first to operate west of the Mississippi River. The railroad reached Jefferson City in 1854, Tipton in 1858, and Sedalia, Mo., 185 miles from St. Louis, in 1860. It was completed to Kansas City, 94 miles farther, in 1865.

In 1866 the road leased the Kansas City, Leavenworth, & Atchison Railway, and in 1869 leased the Leavenworth, Atchison, and Northwestern Railroad, reaching Atchison, Kansas, with the intention of continuing to Omaha.

The Pacific Railroad was built with a state-decreed track gauge of 5 feet 6 inches. When it was begun, a bridge across the Mississippi was considered impossible, so interchange with railroads east of the river was not a consideration.

Missouri Pacific's steam locomotives were generally good-looking machines, and these two 4-8-4s, Baldwin products of 1943, are no exception. They are shown leading a westbound freight through Sandy Hook, Missouri, about 19 miles west of Jefferson City on the River Line. Photo by C. T. Wood.

The Rock Island bridged the Mississippi in 1856, and the Union Pacific and Central Pacific were built to standard gauge; construction of the Eads Bridge at St. Louis had just begun when the Pacific Railroad converted to standard gauge on July 18, 1869. In 1870 the railroad took a new name, Missouri Pacific Railroad, and it was reorganized as the Missouri Pacific Railway in 1876.

Lines south and southwest of St. Louis

Two early railroads formed the nucleus of the southern part of the Missouri Pacific. The St. Louis & Iron Mountain Railroad was chartered in 1851 to build southwest from St. Louis. It was opened in 1858 from St. Louis to Pilot Knob. In 1869 it completed a line from Bismarck southeast to the Mississippi River and a connection by ferry with the Mobile & Ohio. The Iron Mountain was built, like the Pacific Railroad, with a gauge of 5 feet 6 inches, but the connection with the M&O was important enough that the road converted to 5-foot gauge, standard in the South. The Iron Mountain continued building south through Poplar Bluff and reached the Arkansas state line in 1872.

The Cairo & Fulton Railroad was chartered in 1854 to build a railroad from Birds Point, Mo., across the Mississippi River from Cairo, Illinois, to Fulton, Arkansas, near the Texas border. It reached a connection with the Texas & Pacific at Texarkana in 1873. In 1874 the Iron Mountain and the Cairo & Fulton were consolidated as the St. Louis, Iron Mountain & Southern Railway.

Lines in Texas and Louisiana

The Texas portion of the Missouri Pacific system consisted of several entities that at various times owned, controlled, or included each other. The two major ones are the International-Great Northern and Gulf Coast Lines.

The International & Great Northern Railroad was chartered in 1873 to consolidate the Houston & Great Northern Railroad, a railroad between Houston and Palestine, Texas, and the International Railroad, which ran from Longview, where it connected with the Texas & Pacific, through Palestine to Hearne, with the intention of continuing to Laredo to be part of a route to Mexico City. The I&GN underwent reorganization in 1879 and soon afterward was leased to the Missouri, Kansas & Texas (Katy), which had just become part of Jay Gould's empire. In 1883 the I&GN leased the Galveston, Houston & Henderson Railroad.

When the Katy came into financial difficulties in 1888, the lease was canceled, and the I&GN resumed independence, though it remained in the Gould family. In 1895 it "adjusted its debt," in the words of *Poor's Manual of Railroads*, and it entered receivership in 1908. It was succeeded in 1911 by the International & Great Northern Railway. In 1914 the I&GN found itself unable to pay either the principal or the interest due on its bonds. The I&GN's creditors, the executors of the Jay Gould Estate, consented to extend the debt, but were unable to do so because of the unsettled financial situation resulting from the war in Europe and a poor cotton crop that year. The I&GN entered receivership in 1914.

The International-Great Northern Railroad was incorporated in 1922 as successor to the I&GN. The New Orleans, Texas & Mexico (Gulf Coast Lines) purchased the I-GN in 1924.

Gulf Coast Lines was a collection of railroads

Little Rock, Arkansas, was one of the hubs of Missouri Pacific's passenger-train network. While three road diesels await assignments and two EMD switchers shuffle cars, train 220 leaves for Memphis on June 15, 1960, behind MoPac's first two passenger diesels, E3s 7001 and 7000. Photo by J. P. Lamb, Jr.

between New Orleans and Brownsville, Texas, which had been assembled by B. F. Yoakum when he was chairman of the board of the Rock Island and the Frisco. The principal component and parent of GCL was the New Orleans, Texas & Mexico; the biggest of the subsidiaries was the St. Louis, Brownsville & Mexico, a relative latecomer, opened in 1908 from Houston to Brownsville.

The NOT&M, StLB&M, and others were divorced from the Frisco in 1913, at which time they acquired the Gulf Coast Lines name. NOT&M purchased the International-Great Northern in 1924, and acquired control of the San Antonio, Uvalde & Gulf in 1925. Missouri Pacific purchased control of NOT&M in 1924.

The Gould era

Jay Gould bought control of Missouri Pacific in 1879. He soon added to his portfolio the St. Louis, Iron Mountain & Southern; Missouri, Kansas & Texas; International & Great Northern; Texas & Pacific; Galveston, Houston & Henderson; Wabash; and Central Branch, Union Pacific (a railroad running west from Atchison, Kan.).

Gould began an expansion program that extended MP to Omaha, Nebraska, and Pueblo, Colorado; I&GN to Laredo, Texas, on the Mexican border; Iron Mountain to Memphis, Tennessee, Lake Charles, Louisiana, and Fort Smith, Ark.; and T&P west to a connection with Southern Pacific at Sierra Blanca, Texas.

Then his empire fell apart. Wabash entered receivership in 1884, T&P in 1885, MK&T in 1888, and I&GN in 1889. T&P and I&GN remained in the Missouri Pacific family; MK&T became independent; and Wabash eventually became part of the Pennsylvania Railroad family.

Twentieth century

In the early 1900s Missouri Pacific constructed several new lines along rivers to bypass stiff grades on its older routes. Among them were the Illinois Division along the Mississippi southeast of St. Louis and the Jefferson City–Kansas City line along the Missouri. In 1917 the Missouri Pacific Railroad was incorporated to consolidate the Missouri Pacific Railway and the Iron Mountain, which had entered receivership in 1915.

Missouri Pacific acquired control of the New Orleans, Texas & Mexico Railway (Gulf Coast Lines) in 1924, and by 1930 MP owned 92 percent of its stock. MP also owned a 69 percent interest in the Texas & Pacific. The expanded system was known as Missouri Pacific Lines; at times the term included the Texas & Pacific.

MP owned half the common stock of the Denver & Rio Grande Western (Western Pacific had the other half). MP and WP lost their control of the Rio Grande when it was reorganized in 1947.

Mergers

In 1961 MoPac acquired an interest in the Chicago & Eastern Illinois. In 1967 MoPac took control of C&EI, in 1969 sold the Evansville line to Louisville & Nashville, and in 1976 merged C&EI.

In 1923, Texas & Pacific issued preferred stock to Missouri Pacific in exchange for mortgage bonds. By 1930 MP owned all T&P's preferred stock and more than half its common stock. MP merged Texas & Pacific on October 15, 1976. With T&P came the remnants of the Midland Valley and the Kansas, Oklahoma & Gulf, which T&P had acquired in 1964.

In 1968 MP purchased a half interest in Alton & Southern from the Aluminum Corporation of America (Alcoa); Chicago & North Western purchased the other half interest but sold it to St. Louis Southwestern (Cotton Belt). In 1977 MP merged several smaller subsidiaries, among them the Fort Worth Belt and the Missouri-Illinois. That same year MP was reincorporated and became a wholly owned subsidiary of Missouri Pacific Corporation.

Missouri-Illinois Railroad

The predecessors of the Missouri-Illinois were the Mississippi River & Bonne Terre Railway and the Illinois Southern Railway. The MR&BT was incorporated in 1888 and opened in 1890 from a connection with the St. Louis & Iron Mountain at Riverside, about 30 miles south of St. Louis, south into the lead-mining area east of the Iron Mountain line. The MR&BT was owned by the St. Joseph Lead Co.

The Illinois Southern was incorporated in 1900 as successor to the Centralia & Chester, which had a line from Salem, Ill., southwest to Chester on the east bank of the Mississippi. The Illinois Southern planned to extend the line across the Mississippi and on to Kansas City, bypassing St. Louis. The line reached the Iron Mountain at Bismarck, Mo., in 1903, but the ferry crossing of the Mississippi near St. Genevieve, Mo., restricted any serious consideration of the road as a major route. The company underwent reorganization in 1911 and entered receivership in 1915.

The Missouri-Illinois Railroad was incorporated in 1921 to acquire the Illinois Southern. Missouri Pacific acquired control of the M-I in 1929 by acquiring 51 percent of its stock from the lead companies that owned the M-I. At the same time the M-I leased the MR&BT, which it crossed at Derby, Mo. The Missouri-Illinois entered reorganization in 1933, emerged from bankruptcy in 1944, and merged the MR&BT in 1945. The M-I discontinued its ferry operation in 1961. In 1964 Missouri Pacific acquired nearly all the remaining stock of the M-I (total issued, 29,091 shares), and in 1974 acquired the final 16 shares. MP merged the M-I in 1978.

Merger with Union Pacific

The creation of Burlington Northern in 1970 formalized long-established alliances, but Chicago, Burlington & Quincy's acquisition of Frisco stock in 1966 and the opening of merger discussions between BN and Frisco in 1977 in effect put BN in MoPac's back yard. Santa Fe and Union Pacific both considered MoPac as a merger partner in the early 1960s, and in 1966 MoPac purchased a large block of Santa Fe stock, filed an application to control the Santa Fe, then withdrew the application a year or two later.

In January 1980 Union Pacific announced an agreement to acquire Missouri Pacific—then two weeks later made an offer to acquire Western Pacific. The announcement constituted the first significant realignment of railroad alliances in the West since E. H. Harriman had put UP and Southern Pacific together 80 years before.

The merger of UP and MP was consummated on December 22, 1982. Initially, the two railroads were to remain separate in name and image. A year later yellow paint began to replace blue on Missouri Pacific locomotives, and not long after that "Union" replaced "Missouri" in the lettering diagrams.

	1929*	1982
Miles of railroad operated:	9,732	11,167
Number of locomotives:	1,543	1,602
Number of passenger cars:	1,119	17†
Number of freight cars:	55,197	47,825
Number of company service cars:	3,852	3,035

Location of headquarters: St. Louis, Missouri

Notable named passenger trains: *Texas Eagle* (St. Louis to Houston, San Antonio, and Fort Worth), *Colorado Eagle* (St. Louis–Denver, operated north of Pueblo by Denver & Rio Grande Western)

Historical and technical society: Missouri Pacific Historical Society, P. O. Box 330427, Fort Worth, TX 76163

Recommended reading: *Mopac Power*, by Joe G. Collias, published in 1980 by Howell-North Books, 11175 Flintkote Avenue, Suite C, San Diego, CA 92121 (ISBN 0-8310-7117-6)

Subsidiaries and affiliated railroads, 1982:
Alton & Southern (50%)
*1929 figures include Gulf Coast Lines and International-Great Northern
†(1970)

Houston Belt & Terminal (50%)

Predecessor railroads in this book:
Chicago & Eastern Illinois; Kansas, Oklahoma & Gulf; Midland Valley; Texas & Pacific

Successors Union Pacific

Portions still operated:
Arkansas Midland: Helena–Lexa, Ark.
Border Pacific: Rio Grande City–Mission, Texas
Caddo, Antoine & Little Missouri: Birds Mill–Gurdon, Ark.
Delta Southern: McGehee, Ark.–Tallulah, La.; Monroe–Sterlington, La.
Fort Smith Railroad: Fort Smith–Fort Chaffee, Ark.
Georgetown: Kerr–Granger, Texas
Kansas Southwestern: Wichita–Geneseo, Kan.; Wichita–Hardtner, Kan.; Conway Springs–Radium, Kan.
Missouri & Northern Arkansas: Pleasant Hill, Mo.–Diaz Junction, Ark.; Fort Scott, Kan.–Clinton, Mo.; Joplin–Carthage, Mo.
New Orleans Lower Coast: Gretna–Myrtle Grove, La.
Rio Valley Switching: Harlingen–Mission–Hidalgo, Texas
Semo Port: Rush Junction–Capedeau Junction, Mo.
Southeast Kansas: Bartlesville, Okla.–Coffeyville, Kan.–Nassau Junction, Mo.

Mobile & Ohio Railroad

 The original purpose of the Mobile & Ohio was to tap the trade of the Mississippi, Missouri, and Ohio rivers for the port of Mobile, Alabama. It would do this by connecting the city with the Ohio and the Mississippi at their confluence at Cairo, Illinois. Cities, counties, and states along the route bought stock and aided the project financially, and Congress passed a land grant bill in 1850 to aid the M&O (and also the Illinois Central).

The first 30 miles of the M&O, from Mobile to Citronelle, Ala., opened in 1852, and the line was completed to Columbus, Kentucky, on the east bank of the Mississippi a few miles south of Cairo, on April 22, 1861. River steamboats connected Columbus with the south end of the Illinois Central at Cairo, and the St. Louis & Iron Mountain was planning a terminal at Belmont, Missouri, across the river from Columbus.

The road was completed just 10 days after the Confederates fired on Fort Sumter. The Civil War negated any salutary effect the road might have had on the city of Mobile—in addition to pretty much using up M&O's rolling stock and track. The cost of rebuilding the railroad combined with its previous debt sent the M&O into receivership in 1875.

The Iron Mountain did not reach Belmont until 1871, and by then M&O had decided to extend its line north to East Cairo, about 20

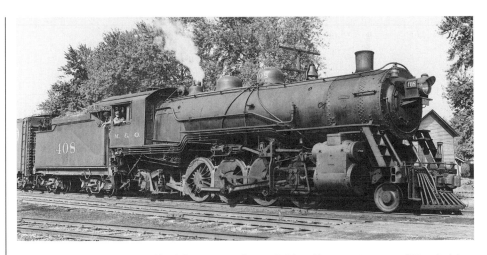

The 2-8-2 was Mobile & Ohio's principal freight locomotive. Number 408, built by Baldwin in 1913, was one of 21 similar light Mikados. Following them on the roster were 37 heavier Mikes of USRA design. Photo by R. J. Foster.

miles. Because of M&O's financial difficulties the extension was not completed until 1882. In 1886 M&O acquired the 3-foot gauge St. Louis & Cairo, which ran between East St. Louis and Cairo, and standard-gauged it. The importance of the terminal at Columbus, Ky., declined, and

soon M&O abandoned the spur to the river there. In 1898 the road opened a line from Artesia and Columbus, Miss., to Montgomery, Ala.

The M&O recognized that it was not as strong a railroad as the Illinois Central or the Louisville & Nashville and accepted Southern

Railway's offer of an exchange of securities in 1901— Southern had its eye on M&O's route between Mobile and St. Louis. Merger of Southern and M&O nearly occurred, but the bill allowing the merger was vetoed by the governor of Mississippi.

Southern control continued, however. In the late 1920s traffic fell off, and deficits appeared on M&O's ledgers in 1930. Southern was unable to provide financial assistance. M&O entered receivership on June 3, 1932.

M&O pursued its own course, but Southern ownership continued until 1938, when Southern had to sell its M&O bonds to meet other financial commitments. The Gulf, Mobile & Ohio purchased the Mobile & Ohio on August 1, 1940, and was consolidated with Gulf, Mobile & Northern a month later.

	1929	1940
Miles of railroad operated:	1,159	1,180
Number of locomotives:	231	119
Number of passenger cars:	112	31
Number of freight cars:	8,368	
Number of company service cars:	361	
Number of freight and company service cars:		3,298

Location of headquarters: St. Louis, Missouri
Reporting marks: M&O
Historical and technical society: Gulf, Mobile & Ohio Historical Society, P. O. Box 2457, Joliet, IL 60434-2457; http://www.tfs.net/~jashaw/rhs/gmo.html
Recommended reading: *The Gulf, Mobile and Ohio,* by James Hutton Lemly, published in 1953 by Richard D. Irwin, Inc., Homewood, IL 60430

Successors:
Gulf, Mobile & Ohio
Illinois Central Gulf
Kansas City Southern

Portions still operated:
Illinois Central: Jackson, Tenn.–Corinth, Miss.
Kansas City Southern: Corinth, Miss.–Mobile, Ala.; West Point, Miss.–Tuscaloosa, Ala.
Norfolk Southern: Tuscaloosa–Montgomery, Ala.
West Tennessee Railroad: Lawrence–Kenton, Tenn.
Map: See page 188

Monongahela Railway

The Monongahela Railway extended south from Brownsville, Pennsylvania, along its namesake river to Fairmont, West Virginia.

The Monongahela Railroad was incorporated in 1900 by the Pennsylvania Railroad and Pittsburgh & Lake Erie to be a jointly owned subsidiary into the coalfields of southwest Pennsylvania and adjacent West Virginia. The Monongahela Railway was incorporated in 1915 as a consolidation of the Monongahela Railroad and the Buckhannon & Northern Railroad. In the 1920s and 1930s it absorbed several shorter railroads in the coal mining area of southwestern Pennsylvania and adjacent portions of West Virginia. On January 1, 1927, the Baltimore & Ohio acquired a one-third interest (one-sixth each from PRR and P&LE) in exchange for some strategic trackage rights.

In 1952 the Monongahela replaced its USRA light Mikes with 27 Baldwin S-12 switchers to be

Baldwin RF-16s 1216 and 1205 lug a train of empty hopper cars alongside the Monongahela River at Alicia, Pennsylvania. The Sharknoses were later purchased by the Delaware & Hudson. Photo by David H. Hamley.

that the Monongahela reached by a steep, curving branch that was unsuitable for long unit coal trains—the principal customer of those mines was Detroit Edison. Monongahela operated the Waynesburg Southern right from the beginning.

Conrail inherited the Pennsylvania's interest in the Monongahela. In 1989 Pittsburgh & Lake Erie sold its interest to Conrail, and in 1990 CSX, successor to Baltimore & Ohio, did the same in exchange for trackage rights that would allow it to abandon its ex-B&O line from Morgantown, W. Va., to Uniontown, Pa. Conrail merged the Monongahela on May 1, 1993.

	1929	1992
Miles of railroad operated:	94	162
Number of locomotives:	69	15
Number of passenger cars:	9	
Number of freight cars (cabooses only):	51	3
Number of company service cars:	33	

Location of headquarters: Brownsville, Pennsylvania

Recommended reading: *Twilight of the Monongahela*, by Harry Stegmaier and Jim Mullison, published in 1994 by H&M Productions II, 193007 45 Avenue, Flushing, NY 11358 (ISBN 0-882608-09-7)

Successor: Conrail

operated singly and in multiple as needed. The Monongahela attracted the attention of rail enthusiasts in early 1968 when it bought eight Baldwin RF-16 freight diesels from the New York Central. They wouldn't multiple with Monongahela's fleet of Baldwin road-switchers, and their carbody configuration wasn't optimal for Monongahela's needs, but they were cheap and, quite important, Monongahela's shop forces understood Baldwin diesels. A year later the railroad ordered five specially ballasted GP38s, the heaviest examples of that model.

In 1968 the Waynesburg Southern Railroad opened to provide an easier route to coal mines

Montpelier & Wells River Railroad

The Montpelier & Wells River was incorporated in 1867 to connect the city of Montpelier, the capital of Vermont, with several Boston & Maine predecessors at Wells River, Vt., and Woodsville, New Hampshire. The railroad was opened in November 1873 and entered receivership almost immediately. It was reorganized by its original officers in 1877. In 1883 the M&WR financed the construction of the Barre Branch Railroad from Montpelier to Barre, six miles, to compete with an existing Central Vermont line. The Barre Branch was opened in 1889 and immediately leased to its parent; it was merged in 1913.

In 1911 Boston & Maine took control of the road through its subsidiary, the Vermont Valley, but in 1926 B&M withdrew from management of the M&WR and returned it to local management, though retaining ownership. By then passenger service, which had once included through trains between Burlington, Vt., and the White Mountains of New Hampshire and through sleepers between Montpelier and Boston, had dwindled to mixed trains. Mail and milk traffic were more important to the road than passengers. The principal item of freight was granite from quarries along the line, particularly on the Barre Branch.

Barre & Chelsea

In December 1944 the properties of the M&WR were acquired by the Barre & Chelsea

Montpelier & Wells River train 1 leads off with an ex-Boston & Maine 2-8-0 built in 1911. Following is a milk car, and bringing up the rear is a wood combine. Photo by William Moedinger Jr.

A Barre & Chelsea 70-tonner switches two granite-laden flat cars near the Rock of Ages quarry. Photo by Jim Shaughnessy.

	1929	1944
Miles of railroad operated:	44	44
Number of locomotives:	9	6
Number of passenger cars:	7	1
Number of freight cars:	9	2
Number of company service cars:	16	19

Location of headquarters: Montpelier, Vermont
Reporting marks: M&WR
Recommended reading: *Vermont's Granite Railroads*, by Robert C. Jones, Whitney J. Maxfield, and William C. Gove, published in 1985 by Pruett Publishing Co., Boulder, Colo. (ISBN 0-87108-695-6)
Successors:
Barre & Chelsea
Montpelier & Barre
Washington County
Map: See page 366 (Rutland Railroad)

Railroad, with which it had long been affiliated and which also was a member of the Vermont Valley family. The B&C had been incorporated in 1913 as a consolidation of the Barre Railroad and the East Barre & Chelsea Railroad. The chief traffic of the B&C was granite from quarries in and around Barre. The road was notable for 5 percent grades, a switchback, and a steam locomotive roster consisting exclusively of saddle-tankers.

After absorbing the Montpelier & Wells River, the Barre & Chelsea dieselized with three GE 70-tonners and continued in existence until 1956, when the ICC authorized abandonment because of operating losses (the Montpelier–Wells River line produced 5 percent of the revenue and was charged with 40 percent of the operating cost). In 1957 the newly organized Montpelier & Barre Railroad, owned by Samuel Pinsly, purchased the portion of the line from Montpelier through Barre to Graniteville, 14 miles, and two of the diesels. In 1958 the Montpelier & Barre purchased the Central Vermont's branch from Montpelier Jct. through Montpelier to Barre and combined that line with its own parallel track.

Montpelier & Barre received ICC permission to abandon in 1980. The state of Vermont purchased the tracks, and operation of the line was taken over by the Washington County Railroad.

Narrow Gauge Railroads

Until about 1870 nearly all railroads in America north of the Mason-Dixon Line and the Ohio River were built with a track gauge of 4 feet 8½ inches—standard gauge. Railroads in the southern states were built with a gauge of 5 feet; they were converted to standard gauge for the most part in 1886.

The origin of the standard track gauge is lost in antiquity. The earliest railways in England were built with cars the same size as the wagons that were in common use. Their wheels were about 4 feet 8½ inches apart. That dimension had been around since Roman times—grooves have been found in Roman pavement that same distance apart. There is a theory that the width of those wagons and chariots was based on the width of two horses working side by side. There is another that it is based on the width of a single horse: A smaller wagon wouldn't efficiently use the pulling power of a horse and a larger wagon would overtax it.

Even if standard gauge is an odd figure (and railroad construction crews have a bar that length; they don't whip out a folding carpenter's rule and count off 56½ inches) it is standard. You can load a car here and send it to there, and it can roll all the way on standard gauge track. If there is a change of gauge along the way, the cargo has to be unloaded, then reloaded into a different car, and that's expensive.

The three-rail track underneath Colorado & Southern 3-foot gauge Mogul No. 8, awaiting departure from Denver Union Station in the 1930s, illustrates the difference between standard gauge and narrow gauge track. Photo by L. C. McClure.

About 1870 the idea of narrow gauge railroads caught on—lighter, smaller, slower trains would be ideal where there wasn't much business. The economics of narrow gauge railroading hinged on the belief that small locomotives and cars were cheaper to build than large ones (I call it the Toyota Fallacy). You can get a 15-inch gauge gasoline-powered locomotive for an amusement-park railroad for a lot less than you'll pay Electro-Motive for an SD70MAC, and it will cost you less to build a park-size railroad from Denver to Salt Lake City than it will to replicate the former Rio Grande line through Moffat Tunnel and along the Colorado River. You couldn't carry much on that railroad, and when you got to Denver you'd have to reload it all into standard gauge cars to ship it to Chicago.

Proponents of narrow gauge railroads also argued that the ratio between the weight of the car and the weight of the load ratio was better for narrow gauge cars than for standard gauge cars, and the narrower the better. Opponents pointed out that you'd need more narrow gauge cars to carry the same amount of freight—and if that argument were carried to its logical conclusion, a wheelbarrow would weigh nothing.

The 1870s were a time when railroads were falling out of favor with the public. Railroads were the first big business, and big business was still in the developmental stage. Every town wanted a railroad, whether or not it made economic sense, and business failures were common. (For most of America, railroads constituted the first improvement in transportation since the corduroy road.) The narrow gauge railroads were proposed by people new to the industry, people untainted by robber-baron railroading. Therein lay some of their appeal.

The narrow gauge boom lasted about 20 years. Most of the narrow gauge railroads were isolated from each other. Only a few major connected systems of narrow gauge railroads were built: the network in Colorado and Utah, the largest component of which was the Denver & Rio Grande; the Grand Narrow Gauge Trunk system, which reached from Toledo, Ohio, to Houston, Texas; and a group of railroads in western Pennsylvania, largest of which was the Pittsburgh & Western.

As the 20th century progressed it quickly became clear that narrow gauge railroads fell into four classes:
• standard gauge railroads—narrow gauge lines that were converted to standard gauge as quickly as possible
• conveyor belts—railroads that carried cargo to a place where it had to be processed before further transportation
• roller coasters—railroads built through rough topography and that would cost more to convert to standard gauge than the cost of transloading freight at the interchange point
• unsuccessful businesses
By the end of the 1940s only a handful of narrow gauge railroad remained in operation in North America:
• Denver & Rio Grande Western's remaining narrow gauge lines in Colorado and the Rio Grande Southern, "roller coasters" if ever there were. Abandonment of the RGS precipitated the standard-gauging of several D&RGW routes.
• The East Broad Top in Pennsylvania, primarily a coal carrier—a "conveyor belt"
• Southern Pacific's line in California's remote Owens Valley
• The White Pass & Yukon in Alaska, British Columbia, and Yukon Territory. It developed containerization techniques to ease the difficulties of transferring cargo to and from ships and trucks. A new parallel highway and closure of mines caused the WP&Y to shut down.
• Canadian National Railways' lines in Newfoundland
• the ore-carrying Coahuila & Zacatecas in Mexico, replaced by a standard gauge line
• National Railways of Mexico's remaining narrow gauge lines, which were in process of being standard-gauged
• United Railways of Yucatan's lines out of Merida

All but the Rio Grande and the East Broad Top dieselized their operations, and remnants of those two lines remain in operation as museum pieces. The White Pass & Yukon has been restored to operation as a tourist attraction. Only the lines in Yucatan remain in service as general-service narrow gauge railroads.

Recommended reading: *American Narrow Gauge Railroads,* by George W. Hilton, published in 1990 by Stanford University Press, Stanford, Calif. (ISBN 0-8047-1731-1)

Nashville, Chattanooga & St. Louis Railway

The Nashville & Chattanooga Railroad was incorporated in 1845. The first nine miles of the line out of Nashville were opened in 1851, and by 1853 the line had crossed Cumberland Mountain and reached the Tennessee River at Bridgeport, Alabama. The next year the N&C arrived in Chattanooga, where a connection to Atlanta was made with the Western & Atlantic, owned by the state of Georgia. Floods in 1862 destroyed much of the N&C before retreating Confederate and advancing Union forces could tear it up, but each army demolished one of the two Tennessee River bridges. The N&C was rebuilt and destroyed again before the Civil War was over. In 1864 and 1865 the United States Military Railroad thoroughly rebuilt the road and returned it to its owners.

In 1870 the road leased from the state of Tennessee the Nashville & Northwestern Railroad, a line from Nashville to Hickman, Kentucky, on the Mississippi River, and in 1873 N&C purchased the line. The N&C was renamed the Nashville, Chattanooga & St. Louis Railway in 1873. During the 1870s the road acquired several short lines which became branches off the N&C's single main line from Hickman through Nashville to Chattanooga.

One of NC&StL's third group of 4-8-4s (they were called Dixies) takes a heavy freight past CTC Tower on the way out of Atlanta. Rail Photo Service photo.

In 1879 the road's president, Edwin W. Cole, attempted to make the NC&StL into a St. Louis–Atlanta route. He obtained control of the incomplete Owensboro & Nashville, which was building a line from Owensboro, on the Ohio River, toward Nashville, and purchased the Illinois and Indiana portion of the St. Louis & Southeastern, which had been in receivership since 1874. Evansville, Ind., the eastern terminus of the StL&SE, was about 30 miles west of (down the Ohio River from) Owensboro, Ky.

Cole initiated negotiations (but didn't complete them) to lease the Western & Atlantic and the Central of Georgia.

Louisville & Nashville reacted quickly to this expansionist policy by buying 55 percent of NC&StL's stock and transferring the East St. Louis–Evansville line to its own system. In 1896 Louisville & Nashville acquired and leased to NC&StL the Paducah, Tennessee & Alabama Railroad (Paducah, Ky.–Bruceton–Lexington, Tenn.) and the Tennessee Midland Railway

(Memphis–Lexington–Perryville, Tenn.). This gave NC&StL a route north to the Ohio River at Paducah and a route southwest to Memphis, a considerably more important destination than Hickman, Ky., which was NC&StL's original western terminal.

In 1917 NC&StL teamed up with the Burlington to build a bridge over the Ohio River between Paducah, Ky., and Metropolis, Ill., and a connecting railroad. In 1924 the two roads sold a one-third interest in the Paducah & Illinois Railroad to the Illinois Central, which used the P&I as part of a freight line (the Edgewood Cutoff) it was building to bypass its own congested Ohio River crossing at Cairo, Ill. IC also participated in another, and unusual, bridge construction project in the 1940s. The Tennessee Valley Authority project widened the Tennessee River at Johnsonville, Tenn., creating the need for a longer, bridge for NC&StL's track. Downstream,

IC's line east of Paducah was rerouted along the top of a dam, rendering its bridge unnecessary. Its spans were barged upstream and raised into place to make a new bridge for NC&StL.

NC&StL was the middle link in several Midwest–Southeast routes, most notably the "Dixie Route" Chicago–Florida passenger trains operated in conjunction with Chicago & Eastern Illinois and L&N north of Nashville and Atlanta, Birmingham & Coast or Central of Georgia, Atlantic Coast Line, and Florida East Coast south of Atlanta.

After nearly 60 years of control, parent Louisville & Nashville merged the Nashville, Chattanooga St. Louis on August 30, 1957.

	1929	1956
Miles of railroad operated:	1,223	1,043
Number of locomotives:	249	132
Number of passenger cars:	219	106
Number of freight cars:	8,510	6,761
Number of company service cars:	775	517

Location of headquarters: Nashville, Tennessee
Reporting marks: N&C
Historical and technical society: Louisville & Nashville Historical Society, P. O. Box 17122, Louisville, KY 40217;
http://www.rrhistorical.com/lnhs
Recommended reading: *Nashville, Chattanooga & St. Louis Ry. History and Steam Locomotives,* by Richard E. Prince, published in 1967 by Richard E. Prince, Green River, Wyo. (LCC 67-26269)
Successors:
Louisville & Nashville
Seaboard System
CSX Transportation

Portions still operated:
Caney Fork & Western: Tullahoma–Sparta, Tenn.
CSX: Dresden–Bruceton, Tenn.; Bruceton, Tenn.–Nashville–Atlanta; Guntersville-Gadsden, Ala.
Huntsville & Madison County Railroad Authority: Huntsville–Norton, Ala.
KWT: Bruceton, Tenn.–Murray, Ky.; Paris–Henry, Tenn.
Sequatchie Valley: Bridgeport, Ala.–Dunlap, Tenn.
South Central Tennessee: Colesburg–Hohenwald, Tenn.
Walking Horse & Eastern: Wartrace–Shelbyville, Tenn.

Nevada-California-Oregon Railway

By 1879 Wadsworth, Nevada, east of Reno, was a major trans-shipment point for supplies going to mines in the area south of there. John T. Davis saw opportunity and formed the Western Nevada Railroad to build a line south from Wadsworth to Walker Lake. When Darius Mills of the Virginia & Truckee heard of Davis's plans, he started planning and building the Carson & Colorado Railroad in the same direction.

Davis moved his base of operations to Reno and on June 1, 1880, organized the Nevada & Oregon Railroad to build south to Aurora (southwest of Hawthorne, almost on the California state line) and north to the California-Oregon state line at Goose Lake in the northeast corner of California. Davis's associates suggested building the railroad in three phases: first south to Carson City and Virginia City (both already well served by the Virginia & Truckee), then north from Reno to Beckwourth Pass, then south beyond Carson City to Bodie, Calif. Davis thought so little of this strategy that he quit and returned to San Francisco.

New management decided to build northward first and broke ground on December 22, 1880. The ground-breaking ceremonies included talk about a main line north to the Columbia River and branches west to Eugene, Ore., and through Klamath Falls to the Rogue River Valley.

Baldwin built 2-8-0 No. 14 in 1906. SP moved several NCO engines to its narrow gauge line in California's Owens Valley when the NCO was converted to standard gauge. Photo from the collection of H. L. Broadbelt.

The Nevada & Oregon was in financial trouble by the time it had graded a mile of roadbed. A new Nevada & Oregon company took over on April 25, 1881, and the first spike was driven on May 28 that year. The line started north on a new alignment 6 miles longer that what had originally been surveyed, and despite further financial problems and another cessation of construction work, regular train operation began to Oneida (or Antelope or Evans), Calif., on October 2, 1882.

On April 17, 1884, the Moran brothers bought the railroad, and by the beginning of 1885 it had a new name—Nevada & California Railroad—and new cars and locomotives. Construction continued north, pretty much following present-day highway U. S. 395, except between Doyle and Wendel, where the railroad went around the east side of Honey Lake, bypassing Susanville, the only settlement of any size in northeastern California. The railhead reached Doyle in 1888 and Amedee in 1890, where it remained for a decade.

At the beginning of 1893 the assets were transferred to a new company, the Nevada-California-Oregon Railway. Construction resumed in 1899.

The line reached Termo in 1900, Madeline in 1902, Likely in 1907, and Alturas in 1908. On January 10, 1912, the line reached Lakeview, Ore., 238 miles from Reno. It was as far as the NCO would go, even though its charter had been altered in 1910 to allow construction north to the Columbia River at The Dalles.

First truncation

The NCO operated profitably from 1899 to 1913. The principal items of freight traffic were cattle, sheep, and lumber. Its passenger trains carried buffet-sleeping cars acquired from the Tonopah Railroad. The berths were not necessary during the 13-hour (more or less) daytime run between Reno and Lakeview, but the buffets provided meal service. In 1901 NCO acquired the Sierra Valleys Railway (later Sierra Valley & Mohawk, consolidated with NCO in 1915), which ran from Beckwourth Pass west to Clio. Other railroads began to penetrate the area. The Western Pacific came up the Feather River Canyon from the west, paralleled the Sierra Valleys as far as Beckwourth Pass, then turned north and paralleled the NCO as far as Hackstaff (present-day Herlong) before turning east. The Southern Pacific built northwest from Wadsworth, crossed the NCO at Wendel, and continued west to Susanville and Westwood.

Western Pacific's charter forbade it to build or acquire branch lines. Receivership and reorganization freed it of that restriction, and it considered a branch to Reno. It first discussed adding a third rail to the NCO from Beckwourth Pass to Reno, then bought the NCO property from Reno north to Hackstaff and the former Sierra Valleys line. The last NCO train departed Reno on January 30, 1918, and the NCO moved its headquarters and shops to Alturas.

Second truncation

Meanwhile, deficits had appeared on NCO's books. NCO management tried to sell the entire road to Western Pacific, without success. In 1921 NCO considered an extension northwest from Lakeview into a lumbering area. WP was involved to the point of providing rails, though there was some debate over that. NCO threated to abandon the line south of Wendel, where it crossed SP's Westwood Branch, but WP invoked a clause in the sale agreement for the Reno line. A year later NCO abandoned the Hackstaff–Wendel part of the line. It had gradually worked north from Reno, and now appeared to be pulling its tail up after it.

Lumber shipments from the north end of the line began to increase, and NCO began to considering standard-gauging its line. Meanwhile Southern Pacific was planning to build a line to connect its Overland and Cascade routes, using part of the Westwood Branch and new construction southeast from Klamath Falls. SP offered to buy the NCO to use the Wendel–Alturas segment as part of that line. SP acquired control of the NCO in October 1926 and began standard-gauging in July 1927. Standard gauge service to Alturas began on October 24, 1927, and to Lakeview on May 27, 1928. SP leased the NCO on September 1, 1929, but until then from the time standard-gauging began it furnished standard gauge locomotives and cars lettered Nevada-California-Oregon.

	1916	1927	1929
Miles of railroad operated:	272	160	155
Number of locomotives:	14	12	3
Number of passenger cars:	18	16*	
Number of freight cars:	257	215	63
Number of company service cars:	47	51	

Location of headquarters: Reno, Nevada, until 1918, then Alturas, California.

Recommended reading: *Railroads of Nevada and Eastern California, Volume I*, by David Myrick, published in 1962 by Howell-North Books, 850 North Hollywood Way, Burbank, CA 91505

Successors:
Western Pacific
Southern Pacific
Union Pacific

Portions still operated:
Great Western Railway (Oregon): Alturas, Calif.–Lakeview, Ore.
Union Pacific (ex-WP): Reno, Nev.–Reno Junction, Calif.
Union Pacific (ex-SP): Wendel–Alturas, Calif.

*2 motor cars)

Nevada County Narrow Gauge Railroad

The Nevada County Narrow Railroad was incorporated in 1874 to connect the gold-mining towns of Nevada City and Grass Valley, California, with the newly constructed Central Pacific at Colfax. The incorporators specified 3-foot gauge after learning of the construction costs of the standard gauge Central Pacific. Construction got under way in early 1875, and rolling stock was ordered. The principal engineering features of the line were tall trestles over the Bear River and Greenhorn Creek. Rails reached Grass Valley in early 1876; regular service began in April of that year to Grass Valley and in May to Nevada City.

In 1908 a line relocation eliminated the trestles and You Bet Tunnel but required a high steel bridge, as impressive as the trestles had been, over the Bear River. The NCNG was also notable in having a woman, Sara Kidder, as president from 1901 to 1913—she inherited the majority of the road's stock from her husband, the previous president.

The railroad went through the usual management crises and competition from trucks, buses, and automobiles. It was reorganized in 1927 under local management. One response to competition was to acquire a number of tank cars to carry oil and gasoline from the Southern Pacific connection at Colfax to Grass

The Bear River Bridge of 1908 was the engineering highlight of the Nevada County Narrow Gauge. When the road was abandoned, the cost of dismantling the bridge exceeded its scrap value, so the bridge remained in place until it was blown up in 1963 to make way for a dam. Photo by Jim Morley.

Valley and Nevada City. NCNG was unusual among narrow gauge railroads in that it purchased two second-hand gasoline-powered switchers in 1936.

On May 16, 1937, the railroad hosted a railfan excursion, first on the West Coast. In 1938 the road discontinued rail passenger service; the road's own buses had taken most of the passengers. The NCNG became profitable in the late 1930s and even paid dividends. As World War II began, though, the scrap value of the railroad outstripped its transportation value, and the federally ordered closing of the gold mines clinched the matter. The last revenue train ran on July 10, 1942.

	1929	1939
Miles of railroad operated:	21	21
Number of locomotives:	4	3
Number of passenger cars:	5	
Number of freight cars:	43	66
Number of company service cars:		3

Location of headquarters: Grass Valley, California
Recommended reading: *Nevada County Narrow Gauge*, by Gerald M. Best, published in 1965 by Howell-North Books, 850 North Hollywood Way, Burbank, CA 91505

Nevada Northern Railway

Mining in Nevada meant gold or silver—until the electrical industry began to grow. Then copper, which had been treated almost as a waste material, became valuable. A large deposit of copper ore was discovered near Ely, in eastern central Nevada many miles from the nearest railroad. One proposal for a railroad to Ely involved standard-gauging the Eureka & Palisade and extending it 75 miles eastward from Eureka to Ely over four mountain ranges.

In 1905 the Nevada Consolidated Copper Co., which had been created the previous year by merger of several mining companies active in the area, incorporated the Nevada Northern Railway to build a line from Ely north through the Steptoe Valley to a connection with the Southern Pacific's line between Reno, Nev., and Ogden, Utah. NN's route was almost twice as long as the proposed line from Eureka, but the only obstacle was sagebrush. The railroad was completed in 1906.

Nevada Consolidated Copper Co. became a subsidiary of Utah Copper Co. in 1909; Kennecott Copper Corp. acquired control in 1923. In the Ely area the Nevada Northern was used by the mine trains of its parent, but the major portion of the road saw only a biweekly freight train. In mid-1983 Kennecott shut down its smelter at McGill, Nev.; for lack of traffic, NN suspended operation.

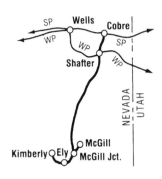

	1929	1981
Miles of railroad operated:	166	149
Number of locomotives:	8	1
Number of passenger cars:	13	
Number of freight cars:	37	58
Number of company service cars:	17	
Location of headquarters: East Ely, Nevada		
Reporting marks: NN		
Portions still operated: Nevada Northern Railway Museum operates on former NN track in and around Ely.		

A freight rolls north toward the Western Pacific connection at Shafter behind Nevada Northern's sole road locomotive, an SD7, near Goshute in September 1976. Photo by Ted Benson.

Newfoundland Railway

The Newfoundland Railway was chartered in 1881. A track gauge of 3 feet 6 inches was chosen both for reasons of economy and because that gauge was traditionally associated with railroads in British colonies. Construction got under way at St. John's, capital of Newfoundland, and the line reached Harbour Grace, almost to its goal, Carbonear, in November 1884. By then it was in financial difficulty and was taken over by the government of the colony.

In 1886 the government began work on a line from Whitbourne to Placentia; it was completed in 1888. The government found that railroad construction was expensive, so for the next extension, 280 miles west, bids were let. Robert Reid won the contract. He received a land grant, and he contracted to operate both the railroad he was to construct and those lines already under government control.

The plans for the railroad were eventually revised to make the western terminal Port-aux-Basques, on the southwest tip of the island, about 110 miles from the mainland port of North Sydney, Nova Scotia. The line was completed from St. John's to Port-aux-Basques in 1898. During the next 20 years several branch lines were added.

In 1920 the Reid Newfoundland Company, as the railroad had become, began to have financial

Newfoundland Railway Mikado 1024 prepares to depart from St. John's with the westbound *Caribou*. The 2-8-2 was built by Montreal Locomotive Works in 1949, just before the road became part of Canadian National Railways. CNR photo.

	1929	1949
Miles of railroad operated:	968	717
Number of locomotives:		63

Location of headquarters: St. John's, Newfoundland

Notable named passenger trains: *Caribou* (Port-aux-Basques–St. John's)

Recommended reading: *Narrow Gauge Railways of Canada*, by Omer Lavallee, published in 1972 by Railfare Enterprises Limited, Box 33, West Hill, ON, Canada M1E 4R4

Successor: Canadian National Railways

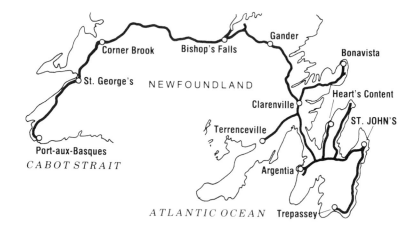

problems. The government took over the railway in 1923, calling it first the Newfoundland Government Railway and later, in 1926, simply Newfoundland Railway. Many of the branches built during the early years of the century were pruned in the 1930s.

The colony itself was nearly bankrupt by the mid-1930s. World War II brought activity and prosperity to Newfoundland, the closest North American point to Europe. Newfoundland became Canada's tenth province in 1949, and the Newfoundland Railway became part of Canadian National Railways.

CNR tried a number of ways to cut the cost of operating its only narrow gauge line: It completed dieselization of the line in 1957, instituted procedures for carrying standard gauge freight cars on narrow gauge trucks, replaced the cross-island *Caribou* (or "Newfie Bullet") with buses in 1969, and in 1979 created a separate organization, Terra Transport, to operate CNR's various Newfoundland services. All Canadian National rail operations in Newfoundland ceased on October 1, 1988.

New Orleans Great Northern Railroad

Like many other railroads in southern Mississippi and adjacent Louisiana, the New Orleans Great Northern began as a logging railroad, but it was constructed to better standards than most logging roads and it was planned to be a permanent railroad.

It was part of the lumbering empire of Frank and Charles Goodyear of Buffalo, New York—another piece of that empire was the Buffalo & Susquehanna Railroad.

The NOGN was incorporated in Louisiana and Mississippi in 1905, and the Mississippi company was merged into the Louisiana one the following year. Also in 1905 the NOGN purchased the East Louisiana Railroad, which had a network of lines in the area north of Lake Pontchartrain and reached New Orleans by trackage rights over the New Orleans & Northeastern (later Southern Railway) from Slidell, La. NOGN opened its line north to Jackson, Miss., in 1909. Passenger traffic on the NOGN declined after World War I, but freight business prospered until the mid-1920s.

New Orleans Great Northern's route between Jackson, Miss., and New Orleans was important to Gulf, Mobile & Northern's traffic agreement with the Burlington. Accordingly, GM&N took control of NOGN on December 30, 1929. NOGN entered receivership on November 7, 1932, with Isaac B. Tigrett, president of GM&N, as receiver.

New Orleans Great Northern 4-4-0 No. 105 stands in Jackson, Mississippi, on September 3, 1927, after bringing train 102 from New Orleans. Photo by Thomas T. Taber; collection of Louis A. Marre.

It was reorganized as the New Orleans Great Northern Railway and leased to GM&N on July 1, 1933. The lease was assumed by Gulf, Mobile & Ohio and later by Illinois Central Gulf.

	1929	1933
Miles of railroad operated:	277	263
Number of locomotives:	28	14
Number of passenger cars:	29	14
Number of freight cars:	1,354	
Number of company service cars:	48	
Number of freight and company service cars:		407
Location of headquarters: New Orleans, Louisiana		

Reporting marks: NOGN

Historical and technical society: Gulf, Mobile & Ohio Historical Society, P. O. Box 2457, Joliet, IL 60434-2457; http://www.tfs.net/~jashaw/rhs/gmo.html

Recommended reading: *The Gulf, Mobile and Ohio,* by James Hutton Lemly, published in 1953 by Richard D. Irwin, Inc., Homewood, IL 60430

Successors:
Gulf, Mobile & Northern
Gulf, Mobile & Ohio
Illinois Central Gulf
Illinois Central

Portions still operated: Illinois Central: Slidell, La.–Wanilla, Miss., Slidell–Covington, La.

Map: See page 188

New York Central System

The New York Central was a large railroad, and it had several subsidiaries whose identity remained strong, not so much in cars and locomotives carrying the old name but in local loyalties: If you lived in Detroit, you rode to Chicago on the Michigan Central, not the New York Central; Conrail's line across Massachusetts is still known as "the Boston & Albany."

NYC's history is easier to digest in small pieces: first New York Central followed by its two major leased lines, Boston & Albany and Toledo & Ohio Central; then Michigan Central and Big Four (Cleveland, Cincinnati, Chicago & St. Louis). By the mid-1960s NYC owned 99.8 percent of the stock of Michigan Central and more than 97 percent of the stock of the Big Four. NYC leased both on February 1, 1930, but they remained separate companies to avoid the complexities of merger.

In broad geographic terms, the New York Central proper was everything east of Buffalo plus a line from Buffalo through Cleveland and Toledo to Chicago (the former Lake Shore & Michigan Southern). NYC included the Ohio Central Lines (Toledo through Columbus to and beyond Charleston, West Virginia) and the Boston & Albany (neatly defined by its name).

The Michigan Central was a Buffalo–Detroit–Chicago line and everything in Michigan north of that. The Big Four was everything south of NYC's Cleveland–Toledo–Chicago line other than the Ohio Central.

The New York Central System included several controlled railroads that did not accompany NYC into the Penn Central merger. The most important of these were (with the proportion of NYC ownership in the mid-1960s):
• Pittsburgh & Lake Erie (80 percent)
• Indiana Harbor Belt (NYC, 30 percent; Michigan Central, 30 percent; Chicago & North Western, 20 percent; and Milwaukee Road, 20 percent)

NYC advertised itself as "The Water Level Route," so "Mountain" would hardly be an appropriate name for its 4-8-2-type locomotives. Thus it's a Mohawk wheeling freight west through Waterloo, Indiana, 367 miles west of Buffalo, in 1948. Photo by Robert A. Hadley.

• Toronto, Hamilton & Buffalo (NYC, 37 percent; MC, 22 percent; Canada Southern, 14 percent; and Canadian Pacific, 27 percent)

New York Central

The Erie Canal, opened in 1825 between Albany and Buffalo, New York, followed the Hudson and Mohawk rivers between Albany and Schenectady. The 40-mile water route included several locks and was extremely slow; in consequence, stagecoaches plied the 17-mile direct route between the cities. In 1826 the Mohawk & Hudson Rail Road was incorporated to replace the stages between Albany and Schenectady.

The railroad opened in 1831; its first locomotive was named *DeWitt Clinton* after the governor of the state when the M&H was incorporated. Within months there was a proposal for a railroad all the way from Albany to Buffalo, but the subject was touchy—the state was still deeply in debt for the construction of the Erie Canal.

One by one, railroads were incorporated, built, and opened westward from the end of the Mohawk & Hudson: Utica & Schenectady, Syracuse & Utica, Auburn & Syracuse, Auburn & Rochester, Tonawanda (Rochester to Attica via Batavia), and Attica & Buffalo. By 1841 it was possible to travel between Albany and Buffalo by train in just 25 hours, lightning speed compared with the canal packets. By 1851 the trip took a little over 12 hours. In 1851 the state passed an act freeing the railroads from the need to pay tolls to the Erie Canal, with which they competed. That same year the Hudson River Railroad opened from New York to East Albany and the New York & Erie (later the Erie Railroad) opened from Piermont, on the Hudson River, west to Dunkirk, N. Y., on Lake Erie.

From the beginning the railroads between Albany and Buffalo had cooperated in running through service. In 1853 they were consolidated as the New York Central Railroad—the roads mentioned above or their successors plus the Schenectady & Troy, the Buffalo & Lockport, the Rochester, Lockport & Niagara Falls, and two unbuilt roads, the Mohawk Valley and the Syracuse & Utica Direct.

The New York & Harlem Railroad was incorporated in 1831 to build a line in Manhattan from 23rd Street north to 129th Street between Third and Eighth avenues (the railroad chose to follow Fourth Avenue). At first the railroad was primarily a horsecar system, but in 1840 the road's charter was amended to allow it to build north toward Albany. In 1844 the rails reached White Plains and in January 1852 the New York & Harlem made connection with the Western Railroad (later Boston & Albany) at Chatham, N. Y., creating a New York–Albany rail route.

The Hudson was a busy river, and the towns along it felt no need of a railroad, except during the winter when ice prevented navigation. Poughkeepsie interests organized the Hudson River Railroad in 1847. In the autumn of 1851 the railroad opened from a terminal on Manhattan's west side all the way to East Albany. By then the road had leased the Troy & Greenbush, gaining access to a bridge over the Hudson at Troy. (A bridge at Albany was completed in 1866.)

By 1863 Cornelius Vanderbilt controlled the New York & Harlem and had a substantial interest in the Hudson River Railroad. In 1867 he obtained control of the New York Central, consolidating it with the Hudson River in 1869 to form the New York Central & Hudson River Railroad. (For simplicity I will refer to the NYC&HR as "NYC," "Central," or "New York Central.")

Vanderbilt wanted to build a magnificent terminal for the NYC&HR in New York. He chose as its site the corner of 42nd Street and Fourth Avenue on the New York & Harlem, the southerly limit of steam locomotive operation in Manhattan. Construction of Grand Central Depot began in 1869 and took two years. The new depot was actually three separate stations serving the NYC&HR, the New York & Harlem, and the New Haven. Trains of the Hudson River line reached the New York & Harlem by means of a connecting track completed in 1871 along Spuyten Duyvil Creek and the Harlem River

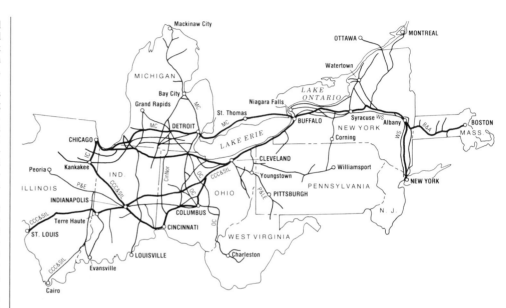

(they have since become a single waterway). That was the first of three Grand Centrals.

The present station, Grand Central Terminal, was opened in 1913. Even in the space age Grand Central remains awesome. Superlatives are inadequate. GCT has a total of 48 platform tracks on two subterranean levels; the project included depressing and decking over the tracks along Park Avenue and electrifying NYC's lines north to Harmon and White Plains. (NYC had two other stretches of electrified line: the Detroit River Tunnel, opened in 1910, and Cleveland Union Terminal, opened in 1930. Diesels put an end to both those electrifications in 1953.)

The Watertown & Rome Railroad was chartered in 1832 to connect Watertown, N. Y., with the Syracuse & Utica, then only a proposal itself. The road opened in 1851, and in 1852 it was extended to Cape Vincent, where it connected with a ferry to Kingston, Ontario. In 1861 the W&R consolidated with the Potsdam & Watertown to form the Rome, Watertown & Ogdens-

NYC wasn't all four-track main lines and glossy streamliners. J-1 Hudson 5340 stops at Lake Orion, Michigan, between Bay City and Detroit, at 3:32 p.m. on June 3, 1949. On the rear of this secondary-line local is a new all-room streamlined sleeping car, which will be in Grand Central Terminal, New York, tomorrow morning. Photo by Elmer Treloar.

burg. The RW&O built a line to Oswego and bought lines to Syracuse and Buffalo. The line to Buffalo was a mistake—it bypassed Rochester, had almost no local business, and was not part of any through route.

The RW&O came under Lackawanna control briefly before a rehabilitation in the 1880s. New management extended the RW&O north to connect with a Grand Trunk line to Montreal and added the Black River & Utica (Utica to Watertown and Ogdensburg) to the system. NYC leased the RW&O in 1893.

Meanwhile, NYC had built its own line north from Herkimer: the St. Lawrence & Adirondack (later Mohawk & Malone) of William Seward Webb, son-in-law of William H. Vanderbilt. NYC merged the Mohawk & Malone in 1911 and the RW&O in 1913.

Lake Shore & Michigan Southern

The Michigan Southern was chartered by the state of Michigan in 1837 to build from the head of navigation on the River Raisin west of Monroe across the southern tier of Michigan to Lake Michigan. Under state auspices it got as far west as Hillsdale, Mich. It was sold to private interests which combined it with the Erie & Kalamazoo (opened in 1837 from Toledo, Ohio, to Adrian, Mich.) and extended it west to meet the Northern Indiana Railroad, which was building east from La Porte, Ind. The line opened from Monroe to South Bend in 1851; by February 1852 it reached Chicago, where it teamed up with the Rock Island to build terminal facilities. (Its successors shared a Chicago station, La Salle Street, with Rock Island until 1968). The roads were combined as the Michigan Southern & Northern Indiana in 1855. By then a direct line between Elkhart, Ind., and Toledo had been constructed.

The railroad situation along the south shore of Lake Erie was complicated by Ohio's insistence on a track gauge of 4 feet 10 inches, Pennsylvania's reluctance to let a railroad from another state cross its borders, and the desire of the city of Erie, Pa., to have the change of gauge within its limits in the hope that passengers would spend money while changing trains there. (Such thinking continues today; oil companies put their gas stations at street corners with traffic signals.)

The NYC controlled the Buffalo & State Line and the Erie & North East railroads by 1853; they were combined as the Buffalo & Erie in 1867. The Cleveland, Painesville & Ashtabula was opened between Cleveland and Erie in 1852. In 1868 the CP&A took its familiar name, Lake Shore, as its official name, and a year later it absorbed the Cleveland & Toledo and joined with the Michigan Southern & Northern Indiana to form the Lake Shore & Michigan Southern. During a business panic about that time Cornelius Vanderbilt acquired control of the LS&MS.

In 1914 the New York Central & Hudson River, the Lake Shore & Michigan Southern, and several smaller roads were combined to form the New York Central Railroad—the second railroad of that name.

West Shore

In 1869 and 1870 several railroads were proposed and surveyed up the west bank of the Hudson River. In 1880 the New York, West Shore & Buffalo Railroad was formed to build a line from Jersey City to Albany and Buffalo, parallel to the New York Central. William Vanderbilt suspected (correctly) that the Pennsylvania Railroad was behind the project. The road opened to Albany and Syracuse in 1883 and reached Buffalo at the beginning of 1884. A rate war ensued. The West Shore entered bankruptcy, as did the construction company that built the line. The West Shore cut its rates to beat those of the NYC, hoping the Central, with its far greater volume of business, would lose a lot more money than the West Shore. The Central, however, had resources to withstand a temporary loss.

In retaliation Vanderbilt decided to revive an old survey for a railroad across Pennsylvania that was considerably shorter than the Pennsylvania Railroad. He enlisted the support of Andrew Carnegie and John D. Rockefeller.

It took J. P. Morgan to work a compromise between the NYC and the Pennsylvania: The Central would lease the West Shore, and the Pennsy would get the South Pennsylvania and its partially excavated tunnels. In 1885 the West Shore was reorganized as the West Shore Railroad, wholly owned by the NYC and leased to it. (The roadbed of the South Pennsylvania was

later used for the Pennsylvania Turnpike.) The Weehawken–Albany portion of the West Shore proved to be a valuable freight route for NYC and more so for its successors Penn Central and Conrail. Most of the West Shore west of Albany has been abandoned. In 1952 NYC merged the West Shore.

Boston & Albany

The Boston & Worcester Railroad opened between the cities of its name in 1835. Its charter had a clause prohibiting the construction of a parallel railroad within 5 miles for 30 years. The Western Railroad opened in 1840 from Worcester west to Springfield and in 1841 across the Berkshires to Greenbush, N. Y., on the east bank of the Hudson opposite Albany. The two railroads shared some directors, but efforts at merging them were futile until 1863, when B&W's protection clause expired and the Western proposed building its own line from Worcester to Boston. The two roads were consolidated as the Boston & Albany Railroad in 1867.

The B&A had several minor branches and a few major ones: Palmer to Winchendon, Mass., Springfield to Athol, Mass., Pittsfield to North Adams, Mass.; and Chatham to Hudson, N. Y.—only short portions of them remain in service.

The B&A's principal connection was the New York Central at Albany, and in 1900 the NYC leased the B&A. The New York Central wanted a route to Boston. It had a choice of the B&A or the parallel Fitchburg Railroad (later Boston & Maine). If NYC chose the Fitchburg, the B&A would be left with only local business, so B&A willingly forsook independence. In 1961 NYC merged the Boston & Albany.

B&A maintained more of its identity than other NYC subsidiaries. It had its own officers, and until 1951 its locomotives and cars were lettered "Boston & Albany" rather than "New York Central Lines," largely to appeal to local sensitivities. B&A's steam power was basically of NYC appearance but with a few distinctive features, such as square sand domes on the Hudsons and offset smokebox doors on Pacifics. The profile of the B&A, definitely not the water level route NYC was so proud of elsewhere, called for heavy power in the form of 2-6-6-2s and 2-8-4s (the latter named for the Berkshires over which the line ran). Nearer Boston, B&A ran an intense suburban service powered by 2-6-6Ts and 4-6-6Ts, the latter looking like condensed, solid-pack NYC Hudsons.

Ohio Central Lines

Ohio Central Lines included the Toledo & Ohio Central Railway and three leased lines (merged in 1938), the Zanesville & Western Railway, the Kanawha & Michigan Railway, and the Kanawha & West Virginia Railroad. They formed a route from Toledo southeast through Columbus, across the Ohio River, and through Charleston to Swiss and Hitop, West Virginia. The Ohio Central began as the Atlantic & Lake Erie, chartered in 1869. After a series of receiverships and a name change to Ohio Central the road managed to link Columbus with the Ohio River at Middleport in 1882. It then pushed into the coalfields along the Kanawha River in West Virginia and extended itself northwest toward Toledo. It was renamed the Toledo & Ohio Central in 1885.

The NYC acquired control of the T&OC by 1910 and began operating it as part of the New

York Central System. NYC leased the road in 1922 and merged it in 1952. In recent years Penn Central revived the road's identity with the "TOC" reporting marks.

Michigan Central

Michigan Central had its beginnings in the Detroit & St. Joseph Railroad, which was incorporated in 1832 to build a railroad across Michigan from Detroit to St. Joseph. Michigan attained statehood in 1837 and almost immediately chartered railroads to be constructed along three routes: the Northern, from Port Huron to the head of navigation on the Grand River; the Central, from Detroit to St. Joseph; and the Southern, from the head of navigation on the River Raisin to New Buffalo.

The state purchased the Detroit & St. Joseph to use as the basis for the Central Railroad. About the time the road reached Kalamazoo in 1846 it ran out of money. It was purchased from the state by Boston interests led by John W. Brooks and was reorganized as the Michigan Central Railroad. Construction resumed in the direction of New Buffalo rather than St. Joseph, and in 1849 the line reached Michigan City, Ind., about as far as its Michigan charter could take it.

To reach the Illinois border the Michigan Central used the charter of the New Albany & Salem (a predecessor of the Monon) in exchange for which it purchased a block of NA&S stock. The MC continued on Illinois Central rails to Chicago, reaching there in 1852.

Vanderbilt began buying Michigan Central stock in 1869. New York Central leased the Michigan Central in 1930.

The Great Western Railway opened in 1854 from Niagara Falls to Windsor, Ont., opposite Detroit, and in March 1855 John Roebling's suspension bridge across the Niagara River was completed, creating with the New York Central a continuous line of rails from Albany to Windsor. The Great Western (which had a track gauge of 5 feet 6 inches) installed a third rail for standard gauge equipment between 1864 and 1866.

Vanderbilt tried without success to purchase the Great Western and turned his attention to the Canada Southern. It had been incorporated in 1868 as the Erie & Niagara Extension Railway to build a line along the north shore of Lake Erie and then across the Detroit River below the city of Detroit. He acquired the Canada Southern in 1876, and Michigan Central leased it in 1882. Conrail sold the Canada Southern to Canadian Pacific and Canadian National in 1985. New York Central leased the Michigan Central in 1930.

Cleveland, Cincinnati, Chicago & St. Louis (Big Four)

The oldest predecessor of the Big Four (and a comparatively late addition to it) was the Mad River & Lake Erie. Ground was broken in 1835, and the line opened from Sandusky to Dayton, Ohio, in 1851. It went through several renamings and became part of what later was the Peoria & Eastern before it was merged into the CCC&StL in 1890.

The Cleveland, Columbus & Cincinnati got its charter in 1836, broke ground in 1847, and opened in 1851 between Cleveland and Columbus. In 1852 it teamed up with the Little Miami and Columbus & Xenia railroads to form a Cleveland–Cincinnati route.

In 1848 the Indianapolis & Bellefontaine and the Bellefontaine & Indiana railroads were incorporated to build a line between Galion, Ohio, on the CC&C, and Indianapolis. The I&B and the B&I amalgamated and became known as "The B. Line." They were absorbed by the CC&C when it reorganized as the Cleveland, Columbus, Cincinnati & Indianapolis in 1868. The nickname of the new road was "The Bee Line."

The Cleveland, Columbus, Cincinnati & Indianapolis reached Cincinnati with its own rails in 1872. That same year it opened a line from Springfield to Columbus. By then the Vanderbilts owned a good portion of the road's stock.

The Terre Haute & Alton Railroad was organized in 1852. Its backers were certain that with a railroad to Indiana the Mississippi River town of Alton, Ill., could easily outstrip St. Louis a few miles south. It soon combined with the Belleville & Illinoistown Railroad (Illinoistown is now East St. Louis) as the Terre Haute, Alton & St. Louis. The Indianapolis & St. Louis was organized to build between Indianapolis and Terre Haute. It leased the St. Louis, Alton & Terre Haute, successor to the Terre Haute, Alton & St. Louis, and came under control of the CCC&I in 1882.

In the late 1840s and early 1850s several railroads were completed forming a route from Cincinnati through Indianapolis and Lafayette, Ind., to Kankakee, Ill., connecting there with the Illinois Central north to Chicago. In 1880 these roads were united as the Cincinnati, Indianapolis, St. Louis & Chicago—which some consider the first "Big Four." Heading the company was Melville Ingalls, and on its board was C. P. Huntington, whose Chesapeake & Ohio formed a friendly connection at Cincinnati.

The Vanderbilts had invested in the first Big Four, and they were firmly in control of the second Big Four, the Cleveland, Cincinnati, Chicago & St. Louis, which was formed in 1889 by the consolidation of the old Big Four (Cincinnati, Indianapolis, St. Louis & Chicago) and the Bee Line (Cleveland, Columbus, Cincinnati & Indianapolis).

In the late 1880s Ingalls and the Vanderbilts gathered in a group of railroads between Cairo and Danville, Ill.; added to them the St. Louis, Alton & Terre Haute, then added them all to the Big Four. The line from Danville north to Indiana Harbor was a comparatively late addition to the system: It was built in 1906 and became part of the New York Central rather than the Big Four.

The Peoria & Eastern was formed in 1890 from several small roads. At one time its predecessor briefly included the former Mad River & Lake Erie and a line from Indianapolis east to Springfield, Ohio, before settling down to be simply a Peoria–Bloomington–Danville–Indianapolis route.

In 1902 the Big Four bought the Cincinnati Northern, a line that had been proposed in 1852 and finally constructed in the 1880s from Franklin, Ohio, between Dayton and Cincinnati, to Jackson, Mich.

In 1920 the Big Four acquired the Evansville, Indianapolis & Terre Haute, a castoff from the Chicago & Eastern Illinois in southwestern Indiana. The New York Central leased the Big Four in 1930.

New York Central System

The New York Central System was the largest of the eastern trunk systems from the standpoint

The Boston & Albany was an exception to NYC's water-level profile. Three Alco freight units are working hard to lift up a westbound freight up Washington Mountain in the Berkshires of western Massachusetts in September 1949. Photo by R. E. Tobey.

of mileage and second only to the Pennsylvania in revenue. It served most of the industrial part of the country, and its freight tonnage was exceeded only by the coal-carrying railroads. In addition it was a major passenger railroad, with perhaps two-thirds the number of passengers as the Pennsylvania, but NYC's average passenger traveled one-third again as far as Pennsy's. NYC did not share as fully in the postwar prosperity because of rising labor and material costs and an

expensive improvement program, especially for passenger service.

In 1946 and 1947 Chesapeake & Ohio purchased a block of NYC stock (6.4 percent), becoming the road's largest stockholder. Robert R. Young gained control of New York Central and became its chairman in 1954 as part of a maneuver to merge it with C&O. One of his first acts was to put Alfred E. Perlman in charge of the Central.

Under Perlman NYC slimmed its physical plant, reducing long stretches of four-track line to two tracks under Centralized Traffic Control, and developed an aggressive freight marketing department. At the same time NYC's passenger operations were de-emphasized. On December 3, 1967, just before NYC and Pennsy merged, the Central reduced its passenger service to a skeleton, combining its New York–Chicago, New York–Detroit, New York–Toronto, and Boston–Chicago services into a single train and dropping all train names (including that of the *Twentieth Century Limited*, once considered the world's finest train) except for, curiously, that of the Chicago–Cincinnati *James Whitcomb Riley*.

The Central's archrival was the Pennsylvania Railroad. West of Buffalo and Pittsburgh the two systems duplicated each other at almost every major point; east of those cities the two hardly touched. Both roads had physical plant not being used to capacity (NYC was in better shape); both had a heavy passenger business; neither was earning much money. In 1957 NYC and Pennsy announced merger talks.

The initial industry reaction was utter surprise. "Who? Why?" Every merger proposal for decades had tried to balance the Central against the Pennsy and create two, three, or four more-or-less equal systems in the east. Traditionally Pennsy had been allied with Norfolk & Western and Wabash; New York Central with Baltimore & Ohio, Reading, and maybe the Lackawanna;

and everyone else swept up with Erie and Nickel Plate. Tradition also favored end-to-end mergers rather than those of parallel roads.

Planning and justifying the merger took nearly ten years, during which time the eastern railroad scene changed radically, in large measure because of the impending merger of NYC and PRR: Erie merged with Lackawanna, Chesapeake & Ohio acquired control of Baltimore & Ohio, and Norfolk & Western took in Virginia, Wabash, Nickel Plate, Pittsburgh & West Virginia, and Akron, Canton & Youngstown. Tradition aside, though, the New York Central and the Pennsylvania merged on February 1, 1967, to form Penn Central.

New York Central, including Boston & Albany and Ohio Central	1929
Miles of railroad operated:	6,915
Number of locomotives:	3,472
Number of passenger cars:	3,866
Number of freight cars:	138,199
Number of company service cars:	9,533
Michigan Central	**1929**
Miles of railroad operated:	1,858
Number of locomotives:	500
Number of passenger cars:	337
Number of freight cars:	16,303
Number of company service cars:	1,187

Big Four, including Peoria & Eastern	1929
Miles of railroad operated:	2,399
Number of locomotives:	925
Number of passenger cars:	615
Number of freight cars:	40,996
Number of company service cars:	1,137
New York Central	**1967**
Miles of railroad operated:	9,696
Number of locomotives:	1,917
Number of passenger cars:	2,085
Number of freight cars:	78,172
Number of company service cars:	2,650
Location of headquarters: New York, New York	

Reporting marks: NYC, B&A, CASO, CCC&StL, MCRR, P&E, P&LE, PMcK&Y, CRI, IHB

Notable named passenger trains: *Twentieth Century Limited, Commodore Vanderbilt, Pacemaker* (New York–Chicago), *Mercury* (Detroit–Cleveland, Detroit–Chicago), *Detroiter* (New York–Detroit), *Cleveland Limited* (New York–Cleveland), *Empire State Express* (New York–Buffalo–Cleveland/Detroit), *New England States* (Boston–Chicago), *Southwestern Limited* (New York–St. Louis), *Ohio State Limited* (New York–Cincinnati), *James Whitcomb Riley* (Cincinnati–Chicago)

Historical and technical society: New York Central System Historical Society, P. O. Box 81184, Cleveland, OH 44181-0184

Recommended reading: *The Road of the Century*, by Alvin F. Harlow, published in 1947 by Creative Age Press, New York, New York

Predecessor railroads in this book: Ulster & Delaware

Successors:
Penn Central
Conrail
Metro-North

Portions still operated:
Major portions operated by roads other than Conrail
Major portions abandoned
(The size and complexity of the NYC calls for a slightly different format here. This is not an exhaustive list of what is gone and what remains. In some cases I have shown an entire line as abandoned, even though short stubs remain where it crossed other lines.)

New York Central
Hannibal–Webster, N. Y.: Ontario Midland
Pittsfield–Saline, Mich.: Michigan Interstate (Ann Arbor)
Litchfield–Hillsdale–Steubenville, Ind.: Hillsdale County
East View–Brewster, N. Y. (Putnam Division);
Millerton–Chatham, N. Y. (New York & Harlem);
Herkimer–Remsen, N. Y.–Adirondack Jct., Que.; Tupper
Lake Jct., N. Y.–Ottawa, Ont.; Philadelphia–Ogdensburg,
N. Y.; Carthage–Cape Vincent, N. Y.; Pulaski–Oswego,
N. Y.; Webster–Niagara Falls, N. Y.; Batavia–North
Tonawanda, N. Y.; Fredonia, N. Y.–North Warren, Pa.,
Litchfield–Lansing, Mich.; Otsego–Grand Rapids, Mich.;
Ypsilanti–Pittsfield, Mich.; Saline–Hillsdale, Mich.;
Jackson–Bankers, Mich.; Steubenville–Fort Wayne, Ind.

West Shore
Kingston–Oneonta (ex-Ulster & Delaware); South
Amsterdam–Utica;
Utica–Rochester; Rochester–Oakfield, N. Y.

Boston & Albany
North Adams Junction–North Adams, Mass.: Boston & Maine
Post Road Crossing–Rensselaer, N. Y.: Amtrak
South Barre–Winchendon; Ludlow–Athol, Mass.;
Chatham–Claverack, N. Y.

Ohio Central
Fostoria–Thurston, Ohio; St. Marys–Peoria, Ohio

Michigan Central
Bay City–Mackinaw City: Detroit & Mackinac
Kalamazoo, Mich.–Michigan City, Ind.: Amtrak
Canada Southern lines: Canadian National and Canadian Pacific
Carleton–Marshall, Mich.; Battle Creek,
Mich.–Shipshewana, Ind.; Monroe–Hillsdale, Mich.
(original Michigan Southern route)

Big Four
Brookville, Ind.–Valley Jct., Ohio: Indiana & Ohio
Sheldon–Kankakee, Ill.: Kankakee, Beaverville & Southern
Mount Carmel–Cairo, Ill.: Southern
Mitchell–Pana, Ill.: Missouri Pacific
Springfield, Ohio –Shirley, Ind.; Greensburg–Nabb, Ind.;
New Castle–Brookville, Ind.; Goshen, Ind.–Niles, Mich.;
Paris–Pana, Ill.; Hillsboro–Alton, Ill.;
Kankakee–Seneca, Ill.
Bloomington–Tremont, Ill. (Peoria & Eastern)
Greenville, Ohio–Jackson, Mich. (Cincinnati Northern)

New York, Chicago & St. Louis Railroad

In 1879 and 1880 a syndicate headed by George I. Seney, a New York banker, assembled the Lake Erie & Western Railway, a line from Fremont, Ohio, to Bloomington, Illinois. After a dispute with the New York Central System about the routing of freight, Seney decided to build a line to connect the LE&W to Cleveland. He incorporated the New York, Chicago & St. Louis Railway in 1881 as a Buffalo–Chicago project. About this time it was referred to by a Norwalk, Ohio, newspaper as the "great double-track nickel-plated railroad" and the nickname stuck. (That's one theory about the name; another hinges on the pronunciation of "NYCL.") The line was completed in August 1882. William H. Vanderbilt offered to buy off Seney during its construction and then threatened to starve it of traffic—from Cleveland to Buffalo it was parallel to Vanderbilt's Lake Shore & Michigan Southern. Jay Gould began to negotiate to purchase the road; to block Gould, Vanderbilt purchased it instead and installed his son William K. Vanderbilt as president in 1883. Then he wondered what to do with it—benign neglect is what happened. Even though it was no more than a secondary line in the Vanderbilt system, it gained a reputation for fast movement of perishables, particularly meat.

In 1916 Cleveland real estate developers Oris Paxton Van Sweringen and Mantis James Van

A westbound Nickel Plate freight rolls along the shore of Lake Erie in April 1957 between Lorain and Vermilion, Ohio. The locomotive, Berkshire No. 779, was the last steam locomotive built by Lima Locomotive Works. Photo by John A. Rehor.

Sweringen bought NYC's interest in the Nickel Plate. NYC recognized that the Clayton Antitrust Act would require selling NKP; selling it to the Van Sweringen brothers would keep it out of the clutches of the Lackawanna or the Pennsylvania. The Van Sweringens were suddenly in the railroad business, and to run their railroad they chose John Bernet of the NYC. Bernet worked a thorough upgrading of NKP's locomotives and track, with the result that by 1925 the road had doubled its freight tonnage and average speed, halved its fuel consumption per ton mile, and led all U. S. roads in car miles per day.

The ICC merger plan of the 1920s grouped NKP with Lake Erie & Western; Toledo, St. Louis & Western; Wheeling & Lake Erie; Lehigh Valley; and Pittsburgh & West Virginia. In 1922 the Van Sweringens acquired both the LE&W, an unprofitable ward of the NYC, and the TStL&W (the Clover Leaf), which was in receivership because it had defaulted on the bonds it issued to gain control of the Chicago & Alton.

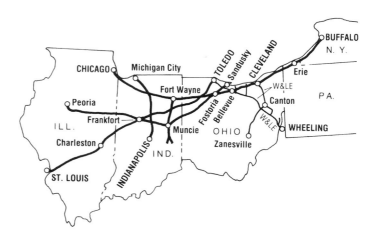

Lake Erie & Western

The Lake Erie & Western Railway was formed in 1879 to consolidate smaller railroads between Fremont, Ohio, and Bloomington, Ill. In 1880 the LE&W extended its line east from Fremont to Sandusky to replace boats on the lower stretches of the Sandusky River and teamed up with the Lake Shore to offer through freight and passenger service. The Lake Shore's lack of cooperation in the matter of westbound traffic was the reason LE&W's backers built the Nickel Plate.

The LE&W nearly died during the 1880s, but the discovery of natural gas and oil along the line

in Ohio and Indiana revived it. In 1887 it was reorganized and extended west to Peoria, Ill. That same year it acquired a Michigan City–Indianapolis line that crossed its main line at Tipton, Ind., and in 1890 it acquired a line from Fort Wayne to Connersville and Rushville, Ind., a line which crossed the Lake Erie & Western at Muncie. In 1895 the LE&W proposed assembling a line to the East Coast by using the Reading, the Buffalo, Rochester & Pittsburgh, and the Pittsburgh, Akron & Western, a former narrow gauge line from Akron to Delphos, Ohio. The

PA&W was reorganized that year as the Northern Ohio and leased to the LE&W.

In 1899 the LS&MS purchased a majority interest in the LE&W and proceeded to let it decline gently. In 1920 LE&W sold the Northern Ohio to the Akron, Canton & Youngstown.

Toledo, St. Louis & Western

The Toledo, Delphos & Indianapolis was organized in 1877 and that year opened a 3-foot gauge line a few miles north from Delphos, Ohio. Two years later it became part of the Toledo,

Delphos & Burlington, a consolidation of four railroads. The TD&B had as its goal a 3-foot gauge line from Toledo to Burlington, Iowa. The line was opened from Toledo to Kokomo, Ind., in 1880. It began extending south, buying up railroads to form a line south through Dayton to Cincinnati and Ironton, Ohio. Then it got caught up in a proposal to assemble a narrow gauge line all the way from Toledo to Mexico City.

The line was opened from Toledo to East St. Louis, Ill., in 1883 and the company collapsed soon afterwards. The lines south of Delphos to Cincinnati and Ironton were spun off to eventually become standard gauge pieces of the Cincinnati, Hamilton & Dayton, the Pennsylvania, and the Detroit, Toledo & Ironton. The Toledo–East St. Louis line was nearly dead when gas and oil were discovered along the line. It was reorganized as the Toledo, St. Louis & Kansas City Railroad, and it adopted a clover leaf as its emblem. Trackage east of Frankfort, Ind., was converted to standard gauge on June 25, 1887; the remainder of the line was converted two years later. The road developed a good freight business, particularly in eastbound livestock and perishables received from connections at East St. Louis.

The TStL&KC went bankrupt in 1893. The court proceedings included William Howard Taft as judge and Benjamin Harrison as counsel. The railroad was sold to its bondholders and became the Toledo, St. Louis & Western. It continued as a fast freight line, particularly in competition with the Wabash. In contrast to many midwestern roads, the TStL&W got along well with neighboring interurbans, even filing joint passenger tariffs. In 1903 the Clover Leaf acquired a half interest in the Detroit & Toledo Shore Line.

In 1907 it purchased control of the Alton. The TStL&W issued bonds to finance the purchase; interest on the bonds brought on another receivership in 1914.

Nickel Plate

In 1923 the Nickel Plate, the Lake Erie & Western, and the Clover Leaf were consolidated as a new New York, Chicago & St. Louis Railroad. On the recommendation of Alfred H. Smith, president of the NYC, the Van Sweringens went after the Chesapeake & Ohio, for its coal traffic, and the Pere Marquette, for its automobile business. In 1925 the New York, Chicago & St. Louis Railway was incorporated to lease and operate the Nickel Plate, C&O, PM, Erie, and Hocking Valley. The railroad industry was in favor of the merger, but a small group of C&O stockholders fought it. In 1926 the ICC rejected the petition on financial grounds—it was in favor of it from the standpoint of transportation. Then the Van Sweringens tried again in 1926—C&O applied to acquire PM, Erie, and Hocking Valley. The ICC rejected that in 1929.

The Van Sweringens moved Bernet to the Erie; taking his place was Walter Ross, who had been president of the Clover Leaf. He engineered an about-face for NKP's passenger service, which for years had been operated on the assumption there was no sense trying to compete with the NYC. Ross went after the long-haul passenger with comfort and personal service. The passenger renaissance lasted only until 1931, when the Depression occasioned cutbacks.

Nickel Plate came under Chesapeake & Ohio management in 1933, and Bernet was back in the presidency. He initiated a scrap drive to

finance rebuilding of the Clover Leaf district, and he ordered the first 15 of a series of big 2-8-4 Berkshires that eventually numbered 80 to upgrade the road's freight power. The design of the new locomotives drew heavily on Chesapeake & Ohio's 2-10-4s. Other improvements of the late 1930s and the war years were strengthening the bridges east of Cleveland, introducing Centralized Traffic Control, and upgrading track and bridges on the Lake Erie & Western and the Clover Leaf to permit the Berkshires to work to Peoria and Madison (East St. Louis), Ill.

Nickel Plate resumed its own management in December 1942; Chesapeake & Ohio attempted merger in 1945, but NKP stockholders objected. Dieselization of passenger service began in the late 1940s, but freight continued to roll behind steam. In 1948 Nickel Plate tested a set of Electro-Motive F3s and immediately ordered 10 more Berkshires (they proved to be Lima's last steam locomotives). A four-unit set of F3s could outperform the 2-8-4s, but fuel costs were greater; a Berkshire developed greater horsepower at speed than a three-unit set—and at speed was where Nickel Plate used most of its horsepower.

NKP also tested General Electric's gas turbine-electric, and EMD painted a pair of F7s blue and gray, like the PAs, for a demonstration on the former LE&W. Freight diesels finally began to arrive in the form of GP7s in 1951, but steam dominated mainline freight service until the business recession of 1957 and 1958. Nickel Plate was one of the last U. S. railroads to operate steam, and two of the Berkshires, 759 and 765, remained active in excursion service.

In 1946 and 1947 NKP purchased about 80

percent of the stock of Wheeling & Lake Erie, and on December 1, 1949, NKP leased the W&LE. The Wheeling served the steel-and-coal area of Ohio and originated much of its tonnage, in contrast to NKP, thus providing balance to the NKP's bridge-route freight business.

For years NKP's principal freight competitors had been the Erie and the Wabash; after 1954 the New York Central under Alfred Perlman began to become a lean, fast railroad. The Lackawanna proposed merger with Nickel Plate; NKP management rejected the union. When Lackawanna merged with Erie, it disposed of a large block of NKP stock. Norfolk & Western merged the Virginian, and the New York Central and the Pennsylvania announced their engagement. Nickel Plate, su^addenly unattached, looked around, set up through freight trains with Lehigh Valley, and began merger negotiations with Norfolk & Western. On October 16, 1964, N&W merged the Nickel Plate.

	1929	1963
Miles of railroad operated:	1,691	2,170
Number of locomotives:	465	408
Number of passenger cars:	159	60
Number of freight cars:	21,625	22,305
Number of company service cars:	832	700

Location of headquarters: Cleveland, Ohio

Reporting marks: NKP

Historical and technical society: Nickel Plate Road Historical & Technical Society, P. O. Box 381, New Haven, IN 46774-0381; nkphts@mail.iac.net;http://www.iac.net/~nkphts/index.html

Recommended reading: *The Nickel Plate Story*, by John A. Rehor, published in 1965 by Kalmbach Publishing Co. (ISBN 0-89024-012-4)

Subsidiaries and affiliated railroads, 1963: Detroit & Toledo Shore Line (50%, jointly with Grand Trunk Western)

Predecessor railroads in this book: Wheeling & Lake Erie

Successors:

Norfolk & Western

Norfolk Southern

Portions still operated:

Norfolk Southern: Buffalo–Chicago; Muncie–Frankfort, Ind.–Peoria, Ill.; Coffeen–Madison, Ill.; Fort Wayne–Muncie–New Castle; Michigan City–Peru; Fort Recovery–Muncie; Arcadia–Lima, Ohio; Douglas–Delphos, Ohio–Decatur–Marion, Ind.; Bellevue–Toledo (ex-W&LE)

Central RR of Indianapolis: Frankfort–Kokomo–Marion, Ind.; Tipton–Kokomo–Peru, Ind.

Indiana Hi-Rail Corp.: New Castle–Rushville, Ind.; Beesons–Connersville, Ind.

Eastern Illinois: Neoga–Metcalf, Ill.

Ohio Central: Zanesville–Harmon, Ohio (ex-W&LE)

R. J. Corman — Western Ohio: South Lima–St. Marys–Fort Recovery, Ohio; St. Marys–Minster, Ohio

Wheeling & Lake Erie (1990): Bellevue, Ohio–Martin's Ferry, W. Va.; Cleveland–Harmon; Huron Junction–Huron, Ohio; Canton–Carrollton, Ohio; Warrenton–Steubenville, Ohio

New York, New Haven & Hartford Railroad

The New York, New Haven & Hartford eventually gathered in nearly all the railroads in Connecticut, Rhode Island, and southeastern Massachusetts. Its four principal predecessors were the Old Colony, the New York & New England, the Central New England, and the New York & New Haven (for simplicity, the "New Haven"), which was the dominant corporation.

Old Colony

The Old Colony Railroad was opened in 1845 between Boston and Plymouth, Mass. In 1854 it was consolidated with the Fall River Railroad, which had been formed in 1845 from three smaller roads to form a route from the port of Fall River, Mass., north to a junction with the Old Colony at South Braintree. In 1876 the Old Colony leased and in 1883 merged the Boston, Clinton, Fitchburg & New Bedford, which extended from New Bedford to Fitchburg, Mass., with a branch from Framingham to Lowell. The final addition to the Old Colony came in 1888 with the lease of the Boston & Providence. The B&P had been chartered in 1831 and completed in 1835 between the Massachusetts and Rhode Island cities of its name.

Most of the railroading in southeastern Massachusetts was now under the control of the Old Colony. The area was rich in industry, and the

Streamlined Hudson 1406 accelerates west out of New London, Connecticut, with the 15 cars of the *Yankee Clipper* in March 1947. Photo by Kent W. Cochrane.

road's traffic included not only raw materials and finished goods but also coal distributed inland from the ports. The Old Colony had an intense passenger business, participating not only in an all-rail route to New York in conjunction with other lines beyond Providence but also connecting with steamers operating on Long Island Sound, principally between Fall River and New York.

New York & New England

Only fragments remain today of the New York & New England, which at its height reached from Boston and Providence through Hartford, Conn., to the Hudson River, with branches to Worcester and Springfield, Mass., and New London, Conn. Its oldest ancestor was the Manchester Railroad, chartered in 1833 to build east from Hartford, Conn., through Manchester to Bolton. The charter lay dormant for some years until a group of Providence, R. I., businessmen sought to build a railroad to the industrial towns of western Rhode Island and eastern Connecticut. The project quickly expanded, first taking over the Manchester charter and then blossoming into a line from Providence to the Hudson River at Fishkill Landing (now Beacon), N. Y. The first part of the Hartford, Providence & Fishkill was opened in 1849, and by 1855 the line was in service between Providence and Waterbury, Conn.

Meanwhile two small railroads were building southwest out of Boston into the area between Providence and Worcester. A combination of the Charles River Branch, the Charles River Railroad, and the New York & Boston assembled a line from Brookline, Mass., on the Boston &

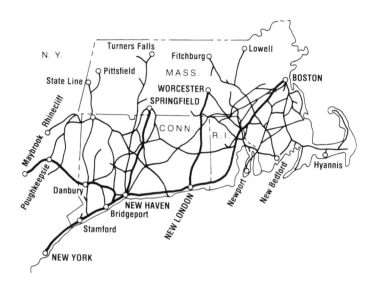

Albany, to Woonsocket, R. I., with the intention of building on through Willimantic, Conn., to New Haven.

The Norfolk County Railroad opened a line through Walpole to Blackstone, Mass., in 1849. It became the Boston & New York Central and also aimed for Willimantic, but to connect there with the Hartford, Providence & Fishkill. It reorganized and changed its name several times. Among its names were Midland and Boston, Hartford & Erie, and under the latter it consoli-

dated with the New York & Boston and the Hartford, Providence & Fishkill in 1864, creating a line chartered all the way from Boston to the Hudson River and in service from Boston to Mechanicsville, Conn. (just north of Putnam), and from Providence to Waterbury.

The BH&E entered bankruptcy in 1870 after a short period of control by the Erie Railroad and emerged as the New York & New England Railroad. NY&NE closed the Mechanicsville–Willimantic gap in eastern Connecticut in 1872

Symbol freight OB-6 is eastbound on the Maybrook line a half mile east of Berkshire Junction in March 1966. Power for the 130-car train is a trio of General Electric U-25-Bs. Photo by John P. Ahrens.

and completed the line west to the Hudson in December 1881. In 1884 the NY&NE inaugurated the *New England Limited*, a Boston–New York express operated in conjunction with the New Haven, which handled the train southwest of Willimantic. The train achieved a place in railroad lore as the "Ghost Train" in 1891 when the cars were painted white (some accounts add that the coal in the tender was sprayed with whitewash before departure each afternoon).

Every few miles NY&NE's route crossed a railroad offering a connection to New York—but nearly all those connections depended on the New Haven. The New Haven, feeling some anxiety about competition from the NY&NE, began

to choke off the connections. The NY&NE turned first to the Housatonic Railroad to form a route to New York that included a ferry across Long Island Sound from Wilson's Point (south of Norwalk) to Oyster Bay and a connection with the Long Island Rail Road. The New Haven took over the Housatonic.

The NY&NE then turned to the New York & Northern, which it met at Brewster, N. Y. The New Haven and the New York Central had previously agreed not to compete with each other, so at the New Haven's request the New York Central acquired the New York & Northern (it became NYC's Putnam Division) to put itself briefly into and out of competition with the New

Haven for Boston–New York business. The New York & New England was squeezed out again.

In 1893 the Philadelphia & Reading acquired control of the NY&NE, which declared bankruptcy by the end of that year. The New Haven acquired control of the New York & New England through J. P. Morgan and in 1898 leased the road.

Central New England

Almost nothing remains of the Central New England. In the early 1890s under the presidency of A. A. McLeod the Philadelphia & Reading put together a group of small railroads as the Central New England & Western to form a New England outlet for anthracite coal. The new road took over the Hartford & Connecticut Western, which had a line reaching from Hartford to the northwestern corner of the state, then consolidated with the Poughkeepsie Bridge & Railroad Co. to form the Philadelphia, Reading & New England. In October 1893 the PR&NE gained control of the New York & New England and the Boston & Maine and even tried to grab the Old Colony. By the end of 1893, the Philadelphia & Reading was bankrupt.

The PR&NE was reorganized as the Central New England in 1899, still under Reading control. In 1904 the New Haven purchased the Central New England, thus acquiring the Poughkeepsie Bridge over the Hudson River (originally backed by the Pennsylvania; opened in 1888). The railroad was operated separately until 1927, when it was fully absorbed by the New Haven. Most of the Central New England other than the portion that formed NH's freight route to Maybrook, N. Y., was abandoned in 1938.

New York & New Haven

The New York & New Haven Railroad was a relative latecomer because of the adequacy of road and water transportation along the Connecticut coast—early railroad activity aimed inland. The Hartford & New Haven Railroad was chartered in 1833 and opened in 1839; by 1844 it had been extended north to Springfield, Mass. The Housatonic Railroad was chartered in 1836 to build up the river of that name from Bridgeport to the Massachusetts state line. In 1842 it reached a connection with the Western Railroad (later Boston & Albany).

It was not until 1844 that the New York & New Haven Railroad was chartered in Connecticut; a New York charter was opposed by the New York & Harlem Railroad until arrangements were made to use the Harlem's tracks into New York City. The line was opened in 1848.

That same year the first portion of the New Haven & Northampton was opened from New Haven north to Plainville, Conn., along the route of a canal. The New York & New Haven promptly leased the Canal Line to use as a competitive weapon against the Hartford & New Haven.

The year 1848 also saw the chartering of the New Haven & New London Railroad, which opened in 1852 and was soon extended to Stonington, Conn., with ferries taking whole trains across the Connecticut River at Saybrook and across the Thames at New London. The NH&NL was reorganized in 1864 as the Shore Line Railway and leased to the New York & New Haven in 1870. The Connecticut and the Thames were bridged in 1870 and 1889, respectively.

Four boxcab 1-B+B-1 electric locomotives lead a New York-bound freight at West Haven, Connecticut. Photo by Kent W. Cochrane.

New York, New Haven & Hartford

On August 6, 1872, the New York & New Haven and the Hartford & New Haven were consolidated as the New York, New Haven & Hartford Railroad. The new road had close affiliations with the Housatonic and Naugatuck lines (the latter followed the river of that name up to Waterbury and Winsted). It acquired control of the Canal Line in 1881 (the lease had ended in 1869), leased the Air Line (New Haven to Willimantic), and bought the Hartford & Connecticut Valley (Hartford to Saybrook) in 1882. In 1892 the New Haven leased the New York, Providence & Boston (which had leased the Providence & Worcester), and in 1893 leased the Old Colony,

completing an all-rail route under one management between Boston and New York.

In 1893 the New York & New England collapsed and NYNH&H began acquisition of its former rival. The New Haven also looked covetously at the concatenation of railroads that stretched up the Connecticut Valley from Springfield but contented itself with an agreement with Boston & Maine to split New England between them along the line of the Boston & Albany (B&M had no lines south of the B&A; NYNH&H had several tentacles reaching almost to the northern border of Massachusetts). By the turn of the century the New Haven had a virtual monopoly on the railroads and the steamboat

A Bridgeport-Waterbury local works northward along the Naugatuck River. The exhaust steam hangs in the below-zero morning air. Photo by Kent W. Cochrane.

lines in Connecticut, Rhode Island, and much of Massachusetts.

Enter Charles S. Mellen, a protege of J. P. Morgan. Mellen set out to gain control of all the railroads in New England. He bought the street and interurban railways in New Haven's territory, then bought control of Boston & Maine and Maine Central and, jointly with New York Central, the Rutland. He reached outside New England for control of the New York, Ontario & Western. He undertook the construction of the New York, Westchester & Boston, an interurban line parallel to New Haven's own line from New York to Port Chester, with a branch to White Plains.

A long battle ensued between the Mellen interests and Louis D. Brandeis, then a Boston lawyer, over what was basically a violation of the Sherman Antitrust Act. A series of wrecks in 1911 and 1912 turned public feeling against the New Haven (and gained it mention in Clarence Day's play Life With Father: "I do wish that those New Haven people would be more careful and not have so many wrecks. If they knew how it upsets your father—").

The costs of electrifying the line between New York and New Haven and of constructing the New York Connecting Railroad and its Hell Gate Bridge to connect with the Pennsylvania Rail-

road would have helped push the road into bankruptcy had it not been taken over by the United States Railroad Administration during World War I.

New Haven's electrification deserves special mention. Before the turn of the century NH electrified several branch lines using low-voltage DC systems, but for its main line between Woodlawn, N. Y., and New Haven the road chose the relatively unproven high-voltage AC system, even though the locomotives would have to be able to use New York Central's low-voltage DC system from Woodlawn to Grand Central Terminal.

The New Haven's situation improved in the late 1920s. The Pennsylvania acquired nearly one-fourth of New Haven's stock and an interest in the Boston & Maine, and New Haven also acquired B&M stock, effectively regaining control of B&M. The New Haven struggled through the Depression as long as it could and entered bankruptcy on October 23, 1935.

In the ensuing reorganization NH pruned much of its branchline network, abandoned its steamship lines and the New York, Westchester & Boston, and upgraded the physical plant and rolling stock on its main lines. It inaugurated piggyback service in 1938 and dieselized many of its mainline trains with a fleet of Alco DL-109s. New Haven's traffic increased greatly during World War II. If the New Haven is remembered for nothing else it will be for a 1942 advertisement, "The Kid in Upper 4." The ad showed a young soldier lying awake in an upper berth on his way to war. The accompanying text, which told of his feelings, was a masterpiece.

The New Haven was heavy-duty, intense railroading as few other roads in North America have practiced it. The main passenger routes came from Pennsylvania Station and Grand Central Terminal to merge at New Rochelle, N. Y., forming a four-track electrified line as far east as New Haven. From there double-track lines continued east to Boston and north to Springfield. The principal freight route was the line east from Maybrook, N. Y., where New Haven connected with Erie, Lehigh & Hudson River, Lehigh & New England, and New York, Ontario & Western; New Haven also interchanged a great deal of freight with the Pennsylvania via carfloats across New York harbor.

The New Haven experimented very early with electrification of branch lines and was the first railroad with a long-distance mainline electrification. The road had four major bridges: the high bridge that carried the Maybrook Line across the Hudson at Poughkeepsie, N. Y., the vertical lift bridge, until 1959 the longest in the world, over the Cape Cod Canal at Buzzards Bay, Mass., the Canton Viaduct across the Neponset River valley at Canton, Mass., and the Hell Gate Bridge (operated by New Haven, but owned by the New York Connecting Railroad, which was jointly owned by the New Haven and the Pennsylvania).

The Dumaines and McGinnis

New Haven's reorganization was completed on September 18, 1947. Frederic C. Dumaine Sr. and others, including Patrick B. McGinnis, gained control in 1948. The experienced executives who had overseen the reorganization were dismissed, new management came in, and the road began another plunge into the depths. Frederic C. Dumaine Jr. took over upon his father's

death in 1951 and immediately set about restoring the condition of the railroad and the morale of the employees.

In 1953 control passed from the preferred stockholders to the common stockholders. A proxy battle ensued and Patrick B. McGinnis won. He slashed maintenance and ordered experimental lightweight trains for Boston–New York service. Another McGinnis contribution was a new image of red-orange, black, and white. New paint or no, Connecticut commuters revolted at the imposition of parking charges at stations. Directors resigned. Hurricanes (not McGinnis's fault) in 1955 washed out a number of lines. Upon McGinnis's departure for the Boston & Maine in 1956 auditors found that New Haven's earnings for 1955 were less than half what McGinnis had been saying they were.

George Alpert became president just as the lightweight trains that McGinnis ordered arrived. One caught fire on the press run, then derailed later that day. The piggyback traffic disappeared as the railroads serving New York initiated their own piggyback service and found that trailers could move into NH's territory by highway, especially the newly completed Connecticut Turnpike that paralleled NH from Greenwich to New London. In 1956 the New Haven decided to buy 60 FL9s, diesel locomotives that could also draw power from third rail in the New York terminals, in order to phase out its electrification—for which it had just taken delivery of 10 new passenger locomotives and 100 new M. U. cars. A few years after the FL9s arrived, the New Haven purchased 11 nearly new electric freight locomotives from the Norfolk & Western.

Government loans guaranteed by the ICC kept the road afloat until July 7, 1961, when the New Haven went back into reorganization. The railroad sought local and state tax relief and petitioned for inclusion in the Pennsylvania-New York Central merger. The initial condition imposed by the two larger railroads was that NH be free of passenger service, but the ICC denied that request and on December 2, 1968, ordered Penn Central (which had come into being on February 1 of that year) to take over the New Haven by the beginning of 1969. On December 31, 1968, PC purchased New Haven's properties.

With all of its problems the New Haven soldiered on. Freight business suffered as much from the change in New England's economy and the shift from heavy industry to high technology as it did from truck competition. Until its inclusion in Penn Central the New Haven offered hourly passenger service between Boston and New York, with parlor and dining cars on nearly all trains, and almost as frequent service between New York, Hartford, and Springfield. Only in the past few years and by virtue of extensive track work has Amtrak managed to equal New Haven's Boston–New York running time.

	1929	1967
Miles of railroad operated:	2,133	1,547
Number of locomotives:	957	332
Number of passenger cars:	2,110	855
Number of freight cars:	24,033	
Number of company service cars:	1,049	
Number of freight and company service cars:		4,200

Location of headquarters: New Haven, Connecticut

Reporting marks: NH

Notable named passenger trains: *Merchants Limited, Yankee Clipper* (New York–Boston); *Colonial, Senator, Patriot* (Washington–New York–Boston, operated jointly with Pennsylvania Railroad); *State of Maine, Bar Harbor* (Washington–New York–Portland–Ellsworth, operated with Boston & Maine and Maine Central), *Washingtonian, Montrealer* (Washington–New York–Montreal, operated with Pennsylvania, Boston & Maine, Central Vermont, and Canadian National)

Historical and technical society: New Haven Railroad Historical & Technical Association, P. O. Box 122, Wallingford, CT 06492

Recommended reading:
The New Haven Railroad — Its Rise and Fall, by John L. Weller, published in 1969 by Hastings House, New York, NY 10016
New Haven Railroad — The Final Decades, by Scott Hartley, published in 1992 by Railpace Company, P. O. Box 927, Piscataway, NJ 08855-0927 (ISBN 0-9621541-5-6)
Connecticut Railroads . . . an Illustrated History, by Gregg M. Turner and Melanchthon W. Jacobus, published in 1989 by The Connecticut Historical Society, 1 Elizabeth Street, Hartford, CT 06105 (ISBN 0-940748-96-7)
Golden Years of Railroading: New Haven Railroad Along the Shore Line, by Martin J. McGuirk, published in 1999 by Kalmbach Publishing Co., P. O. Box 1612, Waukesha, WI 53187 (ISBN 0-89024-344-1)

Subsidiaries and affiliated railroads, 1967:
Boston Terminal Corp. (70%)
New York Connecting Railroad (50%)
Union Freight Railroad (50%)
South Manchester Railroad (100%)

Predecessor railroads in this book: Central New England

Successors:
Penn Central
Conrail
Amtrak
Providence & Worcester
Pioneer Valley
Bay Colony
Massachusetts Bay Transportation Authority
Metro-North

Portions still operated:
Amtrak: Boston–New York (Penn Station); Springfield–New Haven
Bay Colony: Middleboro, Mass., to Hyannis and South Dennis; Braintree to West Hanover and Plymouth; Medfield Junction to Newton Highlands and Millis; North Dartmouth–Watuppa; West Concord–Acton
Conrail: New York–New Haven–Springfield, Mass.; Hartford to Manchester and East Windsor, Conn.; Attleboro–Boston; Attleboro–Middleboro–Braintree, Mass.; Taunton to New Bedford, Mass., and Tiverton, R. I.; Readville–Franklin–Milford, Mass.; Mansfield–Fitchburg, Mass.
Danbury Terminal: Beacon, N. Y.–Hopewell Junction–Derby, Conn.; Berkshire Junction–New Milford, Conn.
Guilford Transportation Industries: Springfield, Mass.–Hazardville, Conn.; Berlin–Waterbury, Conn.; Torrington–Waterbury–Derby, Conn.
Housatonic Railroad: New Milford, Conn.–Pittsfield, Mass.
Massachusetts Bay Transportation Authority: Boston to Providence, R. I., and to Stoughton, Franklin, Middleboro, and Plymouth, Mass.
Metro-North: New York (Grand Central) to New Haven, Waterbury, Danbury, and New Canaan, Conn.
Pioneer Valley: Westfield–Holyoke, Mass.
Providence & Worcester: Providence–Worcester; Groton, Conn.–Worcester; Pawtucket, R. I.–New Haven–South Norwalk–Danbury, Conn.; Plainfield–Willimantic, Conn.
Conrail: New Haven–Portland Conn.; South Norwalk–New Milford. Conn.; Devon, Conn. to Poughkeepsie and Beacon, N. Y.; Highland–Maybrook, N. Y.; Providence–Boston

New York, Ontario & Western Railway

In 1866 the New York & Oswego Midland Railroad was incorporated to build a railroad from Oswego, N. Y., on the shore of Lake Ontario, to New York—or more specifically to the New Jersey state line, then to a point on the Hudson River opposite New York City. The road's first problem was finance. Cities and towns that refused to issue bonds to finance the line found themselves bypassed by the new railroad, with the result that the line went through few established places of any size and made unnecessary contortions, both horizontal and vertical. The state of New Jersey refused to allow such bonding, so the NY&OM struck a deal with the Middletown, Unionville & Water Gap and the New Jersey Midland (forerunners of the Middletown & Unionville and the New York, Susquehanna & Western). One of the incorporators of the railroad boasted that the line would run at right angles to the mountains, and after construction began the railroad discovered just what that meant in terms of bridges and tunnels.

The NY&OM opened from Oswego to Norwich in 1869. In 1871 it opened a line known as the Auburn Branch—it straggled northwest, southwest, and northwest from Norwich through Cortland and Freeville to end at Scipio, about ten miles short of Auburn. In 1872 the NYO&M leased railroads to create branches to

Westbound symbol freight BC-3 rolls past the station at Summitville, New York, in early 1957. Between the diesels and the caboose are only 12 cars — illustrating one reason for NYO&W's demise. Photo by Jim Shaughnessy.

Utica and Rome. The first train ran all the way from Oswego to Jersey City in July 1883.

Operation ceases

Within a few weeks the railroad declared bankruptcy. For a short period in early 1875 the NY&OM ceased operation entirely except for the portion from Sidney to Utica and Rome, which was operated by Delaware & Hudson, in much the same way as designated operators took over portions of the Rock Island a century later. While the line was idle, a number of local residents, fearing they would not be paid for their land, tore up the track and reclaimed their land.

Operation resumed, and the company was reorganized in 1879 as the New York, Ontario & Western Railway. Implicit in the new name was hope of a ferry connection across Lake Ontario and a continuation to the West. Missing from the map was the Auburn branch, dismantled except from Freeville through Cortland to De Ruyter, which became part of the Lehigh Valley.

Soon added to the map was a line from Middletown east to Cornwall, on the Hudson River. NYO&W made arrangements with the West Shore for trackage rights south from Cornwall to West Shore's terminal at Weehawken, N. J. The West Shore soon came under the control of New York Central. NYO&W found NYC amenable to continued use of the Weehawken–Cornwall portion of the West Shore, but NYC's presence put NYO&W firmly in the position of a feeder line, not part of a trunk route—and the through route that NYO&W participated in was hardly competitive with NYC: Rome, Watertown & Ogdensburg from Oswego to Buffalo, and Wabash from Buffalo to Chicago.

Anthracite carrier

More important to NYO&W's future was the opening in 1890 of a 54-mile branch from Cadosia, N. Y., to Scranton, Pennsylvania, to tap the anthracite regions. The road converted a number of its locomotives to anthracite-burners, in the process changing them from conventional configuration to Camelbacks. In 1904 the New Haven purchased control of the NYO&W for its coal business.

In 1912 the New York Central and the New Haven discussed trading their interests in Rutland and NYO&W, respectively; New Haven wound up with part of NYC's Rutland stock but retained its NYO&W control.

The 1920s saw a travel boom on the NYO&W as the Catskill Mountains became a resort area. The Depression killed much of that business. Coal from the Scranton Branch provided a greater and greater portion of the road's revenue, peaking in 1932. It was downhill from there. The coal mines in Scranton failed in 1937, and NYO&W filed for reorganization in May of that year.

Bridge route

The road's trustee, Frederic Lyford, recognized that any future the NYO&W had lay in general merchandise traffic, not coal, and began to change the road into a bridge route between the west end of the New Haven at Maybrook and connections at Scranton. By this time passenger traffic to the Catskills was growing again. NYO&W couldn't afford a streamliner but asked designer Otto Kuhler to do what he could for $10,000 for the 1937 summer season. The result was *The Mountaineer:* streamstyling for a 4-8-2, slipcovers for the seats of the coaches, and maple armchairs replacing wicker in the parlor car, all painted maroon and black with orange trim—and matching uniforms for the crew.

In 1941 NYO&W sold its New Berlin branch to the Unadilla Valley. Dieselization of the NYO&W began in 1941 with five General Electric 44-ton switchers. Several sets of Electro-Motive FTs soon followed for freight service. One pair of FTs was financed by Standard Oil in exchange for detailed performance data over three years of operation.

Demise

The NYO&W enjoyed a brief postwar surge of business, but NYO&W's division of the revenue wasn't enough to keep the rest of the road in business. The originating carrier gets most of the revenue from a freight move. To make money as a bridge carrier you need lots of business and a long haul—longer than the 145 miles from Scranton to Campbell Hall. Passenger service was reduced to a single summer-only Wee-hawken–Roscoe round trip. A booster organization of shippers was formed but little of the road's freight originated on line.

In 1952 the New Haven offered to purchase the road but soon withdrew its offer (and had financial problems of its own). Abandonment was loudly protested by towns along the line, which considered unpaid back taxes as an investment in the railroad. The New York state legislature passed a $1 million aid bill, citing the road as essential for civil defense, but the state civil defense commission rejected it. The federal government recommended liquidation. Finally operation ceased on March 29, 1957. The assets were auctioned off—the diesels found new owners, but everything else was scrapped. None of the road's lines remains in operation.

	1929	1956	
Miles of railroad operated:	569	541	**Location of headquarters:** New York, New York
Number of locomotives:	177	46	**Reporting marks:** OW
Number of passenger cars:	401	12	**Historical and technical society:** Ontario & Western Railway Historical Society,
Number of freight cars:	5,077	152	P. O. Box 713, Middletown, NY 10940; http://idt.net/~nyowrhs/
Number of company service cars:	253	71	**Recommended reading:** *O. & W.,* by William F. Helmer, published in 1959 by Howell-North Books, 850 North Hollywood Way, Burbank, CA 91505

Norfolk & Western Railway

 Norfolk & Western has two distinct images. Before 1964 it was a coal hauler controlled by the Pennsylvania Railroad. It even looked like the Pennsy in places: Tuscan red coaches, position-light signals, and a short electrified district—but no Belpaire fireboxes. In 1964, possibly as a reaction to the proposed merger of the Pennsylvania and the New York Central, N&W merged, leased, or purchased four other railroads. Suddenly the N&W was a midwestern railroad, with a multiplicity of routes from Buffalo to Chicago and St. Louis and terminals on the Missouri River at Kansas City and Omaha.

Norfolk & Western's oldest ancestor was a line from Petersburg, Virginia, to City Point, a few miles away on the James River. In 1850 the Norfolk & Petersburg Railroad was chartered to build a railroad between the cities of its name. It reached Petersburg in 1858 after crossing part of the Dismal Swamp on a roadbed laid on a mat of trees and logs. Other N&W forebears were the Southside Railroad, opened in 1854 from Petersburg to Lynchburg, Va., and the Virginia & Tennessee, completed in 1856 from Lynchburg to Bristol on the Virginia-Tennessee line.

Consolidation and a new name

The Norfolk & Petersburg, Southside, and Virginia & Tennessee were consolidated in 1867 but

Class Y6b 2-8-8-2 No. 2121 pulling a string of empty coal cars west from Roanoke, Virginia. Photo by the Rev. LeRoy Scott.

retained their identities until 1870, when they were organized as the Atlantic, Mississippi & Ohio Railroad.

The AM&O was sold in 1881 to the Clark family, who ran a banking house in Philadelphia and owned the Shenandoah Valley Railroad. The Clarks moved the headquarters of their railroads to a place called Big Lick. The place was soon renamed Roanoke, and the AM&O was renamed the Norfolk & Western Railroad.

The N&W was extended northwest into the coalfields of West Virginia, and in 1890 it began building an extension to the Ohio River. It reached the river in 1892 and bridged it to connect with the Scioto Valley & New England Railroad, which ran north to Columbus, Ohio.

Purchase of the Cincinnati, Portsmouth & Virginia Railroad put the Norfolk & Western into Cincinnati in 1901. The Norfolk–Columbus–Cincinnati main line plus branches to Hagerstown, Maryland, and Winston-Salem and Durham, North Carolina, constituted the major part of the "old" N&W, a coal carrier operating between the Ohio River and tidewater.

Pennsylvania Railroad control

The Pennsylvania Railroad began purchasing N&W stock in 1900, and by 1964 Pennsy owned about one-third of N&W's stock, either directly or through a subsidiary holding company. The Pennsy treated the N&W as an investment, not a fief, despite superficial resemblances—mostly those signals and the red paint.

Between 1915 and 1924 N&W electrified 56 route miles between Iaeger and Bluefield, W. V., to increase the capacity of a line that included 2 percent grades and a 3,014-foot tunnel. A line

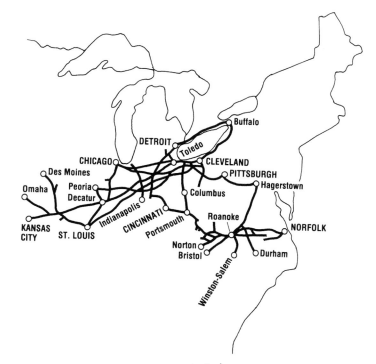

relocation and a new tunnel in 1950 eliminated the need for the electrification, and the line reverted to steam power.

Less than a decade later N&W inherited Virginian's electrified operation; it fell victim to one-way traffic patterns.

Coal

The N&W was the acme of coal railroading, and longer than any other coal road—well into the late 1950s—it burned in its locomotives what it hauled in its hopper cars. N&W built many of its steam locomotives in its Roanoke Shops,

Two GP9s have N&W's *Wabash Cannon Ball* rolling toward Detroit at good speed through Sangamon, Illinois. Photo by Walter A. Peters, from the collection of J. David Ingles.

experimented with a steam turbine-electric locomotive, and explored what modern servicing facilities could do for steam locomotive operating efficiency.

The tide of the coal movement was generally westward to the Great Lakes until the mid-1950s, when there was a demand for high-grade coal in Europe. That change in the direction of the flow may have precipitated the first in a long string of mergers. Eastbound coal on N&W had to cross several summits; on the parallel Virginian Railway it had a gentle descent most of the way. N&W had applied to lease the Virginian in 1925 and was denied permission by the Interstate Commerce Commission. In 1959 the situation was different. There was surprisingly little protest, and the ICC moved quickly. Merger took place on December 1, 1959.

In 1962 N&W purchased the Atlantic & Danville, a line running from Norfolk west to Danville, Va., 211 miles, and reorganized it as the Norfolk, Franklin & Danville. Much of this line has since been abandoned.

Merger and growth

The merger plans of the Pennsylvania and the New York Central created a merger frenzy north of the Ohio River and east of the Mississippi. The situation was like trying to choose some variable and unspecified number of teams on the playground while the usual two team captains were sharing a soda at the corner drugstore.

Norfolk & Western moved quickly and acquired the Nickel Plate, the Wabash, the Pittsburgh & West Virginia, the Akron, Canton & Youngstown, and, to connect them to the N&W proper, the Pennsylvania's line from Columbus to Sandusky, Ohio, which crossed the AC&Y at Chatfield and the Nickel Plate at Bellevue. The merger, leases, and purchases took effect October 16, 1964.

Less than a year later, on August 31, 1965, N&W and Chesapeake & Ohio (plus Baltimore & Ohio and Western Maryland) announced merger plans, offering to include Reading, Central Railroad of New Jersey, Erie Lackawanna, Delaware & Hudson, and Boston & Maine. It would have created a system about the same size as Penn Central. N&W and C&O stockholders approved the merger, and by the end of 1969 there were only two opponents, Penn Central and the state of New York. N&W and C&O were confident that merger would take place within a year.

Ironically, Penn Central had its way. PC's bankruptcy on June 21, 1970, and the ensuing bankruptcies of several other Eastern railroads changed the situation. On April 22, 1971, the boards of N&W and C&O canceled the proposed merger. A residue was the ownership of Erie Lackawanna and Delaware & Hudson by an N&W subsidiary, a holding company named Dereco.

Further discussion of merger was delayed by the formation of Conrail and the question of its ultimate disposition. Spurred perhaps by the formation of the CSX Corporation in 1980, N&W turned to the Southern Railway. On June 1, 1982, N&W and Southern Railway became subsidiaries of Norfolk Southern Corporation, a newly formed holding company.

N&W purchased the Illinois Terminal on September 1, 1981. Corporate existence of the IT and of the Akron, Canton & Youngstown ended in 1982.

At the end of 1990 the Norfolk & Western Railway became a subsidiary of the Southern Railway (it had been a subsidiary of Norfolk Soutern Corporation), and the Southern Railway changed its name to Norfolk Southern Railway.

	1929	1981
Miles of railroad operated:	2,240	7,803
Number of locomotives:	788	1,372
Number of passenger cars:	476	113*
Number of freight cars:	30,222	87,903
Number of company service cars:	2,005	2,978

Location of headquarters: Roanoke, Virginia

Reporting marks: NW, WAB, NKP, ACY, PWV

Notable named passenger trains: Pocahontas and Powhatan Arrow (Norfolk–Cincinnati)

Historical and technical society: Norfolk & Western Historical Society, P. O. Box 201, Forest, VA 24551-0201; http://www.inmind.com/people/shammer

Recommended reading:

The Norfolk & Western: A History, by E. F. Pat Striplin, published in 1981 by the Norfolk & Western Railway, 8 N. Jefferson Street, Roanoke, VA 24042

Golden Years of Railroading: Norfolk & Western in the Appalachians, by E. W. King, Jr., published in 1997 by Kalmbach Publishing Co., P. O. Box 1612, Waukesha, WI 53187 (ISBN 0-89024-316-6)

*(1970)

Subsidiaries and affiliated railroads, 1981:

Akron, Canton & Youngstown

Chesapeake Western

Illinois Terminal

Wabash

Wheeling & Lake Erie (90.89%)

Winston-Salem Southbound (50%)

Predecessor railroads in this book:

Akron, Canton & Youngstown

Atlantic & Danville

Illinois Terminal

New York, Chicago & St. Louis

Pittsburgh & West Virginia

Virginian

Wabash

Successors: Norfolk Southern

Portions still operated: Portions still operated: All of the "old" N&W is still operated by Norfolk Southern, except the south end of the Lynchburg, Va.–Durham, N. C. line; Pulaski–Fries–Galax, Va.; Abingdon, Va.–West Jefferson, N. C.; and Sardinia–Hillsboro, Ohio. See also the entries for the various merged and leased railroads.

Norfolk Southern Railroad

Today's Norfolk Southern is quite a different railroad from the one that is the subject of this entry. True, this railroad is part of the present one but only a small part. Perhaps the problem is the Southern Railway's historical penchant for reusing names.

The Elizabeth City & Norfolk Railroad was chartered in 1870. In 1880 construction began on its line from Berkley, Virginia, now part of Norfolk, along the east edge of the Dismal Swamp to Elizabeth City, North Carolina. The line was opened to Elizabeth City in June 1881 and extended a few miles farther to Edenton, on the shore of Albemarle Sound, in December of that year. There steamers connected with the trains for points up the rivers and along the coast of North Carolina. The road got a new name, Norfolk Southern Railroad, in 1883.

The Norfolk Southern entered receivership in 1889 and was reorganized as the Norfolk & Southern Railroad in 1891. Included in the N&S was the Albemarle & Pantego Railroad, which had been organized in 1887 by the John L. Roper Lumber Co. to build from Mackey's Ferry, across the sound from Edenton, to Belhaven, N. C.

In 1900 the N&S absorbed the Norfolk, Virginia Beach & Southern Railroad. The NVB&S had opened in 1883 as a 3-foot gauge line from Norfolk to Virginia Beach; in 1899 it

In 1940 Norfolk Southern received five light 2-8-4s from Baldwin. They were the road's only steam locomotives with trailing trucks, and they were several orders of magnitude more modern than anything else on the NS. When NS dieselized, the Berkshires were sold to the National Railways of Mexico. Photo by H. Reid.

was standard-gauged and acquired a branch to Munden, in the extreme southeast corner of Virginia. In 1902 Chesapeake Transit Co. opened an electric line from Norfolk to Cape Henry, Va. To meet the competition, N&S built a short branch from Virginia Beach to Cape Henry, electrified its line from Norfolk to Virginia Beach, and bought Chesapeake Transit—and the former management of Chesapeake Transit wound up in control of N&S.

That same year N&S acquired the 3-foot gauge Washington & Plymouth, which connected the North Carolina towns of its name, widened it to standard gauge, built a 10-mile link between Plymouth and Mackey's ferry, and installed the *John W. Garrett*, a ferry that had been on Baltimore & Ohio's roster, on the run between Edenton and Mackey's Ferry.

The Suffolk & Carolina Railway was chartered in 1873. By 1897 its 3 foot 6 inch gauge line reached from Suffolk, Va., to Ryland, N. C. In 1902 it was extended to Edenton; in 1904 it was standard-gauged and it built a branch to Elizabeth City. In 1906 the Suffolk & Carolina was taken over by the Virginia & Carolina Coast. The V&CC bought the Roper Lumber Co. and built a line east from Mackey's Ferry to Columbia, N. C. In 1903 the Raleigh & Pamlico Sound was organized to build lines from Raleigh and New Bern to Washington, N. C., and the Pamlico, Oriental & Western began a line from New Bern to Oriental.

Consolidation

In 1906 the Norfolk & Southern Railway was formed as a consolidation of the Norfolk & Southern Railroad, the Virginia & Carolina

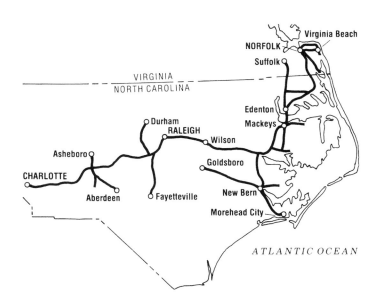

Coast Railroad, the Raleigh & Pamlico Sound Railroad, the Pamlico, Oriental & Western Railway, and the Beaufort & Western Railroad. The new N&S also held the lease of the Atlantic & North Carolina.

Expansion outpaced the railroad's finances in 1908. The road entered the hands of receivers that year and was reorganized as the Norfolk Southern Railroad in 1910. That same year a trestle was constructed across Albemarle Sound to replace the ferry that operated between Eden-

ton and Mackey's Ferry. The expansion program continued. NS bought four railroads and undertook new construction, extending the main line from Raleigh to Charlotte with branches to Fayetteville, Aberdeen, and Asheboro. In 1920 the NS leased the Durham & South Carolina Railroad, gaining access to Durham.

The Depression drove the NS into receivership yet again in 1932. The electric passenger service to Virginia Beach and Cape Henry, primarily suburban in character, was replaced by gasoline-powered cars in 1935 (it was discontinued in 1948). Also in 1935 the Atlantic & North Carolina withdrew its lease for nonpayment, and in 1937 the Beaufort & Western was sold to local interests to become the Beaufort & Morehead. In 1937 NS abandoned much of the Belhaven branch and in 1940 all of the former Virginia & Carolina Coast. The road was sold at foreclosure in 1941.

The Norfolk Southern Railway took over at the beginning of 1942. In 1947 a group of investors headed by Patrick B. McGinnis took control. The railroad acquired a pair of office cars, leased apartments or suites in New York, Washington, and Miami, lavishly entertained its shippers, and got investigated by the ICC. McGinnis resigned and moved on, eventually to the New Haven. New management took over in 1953. In the early 1960s NS constructed a branch to serve phosphate deposits between Washington and New Bern.

The Southern Railway purchased the Norfolk Southern in 1974. Southern merged it with the Carolina & Northwestern under the NS name. In 1981 the name was changed to Carolina & Northwestern so that the Norfolk Southern name could be used for a newly formed holding company as part of the Southern-Norfolk & Western merger.

	1929	1973	Successors:
Miles of railroad operated:	933	622	Atlantic & East Carolina
Number of locomotives:	105	37	Southern
Number of passenger cars:	108		Norfolk Southern
Number of freight cars:	3,282	2,245	**Portions still operated:**
Number of company service cars:	192	50	Aberdeen, Carolina & Western: Aberdeen–Star, N. C.
Number of electric locomotives:	5		Carolina Coastal: Pinetown–Belhaven, N. C.
Number of electric passenger cars:	42		Chesapeake & Albemarle: Chesapeake, Va.–Edenton, N. C.
Number of electric company service cars:	2		Commonwealth Railway: Suffolk–West Norfolk, Va.
Location of headquarters: Norfolk, Virginia; after 1961 Raleigh, North Carolina			Norfolk Southern: Plymouth, N. C.–Charlotte; Norfolk–Virginia Beach;
Reporting marks: NS			Washington–Belhaven; Phosphate Junction–Lee Creek, New Bern–Chocowinity;
Recommended reading: *Norfolk Southern,* by Richard E. Prince, published in 1972 by Richard E. Prince (SBN 9600088-5-3)			Varina–Fayetteville; Goldsboro–Morehead City (A&NC)

Northern Alberta Railways

The Northern Alberta Railways Co. was incorporated June 14, 1929, and was owned half-and-half by Canadian Pacific Railway and Canadian National Railways. On July 1, 1929, NAR purchased from the province of Alberta four railways: the Edmonton, Dunvegan & British Columbia; the Central Canada; the Pembina Valley; and the Alberta & Great Waterways.

Construction of the Edmonton, Dunvegan & British Columbia began in 1912. The line reached Dawson Creek, B. C., in 1930, by way of Smith, Slave Lake, McLennan, and Grande Prairie, Alta. The Central Canada was opened from McLennan north to Peace River, Alta., in 1916 and later extended to Hines Creek. The two roads were built by the J. D. McArthur Co. of Winnipeg. The construction company operated them until financial difficulties caused by World War I caused the provincial government to take control. It leased the ED&BC and the Central Canada in 1920 and contracted with Canadian Pacific to operate the two roads.

The Alberta & Great Waterways was chartered in 1909 and began construction in 1914 at Carbondale, just north of Edmonton on the ED&BC. The line reached Lac La Biche a year later and was completed to Waterways (Fort McMurray), Alta., in 1925. The government

The conductor of Northern Alberta train 2 (Dawson Creek to Edmonton) signals the engineer to back into the siding at Hythe to pick up the dining car from the rear of train 1. The car served dinner, breakfast, and an early lunch to northbound passengers and will now serve a late lunch, dinner, and breakfast to southbound passengers. The grain elevators are typical of Alberta prairie towns; the octagonal enclosed water tank to the right of the track indicates cold winters. Photo by Donald E. Smith.

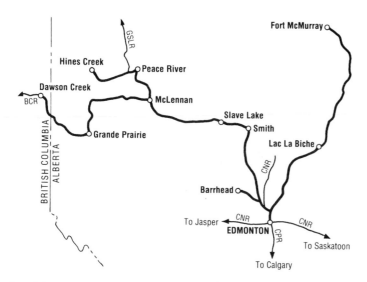

In 1962 the Canadian government began construction of the Great Slave Lake Railway north from Roma Junction, west of Peace River. The line, operated by Canadian National, was opened in 1964. It furnished much bridge revenue to NAR in the form of lead and zinc ores moving south to Trail, B. C., to supplement the grain that was NAR's principal commodity. Another provincially owned, CN-operated road, the Alberta Resources Railway, reached Grande Prairie from the south in 1969.

Canadian Pacific sold its share of NAR to Canadian National in 1980. Northern Alberta's operations were absorbed into CN on January 1, 1981, as part of a new CN operational unit, the Peace River Division.

	1930	1980
Miles of railroad operated:	862	923
Number of locomotives:	27	21
Number of passenger cars:	39	9
Number of freight cars:	225	100
Number of company service cars:	202	

Location of headquarters: Edmonton, Alberta
Reporting marks: NAR
Recommended reading: *The Northern Alberta Railways*, by Colin Hatcher, published in 1981 by the British Railway Modelers of North America, 5124 33 Street N.W., Calgary, AB, Canada T2L 1V4 (ISBN 0-9690798-9-3)
Successors: Canadian National Railways

purchased the A&GW from the McArthur company and operated it through its Department of Railways and Telephones, but later turned it over to CP to operate with the other two provincially owned lines.

The government of Alberta chartered and built the Pembina Valley Railway, opening the 26-mile line from Busby, on the ED&BC north of Edmonton, to Barrhead in 1927.

The provincial government tried without success to sell its railroads to either CP or CN, and in November 1926 it took over operation from CP. In 1928 CP offered to purchase the railroads if CN would go halves. The arrangement was acceptable to the province, and Northern Alberta Railways, jointly owned by the two large roads, began operation.

The construction of the Alaska Highway north from Dawson Creek began in March 1942 and brought a great increase in traffic to NAR. Traffic remained at a high level after World War II. The opening of provincial highway 43 in 1955 provided a shortcut from Edmonton to the Dawson Creek and Peace River areas, and in 1958 the Pacific Great Eastern Railway (now BC Rail) reached Dawson Creek from North Vancouver. Both the highway and BCR siphoned traffic from NAR.

Northern Pacific Railway

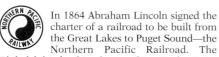

In 1864 Abraham Lincoln signed the charter of a railroad to be built from the Great Lakes to Puget Sound—the Northern Pacific Railroad. The Philadelphia banking house of Jay Cooke & Co. undertook to sell the bonds, which were to yield 7.3 percent interest, and sold $30 million worth. Work began in 1870 at Carlton, Minnesota, 20 miles from Duluth on the Lake Superior & Mississippi Railroad. The LS&M had just been opened between St. Paul and Duluth, and in 1872 Northern Pacific leased the road. By 1873 the NP was completed west to Bismarck, North Dakota, plus an isolated section from Kalama, Washington, on the Columbia River, to Tacoma. The Panic of 1873 wiped out Cooke and work ceased on the railroad.

NP reorganized by converting the bonds to stock, and the Lake Superior & Mississippi was reorganized as the St. Paul & Duluth. In 1881 control of the NP was purchased by Henry Villard, who also controlled the Oregon Railway & Navigation Co. and the Oregon & California Railroad. On September 8, 1883, NP drove a last spike at Gold Creek, Montana, near Garrison, completing a line from Duluth to Wallula Junction, Wash. NP trains continued on the rails of the OR&N to Portland, where NP's own line to Tacoma resumed (it crossed the Columbia River by ferry from Goble, Ore., to Kalama, Wash.

Northern Pacific was the first railroad to use the 4-8-4 wheel arrangement, and the type was named "Northern" for the railroad. NP 2601, second of the first group of Northerns, leads train 407 out of Tacoma on the last leg of its Portland–Seattle trip. Photo by F. Barry Thompson.

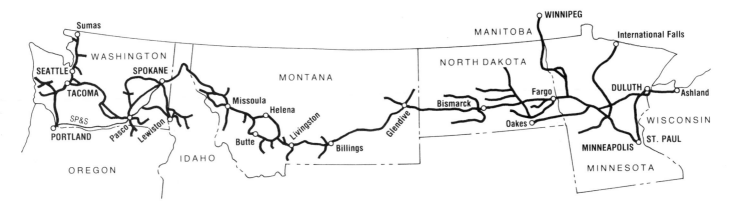

Even before completing the line at Gold Creek, NP began constructing a direct line from Pasco, Wash., over the Cascade Range to Tacoma. The Puget Sound area was beginning to grow, and NP wanted to reach it with its own line rather than rely on OR&N. Indeed, soon after the last-spike ceremonies, Villard's empire collapsed and OR&N became part of Union Pacific (Southern Pacific got the Oregon & California). The Pasco–Tacoma line opened in 1887, with temporary switchbacks carrying trains over Stampede Pass until the opening of Stampede Tunnel in May 1888.

East to Chicago

In 1889 NP contracted with the Wisconsin Central to operate through service to Chicago from the Twin Cities, and in 1890 NP leased the WC. NP organized a terminal company, the Chicago & Northern Pacific, and leased it to the WC. NP entered receivership in 1893 and defaulted on lease payments to Wisconsin Central, which in turned defaulted on the C&NP lease. Wisconsin Central became part of Soo Line, and the Chicago & Northern Pacific became the Baltimore & Ohio Chicago Terminal.

The Superior & St. Croix Railroad, chartered in Wisconsin in 1870, provided the vehicle for the reorganization of the NP. It was renamed the Northern Pacific Railway in July 1896 and on September 1 of that year acquired the properties, rights franchises, and lands of the Northern Pacific Railroad. The reorganization included the absorption of the St. Paul & Northern Pacific Railway (Brainerd and Staples, Minn., to St. Paul). In 1900 NP acquired the properties of the St. Paul & Duluth, and in 1901, the Seattle & International Railway (Seattle to Sumas, Wash.). Also in 1901 NP leased its Manitoba lines (Emerson–Winnipeg–Portage-la-Prairie and Morris–Brandon) to the Province of Manitoba. (They were sold to Canadian National Railways in 1946.)

The beginnings of Burlington Northern

In 1901 Northern Pacific and Great Northern gained control of the Chicago, Burlington & Quincy by jointly purchasing approximately 98 percent of its capital stock. That same year James J. Hill and J. P. Morgan formed the Northern Securities Co. as a holding company for NP and Great Northern. The U. S. Supreme Court dissolved Northern Securities in 1904. In 1905 the two roads organized the Spokane,

Portland & Seattle, which was completed from Spokane through Pasco to Portland in 1908. GN and NP attempted consolidation in 1927, but the Interstate Commerce Commission made giving up control of the Burlington a requisite for approval.

In October 1941 NP purchased the property of the Minnesota & International Railway (Brainerd to International Falls, Minn.), which it had controlled for a number of years.

In image Northern Pacific was the most conservative of the three northern transcontinentals. (Great Northern was a prosperous, well-thought-out railroad; the Milwaukee Road was a brash newcomer.) Bulking large in NP's freight traffic were wheat and lumber. In the 1920s and 1930s NP suffered from smaller than usual wheat crops and competition from ships for lumber moving to the East Coast. Ship competition decreased during World War II, and postwar prosperity brought an increase in building activity and population growth to the area NP served. NP was the oldest of the northern transcontinentals and had been instrumental in settling the northern plains. It served the populous areas of North Dakota, Montana, and Washington. Its slogan was "Main Street of the Northwest," and its secondary passenger train of the 1950s and 1960s was the *Mainstreeter.*

In 1956 NP and Great Northern again studied merger of the two roads, the Burlington, and the Spokane, Portland & Seattle. In 1960 the directors of both roads approved the merger terms. On March 2, 1970, NP was merged into Burlington Northern along with Great Northern; Chicago, Burlington & Quincy; and Spokane, Portland & Seattle.

NP relied on Electro-Motive F units for both passenger and freight service and was one of the few roads to order the F9, last of the type, in significant numbers. Five black-and-gold freight Fs (MP's passenger Fs were green) are shown here lifting a freight up the west slope of the Continental Divide at Elliston, Montana. Photo by R. V. Nixon.

	1929	1969
Miles of railroad operated:	6,784	6,771
Number of locomotives:	1,087	604
Number of passenger cars:	933	192
Number of freight cars:	50,960	34,961
Number of company service cars:	2,924	3,970

Location of headquarters: St. Paul, Minnesota

Reporting marks: NP, NPM

Notable named passenger trains: *North Coast Limited* (Chicago–St. Paul–Seattle and Portland; operated Chicago–St. Paul by Chicago, Burlington & Quincy and Pasco–Portland by Spokane, Portland & Seattle)

Historical and technical society: Northern Pacific Railroad Historical Association, c/o Norm Snow, 13044 87th Place N.E., Kirkland, WA 98034-2649; http://pw2.netcom/~whstlpnk/np.html

Recommended reading: *Northern Pacific Supersteam Era 1925–1945*, by Robert L. Frey and Lorenz P. Schrenk, published in 1985 by Golden West Books, P. O. Box 80250, San Marino, CA 91108 (ISBN 0-87095-0924)

Subsidiaries and affiliated railroads, 1969:

Chicago, Burlington & Quincy (48.59%)

Spokane, Portland & Seattle (50%, jointly with Great Northern)

Camas Prairie (50%, jointly with Union Pacific)

Midland Ry. of Manitoba (50%, jointly with Great Northern)

Walla Walla Valley (100%)

Successors:

Burlington Northern

Burlington Northern & Santa Fe

Portions still operated:

Of the major lines of the Northern Pacific, these have been abandoned: Moose Lake–Duluth, Minn.; Glenwood–Brainerd, Minn.; Wadena–Breckenridge, Minn.; Red Lake–East Grand Forks, Minn., Silesia–Red Lodge, Mont., Livingston–Gardiner, Mont.; St. Regis, Mont.–Mullan, Idaho, Hartford–Sedro Woolley Wash. The remainder, except for the short lines and regional railroads listed below, is operated by Burlington Northern & Santa Fe: Minneapolis–Fargo, N. Dak.–Glendive, Mont.–Huntley, Mont.; Duluth, Minn.–Staples, Minn.; Sanborn–Rogers, N. Dak.; Hannaford–Cooperstown, N. Dak.; McKenzie–Linton, N. Dak.; Mandan–Zap, N. Dak.; Glendive–Circle, Mont.; Nichols–Colstrip, Mont.; Sandpoint, Idaho–Spokane, Wash.–Pasco–Seattle; Gibbon–Zillah, Wash.; Moxsee City–Naches, Wash.; Auburn–Tacoma, Wash.–Portland, Ore.; Renton–Snohomish, Wash.; Sedro Wooley–Sumas, Wash.

Montana Rail Link: Huntley, Mont.–Sand Point, Idaho; Logan–Twin Bridges, Mont.; Missoula–Darby, Mont.; Dixon–Polson, Mont.; DeSmet–St. Regis–Paradise, Mont.

Montana Western: Garrison–Butte, Mont.

Red River Valley & Western: Wahpeton–Oakes–Minnewaukan, N. D.; Casselton–Marion, N. D.; Horace–Edgeley, N. D.; Pingree–Regan, N. D.; Carrington–Turtle Lake, N. D.; Oberon–Esmond, N. D.

St. Croix Valley: Hinckley–North Branch, Minn.

Toppenish, Simcoe & Western: Toppenish–White Swan, Wash.

Northwestern Pacific Railroad

The Northwestern Pacific was a subsidiary of Southern Pacific. It had no locomotives, passenger cars, or interchange freight cars of its own after 1960, and to the casual observer it appeared to be simply another piece of the far-flung SP.

NWP gradually lost its identity in that of its parent but until SP merged it in 1992, it existed as a "paper railroad," which is a railroad that exists only on paper and has no rolling stock of its own. Since most of NWP's rolling stock was gone by the end of 1959, I will use that for an ending date for the mileage statistics. NWP equipment statistics in *Moody's Transportation Manual* for the 1950s and 1960s are as meaningless as the route description that remained constant through the years, at least into the 1984 edition: "Lines extend from San Francisco Bay at Sausalito northward to Eureka connecting by motor coach for the Redwood Empire Tour to Grants Pass, Oregon, where connection is made with Southern Pacific Shasta Route trains for Portland."

San Francisco & North Pacific

The earliest ancestor of the NWP was the Petaluma & Haystack Railroad, which in 1864 opened a three-mile line from Petaluma, California, to a landing on Petaluma Creek and a connection with boats for San Francisco. A boiler explosion destroyed its locomotive in 1866 and the line reverted to horse power.

In the 1860s there were several rival proposals for railroads in Sonoma County, some aimed north at the redwood country and some aimed south toward San Francisco Bay. The San Francisco & North Pacific was the successor to most of these. By 1870 construction was in progress from Petaluma north toward Santa Rosa. In 1871 the California Pacific, which had lines from Vallejo to Sacramento, Marysville, and Calistoga, purchased the SF&NP and completed it to Healdsburg—and then made noises about building a line up the Feather River Canyon and over Beckwourth Pass to connect with the Union Pacific at Ogden. Central Pacific, already smarting because upstart California Pacific had built a shorter, faster route between San Francisco and Sacramento, snapped up California Pacific and considered making Sausalito its San Francisco Bay terminal The SF&NP was extended to Cloverdale in 1872. At the beginning of 1873 Central Pacific sold the SF&NP back to its builder, Peter Donahue.

In 1874 the Sonoma & Marin was organized to build a line from Petaluma south to San Rafael. It purchased the Petaluma & Haystack, surveyed a line to San Rafael, and was taken over by the SF&NP. The S&M opened and closed several times in 1878 and 1879. A tunnel cave-in

Orange-painted electric cars roll along between Larkspur and Kentfield, heading for Manor from the ferry terminal at Sausalito. Photo by Waldemar Sievers; collection of Harre W. Demoro.

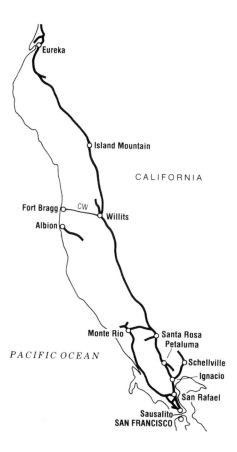

was responsible for one closing, but the SF&NP was responsible for another—the new line in conjunction with the San Rafael & San Quentin and its ferry could provide a much faster trip to San Francisco than SF&NP's own steamer down winding Petaluma Creek. However, the growing commuter trade from San Rafael to San Francisco prompted SF&NP to extend the Sonoma & Marin south to Tiburon on San Francisco Bay. The SF&NP also gained a branch to Sonoma that had been started as a monorail, then converted to narrow gauge. In 1886 a line was completed across the marshes to connect it to the rest of the SF&NP at Ignacio.

In 1886 SP (successor to Central Pacific) built a line to Santa Rosa from Napa Junction, finally establishing a rail connection between the lines north of San Francisco and the rest of the country. Mervyn Donahue, Peter's son and his successor as head of the SF&NP, discovered that SP had an option on the Eel River & Eureka (descendant of an 1877 logging railroad), which Donahue had anticipated using as the north end of the SF&NP. Donahue invoked the prospect of extending his system up the Feather River Canyon, and SP let its option drop. When the younger Donahue died in 1890, the road was sold to new owners who organized the California Northwestern and leased the SF&NP to it.

North Pacific Coast

In 1870 the standard gauge San Rafael & San Quentin Railroad opened from San Rafael to the San Quentin ferry landing, three miles to the southeast. In 1871 the North Pacific Coast Railroad was incorporated to build a line from Sausalito north through San Rafael to Tomales, on the coast, to serve a growing redwood lumber industry. The line was constructed with a gauge of 3 feet and was completed in 1875. Since its line bypassed San Rafael by a couple of miles, the NPC built a branch from what is now San Anselmo to San Rafael. It leased the San Rafael & San Quentin, narrowed its gauge, and made that the main line rather than the route to Sausalito. In 1876 NPC rails reached the Russian River, and the road re-established Sausalito as its principal terminal after boring a tunnel at Corte Madera to replace a stiff climb over the hills, and in 1877 the road extended its rails north of the Russian River to Duncan Mills.

New management took over the NPC in 1902. They renamed it the North Shore Railroad and standard-gauged, double-tracked, and electrified it from Sausalito to Mill Valley and San Rafael.

Northwestern Pacific

In 1903 the Santa Fe acquired the Eel River & Eureka and the Albion & Southeastern (an isolated line extending inland from the coast). Southern Pacific acquired the California Northwestern (by then its northern terminal was Willits) and the North Shore and started talking about building to Eureka. The battle lines were drawn. The principals, E. H. Harriman and Edward Ripley, soon recognized that the Eureka area could not support two railroads, and expensive ones at that. They formed the jointly owned Northwestern Pacific Railway as a compromise; the Northwestern Pacific Railroad soon followed. Construction of a line along the Eel River canyon—inaccessible and prone to flood—was completed in 1914.

Train 3, the overnight to San Rafael, picks its way along the trestle at the base of Scotia Bluff, about 30 miles south of Eureka, on June 20, 1953. Photo by Richard C. Brown.

In 1929 SP assumed sole ownership of the NWP. The former NPC was standard-gauged as far as Point Reyes in 1920; the line from there north to the Russian River remained narrow gauge until its abandonment in 1930. The Manor–Point Reyes line was abandoned in 1933, and the Russian River branch was abandoned in 1935. The NWP bought the Petaluma & Santa Rosa, an interurban connecting the towns of its name, in 1932. P&SR discontinued its passenger service then and ended electric operation in 1947. NWP merged the P&SR in 1985.

NWP's electric suburban service was discontinued on March 1, 1941, a casualty of bus service over the new Golden Gate Bridge. Two San Rafael–Eureka trains remained as NWP's only passenger service. The day train was discontinued in May 1942. The overnight train was replaced by the triweekly daytime *Redwood* in 1956, and that was cut back to a Willits–Eureka run handled by SP's sole RDC in 1958.

During the 1930s NWP began to lease steam locomotives from parent SP. The last of these was returned to SP in August 1953, leaving just five active NWP steamers; the last steam run was September 20, 1953. The diesels that took over were all SP property. NWP's last passenger cars left the roster in 1957, and the last interchange freight cars to carry NWP markings were gone by October 1958. A few cabooses carried NWP lettering until the 1970s.

A tunnel fire north of San Rafael in July 1961 cut off rail access to the south end of the NWP. Traffic was maintained by Santa Fe carfloat to the slip at Tiburon. The tunnel was repaired in 1967 after a long legal battle. Floods in December 1964 washed out more than 100 miles of the

Typical of the diesel freight era on the NWP is this pair of Southern Pacific SD7s leading train 77 south near Scotia in August 1956. Photo by Richard Steinheimer.

	1929	1959
Miles of railroad operated:	477	328
Number of locomotives:	65	
Number of passenger cars:	207	
Number of freight cars:	1,234	
Number of company service cars:	322	

Location of headquarters: San Francisco, California

Reporting marks: NWP

Historical and technical society: Northwestern Pacific Historical Society, P. O. Box 667, Santa Rosa, CA 95402

Recommended reading:
The Northwestern Pacific Railroad, by Fred A. Stindt and Guy L. Dunscomb, published in 1964 by Fred A. Stindt, 3363 Riviera West Drive, Kelseyville, CA 95451
Electric Railway Pioneer, by Harre Demoro, published in 1983 by Interurban Press, P. O. Box 6444, Glendale, CA 91205 (ISBN 0-916374-56-6)

Subsidiaries and affiliated railroads, 1959:
Petaluma & Santa Rosa

Successors:
Southern Pacific
Eureka Southern

Portions still operated:
California Northern: Schellville–Willits
North Coast: Willits–Eureka

line in the Eel River Canyon; replacement took 6 months. A fire in a tunnel north of Island Mountain severed the line again in September 1978; it was reopened a year later. In January 1980 heavy rains washed out the interchange yard at Schellville, NWP's only rail connection. SP closed the NWP north of Willits in April 1983, citing heavy expenses as its reason, In June of that year SP reopened the line but levied a $1200-per-car surcharge on each shipment. Another tunnel fire north of Willits in September 1983 again shut down the line—and SP threatened to make it permanent. A U. S. District Court ordered the line reopened, since it had been closed without ICC approval, and the line was reopened in March 1984. On November 1, 1984, the line north of Willits was sold to a new company, the Eureka Southern. The Eureka Southern declared bankruptcy, and operations were taken over by the North Coast Railroad in April 1992. Southern Pacific continued to operate the NWP south of Willits and merged the NWP in 1992. In 1993 SP leased the Schellville–Willits portion of the NWP to the California Northern Railroad.

Oahu Railway & Land Company

In September 1888 Benjamin F. Dillingham received a franchise from King Kalakaua to build a railroad from Honolulu to a sugar plantation at Ewa, about 20 miles west. Dillingham organized the Oahu Railway & Land Co., and construction of the 3-foot gauge line began. The road opened for service on November 16, 1889—the king's birthday—and the rails reached Ewa in May 1890.

As Dillingham developed more sugar plantations the railroad was extended up the west coast of the island of Oahu, around Kaena Point, then east to Kahuku, 71 miles by rail from Honolulu (26 miles, airline distance).

In 1906 the railroad constructed an 11-mile branch north from Waipahu to a pineapple plantation being developed by James B. Dole at Wahiawa, with a spur added to the U. S. Army base at Schofield Barracks. The new branch included stretches of 3-percent grade.

The road prospered. Between 1908 and 1916 it thoroughly modernized its roster of locomotives and cars and installed block signals along the double-track line between Honolulu and Waipahu. In 1925 the road built a new station in Honolulu, and about that time it acquired four 2-8-2s (nearly identical to Rio Grande's K-28 Mikados) and built four motor cars for passenger service. By 1927 the company had retired all its bonds and was free of debt; the

Oahu Railway No. 70, a Mikado built by Alco in 1925, wheels a Kahuku-bound freight train along the edge of the Pacific east of Kaena Point. Photo by Kent W. Cochrane.

Depression merely reduced the dividend rate.

Passenger business dropped during the 1930s but freight traffic held up. When World War II began, traffic to Army and Navy bases increased, and the bombing of Pearl Harbor on December 7, 1941, brought a complete change of pace. The road found itself running 20-car commuter trains. To accommodate the traffic it acquired used cars and locomotives from the Pacific Coast Railway, the Nevada County Narrow Gauge, and the Boston, Revere Beach & Lynn. A connection was built from Wahiahwa to Waialua in case the Japanese shelled the main line along the coast.

By the end of 1946 the servicemen had gone home and passenger traffic dropped 50 percent.

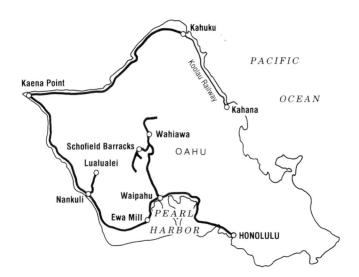

• Kahului Railroad (3-foot gauge), 16 miles of main line along Maui's north shore. It was abandoned in 1966.

The Koolau Railway connected with the Oahu Railway at Kahuku; none of the other common-carrier railroads connected with each other. There were also numerous plantation railroads in Hawaii. One last line deserves mention: The Lahaina, Kaanapali & Pacific Railroad along the west shore of Maui was built in 1970 as a tourist carrier. It can be considered a successor to the Kahului Railway in that it reused the rails of that line. It is still in operation.

	1929	1945
Miles of railroad operated:	88	93
Number of locomotives:	30	26
Number of passenger cars:	64	83
Number of freight cars:	1,033	
Number of company service cars:	7	
Number of freight and company service cars:		1,308
Location of headquarters: Honolulu, Hawaii		
Historical and technical society: Hawaiian Railway Society, P. O. Box 1208, Ewa Station, Ewa Beach, HI 96706		
Recommended reading: *Railroads of Hawaii*, by Gerald M. Best, published in 1978 by Golden West Books, P. O. Box 80250, San Marino, CA 91108 (ISBN: 0-87095-049-5)		

As plantation owners scrapped their railroads and turned to trucks, freight traffic on the Oahu Railway dropped. The railroad abandoned most of its line at the end of 1947. A short portion serving docks and canneries at Honolulu remained in operation until 1971.

The U. S. Navy purchased the main line from Pearl Harbor to Nanakuli and operated it until 1970 to serve ammunition dumps at Lualualei. Some of the locomotives and cars were sold to El Salvador.

Hawaii's other common-carrier railroads were:
• Koolau Railway (3-foot gauge) from Kahuku to Kahana, 11 miles, on the northeast shore of Oahu, absorbed by a plantation railway
• Ahokini Terminal & Railway (30-inch gauge), approximately 12 miles on the eastern shore of Kauai, absorbed by a plantation railway
• Kauai Railway (30-inch gauge), 19 miles along the south shore of the island of Kauai, abandonment date uncertain
• Hawaii Railway (3-foot gauge) on the island of Hawaii, 18 miles, abandoned in 1945
• Hawaii Consolidated Railway (standard gauge), 77 miles of main line along the eastern shore of Hawaii, wiped out by a tidal wave April 1, 1946

Pacific Railroad (Ferrocarril del Pacífico)

The Ferrocarril del Pacífico was built by the Santa Fe in 1881 and 1882 as the Sonora Railway from Guaymas, the principal Gulf of California port in the Mexican state of Sonora, to Nogales, Son., on the U. S. border. In 1897 Santa Fe traded the railroad to the Southern Pacific for the line SP had built between Mojave and Needles, California. It is more fully described in the entry for the Southern Pacific.

In 1951 SP sold the railroad to the Mexican government, and it was renamed Ferrocarril del Pacífico. It developed a considerable business in fruits and vegetables moving northward, in later years in solid piggyback trains at passenger-train speeds, and it teamed up with National of Mexico to operate first-class passenger service from the U. S. border at Nogales to Mexico City.

In the mid-1980s the Mexican government decided to unify its railroad under the banner of the National Railways of Mexico. On June 22, 1987, the FCP became the Pacific Region of the National Railways of Mexico.

In February 1998 Union Pacific and two Mexican partners completed privatization of Mexico's Pacific-North Line. With a final payment of 3.26 billion pesos, UP took control of the line from Nogales to Mexico City, including the former Ferrocarril del Pacífico as far as Guadalajara and the National Railways of Mexico line beyond.

In the 1950s and 1960s the Ferrocarril del Pacífico favored Alco power. A mixed bag of hood and cab units heads up train 4, the secondary Nogales–Guadalajara train, at Navojoa. Display of the train number in the number boards of the lead unit is a trait inherited from Southern Pacific. Photo by Robert P. Schmidt.

322

Pacific Electric Railway

The 1900 census put the population of Los Angeles at 102,479—it had more than doubled in the previous decade and would more than triple in the next. During the 1890s the city acquired a local trolley system, and in 1895 the Los Angeles & Pasadena Railway opened from Los Angeles to Pasadena, 10 miles northeast. The line was successful and its owners opened another line the next year, the Pasadena & Pacific, from Los Angeles to Santa Monica. Both companies were reorganized in 1898 as the Pasadena & Los Angeles and the Los Angeles Pacific, respectively. The Pasadena & Los Angeles was purchased (and along with it the Los Angeles Consolidated Electric Railway) by a group of investors headed by Henry E. Huntington (nephew of Collis P. Huntington, one of the builders of the Southern Pacific).

Huntington incorporated the Pacific Electric Railway in 1901 to build a high-speed interurban line from Los Angeles to Long Beach (20 miles)—it was opened in 1902. PE's tracks quickly spread throughout the Los Angeles area. E. H. Harriman was concerned about the effect the interurban would have on his Southern Pacific. He opposed Huntington at first and then purchased a 45 percent interest in the PE. Huntington, who was at the time a vice-president of SP, then incorporated the Los Angeles Inter-Urban Railway, entirely under his control.

Pacific Electric's stretch of four-track main line from Los Angeles south to Watts is shown on a typical foggy morning at Amoco Tower with two passenger trains and, dimly visible in the distance, a freight. Photo by William K. Barham.

That company soon outgrew the PE. In 1908 Huntington leased the Los Angeles Inter-Urban to PE; in 1909 he sold several traction properties elsewhere in California to SP; and in 1910 he sold his Pacific Electric interests to Southern Pacific. He retained his ownership of the Los Angeles Railway, the 3-foot-6-inch gauge local trolley system.

A new Pacific Electric Railway was incorporated in 1911 to consolidate the old PE, the Los Angeles Pacific, the Los Angeles Inter-Urban, and several other traction companies. It was the largest electric railway in the country. In addition to interurban lines stretching from Santa Monica east to Redlands and from San Fernando south to Balboa, PE operated local trolley service in most of the cities and towns. By 1918 PE was the largest electric railway in the world, according to its advertisement in *The Official Guide*. PE's big red cars went nearly everywhere, and they were responsible for much of the development of southern California.

PE's local lines were gradually abandoned or converted to bus operation, but the interurban lines remained strong into the 1940s, operating from terminals in Los Angeles at Sixth and Main streets and on Hill Street near Fourth at the end of a mile-long subway for trains to Hollywood, Burbank, and Van Nuys. After World War II the interurban lines disappeared one by one. In 1953 PE sold the remaining passenger operations (to Bellflower, Long Beach, San Pedro, Burbank, and Hollywood) to Metropolitan Coach Lines. The Burbank and Hollywood lines were abandoned in 1955. Metropolitan Transit Authority took over the system in 1958; the last line, the Long Beach route, ceased passenger service on April 8, 1961.

Pacific Electric remained in the freight business with diesel power. It was merged with parent Southern Pacific on August 13, 1965.

	1929	1965
Miles of railroad operated:	575	316
Number of locomotives:	64	42
Number of passenger cars:	822	
Number of freight cars:	2,296	29
Number of company service cars:	97	41
Location of headquarters: Los Angeles, California		

Reporting marks: PE

Recommended reading: Numerous books on all aspects of PE have been published by Interurban Press, P. O. Box 6444, Glendale, CA 91205

Successors:
Southern Pacific
Union Pacific

Portions still operated: Major portions of the Santa Monica, El Segundo, Torrance, Long Beach, Santa Ana, Yorba Linda, and San Bernardino lines continued in operation for freight service by Southern Pacific and have passed to its successor, Union Pacific.

Peabody Short Line

Peabody Coal Company, one of the largest producers of coal in the U. S., purchased the St. Louis & Belleville Electric Railway from Union Electric Company of St. Louis in 1956. The railroad was renamed the Peabody Short Line in December 1958 and given a new image of bright yellow and green. The colors were unexpected for a railroad whose business was the traditionally dirty one of moving coal—specifically from Peabody's River King Mine near Freeburg, Illinois, to an interchange with the Terminal Railroad Association of St. Louis at East St. Louis.

The St. Louis & Belleville Electric Railway was at first a freight-only subsidiary and later a survivor of the East St. Louis & Suburban railway, an interurban system that was abandoned in 1932. It was dieselized in 1949.

	1956	1960
Miles of railroad operated:	1414	
Number of locomotives:	1	3
Number of freight cars:	206	180
Location of headquarters: East St. Louis, Illinois		
Reporting marks: PSL		
Successor: Illinois Central		

Yellow-and-green RS-2s negotiate a reverse curve at Belleville, Illinois, with a coal train. Photo by J. P. Lamb, Jr.

Illinois Central acquired stock control of the Peabody Short Line in 1960 and merged it in August 1961. Almost all the track has since been retired, except for that leading to the mine at Freeburg.

Penn Central Company

 Penn Central came into existence on February 1, 1968. More accurately, it was incorporated in 1846 as the Pennsylvania Railroad; changed its name to Pennsylvania New York Central Transportation Co. on February 1, 1968, when it merged the New York Central; and adopted the name Penn Central Company on May 8, 1968. On October 1, 1969, it again changed its name, to Penn Central Transportation Company, and became a wholly owned subsidiary of a new Penn Central Company, a holding company.

The stockholders of the Pennsylvania and the New York Central approved merger of the two roads on May 8, 1962; nearly four years later the Interstate Commerce Commission approved the merger on the following conditions:

• The new company ("Penn Central" for convenience) had to take over the freight and passenger operations of the New Haven. That happened on December 31, 1968.

• Penn Central had to absorb the New York, Susquehanna & Western. PC and the Susquehanna could not agree on price, and NYS&W became part of the Delaware Otsego System.

• Penn Central had to make the Lehigh Valley available for merger by either Norfolk & Western or Chesapeake & Ohio or, if neither of those roads wanted it, merge it into PC. Lehigh Valley

Electro-Motive and General Electric diesels lead a Penn Central freight west on the former Pennsylvania Railroad Pittsburgh–St. Louis line at Mingo Junction, Ohio, in 1976. Photo by Jay Potter.

struggled along on its own and entered bankruptcy only three days after Penn Central did.

The beginnings of failure

The merger was not a success. Little thought had been given to unifying the two railroads, which had long been intense rivals and had different styles of operation. In the previous decade New York Central had trimmed its physical plant and assembled a young, eager management group under the leadership of Alfred E. Perlman. The Pennsy was a more conservative and traditional operation. Many of NYC's management people (the "green team") saw that Pennsy (the "red team") was dominant in Penn Central management and soon left for other jobs.

In addition to the problems of unification, the industrial states of the Northeast and Midwest were fast becoming the "Rust Bowl." As industries shut down and moved away, railroads found themselves with excess capacity. The Pennsylvania was worse than practically anyone else in having four or six tracks where one or two would do—tracks that were no longer needed but were still on the tax rolls. West of the Alleghenies Pennsy and Central duplicated each other's track nearly everywhere. The PC merger was like a late-in-life marriage to which each partner brings a house, a summer cottage, two cars, and several complete sets of china and glassware—plus car payments and mortgages on the houses.

Bankruptcy and reorganization

Pennsy and New York Central came into the merger in the black, but Penn Central's first year of operation yielded a deficit of $2.8 million. In 1969 the deficit was nearly $83 million. PC's net income for 1970 was a deficit of $325.8 million. By then the railroad had entered bankruptcy proceedings—specifically on June 21, 1970. The nation's sixth largest corporation had become the nation's largest bankruptcy.

The reorganization court decided in May 1974 that PC was not reorganizable on the basis of income. A U. S. government corporation, the United States Railway Association, was formed under the provisions of the Regional Rail Reorganization Act of 1973 to develop a plan to save Penn Central. The outcome was that Consolidated Rail Corporation, owned by the U. S. gov-

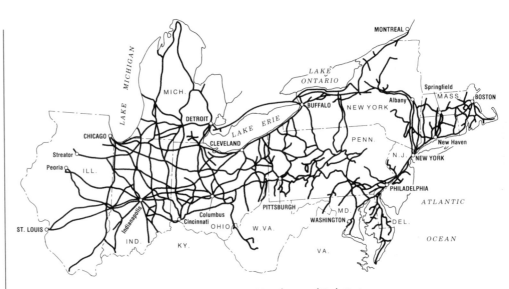

ernment, took over the railroad properties and operations of Penn Central (and six other railroads: Central of New Jersey, Erie Lackawanna, Lehigh Valley, Reading, Lehigh & Hudson River, and Pennsylvania-Reading Seashore Lines) on April 1, 1976. It was a major step toward nationalization of the railroads of the U. S. They had been nationalized briefly during World War I (through the agency of another USRA, the United States Railroad Administration), but the U. S. had held out against a world-wide trend toward nationalization of railroads until the creation of Amtrak, which nationalized the country's passenger trains, on May 1, 1971.

Metroliner and TurboTrain

PC participated in two passenger service experiments in cooperation with the U. S. Department of Transportation. Both were aimed at upgrading passenger service in the Northeast Corridor. Between New York and Washington PC inherited the Metroliner experiment that the Pennsy had begun—fast electric trains that were intended for a maximum speed of 160 mph. The inauguration of service was delayed several times, and when it did begin, it was not shown in *The Official Guide*. While not an absolute success, the Metroliners reversed a long decline in ridership on the New York–Washington run.

On the Boston–New York run PC operated a United Aircraft TurboTrain in an effort to beat the 3-hour, 55-minute running time of the New Haven's expresses of the early 1950s. Information about TurboTrain schedules was even more difficult for the public to obtain than Metroliner timetables.

The combination of untested equipment, track that had been allowed to deteriorate, and the general incongruity of space-age technology and traditional railroad thinking made the services the butt of considerable satire.

PC's intercity passenger service was taken over by Amtrak on May 1, 1971. The Metroliner cars were soon stored, and their schedules taken by Amfleet trains with accelerated timings. The TurboTrains were scrapped. The commuter service, which was already subsidized by local authorities, passed first to Conrail and then to other operating authorities.

Aftermath

The Penn Central bankruptcy was a cataclysmic event, both to the railroad industry and to the nation's business community. The PC and its problems were the subject of more words than almost anything else in the railroad industry, everything from diatribes on the passenger business to analyses of the reason for PC's collapse. Oddly, almost nothing specifically aimed at the railroad enthusiast has been published about the Penn Central.

Few undertakings have had less auspicious beginnings than Conrail—and Conrail surprised everyone with its success.

	1968	1975
Miles of railroad operated:	20,530	19,300
Number of locomotives:	4,411	4,033
Number of passenger cars:	5,046	3,569*
Number of freight cars:	187,423	137 546
Number of company service cars:	5,254	4,354

Location of headquarters: Philadelphia, Pennsylvania

Reporting marks: PC

Recommended reading:
The Wreck of the Penn Central, by Joseph R. Daughen and Peter Binzen, published in 1971 by Little, Brown & Co., Boston, Mass.
No Way to Run a Railroad, by Stephen Salsbury, published in 1982 by McGraw-Hill, Inc., 1221 Avenue of the Americas, New York, NY 10020 (ISBN 0-07-054483-2)
*(1970)

Subsidiaries and affiliated railroads, 1976:
Akron & Barberton Belt (25%)
Ann Arbor (99.5%)
Cambria & Indiana (40%)
Detroit, Toledo & Ironton (100%)
Illinois Terminal (9%)
Indiana Harbor Belt (51%)
Lehigh Valley (97%)
Monongahela (66.7%)
Niagara Junction (75%)
Norfolk & Portsmouth Belt Line (12.5%)
Pennsylvania-Reading Seashore Line (66.7%)
Pittsburgh & Lake Erie (92.6%)
Toledo, Peoria & Western (50%, jointly with Santa Fe)
Toronto, Hamilton & Buffalo (72.9%)
Washington Terminal (50%, jointly with Baltimore & Ohio)

Predecessor railroads in this book:
Pennsylvania
New York Central
New York, New Haven & Hartford

Successors: PC's principal successor in the freight business was Conrail. PC's passenger operations were taken over by Amtrak, Metro-North, Massachusetts Bay Transportation Authority, Southeastern Pennsylvania Transportation Authority, and NJ Transit. The short lines spun off to operate portions of former Penn Central track are too numerous to mention here.

Portions still operated: See the entries for Pennsylvania, New York Central, and New York, New Haven & Hartford

Pennsylvania Railroad System

 The original Pennsylvania Railroad ran from Philadelphia to Pittsburgh. Much of the road's subsequent expansion was accomplished by leasing or purchasing other railroads: the Pittsburgh, Fort Wayne & Chicago, the Pittsburgh, Cincinnati, Chicago & St. Louis, the Little Miami Railroad (to Cincinnati); the Northern Central (Baltimore to Sunbury, Pa.); the Philadelphia, Baltimore & Washington; and the Philadelphia & Trenton and the United New Jersey Railroad & Canal Company (to New York). I will deal with each of these separately.

The Main Line

Philadelphians were slow to recognize that the Erie Canal and the National Road (and later the Baltimore & Ohio Railroad) were funneling to New York and Baltimore commerce that might have come to Philadelphia. A canal opened in 1827 between the Schuylkill and Susquehanna rivers, and another was proposed along the Susquehanna, Juniata, Conemaugh, and Allegheny rivers (along with a four-mile tunnel under the summit of the Allegheny Mountains) to link Philadelphia and Pittsburgh. Parts of that project were declared impractical and it was modified to consist of alternate stretches of railroad and canal. In 1828 the Main Line of Public Works was chartered to build a railroad from

Three Atlantics, a Cole compound (Pennsy class E29, one of two built for PRR in 1905) and two E3a-class 4-4-2s, lift the Pennsylvania Limited up the 1.45 percent grade around Horse Shoe Curve sometime before 1911. Photo from the collection of Albert M. Rich.

Philadelphia to Columbia and another across the mountains, and canals from Columbia and from Pittsburgh to the base of the mountains.

By 1832 canals were open from Columbia to Hollidaysburg and from Pittsburgh to Johnstown; in 1834 a railroad opened from Philadelphia to Columbia and a portage railroad started operation over the mountains. The latter was a series of rope-operated inclined planes; canal

boats were designed to be taken apart and hauled over the mountains.

The Pennsylvania Railroad

The pace of the state's action increased when the Baltimore & Ohio requested a charter for a line to Pittsburgh. The B&O line was chartered, but so was the Pennsylvania Railroad, on April 13, 1846—to build a railroad from Harrisburg to

Pittsburgh with a branch to Erie. B&O's charter would be valid only if the Pennsylvania Railroad were not constructed.

The line was surveyed by J. Edgar Thomson, who had built the Georgia Railroad. His operating experience led him to lay out not a line with a steady grade all the way from Harrisburg to the summit of the mountains, but rather a nearly water-level line from Harrisburg to Altoona where a steeper grade (but still less than that of the Baltimore & Ohio) began for a comparatively short assault on the mountains. This arrangement concentrated the problems of a mountain railroad in one area.

Construction began in 1847. In 1849 the Pennsy made an operating contract with the Harrisburg, Portsmouth, Mountjoy & Lancaster ("Harrisburg & Lancaster" from here on), and by late 1852 rails ran from Philadelphia to Pittsburgh, via a connection with the Portage Railroad between Hollidaysburg and Johnstown. The summit tunnel was opened in February 1854, bypassing the inclined planes and creating a continuous railroad from Harrisburg to Pittsburgh. By then more than half the line had already been double-tracked.

The Main Line of Public Works was constructed with a much smaller loading gauge or clearance diagram than the Pennsylvania, and although the Pennsy was operating the Harrisburg & Lancaster, the road's own management was responsible for maintenance—and not doing much of it. In 1857 PRR bought the Main Line and in 1861 leased the Harrisburg & Lancaster, putting the entire Philadelphia–Pittsburgh line under one management.

To protect its canal the state included a tax on railroad tonnage in PRR's charter. When PRR

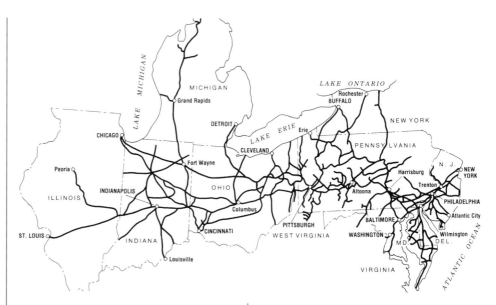

purchased the Main Line, canals and all, it mounted a long battle to have the tax repealed. The charter was amended only to the point that the funds were used to aid short lines that connected with the Pennsy. Most of those railroads eventually became part of the PRR.

PRR also acquired interests in two major railroads, the Cumberland Valley and the Northern Central. The Cumberland Valley was opened in 1837 from Harrisburg to Chambersburg, and it was extended by another company in 1841 to Hagerstown, Maryland. The Baltimore & Susquehanna was incorporated in 1828, not long after the Baltimore & Ohio got under way, to build north from Baltimore. Progress was slowed not by construction difficulties but because of the reluctance of Pennsylvania to charter a railroad that would carry commerce to Baltimore. The line reached Harrisburg in 1851 and Sunbury in 1858. By then the railroad companies that formed the route had been consolidated as the Northern Central Railway. A block of its stock that had been held by John Garrett, president of the B&O, was purchased

GG1 No. 4831 stands at the head of the *Congressional* awaiting departure from Washington Union Station. The big electric was built in 1935; the sans-serif lettering dates from the same era. Photo by H. W. Pontin.

by John Edgar Thomson, PRR's president, about 1860 and transferred to PRR ownership. Pennsy acquired majority ownership of the Northern Central in 1900.

The Pennsylvania Railroad expanded into the northwestern portion of the state by acquiring an interest in the Philadelphia & Erie Railroad in 1862 and assisting that road to complete its line from Sunbury to the city of Erie in 1864. The line to Erie was not particularly successful, but from Sunbury to Driftwood it could serve as part of a freight route with easy grades. The rest of that route was the Allegheny Valley Railroad, conceived as a feeder from Pittsburgh to the New York Central and Erie railroads. The Pennsylvania obtained control in 1868, and in 1874 opened a route with easy grades from Harrisburg to Pittsburgh via the valleys of the Susquehanna

and Allegheny rivers. PRR leased the Allegheny Valley Railroad in 1900.

Pittsburgh, Fort Wayne & Chicago

By 1847 the directors of the Pennsylvania were looking west into Ohio. In 1851 they discussed assisting the Ohio & Pennsylvania Railroad which by then was open from Allegheny, Pa., across the Allegheny River from Pittsburgh (and now part of Pittsburgh), to Salem, Ohio. Projected west from the end of the O&P at Crestline, Ohio, was the Ohio & Indiana, which was building a line to Fort Wayne, with extensions to Burlington, Iowa, and, almost incidentally, Chicago.

In 1856 the Ohio & Pennsylvania, the Ohio & Indiana, and the Fort Wayne & Chicago were consolidated as the Pittsburgh, Fort Wayne &

Chicago Rail Road. The Pennsylvania held an interest in the road, but not a controlling one. In 1858 the Fort Wayne connected its track with the Pennsylvania at Pittsburgh, and at the end of that year its rails reached into Chicago. In 1860 the Fort Wayne leased the Cleveland & Pittsburgh, a line from Cleveland through Alliance (where it crossed the Fort Wayne) to the Ohio River near Wellsville, Ohio, and then upstream to Rochester, Pa., where it again met the Fort Wayne.

In 1869 Jay Gould tried to get control of the Fort Wayne for the Erie, but the Fort Wayne evaded him and was leased by the Pennsy. The lease included the Grand Rapids & Indiana, a line from Richmond, Ind., north through Fort Wayne and Grand Rapids, Michigan. In 1873 the Pennsylvania assembled a route into Toledo; about 50 years later it extended the line to Detroit, mostly on trackage rights.

Pittsburgh, Cincinnati, Chicago & St. Louis

West of Pittsburgh lay a string of railroads—Pittsburgh & Steubenville, Steubenville & Indiana, Central Ohio, Columbus & Xenia, and Little Miami—that formed a route through Columbus to Cincinnati. The Pittsburgh & Steubenville was the last to be opened because the state of Virginia, which held a large interest in the B&O, refused to permit a railroad to be built across its narrow strip of territory (now the panhandle of West Virginia) between Pennsylvania and the Ohio River. The Pittsburgh & Steubenville was sold at foreclosure and a new company, the Panhandle Railway, took over in January 1868. In May of that year the Pennsylvania consolidated the Panhandle and the Steubenville & Indiana as the Pittsburg, Cincinnati & St. Louis Railway, but the nickname "Panhandle" stuck with it and its successors.

West of Columbus the Columbus, Chicago & Indiana Central Railway had a line from Columbus to Indianapolis and another from Columbus through Logansport, Ind., to Chicago. The Pennsy leased the CC&IC in February 1869, snatching it from the clutches of Jay Gould.

Beyond Indianapolis lay the Terre Haute & Indianapolis and the St. Louis, Alton & Terre Haute. Because several roads in the area could not agree about the division of traffic, the St. Louis, Vandalia & Terre Haute was constructed between 1868 and 1870 from East St. Louis to Terre Haute and leased by the Terre Haute & Indianapolis, which then made traffic agreements with the Panhandle and the Columbus, Chicago & Indiana Central. (The St. Louis, Alton & Terre Haute wound up in the New York Central System.)

The Little Miami Railroad was incorporated in 1836. By 1846 it had a line from Cincinnati through Xenia to Springfield, Ohio, and it grew by purchasing and leasing lines to Columbus and Dayton. The Pennsylvania saw it as a route to Cincinnati. To force the issue, the Panhandle got control of the Cincinnati & Zanesville, a secondary line into Cincinnati. The Panhandle leased the Little Miami in 1869.

In 1890 the Pittsburg, Cincinnati & St. Louis and several other lines were consolidated as the Pittsburgh, Cincinnati, Chicago & St. Louis Railway. In 1905 the Vandalia Railroad was incorporated to consolidate the lines west of Indianapolis. The PCC&StL, the Vandalia, and several others were consolidated in 1916 as the Pittsburgh,

Cincinnati, Chicago & St. Louis Railroad. At the beginning of 1921 the PCC&StL was leased to the Pennsylvania Railroad.

Pennsylvania Company

With the leases of 1869 the Pennsylvania suddenly had more than 3,000 miles of line west of Pittsburgh. Rather than try to manage it all from Philadelphia, the PRR organized the Pennsylvania Company to hold and manage the lines west of Pittsburgh. The new company also operated the Fort Wayne and its affiliate roads.

The division of the Pennsylvania system into several more or less autonomous divisions was not altogether successful, partly because the pieces all came together at Pittsburgh, where the yards and terminals were under three managements. In 1918 the Pennsylvania Company ceased to be an operating company and transferred its leases to the Pennsylvania Railroad.

Lines east of Philadelphia

Even with the loyalty to Philadelphia engendered by having its roots and headquarters there, the Pennsy could not ignore New York, both as a city and as a port. Any traffic from the west to New York had to be turned over to the Reading at Harrisburg because there was no through Philadelphia–New York route. In 1863 the PRR contracted with the Philadelphia & Trenton (which was built and opened in 1834), the Camden & Amboy (with lines from Camden to South Amboy and from Trenton to New Brunswick, New Jersey), and the Delaware & Raritan Canal Co. In 1871 it leased the properties of these companies and the United Canal & Railroad Companies of New Jersey, acquiring lines northeast to

Jersey City, south to Cape May, and north along the Delaware River to Belvidere. In the 1880s PRR constructed lines up the Schuylkill Valley into Reading territory and acquired lines from Philadelphia east across New Jersey to the shore. The latter were combined in 1933 with a parallel line owned by the Reading to form the Pennsylvania-Reading Seashore Lines.

The New York Central had long had an advantage in New York: It had a terminal, Grand Central, on Manhattan Island, and all the other roads (except the New Haven, which shared NYC's facilities) had to ferry their passengers to Manhattan. Pennsy's desire for a rail terminal in Manhattan was given added impetus by its acquisition of the Long Island Rail Road in 1900.

After studying proposals for bridges and tunnels, PRR began construction in 1904 of Pennsylvania Station, between Seventh and Eighth avenues and 31st and 33rd streets; two tunnels under the Hudson River; four tunnels under the East River; and a double-track line across the Jersey Meadows to connect it to the main line east of Newark—all electrified. The new station opened in 1910.

In 1917 the New York Connecting Railroad, including the Hell Gate Bridge, was opened, creating a rail route from Bay Ridge in Brooklyn for freight service and from Penn Station for passenger service to a junction with the New Haven in the Bronx.

Lines south of Philadelphia

Baltimore & Ohio had a monopoly on traffic to and from Washington, D. C.—and protection of that monopoly in its charter. B&O refused to make arrangements with the Northern Central

The last stronghold of Pennsylvania Railroad steam was suburban service on the New York & Long Branch, operated jointly with Central Railroad of New Jersey. K4 Pacific No. 3678, once streamlined for the *Broadway Limited,* heads up the *Broker* at Rahway, N. J., as the *St. Louisian* streaks past toward Newark and New York on the main line overhead. Photo by Don Wood.

or the Philadelphia, Wilmington & Baltimore for through ticketing of passengers and through billing of freight. The Pennsy bought the charter of the Baltimore & Potomac. The B&P was to have built a railroad from Baltimore straight south to the Potomac River at Popes Creek, Md., but it had lain dormant since its chartering in 1853. B&P's charter allowed it to build branch lines no more than 20 miles long, and the PRR saw that a 16-mile branch from Bowie could reach Washington nicely. The resulting Baltimore–Washington route, opened in 1872, was only three miles longer than B&O's. Congress authorized the Pennsylvania to continue its line through Washington and across the Potomac to connect with railroads in Virginia.

The Philadelphia, Wilmington & Baltimore opened in 1838 between the cities of its name. The Pennsy was quick to connect it to the B&P in Baltimore (it had had no physical connection with the B&O), and in 1873 through service was inaugurated between Jersey City and Washington. Both Pennsy and B&O saw the strategic importance of the PW&B, which included lines down the Delmarva Peninsula—PRR got it in 1881. PRR soon extended the Delmarva lines southward by construction of the New York, Philadelphia & Norfolk Railroad to Cape Charles, Va., where they connected with a ferry to Norfolk, Va.

In 1902 the PW&B and the B&P were consolidated as the Philadelphia, Baltimore & Washington Railroad. PB&W and Baltimore & Ohio teamed up to form the Washington Terminal Co., which constructed a new Union Station in Washington, opened in 1907. In 1917 the Pennsylvania Railroad leased the PB&W.

After 1900

Major additions to the Pennsylvania at the end of the nineteenth century were extension of the Grand Rapids & Indiana north to Mackinaw City, Mich. (1882); construction of the Trenton Cutoff, a freight line bypassing Philadelphia (1892); control of the Toledo, Peoria & Western (1893, sold 1927); and acquisition of the Western New York & Pennsylvania Railroad, which had lines from Oil City, Pa., to Buffalo, N. Y., and Emporium, Pa., and from Emporium to Buffalo and Rochester.

By 1910 the Pennsylvania had achieved full growth. The PRR has been described as a man with his head in Philadelphia, his hands in New York and Washington, and his feet in Chicago and St. Louis. The metaphor, which is unkind to Pittsburgh, requires for completeness a fishnet spread over the man with pins holding it down at Buffalo, Rochester, and Sodus Point, N. Y., Detroit and Mackinaw City, Mich., Marietta, Cincinnati, and Cleveland, Ohio, Madison, Ind., and Louisville, Kentucky. The hand in New York holds a large fish—Long Island—and resting on the other shoulder is another, the Delmarva Peninsula. Almost everywhere the Pennsy went it was the dominant railroad, the principal exception being the New York Central territory in upstate New York and along the south shore of Lake Erie.

The Pennsylvania was also, by its own declaration, "The Standard Railroad of the World."

The standardization was internal. Passenger trains moved behind a fleet of 425 K4s-class Pacifics. The road had hundreds of P70-class coaches built to a single design. Freight was hauled by 579 Lls-class Mikados (which used the same boiler as the K4s) and 598 Ils-class Decapods; PRR had thousands of X29-class 40-foot steel boxcars. Much of Pennsy's standardization was different from nearly everything else in North America: Belpaire boilers on steam locomotives; position-light signals giving their indications with rows of amber lights at different angles; tuscan red passenger cars instead of olive green.

At the turn of the century under the leadership of Alexander Johnston Cassatt, PRR purchased substantial interests in Norfolk & Western, Chesapeake & Ohio, Baltimore & Ohio, and (through B&O) Reading. Cassatt was vigorously opposed to the practice of rebating (returning a portion of the freight charge to favored shippers) and was in favor of an industry-wide end to the practice. Strong railroads would be able to resist pressure to grant rebates, but weaker ones would not—unless they were controlled by strong railroads. In 1906 PRR sold its B&O and C&O interests but increased its Norfolk & Western holdings.

In 1929 the Pennroad Corporation was formed as a holding company owned principally by PRR stockholders. Pennroad purchased sizable interests in Detroit, Toledo & Ironton; Pittsburgh & West Virginia; New Haven; and Boston & Maine. The Pennsylvania Railroad would have needed ICC approval to purchase interests in other railroads; it was not necessary for the holding company.

Pennsy was by far Baldwin's best diesel customer. A four-unit set of "Shark Nose" freights brings a Mingo Junction–Crestline, Ohio, train under the Nickel Plate at Orrville in June 1960. Photo by Herbert H. Harwood, Jr.

The biggest single improvement accomplished by the Pennsylvania Railroad in the 1920s and 1930s was the electrification of its lines from New York to Washington and from Philadelphia to Harrisburg. The nucleus of the project was the 1915 electrification between Philadelphia and Paoli, Pa. That was extended south to Wilmington in 1928. PRR decided to change the New York terminal third-rail electrification to high-voltage AC to match the Philadelphia electrification. The Philadelphia–New York electrification was completed in 1933.

At the same time the road opened two new stations in Philadelphia, Suburban Station next to Broad Street Station in the city center and 30th Street, on the west bank of the Schuylkill, as the first steps in the elimination of Broad Street Station and the "Chinese Wall" elevated tracks leading to it. Two years later the electrification was extended from Wilmington through Baltimore and Washington to Potomac Yard in Alexandria, Va. Electrification was extended west from Paoli to Harrisburg in 1938, with the thought of eventually continuing it to Pittsburgh.

During World War II Pennsy's freight traffic doubled and passenger traffic quadrupled, much of it on the eastern portion of the system. The electrification was of inestimable value in keeping the traffic moving. After the war Pennsy had the same experiences as many other railroads but seemed slower to react. PRR was slower to dieselize, and when it did so it bought units from every manufacturer.

As freight and passenger traffic forsook the rails for the highways, Pennsy found itself with far more fixed plant than the traffic warranted or could support, and it was slow to take up excess trackage or replace double track with Centralized Traffic Control.

PRR was saddled with a heavy passenger business. It had extensive commuter services centered on New York, Philadelphia, and Pittsburgh and lesser ones at Chicago, Washington, Baltimore, and Camden, N. J. It had gone through the Depression without going bankrupt—and bankruptcy can have a salutary effect on old debt. (The Pennsylvania Railroad had to its credit, though, the longest history of dividend payment in U. S. business history.)

Pennsylvania and New York Central surprised the railroad industry by announcing merger plans in November 1957. The two had long been rivals, and the merger would be one of parallel roads rather than end-to-end. The merger took place on February 1, 1968—and Penn Central fell apart faster than it went together.

	1929	1967
Miles of railroad operated:	10,512	9,538
Number of locomotives:	6,152	2,211
Number of passenger cars:	7,384	2,632
Number of freight cars:	270,653	112,431
Number of company service cars:	3,976	2,489

Location of headquarters: Philadelphia, Pennsylvania

Reporting marks: PRR

Notable named passenger trains: *Broadway Limited, General, Trail Blazer* (New York–Chicago), *Liberty Limited* (Washington–Chicago), *Spirit of St. Louis, Jeffersonian* (New York–St. Louis), *Congressional* (New York–Washington), *Senator* (Boston–Washington, operated north of New York by the New Haven), *South Wind* (Chicago–Miami), *Pittsburgher* (New York–Pittsburgh)

Historical and technical societies:
Pennsylvania Railroad Technical & Historical Society, P. O. Box 389, Upper Darby, PA 19082; http://www.rrhistorical.com/prths
Philadelphia Chapter, Pennsylvania Railroad Technical & Historical Society, P. O. Box 663, Wayne, PA 19087-0663

Recommended reading:
Centennial History of the Pennsylvania Railroad Company, by George H. Burgess and Miles C. Kennedy, published in 1949 by The Pennsylvania Railroad Company, Philadelphia, Pa.
Golden Years of Railroading: Heart of the Pennsylvania Railroad, by Robert S. McGonigal, published in 1996 by Kalmbach Publishing Co., P. O. Box 1612, Waukesha, WI 53187 (ISBN 0-89024-275-5)

Subsidiaries and affiliated railroads, 1967:
Detroit, Toledo & Ironton (99.9%)
Lehigh Valley (97.33%)
Monongahela (33.3%, jointly with Baltimore & Ohio and Pittsburgh & Lake Erie)
Montour (50%, jointly with Pittsburgh & Lake Erie)
New York & Long Branch (50%, jointly with Central of New Jersey)
New York Connecting (50%, jointly with New Haven)
Pennsylvania-Reading Seashore Lines (66.7%)
Toledo, Peoria & Western (50%, jointly with Santa Fe)
Wabash (86.7%)

Washington Terminal (50%, jointly with Baltimore & Ohio)
Successors:
Penn Central
Conrail
Amtrak
Portions still operated:
Major portions operated by roads other than Conrail and *major portions abandoned*:
(The size and complexity of the Pennsy calls for a slightly different format here. This is not an exhaustive list of what is gone and what remains. In some cases I have shown an entire line as abandoned, even though short stubs remain where it crossed other lines.)
New York–Washington (Northeast Corridor) New York–Washington, Philadelphia–Harrisburg: Amtrak
New York–Trenton, N. J.; Princeton Jct. –Princeton, N. J.; Rahway–Bay Head Jct., N. J.: NJ Transit
Philadelphia to Trenton, N. J., and Chestnut Hill, Manayunk, Marcus Hook, Paoli, and West Chester, Pa.: Southeastern Pennsylvania Transportation Authority
Wawa, Pa.–Colora, Md.: Octoraro

Pemberton–Bay Head Jct., N. J.; Hightstown–Fort Dix, N. J.; Kinkora–Fort Dix, N. J.; Newfield–McKee City, N. J.; Manumuskin–Cape May, N J.; Trenton–Lambertville, N. J.

Delmarva Peninsula

Townsend, Del.–Centreville, Md.; Massey–Chestertown, Md.; Seaford, Del.–Cambridge, Md.; Hurlock–Preston, Md.; Frankford, Del.–Snow Hill, Md.: Maryland & Delaware

Pocomoke, Md.–Norfolk, Va.: Eastern Shore

Clayton, Del.–Oxford, Md.; Denton Branch Jct.–Love Point, Md.; Easton–Claiborne, Md.; Easton–Preston, Md.; Hurlock–Ocean City, Md.; Kings Creek–Crisfield, Md.; Snow Hill, Md.–Franklin City, Va.

Philadelphia–Pittsburgh

York–Hanover, Pa.: Maryland & Pennsylvania

Taneytown–Walkersville, Md.: Maryland Midland

Newark–Sodus Point, N. Y.: Ontario Midland

Doe Run, Pa.–Newark, Del.; York, Pa.–Cockeysville, Md.; Hanover, Pa.–Taneytown, Md.; Walkersville–Frederick, Md.; Marion–Mercersburg, Pa.; Williamsport, Pa.–Elmira–Newark, N. Y.; Oil City–Irvineton, Pa.; Warren, Pa.–Salamanca, N. Y.; Cuba Jct.–Rochester, N. Y.; Mayville–Brocton, N. Y.; Bedford–Hyndman, Pa.; Mifflinburg–Snow Shoe, Pa.; Washington–Waynesburg, Pa. (3-foot gauge); New Castle–Franklin, Pa.; Hollidaysburg–Gallitzin, Pa. (Mule Shoe Curve)

West of Pittsburgh

Petoskey–Pellston, Mich.: Michigan Northern

Reed City–Petoskey, Mich.: Tuscola & Saginaw Bay

Grand Rapids–Muskegon, Mich.: Grand Trunk Western

Logansport–Effner, Ind.: Toledo, Peoria & Western

Paris–Decatur, Ill.: Prairie Central

Maroa–Peoria, Ill.: Norfolk & Western (ex-Illinois Terminal)

Warren–Ashtabula Ohio; Coshocton–Loudonville, Ohio; Bellaire–Zanesville, Ohio (Ohio River & Western, 3-foot gauge); Marietta–Oneida, Ohio; Bremen–Washington Court House, Ohio; Wilmington–Morrow, Ohio; Xenia–Cincinnati, Ohio; Cambridge City–Columbus–North Vernon, Ind.; Frankfort–Otter Creek Jct., Ind.; Richmond–Decatur, Ind.; Butler–Logansport, Ind.; South Bend–Logansport, Ind.; Frankton–Kokomo, Ind.; Kendallville–Lagrange, Ind.; Comstock Park–Reed City, Mich.; Pellston–Mackinaw City, Mich.

Pennsylvania-Reading Seashore Lines

 The Philadelphia–Atlantic City, New Jersey, corridor was the setting for one of North America's most intense railroad rivalries—back long before the term "corridor" was applied to railroad routes. The two railroads were the Pennsylvania and the Reading—specifically Pennsy's West Jersey & Seashore Railroad and Reading's Atlantic City Railroad.

The West Jersey & Seashore was formed in 1896 by the consolidation of several Pennsylvania Railroad properties in New Jersey, among them the Camden & Atlantic, which had a direct route from Camden to Atlantic City via Haddonfield and Winslow Junction; the West Jersey Railroad (Camden to Cape May through Newfield and Millville plus several branches to towns west of that line); and the West Jersey & Atlantic, which ran from Newfield to Atlantic City. In 1906 the West Jersey & Seashore electrified the Camden–Newfield–Atlantic City route, which served a more heavily populated area and did more local business than the former Camden & Atlantic, with a 650-volt third-rail system. The Newfield–Atlantic City electrification was dismantled in 1931, but Camden–Millville electric trains lasted until 1949.

The Atlantic City Railroad was built as a narrow gauge line from Camden to Atlantic City through Haddon Heights and Winslow Junction,

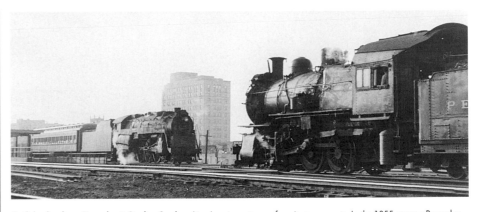

Until the diesel era, Pennsylvania-Reading Seashore Lines' equipment came from its two parents. In the 1955 scene a Pennsylvania B6 0-6-0 watches while train 756, a single Pennsy P70 coach pulled by a 1948-built Reading G3 Pacific, arrives at Camden from Millville. Photo by Philip R. Hastings.

parallel to the Camden & Atlantic and no more than a few miles from it—indeed, within sight much of the way. The narrow gauge line went bankrupt and was acquired in 1883 by the Reading, which standard-gauged and double-tracked it. By the mid-1890s the Reading's subsidiary had reached Cape May, duplicating the West Jersey & Seashore route.

In the 1920s it was clear that the competition and duplication were ruinous, particularly for traffic that could easily be diverted to the highways. Moreover, the business was seasonal—two-thirds of the revenue came from the summer travel to and from the New Jersey shore.

The two railroads agreed in 1932 to consolidate the operations. The Pennsylvania bought

Car 6770 lays over at Millville, the southern terminus of PRSL's third-rail electrification. The horizontal-barred pilot and the round end windows are Pennsy traits. The trolley poles are used for the last 4 miles into Camden, an area with many highway crossings. Photo by Robert W. Hutton.

two-thirds of Reading's Atlantic City stock for $1 (the AC was piling up deficits because of taxes, interest on debt, and equipment rentals), and assigned its lease of the West Jersey & Seashore to the Atlantic City. The consolidation was effective June 25, 1933, and the Atlantic City Railroad was renamed Pennsylvania-Reading Seashore Lines on July 15 of that year. The initial rationalization of the lines resulted in the abandonment of the Reading line east of Winslow Junction and the Pennsylvania line route south of Woodbine. Most of the Newfield–Atlantic City line was abandoned in the early 1960s.

PRSL's business, largely passenger, dwindled to a handful of Camden–Atlantic City and Camden–Cape May RDC runs, which eventually terminated at Lindenwold, end of the PATCO rapid transit line, instead of Camden. (PRSL's Camden– Philadelphia ferries were discontinued in 1952.) On July 1, 1982, the last of those runs were replaced by buses because of a federally imposed track speed limit of 15 mph. PRSL's properties were conveyed to Conrail on April 1, 1976.

	1933	1975
Miles of railroad operated:	413	307
Number of locomotives:	22	14
Number of passenger cars:	216	
Number of motor passenger cars:		10
Number of cabooses:	26	19
Number of company service cars:	53	

Location of headquarters: Camden, New Jersey (officers shared with Pennsylvania and Reading were located in Philadelphia)

Reporting marks: PRSL

Historical and technical society: Pennsylvania-Reading Seashore Lines Historical Society, P. O. Box 422, Bellmawr, NJ 08099

Recommended reading: *Atlantic City Railroad*, by W. George Cook and William J. Coxey, published in 1980 by West Jersey Chapter, National Railway Historical Society, P. O. Box 101, Oaklyn, NJ 08107

Successors:
Conrail
NJ Transit

Portions still operated:
Conrail: Camden–Winslow Junction–Tuckahoe; Camden–Millville; Woodbury–Deepwater; Woodbury–West Swedesboro
NJ Transit: Lindenwold–Atlantic City
Southern Railroad of New Jersey: Winslow Junction–Atlantic City; Pleasantville–Linwood; Tuckahoe–Rio Grande; West Swedesboro–Salem
Winchester & Western (New Jersey): Millville–Dorchester; Bridgeton–Seabrook

Pere Marquette Railway

PERE MARQUETTE

The Pere Marquette Railroad was formed on January 1, 1900, by the consolidation of the Chicago & West Michigan Railway, the Detroit, Grand Rapids & Western Railroad, and the Flint & Pere Marquette Railroad.

The three railroads had been built to serve Michigan's lumber industry, and they were feeling the effects of the decline in lumber production as the forests were logged off. Consolidation would make them into one larger, more powerful road.

The Chicago & West Michigan had a main line from La Crosse, Indiana, north to Pentwater, Mich., opened in 1872, and another line from Holland through Grand Rapids to Bay View, Mich.

The Flint & Pere Marquette had a line completed in 1874 from Monroe, Mich., through Flint and Saginaw, Mich., to the eastern shore of Lake Michigan at Ludington (originally called Pere Marquette). From Ludington the F&PM operated car ferries across Lake Michigan to Kewaunee, Manitowoc, and Milwaukee, Wisconsin. Also part of the F&PM was the former Port Huron & Northwestern, built between 1879 and 1882 as a 3-foot gauge line from Port Huron to Saginaw. The F&PM acquired control of the PH&N in 1883 and merged it in 1889.

The Detroit, Grand Rapids & Western, successor in 1897 to the Detroit, Lansing & Northern, had a line from Detroit to Grand Rapids and a network of branches north and east of Grand Rapids.

The Pere Marquette inherited substantial debt from its predecessors—all three had histories of receivership and foreclosure—and new management concentrated on absorbing short lines in the interior of Michigan rather than the logical step of extending the line to Chicago. Another new management in 1903 leased the Lake Erie & Detroit River Railway, which had lines from Walkerville (Windsor), Ontario, to St. Thomas and from Sarnia to Erieau and acquired trackage rights over the Michigan Central (ex-Canada Southern) from St. Thomas to Suspension Bridge, New York, and over New York Central from Suspension Bridge to Buffalo. The Pere Marquette of Indiana was chartered to build a line from New Buffalo, Mich., to Porter, Ind., 22 miles. That line was opened in 1903, and trackage rights on the Lake Shore & Michigan Southern (NYC) and Chicago Terminal Transfer Railroad (the predecessor of Baltimore & Ohio Chicago Terminal) brought the PM the remaining 52 miles to Chicago.

An era followed in which the PM was tossed around like a volleyball. In July 1904 the Cincinnati, Hamilton & Dayton acquired most of the stock of the Pere Marquette and leased the railroad, but in December 1905 the CH&D annulled the lease. PM purchased the Chicago, Cincinnati & Louisville in 1904 and soon let it go—to eventually become Chesapeake & Ohio's line across Indiana. B&O briefly controlled the PM through the CH&D, and the PM was briefly leased to the Erie. Meanwhile, the PM had entered receivership, from which it emerged in 1907. It again went into receivership in 1912.

Berkshire 1229 darkens the sky as it heads out of Plymouth, Michigan, with a freight for Grand Rapids. Photo by Robert A. Hadley.

The Pere Marquette Railway was incorporated in 1917 to succeed the Pere Marquette Railroad. The automobile industry was beginning to grow, and PM was in the right places to serve it. The Van Sweringen brothers of Cleveland acquired control of the road in 1924, seeing that it could provide markets for coal from their Chesapeake & Ohio. Soon PM's largest source of traffic was the interchange with the Hocking Valley (controlled by C&O) at Toledo. In 1928 the ICC approved control of PM by C&O.

In 1932 Pere Marquette purchased the Manis-

tee & Northeastern Railway, a lumber carrier that reached north from Manistee, Mich., to Traverse City and northeast to Grayling. PM began to develop into a bridge route. Despite the handicaps of a ferry transfer between Walkerville and Detroit and another much longer ferry run on Lake Michigan, the road was able to expedite freight service by avoiding the terminal congestion around Chicago.

Chesapeake & Ohio merged the Pere Marquette on June 6, 1947. For several years thereafter it led an almost autonomous existence as the Pere Marquette District and later as part of C&O's Northern Region. Gradually the Pere Marquette name disappeared and was replaced by "Chesapeake & Ohio" then "Chessie System." (Amtrak revived the Pere Marquette name in 1984 for a Chicago–Grand Rapids train.)

	1929	1945
Miles of railroad operated:	2,241	1,949
Number of locomotives:	388	283
Number of passenger cars:	281	113
Number of freight cars:	16,405	14,335
Number of company service cars:	599	541

Location of headquarters: Detroit, Michigan

Reporting marks: PM

Notable named passenger trains: *Pere Marquette* (Detroit–Grand Rapids)

Recommended reading: *Pere Marquette Power,* by Thomas W. Dixon Jr. and Art Million, published in 1984 by the Chesapeake & Ohio Historical Society, P. O. Box 417, Alderson, WV 24910 (ISBN 0-87012-472-2)

Subsidiaries and affiliated railroads, 1945:
Manistee & Northeastern

Successors:
Chesapeake & Ohio
Chessie System
CSX Transportation

Portions still operated:
CSX: Buffalo–Detroit–Grand Rapids–Chicago; Blenheim, Ont.–Port Huron–Saginaw, Mich.; Monroe–Saginaw, Mich.; Grand Rapids–Baldwin, Mich.; Holland–Montague, Mich.; Berry–Fremont, Mich.; Holland–Hamilton, Mich.; New Buffalo, Mich.–La Crosse, Ind.; Evart–Baldwin–Ludington, Mich.; Walhalla–Manistee, Mich.
Huron & Eastern: Saginaw–Croswell, Mich.; Bad Axe–Kinde, Mich.; Palms–Harbor Beach, Mich.
Mid-Michigan: Elmdale–Greenville, Mich., Saginaw–Alma–Elwell, Mich.
Tuscola & Saginaw Bay: Grawn–Traverse City–Williamsburg, Mich.

Piedmont & Northern Railway

When the American Tobacco Trust was dissolved in 1910 by the U. S. government, its founder, James B. Duke, turned his attention to general industry in the Piedmont area of North and South Carolina. Rivers flowing through the area could provide hydroelectric power, and Duke soon owned several power companies, which in turned owned streetcar systems in area cities.

In 1909 William S. Lee, vice-president of Southern Power & Utilities, proposed an interurban railroad system to connect the cities in the Piedmont area. Two companies were organized, the Piedmont Traction Company in North Carolina and the Greenville, Spartanburg & Anderson Railway in South Carolina, with Duke as president and Lee as vice-president. The railroads were planned for freight service from the outset and would use a 1500-volt DC catenary distribution system. The Piedmont Traction Co. was opened in 1912 as was the Greenwood–Greenville segment of the South Carolina company. The line to Spartanburg was opened in 1914, and in that year the two railroads were consolidated as the Piedmont & Northern Railway.

Even while the railroad was under construction Duke proposed joining the two portions of the system with a 51-mile line between Spartanburg and Charlotte. He also proposed an exten-

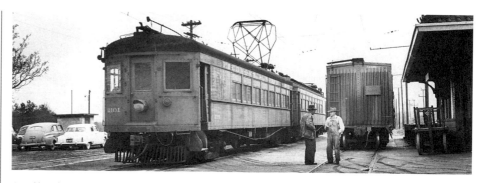

A northbound train stops at Belton, South Carolina, on its run from Greenwood to Spartanburg in April 1951. Photo by A. C. Kalmbach.

sion to Norfolk, Virginia. Through the years there were other proposals for extensions to Raleigh, Winston-Salem, and Atlanta, and even to take over and electrify the Georgia & Florida Railroad.

The P&N was taken over by the USRA during World War I. By the early 1920s the P&N, back under its own management, had rebuilt the line and begun a new emphasis on freight service. The connection between the two portions of the line was again proposed in 1924. The Southern Railway, whose main line ran between Spartan-

burg and Charlotte, opposed it, and the ICC ruled against it. Technically the ICC had no jurisdiction over an electric railway, but it ruled that the P&N was a Class 1 railroad that was electrified (basically, a "steam railroad"). The P&N went ahead with preliminary work; the ICC obtained an injunction, which the Supreme Court upheld.

During the Depression the management of the P&N was combined with that of the Durham & Southern, also owned by Duke interests. P&N dropped most of its passenger service, but

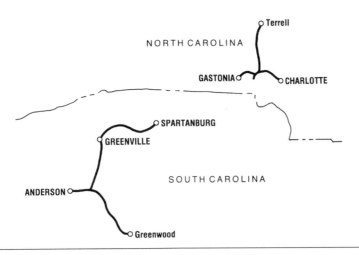

NORTH CAROLINA

Terrell

GASTONIA CHARLOTTE

SPARTANBURG

GREENVILLE

SOUTH CAROLINA

ANDERSON

Greenwood

	1929	1968
Miles of railroad operated:	127	150
Number of locomotives:	17	18
Number of passenger cars:	30	
Number of freight and company service cars:	340	23
Location of headquarters: Charlotte, North Carolina		
Reporting marks: PN		

Historical and technical society: Piedmont & Northern Railway Historical Association, c/o Craig A. Myers, P. O. Box 5481, Greenville, SC 29606

Recommended reading: *Piedmont and Northern,* by Thomas T. Fetters and Peter W. Swanson Jr., published in 1974 by Golden West Books, P. O. Box 80250, San Marino, CA 91108 (ISBN 0-87095-051-7)

Successors:
Seaboard Coast Line
Seaboard System
CSX Transportation

Portions still operated: Seaboard System operates all the former Piedmont & Northern except for the Belton–Anderson, S. C., branch.

because its franchise required that a minimum service be offered, it reduced fares from 3.5 cents per mile to 1 cent per mile. The road had to restore some schedules and buy used passenger cars from the Pennsylvania and the Long Island to handle the resulting surge of business. Later in the 1930s the P&N actively solicited industries to establish plants along the line.

By 1950 the power distribution system needed replacement, and the road turned to diesel power. It dropped all passenger service in 1951 and ended electric operation in South Carolina that year. Mainline electric operation ended in North Carolina in 1954 but a short switching operation at Charlotte remained under wires until 1958.

In 1930 Charleston & Western Carolina and Clinchfield (both controlled by Atlantic Coast Line) and Piedmont & Northern proposed a tunnel under the Southern Railway main line at Spartanburg to connect the Clinchfield directly with the other two without involving the Southern for a half-mile move. The Southern protested, but in 1961 the Supreme Court approved the project and the 750-foot tunnel was opened in 1963.

In 1965 P&N constructed a branch north from Mount Holly, N. C., to a new Duke Power Co. plant at Terrell. That same year the Duke interests decided to divest their P&N holdings and looked for a buyer. Seaboard Air Line was interested but was preoccupied by its merger with Atlantic Coast Line. Once that was accomplished (and over the protests of the Southern) Seaboard Coast Line merged the Piedmont & Northern July 1, 1969.

Pittsburgh & Lake Erie Railroad

 The Pittsburgh & Lake Erie was chartered in 1875 and opened from Pittsburgh, Pennsylvania, to Youngstown, Ohio, in 1879. Cornelius Vanderbilt of the New York Central subscribed to 15 percent of the railroad's stock, because he saw the P&LE as the route by which his New York Central system could enter Pittsburgh to compete with the Pennsylvania Railroad to serve the steel industry. NYC gained control of P&LE in 1889, and from then on it was for all practical purposes a division of the NYC and a highly profitable one.

The portion of the P&LE south of Pittsburgh was incorporated in 1881 as the Pittsburgh, McKeesport & Youghiogheny. It was jointly owned by P&LE and NYC and was operated as part of P&LE. In 1965 P&LE bought NYC's half interest in the PMcK&Y.

When Penn Central, successor to New York Central, went bankrupt in 1970 it owed P&LE $15 million and it owned 92.6 percent of P&LE's stock. Officials who held positions with both PC and P&LE were replaced with new management, and P&LE began to chart an independent course. Local congressmen were persuaded by P&LE management, labor, and shippers to amend the Regional Rail Reorganization Act of 1973 to allow solvent subsidiaries of Penn Central to stay out of Conrail. Later negotiations

In 1948 P&LE received 7 Berkshires, the last steam locomotives ordered by the New York Central System and the last built by Alco. Indeed, Alco was committed to diesels to the point that the tenders had to be built by Lima. The second of the group, No. 9401, is shown on a southbound freight at Beaver, Pennsylvania, on June 20, 1948. Photo by Richard J. Cook.

gave P&LE access to Norfolk & Western's ex-Nickel Plate line at Ashtabula, Ohio, via trackage rights on Conrail north from Youngstown. On February 27, 1979, Penn Central sold the Pittsburgh & Lake Erie Railroad to the new Pittsburgh & Lake Erie Company, which subsequently became a private corporation.

The new P&LE made a good start. It drew up plans to purchase from Conrail some or all of the former Erie main line east of Youngstown. Then the Pittsburgh steel industry went into a sharp decline and Conrail proved to be a sharp competitor. Flooding caused the closure of coal mines on P&LE's Connellsville line and along P&LE subsidiary Montour Railroad, and P&LE abandoned those lines.

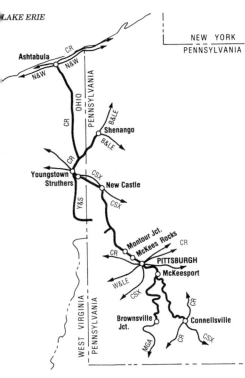

In the late 1980s the road was up for sale. Several prospective buyers came and went while the labor unions fought for income protection. In June 1989 the United States Supreme Court reversed the decision of a lower court and upheld a company's right to sell its business without having to bargain with the unions. In May 1990 P&LE reached agreement with its 14 unions on severance benefits. Railroad Development Corporation bought the P&LE on June 6, 1990.

In July 1991 the P&LE sold 61 miles of its main line—from McKeesport through Pittsburgh to New Castle—to CSX Transportation. Baltimore & Ohio had obtained trackage rights on the route in 1934 to bypass the steep grades and sharp curves of its own line west of Pittsburgh. The sale reversed the owner-tenant relationship and generated some much-needed cash for P&LE.

P&LE continued to decline. P&LE's last day of operation was September 11, 1992. The next day, the remaining rail lines and trackage rights were purchased by Three Rivers Railway, a CSX subsidiary.

P&LE operated few branch lines but had several subsidiary railroads. The Montour Railroad served the area west of Pittsburgh. It was owned jointly with Penn Central; P&LE bought PC's half interest in 1975. The Montour ceased operation in 1983, and abandonment was approved in 1986. The Montour owned the Youngstown & Southern Railway, a 35-mile road running south and east from Youngstown, Ohio. It remains in operation under the ownership of P&LE's parent company. The Pittsburgh, Chartiers & Youghiogheny Railway, a 12-mile switching line between Pittsburgh, McKees Rocks, and Carnegie, is owned jointly by P&LE's parent company and Conrail.

1991

Miles of railroad operated:	404
Number of locomotives:	39
Number of freight cars:	3,174

Location of headquarters: Pittsburgh, Pennsylvania
Reporting marks: PLE
Historical and technical society: New York Central System Historical Society, P. O. Box 81184, Cleveland, OH 44181-0184
Recommended reading:
Pittsburgh and Lake Erie R. R., by Harold H. McLean, published in 1980 by Golden West Books, P. O. Box 8136, San Marino, CA 91108 (ISBN 0-87095-080-0)
"The Little Giant, Free Again," by Lee A. Gregory, in *Trains* Magazine, July 1981, pages 36–47
Subsidiaries and affiliated railroads, 1992:
Lake Erie & Eastern
Pittsburgh, Chartiers & Youghiogheny
Youngstown & Southern
Portions still operated: CSX: Brownsville–McKeesport–Pittsburgh–New Castle–Youngstown

Pittsburgh & Shawmut Railroad

In 1903 the Brookville & Mahoning Railroad was incorporated by Edward Searles, who in 1882 had married the widow of Mark Hopkins (one of the four men who built the Central Pacific) and in 1891 had inherited her fortune. The first portion of the line was built south from Brookville, Pennsylvania, to Knoxdale, 9 miles; soon the railroad also had a line from Brookville east to Brockway. From 1908 to

	1929	1994
Miles of railroad operated:	103	96
Number of locomotives:	24	11
Number of passenger cars:	8	
Number of freight cars:	1,591	675
Number of company service cars:		25

Location of headquarters: Kittanning, Pennsylvania

Reporting marks: PS

Subsidiaries and affiliated railroads, 1994:
Mountain Laurel Railroad
Red Bank Railroad

Portions still operated: Buffalo & Pittsburgh: Driftwood–Brookville–Freeport, Pa.; Brookville–Sligo; Norman–Conifer

Three SW9s team up to bring hopper cars out of the coal-cleaning plant at Ringgold, Pennsylvania. Photo by Richard J. Cook.

1916 the railroad was leased and operated by the Pittsburg, Shawmut & Northern. In 1910 the Brookville & Mahoning changed its name to Pittsburg & Shawmut; "Shawmut" is said to be a reference to a Boston bank that had an interest in the railroad.

The railroad prospered on coal traffic, some of which came from mines of the Allegheny River Mining Co., owned by the railroad. The Shawmut dieselized in 1953 with nine SW9s. To celebrate the nation's bicentennial in 1976 these were repainted, renumbered, and given patriotic names or names of men famous in the gun industry.

Control of the railroad passed from Searles to his secretary, Arthur T. Walker, then to

Walker's estate, then to the Dumaine family, which has long been connected with New England railroading.

In 1990 the Red Bank Railroad was established to operate 10 miles of a former Pennsylvania Railroad branch from Lawsonham to Sligo, Pa. In 1991 another affiliate, the Mountain Laurel Railroad, was formed to operate Pennsy's former Allegheny Valley line from Driftwood through Brookville to Lawsonham, and a former New York Central branch from Brookville to Gretchen (later cut back to Reidsburg; no longer on the map).

The Pittsburg & Shawmut was acquired by Genesee & Wyoming Industries' Buffalo & Pittsburgh Railroad on April 27, 1996.

Pittsburgh & West Virginia Railway

In 1881 Jay Gould acquired control of the barely begun Wheeling & Lake Erie Rail Road. The Wheeling was to be a Toledo, Ohio–Wheeling, West Virginia, link in a chain of railroads to connect the Wabash with the Central of New Jersey—and more than that, a link in the transcontinental system Gould sought to assemble. In the mid-1880s Gould lost much of his railroad empire, but he was able to pass the Missouri Pacific and the Wabash on to his son George.

George Gould saw that the Wheeling & Lake Erie put him within 60 miles of the industries of Pittsburgh. Spurred by a traffic agreement with Andrew Carnegie, who was feuding with the Pennsylvania Railroad, Gould built a railroad into Pittsburgh from the west to form an eastern extension of the Wheeling & Lake Erie and the Wabash. The easy locations for railroads had already been taken, so the new line was built from hilltop to hilltop and finally through Mount Washington in a tunnel, across the Monongahela on an immense cantilever bridge, and into an elaborate passenger terminal in downtown Pittsburgh. It was an expensive railroad.

It was completed in 1904 and the three companies that had built the lines were consolidated as the Wabash Pittsburgh Terminal Railway, though it and the West Side Belt (a coal-hauling line around the southern part of Pittsburgh)

To power its transformation from a coal-and-terminal road to bridge carrier, Pittsburgh & West Virginia bought seven Belpaire-boilered 2-6-6-4s, One is shown here leading a freight across the Monongahela River bridge at Belle Vernon, Pennsylvania. Photo by Ralph E. Hallock.

were operated as an integral part of the W&LE.

By 1904 George Gould had acquired control of the Western Maryland and was trying, as his father had tried, to assemble a transcontinental railroad system. WM planned an extension from Cumberland, Maryland, northwest to Connellsville,

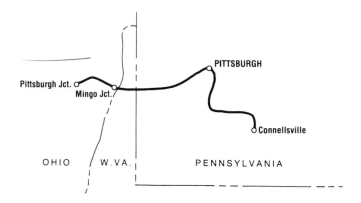

	1929	1963
Miles of railroad operated:	89	132
Number of locomotives:	30	25
Number of passenger cars:	5	
Number of freight cars:	5,589	1,334
Number of company service cars:	55	161

Location of headquarters: Pittsburgh, Pennsylvania

Reporting marks: P&WV

Recommended reading: *Pittsburgh & West Virginia: The Story of the High and Dry*, by Howard V. Worley, Jr., and William N. Poellot, Jr., published in 1989 by Withers Publishing, R. D. 4, Box 170H, Halifax, PA 17032 (ISBN 0-9618503-5-3)

Successors:
Norfolk & Western
Norfolk Southern
Wheeling & Lake Erie (1990)

Portions still operated: Wheeling & Lake Erie: All of the P&WV except for the 6-mile Donora branch and the line into downtown Pittsburgh

Pennsylvania, and WPT projected a 40-mile extension southeast to Connellsville.

The Panic of 1907, the cost of building the WPT, and an accord between Andrew Carnegie and the Pennsylvania put an end to Gould's plans. Both WPT and the Wheeling & Lake Erie entered receivership in 1909.

The Pittsburgh & West Virginia Railway was incorporated as successor under foreclosure to the Wabash Pittsburgh Terminal Railway. In the 1920s Frank Taplin, president of the P&WV, made overtures to control the Wheeling & Lake Erie and the Western Maryland, but the ICC disapproved. In 1931 Taplin completed the extension to Connellsville, where the Western Maryland had been waiting since 1912. About that time, control of the P&WV was acquired by the Pennroad Corporation, a holding company that shared many officers with the Pennsylvania Railroad.

During the last 1930s the P&WV developed into a bridge railroad, part of the "alphabet route" between the Midwest and the East (Nickel Plate, Wheeling & Lake Erie, P&WV, Western Maryland, and Reading). P&WV pulled out of downtown Pittsburgh after its freight house burned in 1946—the fire may well have sparked the redevelopment of downtown Pittsburgh. In 1949 the road tore down its nine-story office building (the passenger terminal in it had lain idle since 1931), dismantled its downtown Monongahela River bridge, and sealed the Mount Washington tunnel.

The Pittsburgh & West Virginia was a natural eastern extension of the Wheeling & Lake Erie (later Nickel Plate), providing access to the industries of Pittsburgh, as George Gould had intended years before. When Norfolk & Western merged the Nickel Plate in 1964 it leased the Pittsburgh & West Virginia.

In 1990 Norfolk Southern sold most of the former Wheeling & Lake Erie to form a new Wheeling & Lake Erie Railway. Included in the deal was the lease of the Pittsburgh & West Virginia.

Pittsburgh, Shawmut & Northern Railroad

The Pittsburg, Shawmut & Northern was incorporated in 1899 to consolidate five small railroads, some standard gauge and some narrow, in southwestern New York and northwestern Pennsylvania. The road's immediate task was to join the five

	1929	1945
Miles of railroad operated:	198	190
Number of locomotives:	33	16
Number of passenger cars:	18	
Number of freight cars:	416	220
Number of company service cars:	34	40

Location of headquarters: St. Mary's, Pennsylvania

Reporting marks: PS&N

Historical and technical society: Pittsburg, Shawmut & Northern Railroad Historical Society, RD 1, Box 361, Alfred Station, NY 14803

Recommended reading: *Pittsburg, Shawmut & Northern,* by Paul Pietrak, published in 1969 by Paul Pietrak, North Boston, NY 14110

Pittsburg, Shawmut & Northern 2-8-0 No. 71 leads a southbound freight train between West Eldred and Corryville, Pennsylvania, in February 1947, just before the road was abandoned. Photo by H. D. Runey.

separate parts with new construction and standard-gauge the narrow ones to form a route from Wayland and Hornell, N. Y., to Hyde, Pa., north of Brockway in the Shawmut area (a tract of coal land which had been named by a group of Boston industrialists).

The PS&N then organized the Brookville & Mahoning (which later became the Pittsburg & Shawmut Railroad) to extend the line southwest toward Pittsburgh (at the time, spelled without the "h"). P&S was leased to and operated by the PS&N until 1916, when it gained independence.

No sooner had the PS&N assembled its railroad than it found it could not pay the interest on the money borrowed to finance construction. It entered receivership in 1905. Even though the road earned a modest income in most years, it could not begin to repay its accrued debt, nor could it formulate an acceptable reorganization plan. The PS&N served no major industrial centers; the few towns of any appreciable size that it reached were well served by other roads. Coal and lumber formed the Shawmut's principal traffic, and both gradually disappeared as the mountains were logged off end the mines played out. In the mid-1940s the courts and the management decided that 40 years of receivership was enough, and the road was abandoned in its entirety in 1947.

Only PS&N's herald survives: In 1978 one-time affiliate Pittsburg & Shawmut began using the diamond-shaped "Shawmut Line" emblem in its advertising.

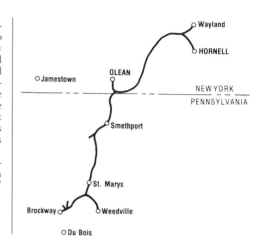

Pullman Company

George M. Pullman did not invent the sleeping car—what he did was develop the construction and operation of sleeping cars into a nationwide institution.

Sleeping cars existed before 1850, but most railroad routes were not long enough to require an overnight journey. But as railroads and railroad trips grew longer, the need developed for cars that combined day and night accommodations. Inventors strove to find ways to change seats into beds and vice versa. During that same period there was a shift in the way the cars were operated. Originally the railroads had operated the sleeping cars; gradually entrepreneurs—often the inventors or builders of the cars—took over their operation, essentially sparing the railroad the problems of running a hotel. Among the better-known sleeping car builders and operators are Theodore and Jonah Woodruff, William D'Alton Mann, and Webster Wagner.

In 1859 George M. Pullman, a cabinetmaker from Brocton, New York, and Benjamin Field remodeled two day coaches into sleeping cars for the Chicago, Alton & St. Louis. In 1863 Pullman decided to go into the sleeping car business

A long train of heavyweight Pullmans — "battleships" — departs Milwaukee on the Chicago & North Western in the summer of 1950. The rear car, Lake James, has 10 sections, 2 compartments, and 1 drawing room. Kalmbach Publishing Co. photo by Bill Wight.

for himself and built a car named *Pioneer* that was larger and more luxurious than most cars of the era. Much legend and myth clings to *Pioneer*; it is fairly certain, though, that the car was part of the train that carried Abraham Lincoln's body home to Springfield, Illinois.

The Pullman Palace Car Company was chartered in 1867 and began its operations with 48 cars. The company grew as it acquired the cars and lines of other operators. The arrangement with the railroads was usually that Pullman pro-vided the cars, fully furnished and staffed, and the railroads hauled them and provided heat and light. The railroad received the regular coach fare for each passenger, and Pullman received a supplement fare plus a charge for berth or seat occupancy. Some railroads owned the cars, either solely or jointly with Pullman.

When George H. Pullman died in 1897 the company had an almost complete monopoly on the operation of sleeping and parlor cars in the U. S. It owned the largest railroad car plant in the world and had, incidentally, an enormous cash surplus.

Robert Todd Lincoln, son of President Abraham Lincoln, succeeded George M. Pullman as head of the company. The company changed its name to Pullman Company. It soon began building steel cars, spurred in part by the prohibition of wood cars in New York's two subterranean terminals. It expanded into the manufacture of freight cars by acquiring other builders, among them Haskell & Barker and Standard Steel Car Company.

Pullman was known for standardization, both in its rolling stock and in its service. Although its car fleet comprised more than a hundred different floor plans, half the cars were of the 12-section-1-drawing-room configuration, and the various floor plans were combinations of a few standard accommodations. Even more standardized was the level of service on board. Everything the black porter and the Filipino lounge attendant did was governed by books of instructions, from the position of the pillows and the folding of the towels to the proper way to serve beer in the lounge car.

Pullman operated sleeping cars in Mexico just as it did in the U. S., but for the most part, the Canadian roads operated their own sleeping car services. Pullman's operations in Canada were limited to international routes and to routes that predated Grand Trunk's absorption into Canadian National Railways.

At the height of the Roaring Twenties about 100,000 passengers slept in Pullman beds each night, but the Depression soon wrote losses in Pullman's ledgers. Grudgingly, Pullman yielded to pressure for streamlined cars and private-room accommodation, but it balked at operating sleeping cars built by the Budd Company.

In 1940 the U. S. Department of Justice filed a complaint against Pullman's monopoly of the sleeping car business. It was a monopoly the railroads tolerated because Pullman's enormous pool of cars could move around the country to handle traffic peaks: to Florida in the winter, to Maine in the summer, to Chicago for a Shriners' convention, to Washington for a presidential inauguration. In 1944 a ruling stated that Pullman must separate its carbuilding and its operating divisions. Separation came in 1947. Pullman became Pullman, Inc., a builder of railroad cars, and sold the sleeping-car operation, the Pullman Company, to the 57 railroads over which its cars ran.

There was still a market for long-distance travel, and business held up for a decade. Then one by one railroads pulled out of the Pullman operation. In 1957 the Pennsylvania Railroad began operating its own parlor cars, and in 1958 New York Central began to operate its own sleeping cars.

A more devastating development in 1958 was the beginning of commercial jet flight, which took away the Pullman passenger just as the interstate highway system had taken away the coach passenger.

First-class passenger business collapsed, and the Pullman Company ceased operation of sleeping cars in the U. S. on December 31, 1968. The railroads took over operation of the few remaining sleeping car lines. Pullman continued to maintain and service the cars until August 1, 1969. Pullman service in Mexico ended about the same time.

Pullman accommodations

The basic Pullman space was the section, which consisted of two facing seats during the day. At night, the lower berth was formed by pulling the two seat cushions toward each other; the backs of the seats dropped down to a horizontal position. The upper berth was swung down from its stowed position against the upper wall of the car. During the day it provided storage space for the lower berth mattress, pillows, blankets, and curtains.

Heavy curtains hung between the berths and the aisle; the passenger buttoned them together after he was in his berth, and that was the extent of privacy. Attached to the inside of the curtains were two coat hangers for each berth, and a net hammock slung lengthwise could hold anything that wouldn't slip through the mesh. The only space for luggage was under the seat (which explains the piece of luggage known as a Pullman case). Toilets and washrooms were at either end of the car. Amtrak's Superliner economy room is much like a Pullman section in its basic principles.

Most sleeping cars had one or more private rooms in addition to the sections. These rooms were wider, forcing the aisle to the side of the car. A compartment had a standard section plus a basin and a toilet. A drawing room had a standard section plus a lengthwise couch along the corridor wall, with toilet and basin in a separate room. The term "bedroom" was originally applied to a room with a bed crosswise of the car, with or without an upper berth above it. The roomette, which first appeared in 1937, was a single-occupancy room that had a bed stowed in the wall behind the seat, plus a toilet and a basin. At night the bed was swung down, filling the room.

Some Pullman cars were part sleeper, part lounge, usually with a buffet or kitchenette for the service of beverages and meals. The terms "lounge car" and "club car" both meant lounge, but the lounge did not necessarily have an accompanying buffet. Nowadays "club car" means daytime first-class accommodation, what used to be called parlor car. Parlor cars were daytime Pullmans that had two rows of big revolving armchairs and often a private stateroom or drawing room.

	1929	1968
Number of passenger cars: (leased)	9,860	765
Number of cars in Mexican service:		387
Location of headquarters: Chicago, Illinois		

Recommended reading:

More Classic Trains, by Arthur D. Dubin, published in 1974 by Kalmbach Publishing Co., 1027 North Seventh Street, Milwaukee, WI 53233

The American Railroad Passenger Car, by John H. White Jr., published in 1978 by Johns Hopkins University Press, Baltimore, MD 21218 (ISBN 0-8018-1965-2)

Quanah, Acme & Pacific Railway

The Acme, Red River & Northern was incorporated May 3, 1902, to build between Acme (five miles west of Quanah, Texas, the southwesternmost end of the Frisco) and Floydada, Texas. The railroad was renamed the Quanah, Acme & Pacific on January 28, 1909. QA&P projected a line west to El Paso, about 500 miles, and, although never built, the extension appeared on route maps as late as 1944.

The Saint Louis-San Francisco guaranteed some QA&P bonds in 1911 and eventually acquired full control of the road. By the early 1960s the QA&P had no rolling stock of its own and relied on parent Frisco for its equipment, although three of Frisco's GP7s bore QA&P lettering when they were delivered.

The QA&P was a bridge line between the Frisco at Quanah (named for the last chief of the Comanches) and the Santa Fe at Floydada for traffic moving to and from the West Coast. In 1973 most of the transcontinental traffic moving over the QA&P was diverted through a direct Frisco-Santa Fe interchange at Avard, Oklahoma. The QA&P was merged with Burlington Northern on June 8, 1981. Merger of the Frisco with Burlington Northern rendered the Quanah Route redundant, and the western half of the line was abandoned in 1982.

Three Frisco GP7s lead a Quanah, Acme & Pacific freight across the open country of the Texas panhandle. Photo by Donald Sims.

	1929	1980
Miles of railroad operated:	126	119
Number of locomotives:	7	
Number of freight cars:	47	
Number of company service cars:	27	
Location of headquarters: Quanah, Texas		
Reporting marks: QAP		
Historical and technical society:		
Frisco Modelers Information Group, 1212 Finnean's Run, Arnold, MD 21012-1876;		

http://www.frisco.org/fmig/fmig.htm
Frisco Railroad Museum, 543 E. Commercial Street, Springfield, MO 65803-2945;
http://www.frisco.org/frisco/frisco.html
Successors:
St. Louis-San Francisco
Burlington Northern
Burlington Northern & Santa Fe
Portions still operated: Burlington Northern & Santa Fe: Acme–Paducah, Texas
Map: See page 374

Railway Express Agency

Express service is the prompt and safe movement of parcels, money, and goods at rates higher than standard freight rates. It is generally considered to have been started by William Harnden, who in 1839 began regular trips between New York and Boston carrying such items. Other early names in the express business are Henry Wells, a leather worker at Batavia, N. Y., and William G. Fargo, a New York Central freight clerk at Auburn, N. Y., who organized Wells Fargo & Co. in 1853; Henry B. Plant, who

formed Southern Express; Alvin Adams; and John Butterfield.

The express business flourished in the latter half of the nineteenth century, and by 1900 there were four principal express companies: Adams, Southern, American, and Wells Fargo. In 1913 the Post Office introduced parcel post, the first major competition for the express companies. Even so, express business continued to increase until 1920, then remained stable for a decade.

Under the USRA the four major U. S. express companies were consolidated as American Railway Express, Inc., except for the portion of

Southern Express that operated over the Southern Railway and the Mobile & Ohio (and that came into the organization in 1938). In March 1929, upon expiration of the initial contracts, the assets and operations of American Railway Express were transferred to Railway Express Agency, which was owned by 86 railroads in proportion to the express traffic on their lines—no one railroad or group of railroads had control of the agency.

REA's arrangement with the railroads was that they provided terminal space and cars and moved the cars at their expense; REA paid its

own expenses and divided the profit among the railroads in proportion to the traffic. Express service in Canada and Mexico was operated directly by the railroad companies.

Express revenues remained at profitable levels into the 1950s, albeit partly because of rate increases—express volume dropped substantially after World War II. The railroads began to view express service as expensive business. REA negotiated a new contract in 1959 that allowed it to use any mode of transportation, and it acquired truck rights to allow continued service after passenger trains were discontinued. It tried piggyback and containers, but without much success.

In 1969, after several years of deficits, REA was sold to five of its officers and renamed REA Express. By then only ten percent of its business moved by rail, and its entire business constituted less than one percent of all intercity parcel traffic. The company sued the railroads and United Parcel Service for various reasons and became involved in suits and counter-suits with the clerks' union. The Civil Aeronautics Board terminated REA's exclusive agreement with the airlines for air express. REA Express terminated operations in November 1975 and began liquidation—which was complicated by the trials of its officers for fraud and embezzlement.

Boxes of merchandise are unloaded from a Railway Express Agency refrigerator car (a converted troop sleeper, and it is being used in non-refrigerated service) at Goldsboro, North Carolina, in July 1966. Photo by Paul Maximuke.

Railway Mail Service

The date mail first moved on trains in the U. S. is disputed, but in 1832 the first official route was authorized by the Postmaster General over the Camden & Amboy Railroad. In 1837 the Post Office Department appointed route agents to accompany mail shipments. In 1838 Congress declared all railroads to be post roads and that same year mail cars in which mail was sorted en route began running between Washington and Philadelphia.

What is generally acknowledged as the first Railway Post Office was established July 7, 1862, on the Hannibal & St. Joseph Railroad to expedite mail handling in connection with the Pony Express. George B. Armstrong of the Post Office Department undertook a reform of the mail service. Part of that reform was the establishment of traveling post offices, to be called United States Railway Post Offices.

The first official RPO was inaugurated between Chicago and Clinton, Iowa, over the Chicago & North Western on August 28, 1864. In July 1869 the Post Office Department established the Railway Mail Service with Armstrong as its first general superintendent. Among Armstrong's early innovations were standard mail cranes and catcher arms and overnight mail trains. Armstrong was followed after three years by George S. Bangs, who is credited with the establishment of fast long-distance mail trains.

Pickup and delivery of mail at speed was a feature of Railway Post Office operation. Here New York Central train 406, the Chicago–Cincinnati *Carolina Special,* picks up a sack of mail from the crane at Sheldon, Indiana, at better than 70 miles per hour in May 1949. Photo by A. C. Kalmbach.

The Congressional declaration that all railroads were post roads or mail routes meant that Railway Post Office cars soon were found everywhere rails went. Most passenger trains carried

Four clerks sort mail aboard Milwaukee Road train 15 between St. Paul, Minnesota, and Aberdeen, South Dakota, in 1968. Photo by Don L. Hofsommer.

mail—and until the 1920s there was no other practical way for mail to move.

In the 1930s trucks began to replace trains for short-distance transportation of mail, and Highway Post Offices—buses or trucks outfitted for sorting mail—were introduced to replace branchline RPOs. The Railway Mail Service oversaw the introduction of air mail and made a few experiments with mail-sorting in flight and even with pickup and delivery literally on the fly.

In 1949 the Railway Mail Service was replaced by the Postal Transportation Service. The change of name forecast changes in service. First-class mail began to move by air, first as space was available, then regularly. The Post Office discontinued RPO runs because passenger trains were being discontinued, and the railroads dropped passenger trains because mail contracts were not being renewed.

In 1963 the introduction of Zip Code and Sectional Center Facilities—in many ways a return to the mail distribution and sorting system in use in the early 1800s—meant the eventual end of sorting in transit. The last RPO route in the U. S., between New York and Washington, made its last run on the night of June 30, 1977. Much mail still moves by rail, but for the most part in containers and trailers on flat cars.

Canada's Railway Mail Service was similar to that of the U. S.; generally speaking, RPO operation in Canada was discontinued before that in the U. S. Mexico's railroads also carried and sorted the mails. The Spanish term for "Railway Post Office" is *Oficina Postal Ambulante,* though the cars were lettered simply *Correo.*

Reading Company

The Philadelphia & Reading Railroad was chartered in 1833 and opened in 1842 from Philadelphia along the Schuylkill River through Reading to Pottsville, Pennsylvania. The purpose of the railroad was to carry anthracite to Philadelphia.

The Philadelphia & Reading grew by acquiring other roads. It assisted construction of the Lebanon Valley Railroad from Reading to Harrisburg; in 1858 the Lebanon Valley was merged into the Philadelphia & Reading. By 1869 the P&R had acquired the East Pennsylvania Railroad between Reading and Allentown. In 1870 the P&R leased the Philadelphia, Germantown & Norristown Railroad, which had been built between 1831 and 1835 from Philadelphia to Germantown and along the east bank of the Schuylkill to Norristown.

In 1869 Franklin B. Gowen became president of the P&R and began buying coal lands for the railroad. The Philadelphia & Reading Coal & Iron Co. acquired about 30 percent of the anthracite land in Pennsylvania, but the cost of the land put the railroad into receivership in 1880. During Gowen's administration the P&R acquired the North Pennsylvania Railroad, which ran from Philadelphia to Bethlehem and Yardley, and built the Delaware & Bound Brook from Yardley to a connection with the Central Railroad

Reading 3012, a 2-10-2, leads a train of anthracite along the bank of the Schuylkill River at Tamaqua, Pa., in July 1953. Reading's K-1-sb Santa Fes, built by Baldwin in 1931, were the world's largest 2-10-2s.

of New Jersey at Bound Brook, N. J. Between 1880 and 1890 the P&R reached out to Shippensburg, Pa., with a line that would eventually carry much of the road's bridge traffic, and extended a line from Bound Brook to a new port, Port Reading, on the New Jersey shore of Arthur Kill (the body of water that separates Staten Island from the mainland).

McLeod's brief empire

Archibald A. McLeod became president of the P&R in 1890. The P&R leased the Central Railroad of New Jersey (P&R had previously leased the CNJ between 1883 and 1887) and the Lehigh

Valley; the three railroads transported more than half of the country's mined coal at the time. To get a better grip on the New England coal market, the P&R acquired control of the Poughkeepsie Bridge route, the Boston & Maine, and the New York & New England. The P&R was reaching out for the Old Colony when it collapsed once again into receivership.

Lines in New Jersey

The Philadelphia & Reading expanded into New Jersey in 1883 by purchasing the Atlantic City Railroad, a narrow gauge line from Camden to Atlantic City, N. J. P&R standard-gauged and

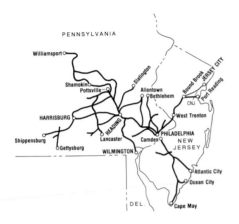

Silverliner multiple unit cars, built by Budd in 1963, approach the huge arched trainshed of Reading Terminal in Philadelphia while a train of Reading's original M.U. cars, built in 1931, awaits departure. Photo by William D. Middleton.

double-tracked the line—Philadelphia–Atlantic City passenger traffic was growing—and extended it to Cape May.

By the 1930s traffic to the New Jersey seashore was declining on the Atlantic City Railroad and also on Pennsylvania Railroad's West Jersey & Seashore, which duplicated the Atlantic City Railroad at almost every point. In 1932 the Reading and the Pennsy agreed to consolidate operations. Pennsy bought two-thirds of Reading's Atlantic City stock and assigned its lease of the West Jersey & Seashore to the Atlantic City, which was renamed Pennsylvania-Reading Seashore Lines. The consolidation took effect June 25, 1933.

The Reading Company

In the reorganization of 1896 the railroad and the coal company both became properties of the Reading Company, a holding company. In 1898 the Reading leased the Wilmington & Northern Railroad, a line from Reading to Wilmington, Delaware, and in 1901 the Reading acquired control of the Central of New Jersey. At that same time the Baltimore & Ohio Railroad purchased a controlling interest in the Reading.

At the end of 1923 the Reading Company merged several of its wholly owned subsidiary railroads (the Philadelphia & Reading chief among them) and became an operating company. Between 1929 and 1933, Reading electrified its Philadelphia suburban service.

Beginning in 1945 the Reading underwent a series of corporate simplifications, merging controlled and leased lines. In 1963 Reading acquired the Lehigh & Susquehanna Railroad from Lehigh Coal & Navigation—Central of New Jersey's lines in Pennsylvania—and in 1968 Reading acquired the Cornwall Railroad, a 12-mile line from Lebanon to Mount Hope, Pa., from Bethlehem Steel.

As the use of coal for domestic heating dwindled, the Reading supplemented its coal traffic with bridge traffic between the Western Maryland at Shippensburg and connections at Allentown for New York and New England. Reading became part of the "alphabet route" between the

Midwest and the East Coast: NKP, W&LE, P&WV, WM, RDG, L&HR. The bridge traffic, though, could not compensate for the fact that the Reading's freight business looked more like that of a switching and terminal railroad than a long-haul, line-haul carrier.

In 1971 Reading's passenger trains were deemed commuter trains and therefore were not taken over by Amtrak. Philadelphia–Reading–Pottsville and Philadelphia–Bethlehem service continued to operate for another 10 years. Philadelphia–New York service, once part of the Royal Blue Route operated in partnership with Baltimore & Ohio and Central of New Jersey, was down to a single Newark–West Trenton train when service ceased in November 1982.

The Reading entered bankruptcy proceedings on November 23, 1971; its operations were taken over by Conrail on April 1, 1976. Southeastern Pennsylvania Transportation Authority subsequently took over operation of Reading's extensive Philadelphia-area commuter service.

	1929	1975
Miles of railroad operated:	1,460	1,149
Number of locomotives:	988	225
Number of passenger cars:	910	176
Number of freight cars:	43,298	12,213
Number of company service cars:	823	168

Location of headquarters: Philadelphia, Pennsylvania

Reporting marks: RDG

Notable named passenger trains: *Crusader, Wall Street* (Philadelphia–Jersey City)

Historical and technical societies:
Anthracite Railroads Historical Society, P. O. Box 519, Lansdale, PA 19446-0519; http://www.rrhistorical.com/arhs
Reading Company Technical & Historical Society, P. O. Box 15143, Reading, PA 19612-5143; http://www.vicon.net/~reading

Recommended reading: *The Reading Railroad: History of a Coal Age Empire,* by James L. Holton, published in 1989 by Garrigues House, P. O. Box 400, Laury's Station,

PA 18059 (ISBN 0-9620844-1-7)

Subsidiaries and affiliated railroads, 1975:
Ironton (50%, jointly with Lehigh Valley)
Central Railroad of New Jersey (49%)
Pennsylvania-Reading Seashore Lines (33%)
Wilmington & Northern

Successors:
Conrail
Southeastern Pennsylvania Transportation Authority

Portions still operated:
Brandywine Valley: Coatesville–Modena, Pa.
Conrail: Philadelphia–Bound Brook–Port Reading, N. J.; Philadelphia–Bethlehem, Pa.; Philadelphia–Reading, Pa.; Winfield–Williamsport–Newberry Jct., Pa.; Norristown–Doylestown, Pa.; Pottsville–St. Clair, Pa.; Schuylkill Haven–Good Spring, Pa.; Allentown–Reading–Harrisburg–Shippensburg, Pa.; Alburtis–Seiple, Pa.; Sinking Spring–Akron, Pa.; Lititz–Columbia, Pa., Lancaster Jct. –Lancaster, Pa.; Lebanon–Cornwall, Pa.

Delaware Valley: Modena, Pa.–Wilmington, Del.
East Penn: Pottstown–Boyertown; Topton–Kutztown; Emmaus–Pennsburg, Pa.
Gettysburg: Gettysburg–Mount Holly Springs, Pa.
Lancaster Northern: Sinking Spring–Ephrata, Pa.
Landisville: Landisville–Silver Springs, Pa.
Middletown & Hummelstown: Middletown–Hummelstown, Pa.
New Hope & Ivyland: New Hope–Warminster, Pa.
Reading, Blue Mountain & Northern: Reading–Port Clinton–Pottsville; Port Clinton–Good Springs; Port Clinton–Locust Summit, Pa.
Shamokin Valley: Sunbury–Locust Summit, Pa.
Southeastern Pennsylvania Transportation Authority: Philadelphia to West Trenton, N. J., and Chestnut Hill, Doylestown, Newtown, Norristown, and Warminster, Pa.
Union County: Milton–New Columbia; West Milton–Lewisburg–Winfield, Pa.

Richmond, Fredericksburg & Potomac Railroad

RF&P The Richmond, Fredericksburg & Potomac was a strategic link in the chain of railroads along the east coast. The Atlantic Coast Line and the Seaboard Air Line both terminated in Richmond, the Baltimore & Ohio reached as far south as Washington, and the Pennsylvania reached just beyond Washington to Alexandria, Virginia. RF&P tied them together and also carried the Southern Railway's trains the last few miles from Alexandria to Washington—Chesapeake & Ohio trains, too, which operated on Southern rails. It was a double-track main line without any branches. It did little local business, and through passenger and freight trains ran at pretty much the same speed up and down the line.

The RF&P was chartered in 1834 to build northward from Richmond, Virginia, to a point on the Potomac River to connect with steamboats to Washington, D. C. The rail route from Richmond to Washington was opened in 1872 with the completion of the Alexandria & Fredericksburg, a subsidiary of the Pennsylvania Railroad, south to a connection with the RF&P at Quantico. The northernmost portion of the route was the Alexandria & Washington, also a Pennsylvania subsidiary.

In 1890 the two Pennsy properties were consolidated as the Washington Southern, and in 1901 the Richmond-Washington Company was

A freight train from the south rolls into Alexandria, Virginia, almost at its destination, Potomac Yard, on December 29, 1949. The three-unit F7 (blue and gray, trimmed in gold) is nearly brand new. The train is on the northbound freight track; the two tracks at the right are the passenger tracks through the Alexandria station. Photo by Charles Wales.

	1929	1990
Miles of railroad operated:	118	113
Number of locomotives:	101	31
Number of passenger cars:	117	41*
Number of freight cars:	1,319	1,876

Number of company service cars: 141

Reporting marks: RFP

Location of headquarters: Richmond, Virginia

Notable named passenger trains: RF&P had no notable trains of its own, but it participated in operating the New York–Florida trains of the Atlantic Coast Line and the Seaboard Air Line.

Recommended reading: *One Hundred Fifty Years of History Along the Richmond, Fredericksburg & Potomac Railroad,* by William E. Griffin, published in 1983 by the Richmond, Fredericksburg & Potomac Railroad (LCC 83-51689)

Successor: CSX Transportation

Portions still operated: CSX: Washington–Richmond

*(1970)

formed to operate the WS and the RF&P as a single railroad. In 1920 the RF&P absorbed the Washington Southern.

The Richmond-Washington Company owned about three-fourths of RF&P's common stock; the remainder of RF&P's common stock was owned by the Virginia Supplemental Retirement System and the public. The Richmond-Washington Company was equally owned until the 1960s by Seaboard Air Line, Atlantic Coast Line, Chesapeake & Ohio, Baltimore & Ohio, Southern, and Pennsylvania. Penn Central relinquished its ex-Pennsylvania share in 1978, and mergers among the owners brought ownership down to CSX Corporation (80 percent) and Norfolk Southern (20 percent). The RF&P became a link between two halves of CSX, the former Chessie System at Washington and the former Seaboard System at Richmond. Because CSX trains ran straight through and much of Norfolk Southern's traffic had been shifted to the Shenandoah Valley line, RF&P's enormous Potomac Yard in Alexandria was no longer necessary—and it was valuable real estate.

CSX offered merger in 1990, but the Virginia legislature rejected the offer. Later that year the Virginia Retirement System (formerly the Virginia Supplemental Retirement System) acquired a block of RF&P stock from Norfolk Southern and got together with CSX on another proposal: CSX would get the railroad and the retirement system would get CSX's shares in the RF&P and be free to develop the real estate. By the end of 1991 CSX had absorbed the RF&P's operation.

Rio Grande Southern Railroad

In 1882 the Denver & Rio Grande completed its line from Durango to Silverton, Colorado, and in 1887 it pushed a line south from Montrose to Ouray, a silver-mining center about 15 miles north of Silverton—straight-line distance, ignoring Red Mountain. Otto Mears surveyed and built a wagon road from Silverton over Red Mountain Pass. He then built the Silverton Railroad on much the same alignment as far as Albany, about 8 miles short of Ouray. To descend from Albany to Ouray the railroad would have to use stairs, not rails, or resort to extremely expensive construction to build a line that would be subject to rockslides part of the year and snowslides during the rest.

Mears knew that the ore-rich area west and northwest of Durango needed transportation, so he had a railroad surveyed from Dallas, north of Ridgway, to Durango by way of Telluride, Rico, and Dolores. The Rio Grande Southern Railroad was incorporated in 1889 and completed in 1891. The route crossed four major summits, highest of which was Lizard Head Pass (10,250 feet), and included innumerable trestles and bridges.

The road basked briefly in the prosperity that resulted from the passage of the Silver Purchase Act in 1890. Repeal of the act in 1893, however, ended the prosperity, and the Rio Grande Southern entered receivership because

Galloping Goose No. 4—more properly, Motor No. 4 of the Rio Grande Southern—rolls north past Trout Lake, between Lizard Head Pass and Ophir. Photo by Otto Perry.

of its construction debt. The Denver & Rio Grande gained control in 1893.

The RGS continued to exist as a separate entity on paper, but it was operated as a division of its parent, eking out an existence carrying ore and livestock and battling snow and slides. Even though it operated at a profit, it never earned enough to cover interest on its bonds or issue a stock dividend. In 1929 it was again placed in the care of a receiver, Victor Miller.

In 1931 RGS assembled a motor rail car from

Buick parts. It was successful enough that the road built a fleet of motor cars from Pierce-Arrow parts. These cars, which acquired the nickname "Galloping Geese," replaced the mixed trains that had previously replaced the passenger trains. They became a symbol of the Rio Grande Southern.

In 1942 the property of the RGS was purchased by the Defense Supplies Corporation—one of the road's cargoes during World War II was uranium ore from mines at Vanadium. In spite of Galloping Geese and uranium, though, the Rio Grande Southern continued to decline. Its ailments and afflictions included floods and washouts, a fire that destroyed a large lumber mill, the explosion of the boiler of its rotary snowplow, a drop in zinc prices, and loss of the mail contract. The imposition of a surcharge on every car of freight drove away business. There were no formal protests to Rio Grande Southern's abandonment petition, and the last train ran on December 27, 1951.

	1929	1951	
Miles of railroad operated:	174	172	**Location of headquarters:** Denver, Colorado
Number of locomotives:	13	5	**Historical and technical society:** Galloping Goose His-
Number of motor cars:		5	torical Society, P. O. Box 297, Dolores, CO 81323
Number of passenger cars:	5		**Recommended reading:** *Silver San Juan*, by Mallory
Number of freight cars:	9		Hope Ferrell, published in 1973 by Pruett Publishing Co.,
Number of company service cars:	33		3235 Prairie Avenue, Boulder, CO 80301 (ISBN
Number of cars:		84	0-87108-057-5) **Map:** See page 144

Rutland Railroad

The Rutland's early history is entwined with that of the Vermont Central (predecessor of the Central Vermont) and with that of New England railroads in general. Two major themes in New England railroad history are the competition between railroads to build lines to the Great Lakes, and the consolidation of the multitude of small railroads into a few major ones.

Rutland's development is easiest to understand considered route by route: the original Bellows Falls–Rutland–Burlington route diagonally across Vermont; the line south from Rutland through Bennington to Chatham, New York; and the tentacle from Burlington across the north end of Lake Champlain and the northern tier of New York to Ogdensburg, on the St. Lawrence River. Not until the turn of the century were the three routes united as one railroad.

Bellows Falls–Rutland–Burlington

The Champlain & Connecticut River Rail Road Company was incorporated November 1, 1843, to build a railroad between Bellows Falls and Burlington, Vt., as part of a route from Boston to Ogdensburg, N. Y. The enterprise was reorganized as the Rutland & Burlington Railroad in 1847, and the line was completed in December 1849. At Bellows Falls there were con- nections southeast to Boston and south down the Connecticut River, but at Burlington the railroad fought and feuded with the Vermont Central for traffic and for connections with the Vermont & Canada at nearby Essex Junction. In 1854 the Rutland & Burlington defaulted on mortgage interest payments. It was reorganized in 1867 as the Rutland Railroad.

The Vermont Central leased the Rutland on December 30, 1870, partly to acquire Rutland's leases of the Vermont Valley (from Bellows Falls south to Brattleboro, Vt.) and the Vermont & Massachusetts (Brattleboro to Millers Falls, Massachusetts), which gave Vermont Central a connection to the New London Northern and a

Rutland train 8, the milk train from Ogdensburg, inches along the trestle across the north end of Lake Champlain between Rouses Point, New York, and Alburg, Vermont. The Rutland and the Central Vermont share the bridge; gantlet track avoids the complication of switches. Photo by Philip R. Hastings.

water route from New London, Connecticut, to New York.

A more pressing reason for the lease was to forestall a move by the Rutland to construct a line around the south end of Lake Champlain, then north along the west shore of the lake to a connection west to Ogdensburg. The terms of the lease were particularly beneficial to the Rutland; the rental was better than the income the Rutland would earn operating independently.

In 1887 Delaware & Hudson gained control of the Rutland, which was still leased to the Central Vermont (the successor in 1873 to the Vermont Central). The Rutland renewed its lease to the CV in 1890. Central Vermont entered receivership in 1896 and terminated the lease of the Rutland; in 1888 D&H had sold its interest in the Rutland to Percival W. Clement, a banker in Rutland (and later governor of Vermont).

Rutland–Bennington–Chatham

The Western Vermont Railroad was char-

tered in 1845 to build south from Rutland to North Bennington, then west to a connection with the Troy & Boston at White Creek, N. Y. The railroad opened in 1853 and was leased to the T&B in 1857, forming a route, if a roundabout one, from Boston to the Hudson River in conjunction with the Rutland & Burlington, Cheshire, and Fitchburg railroads. The Western Vermont was renamed the Bennington & Rutland in 1865.

When the Hoosac Tunnel in western Massachusetts opened in 1875, the T&B gained a direct route to Boston and cast off the Bennington & Rutland. The B&R filed suit against the T&B. There ensued a small railroad war. Then the B&R merged with the Lebanon Springs, a line that meandered north from Chatham, N. Y., to form the Harlem Extension Railroad. It was essentially a northward extension of the New York & Harlem. Vermont Central leased the Harlem Extension from 1873 to 1877. The Harlem Extension emerged from the lease as two railroads, the Harlem Extension South, later the Lebanon Springs, then Chatham & Lebanon Valley, and the Bennington & Rutland. The Rutland purchased the Bennington & Rutland in 1900 and the Chatham & Lebanon Valley in 1901.

Burlington–Ogdensburg

Ogdensburg, N. Y., was at the eastern limit of Great Lakes and St. Lawrence River navigation. A railroad between Ogdensburg and Lake Champlain was discussed as early as 1830 as part of a Boston-to-Great Lakes route, but it was 1850 before the Northern Railroad (of New York) opened between Ogdensburg and Rouses Point.

It was extended east to connect with the Vermont & Canada in 1852, and the company was reorganized as the Ogdensburg Railroad in 1858 and again as the Ogdensburg & Lake Champlain in 1864. A subsidiary, the Ogdensburg Transportation Company, operated a fleet of lake boats between Ogdensburg and Chicago. The O&LC was leased to the Vermont Central in 1870. Like the Rutland, it resumed independent operation after Central Vermont entered receivership in 1896. In 1901 the Rutland purchased the road.

To connect the O&LC with its own line the Rutland chartered the Rutland & Canadian Railroad, which quickly constructed a line from Burlington to Rouses Point. The line used the islands at the north end of Lake Champlain as stepping stones; a 3-mile causeway connected the islands with the mainland north of Burlington. The line opened in 1901 and the company was consolidated with the Rutland that same year.

By 1902 the Rutland extended from Chatham, N. Y., and Bellows Falls, Vt., north through Rutland, where the two lines joined, to Burlington and then west through Rouses Point and Malone, N. Y., to Ogdensburg. It participated in Boston–Montreal and New York–Montreal passenger traffic, and in conjunction with its navigation line on the Great Lakes it offered freight service between New England and Chicago. It did a good business carrying Boston- and New York-bound milk out of Vermont.

New York Central control

Shortly after 1900 the New York Central & Hudson River and William Seward Webb, son-in-law of William H. Vanderbilt of the NYC&HR, began to buy Rutland stock. Webb became president of the Rutland in 1902, and by 1904 NYC interests owned more than half the capital stock of the Rutland. The railroad entered a period of New York Central control and prosperity.

About that same time the New York Central acquired control of the New York, Ontario & Western. The New Haven regarded New England as its own territory and was concerned about New York Central's acquisitions of the Boston & Albany and the Rutland. NYC for similar reasons was wary of NH's interest in the NYO&W. There was discussion of an exchange of subsidiaries. In 1911 the New Haven purchased half of the New York Central interest in the Rutland over the protests of Rutland's minority stockholders, who recognized that NYC control was the best thing that had happened to the road in many years.

The Panama Canal Act of 1915 amended the Interstate Commerce Act to prohibit railroad ownership of a competing interstate water carrier. The Interstate Commerce Commission ruled that Rutland's boats between Ogdensburg and Chicago competed with parent New York Central. The boats were discontinued, and their traffic, which formed a large part of Rutland's freight business, wound up on NYC trains.

Control by the United States Railroad Administration during World War I brought a

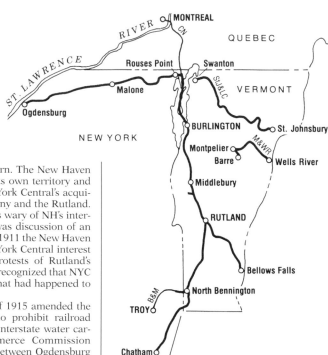

great increase of traffic to the Rutland but at a considerable cost in deferred maintenance. Passenger traffic began to trickle away to the highways, and floods in 1927 washed out much of Rutland's line. The Rutland was strong enough financially to remain solvent through much of the Great Depression, but on May 5, 1938, the Rutland entered receivership.

Economy measures, wage cuts, tax reductions, and a "Save the Rutland" Club kept the railroad going. Symbolic of the effort was a new Bellows Falls-Norwood, N. Y., freight train, *The Whippet*, for which the road streamstyled and painted a 1913-vintage 2-8-0. Many different reorganization plans were proposed and discussed, but it was more than 12 years before a new company emerged—the Rutland Railway, which came into existence on November 1, 1950.

The revived Rutland

Heading the management committee of the new company was Gardner Caverly, a major bondholder. He scrapped 25 miles of sidings and branches, and used the scrap value of Rutland's roster of steam locomotives and the worst of the freight cars as a down payment on 15 diesels. He scrapped the Bennington-Chatham line to pay for 450 new box cars, which wore yellow and green paint and a new herald, plus 70 gondolas and 27 covered hopper cars.

A short strike in the summer of 1953 had the beneficial effect of ridding the Rutland of its passenger trains, which were expensive to operate and ran almost empty. The entire physical plant

of the railroad was modernized and the labor force was thinned. In 1957 the Rutland paid a dividend on its preferred stock.

Through all of this Rutland's employees were being paid less than the national standard, and in September 1960 they walked out. William Ginsburg, Caverly's successor, had cut all the costs he could. Traffic, particularly milk, was declining, and the company had no cash reserve. An injunction brought the employees back to work 41 days after they struck, but the cooling-off period ended on September 25, 1961, and so did all service on the Rutland Railway. Neither management nor labor would compromise, and on December 4, 1961, the Rutland petitioned for abandonment. Hearings and appeals went on for more than a year, but the Rutland was dead.

The state of Vermont bought the Burlington–Bennington–White Creek and Rutland–Bellows Falls lines. The Vermont Railway began operation on the former on January 6, 1964, and the Green Mountain Railroad began freight service between Bellows Falls and Rutland in April 1965 after a season of steam passenger operation on the line by the Steamtown museum at Bellows Falls. Service resumed on the Norwood–Ogdensburg portion of the former O&LC in 1967 following its acquisition by the Ogdensburg Bridge & Port Authority.

	1929	1961
Miles of railroad operated:	413	391
Number of locomotives:	85	15
Number of passenger cars:	138	42*
Number of freight cars:	1,778	
Number of company service cars:	231	
Number of freight and company service cars:		465

Location of headquarters: Rutland, Vermont
Reporting marks: R
Historical and technical society: Rutland Railroad Historical Society, P. O. Box 6262, Rutland, VT 05701
Recommended reading: *The Rutland Road, Second Edition*, by Jim Shaughnessy, published in 1997 by Syracuse University Press, Syracuse, NY 13244-5160 (ISBN 8-8156-0456-4)
Portions still operated:
Green Mountain Railroad: Bellows Falls–Rutland
St. Lawrence & Raquette River: Norwood–Ogdensburg, N. Y.
Vermont Railway: Burlington–North Bennington
*(1953)

Sacramento Northern Railway

At one time Sacramento Northern offered the longest interurban ride in the world, 183 miles from San Francisco to Chico, California. The ride included the Bay Bridge between San Francisco and Oakland, a tunnel through the Oakland hills, a train ferry across Suisun Bay just west of the confluence of the Sacramento and San Joaquin rivers, a fast ride across California's delta country, and a long look at the agricultural Sacramento Valley. In recent years SN abandoned much of its main line, leaving odds and ends of track in the towns and cities it served, and it shared most of its officers with parent Western Pacific (or vice versa, to be more accurate). WP was acquired by Union Pacific in 1982, and by 1984 SN no longer had interchange freight cars of its own and most of its officials were in Omaha. I have used 1971 as an end date for SN because the 1972 issue of *Moody's Transportation Manual is* the last with any information on the road.

Motors 604 and 603 prepare to pull cars off the ferry Ramon at Mallard, on the south shore of Suisun Bay, in 1951. Photo by Reginald McGovern.

Northern Electric

The Northern Electric Company was incorporated in 1905 to build a railroad from Chico to Sacramento, 90 miles. Construction began at Chico, and service began between there and Oroville on April 25, 1906, a week after the San Francisco earthquake and fire. Construction then worked south from Oroville Junction through Marysville, reaching Sacramento, the state capital, in 1907. The extension to Sacramento was built with a 600-volt third rail for power distribution, except in the cities, where it used conventional trolley wire, and in 1909 Northern Electric converted the Oroville–Chico line to third rail. The line soon acquired branches to Hamilton City, Colusa, and Woodland. It proposed an extension north to Redding, and a subsidiary built an isolated line between Vacaville and Suisun as part of a proposed extension from Woodland to Vallejo.

In 1914 Northern Electric entered receivership. The Hamilton branch, which had a pontoon bridge over the Sacramento River, was abandoned in 1915 after only eight years of operation. A new company, the Sacramento Northern Railroad, took over the properties and operations in 1918, and in 1921 Western Pacific acquired control of the SN.

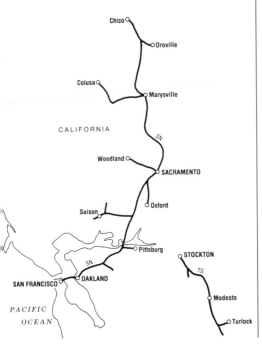

Oakland, Antioch & Eastern

The Oakland, Antioch & Eastern was successor to the Oakland & Antioch Railway, which was incorporated in 1909. By early 1913 the line was open from Bay Point (now Port Chicago) south through the San Ramon Valley towns of Concord, Walnut Creek, and Lafayette to Oakland. The engineering feat of the line was a 3,600-foot tunnel through the Oakland hills. From 40th Street and Shafter Avenue in Oakland the O&A used Key System rails to reach the Key System pier and a ferry connection to San Francisco. In September of that year the line to Sacramento was opened. Trains were ferried across Suisun Bay; the railroad obtained permission from the U. S. War Department to build a bridge, but specifications for height and clear channel put it beyond OA&E's means. From the north shore of Suisun Bay the line made a straight shot through unpopulated country to Sacramento. A branch was constructed as far east as Pittsburg; the line never reached Antioch. DA&E's cars were equipped with pantographs to draw current from Key System's 600-volt overhead wire and trolley poles for DA&E's 1,200-volt overhead.

In 1920 the OA&E was succeeded by the San Francisco-Sacramento Railroad. In 1927 the Western Pacific bought control of the San cisco-Sacramento with the idea of using its line to save 50 miles between Oakland and Sacramento. (WP's own line headed south out of Oak-land, then crossed the Coast Range and reached the Central Valley at a point well south of Stockton.) On December 31, 1928, Sacramento Northern acquired all the properties of the San Francisco-Sacramento, creating a single railroad between Oakland and Chico.

Sacramento Northern

The Sacramento Northern Railway was incorporated in 1921. In 1925 it purchased the properties of the Sacramento Northern Railroad and in 1928 it acquired the San Francisco-Sacramento. SN placed its emphasis on freight. For passengers SN offered no time advantage over Southern Pacific between San Francisco and Sacramento, and the opening of SP's bridge across the Carquinez Strait put SP well ahead. Paved highways began to siphon off SN's passengers, and the Depression put an end to any thought of acquiring additional all-steel passenger cars. Dining car and parlor car service ended in 1936 and 1938, respectively.

The Bay Bridge opened between San Francisco and Oakland for motor vehicles in 1936 and for Key System, Interurban Electric (SP), and SN trains in 1939. San Francisco–Sacramento through service lasted little more than a year before discontinuance on August 26, 1940. San Francisco–Pittsburg commuter service ran less than a year longer. Interurban service north of Sacramento ended October 31, 1940. There was almost no opposition to SN's petitions to cease passenger service. Marysville–Yuba City streetcar service was discontinued in 1942. Streetcar service in Chico ended in December 1947—it was the last Birney car and the last nickel fare in California.

Sacramento Northern's ferry *Ramon* approaches the slip at Chipps with cars bound for Sacramento. Locomotive and caboose await the boat's arrival. Photo by Reginald McGovern.

	1929	1971
Miles of railroad operated:	261	336
Number of locomotives:	24	8
Number of passenger cars:	82	
Number of freight cars:	315	229
Number of company service cars:	64	18

Location of headquarters: San Francisco, California

Reporting marks: SN

Notable named passenger trains: *Comet*, *Meteor* (San Francisco–Chico)

Recommended reading: *Sacramento Northern* (Interurbans Special 26), edited by Ira L. Swett, published in 1962 by Interurban Press, P. O. Box 6444, Glendale, CA 91205

Successors: Union Pacific

Portions still operated:
Western Railway Museum: Rio Vista Junction–Dozier–Cannon
Yolo Short Line: Sacramento–Woodland; Sacramento–Clarksburg

In 1929 SN opened a line south along the Sacramento River to Oxford, and the same year SN connected its isolated Vacaville–Suisun line, by then freight-only, with the rest of the system by building a line from Vacaville Junction east to Creed (construction of Travis Air Force Base later required a relocation of the line and a new junction at Dozier).

In December 1937 floods damaged the Feather River bridge at Oroville, severing the branch line. SN's presence in Oroville changed to that of a switching road for its parent WP. The Oroville line was dieselized in 1954 and discontinued in 1957.

SN dieselized its operation between Sacramento and Marysville in 1946. In 1951 a low trestle at Lisbon collapsed under a trainload of steel. Trains were rerouted over WP and Santa Fe between Sacramento and Pittsburg in an arrangement that became permanent when the ferry *Ramon* failed a Coast Guard inspection in 1954. When the trestle was repaired the line was de-electrified.

Floods in 1955 washed out some of SN's line near Marysville and caused a rerouting to the WP line there. The Oakland–Walnut Creek line with its tunnel through the Oakland hills was abandoned in 1957, and the remaining Pittsburg–Walnut Creek segment was dieselized. SN's last electrified operation was at Marysville; as late as April 1965 it was possible to ride underneath live catenary in the domes of WP's *California Zephyr* and watch SN motors on the adjacent track.

Gradually SN was dismembered, leaving short stubs of its lines where it intersected other railroads. Eventually its affairs were all but indistinguishable from those of Western Pacific. The absorption of WP by Union Pacific spelled the end of any separate existence for Sacramento Northern.

St. Johnsbury & Lake Champlain Railroad

The Bridge Road

In 1869 ground was broken at St. Johnsbury, Vermont, for the Vermont Division of the Portland & Ogdensburg Railroad. The destination was Lake Champlain; the railroad was to be part of a bridge route between Portland, Maine, and the Great Lakes. In 1875 the Portland & Ogdensburg Railroad building northwest from Portland met the independent Vermont Division at Lunenburg, Vt., east of St. Johnsbury on the New Hampshire state line. The line was pushed west to Swanton, Vt., almost to Lake Champlain, in 1877. Receivership followed within months.

The railroad was reorganized as the St. Johnsbury & Lake Champlain by its bondholders in 1880, and it built the last few miles to the shore of Lake Champlain at Maquam that year. In 1883, with the encouragement of the Ogdensburg & Lake Champlain, it built a short extension from Swanton to Rouses Point, New York, to connect with the O&LC, the westernmost link in the Portland-to-Ogdensburg route. In the meantime the Central Vermont took over the O&LC and refused to interchange traffic with the StJ&LC at Rouses Point, prompting abandonment of the now-useless new extension.

In 1880 Maine Central acquired the Portland & Ogdensburg and leased the portion of the StJ&LC that lay east of St. Johnsbury. Boston &

General Electric 70-tonners bring a mixed train into Cambridge Junction, Vermont, on May 30, 1955. In the distance is the road's covered bridge over the Lamoille River. Photo by Jim Shaughnessy.

Lowell obtained control of the StJ&LC in 1885; that control passed to Boston & Maine in 1895.

Independence

Boston & Maine guaranteed StJ&LC's bonds, but in 1925 when the StJ failed to earn enough to pay the interest on them, B&M turned the line over to local management—the same management that later operated the Montpelier & Wells River—in an experiment to see if local management could run the road better than B&M could from its Boston headquarters. The road struggled on into bankruptcy in 1944, and it was reorganized in 1948 as the St. Johnsbury & Lamoille County Railroad.

Boston & Maine soon sold the railroad to local interests. They in turn sold it in 1956 to the H. E. Salzberg Co.; it was sold again in 1967 to Samuel M. Pinsly, who like Salzberg was the owner of a group of short lines. Pinsly's rehabilitation of the railroad included abandonment of the western end of the railroad between Swanton and East Swanton (including the three-span covered bridge over the Missisquoi River at Swanton), purchase of a short piece of Central Vermont track from East Swanton to Fonda Junction, and replacement of two more covered bridges at Cambridge Junction and west of Wolcott with steel bridges. The Fisher Bridge east of Wolcott was preserved by adding concealed reinforcement, retaining its appearance as a covered bridge. It became the emblem of the railroad.

Pinsly had no more financial success with the road than had previous management. He petitioned for abandonment, embargoed the line, and proposed that the state of Vermont purchase it as it had the Rutland Railway. In 1973 the state purchased the railroad from Pinsly and awarded the operating contract to Bruno Loati of Morrisville, Vt. The road began operation as the Lamoille County Railroad, then reassumed its former name. Because of a dispute with the state over track rehabilitation and a strike by maintenance-of-way employees, the state announced that Vermont Northern, a subsidiary of Morrison-Knudsen, would take over in October 1976.

Vermont Northern took over, but the state was still not satisfied with the operation of the railroad and refused to provide long-term subsidy. A local group that included the line's major shippers formed the Northern Vermont Corporation, bid in on the operation, and incorporated the Lamoille Valley Railroad, which took over the railroad on January 1, 1978.

In 1980 the Lamoille Valley and the Central Vermont agreed to interchange traffic at St. Albans rather than Fonda Junction, with LVRC operating between Sheldon Junction and St. Albans on CV track and CV in turn serving the road's customers at Swanton and East Swanton. In the mid-1980s the Lamoille Valley briefly operated excursion trains. In recent years the railroad has operated only between St. Johnsbury and Morrisville.

	1929	1972	Successors:
Miles of railroad operated:	96	98	St. Johnsbury & Lamoille County
Number of locomotives:	9	10	Lamoille County
Number of passenger cars:	5		Vermont Northern
Number of freight cars:	7	47	Lamoille Valley
Number of company service cars:	9	20	**Portions still operated:** Lamoille Valley: St. Johnsbury, Morrisville
Location of headquarters: Montpelier, Vermont			**Map:** See page 366
Reporting marks: SJL			

St. Louis-San Francisco Railway

FRISCO Ground was broken on July 19, 1853, at Franklin (now Pacific), Missouri, for the South-West Branch of the Pacific Railroad (now the Missouri Pacific). The line reached Rolla, Mo., 77 miles from Franklin, in 1860, but the Civil War brought a halt to construction. In 1866 the state of Missouri took over the railroad—separation from the parent road seemed desirable—and sold it to John C. Fremont, who reorganized it as the Southwest Pacific Railroad. Fremont was unable to keep up the payments, and the road was reorganized again as the South Pacific Railroad in 1868. The line continued to inch southwest. It reached Springfield in 1870 and was consolidated with the Atlantic & Pacific that same year.

Atlantic & Pacific

The Atlantic & Pacific Railroad was chartered in 1866 to build a railroad from Springfield, Mo., to the Pacific. Its route lay roughly along the 35th parallel of latitude—west along the Canadian River to Albuquerque, then along the Little Colorado and Colorado rivers and west to the Pacific by a "practicable and eligible route," to quote the language of the act of incorporation. Among the provisions of the act were that the U. S. government would clear up the matter of Indian lands being granted to the rail-

Frisco's overnight *Meteor* from St. Louis swings through a reverse curve about 20 miles east of Oklahoma City, its destination, on October 12, 1946. Photo by Preston George.

road, the Southern Pacific Railroad would connect with it at the Colorado River, and the railroad had to be completed within 12 years to receive the land grant.

Financing was difficult to find, and the A&P entered receivership in 1875. The portion of the A&P within Missouri was sold to become the St. Louis & San Francisco Railway, and the 37-mile portion in Indian Territory (now Oklahoma) from the border to Vinita retained the Atlantic & Pacific name.

The SL&SF began expanding. Lines reached Wichita, Kansas, in 1880, Fort Smith, Arkansas, and Tulsa, Ind. Terr., in 1882, and St. Louis (to replace the use of Missouri Pacific track) in 1883. In 1887 an extension of the Fort Smith line reached Paris, Texas, and in 1888 a line was opened from Wichita to Ellsworth, Kans.

In 1879 Frisco, A&P, and Santa Fe signed an agreement under which Frisco and Santa Fe would jointly build and own the A&P west of Albuquerque. At the time Jay Gould was trying to gain control of the Frisco to head off its extension into Texas—and forestall competition with Gould's Texas & Pacific. Gould and C. P. Huntington acquired control of the Frisco in 1882. The A&P was completed in 1883 from Albuquerque to Needles, California, on the west bank of the Colorado River, where it connected with the Southern Pacific. The Santa Fe would not allow earnings from the completed portion to finance the construction of the line from Sapulpa, near Tulsa, to Albuquerque. In 1886 Congress voided A&P's land grant for the unbuilt part of the line. The Santa Fe purchased the Frisco in 1890, briefly creating the largest railroad in North America (measured in route-miles). During the Panic of 1893, though, Santa Fe entered receivership.

Reorganization

A new St. Louis & San Francisco Railroad, organized in 1896, bought the old Frisco and the Oklahoma portion of the A&P; the A&P from Albuquerque to Needles became part of Santa Fe. The new Frisco extended its main line from Tulsa to Oklahoma City in 1898, and a subsidiary, the Kansas City, Osceola & Southern, completed a Kansas City-Springfield route that same year. In 1901 Frisco put in service a line from Sapulpa, Okla., near Tulsa, to Denison, Tex., a year later the line reached Carrolton, Tex., within striking distance of Dallas and Fort

Worth. Also in 1901 Frisco leased the Kansas City, Fort Scott & Memphis, which with subsidiaries formed a route from Kansas City through Springfield, Mo., and Memphis, Tennessee, to Birmingham, Alabama.

Benjamin F. Yoakum acquired control of the Frisco right after the turn of the century. His holdings included the Rock Island, the Chicago & Eastern Illinois, and a group of railroads stretching from New Orleans through Houston to Brownsville, Tex., later known as Gulf Coast Lines. Yoakum's empire collapsed in 1913, and the Frisco was reorganized in 1916 as the St. Louis-San Francisco Railway.

The new Frisco settled down to become a regional railroad, an X-shaped system with lines from St. Louis through Oklahoma to Texas, including the Quanah, Acme & Pacific, the west

Texas tail of the system, and from Kansas City to Birmingham. In 1925 the Frisco purchased the Muscle Shoals, Birmingham & Pensacola Railway (Kimbrough, Ala.–Pensacola, Florida, successor in 1922 to the Gulf, Florida & Alabama Railway), and constructed a new line from Aberdeen, Mississippi, to Kimbrough. In 1928 Frisco purchased and absorbed the Kansas City, Fort Scott & Memphis and its subsidiaries.

The Frisco again entered receivership in 1932. In 1937 the road sold the Fort Worth & Rio Grande, a line from Fort Worth to Menard, Tex., to the Santa Fe. Revenues from increased traffic during World War II helped boost Frisco out of receivership in 1947. In 1948 SL-SF acquired control of the Alabama, Tennessee & Northern, gaining a second Gulf port, Mobile. (Merger with AT&N occurred January 1, 1971.) Frisco dropped the last of its passenger trains in 1967.

In 1956 Frisco purchased control of the Central of Georgia, but the ICC disapproved and Frisco sold its interest to the Southern Railway in 1961. In 1964 Frisco acquired control of the Northeast Oklahoma Railroad, a one-time interurban—merger of NEO occurred January 1, 1967. About the same time Frisco talked merger with Chicago Great Western, then with Santa Fe, then with Southern. In 1966 the Burlington purchased a sizable block of Frisco stock. For about a decade there was no further substantive news of a Frisco merger, but in 1977 Burlington Northern and Frisco began discussions which led to merger on November 21, 1980.

	1929	1979
Miles of railroad operated:	5,735	4,653
Number of locomotives:	880	431
Number of passenger cars:	669	
Number of freight cars:	34,009	17,392
Number of company service cars:	1,964	933

Location of headquarters: St. Louis, Missouri

Reporting marks: SLSF

Notable named passenger trains: *Texas Special* (St. Louis–San Antonio, operated south of Vinita, Okla., by the Missouri-Kansas-Texas); *Meteor* (St. Louis–Oklahoma City)

Historical and technical societies:
Frisco Modelers Information Group, 1212 Finnean's Run, Arnold, MD 21012-1876;
http://www.frisco.ord/fmig/fmig.htm
Frisco Railroad Museum, 543 E. Commercial Street, Springfield, MO 65803-2945;
http://www.frisco.ord/frisco/frisco.html

Recommended reading:
The St. Louis-San Francisco Transcontinental Railroad, by H. Craig Miner, published in 1972 by the University Press of Kansas, Lawrence, Kans. (SBN 7006-0081-7)
Frisco Power, by Joe G. Collias, published in 1984 by M M Books, P. O. Box 29318, Crestwood, MO 63126 (ISBN 0-9612366-0-4)

Subsidiaries and affiliated railroads, 1979:
Quanah, Acme & Pacific

Predecessor railroads in this book: Alabama, Tennessee & Northern

Successors:
Burlington Northern
Burlington Northern & Santa Fe

Portions still operated:
Burlington Northern & Santa Fe: St. Louis, Mo.–Quanah Tex.; Cuba–Buick, Mo.; Springfield–Kissiek Mo.; Monett, Mo.–Columbus, Kan.; Joplin, Mo.–Columbus, Kan.; Tulsa–Avard, Okla.; Sapulpa, Okla.–Denison, Tex.; Kansas City–Memphis, Tenn.–Birmingham, Ala.; St. Louis, Mo.–Turrell, Ark.; Amory, Miss.–Kimbrough, Ala.; Edward, Kans.–Afton Jct., Okla.

Arkansas & Missouri: Montett, Mo.–Fort Smith, Ark.

Delta Valley & Southern: Delpro–Elkins, Ark.

Grainbelt: Enid–Frederick, Okla.

Kansas Eastern: Beaumont–Augusta, Kan.

Kiamichi: Hope, Ark.–Lakeside, Okla.; Antler, Okla.–Paris, Texas

South Kansas & Oklahoma: Columbus–Beaumont, Kan.

St. Louis Southwestern Railway

The St. Louis Southwestern (usually called the Cotton Belt) was Southern Pacific's principal subsidiary. The reason it remained a separate railroad through more than half a century of SP control was that when the Interstate Commerce Commission approved control of Central Pacific by Southern Pacific in 1923, it imposed the condition that SP solicit freight traffic for movement via Ogden, Utah, and the Union Pacific in preference to its own route across Texas. Cotton Belt traffic offices were not governed by that agreement and could solicit traffic to move over SP and SSW rails all the way to East St. Louis.

The Cotton Belt began as the 3-foot-gauge Tyler Tap Railroad, chartered in 1871 and opened in 1877 between Tyler, Tex., and a junction with the Texas & Pacific at Big Sandy. It was rechartered as the Texas & St. Louis Railway in 1879 under the leadership of James Paramore, a St. Louis financier, who sought an economical way to transport cotton from Texas to St. Louis. The road was extended to Texarkana and a connection with the St. Louis Iron Mountain & Southern in 1880. A year later the west end of the railroad was extended to Waco.

In 1881 Jay Gould purchased the Iron Mountain (he already owned the T&P), returning the Texas & St. Louis to one-connection status, and canceled the Iron Mountain's traffic agreements

During World War II the War Production Board rejected Cotton Belt's request for freight diesels but allowed the construction of five 4-8-4s in the road's Pine Bluff shops, which had built five such machines in 1937. The last of the series, 819, is shown leaving Texarkana in 1951. The locomotive was retired to a park in Pine Bluff in 1955; it was restored and returned to operation in 1985. Photo by R. S. Plummer.

with the T&StL. The T&StL decided to fulfill its name. In 1882 it reached Birds Point, Missouri, across the Mississippi River from Cairo, Illinois. There it connected by barge with the narrow gauge St. Louis & Cairo. By 1885 a continuous line of 3-foot-gauge railroads reached from Toledo, Ohio, to Houston, Tex., with intentions of heading for Laredo and eventually Mexico City.

In 1886 the T&StL was reorganized as the St. Louis, Arkansas & Texas Railway. It converted its lines to standard gauge, built branches to Shreveport, Louisiana, and Fort Worth in 1888, and entered bankruptcy in 1889.

Jay Gould organized the St. Louis Southwestern Railway in 1891 and took over the StLA&T. Shortly thereafter the road gained access to Memphis, Tennessee, by way of trackage rights over the Iron Mountain. Cotton Belt acquired trackage rights over Missouri Pacific from Thebes, Ill., to St. Louis in exchange for letting MP operate over SSW between Illmo, Mo., and Paragould, Ark.; and joined with MP in 1905 to construct a bridge over the Mississippi between Thebes and Illmo. Passenger trains to and from Memphis were moved to Rock Island's Brinkley, Ark.–Memphis line in 1912; freight trains made the change in 1921.

After World War I overhead traffic (also called intermediate or bridge traffic—freight received from one railroad to be turned over to another) began to increase on the Cotton Belt. The Rock Island purchased a controlling interest in the road in 1925 and sold it almost immediately to Kansas City Southern. KCS proposed a regional system to include KCS, SSW, and the Missouri-Kansas-Texas, but the ICC refused approval. KCS lost interest in the Cotton Belt

about the time Southern Pacific was looking for a connection to St. Louis from its Texas lines. SP applied for control and in 1932 took over.

Cotton Belt weathered receivership between 1935 and 1947; in recent years it has been essentially a division of the SP, though its equipment is still lettered "Cotton Belt." The last diesels painted in Cotton Belt's yellow and gray were delivered in 1949; after that they wore SP colors.

Cotton Belt was never a major passenger carrier. The Dallas–Memphis *Lone Star* was discontinued in 1953, all passenger service in Texas ended in 1956, and Cotton Belt's last passenger train, a St. Louis–Pine Bluff coach-only local, made its last run November 30, 1959. As SSW's 4-8-4s had done, the passenger diesels and ten streamlined coaches moved west for service on SP lines.

In 1973 Cotton Belt purchased a half interest in the Alton & Southern, a belt line serving East St. Louis, Ill., from the Chicago & North Western. In 1980 SSW acquired the former Rock Island line from St. Louis through Kansas City to Santa Rosa, New Mexico. (The Tucumcari–Santa Rosa portion of the RI had long been leased to SP.) The reason Cotton Belt purchased the line, not SP itself, is also rooted in the 1923 treaty with the UP. (The St. Louis–Kansas City track apparently was part of a package deal; even when Cotton belt purchased it, it was in no condition for high-speed heavy freight service.) In 1982 SSW obtained another piece of the late Rock Island, the line from Brinkley, Ark., to the Mississippi River bridge west of Memphis.

Union Pacific's merger of Southern Pacific on September 12, 1996, included the Cotton Belt.

	1929	1983
Miles of railroad operated:	1,809	2,375
Number of locomotives:	248	307
Number of passenger cars:	168	
Number of freight cars:	8,458	
Number of company service cars:	898	
Number of freight and company service cars:		17,407

Location of headquarters: St. Louis, Missouri

Reporting marks: SSW

Historical and technical society: Cotton Belt Rail Historical Society, P. O. Box 2044, Pine Bluff, AR 71613-2044; http://www.seark.net/~wbeck/cb819.html

Recommended reading: *Cotton Belt Locomotives,* by Joseph A. Strapac, published in 1977 by Shade Tree Books, P. O. Box 2268, Huntington Beach, CA 92647

Subsidiaries and affiliated railroads, 1973: Alton & Southern (50%, jointly with Missouri Pacific)

Successors: Union Pacific

Portions still operated:

Kansas City Southern: Sulphur Springs–Wylie, Texas

Union Pacific: St. Louis–Texarkana–Sulphur Springs, Texas; Malden–New Madrid, Mo.; Brinkley, Ark.–Memphis, Tenn.; Stuttgart–Dewitt, Ark.; Lewisville, Ark.–Shreveport, La.; Mount Pleasant–Corsicana, Texas

San Diego & Arizona Railway

In 1907 John D. Spreckels broke ground at San Diego, California, for a railroad that would give the city a direct route east. Financial backing for the San Diego & Arizona came for Spreckels and from E. H. Harriman of the Southern Pacific. The new railroad would bring SP into San Diego and break Santa Fe's monopoly there—a reversal of the usual situation in California in those days. The route of railroad was south across the Mexican border to Tijuana, east to Tecate via the sub-

sidiary Tijuana & Tecate Railway, back into the U. S. and north through awesome Carriso Gorge, then east to a connection with SP at El Centro, the principal town in California's Imperial Valley. In spite of revolution in Mexico and a ban on construction of new railroads during World War I, the last spike was driven in 1919.

In 1932 Spreckels sold his interest to Southern Pacific, which formed the San Diego & Arizona Eastern Railway to take over operation on February 1, 1933. In 1951 the SD&AE operated its last passenger train. The slow trip east to a

connection with the secondary trains of SP's Golden State Route—and El Centro was not on the main line—was no match for Santa Fe's frequent *San Diegans* to Los Angeles and the best of Santa Fe, Union Pacific, and Southern Pacific from there.

In 1970 SP sold the Tijuana & Tecate to the Mexican government; it became an isolated part of the Sonora-Baja California Railway. (SP retained trackage rights for through traffic.) A hurricane in September 1976 damaged a 40-mile stretch of the line, and Southern Pacific

East of San Diego is a land of mountains, deserts, rocks, and little else. The hostile topography dwarfs the railroad and its train. Photo by C. D. Whittaker.

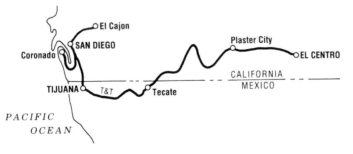

	1929	1975
Miles of railroad operated:	201	199
Number of locomotives:	16	5
Number of passenger cars:	34	
Number of freight cars:	175	3
Number of company service cars:	39	16

Location of headquarters: San Diego, California
Reporting marks: SDAE
Recommended reading: *San Diego & Arizona*, by Robert M. Hanft, published in 1984 by Trans-Anglo Books (Interurban Press), P. O. Box 6444, Glendale, CA 91205 (ISBN 0-87046-071-4)
Subsidiaries and affiliated railroads, 1969:
Tijuana & Tecate Railway
Successors:
Southern Pacific
San Diego & Arizona Eastern Transportation Co.
San Diego & Imperial Valley
Union Pacific
Metropolitan Transit Development Board
Portions still operated:
Metropolitan Transit Development Board: San Diego–San Ysidro; San Diego–El Cajon
San Diego & Imperial Valley: San Diego–Garcia, B. Cfa.; San Diego–El Cajon
San Diego Railroad Museum: Camp–Miller Creek
Union Pacific: El Centro–Plaster City, Calif.

petitioned for abandonment of all but a few miles from El Centro to Plaster City.

In 1979 San Diego's Metropolitan Transit Development Board purchased three portions of the SD&AE: from Plaster City west to the border, from San Diego south to the border at San Ysidro, and from San Diego east to El Cajon. MTDB began construction of a 16-mile transit line from the Amtrak (ex-Santa Fe) station in San Diego to the border. The trolleys began operating in July 1981.

Freight trains were operated on the line first by San Diego & Arizona Eastern Transportation Co., a subsidiary of Kyle Railways, then by the San Diego & Imperial Valley Railway, a RailTex subsidiary (which also operates the former Tijuana & Tecate).

Sandy River & Rangeley Lakes Railroad

The Sandy River was the most extensive 2-foot gauge railroad in Maine. Its ancestry, like that of the state of Maine itself, lies in Massachusetts. In 1875 George Mansfield organized the Billerica & Bedford Railroad to build a 2-foot gauge railroad between the towns of its name. Mansfield had visited the Festiniog Railway, a 23½-inch gauge slate carrier in Wales, and he promoted the narrow gauge as economical. There was no traffic to support the B&B. It operated only from November 1877 through May 1878, then was abandoned and its equipment was sold at auction to a B. F. Brown.

Mansfield went north to Franklin County, Maine, which was having an attack of railroad fever and also had a growing lumber industry. Standard gauge rails, later to become a branch of the Maine Central, had reached the county seat, Farmington, about 80 miles north of Portland, in 1865.

The Sandy River Railroads was organized in 1879 with Mansfield as its manager and a track

The Sandy River turned to motor cars to cut passenger train expenses. Here a gasoline railcar and baggage trailer are nearly ready to depart from Strong in 1934. The local freight and mixed train will follow it out of town behind 2-6-2 No. 24. Photo from the collection of Peter Cornwall.

gauge of 2 feet. Mansfield knew where he could get a complete 2-foot gauge train set, only slightly used, in exchange for Sandy River stock. The first train arrived in Phillips, 18 miles from

Farmington, on November 20, 1879—the town of Phillips had set that date as a deadline in order for the railroad to use the town's credit.

In 1883 the Franklin & Megantic railroad was incorporated to build from Strong, 11 miles north of Farmington, to Kingfield, 15 miles. The line was completed in October 1884. Both the F&M and the Sandy River suddenly were busy hauling lumber. The Phillips & Rangeley Railroad was incorporated in 1890 to build north from Phillips to Rangeley, 28 miles. The P&R organized a subsidiary, the Madrid Railroad, to build a branch into the forests west of Madrid, and in 1903 the Eustis Railroad was chartered to build into the area northeast of Rangeley.

In 1894 the owners of the F&M organized the Kingfield & Dead River Railroad to extend their railroad north to Carrabasset and, in 1900, to Bigelow. In 1897 Josiah Maxcy, a Gardiner, Maine, banker who had purchased the Sandy River in 1892, acquired control of the F&M and the K&DR and began operating the three roads as a single system.

Maxcy's system expanded in 1908. In January of that year he organized the Sandy River &

Rangeley Lakes Railroad, which immediately took over the Sandy River, the F&M, and the K&DR. In June 1908 the SR&RL purchased the Phillips & Rangeley and the Madrid Railroad and leased the Eustis Railroad (and purchased it in 1911).

Maine Central gained control of the SR&RL in 1911. Traffic, chiefly pulpwood, was good on the narrow gauge through World War I, but paved highways began to penetrate Franklin County, and the road's freight and passenger business proved susceptible to diversion to trucks and cars. In the early 1920s the SR&RL's expenses began to outpace income—and a good portion of the expense was interest on the debt owed to the Maine Central for improvements. The SR&RL entered receivership in 1922. In July 1926 the former K&DR was cut back to Carrabasset, and in 1931 service was discontinued north of Phillips. On July 8, 1932, the SR&RL ceased operating and stored its equipment.

Operation resumed on April 17, 1933, with the assurance of traffic from a plywood mill. Operations were briefly profitable at the expense of maintenance—cars and locomotives were

simply run until they could run no more. In June 1935 the railroad was sold to H. E. Salzberg & Co., railroad scrappers. The last day of operation was June 29, 1935.

	1929	1933	Recommended reading:
Miles of railroad operated:	96	43	*The Maine Two-Footers*, by Linwood W. Moody, published in 1959 by Howell-North Books, 850 North Hollywood Way, Burbank, CA 91505
Number of locomotives:	31	10	
Number of passenger cars:	20		*Ride the Sandy River*, by L. Peter Cornwall and Jack W. Farrell, published in 1973 by Pacific Fast Mail, P. O. Box 57, Edmonds, WA 98020
Number of freight cars:	156		
Number of other cars:	140	309	

Savannah & Atlanta Railway

George M. Brinson began constructing a railroad northwest from Savannah, Georgia, in 1906. The railroad—the Brinson Railway—reached Newington, Ga., 43 miles from Savannah in 1909. Brinson then acquired the Savannah Valley Railroad, which had a line from Egypt, Ga., through Newington and Sylvania to Mill Haven. At that point he ran out of money.

Control of the railroad company was acquired by a New York bank, though Brinson remained president. Construction resumed and the road reached Waynesboro and a connection with the Central of Georgia in 1911, and St. Clair and a connection with the Georgia & Florida in 1913. The road was renamed the Savannah & Northwestern in 1914.

The Savannah & Atlanta was incorporated in 1915 to build a connecting link between St. Clair and the Georgia Railroad's main line at Camak. Upon completion in 1916 the combination of the Georgia Railroad and the Savannah & Atlanta formed the shortest route between Atlanta and Savannah. In 1917 the Savannah & Atlanta absorbed the Savannah & Northwestern.

The company entered receivership in 1921 and emerged with its name unchanged in 1929. Its principal business was to serve as a Savannah extension of the Georgia Railroad. It was

Savannah & Atlanta train 2, the southbound mixed, pulls out of Sardis, Georgia, about halfway between Camak and Savannah, behind Mikado 503. Photo by C. M. Clegg.

purchased by the Central of Georgia Railway in 1951 but continued to operate independently until the formation of the Central of Georgia Railroad, a subsidiary of the Southern Railway, in 1971.

In 1961 the S&A abandoned 36 miles of its line between Sylvania and Waynesboro and initiated joint operation with CofG, using S&A track between Savannah and Ardmore and CofG track between Ardmore and Waynesboro.

The S&A is remembered today chiefly for Pacific 750, purchased from the Florida East Coast in 1935 and given to the Atlanta Chapter of the National Railway Historical Society in 1962. For a number of years the locomotive was a regular participant in the Southern's steam excursion program.

	1929	1969
Miles of railroad operated:	142	167
Number of locomotives:	13	11
Number of passenger cars:	7	
Number of freight cars:	58	781
Number of company service cars:	46	23
Location of headquarters: Savannah, Georgia		
Reporting marks: SA		

Recommended reading: *Central of Georgia Railway and Connecting Lines,* by Richard E. Prince, published in 1976 by Richard E. Prince

Successors:
Central of Georgia
Southern
Norfolk Southern

Portions still operated:
Ogeechee Railway: Ardmore–Sylvania, Ga.
Norfolk Southern: Savannah–Ardmore;
Waynesboro–Camak, Ga.

Seaboard Air Line Railway

The Portsmouth & Roanoke Rail Road was formed in 1832 to build a railroad from Portsmouth, Virginia, to Weldon, North Carolina, on the Roanoke River, shortcutting a long, three-sided water route. The line reached Weldon in 1837. The new railroad was not successful, and in 1846 it was purchased by the Virginia State Board of Public Works, leased to the town of Portsmouth, and reorganized as the Seaboard & Roanoke Railroad. In the early 1850s control of the road was acquired by a group of Philadelphians who also controlled the Richmond, Fredericksburg & Potomac and Richmond & Petersburg railroads.

The Raleigh & Gaston Railroad was completed in 1840 between Raleigh and Gaston, N. C.—not present-day Gaston but a town a few miles up the Roanoke River from it. In 1853 the railroad was extended a few miles east to Weldon, connecting there with the Seaboard & Roanoke and several other railroads.

During the Civil War portions of the railroad were torn up by both Union and Confederate troops, and parts were rebuilt and used by both sides, even though it was not a particularly strategic railroad.

In 1871 the Raleigh & Gaston acquired control of a railroad under construction south from Raleigh, the Raleigh & Augusta Air-Line Railroad. (An air-line is a straight, direct, bee-line

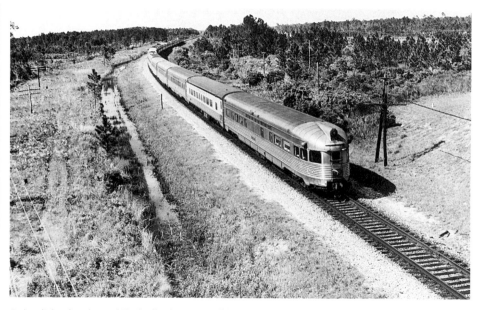

Seaboard's line through central Florida offered a view (it still does to Amtrak passengers) of agricultural country quite different from the resort areas along the coasts. Train 58, the *Silver Meteor*, rolls north near Citra. Even as late in the passenger era at 1965 an observation car brings up the rear of the 21-car streamliner. Photo by David W. Salter.

between two points. Such a line is a wonderful asset in advertising, and even if the railroad is not perfectly, absolutely straight, it can be drawn that way on timetable maps.) By 1877 that line had reached Hamlet, N. C., and a connection with the Carolina Central, a line from Wilmington through Charlotte to Shelby.

Seaboard Air-Line System

The Seaboard & Roanoke and the two Raleigh railroads were by then under the control of John M. Robinson, who was president of the RF&P and the Baltimore Steam Packet Co. In 1881 Robinson gained control of the Carolina Central. Robinson's railroads became known as the Seaboard Air-Line System.

The Seaboard system had had a friendly connection at Charlotte in the form of the Atlanta & Charlotte Air Line Railway. In 1881 that came under the control of the Richmond & Danville, a predecessor of the Southern Railway, and lost its friendly-connection status. The Seaboard began construction in 1887 of a line from Monroe, N. C., between Hamlet and Charlotte, to Atlanta—the Georgia, Carolina & Northern Railway. It reached the Georgia capital in 1892. In the late 1890s the Richmond, Petersburg & Carolina Railroad was completed between Norlina, N. C., and Richmond, Va., and in 1900 it was renamed the Seaboard Air Line Railway.

Florida Central & Peninsular

The Florida Central & Peninsular traced its ancestry to the Tallahassee Railroad, organized in 1834 to build from Tallahassee to the Gulf of Mexico—its 22-mile line was opened in 1836. The Jacksonville–Tallahassee route, opened in 1860, was built by two companies that were eventually united as the Florida Central & Western Railroad.

The Florida Railroad opened in March 1861 from Fernandina through Baldwin and Gainesville to Cedar Key, Fla., to form a land bridge (to use current terminology) from the Atlantic to the Gulf. It became the Atlantic, Gulf & West India Transit company, then the Florida Transit Railroad ("transit" having its older, less-specific meaning, rather than referring to streetcars, nickel fares, and frequent service). In 1883 it was consolidated with two other companies to form the Florida Transit & Peninsular Railroad. In 1884 that company and the Florida Central & Western merged to form the Florida Railway & Navigation Co., which was succeeded in 1889 by the Florida Central & Peninsular Railway. In 1890 a line of the FC&P was extended south to Tampa, and in 1893 the company built a line north to Savannah, where it connected with the recently opened South Bound Railroad to Columbia, S. C.

John Skelton Williams

In 1896 John Skelton Williams of Richmond and a group of associates obtained control of the Georgia & Alabama Railway, a line completed in 1891 between Montgomery, Ala., and Lyons, Ga. Williams leased and built railroad lines to extend the G&A east to Savannah. In 1898 he acquired control of the Seaboard group of railroads, and in 1899 he took over the Florida Central & Peninsular Railroad, which had a line from Columbia, S. C., through Savannah and Jacksonville to Tampa, and another line west from Jacksonville through Tallahassee to a junction with the Louisville & Nashville at the Chattahoochee River.

In 1900, 91 miles of new railroad between Columbia and Cheraw, S. C., connected the Georgia & Alabama (Montgomery–Savannah) and the Florida Central & peninsular with the "old" Seaboard. Williams proposed to build north from Richmond to connect with the Baltimore & Ohio, because the Richmond, Fredericksburg & Potomac was then controlled by the Atlantic Coast Line. The Pennsylvania Railroad and the state of Virginia, both owners of portions of the RF&P, applied pressure, and the Seaboard was allowed to sign a traffic agreement with the RF&P—and with the Pennsy, too.

Twentieth-century expansion

Williams was out at the end of 1903—he went on to assemble the Georgia & Florida—but he had begun an extension west from Atlanta to Birmingham by a combination of new construction and the acquisition of the East & West Railroad.

In the early years of the twentieth century the Seaboard acquired a number of branches and short lines. SAL entered a brief receivership in 1908, and the corporation underwent a reorganization in 1915 when the subsidiary Carolina, Atlantic & Western Railway was renamed the Seaboard Air Line Railway and took over the previous Seaboard Air Line.

In 1918 SAL opened a new line from Charleston, S. C., to Savannah. In conjunction with an existing line from Hamlet to Charleston it formed a freight route with easier grades than the main line through Columbia. About that same time SAL began to gather up short lines in the agricultural and phosphate-mining area of

central Florida: the Tampa & Gulf Coast (Tampa to St. Petersburg and Tarpon Springs), the Charlotte Harbor & Northern (Mulberry to Boca Grande), and the Tampa Northern (Tampa to Brooksville).

SAL's principal project in Florida during the land boom of the early 1920s was a line from Coleman, just south of Wildwood, southeast to West Palm Beach and Miami. SAL's first passenger train arrived in Miami on January 8, 1927. A few months earlier SAL had opened an extension down the west coast to Fort Myers and Naples. In 1928 Seaboard acquired the Georgia, Florida & Alabama Railway, a 194-mile line from Richland, Ga., south through Tallahassee to the Gulf.

The Florida land boom collapsed in 1926, just as SAL was completing its lines to Miami and Naples, and the stock market crashed in 1929. The Seaboard was not a strong railroad, and it was located between the Atlantic Coast Line and the Southern, both prosperous and well-established. Overextended by its expansion program in Florida, SAL collapsed into receivership in December 1930.

Government loans helped SAL undertake a modernization program, and revenues from the busy years of World War II lifted the road back to profitability and permitted it to install block signals and centralized traffic control. The lack of signals on most of SAL's lines had caused several major accidents during the war years. The company was reorganized as the Seaboard Air Line Railroad in 1946.

Postwar prosperity

During the decade after World War II the Seaboard prospered along with nearly every

Some railroads were loyal to a single locomotive builder; others believed in spreading their business around. An assortment of Baldwin, Electro-Motive, and Alco power leads a Seaboard freight out of Montgomery, Ala., in August 1959. Seaboard's winding main line was responsible in part for the design of the Baldwin Centipede in the lead. Ironically, Seaboard's map included the longest tangent in the U. S., nearly 79 miles from Hamlet to Wilmington, North Carolina, and another 57-mile stretch across Florida. Photo by David W. Salter.

other railroad. Its position was bolstered by industrial development in the South and healthy traffic in phosphate rock—one-fifth of Seaboard's tonnage—used in the production of fertilizers. Seaboard's passenger business was also healthy, thanks to heavy traffic between the Northeast and Florida.

In 1958 SAL absorbed the Macon, Dublin & Savannah, which it had long owned, and in June 1959 SAL purchased the Gainesville Midland, a 42-mile line connecting the mill town of Gainesville, Ga., with the Seaboard at Athens.

Merger of the Seaboard with parallel—and rival—Atlantic Coast Line was proposed in 1958. The benefits of the Seaboard Coast Line merger, which took effect July 1, 1967, derived largely from eliminating duplicate lines and terminals.

	1929	1966
Miles of railroad operated:	4,490	4,123
Number of locomotives:	726	551
Number of passenger cars:	474	414
Number of freight cars:	22,483	28,778
Number of company service cars:	1,055	1,003

Location of headquarters: Norfolk, Virginia

Reporting marks: SAL

Notable named passenger trains: *Orange Blossom Special*, *Silver Meteor* (New York–Miami, operated north of Richmond by Pennsylvania and Richmond, Fredericksburg & Potomac)

Historical and technical society: Atlantic Coast Line and Seaboard Air Line Historical Society, P. O. Box 325, Valrico, FL 33595-0325; http://www.visuallink.net/ACLSAL

Recommended reading:

Seaboard Air Line Railway, by Richard E. Prince, published in 1969 by Richard E. Prince (SBN 9600088-1-0)

Seaboard Air Line Railway Album, by Albert M. Langley, Jr., W. Forrest Beckum, Jr., and C. Ronnie Tidwell, published in 1988 by Union Station Publishing, 785 Murrah Road, North Augusta, SC 29841 (ISBN 0-9615257-2-X)

Subsidiaries and affiliated railroads, 1966:

Gainesville Midland

Richmond-Washington Co. (which owned a controlling interest in the Richmond, Fredericksburg & Potomac, 16.7%

Predecessor railroads in this book: Macon, Dublin & Savannah

Successors:

Seaboard Coast Line

Seaboard System

CSX Transportation

Seaboard Coast Line Railroad

In retrospect the Seaboard Coast Line seems to have been an intermediate phase in the creation of Seaboard System. Merger of the Seaboard Air Line and the Atlantic Coast Line was proposed in 1958 and took effect July 1, 1967. Soon after the merger some duplicate routes were rationalized. Among the abandonments were SAL's line between Charleston and Savannah, most of ACL's route into the Norfolk-Portsmouth area, and much of the dense network of branch lines in central Florida.

The most prevalent objection to the creation of SCL was over Atlantic Coast Line's control of Louisville & Nashville. Both Southern Railway and Illinois Central asked to purchase ACL's interest in L&N. The Southern and ACL plus SAL were about the same size, roughly 10,000 route miles, and adding 6,000-mile L&N to either would create a large railroad. Southern presumably felt that if one railroad was to be considerably larger than its competitor, it wanted to be the big one. Southern later dropped its objection when it gained control of Central of Georgia. Illinois Central was about the same size as L&N but had long been eager to penetrate the Southeast. Other protesters were Florida East Coast, which said that ACL-SAL would surround it, and Gulf, Mobile & Ohio.

On July 1, 1969, SCL purchased the Piedmont

Two GP40s lead a fast piggyback train through Neuse, North Carolina, a few miles north of Raleigh on the former Seaboard main line, in June 1979. Photo by Curt Tillotson, Jr.

& Northern, a former interurban line owned by the Duke interests, and on September 1, 1976, SCL purchased the Durham & Southern, obtaining easier access to Durham, N. C.

About 1974 SCL's advertising began to refer to SCL, Louisville & Nashville, Clinchfield, Georgia railroad, and the West Point Route as "The Family Lines," but the title was simply a marketing device, not the name of a corpora-tion. The reference usually included a list of the members of the family. By then two other alliances had been formed south of the Ohio River and east of the Mississippi: Southern-Central of Georgia-Georgia & Florida-"old" Norfolk Southern and Illinois Central-Gulf, Mobile & Ohio. Unification of the members of the Family Lines could proceed. One December 29, 1982, SCL merged the Louisville &

	1967	1982
Miles of railroad operated:	9,306	8,772
Number of locomotives:	1,235	1,255
Number of passenger cars:	729	448*
Number of freight cars:	63,405	59,335
Number of company service cars:	2,156	2,392

Location of headquarters: Jacksonville, Florida

Reporting marks: SCL

Notable named passenger trains: SCL continued to operate the trains of its predecessors and maintain their high standards. When airplanes were being hijacked to Cuba, SCL seized the opportunity to advertise the inability of a train to be hijacked.

Historical and technical society: Atlantic Coast Line and Seaboard Air Line Historical Society, P. O. Box 325, Valrico, FL 33595-0325; http://www.visuallink.net/ACLSAL

Predecessor railroads in this book:
Atlantic Coast Line
Durham & Southern
Piedmont & Northern
Seaboard Air Line

Successors:
Seaboard System, CSX Transportation

Portions still operated: See the entries for the predecessor railroads.

*(1970)

Nashville to form the Seaboard System Railroad.

Further mergers were already in the wind: More than two years earlier, on November 1, 1980, Seaboard Coast Line Industries, corporate parent of Seaboard Coast Line Railroad, and Chessie System, parent of the Baltimore & Ohio and Chesapeake & Ohio, merged to form the CSX Corporation.

Seaboard System Railroad

Seaboard System came into being on December 29, 1982, when the Seaboard Coast Line Railroad merged the Louisville & Nashville Railroad. The Seaboard Coast Line had been formed in 1967 by the merger of the Atlantic Coast Line and the Seaboard Air Line; ACL had controlled the L&N since 1902.

On January 1, 1983, the Clinchfield Railroad became the Clinchfield Division of the Seaboard System. That same year Seaboard System purchased the Georgia Railroad, another member of the ACL-L&N family, and merged it, and took over operations of the Atlanta & West Point Rail Road and the Western Railway of Alabama, both of which had long been affiliated with the Georgia Railroad.

Seaboard System owned 40 percent of the stock of the Richmond-Washington Company, a holding company that owns 63.6 percent of the voting stock of the Richmond, Fredericksburg & Potomac Railroad.

Seaboard System was not destined to have a long life. Two years before its creation, its parent holding company, Seaboard Coast Line Industries, and Chessie System, Inc., merged to form CSX Corporation ("C" for Chessie, "S" for Seaboard, and "X" for a multiplication symbol).

When CSX was formed, the intention was for the component railroads to retain their identities. However, on July 1, 1986, the name of the Seaboard System Railroad was changed to CSX Transportation, and on August 31, 1987, CSX Transportation merged the Chesapeake & Ohio.

Four freshly painted U36Bs lead freight train 461 south at Henderson, North Carolina, on the former Seaboard Air Line main line on April 21, 1985. By 1988 the line will be abandoned just north of here. Photo by Curt Tillotson, Jr.

	1982	1986
Miles of railroad operated:	15,294	13,506
Number of locomotives:	2,426	2,093
Number of freight cars:	117,177	90,753
Number of company service cars:	3,946	3,845

(1982 figures include Clinchfield Railroad)

Location of headquarters: Jacksonville, Florida

Reporting marks: SBD

Historical and technical society: Atlantic Coast Line and Seaboard Air Line Railroads Historical Society (formerly Southeastern Railroad Technical Society), P. O. Box 325, Valrico, FL 33595-0325; http://www.visuallink.net/ACLSAL

Recommended reading: *Locomotives of the Seaboard System*, by Paul Carleton, published in 1987 by D. Carleton Railbooks, P. O. Box 1827, Dunnellon, FL 32630

Subsidiaries and affiliated railroads, 1986: Richmond-Washington Company (40%)

Predecessor railroads in this book: Atlanta & West Point/Western Railway of Alabama/Georgia Railroad

Atlanta, Birmingham & Coast
Atlantic Coast Line
Chicago & Eastern Illinois
Chicago, Indianapolis & Louisville (Monon)
Durham & Southern
Louisville & Nashville
Macon, Dublin & Savannah
Nashville, Chattanooga & St. Louis
Piedmont & Northern
Seaboard Air Line
Seaboard Coast Line

Successor: CSX Transportation

Portions still operated: Most of Seaboard System's routes are operated by CSX Transportation. The only major abandonments during the brief tenure of Seaboard System were: Tullahoma–Sparta, Tenn. (ex-NC&StL, now operated by the Caney Fork & Western) Cowan–Tracy City, Tenn. (ex-NC&StL) Union Point–Athens, Ga. (ex-Georgia Railroad) Milledgeville–Mogul, Ga. (ex-Georgia Railroad) Petersburg, Va.–Norlina, N. C. (ex-SAL main line)

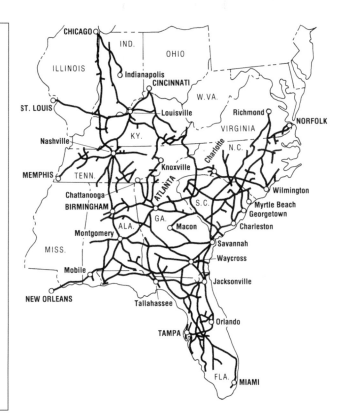

Sonora-Baja California Railway

(Ferrocarril Sonora-Baja California)

The Sonora-Baja California had its beginning in 1923 when a 43-mile line was constructed under the aegis of the Department of Communications and Public Works (Secretaria de Comunicaciones y Obras Publicas) southeastward from Mexicali, the capital of the state of Baja California. No further work was done on the railroad until 1936, when construction resumed across the hot, dry, unpopulated Altar Desert. The line was opened as far east as Puerto Peñasco on the Gulf of California in 1940.

Construction resumed again in 1946. On December 16, 1947, the line was completed to a connection with the Southern Pacific of Mexico (later the Ferrocarril del Pacifico) at Benjamin Hill, Sonora, creating an all-Mexican rail link between the state of Baja California and the rest of the country.

Although the Sonora-Baja California name was applied in 1948, at least until 1956 the railroad was operated by the Department of Communications and Public Works. The Sonora-Baja California developed a respectable passenger business and purchased much of its rolling stock in Europe: German coaches and British-built,

Sonora-Baja California passenger trains meet at Puerto Peñasco, Sonora, on the morning of November 28, 1982. High-nosed boiler-equipped GP40-2 No. 2104 is in charge of the southbound train. Photo by William T. Morgan

Rolls-Royce-powered diesel cars (the latter were abject failures).

In 1970 the Mexican government purchased the Tijuana & Tecate Railway, the Mexican por-

tion of the former San Diego & Arizona Eastern line from San Diego to El Centro. Later its ownership was transferred to the S-BC, but because the T&T was connected only to the former

392

SD&AE, it continued to be operated by the U. S. operator of that line—first the San Diego & Arizona Eastern Transportation Co., then the San Diego & Imperial Valley Railroad.

On April 2, 1987, the Sonora-Baja California became the Baja California Division of the National Railways of Mexico.

	1986
Miles of railroad operated:	379
Number of locomotives:	20
Number of passenger cars:	43
Number of freight cars:	561
Location of headquarters: Mexicali, B. Cfa., Mexico	
Reporting marks: SBC	
Recommended reading: *Baja California Railways*, by	

John A. Kirchner, published in 1988 by Golden West Books, P. O. Box 80250, San Marino, CA 91108-8250 (ISBN 0-87095-100-9)

Subsidiaries and affiliated railroads, 1986:
Tijuana & Tecate Railway
Successors: National Railways of Mexico
Portions still operated: National Railways of Mexico: Mexicali—Benjamin Hill

Minneapolis, St. Paul & Sault Ste. Marie Railway
Soo Line Railroad

In the 1870s the flour millers of Minneapolis sought a new outlet for their products to avoid the exorbitant freight rates charged by existing railroads through Chicago. James J. Hill, who later built the Great Northern, tried to persuade the Canadian Pacific to construct its line to the west through Sault Ste. Marie and Minneapolis, but nationalistic feeling in Canada dictated CP's all-Canada route north of Lake Superior.

In 1883 a group of Minneapolis men incorporated the Minneapolis, Sault Ste. Marie & Atlantic Railway to construct a line from the Twin Cities east to connect with the Canadian Pacific at Sault Ste. Marie. (Sault is pronounced "Soo." The area around the rapids of the St. Marys River is called "the Soo.")

A year later the Minneapolis & Pacific Railway was incorporated by many of the same men to build northwestward into the wheat-growing

areas of Minnesota and North Dakota. In 1888 these two roads and two others were consolidated to form the Minneapolis, St. Paul & Sault Ste. Marie Railway. Canadian Pacific acquired control of the railroad largely to block any attempt by CP's rival Grand Trunk Railway to build toward western Canada via the U. S. In 1893 the Soo Line, as it was nicknamed, built northwest to connect with CP at Portal, N. Dak., and in 1904 completed a line north from

Glenwood, Minn., to a connection with CP at Noyes, Minn.

In 1909 Soo Line leased the properties of the Wisconsin Central Railroad, a 1,000-mile road extending from Chicago to St. Paul, Duluth, and Ashland, Wis. In addition to gaining access to Chicago, Soo Line also obtained routes to the industrial Fox River Valley of Wisconsin and the iron ore deposits in the northern part of the state.

The Duluth, South Shore & Atlantic Railway was formed by the merger of several lines along the south shore of Lake Superior. Its traffic consisted largely of iron ore and forest products. Its line ran east from Duluth along the south shore of Lake Superior to Sault Ste. Marie and to St. Ignace, where it connected via carferry to Mackinaw City at the northern tip of Michigan's lower peninsula. Canadian Pacific obtained control of the DSS&A in 1888 for the same reason it had bought into the Soo Line—to block possible construction by Grand Trunk. By 1930 the DSS&A shared officers with the Soo Line.

Soo Line

In 1961 the Minneapolis, St. Paul & Sault Ste. Marie; the Duluth, South Shore & Atlantic; and the Wisconsin Central merged to form the Soo Line Railroad (the corporate structure was that

Soo Line train 2, an all-day Minneapolis–Chicago local, rolls through Sussex, Wisconsin. The catcher arm of the RPO is in position to pick up a bag of outgoing mail.

Freights for Superior and Sault Ste. Marie await their nocturnal departures from Shoreham Yard, Minneapolis, in the early 1960s. Soo Line photo.

of the 1949 reorganization of the DSS&A). In 1982 Soo Line acquired the Minneapolis, Northfield & Southern Railway, a 74-mile line between Northfield, Minn., and the suburbs of Minneapolis.

Acquisition and divestment

Soo Line purchased the bankrupt Chicago, Milwaukee, St. Paul & Pacific Railroad in 1985 and merged it at the beginning of 1986. By then the Milwaukee, which had once reached west to Puget Sound, had shrunk to three principal routes: Chicago–Milwaukee–Minneapolis; Chicago–Kansas City; and Chicago–Louisville, Kentucky, the last almost entirely by trackage rights. Soo Line also acquired trackage rights on Chessie System (now CSX) from Chicago to Detroit, where it made a connection with parent CP Rail.

Soo briefly tried operating its light-density lines in Michigan and Wisconsin as Lake States Transportation Division (don't confuse it with Michigan's Lake State Railway, the former Detroit & Mackinac Railway). Then Soo Line consolidated its Chicago–Twin Cities operations on the former Milwaukee Road main line and sold what had been its own lines to Wisconsin Central Ltd. in 1987, in many ways re-creating the pre-1909 Wisconsin Central.

For a long time Canadian Pacific owned a little more than half of Soo's outstanding stock. In the late 1980s CP tried briefly to sell off Soo Line, then decided to try for full ownership. By early 1990 CP Rail had acquired full ownership, and in early 1992 the separate listing for Soo Line disappeared from the *Pocket List of Railroad Officials*. CP briefly tried referring to Soo Line as its "Heavy Haul–U. S. Division" but that didn't catch

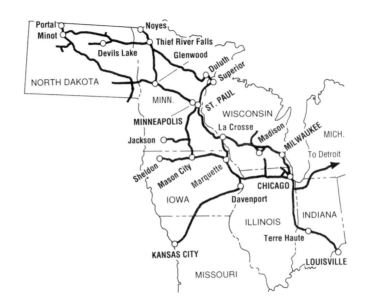

on. By the mid-1990s it was simply part of the CP Rail System—and "CP Rail" soon yielded to a restoration of the full Canadian Pacific name.

In 1990 Soo Line leased two routes in wheat-growing country totaling 293 miles to the Dakota, Missouri Valley & Western Railroad: Flaxton, N. Dak., to Whitetail, Montana, and Oakes, N. Dak., through Wishek and Bismarck to Washburn, N. Dak., plus a branch from Wishek to Ashley. In late 1996 CP sold a group of former Milwaukee Road lines to Montana Rail Link to operate as I&M Rail Link: Pingree Grove,

Ill. (45 miles west of Chicago) to Kansas City branches serving northern Iowa and southern Minnesota.

All that remains of the Soo Line under Canadian Pacific ownership is the ex-Milwaukee Road Chicago–Milwaukee–Minneapolis line and a two-pronged route from Minneapolis to the Canadian border at Noyes, Minn., and Portal, N. Dak., plus a few short branches.

	1929	1991
Miles of railroad operated:	4,412	5,045
Number of locomotives:	276	400
Number of passenger cars:	270	
Number of freight cars:	15,161	12,695
Number of company service cars:	495	

Location of headquarters: Minneapolis, Minnesota

Reporting marks: SOO

Historical and technical society: Soo Line Historical & Technical Society, 3410 Kasten Court, Middleton, WI 53562

Recommended reading: *The Little Jewel,* by Wallace W. Abbey, published in 1984 by Pinon Productions, 781 McCarthy Boulevard, Pueblo, CO 81005 (ISBN 0-930855-00-0)

Predecessor railroads in this book:
Chicago, Milwaukee, St. Paul & Pacific
Duluth, South Shore & Atlantic
Minneapolis, Northfield & Southern

Successors:
Canadian Pacific
Wisconsin Central Ltd.

Portions still operated:
Canadian Pacific: Minneapolis–Glenwood–Noyes, Minn.; Glenwood–Minot–Portal, N. Dak.; Fairmount–N. Dak.–Veblen, S. Dak.; Hankinson–Oakes, N. Dak.; Drake–New Town, N. Dak. Dakota, Missouri Valley & Western: Flaxton, N. Dak.–Whitetail, Mont; Oakes–Wishek–Bismarck–Max, N. Dak., Wishek–Ashley, N. Dak.
Escanaba & Lake Superior: Sidnaw–Nestoria, Mich. (DSS&A)
Northern Plains: Thief River Falls, Minn.–Baker, N. Dak.; Fordville–Kenmare, N. Dak.
Wisconsin Central Ltd.: Chicago–Neenah, Wis.–Superior, Wis.; Neenah–Manitowoc; Neenah–Argonne, Wis.; Spencer–Medford, Wis.; Owen, Wis.–Withrow, Minn.; Withrow–Amery, Wis.; Almena, Wis.–Sault Ste. Marie, Ont.; Prentice–Ashland, Wis.; Marengo, Wis.–White Pine, Mich. (DSS&A); Baraga–Nestoria–Humboldt, Mich. (DSS&A); Ishpeming–Trout Lake, Mich. (DSS&A)

Southern Pacific Lines

Until the supermergers of recent decades, Southern Pacific was one of the largest railroads in the U. S., ranking third behind Pennsylvania and New York Central in operating revenue and second behind Santa Fe in route mileage. SP's lines stretched over a greater distance than any other railroad—from New Orleans west to Los Angeles, then north to Portland, Oregon, east from Sacramento to Ogden, Utah, and before 1951 down the west coast of Mexico to Guadalajara. It dominated transportation in California and was the only large railroad headquartered on the West Coast. Explaining Southern Pacific's history route by route, much as its passenger timetables were arranged years ago, makes it easier to understand.

Overland Route

In 1850 the state of California was admitted to the union. It would need a railroad to connect it to the rest of the country. The route that railroad should take posed a question: south toward the slave states or north toward the free states? The question was answered a decade later by the outbreak of the Civil War.

In 1852 the Sacramento Valley Rail Road engaged Theodore D. Judah to lay out its line from Sacramento east a few miles to Folsom and Placerville. The line was opened in 1856, but Judah had higher goals—a railroad over the Sierra Nevada to Virginia City, Nevada. He scouted the mountains for a route and sought financial backing in San Francisco. That city considered itself a seaport, not the terminal of a railroad, but in Sacramento he obtained the backing of four merchants: Collis P. Huntington, Mark Hopkins, Charles Crocker, and Leland Stanford—collectively, the Big Four. They incorporated the Central Pacific Railroad in June 1861.

In 1862 Congress passed the Pacific Railroad Act. It provided for the incorporation of the Union Pacific Railroad, to build westward (its eastern terminal, Omaha, was decided later); empowered the Central Pacific to build east; and provided loans and land for both efforts.

Construction of the Central Pacific began at Sacramento in January 1863. Its first train operated 18 miles east to what is now Roseville in November of that year. By 1867 Central Pacific had crossed the state line into Nevada, and on May 10, 1869, the Central Pacific and the Union Pacific met at Promontory, Utah, creating the first transcontinental railroad.

California Lines

After meeting the UP at Promontory, the Central Pacific was extended west from Sacramento to San Francisco Bay, first by construction of the Western Pacific Railroad to Oakland over Altamont Pass (don't confuse this Western Pacific with the 20th century railroad of the

The cab-forward articulated was Southern Pacific's solution to the problem of operating through snowsheds and still letting the engine crew see ahead. One is shown here on a southbound freight passing Mount Shasta in northern California some time during World War II. SP photo.

same name over the same pass, now part of Union Pacific), then by acquisition in 1876 of the California Pacific Railroad from Sacramento to Vallejo.

In 1879 Central Pacific completed a line from Port Costa, across the Carquinez Strait from Vallejo, along the shore of San Francisco Bay to Oakland. Train ferries made the connection between Port Costa and Benicia (just east of

Vallejo) until the construction of the bridge across Carquinez Strait in 1929.

The San Francisco & San Jose Railroad opened between the cities of its title in 1864, and in 1865 its owners incorporated the Southern Pacific Railroad to build south and east to New Orleans. History is unclear as to the next few years—who acquired whom, what was incorporated when—but by 1870 the Southern Pacific

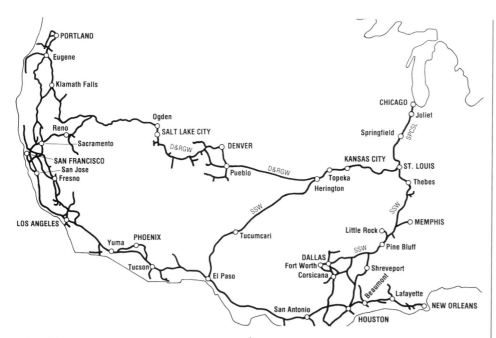

The Tehachapi Mountains form the south end of the San Joaquin valley. To keep the grade over the mountains within limits, William Hood laid out a tortuous line that twists back and forth and at one point crosses over itself. The line reached a summit at Tehachapi, then descended directly to the northwest corner of the Mojave Desert. SP had intended to build southeast across the Mojave Desert to the Colorado River but it was induced to detour through Los Angeles, then barely more than a mission settlement.

The Coast Line, which was (and is) primarily a passenger route between San Francisco and Los Angeles, opened in 1901.

SP's line from Mojave to Los Angeles was a detour. SP returned to Mojave and built east across the Mojave Desert to the Colorado River at Needles, Calif., not with the intention of continuing eastward but to connect with the Atlantic & Pacific—meeting it at the state line and saying, "Welcome to Southern Pacific country." The eventual result of the line across the Mojave Desert was the Southern Pacific of Mexico.

Sunset and Golden State Routes

SP built east from Los Angeles and reached the Colorado River at Yuma, Arizona, in 1877. Further construction, this time as the Galveston, Harrisburg & San Antonio Railway, put the line into El Paso, Texas, in 1881. That same year it connected with the Texas & Pacific Railway at Sierra Blanca, Texas, 90 miles east of El Paso, completing the second transcontinental railroad route.

The railhead was pushed eastward, meeting the line from San Antonio alongside the banks of the Pecos River in 1883. The line at that

(possibly a new Southern Pacific) and the San Francisco & San Jose were in the hands of the Big Four. Construction started southeast from San Jose, and by 1871 the line had reached Tres Pinos, in the mountains east of Salinas and west—a long way west—of Fresno.

There was almost no population to support a railroad beyond Tres Pinos, so Southern Pacific changed its plans and started construction

southeast through the San Joaquin Valley from Lathrop, 9 miles south of Stockton. The rails reached Fresno in 1872 and Sumner, across the Kern River from Bakersfield, at the end of 1874. The line was built by the Central Pacific as far south as Goshen Junction, 53 miles south of Fresno, where it intersected the original Southern Pacific survey. Beyond Goshen Junction it was built by Southern Pacific.

point has since been relocated, crossing the Pecos on the highest bridge of any U. S. common carrier (320 feet).

In the mid-1880s the Rock Island planned a line southwest from Kansas to El Paso. In 1902 the line met the El Paso & Rock Island Railway at Santa Rosa, N. M. The El Paso–Santa Rosa line was the Eastern Division of the El Paso & Southwestern System; the Western Division consisted of a line from El Paso to Tucson, Arizona, roughly parallel to SP's line, but for much of its distance 30 to 70 miles south of it. SP purchased the El Paso & Southwestern in 1924.

Texas and Louisiana Lines

The SP lines east of El Paso grew from the Buffalo Bayou, Brazos & Colorado Railroad and the New Orleans, Opelousas & Great Western Railroad, both chartered in 1850. The BBB&C was reorganized as the Galveston, Harrisburg & San Antonio Railway in 1870. It reached San Antonio in 1877, engaged in some machinations with and against Jay Gould's Missouri Pacific system, and continued building west. The Opelousas, sold in 1869 to steamship magnate Charles Morgan and later resold and reorganized as Morgan's Louisiana & Texas Railroad, built across the bayou country west of New Orleans to form a New Orleans–Houston route in conjunction with the Louisiana Western and the Texas & New Orleans.

In 1934 all these railroads were consolidated as the Texas & New Orleans Railroad. Even after the repeal in 1967 of the article in the Texas constitution requiring railroads operating in Texas to be headquartered there, the T&NO lines were operated as a separate entity.

The *Coast Daylights,* trains 99 (left) and 98, meet at Chorro siding just north of San Luis Obispo, California. The 2-10-2 ahead of the streamlined 4-8-4 will assist the streamliner to Santa Margarita. Photo by Richard Steinheimer.

Shasta and Cascade Routes

In 1870 Central Pacific acquired the California & Oregon Railroad, which had built north from Marysville. It pushed north through Redding, Calif., up the Sacramento River canyon, and over the Siskiyou Range to connect with the Oregon & California Railroad at Ashland, Ore., in 1887. SP acquired the O&C at that time, extending its system north to Portland. In 1909 SP opened a line from Black Butte, Calif., at the foot of Mount Shasta, northeast across the state line to Klamath Falls, Ore.

In 1926 SP opened the Natron Cutoff between Klamath Falls and Eugene, Ore. It had been conceived as a line southeast from Eugene to meet a proposed Union Pacific line west from the Idaho-Oregon border. That linkup never happened, but SP saw that extending this line south through the Klamath Basin might head off the Great Northern, which was constructing a line south from the Columbia River to connect with a Western Pacific line being pushed north from Keddie, Calif. As it turned out, GN wound up on SP rails between Chemult, Ore., and Klamath

Southern Pacific of Mexico

In 1881 and 1882 the Santa Fe built the Sonora Railway north from Guaymas, the principal Gulf of California port in the Mexican state of Sonora, to Nogales, on the U. S. border. The Santa Fe had already built southwest from Kansas to Deming, N. M. Trackage rights over SP from Deming to Benson, Ariz., and the New Mexico & Arizona Railroad, another Santa Fe subsidiary, from there to Nogales connected the Santa Fe to the Sonora Railway—and Pacific tidewater.

The Santa Fe had also built west from Albuquerque to Needles, California, meeting an SP line from Mojave. The SP line would give Santa Fe an entrance to southern California; SP saw in the Sonora Railway access to Mexico. The two roads worked a trade— Santa Fe got the Needles–Barstow–Mojave line, and SP got the Sonora Railway, leasing it in 1898 and purchasing it outright at the end of 1911.

A new SP subsidiary, the Cananea, Rio Yaqui & Pacific, extended the railroad south from Guaymas and built branches east of Nogales. The Southern Pacific Railroad of Mexico (Sud Pacifico de México) was incorporated in 1909 and acquired the CRY&P in 1909 and the Sonora Railway in 1912.

Construction southeast along the coast was hampered by Indian uprisings and the Mexican revolution; by the time those settled down, the railhead was in the wild, rough barranca country southeast of Tepic. The SPdeM finally reached a connection with the National Railways of Mexico at Orendain Junction, 24 miles from Guadalajara in 1927. Further revolutionary activity in 1929 destroyed bridges and interrupted service.

The SPdeM was a consistent money-loser for its parent, and at the beginning of 1940 Southern Pacific withdrew support, forcing the SPdeM to live on its own income. Losses continued, partly because of labor laws and partly because of tariffs imposed by the U. S. on Mexican produce stifled traffic. Mexican authorities operated the line during a strike in 1947 and 1948. The status of foreign-owned holdings in Mexico became questionable, and there was a possibility of expropriation. In December 1951 SP sold the railroad to the Mexican government. It was renamed the Ferrocarril del Pacifico (Pacific Railroad).

	1929	1950
Miles of railroad operated:	1,370	1,331
Number of locomotives:	104	93
Number of passenger cars:	129	88
Number of freight cars:	1,513	618
Number of company service cars:		202

Location of headquarters: Guadalajara, Jalisco, Mexico

Reporting marks: SPM

Recommended reading: *Southern Pacific of Mexico*, by John R. Signor and John A. Kirchner, published in 1987 by Golden West Books.

ISBN 0-87095-099-1

Successors:

Ferrocarril del Pacifico

National Railways of Mexico

Portions still operated:

Grupo Ferroviaria Mexicano: Nogales–Guadalajara

National Railways of Mexico: Nogales–Del Rio, Cananea–Naco

Texas & New Orleans train 13, the *Sunbeam* (a Texas *Daylight*) is shown at Dallas on September 13, 1954, behind a pair of Alco PA-1s. Photo by R. S. Plummer.

Falls. The new route had much easier grades and curves than the original route through Ashland, and it became SP's main route in Oregon.

About the same time SP opened a line from Klamath Falls southeast to the Overland Route at Fernley, Nev. Some of the Modoc Line, as it is called, was new construction; for other portions of it, SP purchased and standard-gauged the 3-foot gauge Nevada-California-Oregon Railway.

Construction of Shasta Dam between 1938 and 1942 required relocation of much of SP's line in the lower Sacramento River canyon. The Pit River bridge, which carries both railroad and highway traffic, was at the time of its construction the highest in the U. S. (433 feet). Subsequent filling of Shasta Lake brought the water level up to just below the girders.

Southern Pacific, Central Pacific, and Mr. Harriman

The four men who controlled the Central Pacific also controlled the Southern Pacific, and the two roads were operated as a unified system. By 1884 it was clear that corporate simplification was necessary. The most logical proposal, consolidating the two companies, was rejected. A new Southern Pacific Company was formed to replace the Southern Pacific Railroad. The Central Pacific Railroad leased its properties to the SP and was reorganized as the Central Pacific Railway.

As the nineteenth century closed, control of SP rested with C. P. Huntington, last survivor of the Big Four. Huntington died in 1900, and his SP stock was purchased by the Union Pacific, which had recently come under the control of E. H. Harriman.

Harriman had acquired a UP that had fallen on hard times. It consisted essentially of lines from Omaha and Kansas City west through Cheyenne to Ogden. Harriman immediately undertook a complete rebuilding of the UP and reacquired the route northwest through Idaho to Portland, Oregon, that UP had lost a few years before. Without ownership or control of the Central Pacific from Ogden to California, though, UP's line to Ogden was worthless.

The Southern Pacific was in good condition, but Harriman soon undertook three major improvements on SP's Overland Route: the Lucin Cutoff across the Great Salt Lake, shortening the Oakland–Ogden distance by 44 miles (and bypassing Promontory), a second track over the Sierra, in many places with an easier grade, and automatic block signaling. One of Harriman's improvements in California was the Bayshore Cutoff south of San Francisco, which replaced a steep inland route with a water-level route along the shore of San Francisco Bay.

Meanwhile President Theodore Roosevelt had begun to consider the problems that big business posed for the free enterprise system. He focused his attention on Harriman, the Union Pacific, and the Southern Pacific (and matters weren't

Southern Pacific Company — Narrow Gauge Lines

The Carson & Colorado Railroad was conceived in 1880 at the height of the Nevada gold and silver boom. It was intended to run from Carson City to the Colorado River. Construction began at Mound House, Nev., east of Carson City on the standard gauge Virginia & Truckee. Its rails reached Keeler, California, 299 miles from Mound House, in 1883. At that point William Sharon, its promoter, asked Darius Mills, its financier, what he thought of it. Mills answered, "Either we have built the railroad 300 miles too long or 300 years too soon."

In 1900 Southern Pacific purchased the line—and the town of Tonopah, Nev., began to boom. The Nevada & California Railway, an SP subsidiary, built a connection from Hazen, on SP's Sacramento–Ogden main line, to Churchill on the C&C, bypassing the Virginia & Truckee, then standard-gauged 137 miles of the C&C from Mound House to Tonopah Junctions. SP merged the C&C into the Nevada & California in 1905.

SP's standard gauge "Jawbone" line from Mojave to Owenyo was completed in 1910, larger to carry construction materials for the Los Angeles Aqueduct. At Owenyo it connected with the narrow gauge. There were proposals to standard-gauge the former C&C from Owenyo to Tonopah Junction to form a route from Los Angeles to Ogden, but uncertainty about the status of Southern Pacific control of Central Pacific kept the project from fruition.

In 1943 SP removed the narrow gauge rails between Mina, Nev., and Laws, Calif., having in 1938 ceased service between Tonopah Junction and Benton. The Laws–Keeler segment of the line was dieselized in 1954 and remained in operation until April 29, 1960, carrying minerals and livestock.

	1929	1959
Miles of railroad operated:	160	71
Number of locomotives:	9	1
Number of passenger cars:	9	
Number of freight cars:	284	222

Location of headquarters: San Francisco, California

Recommended reading: *Southern Pacific Narrow Gauge*, by Mallory Hope Ferrell, published in 1982 by Pacific Fast Mail.

Portions still operated:

Union Pacific: Churchill–Wabuska, Nev.

U. S. Government: Wabuska–Thorne, Nev.

---

helped by Frank Norris's muckraking novel of 1901, *The Octopus*).

The upshot was that UP had to sell its SP stock and SP had to justify its retention of Central Pacific. Divestiture of Central Pacific would have ripped the heart out of Southern Pacific's network of lines in California and Oregon. Central Pacific's principal routes were from Oakland through Sacramento and Reno to Ogden,

from Fernley, Nevada, northwest to Susanville, Calif.; from Hazen, Nevada, down to Mojave (mostly narrow gauge; from Roseville north to Hornbrook, Calif., on the Siskiyou Route and to Kirk, Oregon, north of Klamath Falls; and from Stockton through Fresno to Goshen Junction. The Natron Cutoff and the Modoc line, both built in the late 1920s, were also Central Pacific routes. The process of justifying SP's ownership

of Central Pacific to government agencies continued for years, consuming management time and creating an atmosphere of uncertainty. Central Pacific's corporate existence continued until 1959.

Merger with, um—who's available?

Southern Pacific and Santa Fe announced their merger proposal in May 1980, called it off

El Paso & Southwestern System

Southern Pacific acquired the El Paso & Southwestern system in 1924, a few years too early to merit inclusion in this book. However, its lines were significant enough that the abandonment of the middle of the system provokes curiosity, and its steam locomotives were conspicuous, long-lived members of SP's roster.

The El Paso & Southwestern system was controlled by the Phelps-Dodge Corporation. It comprised several railroads:

• El Paso & Southwestern Railroad, from the Rio Grande bridge at El Paso west through Douglas, Ariz., to Tucson, plus branches to Deming, Courtland, Bisbee, Lowell, Fort Huachuca, Benson, and Tombstone

• El Paso & Southwestern Railroad of Texas, from the Rio Grande bridge through El Paso, then northeast to the New Mexico state line

• El Paso & Northeastern Railway, from the Texas-New Mexico state line northeast of El Paso to Carrizozo, N. M.

• El Paso & Rock Island Railway: Carri-zozo to Santa Rosa, 128 miles (the line from Santa Rosa to Tucumcari was owned by the Rock Island but in later years leased to the Southern Pacific)

• Alamogordo & Sacramento Mountain Railway: Alamogordo and Russia, 32 miles (notable for its climb from 4,320 feet at Alamogordo to 8,600 feet at Cloudcroft, 20 miles out)

• Dawson Railway & Coal Co.: Tucumcari to Dawson, N. M., 132 miles

• EP&SW controlled the Nacozari Railroad, from Douglas, Ariz., to Nacozari, Sonora

The eastern portion of the EP&SW formed an extension of the Rock Island's route southwest across Kansas, Oklahoma, Texas, and New Mexico—the Golden State Route in SP's advertising. West of El Paso the EP&SW was a second main line parallel to SP's own line but some distance south, close to the Mexican border. At Naco the EP&SW turned north to Benson, then turned northwest, crossing and recrossing the SP between Benson and Tucson.

	1923
Miles of railroad operated:	1,140
Number of locomotives:	147
Number of passenger cars:	83
Number of freight cars:	4,326
Number of company service cars:	320
Location of headquarters: El Paso, Texas	
Successors:	
Southern Pacific	
Union Pacific	
Portions still operated: Union Pacific: El Paso–Tucumcari; Douglas–Benson Junction; Mescal–South Line Junction (Tucson)	

later that year, and revived it in 1983. On December 23, 1983, Santa Fe Industries and Southern Pacific Company, the parent companies of the two railroads, were absorbed by the new Santa Fe Southern Pacific Corporation. The two rail-roads remained separate but went so far as to paint and partly letter locomotives for the Southern Pacific & Santa Fe Railway.

The Interstate Commerce Commission turned down the request for merger, rejected the subse-quent appeal, and ordered SFSP to divest itself of one railroad. Offers to buy SP came from Kansas City Southern, Guilford Transportation Industries, SP management, and Rio Grande Industries, parent of the Denver & Rio Grande

Western. On August 9, 1988, the ICC approved sale of the SP to Rio Grande Industries. The sale was completed on October 13, 1988.

The name of the new system was Southern Pacific Lines. The identity and image of the Denver & Rio Grande Western were replaced by those of SP—much like Cotton Belt came to look like its parent, SP.

In 1991 SP sold its San Francisco–San Jose line and the commuter business it operated for the California Department of Transportation to San Francisco, San Mateo, and Santa Clara counties (retaining freight rights). The Peninsula Corridor Joint Powers Board assumed responsibility for funding and operating the service; Amtrak took over actual operation of the Peninsula commute trains on July 1, 1992.

Union Pacific purchased the Southern Pacific on September 12, 1996. SP enthusiasts can take pleasure in knowing that technically SP merged UP, not the other way around. On February 1, 1998, the Southern Pacific Transportation Company (a Delaware corporation) merged the Union Pacific Railroad and was then renamed the Union Pacific Railroad Company.

Cotton Belt

The St. Louis Southwestern Railway (the Cotton Belt) was SP's principal subsidiary. It began as the 3-foot gauge Tyler Tap Railroad, opened in 1877 between Tyler, Tex., and a junction with the Texas & Pacific at Big Sandy. It was rechartered as the Texas & St. Louis Railway and extended to Texarkana and a connection with the St. Louis, Iron Mountain & Southern Railway in 1880. A year later it was extended west to Waco.

In 1881 the T&StL decided to fulfill its name. In 1882 it reached Birds Point, Missouri, across the Mississippi River from Cairo, Illinois. There it connected by barge with the narrow gauge St. Louis & Cairo. By 1885 a continuous system of 3-foot gauge railroads reached from Toledo, Ohio, to Houston, Tex., with intentions of heading for Laredo and eventually Mexico City.

In 1886 the T&StL was reorganized as the St. Louis, Arkansas & Texas Railway. It converted to standard gauge, built branches to Shreveport, Louisiana, and Fort Worth, Texas, in 1888, and entered bankruptcy in 1889. Jay Gould organized the St. Louis Southwestern Railway in 1891 and took over the StLA&T. The road gained access to Memphis, Tennessee; acquired trackage rights over Missouri Pacific from Thebes, Ill., to St. Louis in exchange for letting MP operate over SSW between Illmo, Mo., and Paragould, Ark.; and joined with MP in constructing a bridge over the Mississippi between Thebes and Illmo.

After World War I bridge traffic began to increase on the Cotton Belt. The Rock Island and the Kansas City Southern controlled it briefly before SP applied for control, which it got in 1932. The Cotton Belt essentially became a division of the SP, though its equipment was still lettered "Cotton Belt." (The St. Louis Southwestern Railway—the Cotton Belt—is described fully in its own entry in this book.)

In 1980 SSW acquired the former Rock Island line from St. Louis through Kansas City to Santa Rosa, N. M. (RI owned the line between Santa Rosa and Tucumcari, N. M., but it had long been leased to SP.) and trackage rights on Union Pacific's ex-Missouri Pacific route from Kansas City to St. Louis (the former RI line between Kansas City and St. Louis was part of a package).

SPCSL

Chicago, Missouri & Western Railway purchased Illinois Central Gulf's lines from Joliet to East St. Louis, Illinois, and from Springfield, Ill., to Kansas City on April 28, 1987, essentially resurrecting the old Alton Railroad. Less than a year later, on April 1, 1988, the CM&W entered bankruptcy. Southern Pacific purchased the East St. Louis–Joliet line to operate as SPCSL Corporation (Southern Pacific Chicago St. Louis).

Other subsidiaries

In 1907 SP and Santa Fe formed the jointly owned Northwestern Pacific Railroad, which consolidated several lines north of San Francisco. NWP built north through the redwood country and down the canyon of the Eel River to Eureka, Calif. SP bought out Santa Fe's share in 1929, and sold the line in the 1980s and 1990s. (Northwestern Pacific is described fully in its own entry in this book.)

SP had several subsidiary traction lines. The Portland, Eugene & Eastern served Oregon's Willamette Valley. The Interurban Electric Railway served the East Bay cities of Oakland, Berkeley, and Alameda and for a short period connected them with San Francisco via the Bay Bridge.

The Pacific Electric, largest interurban line in the U. S., blanketed the Los Angeles Basin. In addition, the Marin County suburban lines of Northwestern Pacific were electrified until the Golden Gate Bridge opened and buses replaced the train-and-ferry service. (Pacific Electric is described fully in its own entry in this book.)

	1929	1994
Miles of railroad operated:	13,848	8,991
Number of locomotives:	2,388	1,682
Number of passenger cars:	2,786	407*
Number of freight cars:	80,619	32,363
Number of company service cars:	6,083	1,154

Location of headquarters: San Francisco, California

Reporting marks: SP

Notable named passenger trains: *Coast Daylight* and *Lark* (San Francisco–Los Angeles), *Shasta Daylight* and *Cascade* (Oakland–Portland), *City of San Francisco* (Oakland–Chicago, operated jointly with Union Pacific and Chicago & North Western/Milwaukee Road), *San Joaquin Daylight* (Oakland–Los Angeles), *Sunset Limited* (Los Angeles–New Orleans), *Golden State* (Los Angeles–Chicago, operated jointly with Rock Island)

Historical and technical societies:
Southern Pacific Historical & Technical Society, P. O. Box 93697, Pasadena, CA 91109-3697
Southern Pacific Narrow Gauge Society, 3101 Waldorf, Riverside, CA 92507
*(1970)

Recommended reading:
Blue Streak Merchandise, by Fred W. Frailey, published in 1991 by Kalmbach Publishing Co., 21027 Crossroads Circle, P. O. Box 1612, Waukesha, WI 53187 (ISBN 0-89024-130-9)
The Southern Pacific 1901–1985, by Don L. Hofsommer, published in 1986 by Texas A&M University Press, College Station, TX 77843-4354 (ISBN 0-89096-246-4)
Golden Years of Railroading: Southern Pacific in the Bay Area, by George H. Drury, published in 1996 by Kalmbach Publishing Co. (ISBN 0-89024-274-7)

Subsidiaries and affiliated railroads, 1991:
Central California Traction Co. (33.3%)
Northwestern Pacific Railroad
Pacific Fruit Express
Portland Traction Co. (50%, owned jointly with Union Pacific)
St. Louis Southwestern Railway (99.9%)
Sunset Railway (50%, owned jointly with Santa Fe)
Visalia Electric Railway
Successor: Union Pacific

Southern Railway System

The earliest portion of the Southern Railway was the South Carolina Canal & Rail Road Company, which was chartered in 1828 to build from Charleston, S. C., to Hamburg, S. C., on the north bank of the Savannah River. Its purpose was to bring trade to the port of Charleston from inland points and divert trade that would otherwise move down the Savannah River to the port of Savannah, Georgia. When the 136-mile line was opened in 1833, it was the longest railroad in the world. By 1857 it was part of a line from Charleston to Memphis, Tennessee—at the time the longest connected system of railroads in the world. (Two of the railroads involved, the Georgia Railroad and the Western & Atlantic, are now part of CSX Transportation.)

The Southern Railway system, like many other railroads, grew by merger and acquisition, and the components retained their identities and corporate structure long after most other roads had absorbed their subsidiaries.

Richmond & Danville–Richmond Terminal

The Richmond & Danville Railroad was the nucleus of the Southern Railway. It was chartered in 1847 and completed in 1856 from Richmond, Virginia, west 141 miles to Danville, Va. Its charter allowed it to acquire and control only railroads with which it connected directly.

No steam locomotive typified the Southern Railway more than the green-and-gold class Ps-4 Pacific. Built between 1923 and 1928, these 64 4-6-2s were a modification of the USRA heavy Pacific and constituted the ultimate development of the steam passenger locomotive on the Southern. Number 1395 is shown leaving Alexandria, Virginia, in June 1937, with train 35, the Atlanta–New Orleans Express. Photo by Walter H. Thrall Jr.

In 1880 (to jump ahead briefly) interests connected with the R&D incorporated the Richmond & West Point Terminal Railway & Warehouse Co. ("Richmond Terminal") to acquire railroads that did not connect directly with the R&D. The majority owners of the R&D and the Richmond Terminal decided the existence of the Richmond Terminal was unnecessary (by

then, the R&D's charter had been amended) and in 1886 leased the railroads controlled by the Richmond Terminal to the Richmond & Danville; then the Richmond Terminal acquired the Richmond & Danville. In the following paragraphs, "R&D" can mean Richmond & Danville or Richmond Terminal or the owners of either, depending upon who was on top at the moment.

In 1863 the Richmond & Danville purchased a majority of the stock of the Piedmont Railroad, under construction from Danville to Greensboro, N. C. The line opened in 1864, and the R&D leased it in 1866. In 1871 the R&D leased the North Carolina Railroad, which was opened in 1856 from Goldsboro through Greensboro to Charlotte.

The R&D contracted to construct the Northwestern Railroad of North Carolina from Greensboro to Salem, and assisted the Atlanta & Richmond Air-Line Railroad with the construction of its line between Atlanta and Charlotte. Both those routes were opened in 1873. The Atlanta & Charlotte Air-Line Railway was organized in 1877 as the successor to the Atlanta & Richmond. It was leased to the Richmond & Danville in 1881.

In 1881 the R&D purchased the Virginia Midland Railway from the Baltimore & Ohio to get a direct Danville–Washington route that was about 20 miles shorter than the route through Richmond. The Virginia Midland had begun as the Orange & Alexandria Railroad, opened from Alexandria, Va., across the Potomac River from Washington, D. C., southwest to Gordonsville in 1854. Through trackage rights on a C&O predecessor and further construction it reached Lynchburg in 1860. It came under control of the state of Virginia in 1867, and in 1872 the Virginia & North Carolina Railroad was organized to consolidate the Orange, Alexandria & Manassas Gap (successor to the O&A) and the Lynchburg & Danville Railroad, under construction between the cities of its name. The Baltimore & Ohio obtained control and gave it a magnificent, resounding name: Washington City, Virginia Midland & Great Southern Railroad. The extension to Danville was completed in 1874, and in 1880 a cutoff from Orange to Charlottesville was opened. The company was reorganized as the Virginia Midland Railway in 1881.

In 1886 the R&D leased the Western North Carolina Railroad, which had been constructed under state auspices from Salisbury west through Old Fort (1869) and Asheville (1879) to a connection at the Tennessee state line with the East Tennessee, Virginia & Georgia.

The Georgia Pacific Railway was chartered in 1881 to build a railroad from Atlanta to a connection with the Texas & Pacific at Texarkana. It was opened as far as Columbus, Ala., in 1887.

It was leased to the Richmond & Danville in January 1889, shortly before it completed its line as far as the Mississippi River at Greenville, Miss. The Mississippi portion of the Georgia Pacific, which had remained a separate entity because of state laws, was cast off as the Columbus & Greenville in 1920.

In 1892 the Richmond Terminal and the railroads it controlled (Richmond & Danville; Virginia Midland; Charlotte, Columbia & Augusta; Western North Carolina; Georgia Pacific; and East Tennessee, Virginia & Georgia) were declared insolvent and entered receivership. The banking house of J. P. Morgan came to the rescue.

East Tennessee, Virginia & Georgia

In 1869 two railroads out of Knoxville, Tenn., the East Tennessee & Virginia and the East Tennessee & Georgia, were consolidated to form the East Tennessee, Virginia & Georgia Railroad. The East Tennessee & Virginia was built from Bristol, Va., to Knoxville, 131 miles, between 1850 and 1856. The East Tennessee & Georgia opened a line from Dalton, Ga., to Knoxville, 110 miles, and a branch from Cleveland, Tenn., to Chattanooga in 1859.

In 1881 the ETV&G acquired and constructed lines from Dalton to Brunswick, Ga., and Meridian, Mississippi. Three other major routes were more or less affiliated with the ETV&G: Chattanooga–Memphis, Mobile–Selma, Ala., and Louisville–Lexington, Kentucky.

Southern Railway

The Southern Railway was chartered in 1894 to acquire the properties of the Richmond Terminal. The system comprised lines from

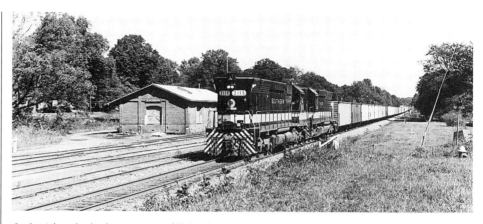

Southern's latter-day diesel image was one of black-and-white diesels with a modest amount of gold trim, running long-hood forward as often as not. Two SD45s have an easy job rolling empty hopper cars north through Blacksburg, South Carolina, but ahead of them is the 4.7 percent grade of Saluda Hill, steepest mainline grade in the U. S. Photo by Curt Tillotson Jr.

Alexandria, Va., to Columbus, Miss.; from Chattanooga through Atlanta to Brunswick, Ga.; from Memphis through Chattanooga to Bristol, Va.; from Selma, Ala., to Rome, Ga.; and from Danville, Va., to Richmond. The Southern began to develop under the direction of Samuel Spencer.

It acquired other railroads just as the Richmond & Danville had done. Among the larger ones were the Georgia, Southern & Florida Railway in 1895 and the Louisville, Evansville & St. Louis Consolidated Railroad in 1898.

The Southern acquired a number of subsidiaries over the years. Many of them retained independent status, and the continued existence of these subsidiaries was attested to by initials on locomotives and cars.

Queen & Crescent Route

The Alabama Great Southern Railway Company, Ltd., and the Alabama, New Orleans, Texas & Pacific Junction Railways, Ltd., were British-owned holding companies that owned five railroads forming the Queen & Crescent Route between Cincinnati (the Queen City) and New Orleans (the Crescent City). The five railroads were the Alabama Great Southern; the Cincinnati, New Orleans & Texas Pacific; the New Orleans & Northeastern; the Alabama &

Vicksburg; and the Vicksburg, Shreveport & Pacific. In 1890 the Richmond & Danville and the East Tennessee, Virginia & Georgia acquired control of the AGS company.

The Alabama Great Southern was incorporated in 1877. It was the successor to the Alabama & Chattanooga Railroad, whose predecessors had been chartered in 1852 and 1853, consolidated in 1868, and opened in 1871. Its main line stretched from Chattanooga to Meridian, Miss., 292 miles; total mileage was 315. Southern acquired the minority interest in AGS in 1969.

The New Orleans & Northeastern Railroad was incorporated in 1868 in Louisiana and in 1871 in Mississippi. It lay dormant until 1881, when control of the company was acquired by the Alabama, New Orleans, Texas & Pacific Junction Railways Ltd. Construction began in 1882, and the line was opened between New Orleans and Meridian, Miss., 196 miles, in 1883. The Southern purchased the NO&NE in 1916. The Alabama Great Southern merged the NO&NE in 1969.

The Cincinnati Southern Railway was incorporated in 1869 to build a railroad south from Cincinnati, Ohio, to Chattanooga, Tenn., 336 miles. It was opened in 1880. The railroad was owned (and still is) by the city of Cincinnati. The Cincinnati, New Orleans & Texas Pacific was chartered in 1881 and immediately leased the Cincinnati Southern for operation. The CNO&TP was controlled by the two British-owned holding companies mentioned above, which also controlled the Alabama Great Southern and the New Orleans & Northeastern. The Southern and the Cincinnati, Hamilton & Day-

ton (Baltimore & Ohio) acquired control of the CNO&TP in 1895, but through its control of the Alabama Great Southern, which held an interest in the CNO&TP, Southern effectively had control. Southern acquired B&O's interest in 1954.

The two Vicksburg railroads, which were controlled by the Alabama, New Orleans, Texas & Pacific company, became part of the Illinois Central system in 1927. The Alabama Great Southern and the Cincinnati, New Orleans & Texas Pacific were considered Class 1 railroads in their own right until recent corporate simplifications took effect.

Georgia Southern & Florida

The Georgia Southern & Florida Railway was incorporated in 1895 under Southern Railway control as a reorganization of the Georgia Southern & Florida Railroad, which had been opened in 1890 from Macon, Ga., through Valdosta, Ga., to Palatka, Fla. It was intended to be part of a route from Birmingham, Ala., to Florida that would bypass Atlanta. In 1902 it purchased the Atlantic, Valdosta & Western Railway line from Valdosta, Ga., to a point near Jacksonville, Fla. Southern acquired control in 1895.

Mobile & Ohio and Monon

The Southern gained control of the Mobile & Ohio in 1901, and went so far as to propose merger. When M&O fell on hard times in 1930, Southern was unable to provide financial help. In 1938 Southern sold its M&O bonds, and M&O became part of the new Gulf, Mobile & Ohio.

In 1902 Southern and the Louisville & Nashville acquired joint control of the Monon (Chicago, Indianapolis & Louisville), but lost

that control in Monon's 1946 reorganization. Both those railroads are discussed elsewhere in this book.

Central of Georgia

The Central of Georgia Railway emerged from Illinois Central control in 1948, and from 1956 to 1961 it was under the control of the Frisco. The ICC rejected Frisco's bid for merger with CofG but approved control by the Southern in 1963. The CofG is discussed elsewhere in this book.

In the 1970s the Southern was notable for staying out of Amtrak, continuing to run its remaining passenger trains and gradually trimming service to just the Washington–Atlanta–New Orleans *Southern Crescent*. Amtrak took over the operation of that train on February 1, 1979. In the past two decades Southern, one of the first large railroads to dieselize, has operated several steam locomotives in conjunction with museums and enthusiast groups.

On March 25, 1982, the Interstate Commerce Commission approved the acquisition by Norfolk Southern Corporation, a newly organized holding company, of two railroads: the Southern Railway and the Norfolk & Western Railway. Merger took place on June 1, 1982. At the end of 1990 the Norfolk & Western Railway became a subsidiary of the Southern Railway (it had been a subsidiary of Norfolk Southern Corporation), and the Southern Railway changed its name to Norfolk Southern Railway.

	1929	1988
Miles of railroad operated:	8,051	9,757
Number of locomotives:	1,802	1,416
Number of passenger cars:	1,037	119
Number of freight cars:	60,423	58,929
Number of company service cars:	2,565	2,678

Location of headquarters: Washington, D. C.

Reporting marks: SOU

Notable named passenger trains: *Crescent Limited* (New York–New Orleans; operated New York–Washington by the Pennsylvania; Atlanta–Montgomery by the West Point Route; Montgomery–New Orleans by the Louisville & Nashville); *Southerner* and *Southern Crescent* (Washington–New Orleans)

Historical and technical society:
Southern Railway Historical Association, P. O. Box 33, Spencer, NC 28159
Southern Railway Historical Society, P. O. Box 204094, Augusta, GA 30917-4094

Recommended reading: *Southern Railway System Steam Locomotives and Boats*, by Richard E. Prince, published in 1970 by Richard E. Prince

Subsidiaries and affiliated railroads, 1988:
Alabama Great Southern
Atlanta & Charlotte Air Line
Atlantic & East Carolina
Central of Georgia
Cincinnati, New Orleans & Texas Pacific
Georgia Northern
Georgia Southern & Florida
High Point, Randleman, Asheboro & Southern
Interstate Railroad
Live Oak, Perry and South Georgia
Louisiana Southern
Memphis & Charleston
Mobile & Birmingham
North Carolina Midland
Tennessee, Alabama & Georgia

Tennessee Railway
Transylvania Railroad
Virginia & Southwestern
Yadkin Railroad

Predecessor railroads in this book:
Atlantic & East Carolina
Atlantic & Yadkin
Central of Georgia
Georgia & Florida
Georgia Northern
Interstate
Norfolk Southern
Savannah & Atlanta
Tennessee, Alabama & Georgia
Wrightsville & Tennille

Successor: Norfolk Southern

Spokane International Railway

The Spokane International was built by D. C. Corbin from Spokane, Washington, north to the Canadian border at Eastport, Idaho, and Kingsgate, British Columbia. There it connected with Canadian Pacific's Kettle Valley route. The southern half of the line, from Spokane to Sandpoint, was parallel and within a few miles of Northern Pacific's main line; from Sandpoint to Bonners

	1929	1958
Miles of railroad operated:	166	150
Number of locomotives:	11	12
Number of passenger cars:	6	
Number of freight cars:	263	
Number of company service cars:	18	
Number of freight and company service cars:		201
Location of headquarters: Spokane, Washington		
Reporting marks: SI		
Successor: Union Pacific		
Portions still operated: Union Pacific: Spokane, Wash.–Eastport, Idaho; Coeur d'Alene Junction–Coeur d'Alene, Idaho		

Most of Spokane International's business was—and is—bridge traffic, but the lumber industry provided much of the road's local business. In this 1951 scene the first three cars behind the RS-1 of Extra 205 are loaded with forest products. Photo by Philip R. Hastings.

Ferry it virtually duplicated Great Northern's main line. The SI began operation on November 1, 1906. It gave CPR a route to Spokane—or in conjunction with Soo Line, which it controlled, a route from St. Paul, Minnesota, to Spokane in competition with James J. Hill's Great Northern and Northern Pacific. CPR purchased control of the SI in 1917.

Spokane International entered bankruptcy proceedings in 1933. Reorganization in 1941 as the Spokane International Railroad wiped out CPR's stock interest. During World War II business increased and revenues climbed to give the railroad Class 1 status (then, revenues of $1 million or more). After the war it needed and got extensive rebuilding and dieselization. More than 80 percent of its business was bridge traffic between CPR and the connecting railroads at Spokane.

Union Pacific acquired control of SI on October 6, 1958, by acquisition of nearly 90 percent of its stock, and gradually acquired the rest.

Spokane, Portland & Seattle Railway

 James J. Hill announced in 1905 that he intended to build a railroad along the north bank of the Columbia River, partly to block the Milwaukee Road from doing the same and partly to invade Oregon, territory that belonged almost exclusively to E. H. Harriman's Union Pacific and Southern Pacific. The Portland & Seattle Railway was incorporated in 1905, and in 1908 Spokane was added to its name. The railroad was completed during 1908 from Pasco, Washington, to Portland, Oregon, along the north bank of the Columbia River. In 1909 the line was opened from Spokane to Pasco. Jointly financing the construction of the SP&S were Great Northern and Northern Pacific, both under Hill's control.

Hill had already acquired a line along the south bank of the lower part of the Columbia River west of Portland; that plus Northern Pacific's line from Portland to Goble, Oregon, formed a route from Portland to Astoria where connection was made with Hill's steamships to San Francisco.

For most of its life the SP&S functioned as an obscure extension of its two parents. Its steam locomotives for the most part were acquired second-hand from GN and NP. The road acquired a distinct identity during the diesel era with its heavy reliance on Alco power and a new

An extra freight west pulls out of Wishram, Washington, in June 1953 behind an FA-1/FB-1/FA-1 trio while an S-2 works the yard — Spokane, Portland & Seattle favored Alco diesels. Photo by David Plowden.

slogan, "The Northwest's Own Railway." SP&S was merged into Burlington Northern along with its parents, Northern Pacific and Great Northern, and Chicago, Burlington & Quincy on March 2, 1970.

Oregon Electric Railway

SP&S acquired the Oregon Electric Railway in 1910, two years after it had opened between Portland and Salem. The main line was extended south to Eugene in 1912; among the several branches was a freight-only line to a logging area on the western slope of the Cascades. The last passenger service was discontinued in 1933, and the road was dieselized in 1945. Like many other parts of the Hill empire, the OE was characterized by head-on competition with Harriman, in this case with Southern Pacific's electric lines in the Willamette Valley.

Oregon Trunk Railway

The Oregon Trunk was incorporated in 1909 and opened in 1911 between Wishram, Wash., on the Columbia River, and Bend, practically in the center of Oregon, 152 miles. Both Oregon Trunk and the Oregon-Washington Railroad & Navigation Co. (Union Pacific) built south up the canyon of the Deschutes River. The two railroads, backed

by Hill and Harriman, respectively, fought over occupancy of the canyon and eventually came to terms—trackage rights over portions of each other's line and abandonment of duplicate track. Oregon Trunk's bridge over the Crooked River north of Bend is tied with Southern Pacific's Pecos River bridge for the honor of highest common-carrier railroad bridge in the U. S.

United Railways

In 1906 the United Railways Company was incorporated and purchased the properties of Oregon Traction Company, which had a line from Linnton to Keasey, 54 miles. The line was operated primarily as a steam railroad and was notable for a 4,100-foot tunnel west of Portland. SP&S absorbed the company in 1943.

	1929	1969
Miles of railroad operated:	555*	922
Number of locomotives:	99	112
Number of passenger cars:	100	54
Number of freight cars:	698	3,216
Number of company service cars:	252	355

Location of headquarters: Portland, Oregon

Reporting marks: SPS

Notable named passenger trains: *Empire Builder* (Portland–Chicago, operated east of Spokane by Great Northern and Burlington; *North Coast Limited* (Portland–Chicago, operated east of Pasco by
*(915 with subsidiaries)

Northern Pacific and Burlington)

Historical and technical society: Spokane, Portland & Seattle Railway Historical Society, 6207 N. Concord, Portland, OR 97217-4736; http://www.teleport.com/~amacha/spsrhs.htm

Recommended reading: *The Northwest's Own Railway*, by Walter R. Grande, published in 1992 by Grande Press, 4243 S.W. Admiral Street, Portland, OR 97221-3669

Subsidiaries and affiliated railroads, 1929:

Oregon Electric Railway (154 miles, 10 locomotives, 76 passenger cars, 25 freight cars, 27 service cars)

Oregon Trunk Railway (152 miles, 3 locomotives, 10 service cars)

United Railways (54 miles, 6 passenger cars, 62 freight cars, 6 service cars)

Successors:

Burlington Northern

Burlington Northern & Santa Fe

Portions still operated:

Burlington Northern & Santa Fe: Pasco, Wash.–Portland, Ore.; Salem–Eugene, Ore.; Lebanon–Foster, Ore.

Portland & Western: Salem–Greton, Ore.; Bendemeer–Banks, Ore.; Hillsboro–Forest Grove, Ore.; Portland–Astoria, Ore.

Staten Island Rapid Transit Railway

The least-known borough of New York City is Richmond, or Staten Island. Geographically it is much closer to New Jersey than to New York, and until the completion of the Verrazano Bridge in 1964, it was connected to the rest of New York—city and state—by ferries from St. George, at the north end of the island.

In 1885 Baltimore & Ohio purchased the Staten Island Rapid Transit Railway, which had a short line of its own between Tompkinsville and Clifton on the northeast shore of Staten Island and leased the Staten Island Railway, a line from Clifton to Tottenville, at its southern tip. (The latter had been completed in 1860 and was one of Cornelius Vanderbilt's early properties.) B&O's intention was to build freight and passenger terminals on Staten Island; purchase of SIRT gave B&O waterfront property on New York Bay.

SIRT built a line west to the Arthur Kill Bridge in 1889 at the same time the Baltimore & New York, another B&O subsidiary, built a connecting line from Cranford Jct. on the Central Railroad of New Jersey. SIRT built a short line from Clifton to South Beach in 1892.

In anticipation of a tunnel under the Narrows to Brooklyn and a connection there with the New York subway system, SIRT electrified its lines in 1925 using third-rail power distribution and cars similar to those of the Brooklyn-

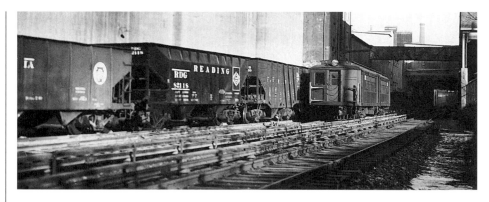

A single electric car operating on the line to Arlington passes through the U. S. Gypsum plant between New Brighton and Sailor's Snug Harbor on State Island's north shore. The standard-size hopper car, small by present-day standards, shows how small the electric car is. Photo by Herman Rinke.

Manhattan Transit Co. The electrification brought no big increase in traffic, and the tunnel was never built.

In 1944 SIRT purchased the property of the Baltimore & New York and merged the Staten Island Railway. In 1948 the road discontinued its ferry service between Tottenville and Perth Amboy, N. J. The terminal at St. George was destroyed by fire in 1946; a modern replacement was opened in 1951. SIRT discontinued passenger service on the lines to Arlington and South Beach in March 1953 because of city-operated bus competition.

On January 1, 1970, New York City's lease of the St. George–Tottenville line was terminated. After that date the city reimbursed the railroad for its passenger deficits. On July 1, 1971, operation of the Tottenville line was turned over to the

Staten Island Rapid Transit Operating Authority, a division of the state's Metropolitan Transportation Authority, and the line itself was purchased by the city of New York. Later that year the name of the railroad was changed to Staten Island Railroad Corporation.

In 1985 the Staten Island Railroad was purchased by the Delaware Otsego System. By the mid-1990s freight service had ceased, but the plans for splitting up Conrail in 1998 included joint service to Staten Island by both CSX and Norfolk Southern.

	1929	1970
Miles of railroad operated:	24	12
Number of locomotives:	4	7
Number of passenger cars:	95	48
Number of freight cars:	1	7*
Number of company service cars:	21	6
Number of ferries:	3	

*(cabooses)

Location of headquarters: New York, New York
Reporting marks: SIR
Historical and technical society: Baltimore & Ohio Railroad Historical Society, P. O. Box 13578, Baltimore, MD 21203
Portions still operated:
Staten Island Rapid Transit Operating Authority: St. George–Tottenville

Sumpter Valley Railway

The Sumpter Valley was incorporated in 1890 to tap the forests of the Blue Mountains of eastern Oregon. Much of the rolling stock for the line came from Union Pacific 3-foot gauge lines in Utah and Idaho that had just been standard-gauged. The first portion of the line from Baker to McEwen opened for service in 1892, and the line reached the town of Sumpter (which was in the midst of a gold-mining boom) in 1897.

The line reached Austin in 1905 and Prairie City, a cattle-raising center, in 1910. There were proposals to extend the line to Burns and also southwest to a connection with the Nevada-California-Oregon, which was building north from Reno, Nevada. The latter would have created a narrow gauge route all the way from California's Owens Valley to Baker, except for a short stretch of the standard gauge Virginia & Truckee, and it would have traversed some of the emptiest country in the U. S. The Sumpter Valley got no farther than Prairie City, but it connected with an extensive network of logging railroads centered on Austin.

Sumpter Valley 2-6-6-2 No. 250 rolls a long train of lumber along the Powder River in the Blue Mountains of eastern Oregon in 1946. Photo by H. R. Griffiths.

free of debt. The last scheduled run was on April 11, 1947, and official abandonment came on August 31, 1948. The articulateds were sold to International Railways of Central America.

A two-mile portion of the railroad at Baker remained in switching service until the end of 1961. The sole remaining locomotive, a 30-ton Davenport diesel switcher built in 1937, was sold to the Denver & Rio Grande Western in 1963 for service at Durango as D&RGW No. 50.

	1929	1945
Miles of railroad operated:	80	58
Number of locomotives:	11	3
Number of passenger cars:	4	
Number of freight cars:	236	
Number of company service cars:	24	
Number of freight and company service cars:		227
Location of headquarters: Baker, Oregon		
Reporting marks: SVRy		

Recommended reading: *Rails, Sagebrush and Pine*, by Mallory Hope Ferrell, published in 1967 by Golden West Books, P. O. Box 80250, San Marino, CA 91108

Portions still operated: Sumpter Valley Railroad Restoration operates a few miles of the line in the mountains west of Baker City.

In 1932 the western 20 miles of the line from Bates to Prairie City were abandoned. In 1940 the SV bought two 2-6-6-2 articulateds from the Uintah Railway. SV converted them from tank engines to tender engines and used them for seven years.

By 1946 a reduction by the U. S. Forestry Service in the amount of timber that could be cut and the necessity to transfer lumber from narrow gauge to standard gauge cars at Baker caused the Sumpter Valley to petition for abandonment, even though it was still profitable and

Tennessee, Alabama & Georgia Railway

TAG ROUTE Construction of the Chattanooga Southern Railway began in 1890 and was completed in 1891, creating a new line between Chattanooga, Tennessee, and Gadsden, Alabama. Backing the project was Russell Sage, a New York financier. The company entered receivership in 1892 and was reorganized as the Chattanooga Southern Railroad in 1896. Receivers again took it over between 1907 and 1910; it was reorganized in 1911 as the Tennessee, Alabama & Georgia Railway—it, too, was reorganized in 1920. During the 1920s the ICC approved a proposal to extend the line southwest to a connection with Seaboard's Atlanta–Birmingham line, but the idea never bore fruit.

The TA&G was sold, reorganized, and sold again, this time to a syndicate headed by W. H. Coverdale of Coverdale & Colpitts, the railroad engineering firm. The new management immediately undertook a long-needed rehabilitation. Much of the line was still laid with the original 56-pound rail; it was upgraded with 100-pound rail. As business increased, TA&G had to replace its small, low-drivered Consolidations with secondhand Mikados and a pair of ex-Boston & Albany Berkshires. The company was reorganized again in 1937.

The original purpose of the road was to tap the iron, coal, and timber resources of northeastern

Tennessee, Alabama & Georgia's entire diesel roster appears in this 1970 scene in the road's Chattanooga yard: GP38 80, GP7 709, GP18 50, and GP7s 708 and 707. Photo by William J. Husa, Jr.

Alabama, but gradually the TA&G's principal purpose came to be serving the steel mills at Gadsden and furnishing a northward outlet for them.

On January 1, 1971, Southern Railway purchased the TA&G. The middle portion of the TA&G was abandoned about 1980, and the south end in the early 1990s. NS sold the northernmost 19 miles of line to the Chattooga & Chickamauga Railway in 1989.

	1929	1970
Miles of railroad operated:	95	87
Number of locomotives:	8	5
Number of passenger cars:	2 (motor)	
Number of freight cars:	8	94
Number of company service cars:	20	8
Location of headquarters: Chattanooga, Tennessee		
Reporting marks: TA&G		

Recommended reading: *Central of Georgia Railway and Connecting Lines,* by Richard E. Prince, published in 1976 by Richard E. Prince

Portions still operated:
Chattooga & Chickamauga: Chattanooga, Tenn.—Hedges, Ga.

Tennessee Central Railway

The Tennessee & Pacific Railroad was organized in 1871 and built eastward from Nashville to Lebanon, Tenn. By 1894 the line had extended east to Monterey with the intention of tapping coal mines; by 1900 the line had been pushed east to a connection with the Southern (Cincinnati, New Orleans, & Texas Pacific) at Emory Gap by the Tennessee Central Railway (the road's history includes several Tennessee Central companies, railroads, and railways). In 1904 the TC was complete, with a 2-mile extension from Emory Gap to Harriman and an 83-mile line constructed from Nashville northwest to Hopkinsville, Kentucky.

The TC was the only direct route from Nashville to eastern Tennessee, albeit through topography requiring 3-percent grades, 10-degree curves, and several spectacular trestles. The road was intended to be a coal carrier—and by 1950 the principal commodity carried by the TC was indeed coal, but more coal was received from connecting railroads than was originated on line. TC provided access to Nashville for Illinois Central from Hopkinsville and for Southern from Harriman. Its tracks formed a belt line around Nashville, a city that was otherwise the exclusive province of Louisville & Nashville and its subsidiary Nashville, Chattanooga & St.

Louis. During World War II TC's traffic was boosted considerably by the Army installation at Fort Campbell, near Hopkinsville.

Between a brief receivership in 1904 and a longer one from 1913 to 1917 the road was divided at Nashville and operated by IC and Southern, but neither IC nor Southern wished to continue the arrangement. The road was reorganized in 1922, and in 1946 control was assumed by a group of investors from Philadelphia. Net operating income moved to the deficit side of the ledgers in 1963; in the decade from 1957 to 1966 the TC posted a net profit for only two years, 1958 and 1959. In May 1968

A westbound extra freight rolls out of a tunnel near Rockwood, Tennessee, at the eastern end of the Tennessee Central. Photo by R. D. Sharpless.

the ICC authorized abandonment of the Tennessee Central.

Portions of Tennessee Central's main line were acquired by other roads: Hopkinsville–Nashville by Illinois Central; Nashville–Crossville by Louisville & Nashville; and Crossville–Harriman by Southern. The Hopkinsville–Nashville segment has had a succession of operators and has been trimmed back to a 19-mile stub out of Nashville. About two-thirds of the line east of Nashville is still in service.

	1929	1966
Miles of railroad operated:	296	280
Number of locomotives:	41	21
Number of passenger cars:	33	
Number of freight cars:	663	
Number of company service cars:	96	
Number of freight and company service cars:		557

Location of headquarters: Nashville, Tennessee
Reporting marks: TC
Recommended reading: *Ghost Railroads of Tennessee*, by Elmer G. Sulzer, published in 1975 by Vane A. Jones Co., Indianapolis, Ind.
Portions still operated:
Central of Tennessee: Nashville–Chapmansboro
Nashville & Eastern: Nashville–Monterey; Stone River–Old Hickory; Carthage Junction–Carthage

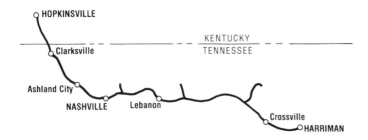

Texas & Pacific Railway

The southernmost of the routes surveyed between 1853 and 1855 for a transcontinental railroad led across central Texas. Although it was the shortest and lowest route between the Atlantic and the Pacific and the one least subject to the rigors of winter, the Civil War eliminated it from consideration.

After the war, though, a transcontinental route between the thirty-second and thirty-fifth parallels was again feasible and desirable. In 1871 Congress chartered the Texas Pacific Railroad to build from Marshall, Tex., to San Diego, California, via El Paso, Texas. The name of the company was soon changed to Texas & Pacific Railway. Its first president was Thomas Scott, who had been vice-president and general manager of the Pennsylvania Railroad, and its first chief engineer was Grenville M. Dodge, former chief engineer of the Union Pacific.

The new road purchased the properties and franchises of two early railroads, including a rail line in operation between Shreveport, Louisiana, and Longview, Tex. Construction west from Longview, begun in October 1872, was plagued by low water in the Red River (hindering the transportation of supplies), an epizootic that killed off the mules used in construction, and yellow fever. Even so, the line reached Dallas in less than a year.

The 2-10-4 wheel arrangement was a natural development of Lima's Super-Power 2-8-4, and it was named "Texas" for the Texas & Pacific, its first user. T&P amassed a stable of 70 of these machines, one of which is shown lifting a freight up Baird Hill in west Texas. T&P photo.

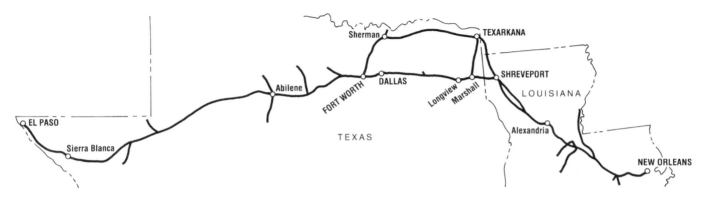

As T&P streamlined and dieselized its passenger trains, the *Eagle* colors were also applied to steam power, such as Pacific 706, shown at Jonesville, Texas, in 1951 on train 24. Photo by Ed Robinson.

By the beginning of 1874 the T&P was operating from Shreveport west to Dallas, from Marshall north to Texarkana, and from Sherman east to Brookston (near Paris). In July 1876 the line from Shreveport reached Fort Worth. (To keep its charter in effect, the T&P had to reach Fort Worth before the state legislature ended its session; Fort Worth's representative kept the session going for several extra days.) Less than a month later the Texarkana–Sherman line was completed.

Fort Worth remained T&P's western terminus for several years. Construction had resumed in 1880, and the line proceeded rapidly across west Texas. On December 15, 1881, at Sierra Blanca, about 90 miles east of El Paso, the T&P met the Southern Pacific, which had been building east from Los Angeles, completing the second transcontinental rail route.

By September 1882 T&P had purchased and built a line east from Shreveport to New Orleans, essentially completing the road. In the decades before and after the turn of the century T&P upgraded some of the hastily constructed portions of its main line and acquired a number of short branches, but did nothing to alter the basic shape of its map.

In January 1880 Jay Gould and Russell Sage joined T&P's board of directors; in April of the next year Scott sold his interests in the T&P to Gould, who became president of the road. The T&P was in receivership from 1885 to 1888 and entered receivership again in 1916. Fortunately for T&P, oil was discovered at Ranger, Texas, in 1918. T&P's revenues from the oil boom underwrote a rehabilitation program and put the road back in the black in 1924. Oil continued to be a major item of traffic until the completion of pipelines in the late 1940s.

In 1962 the Muskogee Co. authorized the sale of all its railroad stocks to the Texas & Pacific. In September 1964 T&P acquired control of the three Muskogee roads but immediately sold the Oklahoma City-Ada-Atoka to the Santa Fe. Midland Valley was merged into T&P on April 1, 1967, and the same happened to Kansas, Oklahoma & Gulf exactly three years later.

During reorganization in 1923 Texas & Pacific issued preferred stock to Missouri Pacific in exchange for mortgage bonds held by MP. By the beginning of 1930 MP owned all T&P's preferred stock and more than half its common stock. After many years of controlling T&P, MoPac finally merged the Texas & Pacific on October 15, 1976.

	1929	1975
Miles of railroad operated:	1,956	2,139
Number of locomotives:	372	153
Number of passenger cars:	234	
Number of freight cars:	9,517	13,366
Number of company service cars:	1,465	263

Location of headquarters: Dallas, Texas
Reporting marks: T&P, TP
Historical and technical society: Missouri Pacific Historical Society, P. O. Box 330427, Fort Worth, TX 76163

Recommended reading: *Texas & Pacific*, by Don Watson and Steve Brown, published in 1978 by Boston Mills Press, R. R. 1, Cheltenham, ON, Canada L0P 1C0 (ISBN 0-919822-83-5)

Subsidiaries and affiliated railroads, 1975:
Abilene & Southern
Fort Worth Belt (60%)
Texas & Pacific-Missouri Pacific Terminal Railroad of New Orleans (50%, jointly with Missouri Pacific)
Texas-New Mexico
Weatherford, Mineral Wells & Northwestern

Predecessor railroads in this book:
Kansas, Oklahoma & Gulf
Midland Valley
Successors:
Missouri Pacific
Union Pacific
Portions still operated:
Acadiana: Opelousas–Bunkie, La.
Texas Northeastern Division, Mid-Michigan Railroad: Texarkana–Sherman–Denison, Texas
Union Pacific: New Orleans–Fort Worth–El Paso; Anchorage–Lettsworth, La.

Tidewater Southern Railway

The Tidewater Southern was conceived as an interurban between Stockton and Fresno, California, although almost from the beginning there was talk of extension south to Los Angeles. Construction began in 1911, and in October 1912 the road began steam passenger service between Stockton and Modesto, 33 miles. The line was electrified in 1913. It was extended to Turlock in 1916, and a branch was built to Manteca in 1918, but these lines were never electrified nor did they offer passenger service. Passenger service ended in 1932, but wires remained over the tracks in Modesto until 1950. The city forbade the operation of steam locomotives in the streets, and electric locomotives (diesels after November 1947) pulled trains, steam locomotive and all, through the city.

The Western Pacific obtained control of the road in 1917. The Tidewater Southern offered WP access to the rich north end of the San Joaquin Valley and became a profitable feeder for WP. Regular operations of the Tidewater Southern were dieselized in 1948. One steam locomotive was retained until 1955 for service during the heavy shipping season—and also out of deference to a bridge remaining from TS's light-rail interurban days.

Tidewater Southern maintained its identity more firmly than did Sacramento Northern, WP's other ex-interurban, and hung on even after WP was absorbed by Union Pacific. It was mid-1983 before the *Official Guide* dropped its listing for Tidewater Southern, and even in 1985 the road was still listed in *The Pocket List of Railroad Officials*, although most of Tidewater Southern's officials were located in Omaha and none were in Modesto.

	1929	1981
Miles of railroad operated:	65	56
Number of locomotives:	1	
Number of passenger cars:	3	
Number of freight cars:	2	
Number of company service cars:	3	

Location of headquarters: San Francisco, California

Reporting marks: TS

Recommended reading: *Western Pacific's Diesel Years,* by Joseph A. Strapac, published in 1980 by Overland Models, Inc., R. R. 12, Box 445, Muncie, IN 47302 (ISBN 0-916160-08-4)

Successor: Union Pacific

Portions still operated: UP operates all the TS except for the long-abandoned passenger trackage into downtown Stockton.

Map: see page 369

The refrigerator cars standing in front of the packing shed at Turner, California, explain Tidewater Southern's value as a feeder to parent Western Pacific. RS-1 No. 747, once on the roster of Spokane International as No. 205, has just picked up three loaded reefers and is ready to leave for Stockton in this 1972 scene. Photo by R. T. Sharp.

Tonopah & Goldfield Railroad

In 1900 the discovery of silver in south-central Nevada created a boom town: Tonopah. The mining boom in turn created a demand for rail transportation. There were several proposals, including a branch of Southern Pacific's narrow gauge Carson & Colorado and southward extensions of the Nevada Central, the Eureka & Palisade and the Nevada Northern.

A preliminary survey was made in early 1903, and on July 25, 1903, the Tonopah Railroad was organized by the Tonopah Mining Co., headquartered in Philadelphia. Work began promptly from Tonopah Junction, 9 miles south of Mina on the C&C, and the 3-foot gauge track reached Tonopah, 60 miles from the junction, on July 23, 1904. One week later a cloudburst washed out part of the line. More rain followed, and it was September 7 before service was restored (the engineer who located the line was one of many Easterners who thought it never rained in the desert).

In October 1904 SP began standard-gauging its line from Mound House, the junction with the Virginia & Truckee, to Mina. The Tonopah Railroad proceeded to standard-gauge its own line. Completion of the job on August 15, 1905, marked the end of one of the shortest-lived narrow gauge operations on record.

Meanwhile, gold had been discovered in 1902 south of Tonopah, creating another boom town,

World War II brought a last surge of business to the Tonopah & Goldfield. Tank cars of aviation gasoline for the air base at Tonopah require the efforts of Consolidations 56 and 57 on the southbound mixed train a few miles out of Tonopah Junction. Photo by C. M. Clegg.

Goldfield. The board of directors of the mining company declared the company had no interest in Goldfield affairs and declined to invest mining company or railroad assets in an extension to Goldfield. As individuals, however, they did—and organized the standard gauge Goldfield Railroad.

On September 12, 1905, the first train rolled into Goldfield. At that point the directors decided that it would be better to have one railroad than two. The Tonopah and Goldfield railroads were consolidated as the Tonopah & Gold-

field Railroad on November 1, 1905. The new railroad did well enough to pay a 30 percent dividend in June 1907, but there were no more dividends for the next five years, and when dividends resumed they were more modest.

Also in 1905 T&G interests organized the improbably named Bullfrog Goldfield Railroad to build south to Beatty to head off the Las Vegas & Tonopah and the Tonopah & Tidewater. It reached Beatty in April 1907, six months after the Las Vegas & Tonopah had arrived. The LV&T pushed north parallel to the BG and reached Goldfield in October 1907, just in time for the collapse of the mining boom and a nationwide business slump. In 1908 the Tonopah & Tidewater took over operation of the Bullfrog Goldfield.

There followed a long period of declining business and belt-tightening through which the T&G continued to operated at a profit, if not a large one. The Las Vegas & Tonopah ceased operation in 1918, and the last Bullfrog Goldfield train departed Goldfield on January 7, 1928, leaving the T&G alone in Goldfield. The T&G endured a receivership from 1932 to 1937, and in 1942 the Tonopah Mining Co. sold its interest in the railroad to Dulien Steel Products of Seattle. Dismantling and scrapping appeared likely.

In 1942 the Army Air Force established an air base at Tonopah. Movements of troops and aviation gasoline suddenly brought boom times to the Tonopah & Goldfield, but management problems prevented the company from taking advantage of the business to put the line and rolling stock into better shape.

When the air base was deactivated at the end of the war and the Army asked for the return of its three Alco RDS-1s, the T&G found itself with no serviceable steam locomotives. The railroad embargoed freight traffic on October 1, 1946, and began handling mail and express by truck. Operators of mines protested the abandonment and promised carloads of ore if the road continued in operation, but the railroad said that it could not exist on an occasional carload of ore with most other commodities moving by truck. The Tonopah & Goldfield was formally abandoned on October 15, 1947.

	1929	1946
Miles of railroad operated:	104	100
Number of locomotives:	7	7
Number of passenger cars:	1	2
Number of freight cars:	104	
Number of company service cars:	7	10
Location of headquarters: Goldfield, Nevada		
Reporting marks: T&G		
Recommended reading: *Railroads of Nevada and Eastern California, Volume I*, by David Myrick, published in 1962 by Howell-North Books, 850 North Hollywood Way, Burbank, CA 91505		

Tonopah & Tidewater Railroad

Francis Marion Smith's Pacific Coast Borax Co. had a borate mine in the Funeral Mountains east of Death Valley, California. The nearest railroad was the California Eastern at Ivanpah, Calif. (That line became a branch of Santa Fe, with which it connected at Goffs; it was abandoned in 1921.) Smith built a wagon road 100 miles north to the Lila C. mine and tried out a steam traction engine as a replacement for his 20-mule teams. The traction engine lasted all of 14 miles. Smith decided a railroad was necessary.

The Tonopah & Tidewater Railway was incorporated on July 19, 1904, to build a railroad to Rhyolite, Calif. After several surveys, construction began on May 29, 1905, at Las Vegas, Nevada, a location suggested by Senator William Clark, the Montana copper magnate and builder of the San Pedro, Los Angeles & Salt Lake (which became Union Pacific's route from Salt Lake City through Las Vegas to southern California). After hearing of the gold and silver discoveries at Tonopah, Clark refused to let the T&T connect with the SPLA&SL and he started his own railroad to Tonopah, the Las Vegas & Tonopah.

Smith moved his base of operations to Ludlow, Calif., on the Santa Fe east of Barstow, and started construction in the fall of 1905. The relocated T&T crossed the SPLA&SL at Crucero, opened a branch from Death Valley Junction to the Lila C. Mine on August 16, 1907, and reached Gold Center on October 30 of that year.

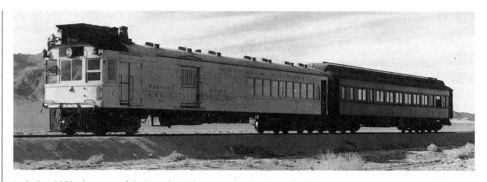

In the late 1920s the owners of the Tonopah & Tidewater tried to develop Death Valley as a winter tourist resort. Part of their program was the purchase of a gas-electric passenger and baggage car, which would cost less to operate than a conventional steam-powered passenger train. Another part of the effort to attract tourists was the operation twice a week of a Pullman sleeping car between Los Angeles and Death Valley Junction. Union Pacific handled the sleeper between Los Angeles and Crucero. The gas-electric car later served the Sonora-Baja California Railway. Photo from the collection of Arthur C. Davis.

The remaining 2 miles to Beatty were on the rails of the Bullfrog Goldfield. By then the Panic of 1907 was in progress and Rhyolite was already losing population. (Except for the former LV&T station and a few scattered buildings in Rhyolite, Beatty is all that remains today of the Rhyolite-Bullfrog-Gold Center-Beatty cluster of mining boom towns.)

In June 1908 ownership of the Tonopah & Tidewater and the Bullfrog Goldfield was transferred to a common holding company, with the blithe hope that the profits and losses of the two railroads would offset each other. In 1914 the Lila C. mine closed and the owners moved the borax operations to a new location at Ryan. The branch to the Lila C. mine was abandoned and a new 3-foot gauge railroad, the Death Valley Railroad, was built from Ryan to the T&T at Death Valley Junction.

Also in 1914 the BG shifted its allegiance to the Las Vegas & Tonopah, and the two roads consolidated their parallel lines between Beatty and Goldfield. When the LV&T ceased operation in 1918, the Tonopah & Tidewater once again took over the Bullfrog Goldfield and in 1920 acquired the majority of its stock.

The borax mines, which provided nearly all the T&T's traffic, were nearly exhausted by the late 1920s. The Bullfrog Goldfield was abandoned in 1928, and the Death Valley Railroad, which had been operated as a branch of the T&T, closed in 1931. Traffic on the T&T continued to decline, but Borax Consolidated continued to pay interest on the bonds and make up the

deficits. In 1933 T&T abandoned the Ludlow–Crucero portion of its line and moved its shop facilities from Ludlow to Death Valley Junction.

Over the years floods had occasionally disrupted service on the line. A major flood in

March 1938 destroyed much of the south end of the T&T, and in December 1938 the road petitioned to discontinue service. Operation ceased on June 14, 1940, and the railroad was scrapped in 1942 and 1943

	1929	1939
Miles of railroad operated:	169	143
Number of locomotives:	5	5
Number of passenger cars:	5	5*
Number of freight cars:	29	29
Number of company service cars:	13	9
Location of headquarters: Los Angeles, California		
*(including a motor car)		

Reporting marks: T&T
Recommended reading: *Railroads of Nevada and Eastern California, Volume I,* by David Myrick, published in 1962 by Howell-North Books, 850 North Hollywood Way, Burbank, CA 91505
Map: See page 425

Toronto, Hamilton & Buffalo Railway

In the 1880s the Canadian Pacific Railway wanted access to the growing industrial city of Hamilton, Ontario, and a connection with U. S. railroads at Buffalo, New York. Moreover, the city of Hamilton wanted the competitive benefits of a second railroad, and existing routes from Hamilton to Buffalo were circuitous. The Toronto, Hamilton & Buffalo was incorporated in 1884 to build a railroad from Toronto through Hamilton to a point on the Niagara River. In 1890, before construction began, the road modified its goal and aimed the line at Welland, Ont., on the main line of the Michigan Central.

Meanwhile the citizens of Brantford, Ontario, which was west of Hamilton and which had been bypassed by the Great Western Railway, incorporated the Brantford, Waterloo & Lake Erie Railway to build a line from Brantford south to a connection with the Michigan Central. The line was in operation by 1889. In 1892 the road undertook an extension from Brantford to Hamilton. Its finances ran out a few miles west of Hamilton, and the TH&B purchased it and began operating trains, even if it still hadn't begun work on its line to Welland.

In 1895 four railroads agreed to buy the TH&B: Canadian Pacific, 27 percent; New York Central, 37 percent; Michigan Central, 18 percent; and

Maroon-and-cream GP7 No. 76 and GP9 No. 402 are power for a Toronto–Cobourg freight train on the rails of parent CP Rail on April 28, 1976. Photo by A. J. Sutherland.

Canada Southern, 18 percent. The last two were part of the New York Central System, so ownership was effectively three-fourths NYC and one-fourth CPR. In April 1896, the CPR was granted trackage rights on Grand Trunk from Toronto almost to Hamilton. The TH&B dropped its plans to build to Toronto and laid a mile and a half of track to connect its Hamilton terminal with the GTR near Bayview Junction, then turned that track over to CPR. In mid-1896 Michigan Central took over operation of the road, but in 1897 TH&B resumed its own operation.

The Hamilton-Welland portion of the TH&B (38 miles) opened in December 1895. It formed the middle third of a Buffalo–Toronto route for its owners. In 1905 TH&B agreed with Michigan Central to pool locomotives and crews between Hamilton and Buffalo, and in 1912 the locomotive pool was expanded to include CPR.

A TH&B subsidiary, the Erie & Ontario Rail-way, completed a line from Smithville to Dunnville, 15 miles, in 1914. The TH&B merged the company in 1915 and extended it another 4 miles to Port Maitland in 1917.

A subsidiary, the Toronto, Hamilton & Buffalo Navigation Co., was incorporated in 1916 to operate a car ferry across Lake Erie between Port Maitland, Ont., and Ashtabula, Ohio. Ferry service ended in 1932.

The TH&B continued as part of a Buffalo–Toronto route through the 1960s. Passenger service diminished little by little until in 1964 just one train was left, the main purpose of which was to convey a New York–Toronto sleeping car. In 1970 the schedule was changed to create a daytime service between New York and Toronto. Freight business grew as passenger business declined.

When Conrail was formed in 1976, majority ownership of the TH&B remained with Penn Central (the ex-New York Central, Michigan Central, and Canada Southern interests in the road). In 1977 CPR purchased the Penn Central interest and assumed sole ownership. The last passenger service, a Toronto–Buffalo RDC (Rail Diesel Car) operated in conjunction with CPR and Conrail, was discontinued April 25, 1981. (Amtrak's *Maple Leaf* began running between New York and Toronto the next day, using Canadian National rails between Niagara Falls and Toronto.)

On January 1, 1987, CPR absorbed the TH&B.

	1929	1979
Miles of railroad operated:	111	110
Number of locomotives:	31	18
Number of passenger cars:	17	
Number of freight cars:	1,357	
Number of company service cars:	43	

Number of freight and company service cars: 1,167
Location of headquarters: Hamilton, Ontario
Reporting marks: THB
Recommended reading: *In the Shadow of Giants*, by Norman Helm, published in 1978 by Boston Mills Press,

132 Main Street, Erin, ON N0B 1T0 (ISBN 0-919822-22-3)
Successor: Canadian Pacific (CP Rail)
Portions still operated: The Hamilton–Brantford portion of the TH&B was abandoned in 1990. The remainder of the TH&B is still on Canadian Pacific's route map.

Uintah Railway

The Uintah Basin in northeastern Utah contains the world's only commercially workable deposits of gilsonite, an asphaltic substance used in paint, roofing materials, sealing compounds, electrical insulation, fuels, and paving materials. In 1885 when it was recognized that gilsonite had commercial possibilities, the nearest railroads were the Rio Grande and the Union Pacific, about 100 miles south and north, respectively.

A railroad into the Uintah Basin was necessary to transport the gilsonite out. General Asphalt Company and a subsidiary, Barber Asphalt Paving Co., approached the Denver & Rio Grande about building a branch. D&RG declined, saying that such a branch would be useless if the market for gilsonite dried up. Barber decided to build its own railroad. Because of the rugged terrain

Uintah 50 and sister 51 carried their water in large rectangular tanks alongside the boiler and their coal in a bunker behind the cab. Sumpter Valley converted them to conventional tender locomotives.

Barber chose to build a 3-foot gauge railroad from Mack, Colorado, on the D&RG west of Grand Junction (by then D&RG's main line was standard gauge).

The Uintah Railway was incorporated in 1903, and the rails reached Dragon, site of the mining operation, in October 1904. The line over Baxter Pass, named for brothers who were the general manager of the railroad and the surveyor who laid out the line, had 5 miles of 7.5-percent grade on the south slope (the grade on the north slope was easier, 5 percent) and curves as sharp as 66 degrees. A 66-degree curve has a radius of 87 feet—12 inches in HO scale. It is a sharper curve than North Shore's *Electroliners* had to contend with. Mainline grades above 2 percent are considered steep.

In 1911 news broke that the Uintah would convert to standard gauge, tunnel under Baxter Pass, extend north to Vernal, Utah (that part of the rumor continued during much of the Uintah Railway's existence), and become an extension of the Colorado Midland. What was constructed was a 12-mile, 3-foot gauge extension to Watson and Rainbow, Utah.

In the early 1920s a business recession reduced the demand for gilsonite and highways penetrated the Uintah Basin, connecting the region with the Denver & Salt Lake at Craig, Colo. In 1923 Lucian Sprague became superintendent of the railroad and in 1924 general manager. He is remembered chiefly for helping design a pair of articulated locomotives with a 2-6-6-2T wheel arrangement to replace Uintah's aging Shays.

The gilsonite business held up fairly well during the Depression, but improved highways began to threaten the line. In 1937 the highway between Vernal and Craig was paved, and that same year the Barber company announced plans to move its mining operations from Rainbow to Bonanza, 15 miles north of the end of the railroad. From Bonanza it was easier to truck gilsonite east to the D&SL than to truck it to the Uintah, lift it over Baxter Pass, and transfer it to standard gauge cars at Mack. By mid-1938 the Uintah Railway had nothing to carry, and the few towns along the line were deserted. In August of that year the road petitioned for abandonment. Colorado's Mesa County was concerned about the abandonment because of the loss of tax revenues for the schools; the ICC examiner stated that taxes were not a sufficient reason to keep a losing business going. In its last few months the railroad operated only one round trip a week, and the last train ran on May 16, 1939. Little remains of the Uintah and the towns it served.

The two articulateds were sold to the Sumpter Valley Railway in eastern Oregon in 1940; they went to Guatemala in 1947.

	1929	1938
Miles of railroad operated:	70	70
Number of locomotives:	10	8
Number of passenger cars:	3	3
Number of freight cars:	123	123
Number of company service cars:	14	14

Location of headquarters: Mack, Colorado
Recommended reading: *Uintah Railway*, by Henry E. Bender, Jr., published in 1970 by Howell-North Books, 850 North Hollywood Way, Burbank, CA 91505
Map: See page 144

Ulster & Delaware Railroad

In 1866 the Rondout & Oswego Railroad was chartered to build west from Rondout, New York (now part of the city of Kingston), the eastern terminal and headquarters of the Delaware & Hudson Canal. Despite the name, the goal of the railroad was not Oswego but Oneonta and a connection with the Albany & Susquehanna Railroad, which later became part of the Delaware & Hudson.

Construction began in 1866, and the rails pushed west — over the Catskills and into the valley of the East Branch of the Delaware River, then up and over into the valley of the West Branch at Stamford. In 1872 the company was reorganized as the New York, Kingston & Syracuse Railroad, and in 1875 it was sold and reorganized again as the Ulster & Delaware Railroad.

The Catskill Mountains were rapidly developing into a summer resort area. The Stony Clove & Catskill Mountain Railroad was organized in 1881 by Ulster & Delaware management to build a 3-foot gauge line from Phoenicia on the U&D to Hunter, with a branch, the Kaaterskill Railroad, to serve the Hotel Kaaterskill and the Catskill Mountain House. Service on the SC&CM began in mid-1882, and the Kaaterskill Railroad opened in June 1883. That same month the West Shore opened between Jersey City and Kingston, giving the Ulster & Delaware a direct rail connection to New York.

It's 10:15 a.m. on August 2, 1947. Both the track and the locomotive are former Ulster & Delaware property as New York Central train 530 stops at Kortright to pick up a box of eggs destined for down-country points. Photo by Charles A. Elston.

In the mid-1880s work resumed to extend the U&D over another divide into the valley of the Susquehanna River. While that was in progress the U&D merged its two narrow gauge subsidiaries in 1893 and standard-gauged them in 1899. In July 1900 the U&D finally arrived in Oneonta, where it connected with the Delaware & Hudson. The D&H Canal had ceased operation only two years before, and the U&D acquired some of its coal traffic. Before long, coal came to provide the bulk of U&D freight revenue.

Ulster & Delaware's peak passenger year was 1913. Paved highways began to penetrate the Catskills, and the huge mountain hotels closed one by one as tastes in vacationing changed. U&D management approached the New York Central, asking if they'd like to buy a nice railroad through the Catskills; NYC replied that they wouldn't. Then the Interstate Commerce Commission added NYC takeover of the U&D (which entered receivership in 1931) to the conditions under which it would approve NYC's absorption of the Michigan Central and the Big Four (Cleveland, Cincinnati, Chicago & St. Louis). On February 1, 1932, the Ulster & Delaware became the Catskill Mountain Branch of the New York Central.

In 1940 the Hunter and Kaaterskill branches, the former narrow gauge lines, were abandoned. Passenger service was discontinued in early 1954. Coal traffic from the D&H disappeared, and in 1965 NYC cut the line back from Oneonta to Bloomville. Conrail completed abandonment of the line in September 1976, but three short portions of the line survive as tourist railroads.

	1929	1931
Miles of railroad operated:	129	129
Number of locomotives:	29	29
Number of passenger cars:	54	53
Number of freight cars:	168	153
Number of company service cars:	12	11

Location of headquarters: Kingston, New York

Recommended reading: *The Ulster & Delaware*, by Gerald M. Best, published in 1972 by Golden West Books, P. O. Box 80250, San Marino, CA 91108

Successors:
New York Central
Penn Central
Conrail

Portions still operated:
Catskill Mountain Railroad: Phoenicia–Mount Pleasant
Ulster & Delaware Rail Ride: Arkville–Fleischmanns
Trolley Museum of New York: Kingston–Kingston Point

Unadilla Valley Railway

The Utica & Unadilla Valley Railroad was incorporated in 1888 to build south along the Unadilla River from the Delaware, Lackawanna & Western's Utica branch at Bridgewater, New York. Construction began in 1889, and the road opened as far as West Edmeston, 9 miles, in 1894. That year the company was reorganized as the Unadilla Valley Railroad. The railroad used Lackawanna rolling stock until it purchased its own locomotive and car in 1895, the same year it was extended another 11 miles to New Berlin and a connection with the New York, Ontario & Western.

In 1904 Lewis Morris obtained control of the railroad and reorganized it as the Unadilla Valley Railway. The railroad became prosperous, and the principal commodity it carried was milk. In the early 1930s Morris purchased a gravel bed, then sold it to the railroad as a potential traffic source. The gravel, however, did not meet the specifications of the state highway department, the intended purchaser of the gravel, and the gravel bed and the quarrying equipment became an expensive millstone around the Unadilla Valley's neck.

In 1936 the railroad (minus the quarry) was purchased by the H. E. Salzberg Co., a scrap dealer and railroad dismantler. Rather than scrap the UV, Salzberg set out to see if it could be made profitable. Among his first actions was to call on shippers and reassure them that the

Unadilla Valley 2-6-2 No. 5 leads a train of Lackawanna milk cars along the Unadilla River at Leonardsville, New York, in June 1947. Photo by John Pickett.

railroad would continue to operate. In the late 1930s the road was the subject of an article in *Fortune* magazine.

In October 1941 the railroad bought the New York, Ontario & Western's New Berlin branch: 29 miles from Edmeston through New Berlin to New Berlin Junction plus trackage rights 3 miles farther on N&O&W's main line into Sidney.

In 1956 the Dairyman's League plant at Mount Upton closed. It had provided 35 percent of the Unadilla Valley's revenue. The UV cut back the south end of the line from New Berlin Junction to Mount Upton and continued to operate while deficits mounted. Its abandonment petition was approved, and the line closed on December 23, 1960.

	1929	1960					
Miles of railroad operated:	19	48					
Number of locomotives:	3	1					
Number of passenger cars:	4						

Number of freight cars: 18 2
Number of company service cars: 7 17
Location of headquarters: New Berlin, New York
Reporting marks: UV

Recommended reading: *Days Along the Buckwheat & Dandelion*, by Fred Pugh, published in 1984 by Fred Pugh, Box 26, West Edmeston, NY 13485 (ISBN 0-914821-04-0)
Map: See page 432

Union Pacific Railroad

Since the first edition of this book appeared in 1985, the number-one question from readers has been "Where's the Union Pacific? I can't find it in the book anywhere." That's because the Union Pacific has not been abandoned or merged out of existence, and this book deals with such railroads.

UP is still doing business at the same stand in Omaha, although it's much larger than it used to be. UP's growth is the reason Western Pacific, Missouri Pacific, Missouri-Kansas-Texas, Chicago & North Western, and Southern Pacific are in this book. A brief description of the UP before those mergers might be useful.

The Union Pacific was chartered by an act of Congress in 1862. The act provided subsidies and land grants to UP, which was to build west from Omaha, and to the Central Pacific, which was to build east from Sacramento, California. Construction began in 1865, and the two roads met at

Union Pacific 9047, a three-cylinder 4-12-2 (a wheel arrangement unique to the UP and named for it) leads a freight east past a lower-quadrant semaphore block signal typical of the Harriman railroads. Photo by A. C. Kalmbach.

The Harriman era

In 1897 E. H. Harriman purchased the UP at a public auction and assembled a system that included Southern Pacific, Illinois Central, and Chicago & Alton. Harriman embarked on an improvement program that included double track from Omaha west to Granger, Wyoming, and a new line over Sherman Hill between Cheyenne and Laramie, Wyoming.

In 1905 the Los Angeles & Salt Lake Railroad was completed between its namesake cities, but severe floods in several successive years in Nevada and western Utah destroyed much of the line in the Meadow Valley Canyon. The line was rebuilt and placed in service in 1912.

After Harriman

In 1912 the federal government required UP to divest itself of its Southern Pacific stock, but close co-operation continued between the two railroads aided by a 1924 agreement that permitted SP to control Central Pacific and required SP to solicit traffic to move via Ogden and the UP.

For the first three-quarters of the twentieth century the map of the Union Pacific remained the same: Omaha to Ogden, Ogden to Los Angeles, Ogden to Butte, Granger, Wyo., to Portland (and on to Seattle, by trackage rights), with a branch to Spokane, and Kansas City through Denver to Cheyenne, plus branches. Chicago, the railroad center of the United States, was 500 miles east of the east end of the main line, but Chicago & North Western's double-track route between Chicago and Omaha had been practically an eastern extension of the UP since before 1900.

Promontory, Utah, on May 10, 1869. Ceremonies and a golden spike celebrated the completion of the first railroad across North America.

The ensuing three decades were difficult for Union Pacific. Bad management, overextension, the effect of the Crédit Mobilier scandal, and the debt owed the federal government took their toll.

During that period affiliated or subsidiary lines were extended north from Ogden, Utah, to Butte, Montana (Utah & Northern), and north-west from Granger, Wyoming, to Portland, Oregon (Oregon Short Line). In 1880 the UP merged the Kansas Pacific Railway, which had opened from Kansas City to Denver in 1870, and the affiliated Denver Pacific, which connected Denver with the UP main line at Cheyenne. About that same time UP gained control of several railroads in Colorado that later became the Colorado & Southern Railway—for a few years until 1893 the UP system reached down into Texas.

The Union Pacific of those years was even then a fast, long-haul, heavy-duty railroad. It had networks of traffic-gathering branches in Kansas, Nebraska, Utah, Idaho (it was the only railroad in the southern part of Idaho), Oregon, and eastern Washington, but its principal business was moving freight across a generally unpopulated area of the West. An hour spent at trackside in Wyoming would demonstrate this: frequent trains running fast on double track. It was equally competent in the passenger department. Its yellow streamliners moved in fleets, and its dining car service was as good as the Santa Fe's—better if you factor in UP's dome dining cars.

In 1955 UP suddenly shifted its streamliners to the Milwaukee Road east of Omaha. Eight years later UP petitioned to merge the Rock Island, primarily for its Omaha–Chicago line. The Rock Island merger case dragged on for 12 years before the parties concerned gave up.

Expansion by merger

While UP was considering the Rock Island, four major railroads got together to form Burlington Northern. That merger was no surprise—it had been sixty-some years in the making. In 1977 Burlington Northern began merger discussions with the Frisco. In early January 1980 Union Pacific surprised the railroad industry by announcing that it intended to acquire the Missouri Pacific—and later that month announced an offer to acquire the Western Pacific.

What might have triggered UP's move? BN's merger of Frisco? Southern Pacific's desire to push toward Kansas City by acquiring part of the

Train 5, a nameless Omaha–Los Angeles mail train (it nonetheless carried sleeping and cafe-lounge cars) and train 36, the *Butte Special* down from Butte, Montana, and Pocatello, Idaho, stand in the morning sun at Salt Lake City about 1960. Photo by Donald Sims.

Rock Island? A hunch that railroads were soon going to choose up sides and UP wanted to be a chooser, not a chosen?

The announcements constituted a major realignment of the western railroads. Union Pacific and Southern Pacific had long been considered logical partners, and Missouri Pacific and Western Pacific were part of the old Gould empire—as was the Denver & Rio Grande Western, which linked MP and WP. More recently, WP and D&RGW had been good friends with the Burlington.

Acquisition of WP would take UP to San Francisco Bay; the MP would give UP access to the oil and chemical industries of Texas and a route to Chicago—Kansas City to St. Louis on MP, then up to Chicago on the former Chicago & Eastern Illinois.

On December 22, 1982, Union Pacific merged the Missouri Pacific and the Western Pacific, more than doubling in size. The name Pacific Rail Systems was used briefly to describe the combined railroads, but it did not catch on. Western Pacific was absorbed immediately. Missouri

Pacific was to remain separate, but within a year later yellow paint began to replace blue on MP locomotives, and not long after that "Union" replaced "Missouri" in the lettering diagrams.

In 1987 Union Pacific Railroad simplified its corporate structure by merging a number of its subsidiaries: Los Angeles & Salt Lake Railroad, Oregon Short Line Railroad, Oregon-Washington Railroad & Navigation Co., St. Joseph & Grand Island, Spokane International, Yakima Valley Transportation Co. (a traction line at Yakima, Wash.), Western Pacific, Sacramento Northern, and Tidewater Southern.

The Interstate Commerce Commission approved the purchase of the Missouri-Kansas-Texas by the Missouri Pacific Railroad on May 16, 1988. UP absorbed the Katy's operations on August 12, 1988. Meanwhile, UP had been buying into Chicago & North Western. UP merged C&NW on April 24, 1995. The transition did not go well: Union Pacific offered buyouts to C&NW employees, and more persons than anticipated took up UP on its offer.

Southern Pacific and Santa Fe began merger processes on the assumption the Interstate Commerce Commission would continue to be as liberal about such matters as it had been—and the ICC rejected their merger proposal. On the rebound, Santa Fe paired up with Burlington Northern and Southern Pacific with Denver & Rio Grande Western—and it was D&RGW that did the acquiring, not SP.

Southern Pacific fell on hard times and obviously had to merge, but not with Burlington Northern & Santa Fe. Been there, done that. On September 11, 1996, Union Pacific announced it would acquire SP, completing what E. H. Harriman had started. Early in the process UP reassured regulatory authorities and shippers that there would not be problems of the magnitude experienced when UP absorbed the Chicago & North Western. They were several orders of magnitude larger, and UP's absorption of SP is still being sorted out 2 years after the date of the merger.

	1929	1981
Miles of railroad operated:	9,878	9,096
Number of locomotives:	1,674	1,665
Number of passenger cars:	1,374	345*
Number of freight cars:	58,214	
Number of company service cars:	4,483	
Number of freight and company service cars:		64,263
Location of headquarters: Omaha, Nebraska		
Reporting marks: UP		

Notable named passenger trains: *City of Los Angeles* (Chicago—Los Angeles), *City of San Francisco* (Chicago—San Francisco), *City of Portland*
*(1970)

(Chicago—Portland), *City of Denver* (Chicago—Denver). All were operated east of Omaha by Chicago & North Western until 1955 and by the Milwaukee Road from 1955 to 1971. The *City of San Francisco* was operated west of Ogden, Utah, by Southern Pacific.

Historical and technical society: Union Pacific Historical Society, P. O. Box 4006, Cheyenne, WY 82003-4006; http://www.uphs.org

Recommended reading: *Union Pacific*, by Maury Klein, published in 1987 (Volume I) and 1989 (Volume II) by Doubleday & Co., 245 Park Avenue, New York, NY 10167 (ISBN 0-385-17728-6 and 0-385-17735-6)

The Golden Years of Railroading: Union Pacific Across Sherman Hill, by George Drury, published in 1999 by Kalmbach Publishing Co., 21027 Crossroads Circle, Waukesha, WI 53187 (ISBN 0-89024-570-3)

Subsidiaries and affiliated railroads, 1981:
Camas Prairie (50%)
Los Angeles & Salt Lake Railroad
Mount Hood Railway (100%)
Oregon Short Line Railroad
Oregon-Washington Railroad & Navigation Co
St. Joseph & Grand Island
Portland Traction Co. (50%)
Spokane International (100%)
Yakima Valley Transportation (100%)

United South Eastern Railways
(Ferrocarriles Unidos del Sureste)

In 1969 the Southeastern Railway (Ferrocarril del Sureste) and the United Railways of Yucatan (Ferrocarriles Unidos de Yucatán) were merged to form the United South Eastern Railways. The railroad consisted of a main line from Coatzacoalcos, in the state of Veracruz, the junction with the National Railways of Mexico, east through Palenque, then northeast through Campeche to Merida, and branches radiating from Merida to Progreso, Valladolid, Tizimin, Peto, and Sotuta. In 1987 the FUS became part of the National Railways of Mexico. The two predecessor railroads are described below.

United South Eastern Railways	1983
Miles of narrow gauge railroad operated:	266
Miles of standard gauge railroad operated:	555
Miles of dual gauge railroad operated:	22
Number of locomotives:	31
Number of passenger cars:	59
Number of standard gauge freight cars:	834
Location of headquarters: Merida, Yucatan	
Reporting marks: FUS	
Successor: National Railways of Mexico	

United Railways of Yucatan 251, a narrow gauge 4-4-0 built by Baldwin in 1916, scurries through a field of sisal on its way to Merida with train 56 from Sotuta in 1964. UdeY's roster included wood-burners until 1960; both standard and narrow gauge 4-4-0s operated until the mid-1960s. Photo by Frank Barry.

United Railways of Yucatan
(Ferrocarriles Unidos de Yucatán)

The first railroad in Mexico's state of Yucatan was the standard gauge Ferrocarril Progreso a Mérida (Progreso to Merida Railway), authorized in 1874 and opened in 1881 between the city of Merida and the port at Progreso, 24 miles north. Most of the railroad's business was in carrying sisal, a fiber from which rope is made.

Two other railroads were begun about the same time, the Ferrocarril Mérida a Valladolid and the Ferrocarril Peninsular, which completed a line to Campeche in the state of the same name in 1898. Both these railroads were 3-foot gauge.

The three railroads were combined in 1902 as the United Railways of Yucatan, and a fourth railroad, the 3-foot gauge Ferrocarril de Mérida a Peto, was added in 1909. A third rail for narrow gauge trains was added to the Merida–Progreso line between 1958 and 1960.

The UdeY was isolated until 1950, when the Southeastern Railway (Ferrocarril del Sureste) was completed from Allende, Veracruz, on the Rio Coatzacoalcos, to Campeche. The UdeY line from Campeche to Merida was standard-gauged in 1962.

A passenger train waits in the siding at Francisco Rueda, in the state of Tabasco, 77 kilometers east of Allende, while a mixed train rolls by on the main line in this 1952 scene. The sides of the Alco FA-2 are lettered for the Sureste; the nose still carries SCOP initials. Kalmbach Publishing Co. photo by Linn H. Westcott.

United Railways of Yucatan	1929	1968
Miles of narrow gauge railroad operated:	535	128
Miles of standard gauge railroad operated:		264
Number of locomotives:	58	49
Number of passenger cars:	119	81
Number of freight cars:	747	294
Number of company service cars:	58	55

Location of headquarters: Merida, Yucatan

Recommended reading: *Mexican Narrow Gauge*, by Gerald M. Best, published in 1968 by Howell-North Books

Successors:
United South Eastern Railways
National Railways of Mexico

Portions still operated: National Railways of Mexico: Merida–Progreso; Merida–Valladolid; Dzitas–Tizimin; Merida–Peto; Ancandeh–Sotuta; Merida–Campeche

Southeastern Railway (Ferrocarril del Sureste)
Mexico's Southeastern Railway was constructed by the Ministry of Communications and Public Works (Secretaria de Comunicaciones y Obras Públicas, abbreviated SCOP). It was completed in 1950 from Allende, Veracruz, on the Rio Coatzacoalcos, to Campeche, where it connected with the United Railways of Yucatan. The railroad opened a bridge across the Rio Coatzacoalcos in 1962, forming an all-rail route to the southeastern part of Mexico.

Ferrocarril del Sureste	1950	1968
Miles of railroad operated:	457	455

Rolling stock figures are unavailable.

Location of headquarters: Coatzacoalcos, Veracruz
Reporting marks: SCOP, SE
Successors:
United South Eastern Railways
National Railways of Mexico

Portions still operated: National Railways of Mexico: Coatzacoalcos–Campeche

Virginia & Truckee Railway

During the California gold rush of 1849 Nevada was simply a place to pass through on the way west. In 1849 the Mormons established a settlement at Genoa, east of Lake Tahoe. Gold placers were discovered nearby, followed by the discovery of the Comstock Lode and the establishment of Virginia City. The boom was on. The miners were hampered by large amounts of a blue rock surrounding the gold, and for some time no one realized that the blue rock was silver ore.

By 1865 the Comstock mines were ready to produce on a larger scale. Machinery and timbers for deeper workings were expensive. William Sharon, local representative of the Bank of California, recognized the need for a railroad to bring in mining machinery and timbers and to take ore to reducing mills located along the Carson River. He asked an engineer if a railroad could be built from Virginia City to the Carson River. The engineer said "Yes."

The Virginia & Truckee Railroad was incorpo-rated on March 5, 1868. Construction began almost a year later, and the first train from Carson City rolled into Gold Hill, just south of Virginia City, on December 21, 1869. A month later the line reached Virginia City. The line from Carson City to Reno and a connection with the Central Pacific was completed on August 24, 1872.

The railroad's fortunes followed those of Virginia City and its mines. The destruction of most of Virginia City by fire in 1875 simply brought more business in the form of building materials, but ore production began to decline toward the end of the decade.

Carson & Colorado

In 1880 the Carson & Colorado was chartered by some of V&T's directors. Its narrow gauge track took off from the V&T at Mound House, northeast of Carson City, to head south 300 miles into California's Owens Valley.

Southern Pacific acquired the C&C in 1900. Two months later silver was discovered at Tonopah, and the C&C became a key link in the route to Tonopah. SP standard-gauged the C&C as far south as Tonopah Junction, and the new Tonopah Railroad did the same. SP considered

	1929	1949
Miles of railroad operated:	67	46
Number of locomotives:	8	3
Number of passenger cars:	19	4
Number of freight cars:	32	9
Number of company service cars:	8	

Location of headquarters: Carson City, Nevada

Reporting marks: V&T

Recommended reading: *The Silver Short Line*, by Ted Wurm and Harre Demoro, published in 1983 by Trans-Anglo Books, P. O. Box 6444, Glendale, CA 91205 (ISBN 87046-064-1)

Portions still operated: Virginia & Truckee (1976) Virginia City–Gold Hill

Map: See page 425

purchasing the V&T as a connection between the C&C and the SP main line at Reno, but V&T's price was too high and SP instead built a connection south from Hazen, bypassing the V&T.

Gentle decline

The V&T was reorganized in 1905 as the Virginia & Truckee Railway. In 1906 it opened a 15-mile extension south from Carson City to Minden, and there was talk of electrifying the Reno–Minden line. Mining continued, but the V&T came to depend more on agriculture.

In 1924 the V&T paid its last dividend. Motor cars and mixed trains replaced the passenger trains, and the Minden line became the main route. Traffic continued to dwindle. Following the death of Ogden L. Mills, sole owner of the road since 1933, the V&T entered receivership. The Virginia City line was abandoned in 1939,

and the V&T sold some of its old-time rolling stock to Hollywood film companies (surplus cars and locomotives had simply been stored and the dry climate of Nevada kept it from deteriorating). Railroad enthusiasts discovered the railroad, and their excursion trains reminded Nevadans that the V&T still existed. More equipment was sold to Hollywood, providing needed dollars in V&T's treasury. The railroad showed a modest profit in 1939, and the scrap value of the Virginia City line kept the road alive through World War II. After the war the V&T was discovered by Lucius Beebe, who romanticized it (and Virginia City and the Comstock Lode) all out of proportion.

It is open to question whether V&T's postwar management was intent on keeping the road alive or abandoning it. That was 50 years ago, and question or no, the V&T ended service on May 31, 1950.

Virginia & Truckee 5, a 2-8-0 purchased from the Nevada Copper Belt in 1947 and V&T's only eight-coupled locomotive, brings the daily-except-Sunday mixed train across the highway at Washoe on August 7, 1948. Photo by Fred H. Matthews, Jr.

Virginian Railway

The Virginian was the creation of one man, Henry Huttleston Rogers, and was a one-commodity railroad—practically a conveyor belt to move coal from the mountains of West Virginia to ships at Norfolk, Virginia.

The Deepwater Railway was incorporated in West Virginia to build a line south into the mountains from Deepwater, W. Va., a station on the Chesapeake & Ohio 30 miles southeast of Charleston. By 1902 Henry Huttleston Rogers, vice-president of Standard Oil, had acquired an interest in the 4-mile line, which served lumber mills and coal mines. Neither C&O nor Norfolk & Western would agree on freight rates, so Rogers decided to build his own railroad from the coalfields to tidewater at Norfolk. He got the Deepwater's charter amended to allow construction to the Virginia state line, and he incorporated the Tidewater Railway in Virginia in February 1904 to build a railroad between Norfolk and the West Virginia state line.

In March 1907 the name of the Tidewater Railway was changed to Virginian Railway; in April of that year the Virginian acquired the property of the Deepwater Railway. The line was completed between Norfolk and Deepwater at the beginning of 1909. From Roanoke to Norfolk the railroad was as close as possible to a straight line, and it had an almost constant

Three-unit electric locomotive 103 rolls downgrade with tonnage at Oakvale, West Virginia, on September 4, 1953. Photo by Richard J. Cook.

gentle descent. West of Roanoke, though, lay the Blue Ridge Mountains, with grades in both directions. The steepest eastbound grade was 2 percent for 14 miles from Elmore to Clarks Gap, W. Va.

The Virginian was built as a heavy-duty railroad. Before World War I, when the normal coal car was a 50-ton hopper, Virginian was using 120-ton, 12-wheel gondolas. In 1909 the road bought 2-6-6-0s, its first Mallets, and within a decade rostered 2-8-8-2s and 2-10-10-2s. It even experimented with a 2-8-8-8-4 that was unable to generate steam fast enough for its six cylinders. In the 1920s the Virginian electrified its line between Mullens, W. Va., and Roanoke. The new electric locomotives could haul heavier trains than the best steam locomotives and move them twice as fast.

In 1925 the Norfolk & Western agreed to lease the Virginian if the Interstate Commerce Commission approved, which it did not. Other suitors included the Pennsylvania, the New York Central, and the Chesapeake & Ohio. In 1929 the Virginian applied to the ICC for permission to build a one-mile line across the Kanawha River at Deepwater to connect with New York Central's Kanawha & Michigan Railway. The ICC approved over the protest of the C&O.

The Virginian was never a major passenger carrier. Even in 1930 mainline service was an all-stops daytime local west of Roanoke and two such trains, one by day and one by night east of Roanoke. Luxury was confined to a Norfolk–Roanoke sleeping car and a Roanoke–Huntington, W. Va., parlor car. Both were gone by 1933, as was the Norfolk–Roanoke night train. January 29, 1956 was the final run of the last passenger schedule, a Norfolk–Roanoke daytime local.

In 1948 Virginian received 4 two-unit electric locomotives to begin replacement of the aging side-rod motors. In 1956 and 1957 12 more

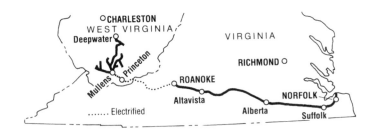

electrics joined the roster. The new units were basically six-axle diesel hood units with Ignitron rectifiers instead of diesel engines. Shortly after they arrived Virginian dumped the fire on its last steam engine. The diesels that replaced steam were all Fairbanks-Morse products, except for a General Electric 44-tonner purchased second-hand in 1954.

The Virginian and the Norfolk & Western had not forgotten the idea of merger. By 1959 the regulatory climate was different. The stockholders of the two railroads and the ICC approved, and on December 1, 1959, the two roads merged. An almost immediate casualty of the merger was Virginian's electrification. N&W developed a one-way traffic pattern to take advantage of the best grades, and the electrics had only eastbound work to do. The electrification was shut down at the end of June 1962.

	1929	1958
Miles of railroad operated:	545	608
Number of locomotives:	175	120
Number of passenger cars:	62	
Number of freight cars:	10,273	17,143
Number of company service cars:	368	184
Location of headquarters: Norfolk, Virginia		

Reporting marks: VGN
Historical and technical society: Norfolk & Western Historical Society, P. O. Box 201, Forest, VA 24551-0201; http://www.inmind.com/people/shammer/
Recommended reading: *The Virginian Railway*, by H. Reid, published in 1961 by Kalmbach Publishing Co. (ISBN 0-89024-558-4)

Successors:
Norfolk & Western
Norfolk Southern
Portions still operated: The only major portion of the Virginian that has been abandoned is the main line from Meherrin, Va., east to Suffolk. The rest is operated by Norfolk Southern.

Wabash Railway

The Wabash seems to have gone through more reorganizations and name changes than most railroads its size. I will use the term "Wabash" to refer to the company in this history, unless clarity requires the full title.

In 1851 the North Missouri Railroad was chartered to build northwest from St. Louis to the Iowa state line at Coatesville, Mo. The railroad, completed in 1858, required a ferry crossing of the Missouri River at St. Charles, 19 miles from St. Louis, until a bridge was completed in 1871. In the 1860s the road acquired a branch to Brunswick; the town of Moberly was established at the junction and became the location of the road's shops. The Brunswick line was extended to Kansas City in 1868. The main route was extended north to Ottumwa, Iowa, in 1870, and construction of a line from Brunswick to Omaha was begun that same year (it reached Council Bluffs, Iowa, in 1879). The North Missouri ran into financial difficulty in 1871. It was succeeded in 1872 by the St. Louis, Kansas City & Northern Railroad.

In 1853 two railroad companies were organized: the Toledo & Illinois to build from Toledo, Ohio, to the Ohio-Indiana state line, and the Lake Erie, Wabash & St. Louis to continue the line across Indiana to Attica, following the route

The Chicago–St. Louis *Blue Bird* was perhaps the ultimate daytime streamliner, with a buffet car up front, a diner in the middle, a round-end observation car at the rear, and five Vista-Domes. However, the other Chicago–St. Louis day train, the *Banner Blue*, shown northbound at Mansfield, Illinois, in 1958, had a certain charm with its assortment of headend cars, comfortable rebuilt coaches, second-hand streamlined diner-lounge, and parlor car with brass-railed observation platform. Photo by J. P. Lamb, Jr.

of the Wabash & Erie Canal. The two companies merged in 1856 as the Toledo, Wabash & Western Railroad, and they were succeeded in 1858 by the Toledo & Wabash Railway. By then the company had absorbed the Great Western of Illinois (a successor to the Northern Cross Railroad, chartered about 1837 to run from Quincy, Ill., east to the Indiana state line) and reached from Toledo to the Mississippi River at Quincy and at Keokuk, Iowa.

Jay Gould

In 1879 Jay Gould obtained control of the Toledo & Wabash and the St. Louis, Kansas City & Northern and merged them to form the Wabash, St. Louis & Pacific Railroad. To the new railroad he soon added the Chicago & Paducah, whose line from Streator to Effingham crossed the Wabash at Bement. Within a year Gould had constructed a line north to Chicago from a point on the Chicago & Paducah, and a line from Butler, Ind., northeast to Detroit.

Gould continued to add to the Wabash. By 1884 it had 3,549 miles of road extending from Detroit to Omaha and from Fonda in northwestern Iowa to Cairo, Ill. Financially the Wabash was overextended, and Gould's frequent rate wars with other railroads reduced the road's income. In May 1884 the Wabash defaulted in interest payments and entered receivership, with Gould as the receiver. The leased lines—like the Des Moines North Western and the Cairo & Vincennes—were returned to their owners. The Wabash itself was reorganized as several separate railroads, which were reunited in 1889 as the Wabash Railroad.

In 1889 the Wabash acquired trackage rights from Detroit through southern Ontario to Buffalo over the rails of the Grand Trunk. The Canadian portion of the system was connected with the rest by ferries across the Detroit River between Detroit and Windsor. A line from Butler to New Haven, Ind., east of Fort Wayne, opened in 1902, allowing Detroit–St. Louis trains to be routed through Fort Wayne, Hunt-

ington, and Wabash, Ind. The older, more direct route along the Eel River was sold to the Pennsylvania Railroad.

Twentieth century

In 1904 the Wabash reached Pittsburgh from Toledo over the rails of the Wheeling & Lake Erie and the Wabash Pittsburgh Terminal (predecessor of the Pittsburgh & West Virginia). The WPT was part of George Gould's plan to assemble the transcontinental system that his father had almost put together. The Wabash wasn't in Pittsburgh very long—receivership overtook it again in 1911, followed by reorganization in 1915 as the Wabash Railway.

The automobile industry was growing, and the Wabash found itself in the middle of it. One of the road's biggest assets was its direct line from Detroit to Kansas City, bypassing Chicago and St. Louis. The key portion of the route was the Decatur, Ill.–Moberly, Mo. line. Decatur was the hub of the Wabash and the site of its principal shops. The Hannibal–Moberly portion of the line was built by the Missouri-Kansas-Texas, but in 1894 the Wabash made arrangements to operate the line jointly, with costs proportionate to use. The Wabash found itself paying 90 percent of the costs and leased the line in 1923.

In 1925 the Wabash acquired control of the Ann Arbor, and by the end of 1962 owned all but a few shares of Ann Arbor's stock. In 1928 the Pennsylvania Company gained control of the Wabash, largely to protect itself after the Wabash and the Delaware & Hudson bought control of the Lehigh Valley.

Wabash passenger service had several distinct personalities. Between St. Louis and Kansas City, Wabash operated the easternmost segment of Union Pacific's *City of St. Louis* and its own *City of Kansas City*. That was also mixed-train territory: Well into the 1960s several mixed trains a day connected the university town of Columbia, Mo., with the main line at Centralia, and in later years the St. Louis–Council Bluffs train was a mixed. On the Chicago–St. Louis run the Wabash competed with Gulf, Mobile & Ohio and Illinois Central and had the best rolling stock—the Vista-Dome *Blue Bird*. The second Chicago–St. Louis train, the *Banner Blue*, was one of the last trains to carry an open-platform parlor-observation car. Between Detroit and St. Louis the night and day trains were not glossy streamliners or extensions of someone else's train or plug locals—they were just plain, comfortable trains. In its last years the daytime run carried a legendary name from folk music, *Wabash Cannon Ball*.

The Wabash was unique in extending across the imaginary line dividing the country—a line from Chicago through Peoria to St. Louis, then down the Mississippi River to New Orleans. The Wabash was more a bridge railroad than an originator of traffic, a paradoxical situation in that most railroads had to shorthaul themselves to turn over traffic to the Wabash. The only major railroads that could give Wabash the long haul without sacrifice were the Union Pacific and the Kansas City Southern at Kansas City, UP at Council Bluffs, Iowa, and the Lackawanna and Lehigh Valley at Buffalo.

Norfolk & Western

At the end of 1963 the Pennsylvania Company owned nearly 87 percent of Wabash's stock. When the Pennsylvania and the New York Central planned their merger it was clear that the Wabash would not be included. Penn Central was large enough, and the Interstate Commerce Commission probably wouldn't allow it anyway. Wabash found a niche in the Norfolk & Western–Nickel Plate merger, but Wabash subsidiary Ann Arbor was kept in the Pennsy family (N&W didn't want it) by selling it to the Detroit, Toledo & Ironton on August 31, 1963.

The expanded Norfolk & Western leased the Wabash on October 16, 1964. On March 31, 1970, N&W acquired control of the Wabash from the Pennsylvania Company; by the end of 1980 N&W had almost complete ownership of the Wabash.

	1929	1963
Miles of railroad operated:	2,524	2,422
Number of locomotives:	660	307
Number of passenger cars:	412	101
Number of freight cars:	26,633	15,028
Number of company service cars:	889	644

Location of headquarters: St. Louis, Missouri

Reporting marks: WAB

Notable named passenger trains: *Blue Bird* (Chicago–St. Louis)

Historical and technical society: Wabash Railroad Historical Society, 813 Ayers Street, Bolingbrook, IL 60440; WabashRR@aol.com; http://members.aol.com/wabashrr/wabash.html

Recommended reading: *Wabash,* by Donald J. Heimburger, published in 1984 by Heimburger House Publishing Co., 310 Lathrop Avenue, River Forest, IL 60305 (ISBN 0-911581-02-2)

Subsidiaries and affiliated railroads, 1963: New Jersey, Indiana & Illinois

Successors: Norfolk & Western

Norfolk Southern

Portions still operated:

Bloomer Line: Gibson City–Strawn, Ill.

Chillicothe-Brunswick Rail Maintenance Authority: Brunswick–Chillicothe, Mo.

Indiana Northeastern: Montpelier, Ohio–South Milford, Ind.

Maumee & Western: Liberty Center–Woodburn, Ohio

Metra: Chicago–Manhattan, Ill.

Norfolk Southern: Detroit–Decatur–Kansas City; South Bend–Pine (NJI&I)–Kingsbury, Ind.; Bement–Gibson City, Ill.; Decatur–St. Louis–Moberly, Mo.

Washington & Old Dominion Railway

The city of Alexandria, Virginia, in 1836 saw the Winchester & Potomac and Baltimore & Ohio railroads suddenly funnel to Baltimore the trade that had been coming down to Alexandria from the Shenandoah Valley. After an initial flurry of excitement and the chartering of a stillborn railroad, Alexandrians in 1853 chartered the Alexandria, Loudon & Hampshire Railroad to build west across the Blue Ridge to Winchester, Va. By 1858 the roadbed reached to Leesburg, and train service began in 1860. During the Civil War the railroad was not of any strategic value, but it suffered as much damage as if it had been.

In 1870 the AL&H set its sights on the Ohio River at Parkersburg, West Virginia, renamed itself the Washington & Ohio, and built a few miles farther to Round Hill, about 50 miles from Alexandria. In 1877 the road slipped into receivership. It went through several more changes of name and goal before being swept into the Richmond & Danville system in 1886. With the rest of the R&D it became part of the Southern Railway family in 1894. In 1900 another 4 miles of track brought the railroad to Snickersville, which was renamed Bluemount when it achieved the lofty status of a town with a railroad.

In the early years of the 20th century John R. McLean (owner of the Washington *Post*) and

By the 1950s the Washington & Old Dominion had shaken off the image of its interurban past and looked like most other short lines, right down to its GE 70-tonners, both of which are shown leading a freight through Sunset Hills, Virginia. Photo by Herbert H. Harwood, Jr.

Senator Stephen B. Elkins (developer of a coal, lumber, and railroad empire in West Virginia) bought a plot of land at the Great Falls of the Potomac, west of Washington, to develop as a park. They built the Great Falls & Old Dominion Railroad, a trolley line, to connect it with Washington. Both park and trolley line opened in 1906.

The enterprise prospered, and McLean and Elkins looked to expand. In 1911 McLean with Elkins's heirs (the senator had died earlier that years) organized the Washington & Old Dominion Railway to include the GF&OD, the Alexandria–Bluemont line (leased from the Southern), and a new connecting link. The W&OD hung trolley wire over most of the Alexandria–Bluemont line and began operating in 1912 as a partly electric, partly steam railroad, and partly rural, partly suburban. It quickly acquired a reputation for random and casual operation.

In the 1920s freight began to replace passengers as the principal revenue item, but the onset of the Depression put the road into receivership. In the mid-1930s it cleaned house—scrapped old equipment, abandoned the park at Great Falls and the line to it, and reorganized as the Washington & Old Dominion Railroad. The Purcellville–Bluemont segment of the line was taken up in 1938, and the trolley wires came down in 1941 with the end of passenger service.

Replacing the electrics were three 44-ton diesels. Passenger service resumed during World War II, first with a two-car streamlined gas-electric train from the Pennsylvania (originally one of Budd's early rubber-tired experimentals), then with assorted secondhand gas-electrics. Passenger service ended again in 1950 when the mail contract expired.

W&OD bought its Alexandria–Purcellville line from the Southern Railway in 1945 and in the early 1950s became solvent, almost prosperous. On November 6, 1956, Chesapeake & Ohio bought the W&OD because of the prospect of a power plant being constructed near its line (it did not materialize). Between

1959 and 1961 business flourished, largely in construction material for Dulles International Airport, although far more material came by truck than by train—and the same was true for the construction of the community of Reston, built in the early 1960s.

W&OD sold its Rosslyn branch in 1962 for highway use and in 1965 petitioned to abandon the rest of the line, in order to sell the right of way for highway and power-line use. The Washington & Old Dominion ceased operation on August 27, 1968. Most of the line has been rebuilt as a hiking-biking trail and bridle path.

	1929	1967
Miles of railroad operated:	72	48
Number of locomotives:	4	3
Number of motor passenger cars:	12	
Number of motor freight cars:	1	
Number of freight cars:	12	
Location of headquarters: Rosslyn (Arlington) Virginia)		
Recommended reading: *Washington & Old Dominion Railroad*, by Ames W. Williams, published in 1970 by Captial Traction Quarterly, Springfield, Va.		

Washington Central Railroad

In 1887 the Northern Pacific Railway opened a line from Pasco, Washington, on the Columbia River, northwest over Stampede Pass in the Cascade Range to Tacoma. The new line cut off a long dogleg through Portland, Oregon, and it became NP's main line.

Burlington Northern was created in 1970 by the merger of Northern Pacific; Great Northern; Spokane, Portland & Seattle; and Chicago, Burlington & Quincy. The new railroad had two routes from the Twin Cities to Puget Sound (plus bypasses, cutoffs, and alternates) and in a few years began to rationalize its map. The Great Northern route over the Cascades was newer and easier than NP's line over Stampede Pass, and between Spokane and Seattle it was 67 miles shorter. If the former NP line were severed, any Pasco–Seattle traffic could move via Vancouver, Washington, with the water-level route along the Columbia River more than compensating for the extra distance. The Stampede Pass route became a candidate for spinning off.

BN closed the Stampede Pass line on August 13, 1983. In October 1986 Washington Central Railroad acquired 149 miles of the former Northern Pacific main line from SP&S Junction in Kennewick, across the Columbia River from Pasco, northwest to Cle Elum (well east of the pass), plus branches to Granger, White Swan, Moxee City, and Naches. Two months later

Washington Central GP9 No. 301 has a short freight in tow at Ellensburg, Washington, on June 10, 1987. Photo by Jim Shaw.

Washington Central acquired a cluster of former NP and Milwaukee Road lines in the wheat-growing area of central Washington, from Connell to Moses Lake, Royal City, Wheeler, and Schrag. Washington Central also took over operation of the U. S. Government Railroad from Richland Junction to Hanford Works.

The traffic surge of the early 1990s began to create congestion on the former Great Northern route across Washington. Train movements

through the 7.8-mile single-track Cascade Tunnel were limited by the time it took for the ventilation apparatus to clear the diesel exhaust fumes. Possible solutions to the problem included double-tracking the line and re-electrifying the line through the tunnel, both astronomically expensive. In 1996 Burlington Northern & Santa Fe purchased the Washington Central and reopened the line over Stampede Pass.

Washington, Idaho & Montana Railway

In 1905 the Potlatch Lumber company moved its mill from Palouse, Washington, to Potlatch, Idaho. The Oregon Railway & Navigation Co. (Union Pacific) was reluctant to build a line to follow the lumber company, so Potlatch built its own line—through towns named Harvard, Yale, Princeton, Vassar, and so on. In 1908 construction reached Purdue, Idaho, which remained the end of the line, despite the goal implied by the railroad's name.

In the early 1950s Potlatch Forests, successor to Potlatch Lumber, was using trucks to carry logs and had little further need for the railroad. However, other business had developed along the line. To tap this traffic source, the Milwaukee Road, which connected with the WI&M at Purdue, purchased the road in 1962. Burlington Northern purchased and absorbed the WI&M in March 1981 after Milwaukee Road abandoned its lines west of the Missouri River. BN spun line to the Palouse River & Coulee City in September 1996.

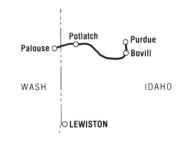

	1929	1980
Miles of railroad operated:	49	50
Number of locomotives:	5	1
Number of passenger cars:	4	
Number of freight cars:	266	
Number of company service cars:	3	

Location of headquarters: Potlatch, Idaho
Successors:
Burlington Northern
Burlington Northern & Santa Fe
Palouse River & Coulee City
Portions still operated:
Palouse River & Coulee City: Palouse, Wash.–Bovill, Idaho

There is little question about the principal item of Washington, Idaho & Montana's traffic. Number 21, an oil-burning 2-8-0, approaches Potlatch in May 1947 with a train carrying forest products. Photo by Philip C. Johnson.

Washington Terminal Company

The Washington Terminal Co. was incorporated in 1901 by an act of Congress to build a station for the Baltimore & Ohio in Washington, D. C. and at the same time eliminate grade crossings and street trackage. At the same time Congress directed the Baltimore & Potomac (Pennsylvania Railroad) to remove its tracks from the streets of Washington and also build a station. Further legislation in 1903 turned the project into a union station jointly owned by B&O and PRR.

The combination stub and through station opened on October 27, 1907. The 20 stub tracks served Pennsylvania and Baltimore & Ohio trains from the north, and 12 lower-level tracks at the east end of the station passed underneath the station to the Capitol Hill tunnel for trains of the Richmond, Fredericksburg & Potomac, the Southern Railway, and the Chesapeake & Ohio.

In the 1970s the station was partly converted to a visitor center for tourists visiting Washington. The incomplete visitor center was grossly unsuccessful, and the project hindered the use of the building as a station—indeed, station functions were moved to a temporary building out back. The whole project became an embarrassment to Amtrak, the city, and particularly the federal government—the Capitol is only four blocks away. In 1981 Congress passed the Union Station Redevelopment Act, and the

In this pre-World War II view of Washington Union Station, note that the five platforms at the near (east) end of the concourse are lower than the others. Tracks serving these platforms lead to the tunnel under Capitol Hill for trains to and from the South. American Association of Railroads photo.

restoration project got under way in 1984. In 1988 the U. S. Department of Transportation bought the station from the real estate susidiaries of the B&O and PRR.

On September 29, 1988, an elegant renovated, redeveloped Union Station opened, a combination of railroad terminal and shopping and restaurant complex. It serves the trains of Amtrak, Maryland Rail Commuter (MARC), and Virginia Railway Express; the Washington Metro has a subway station under the west end of the building. Amtrak's general offices are in the building.

In 1981 Amtrak purchased Washington Terminal Company and over the next three years absorbed its operations.

	1929	1980
Miles of track operated:	54	29
Number of locomotives:	18	8
Number of company service cars:	26	8
Location of headquarters: Washington, D. C.		
Reporting marks: WATC		
Successor: Amtrak		

Waterloo, Cedar Falls & Northern Railway

The Waterloo & Cedar Falls Rapid Transit Co. was incorporated in December 1895. In 1896 it purchased the Waterloo Street Railway. Faced with difficulty obtaining a franchise to operate in Cedar Falls, it arranged to electrify and operate a branch of the Chicago Great Western. The CGW and the electric line were closely associated for several years.

In 1904 the company changed its name to Waterloo, Cedar Falls & Northern Railway. It expanded to the southeast in 1913 with a line to Cedar Rapids, and built a freight belt line around Waterloo to serve such industries as John Deere and Rath Packing Co. The WCF&N early recognized the benefits of interchanging carload freight with the steam railroads— indeed, it handled much of its freight with steam locomotives until 1915, and it actively promoted industrial development in Waterloo.

By 1927 WCF&N's freight revenue exceeded its passenger revenue. The road's passenger service was notable for its steam-road-size parlor-observation cars, which were later rebuilt as coaches, though they retained the observation platform.

A fire in the Waterloo roundhouse in October 1954 destroyed most of the passenger equipment, several locomotives, and the shop machinery that was necessary to maintain the electric cars and locomotives.

WCF&N discontinued passenger service in 1956. (The Waterloo city cars were replaced by buses in 1936; WCF&N operated the buses until 1953, when the city took over the service.) In March 1955 the stockholders approved sale of the line to the Waterloo Railroad, which had recently been organized by the Illinois Central and the Rock Island.

The Waterloo Railroad took over the property of the WCF&N on July 1, 1956. Diesel operation was phased in gradually, and electric operation ended in August 1958. Illinois Central purchased Rock Island's half interest in July 1968, and in 1970 the Waterloo Railroad became simply a part of IC's Iowa Division. Most of WCF&N's line was later abandoned, and in 1985 IC used the corporate structure of the Waterloo Railroad for a subsidiary line in Mississippi.

Waverly

Cedar Falls WATERLOO

I O W A

CEDAR RAPIDS

	1929	1955
Miles of railroad operated:	138	98
Number of locomotives:	7	10
Number of passenger cars:	41	2
Number of freight cars:	120	28
Number of company service cars:	44	67

Location of headquarters: Waterloo, Iowa
Reporting marks: WCF&N
Recommended reading: *Iowa Trolleys*, edited by
Norman Carlson, published in 1975 by Central
Electric Railfans; Association, P. O. Box 503, Chicago,
IL 60690
Successor: Waterloo Railroad

Freight motor 182 leads a train across the Cedar River bridge south of Waterloo. The first car is a refrigerator car from the Rath plant in Waterloo. Photo by William D. Middleton.

Wellsville, Addison & Galeton Railroad

The Wellsville, Addison & Galeton Railroad was incorporated in October 1954 by Murray M. Salzberg to puchase a segment of the B&O from Galeton, Pennsylvania, to Wellsville, New York, Addison, N. Y., and Ansonia, Pa. Salzberg took possession on January 1, 1956.

Salzberg acquired seven center-cab General Electric units built between 1937 and 1940 for Ford Motor Company's River Rouge works.

	1956	1978
Miles of railroad operated:	91	40
Number of locomotives:	4	6
Number of freight cars:	3	17

Location of headquarters: Galeton, Pennsylvania

Reporting marks: WAG

Recommended reading: *Wellsville, Addison & Galeton Railroad*, by Edward A. Lewis, published in 1971 by Short Tracks Development Corp., 14 East Main Street, Arcade, NY 14009

Predecessor railroads in this book:

Buffalo & Susquehanna

Baltimore & Ohio

Map: See page 56

WA&G also gathered a fleet of several hundred interchange freight cars from Boston & Maine. They were rebuilt and repainted and lettered with WA&G's slogan, "The Sole Leather Line," a reference to the tanneries sited along the railroad.

In 1959 the line to Addison was abandoned north of Elkland, Pa., because of a weakened bridge; the interchange at Addison was with the same railroad—Erie—as the interchange at Wellsville. In 1964 Salzberg purchased the 26-mile Coudersport and Port Allegany, which connected with the Wellsville line.

The GE diesels began to wear out and in 1968 and 1969 WA&G acquired a fleet of former Southern Pacific F7s. About the same time, the per diem rules changed and revenue from WA&G's fleet of box cars dropped. WA&G petitioned to abandon the Wellsville line and rely solely on interchange with Penn Central at Ansonia. (The C&PA ceased operation in December 1970.) Floods in 1972 ended service on the Wellsville Line, and it was officially abandoned in 1973.

The road petitioned the Interstate Commerce Commission to discontinue service on the remainder of the line, and the last run was on March 16, 1979. GE center-cab diesel 1700, the last of its type, has been preserved by the Lake Shore Railway Historical Society in North East, Pa.

Wellsville, Addison & Galeton GE center-cab diesel 1700 has a string of the road's wood box cars in tow at Ansonia, Pennsylvania, in March 1970. Photo by David H. Hamley.

Western Maryland Railway

On May 27, 1852, the Maryland General Assembly granted a charter to the Baltimore, Carroll & Frederick Rail Road to build a line from Baltimore northwest through Westminster, then west toward Hagerstown, Md. The name of the enterprise was soon changed to Western Maryland Rail Road.

The line opened to Union Bridge in November 1862, and it was seized briefly by the Union Army during the Battle of Gettysburg in July 1863. Construction resumed in 1868. The line reached Hagerstown in 1872 and was extended a few miles to a connection with the Chesapeake & Ohio Canal at Williamsport in 1873.

In 1881 WM leased a line north to Shippensburg, Pennsylvania, and in 1886 established a connection there with a predecessor of the Reading. Also in 1886 WM gained a branch north from Emory Grove to Hanover and Gettysburg, Pa. That line was soon extended southwest from Gettysburg to meet WM's main line at Highfield, Md.

The main line was extended from Williamsport to Big Pool, Md., and across the Potomac River to Cherry Run, West Virginia, where it connected with the Baltimore & Ohio. B&O, WM, and Reading joined forces to operate a through freight route between Cumberland, Md., and Allentown, Pa., via Harrisburg.

Challengers pull and push Western Maryland tonnage around Helmstetter's Curve a few miles west of Cumberland. Photo by George C. Corey.

The Gould era

WM's stock was largely owned by the city of Baltimore, which also held its mortgage bonds. By the turn of the century WM's debt to Baltimore was substantial and the city sought a buyer for the railroad. Bids were submitted in 1902. The syndicate representing George Gould was the lowest bidder but guaranteed full payment of WM's debt, extension west of Cumberland, and creation of a major tidewater terminal at

Baltimore. On May 7, 1902, the city accepted the Gould syndicate's offer.

WM immediately built the marine terminal, Port Covington, and began construction westward along the Potomac (where all the good locations had been taken by the Baltimore & Ohio Railroad, the Chesapeake & Ohio Canal, and the National Turnpike). The line reached Cumberland in 1906. There it met the Cumberland & Piedmont Railway, which with the West Virginia Central & Pittsburg, another Gould road, formed a route southwest from Cumberland through Elkins to Durbin and Belington, W. Va. In 1907 Gould acquired control of the Georges Creek & Cumberland Railway, which had a line from Cumberland north through the Cumberland Narrows.

B&O and Reading broke their traffic agreement with WM in 1902, with the result that coal from Gould's West Virginia Central bypassed the WM and went instead over the Pennsy, which at the time controlled the B&O. The rest of Gould's empire was in trouble too, and in 1908 the Western Maryland entered receivership, as did the Wabash Pittsburg Terminal and the Wheeling & Lake Erie.

The Western Maryland Railway took over the Western Maryland Rail Road at the beginning of 1910 and immediately began constructing an 86-mile extension northwest from Cumberland to a connection with the Pittsburgh & Lake Erie at Connellsville, Pa.

B&O ownership

When the Gould empire collapsed John D. Rockefeller acquired control of the Western Maryland. Because the ICC merger plan of 1921 grouped WM with Baltimore & Ohio, in 1927

B&O bought Rockefeller's WM interest and soon increased its WM holdings to 43 percent. Frank Taplin, who controlled the Pittsburgh & West Virginia, protested B&O's action. The Interstate Commerce Commission charged B&O with violating antitrust laws—in its effort to carry out the ICC's own merger plan. Pennsylvania Railroad interests offered to help the B&O out of its difficulty by purchasing its WM interests (the PRR had recently acquired the P&WV), but B&O refused to sell and placed its WM holdings in a nonvoting trust.

In 1944 WM acquired the Cumberland & Pennsylvania, a short coal carrier out of Cumberland. WM began dieselization in 1949, starting with the east end of the system, farthest from the coalfields. Passenger service, which consisted of coach-only local trains, lasted barely long enough to be dieselized.

As the large railroads of the East formulated their merger plans WM could envision its traffic disappearing. Merger of the Pennsylvania and New York Central could shift traffic from the Pittsburgh & Lake Erie (part of the NYC) to the Pennsy. Norfolk & Western could easily move traffic off the P&WV onto its own lines, circuitous though they were, right into Hagerstown. WM decided to forsake independence and join the Baltimore & Ohio-Chesapeake & Ohio alliance—after all, B&O was almost a half owner of WM. B&O and C&O applied to control WM, and the ICC approved their bid in 1967.

There was little evidence of C&O-B&O control until 1973, when the Chessie System was incorporated to own C&O, B&O, and WM. In 1973 WM applied to abandon 125 miles of main line from Hancock, Md., to Connellsville, Pa., parallel to the B&O. WM's single track had better clearances and easier grades than B&O's double track, but the expense of maintaining the line and building connecting lines outweighed any saving that might result from lower operating costs. That same year WM's Port Covington coal terminal was abandoned in favor of B&O's newer pier in Baltimore. Gradually B&O absorbed WM's operations and in late 1983 merged WM.

	1929	1982
Miles of railroad operated:	878	1,152
The increase is due to operation over B&O on trackage rights.		
Number of locomotives:	259	109
Number of passenger cars:	78	
Number of freight cars:	11,481	6,836
Number of company service cars:	159	145

Location of headquarters: Baltimore, Maryland

Reporting marks: WM

Historical and technical society: Western Maryland Railway Historical Society, P. O. Box 395, Union Bridge, MD 21791

Recommended reading: *The Western Maryland Railway,* by Roger Cook and Karl Zimmermann, published in 1981 by Howell-North Books, 850 North Hollywood Way, Burbank, CA 91505 (ISBN 0-8310-7139-7)

Predecessor railroads in this book: Cumberland & Pennsylvania

Successors:
Chessie System
CSX Transportation

Portions still operated:
CSX: Baltimore–Gettysburg–Hagerstown, Md.; Hagerstown–Shippensburg, Pa.; Lonaconing, Md.–Piedmont, W. Va. (C&P); Luke, Md.–Bayard, W. Va.
Maryland Midland: Emory Grove–Highfield, Md.
Western Maryland Scenic Railroad: Cumberland–Frostburg, Md.
Yorkrail: Porters–York, Pa.

Western Pacific Railroad

In 1900 the Gould railroads (Western Maryland, Wabash, Missouri Pacific, and Denver & Rio Grande chief among them) stretched from Baltimore, Md., to Ogden, Utah, with only a short gap in Pennsylvania. The Southern Pacific connection at Ogden furnished considerable traffic to the system until E. H. Harriman obtained control of the Union Pacific and the Southern Pacific, effectively shutting Denver & Rio Grande out of the Ogden Gateway. At the same time California shippers and merchants considered themselves at the mercy of Southern Pacific, which had a near-monopoly in the state.

From time to time railroads had been proposed and surveyed across the Sierra Nevada, the mountain range along much of the eastern border of California. Some of those routes followed the canyon of the Feather River to Beckwourth Pass, which was 2,000 feet lower than the Central Pacific (later Southern Pacific) route over Donner Pass.

One such survey had been made by W. H. Kennedy, assistant to the chief engineer of the Union Pacific when Jay Gould controlled UP. Arthur Keddie used the Kennedy survey to obtain a franchise for a railroad along that route. Keddie's partner, Walter J. Bartnett, signed an agreement with George Gould, Jay Gould's eld-

The steam era was ending as Mikado 308 waited with an eastbound freight train at Altamont, California, summit of WP's climb over the hills between San Francisco Bay and the Central Valley. WP Photo by Arthur Lloyd.

est son and successor, to take over the surveys, franchises, and incorporations.

The Western Pacific Railway was incorporated in 1903 to build a railroad from Salt Lake City to San Francisco (the name chosen was also that of the railroad that originally extended the Central Pacific from Sacramento to Oakland). Gould's Denver & Rio Grande underwrote $50 million in bonds for construction. The last spike was driven in 1909 on the Spanish Creek trestle at Keddie, Calif.

The new railroad had no branches to feed traffic to it, and revenue didn't cover operating expenses and construction costs. WP entered bankruptcy in 1915 and pulled the Rio Grande in with it. At the same time the eastern end of Gould's empire collapsed as the cost of building the Wabash Pittsburgh Terminal (later the Pittsburgh & West Virginia) bankrupted the Wabash.

Reorganization and expansion

The Western Pacific Railway was sold in 1916 and reorganized as the Western Pacific Railroad. In 1917 the WP purchased control of the Tidewater Southern, an interurban that ran south from Stockton, Calif., and took over the south end of the narrow gauge Nevada-California-Oregon to gain entry to Reno, Nevada. With the payment it received from the government for damages during the period of operation by the United States Railroad Administration—chiefly the result of lack of maintenance—WP purchased control of the Sacramento Northern, an electric railroad from Sacramento to Chico, Calif. In 1927 WP bought the San Francisco-Sacramento Railroad, an interurban between the two cities of its name, and merged it with Sacramento Northern.

The USRA introduced paired-track operation with Southern Pacific between Winnemucca and Wells, Nev., 182 miles. The arrangement was discontinued after the USRA relinquished control, but resumed in 1924.

In 1926 Arthur Curtiss James acquired control of WP; he already had large holdings in

Great Northern, Northern Pacific, and Burlington. WP built a line to link up with the Great Northern at Bieber, Calif. The completion of the project on November 10, 1931, created the Inside Gateway route and made the WP a north-south carrier in conjunction with the GN and Santa's line in the San Joaquin Valley.

In 1935 WP underwent voluntary reorganization. In 1939 WP teamed up with Rio Grande

and Burlington to operate the *Exposition Flyer* between Chicago and Oakland, Calif. The railroads made plans to upgrade the train, but the war postponed their realization.

In 1949 the three railroads inaugurated the *California Zephyr*, a Chicago–Oakland streamliner. It was scheduled to traverse the most scenic parts of the trip by day and was equipped with Vista-Domes—five per train—so passengers

The *California Zephyr* climbs eastward out of Oroville, California, heading for the Feather River Canyon. Vista-Domes gave passengers an over-the-engineer's-shoulder view. Photo by Richard Steinheimer.

could enjoy the scenery. The train was an immediate success. Soon afterward WP equipped the secondary train on its line with Budd Rail Diesel Cars called *Zephyrettes* (not to be confused with the *CZ*'s train hostess, who had the same title).

	1929	1981
Miles of railroad operated:	1,055	1,436
(1981 figure includes Tidewater Southern and Sacramento Northern)		
Number of locomotives:	169	144
Number of passenger cars:	86	
Number of freight cars:	9,470	6,077
Number of company service cars:	396	219

Location of headquarters: San Francisco, California
Reporting marks: WP
Notable named passenger trains: *California Zephyr* (Chicago–Oakland, operated jointly with Denver & Rio Grande Western and Chicago, Burlington & Quincy)
Historical and technical society: Western Pacific Railroad Historical Society, P. O. Box 608, Portola, CA 96122
Recommended reading:
Portrait of a Silver Lady, by Bruce A. MacGregor and Ted Benson, published in 1977 by Pruett Publishing Co., 3235 Prairie Avenue, Boulder, CO 80301 (ISBN 0-87108-509-7)
Western Pacific's Diesel Years, by Joseph A. Strapac, published in 1980 by Overland Models, RR 12, Box 445, Muncie, IN 47302 (ISBN 0-916160-08-4)
Subsidiaries and affiliated railroads, 1981:
Alameda Belt Line (50%)
Central California Traction (33.3%)
Oakland Terminal (50%)
Sacramento Northern
Tidewater Southern
Successor: Union Pacific
Portions still operated:
Burlington Northern & Santa Fe: Keddie–Bieber, Calif.
Union Pacific: Salt Lake City–Oakland, Calif.; Reno Junction–Reno, Nev.

Independence and merger

In 1962 Southern Pacific and Santa Fe sparred for control of Western Pacific. Neither won, and WP remained independent. The road dropped its segment of the *California Zephyr* on March 21, 1970. WP continued to roll along as it had, very much a regional-size railroad with giants as neighbors (Union Pacific, Southern Pacific, and Santa Fe). In January 1980 Union Pacific surprised the railroad industry by announcing in quick succession its impending mergers of Missouri Pacific and Western Pacific. On December 22, 1982, WP became the Fourth Operating District of Union Pacific. In 1985 in response to employee requests it was renamed the Feather River Division of the new Western District.

WP owned two switching roads on the east short of San Francisco Bay jointly with the Santa Fe: the Oakland Terminal Railway and the Alameda Belt Line. WP, Santa Fe, and Southern Pacific jointly owned the Central California Traction Co., which ran between Stockton and Sacramento.

Wheeling & Lake Erie Railway

The Wheeling & Lake Erie Rail Road was incorporated in 1871 to build a line from Martins Ferry, Ohio, near Wheeling, West Virginia, through the coalfields of southeastern Ohio to the Lake Erie ports of Sandusky and Toledo. Construction began in 1873. The company was unable to raise much capital, and the directors chose narrow gauge. In 1877 a few miles of track were completed between Norwalk and Huron, Ohio, but the only traffic was excursion trains for the stockholders. Construction ceased and the W&LE petitioned for dissolution.

Construction resumed in 1881, this time to standard gauge and with the backing of Jay Gould. In 1882 the W&LE acquired the Cleveland and Marietta Railroad and began service between Toledo and Marietta. A year later, the C&M was in receivership and back on its own.

The W&LE reorganized in 1886 and continued construction eastward, reaching Wheeling in 1891. The road prospered until a depression and a long strike by coal miners in 1896 threw it into receivership.

Myron T. Herrick, a Cleveland banker, was appointed receiver of the W&LE in 1897. He added to it the Cleveland, Canton & Southern, a run-down, former narrow gauge line from Cleveland to Zanesville, Ohio. The shape of the map of the W&LE got it the nickname "Iron Cross."

Turn-of-the-century prosperity embraced the new W&LE, largely because of coal traffic. In 1906 the W&LE chartered the Lorain & West Virginia Railway to build a branch from Wellington, on the W&LE, to Lorain, on Lake Erie.

In 1907 the Gould empire collapsed. The W&LE fell once again into receivership, and in 1912 William McKinley Duncan (nephew of U. S. president William McKinley) was appointed receiver. His management style was conservative, allowing only improvements that promised a good return on investment. The road returned to profitability, but at the expense of unpainted buildings and unsignaled main lines.

The growth of the automobile industry deserves most of the credit for bringing the W&LE up from the depths. While coal continued to be the mainstay of W&LE's traffic, Detroit's factories were hungry for steel from mills at Canton and Massillon, roller bearings from the Timken plant at Canton, and other such goods.

In 1927 the Nickel Plate, Baltimore & Ohio, and New York Central teamed up to buy the W&LE stock held by John D. Rockefeller. The Van Sweringen brothers, who controlled the NKP, bought more stock on their own to ensure that the W&LE would remain out of the reach of Leonor F. Loree of the Delaware & Hudson, who was trying to build a rail system, and to keep the Pittsburgh & West Virginia from buying the W&LE.

Wheeling & Lake Erie Berkshire 6430 has the 75 cars of train 95 rolling toward Toledo along the bank of the Sandusky River north of Fremont, Ohio, on June 20, 1950. Photo by Bob Lorenz.

	1929	1948
Miles of railroad operated:	512	506
Number of locomotives:	185	161
Number of passenger cars:	66	
Number of freight cars:	11,626	13,646
Number of company service cars:	273	151

Location of headquarters: Cleveland, Ohio
Reporting marks: WLE
Historical and technical society: Nickel Plate Historical and Technical Society, P. O. Box 381, New Haven, IN 46774-0381; nkphts@mail.iac.net;http://www.iac.net/~nkphts/index.html

Recommended reading: *The Nickel Plate Story*, by John A. Rehor, published in 1965 by Kalmbach Publishing Co. (ISBN 0-89024-012-4)
Successors:
Nickel Plate
Norfolk & Western
Portions still operated:
Norfolk Southern: Bellevue–Toledo, Ohio
Ohio Central: Harmon–Zanesville, Ohio
Wheeling & Lake Erie: Martin's Ferry, Ohio–Bellevue, Ohio; Cleveland–Harmon; Canton–Carrollton, Ohio; Warrenton–Steubenville, Ohio

The Interstate Commerce Commission investigated the matter and ordered NKP, B&O, and NYC to sell their W&LE stock. The Van Sweringens' Alleghany Corporation bought NYC's shares and traded its interest in the Buffalo, Rochester & Pittsburgh for B&O shares. By 1929 the Van Sweringens owned the W&LE but were not allowed to exercise control.

The W&LE was one of the first railroads to drop passenger service—because of the automobile, which was so beneficial on the freight side of W&LE's ledgers. The road became freight-only in July 1938 when it discontinued its last passenger train, a Cleveland–Wheeling run.

In 1946 and 1947 the Nickel Plate purchased approximately 80 percent of the stock of the W&LE, and on December 1, 1949, the Nickel Plate leased the W&LE. NKP's control and lease passed to the Norfolk & Western in 1964.

On April 9, 1988, the Ohio Central Railroad began operating freight and excursion service between Harmon and Zanesville. On September 16 of that year, the N&W merged the W&LE. On May 17, 1990, a new Wheeling & Lake Railway leased and began operation on most of the rest of the old W&LE (plus the Akron, Canton & Youngstown and the Pittsburgh & West Virginia).

White Pass & Yukon Railway

 The White Pass & Yukon was born in the Yukon gold rush of 1898. A railroad was necessary to carry machinery and supplies from tidewater at Skagway, Alaska, over the Coast Mountains to the Yukon River in Canada's Yukon Territory.

Construction of the 3-foot gauge railroad began in 1898, and crews working from Skagway and from Whitehorse, Y. T., met at Carcross, Y. T., on July 29, 1900. The road's destination at one time was Fort Selkirk, Y. T., at the confluence of the Pelly and Lewes (or Upper Yukon) rivers.

WP&Ys corporate structure encompassed three railroads: the Pacific & Arctic Railway & Navigation Co. (Alaska, 20.4 miles), the British Columbia-Yukon Railway (British Columbia, 32.2 miles), and the British Yukon Railway (Yukon Territory, 58.1 miles), all three operated by the White Pass & Yukon.

The WP&Y prospered for a few years, then gold mining slackened and the company entered reorganization. The belligerence of Japan and the approach of World War II roused the economy of the Yukon. The railroad's business increased and in 1937 it even inaugurated air services (WP&Y had operated steamboats for many years between Whitehorse and Dawson and between Carcross and Atlin).

The bombing of Pearl Harbor in 1941 triggered

An 800-hp GE diesel leads a string of heavyweights across the trestle at Glacier Gorge. Photo by George A. Forero Jr.

	1980
Miles of railroad operated:	111
Number of locomotives:	20
Number of passenger cars:	34
Number of freight cars:	399
Number of company service cars:	36

Location of headquarters: Seattle, Washington
Reporting marks: WPY
Recommended reading: *The White Pass: Gateway to the Klondike*, by Roy Minter, published in 1987 by University of Alaska Press, Fairbanks, AK 99775-1580 (ISBN 0-912006-33-1)

Subsidiaries and affiliated railroads, 1980:
Pacific & Arctic Railway & Navigation Co.
British Columbia-Yukon Railway
British Yukon Railway
Portions still operated: Skagway–White Pass Summit

the construction of the Alaska Highway. One of the jumping-off places for construction crews was Whitehorse, the northern terminus of the railroad. The WP&Y found itself with too big a job to do, so the U. S. Army's Military Railway Service moved in to operate the railroad. The Army purchased locomotives from several narrow gauge lines in the U. S. to handle the increased traffic—in 1943 the road handled the equivalent of 10 years' worth of prewar tonnage.

After the war the WP&Y returned to its primary business of bringing the necessities of life into the Yukon and carrying out silver, lead, and zinc. In addition the railroad developed a tourist business, connecting with cruise ships calling at Skagway. In 1951 the White Pass & Yukon Corp. was chartered to acquire ownership of the subsidiary companies.

To reduce the cost of transferring cargo between ships, trucks, and trains, the White Pass developed a container that would fit on the narrow gauge cars and flatbed trucks. In 1954 WP&Y designed and bought a ship, the *Clifford J. Rogers*, to carry the containers between Vancouver, B. C., and Skagway. The company also acquired a trucking operation and a pipeline parallel to the railroad.

In 1983 a slump in the mining industry and the construction of a highway between Skagway and Whitehorse caused the railroad to shut down. The southern portion of the line, from Skagway to the summit of White Pass, has been reopened for excursion trains.

Winston-Salem Southbound Railway

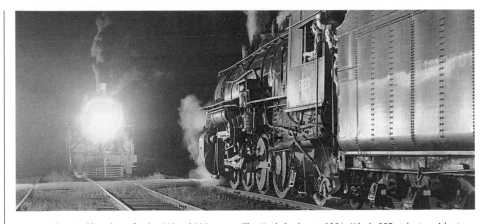

The Winston-Salem Southbound was incorporated in 1905—late as North American railroad history goes—to build a railroad from Winston-Salem, North Carolina, to the South Carolina state line. Construction began in 1909 after the railroad's principal connections, Norfolk & Western and Atlantic Coast Line, guaranteed its bonds and became its joint owners.

The reason for the road's existence was probably to form a shortcut for coal moving south to fuel ACL locomotives and U. S. Navy ships at Charleston, S. C. WSS's rails reached Whitney in December 1910. A few months later the line was extended to Wadesboro, where it connected with ACL.

WSS depended on parent Norfolk & Western for maintenance of its line and for supervision of its operations. It relied on Atlantic Coast Line for accounting and marketing. In the early 1950s WSS's motive power fleet consisted of two half-century-old ex-N&W 2-8-0s, two ex-ACL Mikados, and two similar 2-8-2s purchased new. In 1957 the Southbound replaced steam with four GP9s, two delivered in WSS's gray and maroon and two in ACL black. In 1960 WSS acquired control of the High Point, Thomasville & Denton Railroad, a 34-mile line from High Point to a connection with the WSS at High Rock.

Winston-Salem Southbound time freights 209 and 212 meet at Eller, North Carolina, in 1956. Mikado 827, right, is ex-Atlantic Coast Line, but its tender is ex-Norfolk & Western. Mikado 300, approaching, was built for WSS to ACL specifications—the N&W pilot is a later modification. Photo by Philip R. Hastings.

About 1967 the GP9s disappeared, two each, into the rosters of N&W and Seaboard Coast Line. Thereafter WSS leased power from its parents. About the same time WSS no longer had any interchange freight cars of its own, although three cabooses remained in service into the mid-1980s. I will use 1967 as the end date for the rail-road, but it really marks the transition to paper-railroad status. WSS maintains a degree of independence even though its allegiance is split between the two giants of southeastern railroading, Norfolk Southern and CSX Transportation.

	1929	1967
Miles of railroad operated:	98	95
Number of locomotives:	11	
Number of passenger cars:	3	
Number of freight cars:	203	
Number of company service cars:	17	8

Location of headquarters: Winston-Salem, North Carolina

Reporting marks: WSS

Subsidiaries and affiliated railroads, 1967: High Point, Thomasville & Denton

Portions still operated: Winston-Salem Southbound: Winston-Salem to Wadesboro, N. C.; Whitney—Badin, N. C.

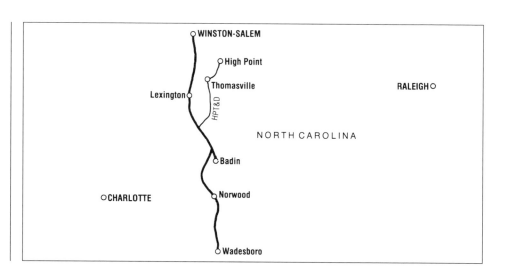

Wrightsville & Tennille

Tennille, Georgia, 55 miles east of Macon on the Central of Georgia, was the starting point for the Wrightsville & Tennille. In 1884 the W&T began and completed a 16-mile line south to Wrightsville. By furnishing material for the construction of the road, the Central Railroad & Banking Company gained control of the short line. In 1886 the W&T merged the Dublin & Wrightsville, which reached to the bank of the Oconoee River opposite Dublin. In 1891 it bridged the Oconee, and in 1899 it acquired the Oconoee & Western Railroad, from Dublin to Hawkinsville. In 1908 the W&T filled out its map by taking over the Dublin & Southwestern Railroad, which had a line from Dublin to Eastman.

The lines west and south of Dublin were abandoned in 1941. The Wrightsville & Tennille was merged with the Central of Georgia

Wrightsville & Tennille train 1, the daily-except-Sunday mixed train from Tennille to Dublin, pauses at Brewton on Washington's birthday, February 22, 1954. Photo by W. F. Beckum, Jr.

Railroad, a new Southern Railway subsidiary, along with its parent, the Central of Georgia Railway, on June 1, 1971. The Tennille–Dublin portion of the line is still in service.

The Wrightsville & Tennille was the largest of Central of Georgia's subsidiary short lines. The others were:

• Wadley & Southern, formed in 1906 to consolidate several railroads with lines from Wadley to Collins, 53 miles, and Wadley to Rockledge, 37 miles. By 1930 the road was down to a 20-mile route from Wadley to Swainsboro; it was abandoned in 1964.

• Louisville & Wadley Railroad, built in 1879 from Wadley north to Louisville, 10 miles. It was reorganized in 1961 was the locally owned Louisville & Wadley Railway. It is still in operation.

• Sylvania Central Railway, built in 1885 from Rocky Ford, of CofG's Savannah line, to Sylvania, on the Savannah & Atlanta, 15 miles. It was independent during some years of its history and a CofG subsidiary at other times. It was abandoned in 1954.

	1929	1970
Miles of railroad operated:	104	36
Number of locomotives:	7	1
Number of passenger cars:	10	
Number of freight cars:	33	1
Number of company service cars:	3	1

Location of headquarters: Dublin, Georgia
Reporting marks: WT
Recommended reading: *Central of Georgia Railway and Connecting Lines*, by Richard E. Prince, published in 1976 by Richard E. Prince
Successors:
Central of Georgia
Southern
Norfolk Southern
Portions still operated: Norfolk Southern: Tennille–Dublin, Ga.
Map: See page 383

Yosemite Valley Railroad

Yosemite National Park was established in 1890, and soon afterward railroad routes were surveyed into the valley. A group of men from San Francisco and Oakland incorporated the Yosemite Valley Railroad in 1902 and chose a route that simply followed the Merced River Canyon into the park. Grading got underway in 1905 from the city of Merced, California, and early in 1906 service began as far as Merced Falls.

In May 1907 the railroad reached a point about 12 miles from the east end of the valley and established a station named El Portal. From there the railroad built a wagon road into the park. Service over the full length of the line began on May 15, 1907.

By 1910 Pullmans were being operated over Southern Pacific from Los Angeles and Oakland to Merced. In 1912 the Yosemite Lumber Co. opened a sawmill at Merced Falls and a logging operation across the river from El Portal. The tourist business grew, and visiting royalty and Hollywood stars rode the YV.

Construction of a dam on the Merced River in the 1920s required a major line relocation. Business peaked in 1925—paved roads reached El Portal in 1926. Passenger traffic dropped 78 percent from 1925 to 1928, and the Yosemite Lumber Co. suspended operations in 1927.

The Depression drove YV into bankruptcy in

In 1940 Yosemite Valley train 3, a 4-4-0 trailing a steel baggage-mail car and a wood observation car, stands at El Portal, ready to carry passengers down the Merced River Canyon. Photo by Millard Brown, from the collection of Harre W. Demoro.

CALIFORNIA

SAN FRANCISCO

To Stockton

AT&SF El Portal

Yosemite
National
Park

Merced Falls

MERCED

SP

AT&SF

SP

To Bakersfield

	1929	1945
Miles of railroad operated:	78	78
Number of locomotives:	8	8
Number of passenger cars:	8	7
Number of freight cars:	255	73
Number of company service cars:	10	8

Location of headquarters: Merced, California

Recommended reading: *Railroads of the Yosemite Valley,* by Hank Johnston, published in 1963 by Johnston-Howe Publications, 1233 Long Beach Boulevard, Long Beach, CA 90813

1935. The company was reorganized as the Yosemite Valley Railway. Freight traffic increased and the railroad showed a small profit, but a flood in December 1937 wiped out 30 miles of line in the Merced River canyon.

Service resumed in 1938. The lumber company, which had resumed operations, closed permanently in 1938, and passenger traffic dropped to almost nothing during World War II. The trustees petitioned for abandonment on August 31, 1944.

Another flood in 1945 further weakened the road's finances, and a bridge fire in August of that year marooned some of the rolling stock. The last run was on August 24, 1945.

The railroad made a profit before fixed charges in 32 of its 38 years of operation. With proper financing it might have endured long enough to take advantage of California's postwar boom. Now, as the crush of automobile traffic threatens to destroy Yosemite National Park, many wish the railroad were still operating.

John W. Barriger III

JOHN W. BARRIGER III (1899–1976) was born in Dallas and grew up in St. Louis. He began railroad service as a laborer in the Pennsylvania Railroad shops at Altoona. He attended the Massachusetts Institute of Technology but continued to work for the Pennsy during vacations. After graduation in 1921 he returned to the Pennsy full time in various capacities until 1927 when he joined the financial firm of Kuhn, Loeb & Co.

From 1933 to 1941 Barriger was chief of the railroad division of the Reconstruction Finance Corporation. By the time he came to the Monon he had been reorganization manager of the Chicago & Eastern Illinois, federal manager of the Toledo, Peoria & Western, vice-president of the Union Stock Yards in Chicago, and manager of the Diesel Locomotive Division of Fairbanks-Morse.

After rebuilding the Monon Barriger was vice-president of the New Haven and the Rock Island, and from 1956 to 1964 he was president of Pittsburgh & Lake Erie, which came as close to his concept of super railroad as any of his railroads.

At the end of 1964 Barriger retired from that post, and in March 1965 he became chairman and chief executive officer (his business card read "Traveling Freight Agent and President") of the Missouri-Kansas-Texas.

After retirement from the Katy at age 70, Barriger briefly became chief executive officer of the Boston & Maine, and then in 1973, a consultant for the Federal Railroad Administration, retiring in 1975. (In 1984 Federal Railroad Administrator John Riley said "You didn't worry about missing one of JWB's retirement parties. You knew there'd be another.") He then was asked to return to the Rock Island as Senior Traveling Freight Agent, the position he held at the time of his death.

In 1976 when Barriger went to the Rock Island, he said, "They could charge me money to let me work as a railroader and I'd still do it. For me, railroading comes under the heading of organized sport." During his life he amassed an excellent railroad library, which his family donated in 1982 to the Mercantile Library of St. Louis to create the John W. Barriger III Railroad Library.

Henry Morrison Flagler

HENRY MORRISON FLAGLER (1830–1913) was born in Hopewell, New York. At the age of 22 he began a business career in Ohio, though he had little education or money. His success led to a partnership with John D. Rockefeller. They formed the Standard Oil Company, and soon the two men controlled much of the oil industry in the U. S.

In 1878 (some accounts say 1883) Flagler went to Florida hoping the climate there would help his ailing wife, Mary. He recognized the Florida's potential as a tourist attraction. To open Palm Beach and Miami to winter vacationers he built the Florida East Coast Railway. He took over a narrow gauge line between Jacksonville and St. Augustine (where he built a hotel, the Ponce de Leon), standard-gauged it, and extended it south, reaching Miami in 1896. Flagler doubled his efforts to develop Florida and lived out the last years of his life at Palm Beach. He died in May 1913.

Fred Harvey

FRED HARVEY (1835–1901) was born in London. In 1850 he arrived in New York and took a job in a restaurant; in 1859 he opened his own restaurant in St. Louis. He eventually left the restaurant business, and by 1876 he was general western freight agent of the Chicago, Burlington & Quincy. He traveled a lot, and his poor health and his memory of the restaurant business rendered him intolerant of the food and lodging he had to endure.

He proposed a system of restaurants along the Burlington's lines. The Burlington, an old, well established company, was unimpressed and sent him to the young, upstart Santa Fe. At the Santa Fe he encountered sympathetic ears—officials who had also encountered poor food and lodging. The railroad agreed to put Harvey in charge of the station restaurant in Topeka. He cleaned it up and turned it into a first-class eating facility that catered not only to passengers and rail-road officials but to townspeople.

Before long Harvey had facilities every 100 miles along Santa Fe routes and "Meals by Fred Harvey" was the best advertising slogan possible for Santa Fe's passenger service.

The usual meal stop was half an hour. Conductors telegraphed ahead the number of passengers for the lunch counter and the dining room. As the train stopped, the restaurant manager directed passengers to the lunch counter and the dining room—men were required to wear a jacket in the dining room. Waitresses worked in teams to serve the passengers quickly. The waitress who took the order would move the coffee cup slightly to indicate coffee, black or with cream, tea, water, or milk, so that the waitresses who followed with the pots and pitchers would not have to ask again. Menus were arranged so passengers wouldn't encounter the same items more than once during the course of a trip.

Harvey's linen, silver, and excellent food received some credit for civilizing the West. The "Harvey girls" also got credit for the job. In 1883 Harvey fired the waiters of the restaurant at Raton, New Mexico, for fighting and replaced them with young women. The women worked so well that he began advertising for women between 18 and 30 to come west to work for him—the Harvey girls.

In 1889 Harvey and the railroad made a new contract that gave him exclusive rights to operate restaurants, lunch counters, and hotels along the lines of the Santa Fe. The railroad would provide utilities and haul supplies and employees free of charge; profits would go to Harvey.

Harvey died in 1901 after a long bout with cancer. By then his entire restaurant and hotel system was in place (also dining cars) and had a world-wide reputation.

Many of Harvey's meal houses were also hotels. In the years before air-conditioning when travel between Chicago and Los Angeles required three or four nights, passengers welcomed a night or two in a comfortable hotel to break the journey. After 1900 the Harvey system began building luxury hotels, like La Fonda in Santa Fe and El Tovar at Grand Canyon, to stimulate tourist traffic, and in 1925 the Harvey organization began operating automobile tours that gave passengers a closer look at the Southwest.

Harvey House patronage fell off in the 1930s as more trains began to carry dining cars and the trains themselves were accelerated and air-conditioned; the Depression and improved highways also took their toll. By the late 1940s most of the Harvey Houses and hotels along the Santa Fe's lines had been torn down.

Recommended Reading: *The Harvey Girls*, by Leslie Poling-Kempes, published in 1989 by Paragon House, 90 Fifth Avenue, New York, NY 10011 (ISBN: 1-55778-064-1)

David H. Moffat Jr.

DAVID H. MOFFAT JR. (1839–1911) was born in Washingtonville, Orange County, New York, a town founded by his grandfather. At the age of 12 he went to New York City, began working as a bank messenger, and quickly rose to the post of assistant teller. In 1855 the Moffat family moved to Des Moines, Iowa. David found a job in a bank there, but a year later moved west to the new city of Omaha, Nebraska.

Moffat prospered until a business panic in 1860 wiped out both his bank and his real estate speculation. He moved farther west to Denver (which had just been settled) where he established a book and stationery store. In 1861 he moved the store to larger quarters, became postmaster, and traveled back to Washingtonville to marry Frances Buckhout. Moffat prospered and entered the banking business in Denver. He soon became involved with Denver's railroads, and gradually the creation of a railroad directly west from Denver became the goal of his life.

Moffat had been involved with a proposed railroad up Clear Creek—the main purpose of the road had been to spur the Colorado Central into action—and he was one of the organizers of the Denver, South Park & Pacific, which had been diverted from the goal of its name to Leadville by news of the discovery of silver there. In 1880 Moffat sold his holdings in several Denver railroads and invested in the Denver, Utah & Pacific, which was to build west over Rollins Pass and then follow the Fraser and Colorado rivers west to connect with the Rio Grande Western at Grand Junction. The Burlington bought the DU&P but abandoned the proposed road in 1886. In 1885 Moffat became president of the Denver & Rio Grande. To counter the construction of the Colorado Midland west from Colorado Springs, he extended Rio Grande's Leadville line over Tennessee Pass and down to the Colorado River, and he surveyed the mountains west of Denver for a pass that would allow a direct line from Denver to Leadville. The directors of the Rio Grande were not interested in such a project and discharged Moffat in 1891.

Moffat's association with the Denver streetcar system had acquainted him with the potential of electric motive power. In 1901 he and others incorporated the Denver & Northwestern Railway, to be an electric railroad to coal mines a few miles west of Denver and eventually into northwestern Colorado. In 1902 Moffat decided to build a steam railroad west from Denver, the Denver, Northwestern & Pacific, predecessor of the Denver & Salt Lake. In the next decade Moffat spent most of his fortune building and maintaining the railroad and battling for its survival. On March 17, 1911, he was in New York and received a promise of the financing he needed to complete his railroad west to Salt Lake City. Word leaked back to Union Pacific (the stories are unclear and conflict with each other) and the help was withdrawn the next morning. Moffat died shortly after learning of the broken promise.

Recommended reading: *The Giant's Ladder*, by Harold A. Boner, published in 1962 by Kalmbach Publishing Co., 1027 North Seventh Street, Milwaukee, WI 53233

William Jackson Palmer

WILLIAM J. PALMER (1836–1909) was born near Leipsic in Kent County, Delaware, and grew up in Philadelphia. He began his railroad career as a surveyor at the age of 17, and eventually became the private secretary of Pennsylvania Railroad president J. Edgar Thomson. During the Civil War he rose to the rank of brigadier general in the Union army.

After his Civil War service was over, Palmer decided on a career with a western railroad and selected the Union Pacific Eastern Division (later Kansas Pacific). He was in charge of surveying parties that were investigating routes westward from El Paso and Albuquerque, and he became fascinated with the Southwest and its mineral wealth.

Kansas Pacific's rails arrived in Denver in 1870, and Palmer set off on his own. Even before then, he had espoused the idea of a railroad south from Denver along the Front Range of the Rockies. A chance encounter with New York attorney William Proctor Mellen resulted in both financing for the railroad and a wife—Mellen's daughter.

Palmer incorporated the Denver & Rio Grande Railway in 1870 as a Denver–El Paso railroad. To exploit coal deposits near Canon City and Walsenburg, Palmer incorporated a coal company which became Colorado Fuel & Iron Co. (now CF&I Steel). Palmer left the D&RG in 1883 because of stockholder dissatisfaction and subsequent changes in the board of directors. He continued as president of the Denver & Rio Grande Western Railway, which was building the western extension of the Denver & Rio Grande from the Colorado-Utah border to Salt Lake City. In 1889 Palmer organized the Rio Grande Western Railway to acquire and standard-gauge the D&RGW.

Meanwhile Palmer had received concessions from the Mexican government to build railways from Mexico City to the Pacific coast and to the U. S. border at Laredo, Texas. In 1881 he began work on the Mexican National Railway, a narrow gauge railroad from Laredo to Mexico City. Palmer sold his Mexican interests in 1902.

In 1901 George Gould, who controlled the Denver & Rio Grande, acquired the Rio Grande Western. Palmer retired from railroading and closed out his life with a period of quiet philanthropy in Colorado Springs, the city he had founded. Despite a riding accident in 1906 that left him paralyzed below the waist, he remained active to the point of hosting a reunion of the Fifteenth Pennsylvania Cavalry and traveling once more to England before his death in 1909.

Recommended reading: *A Builder of the West*, by John S. Fisher, published in 1939 by The Caxton Printers Ltd., Caldwell, ID 83605

Samuel M. Pinsly

SAMUEL M. PINSLY (1899–1977) was born in Cambridge, Massachusetts, and attended Northeastern University in Boston, where he received degrees in engineering and law. He served in the Army during World War I, then worked in the automobile business.

In 1923 he married Jessie Salzberg, daughter of H. E. Salzberg, and six years later he joined Salzberg's company, which dealt in used railroad equipment. Salzberg bought the Hoosac Tunnel & Wilmington Railroad in 1936 and sold it in 1938 to Pinsly, who brought it to profitability. His group of railroads eventually included several short lines cast off by the Boston & Maine:

• Saratoga & Schuylerville (Mechanicville to Saratoga and Schuylerville, New York—purchased 1945, abandoned 1956)
• Sanford & Eastern (Rochester, New Hampshire, to Westbrook, Maine—purchased 1949, abandoned 1961)
• Montpelier & Barre (Montpelier Jct. to Graniteville, Vermont—purchased 1957, sold 1980)
• Claremont & Concord (Claremont Junction to Concord, N. H.—purchased 1954, still in operation from Claremont Junction to Claremont)
• St. Johnsbury & Lamoille County (St. Johnsbury–Swanton, Vt.—purchased 1967, sold 1973)

Appropriately enough, Pinsly's headquarters for many years were located in Boston & Maine's general office building in Boston. He also owned two non-B&M lines, the Greenville & Northern (Greenville to Travelers Rest, South Carolina—purchased 1957, still in operation) and the Frankfort & Cincinnati (Frankfort to Elsinore, Kentucky—purchased 1961, abandoned 1985).

In 1956 Pinsly attempted to purchase the New York, Ontario & Western, and in 1958 he proposed to purchase the Old Colony lines of the New Haven to operate them for freight service. Neither project came to fruition. Pinsly was active in the American Shortline Railroad Association, several regional railroad associations, and numerous civic organizations.

After his death in 1977 the Pinsly organization continued in business. It expanded in 1982 with the acquisition from Conrail of former New Haven lines from Westfield to Easthampton and Holyoke, Mass., now operated as the Pioneer Valley Railroad.

Cornelius Vanderbilt

CORNELIUS VANDERBILT (1794–1877) was born into a farming family on Staten Island. He received little education and went to work early. At 16 he bought a small boat and began ferry service between Staten Island and Manhattan. In 1813 he married Sophia Johnson, a cousin, and began to build a family that eventually numbered nine daughters and four sons (one of whom died in infancy). Vanderbilt's ferry business expanded and prospered, first to a New York–New Brunswick (New Jersey) line, then out Long Island Sound to Stonington, Connecticut. His shipping interests later included a system of ships and stagecoaches from New York to California via Nicaragua and a transatlantic route. Vanderbilt's shipping activities got him the nickname "Commodore."

His shipping activities also brought him into contact with railroads, and he held directorships of several of the railroads that connected with his boats. In 1857 he acquired control of the New York & Harlem Railroad. It was a weak railroad; its chief asset was its line the length of Manhattan Island. In 1863 Vanderbilt bought control of the Hudson River Railroad, which competed with the New York & Harlem, and in 1864 he bought a block of New York Central stock. Vanderbilt attempted to gain control of the Erie in 1867 but failed; the event was his only unsuccessful bid to acquire a railroad. Throughout his later years he continued to buy NYC stock to maintain control of the road.

In his declining years the Commodore took up a belief in spiritualism, attending seances and asking the spirits for information on the future of the stock market. His wife Sophia died in 1868 after a long period during which they had grown apart. Not long afterward the Commodore married Miss Frank Crawford, thirtyish, of Mobile, Alabama. The hero of the Commodore's early years, William Henry Harrison, had been replaced in his esteem by George Washington. Vanderbilt proposed an enormous monument to Washington in New York's Central Park, but his wife's pastor suggested to him that it would be more practical to endow a university. In 1873 Vanderbilt gave a million dollars to Central University in Nashville, Tennessee; the university changed its name to Vanderbilt in his honor.

The Commodore was concerned about the future of his railroad empire, and he arranged his will so that nearly all of his $100 million estate went to his son William H. and to William's sons, in particular Cornelius II. The Commodore died in 1877 and was buried in the family vault in a Moravian cemetery on Staten Island.

Recommended reading: *Commodore Vanderbilt*, by Wheaton J. Lane, published in 1942 by Alfred A. Knopf, New York, N. Y.

Daniel Willard

DANIEL WILLARD (1861–1942) was born in North Hartland, Vermont. He was educated in the local schools, taught school in his hometown, and attended Massachusetts Agricultural College for a year before going to work for the Central Vermont as a track laborer in 1879. He soon hired on as a fireman with the Connecticut & Passumpsic Rivers Railroad, later becoming an engineer.

In 1883 and 1884 he was a locomotive engineer for the Lake Shore & Michigan Southern at Elkart, Indiana, and from 1884 to 1898 he rose from brakeman to superintendent of the Soo Line. There he met F. D. Underwood, general manager of the Soo. Willard followed Underwood to the Baltimore & Ohio in 1899 and became assistant general manager. In 1901 he went to the Erie as Underwood's assistant. From 1904 to 1910 Willard was second vice-president in charge of operation and maintenance of the Burlington. He returned to the B&O in 1910 to become its president.

Willard served as president or chairman of numerous railroad industry boards and committees, among them the American Railway Association, Eastern Railroads' President's Committee, Railroad War Board, and the War Industries Board.

In 1931 Willard, then 70 years old, offered his resignation; the board of directors of the B&O continued to elect him president. He resigned as president on June 1, 1941, and was elected chairman of the board. He died on July 6, 1942, and was buried in the cemetery of the Federated Church, Hartland, Vt., between the graves of his two sons.

Willard was best known for his liberal position on labor relations, a blend of innovation and conservatism in the passenger business (B&O was one of the first railroads to adopt air-conditioning and diesel power, but rejected lightweight cars), and the Fair of the Iron Horse at Baltimore in 1927 (a celebration of B&O's centennial). He had an industrywide reputation for fairness, honesty, and sincerity.

Recommended reading: *Daniel Willard Rides the Line*, by Edward Hungerford, published in 1938 by G. P. Putnam's Sons, New York

Glossary

Abandon: to cease operating all or part of a route or service, especially with the intent of never resuming it again.

Affiliate: a company effectively controlled by another or associated with others under common ownership or control.

ARA: American Railway (or Railroad) Association, a predecessor of the Association of American Railroads

Association of American Railroads (AAR): the coordinating and research agency of the American railroad industry. It is not a government agency but rather an organization to which railroads belong, much as local businesses belong to a chamber of commerce.

Baldwin: Baldwin Locomotive Works; also a locomotive built by Baldwin.

Bankrupt: declared legally insolvent (unable to pay debts as they fall due) and with assets taken over by judicial process to be distributed among creditors.

Beebe, Lucius: (1902–1966) socialite, newspaper editor (the Virginia City *Territorial Enterprise*), and author of several railroad books that brought respectability to the hobby.

Bridge route, bridge traffic: Bridge traffic is freight received from one railroad to be moved by a second railroad for delivery to a third; for example, lettuce from California received by the Cotton Belt from Southern Pacific at Corsicana, Texas, for delivery to New York Central at East St. Louis. A bridge route is a railroad with more bridge traffic than traffic originating or terminating on line.

Broad gauge: any track gauge greater than 4′8½″. The Erie Railroad was built with a gauge of 6 feet; contemporary examples include BART (5′6″); Toronto Transit Commission (4′10″); and SEPTA (5′2¼″). Elsewhere in the world gauges greater than standard are found in Spain, Portugal, India (5′6″); Ireland and New South Wales, Australia (5′3″); and Russia (5′).

Budd, Edward G.: founder of the Budd Company, best known for its stainless steel passenger cars.

Cab-forward: a type of articulated locomotive unique to Southern Pacific. They were essentially back to front, with enclosed cabs; fuel oil was piped from the tender all the way forward to the firebox. The reason for the odd configuration was to put the engine crew ahead of the exhaust gases and to improve visibility in tunnels and snowsheds.

Camelback: a steam locomotive with the engineer's cab astride the middle of the boiler and, where the cab would normally be, a minimal shelter for the fireman stoking the wide anthracite-burning firebox.

Capitalization: the total par value or stated value of the capital of a company. Overcapitalization means the value of the stocks and bonds exceeds the value of the physical properties of the railroad; conservative capitalization means the two values are close.

Catenary: a system of overhead trolley wires in which the contact wire is hung from another wire which hangs in a catenary curve; also, any or all of the overhead trolley wire system.

Centralized Traffic Control (CTC): a traffic control system whereby train movements are directed through remote control of switches and signals from a central control panel. The trains operate on the authority of signal indications instead of the authority of a timetable and train orders.

Charter: an instrument in writing from a state or country granting or guaranteeing rights, franchises, and privileges to a corporation. Obtaining a charter is a necessary part of incorporation.

Clearance diagram: a diagram showing the maximum size of cars and locomotives that may use a line or a track.

Common carrier: a transportation company that offers—indeed, must offer—its services to all customers, as differentiated from a contract carrier, which carries goods for one shipper. The difference is like that between two buses, one signed "Main Street;" the other, "Charter."

Commuter service: passenger service that takes people to and from work. Characteristics include morning and evening peak periods, fares with multiple-ride discounts, the same riders Monday through Friday, and luggage consisting mostly of briefcases.

Company-owned railroad: a railroad whose stock is held by a company, not by individuals.

Consolidation: the unification of two or more corporations by dissolution of existing ones and creation of a single new corporation.

Control: ownership by a railroad or by those sympathetic to its interests of enough of the securities of a second road to control its traffic policies.

Controlling interest: sufficient stock ownership in a corporation to exert control over policy.

Degree: a measure of the sharpness of a curve. It is the angle through which the track turns in 100 feet of track. The number of degrees is equal to 5729 divided by the radius of the curve in feet.

Directed Service Order: an order issued by the Interstate Commerce Commission directing one railroad to handle the traffic of another, if the second is unable to by reason of strike, damage, abandonment, or other emergency.

Duplex-drive: a non-articulated steam locomotive with two sets of cylinders and drive wheels

Embargo: an order issued by a common carrier or public regulatory agency that prohibits the acceptance of some or all kinds of freight for transportation on the carrier's lines or between specified points or areas because of traffic congestion, labor difficulties, or other reasons.

Federal Railroad Administration (FRA): the agency of the U. S. Department of Transportation that deals with transportation policy as it affects railroads.

Financial interest: ownership of enough securities of a second road, short of control, to influence its traffic policies.

Foreclosure: a legal proceeding that bars or extinguishes a mortgagor's right of redeeming a mortgaged estate. In domestic terms, you mortgage your house as security on a loan for its purchase. If you fail to keep up payments, the mortgagee—the bank—can foreclose, which means the bank gets the house and you no longer have it. It's the same with a loan for construction of a railroad.

Gauge: the distance between the running rails of track.

Grade: the inclination or slope of the track. It is usually measured as a percent (the tangent of the angle of inclination)—for example, a rise of 2 feet in 100 feet of track is 2 percent. Occasionally it is expressed as "1 in n," where n is the number of feet in which the track rises 1 foot. Both measures are ratios—1 in 50 is the same as 2 percent. The steepest mainline grade in North America is 4.7 percent on a Norfolk Southern Railway line near Saluda, North Carolina. The usual maximum for a main line in mountainous territory is about 2 percent.

Granger roads: the midwestern railroads that derived most of their revenue from transporting the products of agriculture

Harvey, Fred: (1835–1901) an Englishman who established a chain of restaurants and hotels along the route of the Atchison, Topeka & Santa Fe Railway and later also operated Santa Fe's dining car service.

Haulage: movement of one railroad's traffic by a second road between specific points under the terms of a contract. The hauling road exercises no control over the traffic, is not shown in the route for the traffic, and does not get a division of the revenue.

Head-end cars: mail, baggage, and express cars, so called because they were usually positioned at the head end of the passenger trains they moved in.

Holding company: a company that owns other companies for purposes of control. The charter of one such company empowered it to acquire, hold, and dispose of stocks, bonds, and securities issued by corporations and government, state, and local authorities.

Hood unit: a diesel locomotive with a long hood covering the engine, a short hood enclosing some auxiliary gear, and a cab near one end of the frame; as opposed to cab unit, a streamlined locomotive with a full-width body

Hump yard: a yard in which freight cars are pushed over a low hill and roll down into different tracks singly or a few at a time.

Incentive per diem: To alleviate a shortage of box cars in the mid-1970s, the railroad industry encouraged the railroads to put new cars into service by offering an incentive payment—basically almost double the daily rental for new box cars in good condition. Investors teamed up with short lines to take advantage of incentive payments, accounting regulations, and tax laws; shortline box cars blossomed forth. Then the recession of 1978 hit, followed by truck deregulation. The box cars were soon idle; eventually many of them were sold to other railroads.

Incorporate: to form into a corporation recognized by law as an entity.

Industrial railroad: a railroad owned and operated by an industry to move cars within a factory, plant, or mill and to and from a common-carrier interchange; in somewhat more colloquial terms, a railroad behind a chain-link fence. Industrial railroads are usually not common carriers.

Interchange: a junction of two railroads where cars are transferred from one road to another.

Intercity passenger service: as distinguished from commuter service, the passengers don't make the trip every day, tickets are for single trips, and the luggage contains clothing, not the newspaper and work to do at home. Intercity passenger trains usually include such amenities as sleeping cars and food service.

Intermodal: traffic moving by more than one mode on its trip from shipper to receiver. The term is most frequently used for piggyback or trailer-on-flat-car traffic but it includes containers transferred from seagoing ships to special rail cars.

Interstate Commerce Commission (ICC): the agency of the federal government that carried out the provisions of the Interstate Commerce Act and other federal laws regulating interstate transportation. The agency went out of existence at the end of 1995, and some of its functions were taken over by the Surface Transportation Board of the Department of Transportation.

Interurban: an electric railroad running between cities, often of lighter construction than "steam" railroads and often operating in the streets of cities and towns instead of on private right of way. Interurbans had their rise and fall during the first four decades of the twentieth century.

Joint operation: operation of two railroads as one unit under two separate boards of directors.

Lease: the handing over of the property of a railroad in return for a specified yearly payment. The railroad must be returned in as good condition as when it was handed over. The most prevalent form of lease calls for the guarantee of the interest and principal of outstanding bonds of the lessor and a guaranteed percentage on the stock. The lessor company continues to exist and to retain ownership of its railroad property.

Lignite: low-grade coal

Line-haul railroad: a railroad that performs point-to-point service, as distinguished from a switching or terminal railroad. For line-haul railroads, interline revenue is usually some portion of the through rate.

Mallet: an articulated steam locomotive with two sets of cylinders, rods, and drive wheels under one boiler. Strictly speaking, a Mallet is a compound. The non-swiveling rear engine works at boiler pressure, and the swiveling front engine uses exhaust steam from the rear engine.

Merger: the issuing of additional securities by a major company in payment for the securities of a minor company whose corporate existence is then ended; absorption by a corporation of one or more others. In precise terms, Northern Pacific, Great Northern, and Burlington were not merged to form Burlington Northern but were merged by Burlington Northern. Sometimes a new name is involved: Seaboard Air Line merged Atlantic Coast Line and simultaneously adopted a new name, Seaboard Coast Line.

Metroliner: originally a high-speed electric passenger car developed by the Pennsylvania Railroad and the U. S. Department of Transportation to improve service between New York and Washington.

Mixed (train): a train carrying both freight and passengers, the latter either in passenger cars or in the caboose.

Official Guide: *The Official Guide of the Railways and Steam Navigation Lines of the United State, Porto Rico, Canada, Mexico, and Cuba*, a monthly compilation of all the passenger train schedules for North and Central America—and essentially a directory of the railroad companies

Operating contract: operation of a minor road in return for a payment to the major road for the service rendered. The minor company continues to exist and to retain ownership of its property.

Operating ratio: the ratio of operating expenses to revenue from operations. A railroad with an operating ratio of 80 or lower is doing nicely; a railroad that has an operating ratio over 100 is in trouble or soon will be.

Per diem: the daily rental paid by one railroad for the use of the cars of another.

Percent: the measure of slope or inclination of track—see Grade.

Pooling agreement: Under a pooling agreement railroads are operated separately but all income is divided arbitrarily, irrespective of traffic carried.

Pound (rail): The unit of measure of rail size is weight per yard—a 3-foot length of 90-pound rail, for example, weighs 90 pounds.

Proprietary company: a corporation owning all or a controlling portion of the shares of another.

Purchase: payment of cash outright for all the property of a railroad, which may divide such proceeds as it wishes among its owners and then cease to exist as a corporation.

Receiver, receivership: a person appointed by a court to manage a corporation during a period of reorganization—receivership—in an effort to avoid bankruptcy.

Regional railroad: a railroad bigger than a short line but smaller than a major railroad, usually a Class 2 railroad, such as the Bangor & Aroostook.

Reorganization: the rehabilitation of the finances of a business under procedures prescribed by federal bankruptcy legislation.

Right of way: the track, roadbed, and property along the track owned by the railroad. On a model railroad, the term refers to track, roadbed, and subroadbed.

Route mile: a mile of railroad line without regard to the number of tracks on that line. For example, the Soo Line route from Chicago to Milwaukee is 85 route miles. The line is double track, so it includes 170 track miles for main track alone, not counting sidings and spurs.

Short line: a railroad with less than 100 miles of mainline track. There is no official or legal definition of the term; this is the criterion used by the railroad industry and the American Short Line Railroad Association.

Shorthaul: to move traffic a shorter distance than the maximum possible for a given railroad between two points. For example, Burlington Northern shorthauls itself if it turns over Seattle–Chicago traffic to Wisconsin Central at St. Paul instead of taking it all the way to Chicago on its own rails.

Staggers Act: The Staggers Rail Act, named for Rep. Harley O. Staggers of West Virginia, was signed into law by President Jimmy Carter on October 14, 1980. It was massive deregulation of the railroads, including provisions to raise any rate that falls below 160 percent of out-of-pocket coasts (later 180 percent) and to enter into contracts with shippers to set price and service, both without ICC approval.

Standard gauge: a track gauge of 4'8½".

Steam railroad: a term still used by regulatory bodies to differentiate ordinary railroads from "electric railways"—interurbans and streetcar companies.

Subsidiary: a company wholly controlled by another that owns more than half its voting stock.

Switching district: an area within which a shipper located on one railroad has equal access to other railroads, either through a terminal or switching railroad or through reciprocal switching agreements among the line-haul railroads.

Switching railroad or terminal railroad: a railroad whose business is not point-to-point transportation but pickup and delivery service for a connecting line-haul road. Switching and terminal companies usually receive a flat per-car amount for their services.

Terminal railroad: same as switching railroad.

Track gauge: the distance between rails.

Track mile: a mile of track—see Route mile.

Trackage rights: rights granted by a railroad to another to operate on the tracks of the first, usually for a fee and usually without rights to service customers along that line.

Traffic department, traffic solicitors: the sales staff of a railroad

Transit: short-distance, high-density passenger service usually characterized by electric propulsion, fare payment by token, magnetic card, or cash, and operation under, above, and on streets.

Unit train: a train carrying a single bulk commodity, usually coal or grain, from shipper to consignee without any switching or classification en route.

USRA: United States Railroad Administration, the federal agency that took over operation of almost all U. S. railroads during World War I, or the United States Railway Association, a U. S. government corporation formed about 1973 to develop a plan to save the bankrupt Penn Central.